THE GREAT AWAKENING

THE GREAT AWAKENING

The Roots of Evangelical Christianity in Colonial America

Thomas S. Kidd

Yale University Press
New Haven & London

Published with assistance from the Mary Cady Tew Memorial Fund.

Designed by Nancy Ovedovitz and set in
Electra by Tseng Information Systems, Inc.
Printed in the United States of America.

The Library of Congress has cataloged the hardcover edition as follows:
Kidd, Thomas S.
The great awakening : the roots of evangelical Christianity in
colonial America / Thomas S. Kidd.
p. cm.
Includes bibliographical references and index.
ISBN 978-0-300-11887-2 (cloth : alk. paper)
1. United States—Church history—To 1775. 2. Great Awakening.
3. Revivals—United States—History. I. Title.
BR520.K53 2007
277.3'07—dc22   2007015816

ISBN 978-0-300-15846-5 (pbk.)

A catalogue record for this book is available from the British Library.

10 9 8 7 6 5 4

To George Marsden

CONTENTS

Acknowledgments

Many friends and colleagues helped me write this book. Thanks to Douglas Winiarski for frequent discussions about research and sources for the book. Thanks to David Bebbington for his friendship, encouragement, and his review of the manuscript. Thanks to Catherine Brekus for her thorough reading of the manuscript and many helpful suggestions. The same goes for Yale University Press's anonymous second reader. Stephen Marini read parts of the manuscript and gave very insightful comments. Many others offered advice on the project along the way, including Barry Hankins, Thomas Little, Kenneth Minkema, Mark Noll, Erik Seeman, and Stephen Stein.

Thanks to my department chair, Jeff Hamilton, and to the members of the history department at Baylor University for their support of my work. For their tireless efforts as my research assistants at Baylor, I want to thank Logan Simmons, Ethan Sanders, and Jonathan Reid. Each contributed a great deal to building the base of sources used here, and the book is much stronger for their exemplary work. Thanks to all my Baylor students who discussed the project with me, but particularly to members of my spring 2005 seminar on the First and Second Great Awakenings. The students there helped me hash out my muddled thoughts about evangelicals, and particularly the issue of egalitarianism.

Thanks to Deacon Oscar L. Kemp of the Storm Branch Baptist Church, Clearwater, South Carolina, for his impromptu conversation with me in December 2002 about his church and for the generous gift of his coauthored history of the church.

This book was supported in part by grants from the Baylor University Research Committee, the Office of the Vice Provost for Research, and the Institute for Faith and Learning at Baylor University. The generosity of the National Endowment for the Humanities, including a NEH summer stipend in 2004 and a 2006–7 NEH fellowship made the completion of the book possible. Any views, findings, conclusions, or recommendations expressed in this publication do not necessarily reflect those of the National Endowment for the Humanities or any other financial supporters.

Material from several chapters has appeared elsewhere. A portion of chapter 11 appeared in "The Healing of Mercy Wheeler: Illness and Miracles among Early American Evangelicals," *William and Mary Quarterly*, 3d ser., 63, no. 1 (January 2006): 149–70. An earlier version of chapter 6 appeared as "'A Faithful Watchman on the Walls of Charlestown': Josiah Smith and Moderate Revivalism in Colonial South Carolina," *South Carolina Historical Magazine* 105, no. 2 (April 2004): 82–106. A revised version of chapter 1 will appear in Kenneth Stewart, ed., *Continuities in Evangelical History: Interactions with David Bebbington* (Downers Grove, Ill.: InterVarsity Press, 2007). Portions of chapters 15 and 16 will appear in David Bebbington, ed., *Baptists and Mission* (Carlisle, Eng.: Paternoster Press, forthcoming). Portions of several chapters appeared in "Daniel Rogers' Egalitarian Great Awakening," *Journal of the Historical Society* 7, no. 1 (March 2007): 111-35. I gratefully acknowledge permission to reprint these selections.

Special appreciation goes to the members of Baylor's Interlibrary Loan Department, especially Janet Jasek, for their continual assistance. Thanks to Glen Clayton, Carolyn Lancaster, and the staff at the Furman University Special Collections Library, and Darlene Herod at the Virginia Baptist Historical Society, for delightful and productive visits to their archives. Thanks also to the staffs at the Phillips Library, Peabody-Essex Museum, Salem, Massachusetts; the Pocumtuck Valley Memorial Association Library, Deerfield, Massachusetts; the Beinecke Rare Book and Manuscript Library, Yale University; the Connecticut Historical Society, Hartford, Connecticut; the Massachusetts Historical Society, Boston; the Presbyterian Historical Society, Philadelphia; the Historical Society of Pennsylvania, Philadelphia; the South Caroliniana Library, University of South Carolina; the South Carolina Historical Society, Charleston; and the Southwestern Baptist Theological Seminary (Fort Worth) Library, all of which I visited to research this book. Thanks to the Amherst College library; the Bryn Mawr College library special collections; the Duke University library; the Harry Ransom Humanities Research Center (University of Texas at Austin); the Newberry Library; and the Long Island Historical Society for assisting me with copies of items in their collections.

Thanks to current and former staff at Yale University Press, including especially Chris Rogers, Lara Heimert, Laura Davulis, Molly Egland, and Ellie

Goldberg, for their interest in the project and kind support during its completion. Eliza Childs did a wonderful job of copyediting the manuscript.

I am dedicating this book to my mentor, George Marsden, who continues to be a source of wise advice and counsel. He read the whole manuscript and offered many keen insights, as usual. No one has had more influence on my scholarly development than George, and few people reading a book like this will need to be reminded of his enormous influence on American religious history and Christian scholarship.

Thanks, as always, to good friends from Notre Dame days, including Bryan Bademan, Mike DeGruccio, Darren Dochuk, Patrick Mason, and Kurt Peterson. Thanks to Soren McMillan for his continuing friendship and for many conversations on the state of evangelicalism and Clemson football. Thanks to friends at Highland Baptist Church for being a constant reminder of what matters most. Thanks to my parents, Michael and Nancy Kidd, for their ongoing support and encouragement.

I want to give special thanks to my family, including my boys, Jonathan and Joshua. They are always a delight to me. And finally, thanks to Ruby, my best friend and enduring inspiration.

INTRODUCTION

Everywhere in early twenty-first-century America, signs point to the influence of evangelical Christianity. According to one survey, 40 percent of Americans claim to have been "born again" or to have accepted Jesus as their personal savior. Each of the five most recent presidents of the United States, from Jimmy Carter to George W. Bush, either have been evangelicals or have closely aligned themselves with evangelical leaders. When campaigning for president, George W. Bush famously declared that Jesus was the philosopher who had influenced him most deeply, "because he changed my heart." Yet it is not only in the United States that one sees evangelicalism thriving, for evangelicalism and Pentecostalism have in recent decades swept across Latin America, Africa, and Southeast Asia in ways that Americans are only beginning to comprehend.[1]

How did evangelicalism begin? Many evangelicals assume that their movement originated with Jesus and continued through the great missions of the early church. As the story goes, the church then sank into the "Dark Ages" of medieval Catholicism, only occasionally illuminated by true believers, such as Augustine or Thomas à Kempis. With the Reformation in the sixteenth century, light began to dawn once again. Early evangelicals believed that the Reformation did not complete God's purifying work among Christians. The Reformation marked the beginning of that task, but heavy storm clouds still obscured the brightness of the gospel. Episodic bursts of sunlight pierced the darkness in the form of great revivals, presaging the noonday sun of the millennial Kingdom. Evangelicals presented the gospel of salvation through Christ to as many people as possible, with the hope of seeing them delivered from God's wrath. Evangelical proselytizing would fill up the church universal until all the chosen sheep had been gathered and the True Shepherd could return.

   Most early Protestants shared these beliefs, but the American evangelical tradition that began to take shape in the late seventeenth and early eighteenth centuries was a new elaboration of the Reformation. Its chief tributaries were Continental Pietism, Scots-Irish Presbyterianism, and Anglo-American Puritanism. Historian David Bebbington has identified four characteristics of evangelicalism: conversionism ("the belief that lives need to be changed"), activism ("the expression of the gospel in effort"), biblicism ("a particular regard for the Bible"), and crucicentrism ("a stress on the sacrifice of Christ on the cross"). This definition remains quite serviceable for evangelicals generally, but Bebbington's "quadrilateral" does not adequately distinguish early evangelicalism from movements that preceded it. Evangelicalism did, no doubt, inaugurate new emphases on the discernible moment of an individual's conversion, or the "new birth," and the simultaneous conversion of many individuals during revivals. Activism, biblicism, and crucicentrism, however, characterized many Protestant movements of the sixteenth to eighteenth centuries, including evangelicalism. Missing from Bebbington's definition is early evangelicalism's new attention to the person of the Holy Spirit, particularly in revival. Early American evangelicalism was distinguished from earlier forms of Protestantism by dramatically increased emphases on *seasons of revival,* or *outpourings of the Holy Spirit,* and on *converted sinners experiencing God's love personally.* Both the role of the Spirit and the methods of revival were hotly contested among early American evangelicals.[2]

   Because evangelicalism is a movement, we cannot create tightly sealed categories for who counts as an evangelical and who does not. Moreover, evangelicals themselves bitterly argued about the nature of their movement, and some tried to portray other evangelicals as beyond orthodox boundaries. Historians have often described the "Great Awakening" of the 1740s as a battle between "Old Lights" and "New Lights," with the former opposing the revivals and the latter supporting them. But a close look at early American evangelicalism shows how oversimplified the Old Lights versus New Lights framework is. In this book I present evangelicalism as having fluid boundaries that changed over time. Instead of Old Lights and New Lights, we should think of the debates over this movement in terms of three points on a continuum. On one end were the *antirevivalists,* who dismissed the revivals as religious frenzy or "enthusiasm." In the middle were the *moderate evangelicals,* who supported the revivals at their outset but became concerned about the chaotic, leveling extremes that the awakenings produced. Finally, on the other end were the *radical evangelicals,* who eagerly embraced the Spirit's movements, even if social conventions had to be sacrificed.[3]

Viewed in terms of this continuum, the controversy generated by the revivals was not just a disagreement over tactics and emotions, but over social order. To understand the deep anxieties generated by revivalism, it is important to remember how profoundly stratified eighteenth-century American society was. Landowning white men ruled over their families, social inferiors, servants, and slaves. The elites integrated all these people into a vast system of dependencies. Authorities tried to suppress irregularities that might challenge their hegemony.[4]

One can appreciate, then, why many might have viewed radical evangelicals as a threat to a well-ordered society. Radical evangelicals ordained untutored, and occasionally nonwhite, men as pastors. They sometimes allowed women and nonwhites to serve as deacons or even as elders. They led crowds of the poor, children, and nonwhites singing through the streets. They permitted Native Americans, African Americans, and women to exhort in mixed congregations, and they commended their words as worthy of white male attention. They endorsed the visionary, ecstatic experiences of the disenfranchised. They believed that individuals could have immediate assurance of salvation by the indwelling witness of the Spirit. They affirmed laypeople's right to critique their pastors and founded new churches fully committed to radical revival. While to modern eyes, the radicals' innovations may seem modest, they were for their time well-nigh revolutionary. In the revivals, the world seemed to turn upside down as those with the very least agency in eighteenth-century America felt the power of God surge in their bodies.[5]

Once evangelist George Whitefield arrived in America in 1739, the religion of the new birth became a permanent fixture of American religious life. The Old Lights could protest, but for better or worse, evangelicalism was here to stay. The most interesting question in the first generation of American evangelicalism, then, was what kind of movement it would become. How socially radical would it be? Would it tolerate the dramatic mystical experiences of laypeople? Would it reaffirm traditional boundaries set by race, class, gender, education, and age? Or would it lead to a substantially new egalitarianism for those who embraced the idea of individuals' equality before God? The struggle over these questions played out chiefly between moderate and radical evangelicals, not between Old Lights and New Lights. Evangelicalism's social implications were always deeply conflicted. Though many leading evangelicals defended the social status quo, the movement also held within it an opportunity for socially transformative egalitarianism. From its beginnings, evangelicalism contained the potential to become populist or even democratized. Contrary to the thesis of Nathan Hatch's celebrated *The Democratization of American Christianity*, evangelicalism did not need the American Revolution to give it deep, if controversial, egalitarian possibilities.[6] Indeed, much of the best recent writing on eighteenth-century evangelicalism has analyzed its socially radical manifestations.[7]

Other scholars have shown definitely that early evangelicalism was an international movement spanning the Atlantic world. Led by such books as W. R. Ward's *The Protestant Evangelical Awakening* (1992) and Mark Noll's *The Rise of Evangelicalism* (2003), historians have realized how tightly connected American evangelicals were with colleagues of similar predilections in Continental Europe and Great Britain. In this book I affirm that international interpretation, with early chapters describing how American evangelicalism grew out of English Puritanism, Scots-Irish Presbyterianism, and Continental Pietism. Readers will note, however, that once the American revivals begin in earnest, around 1740, the international perspective fades from my narrative. My closer focus on internal American developments does not imply that the international influences had ceased to be important, but as I wrote the book, I found myself drawn to the domestic contest (repeated outside America, to be sure) between radical and moderate evangelicals. I was also constrained by length to maintain my focus on the internal dynamics of the American side of the story. The regional growth of early evangelicalism in America provided more than enough material for a book of this size, but I would heartily commend efforts to locate this story in a more adequately international context or to test its themes in the European setting.

Some readers might also notice that not only does this book concern itself less than it might with international connections, but within America it also focuses heavily on New England. New England has always been the most studied part of colonial America. During the early phase of the Great Awakening, New Englanders formed the center of revivalist action, likely because their strong Puritan heritage prepared them for intense periods of religious excitement. New Englanders have also saved by far the richest collections of primary sources on early evangelicalism, so the history of the movement in New England is relatively easy to document. In this book I make a serious attempt to weave together the history of early American evangelical Christianity from Nova Scotia to Georgia, but the narrative is admittedly oriented toward New England. I hope that this will only give the impression that New Englanders were deeply influenced by evangelicalism and not the sense that evangelicalism was specific to New England.

Clearly, it would not have been possible to write this book without the generations of excellent scholarship on America's Great Awakening that preceded it. Fine comprehensive treatments of evangelicalism in Virginia, the Middle Colonies, and New England exist, but those studies by Wesley Gewehr, Charles Maxson, and Edwin Gaustad are all at least fifty years old. In the intervening decades, a veritable deluge of scholarship has poured forth, analyzing eighteenth-century religion with attention to social history, the history of race and gender, imperial war and politics, and many other subjects. Our understanding of the Awakening's key evangelist, George Whitefield, has been revolutionized through outstanding biographies by Frank Lambert and Harry Stout. The study of Jonathan Edwards is an industry unto itself, highlighted by wonderful recent biographies by George Marsden and Philip Gura and the imminent completion of the Works of Jonathan Edwards series by Yale University Press. All this scholarly ferment has vastly improved our understanding of the period, and I have undeniably benefited from it. The study of the Great Awakening, however, still seems fragmented by regions and personalities. By revisiting the enormous body of primary sources, including some sources previously neglected, I provide, in this book, a single, coherent narrative of evangelicalism's development in America over its first fifty years.[8]

One question readers may ask at the outset is why the Great Awakening happened. It is difficult to answer this question with much specificity because any truly adequate explanation would have to account for regional differences between and within North America, Britain, and Continental Europe. There are, however, major themes that reappear regularly that may help us understand the timing of the revivals. First, we should acknowledge that participants, as I indicated above, believed that the revivals happened because God had graciously poured out the Holy Spirit. At a minimum, this new emphasis on the Holy Spirit tells us how many pastors and laypeople interpreted what was happening to them at the time. Even if one accepts some kind of supernatural causation for the revivals, one must also acknowledge that earthly means, more accessible to an historian's view, played a major role in spurring the awakenings. One of these factors was the ongoing tensions between Protestant Britain and Catholic France and Spain. As I demonstrated in my previous book, *The Protestant Interest: New England after Puritanism* (2004), British nationalism, Protestant internationalism, and anti-Catholicism shaped New England's public religious culture after the Glorious Revolution of 1688. Between 1688 and 1763, Britain and France, and sometimes Spain, fought a series of wars that routinely spilled into the North American colonies, creating fears among many colonists that Catholic powers would overwhelm and destroy them. Revival, then, became a means by which the churches could return to true godliness and, it was hoped, be delivered from the Catholic menace.[9]

Another key development that helped birth the evangelical movement was the so-called consumer revolution of the eighteenth century and, in particular, the advent of new media sources and techniques. As Frank Lambert showed in his *Inventing the "Great Awakening"* (1999), widespread newspaper and book distribution helped create the idea of a Great Awakening. Evangelicals from George Whitefield and Jonathan Edwards to Billy Graham and Rick Warren have always used the latest media technology and techniques to promote revival. Thus, the circulation of books like Edwards's *A Faithful Narrative* and Whitefield's *Journals* and of Thomas Prince's magazine the *Christian History* was critical for generating excitement about the revivals and expectations that awakenings could happen in towns receiving those publications, too. One also cannot discount the role that simple hard work played in generating the awakenings. Revivalists traveled unbelievable distances and risked health and comfort in order to preach the gospel to thousands across the Atlantic world.

A final salient question that this book must address is whether there actually was a Great Awakening in the eighteenth century. Until 1982, historians took the Great Awakening as a given, but then historian Jon Butler argued that it was only an "interpretative fiction" invented by nineteenth-century Christian historians. Although Butler's argument was overextended, it helpfully provoked a reevaluation of what we actually mean by "the Great Awakening." He contended that the event really amounted to just "a short-lived Calvinist revival in New England during the early 1740s." No doubt the eighteenth-century awakenings were centered in New England, but over time they came to influence parts of all the colonies, and more important, they helped birth an enormously important religious movement, evangelicalism, which shows no sign of disappearing today.[10]

Butler also asserted that the "revivals had modest effects on colonial religion" and that they were "never radical." But if the revivals helped create evangelicalism, then not only did the awakenings make a profound change in colonial religion, but they began a major alteration of global Christian history. Moreover, as I will demonstrate in this book, the revivals featured all manner of radical spiritual manifestations, unnerving antirevivalists and moderate evangelicals alike. Butler's critique does show, however, that it is not enough to evaluate evangelicalism as a homogenous whole. It had radical implications, but those implications were hotly contested by moderates, and its social potential often came to naught for women, African Americans, and Native Americans. Some evangelicals also began a great assault on the churchly establishments of colonial America, and the revolutionary move for disestablishment on the federal and state levels can largely be attributed to evangelical and deist cooperation in favor of the separation of church and state.[11]

Butler finally claimed that, contrary to the suggestions of previous scholars, "the link between the revivals and the American Revolution is virtually nonexistent." As I indicate in chapter 18, "'The God of Glory is on Our Side,'" I am in substantial agreement with Butler on this point. Moreover, evangelicals' responses to the Revolution covered the whole range of opinions from enthusiastic Patriotism to staunch Loyalism. But we should also note that evangelical rhetoric and ideology helped to inspire and justify the Patriot cause for both evangelical and nonevangelical leaders. Evangelicalism did not start the Revolution, but the Patriot side certainly benefited from the support of many evangelicals.[12]

In sum, in this book I contend that there was, indeed, a powerful, unprecedented series of revivals from about 1740 to 1743 that touched many of the colonies and that contemporaries remembered for decades as a special visitation of the Holy Spirit. Calling this event "the" Great Awakening does present historical problems. Chief among them is that the standard framework of the "First" and "Second" Great Awakenings may obscure the fact that the evangelical movement continued to develop after 1743 and before 1800. There were important, widespread revivals that happened before the First, and between the First and Second, Great Awakenings. Additionally, when one recognizes that evangelicalism was a movement not defined just by revivals, then a whole range of missions, agendas, and less celebrated developments open to our view. Thus, this book is not solely about "the" Great Awakening of the 1740s, though those revivals form an indispensable part of our story and roughly half of this text's content. In the book I examine, instead, what we might call the *long* First Great Awakening and the contest to define its boundaries. Although many revivals, including the major season from 1740 to 1743, happened during this period, revivals alone did not delineate the early evangelical movement. Instead, persistent desires for revival, widespread individual conversions, and the outpouring of the Holy Spirit distinguished the new evangelicals. The long First Great Awakening started before Jonathan Edwards's 1734–35 Northampton revival and lasted roughly through the end of the American Revolution, when disestablishment, theological change, and a new round of growth started the (even more imprecise) "Second" Great Awakening. The controversial emergence of the religion of the new birth demarcated the long First Great Awakening and the first generation of American evangelical Christianity.

"Prayer for a Saving Issue": From Puritans to Evangelicals

To expect revival, one had to experience despair, a mood in which the New England Puritans specialized. Puritan church leaders began lamenting the decline of their godly experiment beginning in the 1660s and 1670s. Michael Wigglesworth's poem "God's Controversy with New England" (1662) featured God warning formerly devout New Englanders that

> Your sinns me press as sheaves do load a cart,
>> And therefore I will plague you for this geare
> Except you seriously, and soon, repent,
>> Ile not delay your pain and heavy punishment.

Calls for moral reformation seemed not to stanch a perceived flood of immorality and divine judgments.[1] In the 1670s, Puritan leaders began calling for an outpouring of the Holy Spirit to revive their languishing churches, and some also began experimenting with new measures that raised the possibility of corporate renewal of individual churches and towns.

With regard to the theology of revival, Samuel Torrey, pastor of Weymouth, Massachusetts, might be considered the first evangelical in New England. Torrey became the minister at Weymouth in 1666. There he rose to a sufficiently prominent position to be offered the presidency of Harvard in 1682 and 1684, declining both times. In 1757, Boston's evangelical minister Thomas Prince Sr. recalled Samuel Torrey as a powerful, emotional speaker: "His Sermons were very scriptural, experimental, pathetical, sensibly flowing from a warm and pious Heart . . . with most awakening Solemnity." Given Torrey's rhetoric and theology, he may be regarded as the earliest evangelical spokesman in New England.[2]

In three Massachusetts election day sermons, delivered in 1674, 1683, and 1695, Torrey raised doubts as to whether the churches' reform efforts could ever succeed without an effusion of the Holy Spirit. Certainly, Torrey continued to emphasize the "Work of Reformation," but he thought each person's more pressing need was a "Heart-reformation, or making of a new heart." The churches would not revive through their moral efforts, Torrey argued, but only when God would pour "out [an] abundance of converting grace, and so revive and renew the work of Conversion." Too many congregants had no vital experience of the Spirit, and "if ever these Churches be thoroughly recovered, it will be, it must be by such a dispensation of converting grace, unto an unconverted generation." By 1674 Torrey was already proclaiming the need for revival among pastors and congregations, arguing, "If God make this Ministry a Converting Ministry, the Work of Reformation will be again revived." He called for "Prayer unto God for a dispensation of Converting grace by their Ministry, that the Work of Conversion, and so the Work of Reformation, may be revived." In Torrey's formula, the work of reformation began with the work of conversion.[3]

Torrey and Josiah Flint wrote the preface to William Adams's 1678 sermon *The Necessity of the Pouring Out of the Spirit from on High upon a Sinning Apostatizing People* and continued to beat the drum for revival. The mood in New England following King Philip's War (1675–76) was bleak and raw, and Torrey and Flint thought it obvious that "we are a people in extream danger of perishing, in our own sins and under Gods Judgements." Moreover, "all ordinary means" of promoting moral reformation had failed, making them wonder whether "our degeneracy and apostacy may not prove . . . perpetual." Perhaps, they thought, God had condemned New Englanders to damnable sinfulness because of their intransigence. If so, then no one could reverse the downward slide except for the Almighty. "Truly then it is high time for all orders, degrees & societies of men in New-England, by faith in prayer, to seek the Lord until he come and rain righteousness upon us." Evangelicals like Torrey always assigned a proactive role for the people's prayers in seeking revival.[4]

Torrey continued these pleas in his 1683 and 1695 election sermons. He thought that if only New Englanders would mourn for their sins, God would revive pure religion. In fact, he thought godly grieving would be a sign of the coming revival: "We must follow God mourning . . . this is the way wherein God promiseth to revive his People, ... Such a Mourning is the certain effect of the saving dispensation of the Spirit and converting Grace." In the greatest of Torrey's sermons promoting revival, *Mans Extremity, Gods Opportunity* (1695), he argued that the New Englanders' sin was so severe that hope for ordinary reformation had vanished. Providential history offered hope, however, because "there are certain times, and extraordinary cases, wherein God . . . Saves his People by Himself." The Puritan colonies had once been godly showcases for the Reformation but had forgotten their first love. Torrey thought that God would reclaim New England through unilateral intervention, and "O when God comes to Save New-England by himself, we shall see and feel wonderful effects & changes." Hearkening back to Governor John Winthrop's vision for New England in *A Model of Christian Charity* (1630), Torrey assured his audience that God "will magnifie New-England again before the world . . . God will . . . Save us from our sins & apostasy, by the power of his Spirit, in a general work of Conversion and Reformation; and by a glorious resurrection of Religion."[5] God indeed had a controversy with New Englanders because of their lack of repentance, but God himself would set them right when he sent the revival.

It is one thing, of course, to discuss revival and another to see it happen. When did the evangelical revivals begin? The first clear antecedents in New England to the revivals of the 1740s were covenant renewals that began in the 1670s. Historian Perry Miller once argued that the Great Awakening was "nothing more than an inevitable culmination" of the covenant renewals. These rituals had roots in English Puritanism, but after King Philip's War, New England saw what one might call a revival of renewals: a great new interest in corporate commitments to God and the covenant. The war had created a new sense of desperation among pious New Englanders, making the time right for widespread repentance.[6]

As promoted by Boston's Increase Mather, the covenant renewal usually featured the pastor reminding all church members of their promises to God and each other. The assembly included "halfway" members, or baptized congregants who had not experienced conversion. A major reform, the Halfway Covenant of 1662, had allowed growing numbers of those New Englanders who were baptized and moral, but not converted, to have their own children baptized. Normally only full members had received this privilege before 1662, so the Halfway Covenant extended the right of baptism, but not the Lord's Supper, to many of the unregenerate. The halfway system ensured that the churches would be filled with substantial numbers of pseudo-members waiting for their conversion. That situation set the stage for episodes of spiritual excitement that precipitated mass numbers of conversions. The covenant renewal presented an opportunity for all to consider whether they were truly right before God and also for halfway members to seek conversion and full admission into church membership. The covenant renewal ceremony was often followed by weeks of preaching on salvation, which led to many new conversions. Pastor James Fitch of Norwich, Connecticut, led the first of these renewals in March 1676, and his was followed by hosts of others over the next four years. Thomas Prince later recalled these events as the first "Instances of the transient REVIVAL of Religion."[7]

During King Philip's War, John Cotton Jr. of Plymouth, Massachusetts, also led his congregation in covenant renewal. He addressed the church's forsaken duties to God and pled with the "children of the church" (members who had been baptized but not admitted to the Lord's Supper) to own the covenant and to come to the Lord's table. On July 18, 1676, Cotton implored all to consider their commitment to God and made a special plea for the children of the church to put their faith in Christ and secure the rising generation's fidelity to the Lord. In coming years, Cotton followed up the renewal by hosting catechetical small group meetings for fathers in the church, and by these means he successfully brought much of the next generation into full church communion.[8]

Likewise, in 1680, covenant renewals occurred in the North and Old South churches in Boston, and in Salem and Haverhill. Members of the Salem church acknowledged that they could not "perform any spiritual duty unless the Lord enable us thereunto by the Grace of his Spirit," but they were "awfully sensible that in these times by the loud voice of his judgements both felt and feared, the Lord is calling us all to Repentance and Reformation." The 1679 Reforming Synod had identified a litany of provoking sins and called for increased moral discipline and attention to the church covenants. The Salem church responded to the synod's catalogue of New England's sins with a cry for "pardoning mercy."[9]

Samuel Willard, one of the leaders of the Reforming Synod, directed Boston's Old South Church in covenant renewal in 1680. Early that year a number of children of the church approached Willard about publicly embracing the responsibilities of their baptismal covenant, and that summer Willard led the whole church through the renewal. More than a hundred owned the baptismal covenant, with many of those also eventually becoming full communicant members. The year 1680 proved to be the greatest harvest time of Willard's distinguished ministry. The revival of 1680 "soon pass'd away," according to Prince, and the pastors were left again to worry over the provoking sins of New England.[10]

The key covenant renewal in New England, however, and the most publicized, was the 1705 ceremony at Taunton, in southeastern Massachusetts, led by Samuel Danforth Jr. Danforth's covenant renewal received attention in the 1706 *A Help to a National Reformation*, printed in London, and Danforth published his renewal sermon and the covenant itself in *Piety Encouraged* (1705). Thomas Prince presented the Taunton event as "a second Instance" of revival following the 1680 renewals and reprinted in his magazine the *Christian History* a passage from *A Help to a National Reformation* and letters from Danforth. Taunton's church had held a covenant renewal during King Philip's War in 1676, and Danforth sought to use the renewal again as a means to awaken his congregation, especially the halfway members. Danforth had received accounts of lay reformation societies in England and thought that these might prove useful models for the promotion of authentic piety in Taunton. In 1704 he began meeting monthly with lay leaders in the church "to consult what might be done to promote a Reformation of Disorders there." This group began organizing fathers in the town for regular family worship. Danforth also began hosting young people's meetings, mimicking recent ones in London and Boston. Danforth, like future evangelicals, saw reforming his town's youth as a top priority of revival, and the gatherings put "an End to & utter Banishment of their former disorderly and profane Meetings to drink, &c."[11]

Danforth reported in February 1705 that "we are much encouraged by an unusual and amazing Impression, made by GOD'S SPIRIT on all Sorts among us, especially on the young Men and Women." The young people had become sober as a result of the meetings and some "awful Deaths and amazing Providences." He hoped that their sobriety was not temporary and asked for "Prayer, that these Strivings of the SPIRIT, may have a saving Issue." On March 1, Danforth led the covenant renewal itself. The covenant of 1676 was read aloud, and "We gave Liberty to all Men and Women Kind, from sixteen Years old and upwards to act with us," and three hundred people added their names to a list forsaking sin. He thought perhaps a hundred more would soon submit their names. Danforth also noted a number of new full memberships, as well as some adult baptisms. Later that month Danforth reported that he had no time for his regular pastoral duties because of his constant visits from young people seeking salvation. He believed that this commotion might be a sign of something greater at hand: "I think sometimes that the Time of the pouring out of the SPIRIT upon all Flesh, may be at the Door. Lets be earnest in Prayer that CHRIST's Kingdom may come." Boston's Cotton Mather noted that "the Spirit of Grace has of late been doing wondrously in our Taunton" and commended the late "astonishing Harvest." Mather ended his preface to Danforth's *Piety Encouraged* (1705) with a cautionary note against Satanic excesses. Although it is not clear whether he had heard of such excesses already, Mather wrote in his diary that he warned the Taunton renewers against the devil's schemes to hurt "a glorious work of God which has lately been done, in bringing that popular and vicious Town to a wonderful Reformation."[12]

Taunton's renewal was only one of many revivals before the "First" Great Awakening. In the 1710s and 1720s these episodes became more frequent in New England.[13] Much of the earliest revival activity, in the form of covenant renewals, was in eastern Massachusetts, but the trend toward revivalism was also growing in the Connecticut River valley, particularly under the ministry of Solomon Stoddard of Northampton, Massachusetts, the grandfather of and ministerial predecessor to Jonathan Edwards. Stoddard passed on a considerable evangelical heritage to Edwards, as Edwards noted in his *A Faithful Narrative of the Surprising Work of God* (1737). He described Stoddard as "renowned for his gifts and grace; so he was blessed, from the beginning, with extraordinary success in his ministry in the conversion of many souls. He had five harvests, as he called them." These "harvests" came in 1679, 1683, 1690, 1712, and 1718. Stoddard himself told his congregation in 1687, "I have made it my business to gain Souls to Christ," and in this business he may have been the most successful New England preacher in his generation. Stoddard relied on the Lord's Supper as a "converting ordinance," or a preparatory ritual that could lead unconverted seekers to Christ. On this point Stoddard differed from his colleagues in the Boston area, who believed that the Supper was meant only for the converted.[14] Stoddard had to defend his policy of open communion against various attacks from the eastern establishment, and he argued that he would not hesitate to "clear up a Truth that has not been received, whereby a door is opened for the revival of Religion." Edwards was particularly impressed that during each harvest, "the bigger part of the young people in the town seemed to be mainly concerned for their eternal salvation."[15]

Stoddard developed the most elaborate evangelical theology of conversion prior to Edwards. As an orthodox Calvinist, Stoddard believed that the Spirit of God drew sinners to salvation, but he also considered powerful preaching the means that God often used to draw people. Thus Stoddard recommended that preachers should warn of the threat of damnation, on one hand, and offer the hope of salvation through Christ's grace, on the other. This view no doubt heavily influenced his grandson Edwards. Stoddard argued that the dread of damnation was the most, and perhaps the only, effective means to lead sinners to true "humiliation," or a sense that their sin was deplorable in light of God's holiness. God awakened conviction of sin in the elect, followed by the hope that Christ's grace was sufficient to deliver them from the judgment of God. The brutal wars that plagued the Connecticut River valley during his ministry in Northampton surely colored Stoddard's preaching on damnation. Although the Puritans had originally come to New England with the supposed intent of evangelizing local Native Americans, they tended more often to provoke and bully the Indians over land rights and other issues. When Native Americans resisted, as they did during King Philip's War of 1675–76, the English colonists used the most brutal practices of war imaginable to subdue them. Understandably, many Indians in northern New England allied with the French and periodically raided frontier towns in western and northern New England. The Deerfield raid of 1704, for instance, decimated Northampton's close neighbors to the north. Northamptonites, faced with the ever-present threat of French Catholic and Native American attacks, could easily accept Stoddard's reminders of their imminent peril.[16]

Following ideas similar to those of his contemporary Samuel Torrey, Stoddard insisted that conversions would not happen without the catalyst of the Holy Spirit. Stoddard noted in *The Efficacy of the Fear of Hell, to Restrain Men from Sin* (1713) that in times of languishing piety, "The Spirit of the Lord must be poured out upon the People, else Religion will not revive." Apparently Stoddard had just seen such a pouring out, as one of his "harvests" occurred in 1712. In Stoddard's model, the Spirit poured through the ministers. He still held a church- and community-based theology of conversion, different from some of the more individualistic and anticlerical tendencies many later evangelicals would embrace. Stoddard argued that the Spirit allowed ministers to preach effectively the threat of God's judgment, making sinners fearful of death, and "if the Consciences of Men be terrified, that makes way for their Conversion."[17]

Stoddard also posited that the church should expect seasons of revival, characterized by special outpourings of the Spirit. In times of revival, the Spirit would quicken believers' faith, convert grieving sinners, and make careless sinners more interested in things of God. Stoddard thought that revival could be either general or particular. For instance, he saw the Reformation as a general revival, "when some Nations broke off from Popery, and imbraced the Gospel." He also believed, however, that revival sometimes visited individual towns or congregations, as it had at Northampton during his church's harvests. God determined the time and extent of revivals, but God also chose to respond to people's prayers for revival. Thus, Stoddard insisted, "we should beg of God, that Religion may revive in this Land." Stoddard, with the endorsement of Increase Mather, helped build the foundation for evangelical piety when he wrote *A Guide to Christ* in 1714, which became a standard treatise on conversion in Anglo-American evangelical circles through the early nineteenth century. The itinerant George Whitefield, for one, thought highly of Stoddard's work and recommended *A Guide to Christ* as a devotional text.[18]

Stoddard also promoted the evangelization of Native Americans and the expansion of the gospel across the globe. If religion languished among the Christian churches of New England, then who would bring the message of Christ to the pagan Indians? Stoddard knew the answer: the Roman Catholics and specifically the Jesuits would enter the vacuum and lead the Indians astray with their false gospel. He expressed embarrassment about New England's near-total failure to evangelize Native Americans. In *An Answer to Some Cases of Con-*

science Respecting the Country (1722) and *Question Whether God Is Not Angry with the Country for Doing So Little towards the Conversion of the Indians?* (1723), as new war raged with the northern Wabanakis and their Jesuit supporter, Father Sebastien Rale, Stoddard chastised New Englanders for their failures to proselytize the Indians. Appended to *An Answer* was a hopeful poem he penned in 1701, which asked God to "Give the poor INDIANS Eyes to see, The Light of Life: and set them free." He anticipated the millennial era in which "ASIA, and AFRICA, EUROPA, with AMERICA: All Four, in Consort join'd, shall Sing, New Songs of Praise to CHRIST OUR KING." For that time to arrive, and for the Roman Catholic powers to be destroyed, Protestants needed a great outpouring of the Holy Spirit. Stoddard passed this hope on to many Anglo-American evangelicals who for the next hundred and fifty years would read his works. Not least among these successors were Stoddard's son-in-law Timothy Edwards and his grandson Jonathan Edwards.[19]

Like Stoddard, many early evangelicals believed that they were participating in the worldwide spreading of the gospel. Some Protestants thought this growth might lead to the destruction of Roman Catholicism and Islam, the mass conversion of the Jews to Christianity, and the coming of the millennium. No one was more interested in these eschatological developments than Increase and Cotton Mather, who received every piece of news of successful evangelism from overseas as a sign of the approaching last days. For instance, in Increase Mather's treatise *A Discourse Concerning Faith and Fervency* (1710), he cited news of Dutch missionaries winning converts in the East Indies and reports of Jewish conversions in Europe. Although he thought that the Spirit alone brought conversions, he believed that God chose to send the Spirit in response to believers' prayers. The more news became available about missions, as well as the persecution of European Protestants, the more urgently writers like Mather called for prayers supporting the expansion of the global church and the hastening of the last days. "We should therefore Pray that there may be a plentiful Effusion of the Holy Spirit on the world. Then will Converting work go forward among the Nations." He dreamed of the millennial age: "Oh that the Jewish Nation were Converted! Oh that the fullness of the Gentiles were come in! Oh that our Lord Jesus Christ would Come and take possession of the World for himself!"[20] Following writers like Mather, early evangelicalism was born in a religious culture expecting widespread, nearly simultaneous conversions in the last days.

Stoddard helped foster a sense that churches along the Connecticut and Thames rivers in western New England could begin a great new revival of religion, and a number of his younger colleagues began to promote awakenings in the 1710s and 1720s. The key early evangelical minister in Connecticut, Eliphalet Adams of New London, took the lead. Though later a target of radical evan-

gelical attacks because of his moderation and opposition to unrestrained itinerancy, Adams became in the early decades of the eighteenth century a great
proponent of both the new revivalism and increased clerical authority.[21] He
thought that beginning a revival in Connecticut could spark a larger revival fire,
which might ultimately consume the globe. Adams, along with East Windsor's
Timothy Edwards, Norwich's Benjamin Lord, Windham's Samuel Whiting, and
Windsor's Jonathan Marsh, formed the most activist contingent yet of evangelical ministers in New England. This group helped lead a series of revivals in the
Connecticut River valley in the 1710s and 1720s.

Timothy Edwards, husband of Stoddard's daughter Esther, was "an expert
on the science of conversion," according to historian George Marsden. Unlike
Stoddard, Edwards still required applicants for full membership to give a public
"relation" of their conversions, some of which have survived as testimonies to
his revival ministry. He led four or five revivals in his East Windsor congregation
before the 1734–35 Northampton awakening, according to Jonathan Edwards's
adult memory. At least two of these took place in the 1710s and profoundly affected Jonathan. In 1716 the young Jonathan wrote to his sister Mary, "There
hath in this place been a very remarkable stirring and pouring out of the Spirit of
God. . . . About thirteen have been joined to the church."[22] Timothy Edwards's
awakenings were followed by more regional revivals in the coming years, punctuated especially by a prodigious stir in towns along the Connecticut and Thames
rivers from 1720 to 1722.

Samuel Whiting's Windham church saw one of the largest awakenings in
1721, with eighty people joining the church in about six months. Eliphalet
Adams gave a thanksgiving sermon at the church in July 1721 to commend Whiting's ministry and celebrate the "greater Stirring than Ordinary among the dry
bones." He hoped that the Windham revival might inspire others: "Oh! That the
same Good Spirit from on High were poured out upon the rest of the Country."
Adams also used the imminence of the last days as a motivation for revival: "WHO
can tell but that as he hath begun to pour out of His good Spirit . . . and cause
the Good favour of his Knowledge to spread far and wide . . . seeing the Times
are drawing near." He exhorted Christians to "Pray for the Success of the Gospel
in other Places & for the Peace of Jerusalem." Lay prayer was key to the revival
of piety in New England and to the coming of the eschatological mass conversions. Therefore, he called on the people to "Pray that the Spirit may be poured
out from on High upon every part of the Land, that the work of Religion may
not die among Us where it once so remarkably flourished."[23] Early evangelicals
celebrated current revival activity, but they never saw it as complete because
they knew that a greater revival always remained on the horizon.

The Connecticut revival of 1720–22 was the first major event of the evangelical era in New England. It touched congregations in Windham, Preston, Franklin, Norwich, and Windsor, Connecticut. It seems to have resulted in several hundred new memberships and perhaps even more conversions, but its significance has been obscured because of the lack of print coverage surrounding the revival. Revivals had begun in force, but printers did not yet fully back the creation of awakenings as major media events the way they would in the early 1740s. Because it received little contemporary notice, the Connecticut revival has not only been largely forgotten, but at the time it remained a regional revival and did not flow to other parts of the colonies.[24]

The most significant stir before the one led by Jonathan Edwards in Northampton in 1734 and 1735 came in response to the 1727 earthquake in New England. This 1727 revival marked the beginning of the trend of publicizing awakenings on a massive scale in order to promote further revivals. No doubt the dramatic and frightening nature of the event added to its marketability in print, and some thirty sermons concerning the earthquake were eventually published.[25]

On Sunday evening, October 29, a terrible earthquake shook the homes of New Englanders, awakening many both physically and spiritually. This was followed by a long series of aftershocks, which kept the threat fresh in the minds of penitents. Immediately churches filled with seekers anxious to secure their salvation, lest they be caught unprepared for their own death. Jonathan Pearson, a layman in the Lynn End, Massachusetts, church, reported, "God has by the late amazing Earth-quake Layd open my neglect before me that I see no way to escape. But by fleeing to Christ for refuge. God in that hour Set all my Sins before me. When I was Shaking over the pit looking every moment when the earth would open her mouth and Swallow me up and then must I have been miserable for ever & for ever." His experience seems to have been common in 1727 and 1728, as the pastors preached revival with a most striking object lesson at hand: an earth that seemed ready to swallow up the people. The earthquake helped spark revivals in the Merrimac valley towns of Haverhill, Hampton, Newbury, Bradford, and Andover, where the earthquake had been centered. Andover and Malden, Massachusetts, both held covenant renewal services on December 21 in response to the earthquake.[26]

Haverhill's church, in particular, witnessed a large revival after the earthquake, as documented by pastor John Brown in a letter to Newton's John Cotton. Brown told Cotton that his church, often joined by the Bradford, Massachusetts, church, met in a series of fervent meetings after the first earthquake. Many came to Brown seeking full membership, baptism, or renewal of their baptismal covenant: 154 people in all. Brown noted that most of these were youths. Many gross sinners had come under deep conviction and now sought salvation. "There seems to be in the Town, a General Reformation," he wrote. He had heard that the revival had spread to Exeter also, with 40 baptized there since the earthquake. Someone also told him that at Almsbury, "they were willing to spend their whole time in the Worship of God."[27]

Brown thought that God had sent the earthquake to help precipitate the revival, but he did not believe that the earthquake was the sole cause. Since spring 1727 he had seen a new religious interest in his congregation, and the earthquake only served to sharpen that already-existing appetite. Brown wanted to correspond with Cotton in order to hear of the revival's extent elsewhere and to learn "what are the thoughts of the most Judicious about the Signs of the Times." Eschatological speculations were never far away when awakenings came. He asked Cotton to send him "the best accounts and communicate this where you think proper."[28] Brown here suggested methods of promoting revival that would become critical in the 1730s and 1740s: ministerial correspondence and printers would publicize the revivals, making what formerly might have remained localized stirs into regional, continental, and transoceanic explosions of revivalist religion. Cotton responded to his friend's request by arranging for Brown's letter to be published along with Cotton's own sermon *A Holy Fear of God.* Brown led his congregation in a covenant renewal in March 21, 1728, substantially repeating the ceremony that church had held in 1680.

The leading pastors of New England responded to the earthquake with calls for repentance, arguing that the trembling earth was a divine providence that God might pair with a new outpouring of the Spirit. At the opening of the General Court in Boston three weeks after the initial earthquake, Thomas Foxcroft tried to show how God spoke through the earthquake. He thought "it is a hopeful Symptom of the Spirit's co-operating with Divine Providence, that we hear so many, in great fear & concern for their Souls, crying out . . . What must I do to be saved?" He believed that God brought both a punishing and a winsome message in the earthquake. The punishment was against the provoking sins of New England. He particularly noted people's waste and overindulgence: "the Superfluities of their voluptuous Tables," sexual immorality, lying, Sabbath-breaking, financial oppression, and extortion being their worst sins. These "expose the Land to shaking Dispensations." But the Lord also sent a message of hope in the earthquake. No one had died, and thus it was not too late to find salvation in Christ. Foxcroft called on the ministers to seize the moment of spiritual receptivity. "After Men have been so terrify'd by Earthquake and great Noise, what more likely to melt and charm their Souls, than the still small Voice of the preached Gospel?" He prayed that God would "pour out his Spirit upon us, that we may give ourselves wholly to these things" and see New England revive.[29]

Thomas Prince of the Old South Church thought that the earthquake was worth the damage caused, if accompanied by revival. After noting the path of the earthquake in the appendix to *Earthquakes the Works of God* (1727), he rejoiced that the terrible shaking had led to a "wonderful Reformation." People had abandoned their grievous sins and had "vastly thronged" the churches. Many hundreds had come forward for baptism, covenant renewal, or admission to communion. The terror of the earthquake had become the delight of revival: "What an happy Effusion of the HOLY SPIRIT!." Later, as the revival cooled, the ministers may have felt slightly embarrassed that the first major awakening in the evangelical era had been prompted by a natural disaster. Most other revivals led by early American evangelicals were not so obviously precipitated by external events. Prince gave little attention to the earthquake revival in the *Christian History,* citing only the Boston ministers' introduction to the third edition of Edwards's *Faithful Narrative,* where they noted that God in 1727 was "present to awaken many." But the fear of the earthquake did not last, and "there has since been great Reason to complain of our speedy Return to our former Sins." This became a familiar cycle for evangelicals: bursts of revival would invariably be followed by a waning of fervor and a waxing of worldliness. Nevertheless, they never gave up hope that a greater, or even the final, revival of religion might soon appear. According to Prince, the next New England awakening was "more remarkable" than the earthquake revival, for it came in a "Time of great Security; when there was no terrible Dispensation of Providence." This was the Northampton revival led by Solomon Stoddard's bookish grandson, Jonathan Edwards. Despite its limitations, the earthquake revival helped New England's growing evangelical cohort to think collectively about the potential for massive, publicized revival.[30]

Clearly, Puritanism helped shape early American evangelicalism. Despair over perceived immorality led to some Puritan ministers to believe that only revival could deliver the churches from their sins, and that the advent of great new awakenings might herald the last days. Among the first tactics used to revive religion in New England's churches was the covenant renewal, which emerged in the 1670s and 1680s. The covenant renewals raised the prospect of seeing large numbers of halfway members convert simultaneously, but the renewals differed from later evangelical revivals because they were deliberately planned to take place at particular times. As emphasis grew on the outpouring of the Holy Spirit for conversions, so also did a sense develop that revivals usually occurred unexpectedly. They were, indeed, "surprising."

"A SHOWER OF DIVINE BLESSING": JONATHAN EDWARDS AND *A FAITHFUL NARRATIVE*

"And then a concern about the great things of religion began, about the latter end of December and the beginning of January, to prevail abundantly in the town, till in a very little time it became universal throughout the town, among old and young, and from the highest to the lowest. All seemed to be seized with a deep concern about their eternal salvation."[1] So Jonathan Edwards described the beginnings of what became the most influential revival in the history of evangelicalism, the Northampton awakening of 1734–35. Edwards was not the most important preacher of his era. Surely that distinction rests with George Whitefield. But Edwards's deep roots in the Reformed and Puritan spiritual tradition, combined with his uncanny brilliance, made him the greatest American articulator of the evangelical view of God, man, and revival.

Edwards's background prepared him to become the evangelical giant that he was. His father Timothy was a formidable revivalist, and Jonathan converted under his ministry. Jonathan's "Personal Narrative" traced the beginnings of his own conversion to "a time of remarkable awakening in my father's congregation" when he was nine years old. He began to pray fervently, five times a day, and met with other boys in the congregation to pray. Edwards and his friends "built a booth in a swamp, in a very secret and retired place, for a place of prayer." Though one can see that this was no ordinary boy, Edwards never considered his piety a natural inclination, and soon the immature fervor dulled. As he bluntly put it, he "returned like a dog to his vomit, and went on in the ways of sin."[2]

Edwards saw conversion as the experience of waking out of spiritual deadness and embracing the joy of being chosen by God for salvation. Obviously, this was not something all could do, for not all were chosen. For the elect, rejecting the misery of self-glorification was a long process, punctuated by moments of

John Ferguson Weir, *Reverend Jonathan Edwards*
(*1703–1758*), B.A. *1720*, M.A. *1723*. Yale University Art
Gallery. Gift of Arthur Reed Kimball, B.A. 1877.

spiritual breakthrough. One of those breakthrough moments might be described
as "conversion," but not in the sense that it settled all questions of eternal destiny. Instead, if one takes Edwards's own recollection of his spiritual travels as a
model, the saint was likely to have several critical conversion moments, each followed by seasons of deadness. There was a single point in time, however, when
God regenerated a saint's soul. The believer might not be able definitively to
pinpoint that moment, but for the truly saved, the spiritual trajectory was always
upward, toward delighting in the ways of God and away from idolatry.[3] So it was
for Edwards.

Even as he attended Yale for his pastoral training, Edwards was not convinced
of his own salvation. The main problem blocking Edwards's conversion was his
inability to accept the doctrine of God's sovereignty, especially in salvation.
If God was entirely sovereign over the created order, then certainly that must
mean that he controlled the eternal destiny of humans, the pinnacle of creation.
To Edwards this was no mere theological proposition, for it was intimately in-

volved with the question of his own fate. His salvation came through an admission that he would no longer contest God's supreme authority. This was not an assent to dry doctrine, but an emotional repudiation of sin and embracing of God's ultimate power. The elect enjoyed God's sovereignty, and pursuing salvation meant seeking a "delightful conviction" of the omnipotence of God.[4]

When he was seventeen, and still an intense, unpopular student at Yale, Edwards had the first of his spiritual breakthroughs. He recalled reading I Timothy 1:17—"Now unto the King eternal, immortal, invisible, the only wise God, be honor and glory forever and ever, Amen"—upon which "there came into my soul . . . a sense of the glory of the Divine Being." Overwhelming feelings of joy concerning God's omnipotence stirred him. Soon he went to his father and told him about his experience, and Timothy encouraged his son to feed this new spiritual sensitivity. Jonathan then walked out to his father's pasture, and as he "looked up on the sky and clouds; there came into my mind, a sweet sense of the glorious majesty and grace of God, that I know not how to express. I seemed to see them both in a sweet conjunction: majesty and meekness joined together: it was a sweet and gentle, and holy majesty; and also a majestic meekness; an awful sweetness; a high and great, and holy gentleness." Edwards had stepped out of his father's house and into a wonderful new world of spiritual delights in God.[5] He earnestly devoted himself to bringing others into this new world.

At twenty-six, Edwards took over the Northampton pulpit, following his deceased mentor Solomon Stoddard. Stoddard, like Timothy Edwards, had helped Jonathan develop an expectation of revivals in the congregation. Northampton had gone through five or six significant harvests under Stoddard, the most recent only two years earlier as part of the earthquake revival of 1727, when "there were no small appearances of a divine work amongst some," and perhaps twenty people converted, but "nothing of any general awakening."[6] But when Edwards assumed the Northampton pastorate many congregants were neglecting their spiritual duties. Edwards was concerned about the state of the church's youth, despite being fairly young himself. He seemed unable to identify with their indulgences or frolics. Certainly Edwards was a kind of killjoy in an earthly sense, but in a spiritual sense nearly all he cared about was people's joy and happiness. Edwards believed that true delight was found in God. In 1729, many young people in his congregation did not seem concerned about their intense pastor's pleas for them to forsake carousing for the holy ways of the Lord.[7] These same youths would in several years become pliant in Edwards's pastoral hands, but only temporarily.

In the meantime, when theological liberalism was seeping into certain New England pulpits and Harvard classrooms, Edwards's brilliant orthodoxy made him a favorite among the emerging evangelical cohort in Boston. Edwards's debut as a leading Anglo-American evangelical came in July 1731 when he delivered a public lecture in Boston during the week of Harvard's commencement. His sermon, soon published as *God Glorified in the Work of Redemption*, offered little that was new, but it took a clear stance against the enticements of rationalist Arminianism. Arminians had won many fashionable Anglo-American pulpits, arguing that man had free will to choose salvation. Surely God would not predestine anyone to damnation, the rationalists said. We must have the moral ability to choose God, even if our sin does earn us damnation when we reject God. Without free will, human salvation and damnation seemed not only irrational, but immoral.

Edwards would have none of this "rationality," and *God Glorified in the Work of Redemption* made clear that redemption (and by implication, the renewal of hearts in revival) depended totally on God. The way of salvation in Christ, the faith to believe, and the power for holiness all came from God alone. Thus, God, not man, got all the credit for the great things he accomplished in the salvation of the elect. Moreover, God chose not to redeem some, and because all deserved damnation in the first place, God's free choice was not immoral. "When man is made holy, it is from mere and arbitrary grace; God may forever deny holiness to the fallen creature if he pleases, without any disparagement to any of his perfections."[8] For Edwards, the conversion of any soul depended on God's decision, and the pastor's duty was to remain available for God to use as a tool in the work of redemption.

As a pastor, Edwards's first great moment of usefulness came in 1734. His published account of the revival, *A Faithful Narrative of the Surprizing Work of God*, is our best record of what happened. Although the narrative is heavily colored by Edwards's perspective, it nevertheless gives a fairly systematic account of what seems to have been a stupendous stir. In 1733 Edwards began to notice that the congregation's young people had adopted a new "flexibleness" in their attitudes toward his preaching. He insisted that they give up their "mirth and company-keeping" on Sunday evenings, and he began to see in them a willingness to comply. At the time Edwards also organized neighborhood meetings (the settlements encompassed by the Northampton congregation were far-flung) of fathers concerning the governance of their children. Surprisingly, the fathers reported that their children needed no extra chastening to get them to remain faithful to the Sabbath. The youths themselves were convinced by Edwards's preaching.[9]

The first trickle of the revival torrent began in the village of Pascommuck, about three miles from Northampton but still part of Edwards's parish. There, several people "seemed to have been savingly wrought upon." The catalyst needed to make a serious breach in the people's complacency came in the form

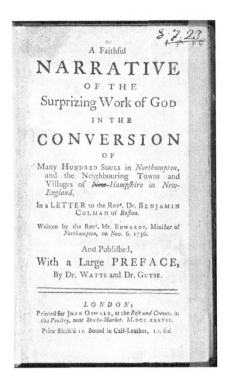

Jonathan Edwards, A *Faithful Narrative
of the Surprizing Work of God* (London,
1737). Beinecke Rare Book and
Manuscript Library, Yale University.

of untimely deaths. A young man "in the bloom of his youth" was stricken with "a pleurisy" and died in two days. Then a young married woman fell ill, but before dying she secured assurance of her salvation and passed away "very full of comfort." Edwards determined to strike while the iron was hot and began encouraging dismayed young people to organize into small group meetings for "social religion."[10]

In December 1734 the excitement broke loose with numbers of conversions that Edwards found surprising. One young woman, "one of the greatest company-keepers in the whole town," came to Edwards with the news that God had converted her. He thought that "what she gave an account of was a glorious work of God's infinite power and sovereign grace; and that God had given her a new heart, truly broken and sanctified." Edwards initially was not sure what effects this transformation might have on her friends, but it produced better results than he could have imagined: "God made it . . . the greatest occasion of awakening to others, of anything that ever came to pass in the town." She received visits from many of the young people inquiring about what happened to her, and many of these friends also were converted.[11]

What had begun as a movement of God among the young people became "universal," and everyone, young and old, seemed to talk only of religion and salvation. Many more began attending the private meetings in homes for discussing spiritual topics, and church assemblies became energized with fervent singing. The fleeting pleasures of carousing and joking were replaced by what Edwards called "spiritual mirth." Northampton also became a regional revival center, a necessary feature of most sizable revivals. Edwards reported that visitors from elsewhere in New England began coming to Northampton, either on business or out of curiosity. Some of these were scoffers, but when they saw the sincere devotion of the Northamptonites they were awakened, and some saved. These then went back to their hometowns and reported on what they saw, helping to create a regional awakening. We should remember, however, that the awakening emanating from Northampton was not unprecedented. It ran along many of the same revival tracks first cut in the Connecticut revival of 1720–22.

Edwards's account mentioned thirty-two communities besides Northampton that experienced awakening in 1734–35. About half were in Massachusetts and half in Connecticut, as the revival ran north and south along the course of the Connecticut River, in communities that depended on the river for trade and transportation. Churches at Windsor and East Windsor, including Timothy Edwards's church, which had experienced awakening in 1720–22, again felt the Spirit move in 1735.[12] "In every place," Edwards wrote, "God brought saving blessings with him, and his Word attended with his Spirit . . . returned not void." He thought that this revival was part of a larger movement of the Spirit:

> This shower of divine blessing has been yet more extensive. There was no small degree of it in some parts of the Jerseys; as I was informed when I was at New York (in a long journey I took at that time of the year for my health) by some people of the Jerseys, whom I saw: especially the Rev. Mr. William Tennent, a minister who seemed to have such things much at heart, told me of a very great awakening of many in a place called The Mountains, under the ministry of one Mr. Cross; and of a very considerable revival of religion in another place under the ministry of his brother, the Rev. Mr. Gilbert Tennent; and also at another place, under the ministry of a very pious young gentleman, a Dutch minister whose name I remember was Freelinghousa.[13]

Edwards constructed the revival as an intercolonial event. The Tennent family and Theodorus Frelinghuysen were preaching the new birth in New Jersey even as the revival was developing in Northampton.

The results in Northampton itself were stunning enough. Edwards was always cautious about definitively pronouncing anyone "saved," but he guessed that about three hundred people had been converted in six months. This meant that the church had grown to 620 communicant members, almost all the adults in Northampton. Truly this awakening had become "universal," as Edwards put it, for it touched all ages of men and women. Edwards noted that Stoddard's revivals had often affected disproportionate numbers of young women, but now the numbers of men and women, young and old, were remarkably even. The revival had jumped racial boundaries, too, as Edwards noted that "several Negroes . . . appear to have been truly born again."[14]

The Northampton revival featured miraculous and ecstatic manifestations of the Holy Spirit that some critics would use to denounce the revival as rank enthusiasm. As historian Leigh Eric Schmidt has noted, "the bodily exercises of early American Protestants . . . have been more often the object of snickers than serious analysis." Yet emotional ecstasies, sometimes along with the more mysterious "signs and wonders" such as visions and healings, accompanied most of the major revivals of the eighteenth century. Edwards always tried to maintain balance regarding emotional expressions because he firmly endorsed the role of the affections in revival, but he also knew that too much spiritual passion could lead to charges of excess. He mentioned that worship services had become much more emotional. Edwards's Anglican opponent Timothy Cutler of Boston also intimated that the fervor of Edwards's revival had been marked by outbreaks of laughter during the services: "they feel an inward joy, and it first shows itself in laughing at meeting." Edwards might have been referring to this behavior when in *Distinguishing Marks* (1741) he recalled the Northamptonites of 1735 forgetting "their distance from God, and were ready . . . to talk with too much of an air of lightness, and something of laughter . . . those who laughed before, weep now."[15]

There had also been visions, or what Edwards called "impressions . . . on persons' imaginations." Again, critics pointed to these as evidences that the revivals had gone wild, but Edwards cautiously defended the visionaries. They had not seen their visions "with their bodily eyes," he wrote, but had only apprehended dramatic pictures in their minds. For example, when some fell into fear of hell, they pictured a great fiery furnace. Others, deeply touched by the sacrificial love of Christ, "have at the same time a lively idea of Christ hanging upon the cross, and of his blood running from his wounds." Some of the visionaries had mystical experiences that Edwards confessed he did not understand. "I have been at a loss about them," he wrote. But even these Edwards was not ready to dismiss because they seemed accompanied by "a great sense of the spiritual excellency of divine things." This was always Edwards's test for ecstatic expressions in worship: did they lead the worshipper to a greater appreciation of God's glory? Or did they encourage self-glorification? If the former, then the usually staid Edwards had to agree that the expressions were likely incidental operations of the Holy Spirit in persons receptive to them because of their particular mental constitution. He continued, however, to warn the visionaries not to mistake the vain and imaginary for the truly spiritual.[16]

Timothy Cutler used the visions as clear evidence of the revival's illegitimacy, writing to a colleague in England that at the same time as Edwards's Northampton revival, "there was a number of Visionaries at Cambridge, and in the College there." The ringleader of the Cambridge visionaries was one M. Louis Hector Piot de l'Angloiserie, who seems to have been a Huguenot employed by Harvard to teach French. Cutler associated him with all manner of excesses and heresies and noted that he was promoting apocalypticism in Cambridge. Without citing any specifics, Cutler wrote that l'Angloiserie's "Perswasion that the World would soon come to an end got up to Northampton-parts, and wrought much on the People's Spirits." Cutler also thought that the evangelical pastors supporting Edwards's narrative were "men of the lowest Form in Learning and Judgement, contracted in their Thoughts, and very apt to fall in with any thing whimsical and visionary." Edwards had to work hard to disavow enthusiastic excesses, while at the same time not endorsing a naturalistic approach to revival.[17]

Edwards also briefly noted that because "Satan . . . seemed to be unusually restrained," a remarkable season of healing accompanied the revival. "Persons that had been involved in melancholy, seemed to be as it were waked up out of it." Edwards saw melancholy, or depression, as both a disease and a Satanic affliction. He and his wife Sarah both seem to have been at least moderately depressive, and he knew that melancholy was a serious problem for some in his flock. Now God had taken it away, but this was not the only sign of healing in the revival. In fact, Edwards thought "it was the most remarkable time of health, that ever I knew since I have been in the town." Prayer requests for sick relatives had previously been common, but during the revival these bids ceased to come in for "many Sabbaths together."[18] Edwards did not present these evidences as clear proof of the authenticity of the awakening, but neither did he shy away from mentioning them.

Sickness returned to Northampton, though, as a sign that the revival was over. A darker side of the visions and ecstasies began to take over. One man was overcome with "violent temptations to cut his own throat" and tried to do so but did not kill himself. The despondent man remained "overwhelmed with melancholy" for a long time, though he eventually overcame his depression through divine deliverance. Edwards's uncle Joseph Hawley, however, was not rescued from similar afflictions, and on June 1, 1735, he slit his throat and died. Edwards, along with all Northampton, was stunned by the suicide of this popular and devout merchant, who had in recent months been declining into a debilitating depressive state, exacerbated by fears that he would be damned to hell. Others confessed to Edwards that Satan had approached them too with the temptations to end their lives, hearing the devil saying "Cut your own throat, now is good opportunity: *now*, NOW!" Similar torments affected people across the Connecticut River valley. Although sparks of revival continued to appear occasionally, by mid-1735 there was no doubt that the fire was cooling. "In the main there was a gradual decline of that general, engaged, lively spirit in religion, which had been before."[19]

The revival in Northampton had waned, but the effects of the awakening would continue to bear fruit for centuries through the mediation of print. Edwards's *Faithful Narrative* would become the first, and most important, text of the new genre of revival narratives. It took a circuitous path into print. Benjamin Colman, the leading evangelical pastor in Boston during the 1730s and 1740s, was the key broker for the narrative in the Anglo-American evangelical community. Actually, Edwards's was not the first narrative of the Connecticut River valley awakening that Colman received. William Williams, pastor at Hatfield, Massachusetts, just up the river from Northampton, had sent him a report on the revival. Colman had excerpts from Williams's report published in the *New England Weekly Journal* in May 1735, but he asked Edwards to send him an account as well. Edwards delivered an eight-page letter about the revival at the end of May, which Colman forwarded to other Boston evangelicals, as well as to the minister John Guyse and the celebrated hymn-writer Isaac Watts, both prominent evangelicals in London. With this step, Edwards became something of a religious celebrity in Britain. Watts and Guyse were elated to hear of the revival and asked for more details.[20]

Edwards wrote a longer account for Colman (much too long, it turned out), and Colman had an abridged version of it published in 1736. Colman sent this narrative on to Watts and Guyse. They wrote back, requesting the whole narrative, with the intention of publishing it in London. In early 1737, Watts put the Northampton revival in the context of his eschatological expectations in a letter to Colman: "These [revivals] are certainly little specimens of what Christ and his grace can do when he shall begin to revive his own work and to spread his Kingdom thro the earth; and if he begins in America, I adore his good pleasure and rejoice, but wait for the blessing in European countrys." Revival was not all that he expected, however, believing that "the same power can subdue all the opposition that is made by earth and hell, and can change heathens and papists as well as formal Protestants into lively Christians." Watts hoped, then, that the account of the revival might help promote these inevitable events of the last days.[21]

A full, stand-alone edition of A *Faithful Narrative* finally appeared in 1737 in London. In an effusive preface, Watts and Guyse wrote, "never did we hear or read, since the first ages of Christianity, any event of this kind so surprising as the present narrative." They thought that readers should take from the narrative a lesson on the power of God, both for the conversion of sinners and for the expected eschatological revival. "We are taught by this happy event how easy it will be for our blessed Lord to make a full accomplishment of all his predictions concerning his kingdom, and to spread his dominion from sea to sea, through all the nations of the earth." Northampton's experiences would one day cover the globe: "Salvation shall spread through all the tribes and ranks of mankind, . . . and his faithful and obedient subjects shall become as numerous as the spires of grass in a meadow newly mown." The Northampton narrative was interesting in and of itself, but Watts and Guyse hoped it would begin the last great revival for Britain, as they prayed that likewise a "plentiful effusion of the blessed Spirit also descend on the British Isles and all their American plantations, to renew the face of religion there!"[22] The print medium gave Watts and Guyse a new means of spreading revival, as the narrative provided a model for what other communities might expect to experience. The text became both a commodity in the Atlantic world's markets and a vehicle for spreading the eschatological revival. The narrative no doubt contributed to a growing revival movement in Britain, as it came out in a second London edition in 1738. The newly converted John Wesley read A *Faithful Narrative* in late 1738, and it made a deep impression on him concerning the kinds of revivals that he might generate through his own ministry. The text was published in its first complete Boston edition in 1738, as evangelical leaders there continued to contemplate what they might do to promote a massive revival.

A *Faithful Narrative* heavily colored the telling, if not the actual experience, of the coming revivals in New England, the Middle Colonies, and Scotland. Many pastors cited the news of the Northampton revival as inspiration for their own. At Durham, New Hampshire, pastor Nicholas Gilman went so far as to read the *Narrative* publicly to steer his church's revival in November and December 1741.[23] Most of the twenty-five revival narratives printed in North America from 1741 to 1745 (mostly printed in the new evangelical magazine the *Christian History*) followed Edwards's model fairly closely. Prominent features in these narratives, like Edwards's, included a spiritual history and assessment of the town in question before the revival, a description of the beginnings and effects of the revival, detailed accounts of individual converts' experiences, and a report on the continuing/declining state of the revival. Pastors William McCulloch and James Robe in Scotland borrowed heavily from Edwards's framework to publicize the extraordinary revivals at Kilsyth and Cambuslang in 1742. John Wesley made great use of *A Faithful Narrative*, despite his reservations about Edwards's Calvinism. Expanding its influence to the Continent, *A Faithful Narrative* was published in German in 1738 and Dutch in 1740.[24]

Samuel Buell, one of the key leaders of the 1762–65 revival in New England and the Middle Colonies, would attempt to take up Edwards's mantle with his 1766 *A Faithful Narrative of the Remarkable Revival of Religion, in the Congregation of East-Hampton, on Long-Island.* Edwards's *A Faithful Narrative* would, if anything, become more popular among nineteenth-century American evangelicals. The New England and American Tract societies saw fit to print an excerpt from Edwards's *A Faithful Narrative*, recounting Abigail Hutchinson's conversion and saintly death; that tract went through eight editions beginning in 1816. Edwards's text has remained popular among evangelicals globally, through the present, as a model for what might be expected to happen in revival. For instance, a Korean translation of *A Faithful Narrative* was published in 1997, serving the thriving evangelical community in South Korea. Guy Chevreau's *Catch the Fire* (1995) used Edwards's revival narrative to help justify the outbreak of so-called holy laughter at the Toronto (Canada) Airport Fellowship, a key center of global charismatic renewal in the 1990s.[25] Though it followed in the train of earlier New England awakenings, Northampton's 1734–35 awakening has become *the* model revival of evangelicalism. Its publicity dramatically heightened expectations in Britain and America for new awakenings, and it provided a framework for local pastors to use to promote revival in their own congregations.

"Soul-Satisfying Sealings of God's Everlasting Love": Continental Pietism, Scots-Irish Presbyterianism, and Early Evangelicalism

In early 1720 a young Reformed minister disembarked from the *King George* in New York City and immediately began causing trouble in the Dutch Reformed churches of the Middle Colonies. He was Theodorus Jacobus Frelinghuysen, called to minister in the Raritan Valley of New Jersey. Frelinghuysen was not impressed with the established Reformed clergy of New York, just as he had not been with the Reformed clergy of Holland. In fact, he suspected that many pastors on both sides of the Atlantic remained unconverted, despite their cultivated religiosity. When Dominie Gualtherus DuBois invited Frelinghuysen to his home, Frelinghuysen commented unfavorably on the pastor's large wall mirror, saying that even "by the most far-stretched necessity" it could never be an appropriate indulgence for a minister of the gospel. The ascetic Frelinghuysen was willing to make enemies when he sensed hypocrisy. Moreover, he was prepared to assess whether anyone, even fellow pastors, had truly experienced the converting work of the Holy Spirit. In the 1720s and 1730s, the Middle Colonies in North America—New Jersey, Pennsylvania, and New York, in particular—began to see more and more clergy like Frelinghuysen arrive from the Continent and cultivate a new affective Christianity. The Pietist "religion of the heart" and New England's developing expectation of revival became two of the three most important influences on early evangelicalism.[1]

Forms of European Continental Pietism flourished in the North American colonies during the eighteenth century, as its spiritual intensity combined with the relative freedom of many colonies that allowed Pietist churches proliferate. The two main branches of European Pietism, Reformed and Lutheran, were among the many religions of the heart generated by the Protestant Reformation. Holland had been an important seedbed for both English Puritanism and Reformed Pietism, with cross-fertilizing performed by English pastors like William Ames and Dutch clerics like Willem Teellinck, both of whom worked in England and Holland in the early seventeenth century. They helped develop the ideal of the individual's Christian life as fervently devoted to God and to self-sacrificial ministry. Faith did not equal assent to propositions about God; it was an affective commitment of one's whole being to God. True faith, as opposed to formal religiosity, was only given by God as a miraculous gift to the sinner. In these emphases, early Reformed Pietism and Puritanism shared much in common. In the mid-seventeenth century, however, New England Puritanism and Reformed Pietism began to take somewhat different, if still friendly, paths. Roughly speaking, Reformed Pietism became more concerned with heart religion and Christian practice, whereas Puritanism became more focused on doctrinal and ecclesiastical purity. In New England, Puritans became heavily invested in creating a sustainable church-state order that would preserve the faithfulness of succeeding generations and the favorable political systems of Massachusetts and Connecticut. The Pietist strain remained within Puritanism, however, and such figures as Richard Baxter and Cotton Mather cultivated personal and intellectual connections between English Puritanism and Continental Pietism.[2]

The fountainhead for Lutheran Pietism was Philipp Jakob Spener's *Pia Desideria* (1675). Spener was a German Lutheran pastor who became deeply concerned about the lack of sincere devotion in the church. He read widely in devotional sources and was especially influenced by the work of the Lutheran Johann Arndt, who had written in the early seventeenth century about the necessity of heart renewal in true Christianity. Spener was also familiar with Puritan devotional works, such as Lewis Bayly's *Practice of Piety.* During a stint in Geneva in 1656, Spener met the controversial Jean de Labadie, a radical seventeenth-century cleric who was raised a Catholic and exposed to the Augustinian reform movement of Jansenism before eventually converting to Protestantism. Labadie originally attempted to purify the Reformed churches, but he eventually decided that those churches were so corrupt that true believers should separate from them. In Geneva, Spener became an avid reader and promoter of Labadie's works on transformation in the churches. Out of this rich mix of Reformed and Lutheran sources, Spener helped develop two of the most influential ideas that would soon become central to evangelicalism.[3]

The first of these ideas was that devotional meetings should be used to encourage spiritual development outside of normal church meetings. Labadie had already begun holding these sorts of gatherings, but under Spener the small-group meetings expanded significantly. In 1670, at Frankfurt am Main, Spener inaugurated the *collegia pietatis* (gatherings for piety). During these, Spener would open with prayer, then read and speak on a passage from a devotional book, and finally lead group discussions. He tried to keep the conversations focused on edifying, devotional topics, not on theological controversies. As the group expanded, Spener increased lay participation, and soon the same type of assemblies began to appear in neighboring towns. Spener had successfully launched a method of small-group ministry that would become critical to the future of evangelicalism and in particular would shape John Wesley's Methodist movement.[4]

Related to the idea of the devotional group was Spener's advocacy of church transformation through the renewal of individual hearts. Pastors had allowed their congregations to grow spiritually dull, and they should train their flocks in authentic spiritual development, Spener argued. The key to this new ministry would be the *collegia pietatis*. Spiritually languishing people needed a pastoral touch, and Spener suspected that the clergy's failure to lead them to renew their hearts revealed that the clergy themselves might not comprehend true faith. He thought that a new emphasis on the practice of piety for all believers would reform the Lutheran church, but the results would not end there. Spener suspected that the corruption of the church delayed the coming of the millennium. If the church revitalized, it would be able to accomplish two things that seemed necessary before the return of Christ: the conversion of the Jews to Christianity, and the destruction of the Roman Catholic Church. A church full of passionate individual converts would certainly be better prepared to take on both of those tasks. "It is incumbent on all of us," he wrote, "on the one hand, to convert the Jews and weaken the spiritual power of the papacy and, on the other hand, to reform our church." Spener's vision for change was remarkably ambitious: the renewal of individual hearts would, collectively, lead to a revived Protestant church, which in turn could help inaugurate the end of days.[5]

Spener not only influenced German Pietism, but he also impressed a number of Anglo-American clerics as an exemplary leader of a new German Reformation. Increase Mather wrote in 1708 that a "New Reformation has obtained a footing in divers Provinces in Germany. . . . The chief instrument in Promoting this work was, that Excellently Learned, and Holy Man Dr. Spener." Spener had recently died (1705), and Mather thought that "next to him, Dr. Frank has been an Eminent Instrument." He was referring to August Hermann Francke, professor of theology at the University of Halle, the Lutheran Pietist who most directly influenced the North American churches, especially in the Middle Colonies. Partly through Spener's influence, Francke experienced a dramatic conversion in 1687, which would color his later emphases on the new birth and fervent service to God. He made Halle into the key center of Continental Pietism, with all manner of programs devoted to spreading the Pietist gospel, including publishing, charitable works, an orphanage, medical training, and pharmaceutical manufacturing and sales.[6]

Francke heavily influenced a number of German and Dutch pastors, many of whom would eventually make their way to North America. Francke's writings helped shape the post-Puritan English dissenting movement, as well, influencing such leaders as Philip Doddridge and Isaac Watts. His example would also guide the early development of English Methodism. The Mathers corresponded with Francke and his Halle associates for many years, and Cotton Mather wrote in 1715 that "Dr. Franckius is a Person truly Wonderful for his vast Erudition; but much more so for his most shining Piety . . . and most of all so, for the Astonishing Blessing of God upon his Undertakings to advance His Kingdom in the World." Mather considered the missionary, charitable, and evangelistic work of Halle to be among the brightest signs of revival around the globe in the early 1700s. Thomas Prince's *Christian History* would later excerpt Francke's *Pietas Hallensis* (London, 1705), wedged between reports of new revivals in Pennsylvania and New Jersey.[7]

Theodorus Frelinghuysen was a Pietist of a more rigidly Calvinist strain than the Franckians, though it seems certain that he was familiar with the Lutheran Halle school's teachings. He was also shaped by the thought of the Utrecht theologian Gysbertus Voetius. Voetius was a protégé of Willem Teellinck, both of whom helped Dutch Pietism develop along parallel tracks with English Puritanism in the seventeenth century. Voetius's Pietism was scholarly but also borrowed from medieval and Puritan devotional sources to forge a learned religion of the heart. Voetius's writings had been used at Harvard in the seventeenth century. Frelinghuysen was born in 1692, the son of a Reformed pastor in Westphalia, and in 1711 he entered the University of Lingen, which was then controlled by disciples of Voetius. At Lingen, Frelinghuysen received rigorous instruction not only in the biblical languages and doctrine, but also in fervent preaching of heart religion. He studied Greek, Hebrew, Aramaic, Syriac, and Rabbinic Hebrew. Frelinghuysen also learned to speak Dutch fluently and began preaching in that language, which would become central to his North American ministry.[8] Although Frelinghuysen would preach heart religion, one should hardly think of him as anti-intellectual.

After taking his first pastoral position in Germany, Frelinghuysen received an offer from the Dutch Reformed Church to take a position in "Rarethans," which he apparently assumed was somewhere in Flanders or Brabant. He accepted the offer, and much to his surprise he found that the church meant to send him across the Atlantic to New Jersey. Frelinghuysen cheerfully received the news as providential and accepted the pastorate, along with ordination from the Classis of Amsterdam. In September 1719 Frelinghuysen boarded the *King George* and set out for North America.[9]

Frelinghuysen's call was to New Brunswick, on the central New Jersey frontier in the Raritan River valley. In 1720, New Brunswick stood on the outer limits of European settlement in North America. Frelinghuysen faced a relatively un-churched people there, but he saw in his new setting an opportunity to forgo the usual ministerial niceties in favor of rigorous Pietist preaching.[10] Frelinghuy-sen, as shown in the mirror incident with Dominie DuBois, did not get off to a good start with the New York authorities, and more conflicts ensued in the Rari-tan Valley. But it would be a mistake to read his publicly tumultuous ministry as unsuccessful. Though the numbers are difficult to trace, it seems that many hundreds of people were converted and admitted to full membership under his ministry, and he planted a number of new churches. He also offended a great number of people along the way, primarily because he did not hesitate to judge the spiritual state of individual congregants, regardless of their social or religious position. Thus, the 1720s and 1730s saw a number of public complaints against Frelinghuysen, as well as attempts by the authorities in New York City to rein him in. Frelinghuysen suffered through these sometimes deserved attacks, and his labors contributed a great deal to the tone and successes of the 1740s awaken-ings.

The growing resentment against Frelinghuysen took full bloom with the 1725 publication of the *Klagte* (the "complaint") by Dominie Henricus Boel and his brother Tobias. In it, the Boels painted Frelinghuysen as a troublemaking ex-tremist who delighted in causing schism. "We welcomed him with joy and love," they wrote, "hoping that his services would be to our edification. But alas! To our sorrow, we soon found . . . that the results were otherwise." They recalled Frelinghuysen's "bitter denunciations" against the congregations "to the effect that we were, all of us, unconverted; and we were discouraged from approach-ing the Lord's Table." Frelinghuysen reportedly insisted that ministers should be able to judge whether a congregant was converted or not. If a minister could not do this, then perhaps the minister himself was not converted.[11]

The appearance of the *Klagte*, predictably, generated a pamphlet war among Frelinghuysen's supporters and critics, and the feuding continued, basically over the same issues, for the next thirteen years. The previously offended Dominie DuBois finally arranged a settlement between the two sides, just in time for the arrival of English itinerant George Whitefield. In the meantime, perhaps partly from the stress of the controversies, Frelinghuysen suffered the first of several apparent psychological breakdowns, which incapacitated him for some time in the late 1720s and early 1730s.[12]

Undeterred by his opponents or by his psychological troubles, Frelinghuysen continued to cultivate Pietism in the Raritan Valley once he recovered from what he called his "severe affliction." He issued a series of sermons in 1733 (published in Amsterdam in 1736) that aspired to achieve the awakening power of Reformation-era sermons. Then, preachers, who were often "uneducated men" who did not know "how to gratify their hearers with far-fetched or inflated words of human wisdom, sought to reach the heart by speaking the words of God in demonstration of the Spirit and with power."[13] He tried to preach awakening by warning the unconverted of the impending judgment of God.

Such preaching clearly helped pave the way for the great Middle Colonies revivalists of the 1740s. Frelinghuysen's influence was most obvious in the case of Gilbert Tennent. Tennent was the oldest son of the Ulster Scottish Presbyterian pastor William Tennent, who moved his family to North America in 1718. After attending Yale, Gilbert was asked to pastor a newly organized Presbyterian church in New Brunswick. This was at the center of Frelinghuysen's parish, and ironically, Frelinghuysen originally resisted Tennent and the new church. Once the church was established, however, the two began a deep and lasting friendship, bound by a common commitment to revivals of piety.[14]

Tennent apparently experienced his own conversion in 1723, but when he arrived in New Brunswick, he was not yet ready to preach the new birth. By his own testimony, he learned this emphasis from Frelinghuysen. In New Brunswick, Tennent recalled, "I had the Pleasure of seeing much of the Fruits of his Ministry." Soon after his arrival, Frelinghuysen initiated contact with Tennent in a "kind Letter" that pressed on him "the Necessity of dividing the Word aright, and . . . excited me to greater Earnestness in ministerial Labours." In comparison to Frelinghuysen, Tennent felt himself inadequate for the ministry, and after a half a year no one had been converted under his preaching. Tennent soon fell extremely sick, and as a result he "had affecting Views of Eternity." This visionary experience convinced Tennent that the conversion of souls should become the one and only point of his ministry. In this work Tennent could find no more enthusiastic partner than Frelinghuysen.[15]

Frelinghuysen and Tennent began working together after Tennent's sickness, sharing pastoral duties that flouted the ethnic barriers of Dutch Calvinism and Scots-Irish Presbyterianism. Frelinghuysen's Dutch opponents complained to the Classis of Amsterdam about the "collusion" between the two in "conjoint services." During these, the two alternated between Dutch and English, and, according to an observer, "Frelinghuysen preaches and Tennent prays and baptizes; and then together they administer the Holy Supper." Critics thought that integrating an "English Dissenter" into Dutch services was a travesty: "we must . . . be careful to keep things in the Dutch way," they reminded the Classis.[16] Here one sees a defining characteristic of early evangelicalism: the tendency to take ethnic and racial boundaries lightly. Just *how* lightly to take them was an easier matter between English, Scots-Irish, German, and Dutch than it would be between European and African, or European and Native American. The religion of the heart tended, however, to bring people together across all manner of boundaries.

After his near-death experience and encounter with Frelinghuysen, Gilbert Tennent began ministering with greater effectiveness, and he reported to the *Christian History* in 1744:

> Frequently at Sacramental Seasons in New-Brunswick, there have been signal Displays of the divine Power and Presence: divers have been convinced of Sin by the Sermons then preached, some converted, and many much affected with the Love of GOD in JESUS CHRIST. O the sweet Meltings that I have often seen on such Occasions among many! New-Brunswick did then look like a Field the LORD had blessed: It was like a little Jerusalem, to which the scattered Tribes with eager haste repaired at Sacramental Solemnities; and there they fed on the Fatness of God's House, and drunk of the River of his Pleasures.[17]

The combined influence of Continental Pietism and Scots-Irish Presbyterianism were making Tennent one of the awakenings' most compelling revivalists.

Scots-Irish Presbyterianism, as represented by Tennent and his father, was the third of the chief tributaries and joined with New England Puritanism and Continental Pietism in forming the headwaters of American evangelicalism. Scots-Irish Presbyterian piety heavily shaped evangelicalism in Pennsylvania, New Jersey, and the southern backcountry. Hundreds of thousands of immigrants came to North America from Scotland and Ulster in the century before the American Revolution, and many of them embraced a style of Presbyterianism that focused on heart religion. Many came prepared to re-create the "holy fairs" of Scotland and Ulster, regional communion festivals that for a century had stirred the souls of Scots-Irish penitents. Many of these immigrants, like their Dutch and German counterparts, tried to replicate traditional practices of piety in their new lands, using the "old" ways to create a new Scots-Irish Presbyterian identity as an American denomination. Some Scots-Irish evangelicals, more controversially, diluted their ethnic commitments by making common cause with non-Scots-

Irish revivalists, such as Frelinghuysen or Whitefield. Scots-Irish Presbyterians emerged in the mid-eighteenth century with a fractious but distinct identity, one not swallowed up in the American sea of faith. The communion season and periodic revivals were fixed features of Scots-Irish Presbyterian piety that would influence the course of the awakenings in North America, as well as continuing revivals in north Britain.[18]

Religious and economic difficulties led a number of Ulster Scots to immigrate to North America beginning in the 1710s. Hundreds of thousands of them poured through the Delaware River ports of New Castle, Delaware, and Philadelphia. Many of these new immigrants carried with them a fervent Presbyterian piety and an expectation of revivals. Though Scots came in considerable numbers too, the Ulster Scots dominated the Presbyterian church membership rolls of the Middle Colonies. As Samuel Blair wrote in 1744, "All our congregations in Pennsylvania except two or three chiefly are made up of people from Ireland."[19]

The Tennents arrived amidst this flood of Ulster immigrants. They would become the single most influential family in creating Middle Colonies revivalism. William Tennent Sr. was born in Ireland and educated at the University of Edinburgh.[20] Tennent was ordained as an Anglican priest in 1704, perhaps for political expediency, but he never felt comfortable as an Anglican. He never worked in a parish church, but only as a chaplain for an Irish nobleman. Tennent's wife, Katherine, was the daughter of Gilbert Kennedy, an important Ulster Presbyterian.

In 1718 the Tennents left Ireland for Pennsylvania, and upon arrival William promptly approached Philadelphia's Presbyterian Synod for membership. When the skeptical synod asked his reasons for renouncing the Anglican communion, he responded by criticizing the Anglicans' church polity and their leanings toward Arminianism. William was accepted into the synod, but finding a permanent pastorate proved difficult. He became friendly with a number of Yale-trained pastors, and in 1725 there were rumors that he might become the rector at Yale. This arrangement never worked out, however, and the Tennents moved to Bucks County, Pennsylvania, and were settled at Neshaminy in 1726. Soon after his arrival Tennent began training candidates for the ministry at the celebrated "Log College" seminary, a forerunner of the College of New Jersey (later Princeton University). Tennent trained nineteen young men at the seminary, and all of them except one became Presbyterian revivalists.[21]

Many Scots-Irish and English Presbyterians in the Middle Colonies established these sorts of seminaries. The academies, sometimes comprising little more than a learned pastor meeting with a small group of young men, cultivated a domestic base for recruiting evangelical Presbyterian pastors. Among the

most significant schools besides Tennent's were those of Log College graduates
Samuel Blair, at Fagg's Manor, Pennsylvania (founded 1739), and Samuel Finley, at West Nottingham, Maryland (1744). The New England-born Jonathan
Dickinson likewise trained young men at his Elizabethtown, New Jersey, home
for years. In 1746, to renew the languishing Log College, Dickinson, along with
Aaron Burr, Ebenezer Pemberton, Gilbert and William Tennent Jr. founded the
College of New Jersey. Dickinson became the first president, and it seems likely
that many of the first students came from Dickinson's academy, especially since
the college first met in Elizabethtown. Dickinson died soon after the college's
founding, and the presidency transferred to Aaron Burr of Newark, who likewise
had run an academy for several years. Presbyterian revivalist and future Princeton president Samuel Davies had trained at Blair's Fagg's Manor academy, demonstrating the interconnectedness of the academies inspired by Tennent's Log
College and the early leaders of Princeton.[22]

Gilbert Tennent's work proceeded with some success in New Brunswick,
though Tennent could not remember any "great Ingathering of Souls at any one
time." His early ministry seemed more like a slow burn, resulting in a "considerable Number" of conversions during his tenure there. Once, around 1728, he
did lead a large revival on Staten Island. He recalled that as he preached there
on Amos 6:1 ("Woe to them that are at ease in Zion"), "the SPIRIT of GOD was
suddenly poured down upon the Assembly." He thought the audience had previously been complacent, but now several began to fall on their knees in the
church, praying for mercy. Some cried out "both under the Impressions of Terror and Love," depending on their stage of conversion.[23]

Gilbert's brothers also shared in the growing revival movement in New Jersey. John Tennent seemed destined to become a great revivalist until his early
death in 1732, and contributed to an awakening at Freehold, New Jersey, during
a brief tenure there. Gilbert used John's conversion narrative as a model. In 1735,
Gilbert described John's conviction of sin as "the most violent in Degree, of any
that ever I saw." Gilbert remembered John crying out, "O my poor soul! O my
bloody lost soul! What shall I do? Have Mercy upon me, O God, for Christ's
sake!" John had committed no grievous sins; Gilbert thought that the worst of-
fense John had ever committed was rash anger. John knew that even this was
enough to earn him eternal damnation, however, and "his Passionateness cost
him many a deep Sob, heavy Groan and salt Tear." Gilbert shepherded him
through his torments, telling him that his deep conviction was warranted, but
that God offered him mercy, too.[24]

The moment of regeneration came for John after a night of desperate sickness, when observers thought that he might have died. Instead, when morning

came Gilbert noticed a "great Alteration in his Countenance," and John told him that after all his begging for mercy, "Christ has told me he would give me a Crumb." This indicated enough faith for salvation, and John was so excited that he walked to see his brother William Jr. who was also terribly sick nearby. When he reached his brother's room, he cried, "O Brother! The Lord has looked in Pity upon my Soul, let the Heavens, Earth and Sea, and all that in them is, praise God!" Gilbert noted that John soon fell ill again, resulting in some more doubts, but there was no turning back for John after his conversion experience. He was licensed by the presbytery of Philadelphia in 1729, after which he began to preach in Freehold.[25]

At Freehold, the evangelistic style John Tennent inherited from his father and older brother began to bear fruit immediately. William Tennent Jr. remembered that the Freehold church "crouded with People of all Ranks and Orders" to hear John's passionate preaching. He recalled congregants "sobbing as if their Hearts would break, but without any public Out-cry; and some have been carry'd out of the Assembly (being overcome) as if they had been dead."[26] William Jr. seems to have approved of emotional expressions during public services, but not of crying out, showing the complex responses to fervent emotions displayed in revival meetings. Some pastors considered excessive any outburst that disrupted their preaching.

When John died in 1732, William Jr. was prepared to assume his duties, for he had been substitute preaching at Freehold regularly in John's last months. Like Gilbert and John, William Jr. considered a near-death experience as key to his development as a believer. It was not unusual for prominent early evangelicals to look back to a desperate illness as the starting point of their ministerial calling. William Jr. studied under his father, as well as under his older brother Gilbert, preparing for ordination. But around 1728 he fell dangerously ill, and slipped into a coma. The family thought he was dead and began inviting friends and family to his funeral. For days the only person who thought he remained alive was the family doctor. Just before William Jr. was to be buried, he awoke with a start, groaned loudly, and then sunk back into the coma. "This put an end to all thoughts of burying him," his biographer wrote. He eventually revived and began recovering, although he had a temporary bout of amnesia. To some observers, it seemed that William Jr. had been raised from the dead, and this would have created enough interest by itself had he not also claimed that during his unconsciousness he was transported to heaven.[27]

In his memoir of the life of William Jr., his friend Elias Boudinot recorded this mystical experience. Tennent had told him that when he lost physical consciousness, he entered "another state of existence, under the direction of a superior being." This angelic person instructed him to follow, and Tennent eventually "beheld at a distance an ineffable glory. . . . I saw an innumerable host of happy beings, surrounding the inexpressible glory . . . but I did not see any bodily shape or representation in the glorious appearance." His joy and rapture was indescribable, and William Jr. asked his guide's permission to "join the happy throng." The guide told him that he must "return to the earth" instead, and at that moment he woke to find the doctor and Gilbert arguing about whether he should be buried or not.[28] This was not the last of William Jr.'s visions.

William Jr. took over at Freehold after John's death and carried on the revival movement there. Like Gilbert at New Brunswick, conversions under his pastorate appear to have come slowly but steadily, punctuated by some significant outbreaks of awakening. Visions were apparently common in his ministry, and at Freehold his mystical experiences heightened religious concern or conversions. In one episode, William Jr. retired to the woods for contemplation one Sunday afternoon, before the evening sermon. While reflecting on Christ's death, the "subject suddenly opened on his mind with such a flood of light, that his views of glory, and the infinite majesty of Jehovah, were so inexpressibly great as entirely to overwhelm him, and he fell, almost lifeless, to the ground." As he lay motionless for a long time, the elders came to find him, and escorted the weakened pastor back to the church. Once he regained his ability to speak, he "began the most affecting and pathetic address that the congregation had ever received from him."[29]

Tennent's nephew William M. Tennent reported that during Whitefield's revivals, William Jr. had a similar experience with more impressive results. This time, he was wracked with skeptical thoughts about the authority of Scripture. Severely agitated, he nevertheless attempted to perform his next service, and when the time came for him to pray, all he could utter was *"Lord have mercy upon me!"* With this, his doubts flew away, "and an unspeakably joyful light shone in upon his soul, so that his spirit seemed to be caught up to the heavens, and he felt as though he saw God, as Moses did on the Mount, face to face, and was carried forth to him." Moreover, "on every page of the scriptures [Tennent] saw [God's] divinity inscribed in brightest colours." The sermon he gave resulted in the conversion of about thirty people, and William Jr. remembered this as his "harvest-day."[30]

He also reported a recent upswing in conversions at Freehold in a letter to Thomas Prince Jr. in 1744. He was reluctant to give numbers because he needed more time to discern the authenticity of conversions, but he wrote, "to all Appearance, both Old and Young, Males and Females, have been renewed. . . . Some Negroes I trust are made free in CHRIST; and more seem to be unfeignedly seeking after it."³¹ Like many early white evangelicals, William Tennent Jr. wrote about African American converts as a discrete category in the revivals. The revivalists conceded that African Americans shared in all humanity's need for renewal by Christ, but their separate mention reminds us of their profoundly unequal status, even if the radical implications of the gospel might suggest a spiritual kind of equality with European Americans.

William Jr. defended the Freehold revivals as bearing good fruit. He also insisted that the revivals had been "quite free from Enthusiasm." What could William Jr., the visionary, have in mind by claiming that these awakenings were not enthusiastic? He thought that the congregation had remained faithful to the guidance of Scripture in all their actions and refused to follow "the Impulses of their own Minds." His assessment of visions was fascinating: "There have not been, that I know of among us, any Visions except such as are by Faith, namely clear and affecting Views of the new and living Way to the FATHER, through his dear Son JESUS CHRIST: Nor any Revelations but what have been long since written in the sacred Volume: Nor any Trances but such as all Men now living shall meet with, for it is appointed for all Men once to die."³² William Jr. considered visions normal and acceptable, so long as they affirmed orthodox doctrine, reprised visions seen in the Bible, or gave a person an early taste of heaven or hell. He himself had experienced all of these, and he certainly believed that his own visions could not count as common enthusiasm.

It is not clear how often the Tennent brothers' revivals involved communion seasons, but several references in the revival magazine the *Christian History* lead one to believe that they saw these services as standard features of their ministries. William Jr. saw the communion season as a critical means to revival in Hopewell and Maidenhead in 1744, where he helped gather a new church. "The Sacramental Season was blessed to the refreshing of the LORD's dear People there, as well as to others of them which came from other Places. So that some who had been much distressed with Doubts about their State, received Soul-satisfying Sealings of GOD's everlasting Love: Others were supported and quickned, so that they returned Home rejoicing and glorifying GOD."³³

Gilbert and William Tennent Jr., along with the growing ranks of the Log College graduates, represented a formidable revivalist contingent in the Philadelphia Synod, based primarily in northeast Pennsylvania and east New Jersey. It seemed for a time that the Tennents' brand of conversionist piety might take hold among all the ministers of the Philadelphia Synod, as in 1734 Gilbert won unanimous approval for two measures designed to revitalize the churches represented at the synod. The overtures asked ministers to examine candidates for the Lord's Supper for signs of grace, and for presbyteries to make sure that their ministers were preaching a conversionist gospel that sought "to convince his hearers of their lost and miserable state whilst unconverted." Some in the synod began to grumble about Tennent, however, when in 1737 he began crossing presbytery lines to preach in Maidenhead, which had no settled pastor at the time. The synod considered a resolution that would require any minister visiting another presbytery's church to gain the permission of that presbytery first. Tennent apparently thought this idea was ridiculous, for he again visited Maidenhead before the matter of permission had been decided.[34]

In 1738 the synod finally passed a complicated resolution basically giving local presbyteries authority over the right to itinerate. At the same time, the synod voted to create a new presbytery under its jurisdiction, the New Brunswick Presbytery. The new presbytery included the parishes of Gilbert and William Tennent Jr., John Cross, Samuel Blair of Shrewsbury, and Eleazar Wales of Kingston. All five were friends of Tennent-style evangelicalism, and the fact that the synod now gave them their own presbytery was a critical turn. The presbytery remained under the authority of the Philadelphia Synod, but nevertheless the Presbyterian evangelicals now had east Jersey all to themselves. The next year Whitefield would note, "It happens very providentially, that Mr. Tennent and his brethren are appointed to be a Presbytery by the Synod, so that they intend breeding up gracious youths, and sending them out into our Lord's vineyard."[35]

The busy synod also agreed, surely over protests from the Tennent camp, to form committees that would test ministerial candidates who did not have degrees from Harvard, Yale, or one of the usual European universities. The Tennents suggested that a pastor's spiritual qualifications mattered more than formal education, though they never suggested that education was unimportant. The Tennents simply thought that an education at an institution like the Log College was sufficiently rigorous. The majority of the synod believed that if a candidate did not have a degree from a formally recognized college, he should be tested on his knowledge of philosophy, theology, and the biblical languages. The Tennents suspected, however, that this test might be used by the synod to exercise more control over pastoral candidates and jeopardize the power of local presbyteries to ordain ministers.[36]

The questions of ministerial qualifications, and of the locus of authority for approving candidates, quickly came to a head when Log College graduate John Rowland applied to the New Brunswick Presbytery for ordination. The presbytery records indicated that the ministers and elders took "serious Consideration" of the synod's desire for candidates like Rowland to be examined by committee, but they came to the unanimous conclusion that "they were not in point of Conscience restrained by said Act from using the Liberty and Power which

Presbyteries have all along hitherto enjoyed," so they proceeded with Rowland's trials themselves and licensed him. Rowland soon received a call from the evangelically inclined Maidenhead congregation, but the Philadelphia Presbytery blocked this call, citing the act against itinerancy. The synod chastised the New Brunswick Presbytery, the Maidenhead congregation, and Rowland for being "disorderly" and "divisive," and they revoked Rowland's license. Not to be outdone, the New Brunswick Presbytery in November 1739 ordained Rowland "to the ministry of the Word in general."[37]

As the Philadelphia Synod squabbled about itinerancy and licensing, signs of a large revival began to appear in New Jersey, especially at Aaron Burr's Newark congregation and those churches in which John Rowland ministered. Rowland's ministry in 1738–39 helped define the terms of the growing debate between what would be called the "New Side" (prorevivalist) and "Old Side" (antirevivalist) Presbyterians. Many in the Philadelphia Synod doubted the sufficiency of his Log College education, but Rowland and the Tennents thought that a basic education combined with the power of the Spirit were more than enough to qualify a man to minister. Many, moreover, recoiled at Rowland's and Gilbert Tennent's loose handling of presbytery boundaries. Some also worried that the sort of emotional outbreaks that Rowland encouraged led not to solid piety but to dangerous enthusiasm.[38]

When Rowland arrived in Hopewell and Maidenhead, he found split congregations. Those who opposed Rowland and the "Brunswick Ministers" kept Rowland out of the meetinghouses for some time, meaning that he had to hold meetings in barns. He seemed to relish these rustic settings, and proudly noted that so many people came to the assemblies that "the largest Barns amongst us were chosen to worship God in." Soon Rowland also received an invitation from nearby Amwell to preach there "one Sabbath in three," so the popular Rowland had three towns in his parish, despite the ongoing protests of the synod.[39]

Rowland estimated that very few of his congregants "knew the Lord Jesus" upon his arrival, but some of those were "earnest in Prayer Night and Day to have the Gospel in Power among them." When Rowland began preaching in 1738, he focused almost exclusively on "Conviction and Conversion." Revival began at once, as "the Lord began to accompany his Word in a measure from the very first." He began to see one or two people at a time come under sharp conviction, and slowly the number of converts began to multiply. He thought the effects of the growing awakening were general, as "Fathers, Mothers and the Youth, some Negroes also" (again separately mentioning African Americans) began to seek their salvation. Some Scots-Irish revivalists seemed more comfortable than other evangelicals with viewing conversion as a process, sometimes

taking months or even years. Thus, Rowland was not concerned that many instantaneous conversions did not attend his preaching at first.[40]

The revival in southwest New Jersey escalated in May 1739 when Rowland
turned his preaching to "inviting and encouraging Subjects," which would help
those grieved by their sins. During a sermon on John 11:28–29 ("The Master
is come and calleth for thee. As soon as she heard that, she arose quickly and
came unto him"), the "Divine Influence" caused "Solemn Weeping and deep
Concern" to appear. Rowland supplemented his preaching with many personal
conversations and home visits, "an excellent Mean to lay them open to Conviction under the publick Word." Rowland was particularly impressed with a small
meeting in October 1739, even though only fifteen people attended. During
the service "some of them cry'd out so very awfully, that I was constrain'd to
conclude." When he asked the affected listeners why they cried out, they told
him that "they saw Hell opening before them, and themselves ready to fall into
it." The next month at Maidenhead Rowland met George Whitefield, who commented that "Much of the simplicity of Christ was discernible in [Rowland's]
behaviour. Blessed be God for sending forth such burning and shining lights in
the midst of the thick darkness."[41]

We can see from Rowland's experience that the revivals in southwest New
Jersey were well under way before Whitefield's arrival. Whitefield's presence no
doubt energized ongoing revivals, and sometimes he helped start new awakenings, too. But we should realize that evangelicalism had begun to take shape lo-
cally in North America without Whitefield, and he never stayed long enough to
put a permanent stamp on any particular place. Instead, local ministers like Rowland welcomed Whitefield but rarely expected Whitefield to do anything more
than to generate excitement. The high point of Rowland's revival began on July
24, 1740 (Whitefield was then in South Carolina), which he called the "Times
of most remarkable Power that I observed in these Towns." He thought that the
worship of that day was unusually passionate, and as the people left the service,
many stopped at what he called "one of the Christian Houses" in town. There
the worship and instruction continued, and soon "the Love of God's People that
were present, was uncommonly inflamed to Jesus Christ." Weeks of deeply emotional services followed in all three of Rowland's churches, and though Rowland
hesitated to count converts, he thought that many people came to a saving faith.
The converts were characterized by a very precise and affecting conviction of
sin, a new desire for Christ, and a consistent practice of faith "steady in the Ways
of God, and not unconstant and uneven."[42] Rowland, like Jonathan Edwards,
was impressed with shows of emotion only if they indicated a deeper transformation of a sinner into a humbled, loving saint.

Continental Pietism and Scots-Irish Presbyterianism helped condition the faith and practices of early American evangelicalism, just as English Puritanism did. Pietism contributed an intense focus on the heart, often in conflict with the decayed state of formal, established religion. Scots-Irish Presbyterianism supplied legions of pious immigrants, who often came expecting revival to occur, especially at communion field services. These traditions helped forge a new multiethnic revivalist cohort in the Middle Colonies. The Pietists and Presbyterians of those colonies had begun striving for awakenings well before the Grand Itinerant George Whitefield came on the scene.

4

"PLENTIFUL EFFUSIONS OF GOD'S SPIRIT IN THESE PARTS": GEORGE WHITEFIELD COMES TO AMERICA

George Whitefield has been described as a "pioneer in the commercialization of religion" and "Anglo-America's first religious celebrity, the symbol for a dawning modern age."[1] These characterizations are undoubtedly true, and Whitefield was the most important figure in fomenting the massive awakenings of the 1740s in Britain and North America. His willingness to work with members of non-Anglican denominations marked a key innovation of the evangelical movement: deemphasizing denominationalism to serve the priority of the new birth. All the attention given to Whitefield, however, may have given the impression that without Whitefield, there would have been no awakenings. Instead, we should see Whitefield as a catalyst reacting with already existing materials to help initiate the Great Awakening. The tributaries feeding the creation of Anglo-American evangelicalism hardly originated with Whitefield, but perhaps he helped their confluence arrive earlier and more forcefully than it otherwise would have. On one hand, Whitefield was enormously influential, but, on the other, most of those affected by the eighteenth-century awakenings did not convert under his preaching. Nevertheless, Whitefield's ministry and writings are an indispensable part of the story of early evangelicals.

Much of what we know about Whitefield comes from his popular *Journals*, which are among the best primary sources on the early revivals in Britain and America. But we have to approach any such autobiographical sources with some skepticism, as the *Journals* were clearly intended for the publishing market and as such to augment Whitefield's fame and the attraction of his meetings. Whitefield probably exaggerated the number of attendees at his meetings, but whether he intended to mislead readers is hard to say. Documents like Whitefield's *Jour-*

James Moore, *George Whitefield.* National Portrait
Gallery, Smithsonian Institution.

nals serve as generally reliable sources of information about the revivals, but they
also promoted the awakenings and shaped Whitefield's public profile.

As he explained at the beginning of the *Journals,* Whitefield was born in
Gloucester, England, in 1714, and his father died when he was two. His mother
ran the Bell Inn, and Whitefield's background (unlike Edwards's) hardly seemed
to prepare him to become a celebrated preacher. Whitefield's mother raised him
and his siblings in a nonevangelical environment of fairly regular observance in
the established Church of England. The young Whitefield enjoyed playing in
the theater and developed a love for the stage. He later denounced the theater as
immoral, but his passion for performance remained.[2]

Whitefield started seriously to contemplate the things of God during a brief
stay in Bristol as a teenager. There Whitefield began to receive visions and dreams.
"Here God was pleased to give me great foretastes of His love, and fill me with
such unspeakable raptures, particularly once in St. John's Church, that I was

carried out beyond myself." Whitefield began reading *The Imitation of Christ* by Thomas à Kempis and thinking that he might enter the priesthood. Soon, however, Whitefield went back to "reading plays, and . . . sauntering from place to place." Even as he dove into theater culture, he believed that God kept drawing him. Once, as he read a play to his sister, he abruptly proclaimed, "Sister, God intends something for me which we know not of. . . . I think God will provide for me some way or other that we cannot comprehend." He did not know why he said these words, but "God afterwards showed me they came from Him."[3] As with a number of his more controversial memories, Whitefield later edited this episode out of the revised version of his conversion narrative, but it is clear from the early version that Whitefield thought God had actively intervened in his mind, thoughts, and words to convert him.

When he was seventeen, Whitefield began preparing for his entrance into Oxford by practicing rigorous spiritual disciplines, including attending services twice a day and fasting. Again, he had a powerful dream, writing of it, "I was to see God on Mount Sinai, but was afraid to meet Him. This made a great impression upon me; and a gentlewoman to whom I told it, said, 'George, this is a call from God.'" The dream sobered him, but he continued to struggle desperately with hypocrisy. Soon thereafter, while on an errand, "an unaccountable, but very strong impression was made upon my heart that I should preach quickly." He shared this impression with his mother, but she rebuked him. For many leaders in the developing evangelical movement, dreams, visions, and impressions became ways to sanction radical departures in self-definition. Often these experiences helped new evangelicals break away from the pressures of a scoffing family.[4]

Whitefield made his way to Oxford, where he resisted the "excess of riot" practiced by his mates, who began to consider him "a singular odd fellow." Whitefield became even more intense as a poor, ascetic college student. Whitefield then made the acquaintance of the Oxford Methodists, including Charles and John Wesley. "My soul . . . was athirst for some spiritual friends to lift up my hands when they hung down," he wrote, and he found them in the Methodists. Charles Wesley recommended to him August Hermann Francke's *Against the Fear of Man* and Henry Scougal's *The Life of God in the Soul of Man*. Whitefield wrote that he "never knew what true religion was" until he read Scougal, a leading Scottish divine of the late seventeenth century. True religion, he learned from Scougal, consisted of becoming a "new creature." He was so impressed that he began sending copies of the book to friends. Whitefield heatedly sought the new birth from that point on.[5]

Whitefield lurched from one extreme to another in his spiritual quest. He began living in an austere and unhealthy manner and worried that Satan meant to destroy him, fearing sometimes at night that any turned corner might bring him face to face with the devil. He often prayed for the devil to depart from him, and he slept very little. He ate only the "worst sort of food" and dressed in ragged clothes. He fell behind in his assignments and became quite ill. Whitefield thought his time of sickness was a "glorious visitation," for God was "purifying my soul." Finally, his breakthrough came. As he suffered through a thirst induced by his sickness, he remembered that on the cross Christ had been thirsty just before his death. "Upon which I cast myself down on the bed, crying out, 'I thirst! I thirst!' Soon after this, I found and felt in myself that I was delivered from the burden that had so heavily oppressed me. . . . Now did the Spirit of God take possession of my soul, and, as I humbly hope, seal me unto the day of redemption."[6]

Whitefield took Anglican orders as a deacon in 1736, at the age of twenty-one. His decision to remain an Anglican, which seems never to have seriously troubled him, was momentous for the transdenominational nature of Anglo-American evangelicalism. In the generation before the awakenings of the 1730s and 1740s, the rivalry between Anglicans and dissenters was sharp. Dissenters were the subject of discrimination and even violence in England, highlighted by London's Sacheverell Riots in 1710 when dissenting meetinghouses were targeted for burning.[7] Tories in Parliament occasionally pushed for the revocation of Massachusetts's charter in the early eighteenth century, trying to terminate the oxymoronic dissenting establishment there. Dissenters in Anglo-America often associated high-church Anglicans, fairly or not, with Jacobitism, the desire to return the Catholic Stuarts to the throne of England. Whitefield's ministry would help alleviate these tensions, as would a growing spirit of latitudinarianism among both leading dissenters and low-church Anglicans. If the point of evangelical ministry was to preach the new birth, then denominational distinctions mattered less. After his ordination, Whitefield began his touring ministry, preaching in pulpits in Bristol and London. His dramatic flair made him an instant sensation, and the press quickly caught on, reporting widely on his fervent preaching. He also began publishing a number of his sermons, which sold quickly. A letter from the Wesleys convinced him to go to North America, to the new colony of Georgia.

Whitefield arrived in the tiny outpost of Savannah in 1738 and found the Wesleys' mission there in shambles. The brothers had departed before Whitefield arrived, leaving a great deal of ill will toward Methodism because of their demanding style and also because of a romance of John's that had turned publicly ugly. Whitefield cheerfully picked up the pieces of the mission and soon realized that desperate conditions in Georgia demanded relief for the poor, including a new orphanage. Charles Wesley had earlier thought of founding an orphanage based on the Halle school model, and Whitefield made that idea central to his ministry. At Ebenezer, Georgia, Whitefield met Johann Martin Bolzius, a Salzburg Lutheran disciple of Halle, who had founded an "Orphan House, in which are seventeen children and one widow." Whitefield hoped to match the Ebenezer home with a new orphanage in Savannah. "I cannot help thinking there are foundations being laid for great temporal and spiritual blessings in Georgia," he wrote, and he devoted his labors to bringing those blessings about.[8] He would not do this by staying in Georgia: it was far too small a stage. Instead, Whitefield would establish the Bethesda orphanage there and then raise funds for the project throughout the British Atlantic world. After three months in Georgia, he returned to England.

Back in England, Whitefield received a warm welcome from his Methodist friends and received ordination as a priest. He commented often on his affecting sense of the Spirit within him: "God fills me with love, peace, and joy in the Holy Ghost. . . . Oh how does the Holy Ghost cause me to joy in God!" Whitefield would attribute much of his success to this invisible spiritual presence within him.[9] He disputed with Anglican opponents of the Methodists and began to believe that though they shared a common ordination, they did not share the same Christ. He and John Wesley stayed up late one night in January 1739 talking with some of these "opposers of the doctrine of the New Birth." He thought the rift between them was wide indeed: "I am fully convinced there is a fundamental difference between us and them. They believe only an outward Christ, we further believe that He must be inwardly formed in our hearts also. But the natural man receiveth not the things of the Spirit of God." The problem his enemies had, Whitefield thought, was that they had never experienced the new birth.

Whitefield began to prepare for an innovative style of preaching this new birth: the field meeting. Whitefield thought that open-air preaching would allow him to reach many thousands more than he otherwise could, and it would give him the independence and latitude that he craved. He knew, moreover, of Wales's Howell Harris, who had been successfully field preaching since his conversion in 1735. Harris was becoming the key figure in Welsh evangelicalism, corresponding with representatives from the Halle school and eagerly reading Edwards's *Faithful Narrative* when it was published in London in 1737. Whitefield admired Harris, writing in January 1739, "May I follow him, as he does JESUS CHRIST. How he outstrips me!" Whitefield first began field preaching in the mining community of Kingswood, near Bristol, in February 1739, and the results were amazing. Within a week he had attracted a crowd he estimated at ten thousand. By May he saw crowds of fifty and sixty thousand in London. Critics always suspected that Whitefield exaggerated his crowds' numbers, but Ben Franklin, a friendly skeptic, once estimated that twenty-five thousand could hear Whitefield preach at one time. Perhaps Whitefield and his publicists overstated the numbers, but interested observers may have stayed even if they could not actually hear Whitefield speaking. Whatever the case, Whitefield was a controversial sensation. He rejoiced when his requests to be admitted to local pulpits were turned down by suspicious priests. "Lord, why dost Thou thus honour me?" he wrote upon receiving a denial from Bristol's Anglican bishop in February.[10] He took this to be a sign of persecution, which he thought surely would be followed by God's blessing on his work.

He continued to develop his field ministry in Bristol, Cardiff, London, and surrounding towns, all the while raising large amounts of money for the Georgia mission. He took the cities between Cardiff and London by storm, but he would not rest on these successes. Leaving Gravesend, England, in August 1739, he prepared to bring his itinerant preaching to the cities of North America. He arrived at Lewes, Delaware, about a year after he had left Savannah. He made his way north to Philadelphia, arriving on November 2. He then began his first major preaching tour in North America.

Philadelphia in 1739 was the second largest town in the colonies but still small at about thirteen thousand people. It was a fast-growing node of imperial commerce, receiving all manner of trade goods and immigrants every year. Although the pacifist Quaker politicians did not approve of Pennsylvania becoming directly involved with the War of Jenkins' Ear, which was declared a month before Whitefield's arrival, the Philadelphia traders made a good deal of money by providing supplies to the West Indies.[11] The town was originally the centerpiece of William Penn's Quaker colony, but its free conditions led to quick religious pluralization. It became a particularly vital center for colonial Presbyterianism, but Philadelphia's Presbyterian Synod was not always friendly to revivalism.

Whitefield brought William Seward with him to Philadelphia. Seward was a new convert who became the brains behind Whitefield's newspaper publicity. He was formerly the treasurer of the South Sea Company, which had used media promotion to grossly inflate its stock prices before their terrible crash in 1721. Seward had sworn off such practices, but he brought a businessman's savvy to marketing Whitefield's revivals. Both the *Pennsylvania Gazette* and the *American Weekly Mercury*, Philadelphia's two newspapers, covered Whitefield's departure from England. As in Britain, newspaper articles, both friendly and unfriendly, contributed to the Whitefield frenzy. Even during Whitefield's

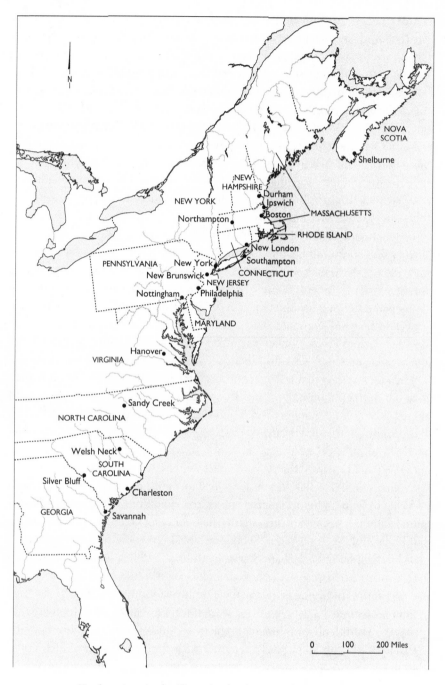

Key locations in the Great Awakening. Map by Bill Nelson.

later visits to North America, when his role in American evangelicalism had become much less significant, newspapers continued to follow his every move. Although publicity alone cannot account for Whitefield's unprecedented success, the media no doubt helped create his widespread attraction. Works by or about Whitefield caused the number of printed texts produced in America to almost double between 1738 and 1741.[12]

Whitefield's first order of business in Philadelphia was to meet the leaders of the Anglican Christ Church, where he "read prayers and assisted at the Communion" on his first Sunday morning in Philadelphia. Whitefield would grow increasingly frustrated with the Anglican leaders' hostility toward him (as would Anglican leaders grow disgusted at Whitefield's incessant attacks), but it is instructive to see him seek out the Anglicans upon his arrival. He also attended the Quakers' meeting on Sunday night, perhaps wanting to touch base with all the religious power brokers in Philadelphia before beginning his field preaching. He did not relish the Quakers' devotion, however, and he was suspicious of their doctrine of the "inward Christ." He also began meeting with the city's Presbyterian and Baptist ministers.[13]

Having warmed up in Christ Church, Whitefield began preaching outdoors; on November 8 he "preached at six in the evening, from the Court House stairs to about six thousand people," or almost half the city's population. He thought that the people of Philadelphia were less formal than their countrymen in England, for they seemed to prefer his outdoor preaching. "There, the generality of people think a sermon cannot be preached well without; here, they do not like it so well if delivered within the church walls." These were just the sort of people Whitefield was looking for. The next night Whitefield preached again, to perhaps eight thousand people.[14]

Soon Whitefield met William Tennent Sr., who had arrived from nearby Neshaminy. Whitefield noted that Tennent was a friend of Scottish revivalist John Erskine, and that Tennent and his sons "are secretly despised by the generality of the Synod," just as Erskine was despised in Scotland and the Methodists were in England. Whitefield took this as a lesson: "we are but few . . . yet I doubt not, but the Lord will appear for us." He saw Tennent, Erskine, and himself as part of a broader Atlantic evangelical movement, subject to persecution at every turn but chosen for a godly, controversial ministry. He continued to preach to large crowds, and he thought that many "have been quickened and awakened to see that religion does not consist in outward things, but in righteousness, peace, and joy in the Holy Ghost."[15]

After a week of ministry, Whitefield began to complain publicly about the Anglican priests' opposition to his work. He wrote that he heatedly bore "testimony against the unchristian principles and practices of our clergy." Three Anglican priests attended this sermon, but he did not know "whether they were offended." He thought that he must question the motives of the priests who opposed him, for "were I to convert Papists, my business would be to shew that they were misguided by their priests; and if I want to convince Church of England Protestants, I must prove that the generality of their teachers do not preach or live up to the truth as it is in Jesus." Whitefield did not care if this tactic affronted many of his fellow priests.[16]

Whitefield never intended to stay long in one place, and he showed little interest in anything but itinerant preaching. This gave him the decided advantage of never having to deal with the messiness of pastoral ministry nor with the enormous controversies his preaching generated. These tasks were left to local ministers. Thus, Whitefield left Philadelphia on November 12, a little more than a week after his arrival, to go to New York. He traveled through southern and central New Jersey, and in New Brunswick he met Gilbert Tennent. The two liked one another immediately, and Tennent, ten years senior, began accompanying Whitefield in his travels. As they traveled north, they swapped conversion testimonies. From Elizabethtown, they crossed by boat to New York City. Whitefield quickly made enemies with New York's Anglican Commissary, who denied him the use of his pulpit, so Tennent and Whitefield secured the use of Ebenezer Pemberton's meetinghouse, the Wall Street Presbyterian Church.[17]

In New York, Tennent's preaching affected Whitefield, who wrote that Tennent "convinced me more and more that we can preach the Gospel of Christ no further than we have experienced the power of it in our own hearts." Tennent was "a son of thunder, and does not fear the faces of men." Whitefield knew that New York did not have the cultivated revival tradition that New Brunswick or Boston did, but he preached to large crowds nonetheless, both at Pemberton's church and in the fields. Whitefield felt very confident about his ability to conquer New York, writing, "I have not felt greater freedom in preaching, and more power in prayer, since I came to America." He continued dutifully to attend Anglican services on Sundays, though as he listened he stewed over the church's faithlessness. "Her prophets prophesy lies, and I fear many of the people love to have it so," he mourned.[18]

An anonymous observer of Whitefield's New York campaign, likely Ebenezer Pemberton, wrote a letter that appeared in several colonial newspapers as well as in Prince's *Christian History*, describing his preaching. This observer had been concerned that Whitefield was promoting enthusiasm, but the young preacher won him over.

I came home astonished. Every scruple vanished; I never saw or heard the like; and I said within myself, Surely God is with this man of a truth! . . . Mr. Whitefield is a man of middle stature, of a slender body, a fair complexion and a comely appearance. He is of sprightly cheerful temper and acts and moves with great agility. The endowments of his mind are very uncommon. . . . He has a most ready memory and, I think, speaks entirely without notes. He has a clear and musical voice, and a wonderful command of it. He uses much gesture, but with great propriety. Every accent of his voice, and every motion of his body, speaks, and both are natural and unaffected. If his delivery be the product of art, 'tis certainly the perfection of it, for it is entirely concealed. He has a great mastery of words, but studies much plainness of speech.[19]

Whitefield was simply a brilliant preacher, but he was also young and attractive, and all of this fed into his growing fame. As many of his portraits show, Whitefield also was cross-eyed, perhaps from a facial tic. His opponents sometimes used this feature to lampoon him, but some supporters seem to have associated this characteristic with spiritual power.[20]

Whitefield and Tennent left New York after five days, returning to New Jersey. Whitefield preached at Elizabethtown's Presbyterian church by invitation of its minister, Jonathan Dickinson. Showing that he did not reserve criticism only for the Anglicans, he wrote that before seven hundred people, he preached against dissenters "who hold the truth in unrighteousness, consenting themselves with a bare, speculative knowledge of the doctrines of grace, but never experiencing the power of them in their hearts." Doctrine was not enough, although conversion presupposed proper doctrine. The doctrines of grace had to transform the heart, or a person could have no hope of salvation. Whitefield's preaching thrilled Dickinson, who inclined toward moderate evangelical Presbyterianism. Dickinson began to preach revival himself in the weeks following the visit.[21]

Whitefield and Tennent returned to New Brunswick, the citadel of Middle Colonies revivalism. Several major revival luminaries attended Whitefield's preaching. "One was a Dutch Calvinistic minister, named Freeling Housen," Whitefield wrote. "He is a worthy old soldier of Jesus Christ, and was the beginner of the great work which I trust the Lord is carrying on in these parts." The next day Whitefield traveled to Maidenhead and met with John Rowland.[22] He gravitated toward those people who had already begun the revival movement in America.

With this pull in mind, Whitefield crossed the Delaware River and visited William Tennent Sr. in Neshaminy, Pennsylvania. Three thousand people gathered in the meetinghouse yard to hear him preach, and though "at first the people seemed unaffected, . . . in the midst of my discourse, the hearers began to be melted down, and cried much." Gilbert exhorted the crowd, too. Whitefield noticed the Log College on the property, describing it as a "log-house, about twenty feet long, and nearly as many broad; and, to me, it seemed to resemble the school of the old prophets." He thought that "carnal ministers" hated the Log College ministers because of their success and because they sometimes suggested that fellow ministers were unconverted. "The poor gentlemen are loaded with contempt, and looked upon as persons who turn the world upside-down." Before returning to Philadelphia, he preached in Abington "to above two thousand people from a porch-window belonging to the meeting-house." Later that day, he arrived in Philadelphia and thanked God for "this little excursion!" The preaching successes in the fields and churches of Britain had transferred now to British North America, becoming what Boston's Thomas Foxcroft called Whitefield's "imported divinity."[23]

Whitefield continued his revival work in and around Philadelphia for another five days, noting that people were approaching him, "inquiring about inward feelings and receiving the Holy Ghost." He preached by appointment in Germantown on November 27 to a crowd he estimated at six thousand. Whitefield loved Germantown, not only because the people responded emotionally to his preaching, but also because the town had so many Protestant refugees of one sort or another from the Continent. He thought that at least fifteen denominations were represented there, and yet to Whitefield they seemed remarkably cooperative and committed to true Christianity.[24] The next day Whitefield announced that he would leave Philadelphia for Georgia, and he preached a farewell sermon to a crowd estimated at ten thousand. With this, Whitefield set out for an overland trip to the southern colonies.

He came to Wilmington, Delaware, and met a Tennent brother that he identified in his journal as William Tennent Jr., but it seems likely that this was actually Charles Tennent, the least known of the four preaching brothers. His congregation was at Whiteclay Creek, Delaware, where Whitefield preached under a tent set up near the meetinghouse. Despite some December rain, approximately ten thousand came to hear him. One account reported that Whitefield led a field communion service on this occasion. At Whiteclay Creek Whitefield also met a future opponent, George Gillespie of Christiana Creek, Delaware. Whitefield called him "another faithful minister of Jesus Christ," but Gillespie would later pen *Remarks upon Mr. George Whitefield, Proving Him a Man under Delusion* (1744).[25]

Whitefield moved south into Maryland, where he found the spiritual soil harder to plow. He would eventually spend a great deal of time preaching in Maryland, especially in 1746–47, when his sustained attention seems to have borne significant results. But in 1739 he noted, "Maryland . . . seems to be a place as yet unwatered with the true Gospel of Christ, and with no likelihood of much good being done in it, unless one could abide there for some time. . . . I trust the time will come when God will visit these dark corners of the earth." Whitefield entered Maryland at Cecil County, where he met with a considerable but localized response among Scots-Irish Presbyterians. Cecil County, and Bohemia Manor in particular, had more in common with eastern Pennsylvania than tidewater Maryland, and it became the locus of Whitefield's greatest successes in Maryland.[26]

He proceeded to Annapolis, where he made the acquaintance of Governor Samuel Ogle, who would consistently support Whitefield in the coming years. The town leaders received him warmly, but he thought that the townspeople were distracted by godless entertainments. As was becoming typical, he challenged the leading Anglicans of Annapolis concerning their worldliness, and they did not respond well, or at least so it seems from a letter on December 11, 1739, written by Stephen Bordley, a member of the St. Anne's Parish vestry.

Whitefield's effective style and appearance Bordley could hardly dispute: "His voice is strong and Clear, but not Musical, & he has a little of the West Country twang. He is very Young, has a well turned person, a fine sett of teeth, which is a great ornament in a Speaker & a Sweet and Agreeable turn of Countenance, but the beauty of this is somewhat lessened by a prodigious Squint wth his left Eye. . . . I freely own I never in my life saw any one man that arrived to so great a prefeccion in the art of Pronounciation as he has done." Bordley, however, thought the evangelist's faults were many: "his language is mean & Groveling, without the least Elegance; & his method of discourse is ten times worse than his language, or rather he has no method at all." The only "divinity" Whitefield promoted was "the particular of the Holy Spirit, whose Operations are so violent & powerfull in those who are possessed with it, as, according to his Account of it, to enable them to do any thing but work miracles." He thought that Whitefield's message exclusively concerned the work of the Holy Spirit and the failings of his fellow Anglicans: these were the "great hinges" of his preaching. Bordley believed that his preaching had affected some in Annapolis, writing "He has putt some among us here on a Wild goose Chase, in quest of that degree of the Spirit Which perhaps they never will find. Others he has thrown into the Vapours & Despair . . . , & into a full perswasion that the Good man, as he would have them believe, is miraculously Inspired." Whitefield "has the best delivery wth the Worst Divinity that I ever mett with," Bordley concluded.[27]

The journey continued south, and Whitefield's band crossed the Potomac River. They passed through the very lightly populated Tidewater and reached Williamsburg in three days. There Whitefield met the Anglican Commissary of Virginia, James Blair, whom Whitefield admired a great deal, particularly because he had founded William and Mary College in 1693. Whitefield thought that the college "may be of excellent use, if learning Christ be made one end of their studies, and arts and sciences only introduced and pursued as subservient to that." Because the English universities had failed to promote Christ, they had become "seminaries of paganism." Whitefield would no doubt have been disappointed that William and Mary came to produce the likes of the Deist Thomas Jefferson. But for now, Whitefield showed that his hostility toward Anglican leaders was not universal. He fancied himself a friend to any friend of Christ.[28]

Moving briskly, his party entered North Carolina. He marveled at the desolate, warm, and exotic countryside. Though it was late December, he thought it was as hot as "Midsummer in England," and one of his companions wondered how people lived "in such a howling wilderness, surrounded with those many wolves, bears, and tigers, which come forth at night roaring upon him?" He did find a small church in Bath at which to preach, and a hundred people came to hear him, five times the usual attendance. The church had suffered a long time with no priest, and Whitefield told the people that "God was angry with them, because He had sent a famine of the Word among them." A woman approached him after the sermon asking for prayer, saying she had not previously met a minister who understood divine things. He glumly noted: "This case is not uncommon. Most that handle the law know not what they say, nor whereof they affirm." He longed for the day when Britain and America would be populated with twice-born ministers prepared to preach the true gospel.[29]

Whitefield celebrated Christmas in New Bern. It is worth noting that he did, in fact, celebrate Christmas, a holiday many of his dissenting colleagues frowned upon as smacking of Catholicism. He sought to focus on the "glad tidings of salvation by Jesus Christ" by receiving the sacrament at the Anglican service, but he lamented that the congregation performed the liturgy in an "indifferent manner." He prayed by himself and preached that afternoon, with great results: "I scarcely know when we have had a more visible manifestation of the Divine Presence since our coming into America." The sermon reduced many to tears, and Whitefield wrote that "this unexpected success rejoiced me the more, because I looked upon it as an earnest of future and more plentiful effusions of God's Spirit in these parts." The revivals, however, would not take hold in North Carolina until 1755 when the New Englanders Shubal Stearns and Daniel Marshall brought Separate Baptist missions to the colony, which began to turn many in the North Carolina backcountry toward evangelicalism.[30]

South of the Trent River, Whitefield came to a home with slaves, and he noted that he "went, as my usual custom is, among the negroes belonging to the house." He prayed with two of the children, who he thought spoke well. "This more and more convinces me," he concluded, "that negro children, if early brought up in the nurture and admonition of the Lord, would make as great proficiency as any white people's children. I do not despair . . . of seeing a school of young negroes singing the praises of Him Who made them." Whitefield, the future slave owner, here revealed his growing ambivalence about the status of African Americans under his ministry. He made it his "custom" to speak to blacks, but the self-congratulatory tone implies that he thought himself noble for relating to them. Whitefield operated in a world that assumed all kinds of social, gender, and racial hierarchies, and as an Oxford-educated priest, and white male, he stood high on most scales. But to Whitefield, blacks and whites had a common Creator, and the gospel of the new birth applied to them equally. Equality before God could mean equality among people, or at least the potential for equality. With training in godliness and proper education, African Americans and European Americans could be on level footing in some social spheres. Whitefield was no social radical, but neither did he discourage all the egalitarian implications of the gospel.[31]

Whitefield also shared the fear, common to many elite European whites in the colonies, of slave insurrection. This concern became a dangerous reality when he crossed into South Carolina on January 1, 1740. South Carolinians had witnessed the Stono slave revolt in 1739, and many slaves still longed to flee from the brutal Carolina plantations, if not rise up in open rebellion. Whitefield's party became lost in the night as they looked for their next host home, and as they wandered down the road they happened upon "a hut full of negroes." When Whitefield's companions asked them if they knew the host's location, "the negroes seemed surprised, and said they knew no such man, and that they were newcomers." Whitefield's men thought this was suspicious and thought they "might be some of those who lately had made an insurrection in the province, and had run away from their masters." The party felt it best to move quickly down the road. When they soon saw another campfire, they suspected it was "another nest of such negroes," and one man thought he saw blacks dancing around a fire. When they finally reached a friendly planter's house and related their story, the planter seemed to know who the slaves along the road were. Whitefield thanked God for their deliverance.[32] For him, evangelizing the slaves was a noble goal, but the thought of marauding bands of slaves hiding in the woods made him long for the order of the cities. On January 5, Whitefield arrived in Charleston, no doubt happy to be through the lonely tracts from Maryland to South Carolina.

By early 1740, Whitefield had firmly established himself as an evangelical superstar and the primary worldly agent catalyzing the growing revivalist movement up and down the Atlantic coast. His clever use of the media, powerful preaching techniques, ecumenism, and single-minded focus on the new birth all helped foster the sensation his tours created. Nevertheless, Whitefield's approach also caused controversy everywhere he went, especially concerning the operations of the Holy Spirit, the authority of established ministers, and the right of itinerancy. Eventually many ministers would rue the eager welcome Whitefield received in America in 1739 and 1740.

THE DANGER OF AN UNCONVERTED MINISTRY: FRACTIOUS REVIVALISM IN THE MIDDLE COLONIES

While Whitefield was in the South, the energized evangelical movement in the Middle Colonies continued to spark controversy. Another large revival began in early 1740 at Samuel Blair's church in Fagg's Manor, Pennsylvania. Blair was a native of Ireland and a Log College graduate. He settled in Fagg's Manor (New Londonderry) in 1739 and began an academy like the Log College, which trained a number of influential Presbyterian ministers, including Samuel Davies. Blair's congregation was composed almost entirely of Ulster immigrants. He recorded one of the most comprehensive accounts of any revival, deliberately similar to Edwards's *Faithful Narrative*, in *A Short and Faithful Narrative, of the Late Remarkable Revival of Religion in the Congregation of New-Londonderry* (1744). Blair recalled that when he arrived at Fagg's Manor, the "Nature and Necessity of the New Birth was little known or thought of." Professing Christians thought that morality was the essence of true religion, but many did not live up even to this standard, as "in publick Companies, especially at Weddings, a vain and frothy Lightness was apparent in the Deportment of many Professors: and in some Places very extravagant Follies, as Horse-running, Fiddling and Dancing, pretty much obtain'd on those Occasions."[1] True religion was dying in Fagg's Manor.

In spring 1740, however, "the GOD of Salvation was pleas'd to visit us with the blessed Effusions of his HOLY SPIRIT." In early March Blair traveled to east New Jersey, perhaps to visit New Brunswick Presbytery members, and while he was gone an unnamed preacher gave a sermon that began to produce "much Soul-concern" in Fagg's Manor. Some people began crying with "audible Noise," which Blair had never before heard in his congregation. When Blair returned, he began preaching to the unconverted, and some "burst out in the most bitter mourning." The narrative devoted a great deal of attention to these outward manifestations, offering them as proofs of the revival's intensity, but also cautioning readers that such displays could get out of hand. He constantly counseled moderation: "I desir'd them as much as possible, to restrain themselves from making any Noise, that would hinder themselves or others from hearing what was spoken . . . I still advis'd People to endeavour to moderate and bound their Passions, *but not so as to resist or stifle their Convictions.*" Blair's ideal penitence was an affective, but controlled, outward response to conviction of sin. Cold passivity in the face of God's impending judgment was a sure sign of damnation, but overheated emotions accompanying the new birth could lead to delusions and disorder.[2]

Church meetings in Fagg's Manor became quite large during the spring and summer. The commotion attracted visitors from "almost all Parts around inclining very much to come where there was such Appearance of the divine Power and Presence." The "manifest Evidences of Impressions" continued as well, and sometimes they would overwhelm the whole congregation: "several wou'd be overcome and fainting; others deeply sobbing, hardly able to contain: others crying in a most dolorous Manner; many others silently weeping." Most provocatively, "sometimes the Soul-Exercises of some (tho' comparatively but very few) would so far affect their Bodies as to occasion some strange unusual bodily Motions." By 1744, critics routinely highlighted these manifestations in order to denigrate all the revivals, but to Blair the physical effects appeared to result from "a rational fixt Conviction of their dangerous perishing Estate." In other words, if someone really believed that God was going to damn them to hell for all eternity, then it was reasonable for that person to exhibit signs of that fear, including physical motions. Blair warned his congregants, however, that they should not try to find assurance of salvation in "extraordinary Ways, by Visions, Dreams, or immediate Inspirations," but only by accepting Christ as their savior.[3]

Blair hesitated to give a number of total converts, for he did not believe that he could always discern a true conversion from a false one. For the historian, this hesitancy makes counting the number of converts in many revivals, or during the awakenings generally, quite difficult. Blair preferred to describe promising results and leave the final judgment to God. Many, he wrote, developed an "enflamed Desire . . . to live to him for ever according to his Will; and to the Glory of his Name," and experienced "remarkable Relief and Comfort" from their fear of judgment. These, he thought, were encouraging signs of authentic conversions. He worried more about those who placed confidence in their outward manifestations. A few "had a very obscure and improper Way of representing their Case . . . : they would chiefly speak of such Things as were only the Effects of their

Soul Exercise upon their Bodies from Time to Time, and some Things that were purely imaginary." With anthropological zeal, Blair pursued the exact nature of these experiences and wrote that at times "they felt, perhaps, a Quivering come over them, . . . or a Faintness, or tho't they saw their Hearts full of some nauseous Filthiness; or when they felt a heavy Weight or Load at their Hearts, or felt the Weight again taken off and a pleasant Warmness rising from their Hearts." When the penitents would explain their conversion this way, which seemed overtly sensual, Blair would push them for a more theologically precise description, and at his urging several gave "a pretty rational Account of solemn and spiritual Exercises."[4] Blair knew that for many critics rationality was the standard for legitimate religious experience, but he tried to show that emotional or bodily expressions could be rational. Like most of the moderate awakeners, Blair never seemed to question whether the ideal of rationality, born out of recent trends in elite European Enlightenment thought, was the appropriate standard for weighing the spiritual experience of his congregants.

Some of the supposed converts, the minister believed, had not been touched by the Spirit at all, but instead were trying to jump on the revival bandwagon by creating their own fleshly religious experiences. These people desired to be converted, but the Spirit was not convicting them. As a Calvinist, Blair believed that the Holy Spirit had to awaken people, or spiritual resurrection would not happen. False converts whipped themselves up into emotional ecstasy and called that conversion. They saw others crying, so "they endeavoured just to get themselves affected by Sermons," and if they could start crying, and focus on some Scripture passage promising salvation, then they thought they were saved. Blair believed these people were "pleasing themselves just with an imaginary Conversion of their own Making."[5] As the shepherd of a revival, he sensed the delicate responsibility of distinguishing between authentic conversions, emotional byproducts of authentic conversions, and illegitimate conversions. Many of the Calvinist revivalists would find this discriminating work a burdensome task, especially as critics tried to paint the revivals as fatally corrupted by enthusiasm.

From his perspective in 1744, Blair regretted that a number of apparent converts had fallen away into sin, but others had remained faithful. Even true converts struggled to maintain their fervor, but that wrestling was a promising sign of long-lasting fidelity. The vital tradition of the Scots-Irish communion season helped many of these believers, who often "meet with some delightful Enlivenings of Soul; and particularly our sacramental Solemnities for communicating in the Lord's Supper have generally been very blessed Seasons of Enlivening and Enlargement to the People of GOD."[6]

To provide a guiding example of real conversion, Blair gave an account of one unnamed young woman's experience. She became convinced that she had neglected Christ and began to pursue salvation with deep concern. The young woman found a Spenerian-style "Society of private Christians" who met in her neighborhood for reading, prayer, and discussion, and their meetings powerfully effected her. "While she was there she got an awful View of her Sin and Corruption, and saw that she was without CHRIST and without Grace." This apprehension produced a dramatic bodily reaction in her, as "her Exercise and Distress of Soul was such that it made her for a while both Deaf and Blind."[7]

Despite being deprived temporarily of her sight and hearing, the woman testified that she still "had the ordinary Use of her Understanding," and she continued to hotly pursue salvation. She broke through at a communion season, "in a House where she was lodged during the Time of a Sacramental Solemnity, while the Family were singing the 84th Psalm, her Soul conceiv'd strong Hopes of Reconciliation with GOD thro' JESUS CHRIST." As she sang, it seemed "as if she had sung out of her self," and "it was as if the LORD had put by the Veil and shewed her the open Glory of Heaven. . . . she saw that GOD could well be reconcil'd to all elect Sinners in HIS SON; which was a most ravishing delightful Scene of Contemplation to her." The woman's conversion sharply engaged her senses: the transporting singing (with aural and verbal effects) led to a visual apprehension of heaven's glory, and a "ravishing delightful" sight it was. The language of "ravishment" was very common in eighteenth-century conversion narratives, particularly among evangelical women, and suggested a sexual dynamic in the relationship between the believer and God.[8]

Blair's young woman continued to seek assurance of salvation and found much comfort at the Lord's Supper. For two years, she alternated between hope and despair, but then "the Sun of Righteousness at last broke out upon her to the clear Satisfaction and unspeakable Ravishment of her Soul, at a Communion Table." There she was raised to new heights of contemplation of Christ's ministry to and suffering for her. From then on she had much more confidence that she was truly saved, and the "LORD condescended to be much with her by his enlivening and comforting Presence, and especially Sacramental Seasons were blessed and precious Seasons to her." The seasons of communion led her to ever-higher spiritual transports, so that it seemed to her that her body was nearly vanishing: "she said it seem'd to her that she was almost all Spirit, and that the Body was quite laid by; and she was sometimes in Hopes that the Union would actually break, and the Soul get quite away."[9] Blair's young saint experienced Christ in the physicality of the Supper, but the sensations that the Supper produced seemed almost to negate her body. We do not know how much Blair edited her account, but the vital mysticism described in this experience seems

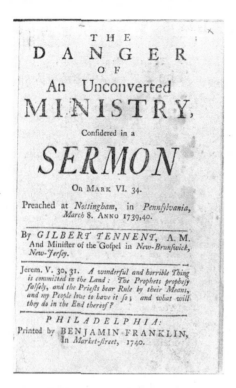

THE
DANGER
OF
An Unconverted
MINISTRY,
Confidered in a
SERMON
On Mark VI. 34.

Preached at *Nottingham*, in *Pennfylvania*,
March 8. Anno 1739,40.

By *GILBERT TENNENT*, A.M.
And Minifter of the Gofpel in *New-Brunfwick*,
New-Jerfey.

Jerem. V. 30, 31. *A wonderful and horrible Thing
is committed in the Land : The Prophets prophefy
falfely, and the Priefts bear Rule by their Means,
and my People love to have it fo ; and what will
they do in the End thereof ?*

PHILADELPHIA:
Printed by BENJAMIN FRANKLIN,
In *Market-ftreet,* 1740.

Gilbert Tennent, *The Danger of an
Unconverted Ministry* (Philadelphia, 1740).
Library of Congress.

likely to have been a fair representation of what this young woman and other penitents like her experienced during their conversions.

Blair noted that the awakening that had begun in March spread to other congregations near Fagg's Manor, including Nottingham, Pennsylvania. Nottingham was in the Donegal Presbytery, which was bitterly divided over revivalism. Nottingham's minister had died in 1739, leaving the church open for a contest over the revivals. Blair worked to get Nottingham to call a revivalist minister, and on March 8, 1740, Gilbert Tennent joined the fray there with his most famous and controversial sermon, *The Danger of an Unconverted Ministry*. Benjamin Franklin quickly realized the interest that this sermon would generate and printed two editions in Philadelphia by year's end. It also was translated into a German edition in Germantown, Pennsylvania, in 1740 and was printed again in Boston in 1742.

In the dedication to the Nottingham church, Tennent expressed his desire "that you might be directed in the Choice of a Minister." Tennent then launched one of the most vicious attacks of these awakenings, as he called supposedly unconverted "hireling" ministers just about every bad name he could use in religious company. Charles Chauncy of Boston's First Church, the most articulate opponent of the revivalists, later listed every such name in his *Seasonable Thoughts* (1743). Among other things, these "Pharisee-Teachers" were "hypocritical Varlets," "dead Dogs, that can't bark," "moral Negroes," "murderous Hypocrites," and "Swarms of Locusts." Tennent thought that many ministers had adopted the old ways of the Pharisees, putting on a great show of religiosity but actually having no saving faith themselves. These blind guides certainly had nothing of value to pass on to their perishing congregations. They preached easy, human-centered doctrines: "The Doctrines of Original Sin, Justification by Faith alone, and the other Points of Calvinism are very cross to the Grain of unrenewed Nature."[10]

What should true believers do in light of the threat of the unconverted ministers? Tennent had two answers. First, the converted should found more schools like the Log College for the training of converted young men. These academies would help supply the dire need for godly ministers in places like Nottingham. He called on believers to support these "Private Schools of the Prophets." Second, and more controversially, Tennent advocated the right of parishioners to go to hear whatever minister they thought could most help them spiritually. He thought that offering many church and ministerial options, like a spiritual market, would eventually run the unconverted out of the ministry, for who would choose to sit under the teaching of a blind guide? "If the Ministry of natural [unconverted] Men be as it has been represented; Then it is both lawful and expedient to go from them to hear Godly Persons." Christians should want to grow spiritually, and surely they profited more under the teaching of a converted minister: "Poor Babes like not dry Breasts," he said. Evangelicals often used the imagery of wet and dry breasts to contrast converted and unconverted pastors. Because the young Christian was as fragile as a newborn baby, there was no point in respecting the "Parish-line" when spiritual health was at stake. Tennent proposed not only the right of ministers to itinerate, but perhaps more subversively, the right of congregants voluntarily to attend church elsewhere if they did not like their pastor's preaching. One could hardly escape the implication that those ministers who opposed the revivalists were themselves unconverted. *The Danger of an Unconverted Ministry* was like a dry wind to a smoldering fire, and from then on the enemies within the Philadelphia Synod seemed extremely unlikely to reach a state of peaceful coexistence.[11]

During the time of the Nottingham controversy, George Whitefield had been in Charleston and Savannah, stoking the revival fires in the coastal South and also beginning the construction of the Bethesda Orphanage. By the time he left, forty children had come under the care of the orphanage, but Whitefield could never stay in one place very long. He went back to Pennsylvania, this time by boat up the Atlantic coast. He arrived in New Castle, Delaware, on April 13 and was welcomed by Charles Tennent and much of his Whiteclay Creek congregation. He went to Philadelphia the next day and received a number of reports of ongoing revivals. In his journal Whitefield mentioned an account of revivals by the Welsh Baptist minister Jenkin Jones, who "recounted to me many noble instances of God's power of free grace, shewn in the conviction and conversion of some ministers, as well as common people." Whitefield had angered the Anglican Commissary Cummings because of the indelicate comments about the priests, and he was now denied the pulpit at Christ Church. Undaunted, he continued to preach to crowds as large as fifteen thousand on Society Hill.[12]

Whitefield expressed growing awareness and concern for the plight of African Americans in both the North and South. In late April, after noting that "many of the negroes" had again received his preaching well, he bought a large tract of land on the Delaware River outside of Philadelphia "and ordered a large house to be built thereon, for the instruction of these poor creatures." He called the place Nazareth. Whitefield's lofty hopes never materialized in Nazareth, however, and after some financial problems and lack of management the property was sold to the Moravians, whom Whitefield had commissioned to survey and build up the property in the first place.[13]

Whitefield's temporary friendliness with the Moravians continued as he set out for a brief tour north of Philadelphia where many Germans lived. Touring with him was the Moravian deacon Peter Böhler, whom Whitefield had met in Georgia. At Skippack, "a very wilderness part of the country," they preached to a crowd of two thousand, with Whitefield speaking English and Böhler German, or what Whitefield called "Dutch." Whitefield initially appreciated the Moravians' evangelical style, but he soon grew concerned about what he considered their antinomian and perfectionist theology.[14]

From Skippack, Whitefield made his way east to Amwell, New Jersey, one of John Rowland's congregations. There he met with Rowland and Gilbert Tennent. They made their way to New Brunswick, where he preached from a wagon in front of Theodorus Frelinghuysen's church. The next day he preached to perhaps eight thousand people in both morning and evening. That night, a struggling woman came to him with hopes that God was finally about to save her. "She cried out, 'I can see nothing but hell!' Oh that all were in as good a way to Heaven," he wrote. He quickly returned to New York City, meeting there

William Tennent, who reported on a revival up the Hudson River "in the High-lands." In New York he preached from a scaffold, with ministers Frelinghuysen, Gualtherus DuBois, and Ebenezer Pemberton sitting behind him in support.[15] Whitefield continued to capitalize on the ongoing revival fervor of the Tennents and others.

On May 1, Whitefield took a ferry to Flatbush on Long Island. As White-field noted, eastern Long Island had become a hotbed for revivals, a reputation it would keep for decades. He attributed the work to "two young Presbyterian ministers," at least one of whom, James Davenport of Southold, he met on this visit. The other was Jonathan Barber of Oysterponds, who would soon accept a position as the superintendent at Whitefield's Bethesda orphanage. Davenport and Barber met at Yale, where Davenport first tasted radical evangelicalism as part of an intense student group led by David Ferris of Milford, Connecticut. Charles Chauncy thought the group had been dangerously enthusiastic: "They laid great Stress upon Impressions and Impulses; particularly, upon any Sense of Scripture that was suddenly and strongly suggested to their Minds."[16] Davenport became acquainted with some in the Philadelphia Synod after his graduation and received an invitation to preach at Hopewell and Maidenhead, New Jersey, the pulpits that John Rowland would eventually take. Instead of going to New Jersey, however, Davenport took a position at Southold in 1738.

News of Whitefield's revivals energized both Davenport and Barber, and Bar-ber began to receive revelations from God about his coming role in the awaken-ings. He felt a strong impression upon reading Habakkuk 2:3, "For the vision is yet for an appointed time, but at the end it shall speak and shall not lie: though it tarry, wait for it; because it will surely come; it will not tarry." In March 1740, Barber stayed up one night meditating, and again he was deeply moved, this time by Psalm 102:13: "Thou shalt arise and have mercy upon Zion; for the time to favor her, yea, the set time, is come." He took this as a direct order from God and promptly fainted. Barber recovered and set out from Oysterponds, de-pending on the Spirit alone to tell him where to go. He visited Davenport and preached at his church. At Oldmans, Barber stalled out, finding no more guid-ance from the Spirit, and according to historian Joseph Tracy, he went nowhere for months "till he grew fat and ragged." He then traveled to Rhode Island and met with Whitefield.[17]

Barber's visionary wanderings seem to have stimulated Davenport's penchant for religious extremes, as Davenport began holding meetings in his home and once apparently tried to preach for twenty-four hours straight. Finally, he too collapsed. When he recovered, Davenport began to run the church in a sepa-ratist style, picking only certain holy "friends" to admit to communion. Eleazar Wheelock, Davenport's brother-in-law, wrote from Southold in April, "Our Dear Br. D. . . . has had indeed a most wonderfull Visitation of God and is full of Life and Zeal & God is in an Extraordinary manner at work with his People here there are many I think Savingly wrought upon." Yale junior Samuel Buell also wrote to Wheelock and commented favorably on the "Glorious Tidings from Long-Island." In May and June, however, Wheelock wrote to Stephen Williams of Longmeadow, Massachusetts, denying reports that Davenport was delirious: "I was with him about a fortnight & perceived nothing of it," he said. It was the "extraordinary impressions he has had upon his mind" that put him in poor health, Wheelock thought. In early May, when they met, Whitefield noted that God had "lately highly honoured" Davenport, "by making use of his ministry for the conversion of many at the east end of Long Island." Whitefield had caught wind of some of Davenport's eccentric behavior, writing "he is looked upon as an enthusiast and a madman by many of his reverend pharisaical brethren." Whitefield thought this skepticism revealed only the great hostility that many pastors held toward the awakenings.[18]

Davenport himself wrote in July to Eleazar Wheelock, reporting that on his recent itinerant tours he had preached to "Very Large Congregations, So yt I was obliged mostly to preach in ye open Air & Highways." Like Whitefield, Davenport had gone out-of-doors to accommodate the people. Davenport particularly noted the ongoing revivals at Fagg's Manor and Philadelphia, "where there is a wonderful work indeed." At Philadelphia, Davenport had seen people falling down as dead who had to be carried out of the meetings. He was much impressed by the "Dear Brethren Tennents" and thought that the "opposing & unconverted Ministers seem afraid." The revivals continued in Southold, as well, where Wheelock had recently visited. Davenport specifically noted that his slave Flora had likely been saved, having been awakened partly by a conversation with Wheelock.[19]

After seeing Davenport, Whitefield returned to New Jersey in the company of the Tennent brothers and then proceeded to Philadelphia, where he soon began to reach the apex of his ministry in that city. "Though God has shewn me great things already in this place, yet to-day I have seen greater." That day he preached twice to crowds he described as "larger congregations than ever." In the evening, he spoke to a society of young women, and there the spiritual ecstasies went to new heights in a very charged environment. Whitefield tried to pray to open his message, but "my soul was so carried out, that I had no time to talk at all. A wonderful power was in the room, and with one accord, they began to cry out and weep most bitterly for the space of half an hour." Whitefield spoke to them and then left, but the women kept on praying for more than an hour, "confessing their most secret faults." Then physical manifestations commenced. "At length, the agonies of some were so strong, that five of them seemed affected as those who are in fits." Revealing the limits of his radicalism, Whitefield thought that the fits were too extreme: "Such-like bodily agonies, I believe, are from the devil," he wrote.[20]

Whitefield preached to enormous crowds that he estimated at fifteen thousand the next morning and twenty thousand at an afternoon farewell sermon, in which he recommended to the crowds, "Messrs. Tennent and their associates, being most worthy preachers of our Lord Jesus." In the squabbles dogging the Philadelphia Synod, Whitefield made his own position very clear. Upon his departure, Whitefield marveled at the Philadelphia area's revival: "I never saw a more general awakening in any place," he wrote. The evening before he left, he stopped again at the young women's meeting, but soon "two of them fell down in violent fits, so that I was obliged to leave them." He loved the emotional responses his ministry generated, but he knew emotions had to be contained within proper limits, and the fits were beyond his.[21]

Whitefield left Philadelphia and headed south for a few more days of preaching in southeast Pennsylvania and northern Delaware. He spoke at Wilmington and at Whiteclay Creek, where Charles Tennent's congregants were among his most devoted followers. He met with Alexander Craighead and Samuel Blair and rode with them to Nottingham. Whitefield recognized that the revival had already begun there "by the ministry of Mr. Blair, the Messrs. Tennents, and Mr. [John] Cross, the last of which had been denied the use of the pulpit by one of his own brethren, and was obliged to preach in the woods." Despite a small population and short notice, twelve thousand came to hear Whitefield preach at Nottingham. Thousands cried out during his sermon, almost drowning it out. Whitefield, joining in the ecstasies of the assembly, was himself "pierced" after the sermon, such that he thought he might die on the spot. "How sweetly did I lie at the feet of Jesus! . . . It almost took away my life." He revived, however, and his entourage retired to Blair's house.[22]

His final stop in Pennsylvania was an obvious one: Fagg's Manor, the site of Blair's great awakening. Whitefield's preaching unleashed a "greater commotion" than even the one at Nottingham. Many cried, while others laid on the ground, fainted, or looked up to the sky and called out for God's mercy. Whitefield thought the scene suggested the Day of Judgment. "One would imagine," he wrote, "none could have withstood the power, or avoided crying out," but one person did. Francis Alison, a hostile member of the Philadelphia Synod, approached Whitefield after the sermon, even as many still were crying in the congregation, and challenged him to a public debate. Whitefield hesitated, thinking the time was not right, but he reluctantly accepted. Alison asked him why he taught that those who did not have full assurance of salvation were "in a damnable condition." Whitefield argued that he taught no such doctrine, but only that believers should seek full assurance. When the crowd realized that Alison meant to shame Whitefield, they became testy, and one man yelled that he would drag Alison out of the meetinghouse. Whitefield scolded this man, but he also told Alison that he had come at a bad time. Alison apparently realized that he had put himself in some danger and so politely withdrew. There can be no doubt that this event signaled a key turning point; the anti-Whitefieldians had begun to muster their forces. Whitefield, though, made his way to Newcastle, Delaware, where he boarded a ship for Georgia.[23]

Three days after Whitefield's departure, the Philadelphia Synod met, churning with controversy over the Grand Itinerant's tour. The synod revisited the 1738 acts against itinerancy and unlettered ministers but could not come to a decision on alternative policies before Samuel Blair and Gilbert Tennent made the atmosphere unworkably tense by airing grievances against the antirevivalist ministers. Blair later claimed, "what I aimed at, was the faithful Discharge of Duty, and a conscientious Testimony against those Evils, for the Good of the Brethren guilty of them, and the Good of the Church, and to shew the Reasonableness of Encouraging rather than Hindering of Ministers to preach Christ's Gospel as they had Opportunity." Opponents, such as John Thomson, saw these complaints as attempts by the New Brunswick men to slander the anti-Whitefieldians without mentioning any specific names or facts. Intentionally or not, Blair and Tennent clinched the synod's inability to reach a compromise on itinerancy and ministerial credentials and set the stage for a full-fledged schism, which came in May 1741.[24]

The New Brunswick preachers could not be bothered for long by the synod's squabbling, however, and they regularly returned to Philadelphia to preach before large crowds. Tennent and Blair were joined there by James Davenport and John Rowland. They also addressed special services at the Presbyterian and Baptist churches. The *Pennsylvania Gazette* remarked that "the Alteration in the Face of Religion here is altogether surprizing. . . . Religion is become the Subject of most Conversations . . . All which, under God, is owing to the successful Labours of the Reverend Mr. Whitefield." To the north, Jonathan Dickinson began to see signs of revival in Elizabethtown in June, when "a remarkable manifestation of the divine presence" appeared. It chiefly began among the youths who had gathered for a special sermon. Dickinson, ever the moderate when it came to outward expressions, noted with satisfaction that "there was no crying out or falling down (as elsewhere has happened) but the inward distress and concern of the audience discovered itself by their tears and by an audible sobbing and sighing in almost all parts of the assembly." Those inclined toward "Enthusiastick Heats" were "easily and speedily regulated." Youths gave up their frolics and became interested in religion, and the church thronged with seekers of all ages. Three years later it appeared that perhaps sixty people were saved during the Elizabethtown awakening.[25]

Some began to complain publicly about the enthusiastic preachers. Philadelphia Baptist pastor Jenkin Jones's assistant, Ebenezer Kinnersly, proclaimed to the *Pennsylvania Gazette* that John Rowland's guest sermons at the Baptist meetinghouse were full of "Enthusiastick Ravings" and "whining, roaring Harangues" about the threat of damnation. The "deluded Creatures" who followed him had alarming responses to his sermons: some became "terrified to Distraction; others drove into Dispair." Others had more mystical responses: they "are fill'd brim-full of Enthusiastical Raptures and Extasies, pretending to have large Communications from God; to have seen ravishing Visions; to have been encompass'd, as it were, with Flames of Lightning, and there to have beheld our Blessed Saviour nail'd to the Cross, and bleeding before their Eyes in particular for them!" When Kinnersly spoke against Rowland at the Baptist church, a group of Rowland's supporters "shewed their Resentments by Running out of the Place of Worship in a most disorderly and tumultuous Manner." Kinnersly was particularly troubled by the types of people who protested: "The Foremost of the Gang, I am inform'd, was a Woman, who supports such a Character as Modesty forbids to mention; and as one Fool has often times made many, so this infamous Leader was followed by a Multitude of Negroes, and other Servants, among whom were some few of higher Stations, but not over-burthen'd with Discretion." Servants, slaves, and women leading a church walk-out seemed to Kinnersly evidence enough to show what consequences this enthusiastic religion could bring. Kinnersly's vigorous opposition earned him a public rebuke from his superior, Jenkin Jones.[26]

In the late summer, Gilbert Tennent began itinerating through south Jersey, Delaware, and Maryland. In south Jersey, there were only two settled ministers, and both opposed the revivalists. Apparently some evangelical congregants made a special plea for Tennent to visit. Like Whitefield, Tennent seems to have preached to friendly congregations, particularly at Bohemia Manor, Maryland, and at his brother Charles's church in Whiteclay Creek. In Tennent's absence, the controversy in the synod continued to stew, and the Donegal and New Castle Presbyteries began to take formal actions against Blair, Tennent, and Whitefield, complaining about the roaming preachers, their unorthodox theology, and their toleration of antinomian ecstasies. Some in the New Castle Presbytery would soon print the first major attack against Whitefield, *The Querists*. Tennent, however, could hardly pay attention to the growing feud in the Presbyterian ranks, as in November the returning Whitefield asked him to join him on a preaching tour of New England.[27]

The situation in the Middle Colonies exemplified the growing divisions over the evangelical movement. Antirevivalists within the Philadelphia Synod feared the effects of unrestrained itinerancy and enthusiasm. Moderate evangelicals like Samuel Blair and Jonathan Dickinson celebrated the awakenings but sought to restrain their noisy excesses. Some radical evangelical clerics like Gilbert Tennent publicly questioned the salvation of their ministerial colleagues. Lay radical evangelicals, like the women driven to fits by Whitefield's preaching, experienced a Spirit-filled awakening that brought frowns of concern from moderates. Some radical laypeople even led a walk-out from Philadelphia's Baptist church. Moderate evangelicals wanted to shelter the awakenings from the charges of critics like Charles Chauncy, but they defended the revivals in part by attempting to regulate lay enthusiasm and initiative. Rifts had begun to grow not only between Old Lights and evangelicals, but also between radical and moderate evangelicals.

"A Faithful Watchman on the Walls of Charlestown": Josiah Smith and Moderate Revivalism in South Carolina

In 1740, Charleston was the largest town in the southern colonies at about 6,500 residents. Mid-eighteenth-century South Carolina society was becoming more stratified between rich and poor, and black and white. Charleston's elites, like those of Philadelphia, Boston, and New York's, were becoming much more concerned with mimicking the styles and fashions of metropolitan London, a trend that evangelicals viewed with considerable unease, even though the processes associated with commercialization and Anglicization also helped create the transatlantic evangelical movement.[1]

Charleston's whites also had reasons to be nervous in 1740. South Carolina faced threats from epidemic disease, the Spanish empire, and, most disturbingly, its own slave population. Although one must exercise caution in looking for psychological causes of revivalism, it does not require much of a leap to imagine that these combined factors nicely prepared the religious communities of Charleston to receive Whitefield in 1740. Beginning in 1738, smallpox ravaged the town, followed by a yellow fever epidemic in summer 1739, which took the lives of half a dozen Charlestonians daily. Then, on September 9, 1739, just as word arrived that hostilities had begun between Britain and Spain, the Stono slave revolt began. Rebel slaves eventually killed more than twenty whites but were stopped as they headed south for the safe harbor of St. Augustine, Florida. The surviving rebels were brutally killed by vengeful whites. Another large conspiracy was apparently foiled north of Charleston in summer 1740. Anxious Carolinians resolved to stop provoking their slaves and to try and balance the black majority by restricting the importation of new slaves and recruiting more white settlers. They also passed a harsh Negro Act in May 1740. The anxiety in South Carolina society could not be placated by these steps alone, however.[2]

George Whitefield saw the tension of the time as a possible opening for the gospel. English newspapers kept him informed of the progress of the war between Britain and Spain, which made him hope that God would "bring mighty things to pass, whilst the world was busied in wars and rumours of wars." With these thoughts in mind, Whitefield took the pulpit at Josiah Smith's Independent meetinghouse on January 6, 1740. Smith was to become Whitefield's key ally in Charleston. Whitefield accused the audience of sin and worldliness, but he found them "polite" and unaffected. Whitefield was aware of the "Divine judgments lately sent amongst them," and he reminded the congregation of them in his sermon. They only squirmed at the reminder, and Whitefield could not convince them of the impropriety of their "affected finery, gaiety of dress, and a deportment ill-becoming" ones who had so recently tasted God's wrath. "Nothing is a greater sign of a people's being hardened," lamented Whitefield, "than their continuing unreformed under Divine visitations."[3]

The next day, Whitefield met with more success at the city's Huguenot church, and then returned to Smith's pulpit and addressed supporters who pleaded for another sermon before he left Charleston. He felt that many had broken under his preaching, but many others remained only polite. "It grieves me," he said, "to see people humane, hospitable, willing to oblige, and in every way accomplished, excepting that they are yet ignorant of *the one thing needful*."[4]

Whitefield, always on the move, was back in Charleston in March 1740, at which point he began a feud with Charleston's Anglican Commissary, Alexander Garden. He had met Garden in January and had pleasant rapport with him, but now their relationship turned ugly as Garden accused Whitefield of preaching publicly against him and the "generality of the [Anglican] clergy." He forbade Whitefield from continuing his tour in Charleston and threatened him with suspension if he did. Whitefield told Garden he would "regard that as much as I would a Pope's bull," and Garden eventually tossed Whitefield and his entourage out of his house. That afternoon Whitefield "drank tea" with Smith and preached at his meetinghouse.[5]

The next day Whitefield preached first at the Baptist church then again at Smith's, where he found his most receptive audience yet. On the Sabbath, Whitefield went and heard Garden paint him as a Pharisee, then spoke at Smith's church in the late afternoon, this time using the churchyard because the crowd was so large. On Monday, Whitefield was at Smith's church again, preaching more explicitly "than ever against balls and assemblies," and that night he took up his largest collection yet for the Bethesda orphanage. With his departure from the city, Whitefield noted hopefully that "God intended to visit some in Charleston with His salvation."[6]

Although South Carolina had little of the evangelical background of New England or the Middle Colonies, Josiah Smith's settlement there in 1728 heralded the beginnings of Charleston's connection to the international revivalist movement. Smith played a crucial role in promoting Whitefield's reputation and in handling the early awakenings in and around Charleston. While Smith was a thoroughgoing evangelical, he also preached a moderate revivalism that would restrain excesses, be they egalitarian, enthusiastic, or commercial. Smith promoted a form of Christianity that would come to define much of white South Carolina's religion: an evangelicalism that might threaten the planter class's consumer excesses but not the southern colonies' racial order.

Smith's southern colonial origins are striking. He was born in 1704 into the elite Smith clan of Charleston. His grandfather, Landgrave Thomas Smith, had served briefly as South Carolina governor in 1693–94. His father, Dr. George Smith, a prominent dissenter and graduate of the University of Edinburgh, moved the family to Bermuda, apparently soon after Josiah's birth. This placed Josiah and his family in the mainstream of the Atlantic trading system that used Bermuda as an entrepôt, shipping service center, and seasonal resort. Its location off the east coast of southern North America and favorable, healthful climate made the small island a good stopover in the Atlantic trades, and its residents often had connections to English movements designed to settle the Caribbean basin and counter the Spanish threat. In spite of the fact that Anglo-Bermudans were becoming predominantly Anglican, Smith and his family remained part of the smaller dissenting cohort in the town under the influence of Boston's powerful Congregationalists. Smith's father, lamenting the lack of proper ministers in Bermuda, eventually concluded that his own son would make a fine candidate and decided to send him to Cambridge, Massachusetts, to receive proper training.[7] Smith graduated from Harvard in 1725 and returned to the Independent church in Bermuda, which received his plain but vigorous preaching well and arranged for his ordination in Boston.

Benjamin Colman of the Brattle Street Church in Boston gave Smith a hearty endorsement in the preface to Smith's ordination sermon. "No one has risen among us & gone from us, so suddenly, with like esteem, affection & applause, as Mr. Smith has done. . . . It is an honour to our College to have such a Son to boast of among the Islands." Colman praised the propriety of Smith's sermon, saying that it did not strain the truth but instead was "natural & familiar, proper & pertinent," a high compliment from Boston's most influential pastor. Smith held up the dignity of Christ's prophetic office and asserted that those who mistreated Christ's ministers abused Christ himself: ministers "may claim the regards due to them that represent his Person and come cloth'd in his Authority, and the indignities you offer them terminate in Christ." Smith meant to challenge his flock to obey scriptural demands, no matter whom he might offend, vowing not to seek "repute from men of parts and distinction." He did not mention that he was one himself.[8]

In another sermon delivered the same weekend as his ordination, Smith argued that "the greater part of the World quench the Spirit" because of their affection for other things besides Christ. Here Smith signaled his intention to confront polite colonial southern society, lamenting "how many indulge themselves in a licentious course of the blackest impurity," including sexual sins and "vile affections." Many also "cringe to the golden Image, and idolize Mammon." The "indulgent pleasures" of the outwardly religious belied their pretensions to godliness, and Smith intended to expose their hypocrisy.[9]

With this mission in mind, Smith returned to Bermuda, but his work there was apparently hampered by two hurricanes that diminished the Independent congregation's resources. Whether because of financial want or other reasons, Smith traveled briefly to Boston with his father in 1727 and the next year moved to Cainhoy, South Carolina, on the Wando River near Charleston. There Smith began his long South Carolina ministry, which would last through Whitefield's awakenings and to the American Revolution. Smith became associate pastor at Charleston's Independent church in 1734 and then assumed his position of leadership because of the early death of his colleague Nathan Bassett in 1738. Smith had attracted the notice of British dissenting luminary and hymn-writer Isaac Watts by October 1739, who wrote to Smith's patron Colman that he appreciated Smith's sermon memorializing Nathan Bassett. Smith's writings had given Watts "a considerable idea of his pious and learned character." Watts wished that the dissenters in England could, like the Bostonians, send effective ministers among the Carolinians, but he feared that the London nonconformists were hamstrung by theological liberalism. Watts thought it more likely that Harvard would continue to supply most of the pulpits in the western Atlantic colonies.[10]

Smith and Alexander Garden, in Whitefield's absence, became embroiled in a print controversy concerning Whitefield's character, and Smith emerged as the key manager of Whitefield's revivals and reputation in Charleston and one of the main links in Whitefield's Atlantic correspondent network. In the January 12 edition of the *South-Carolina Gazette*, Smith began his defense of Whitefield in a letter to a Boston minister, presumably Colman. In it, Smith portrayed himself as an impartial judge, ready to criticize Whitefield if warranted. He claimed to have reserved assessment until he had actually seen and conversed with Whitefield, and now that he had, he heartily approved his work.

The "famous Son of Thunder" had "acquitted himself, if not to universal, yet to general Satisfaction" in his early ministry in Charleston. Smith knew that some had accused Whitefield of enthusiastic excesses, and this charge troubled Smith, too. He attributed the ecstatic manifestations to Whitefield's keen apprehension of the wrath of God, and he believed that Whitefield was a fine example of a tolerant and broad-minded spirit developing in the churches. Smith thought that Whitefield might lack some charity toward other ministers, but the two shared the same essentials in theology, and he was "not displeas'd to hear a Gentleman of the Establishment" preaching doctrines such as original sin. He commended Whitefield's attacks against Charleston's "BALLS and MID-NIGHT ASSEMBLIES, especially in the present Scituation of our Province."[11]

A long letter by "Arminius," generally thought to have been Garden, replied to Smith in the *South-Carolina Gazette*. The letter's main charge against Smith and Whitefield was immoderation. Arminius thought it strange that Smith's letter essentially conceded that Whitefield was an enthusiast, and yet it gave Whitefield the most effusive praise, comparing him to Isaiah or even Christ. "Who can think the Letter Writer, if he had not something in him bordering on Enthusiasm and an heated Imagination, could suppose . . . Mr. Whitefield to resemble Jesus Christ, cloathed in Flames, & coming to Judgment." Smith, following Whitefield, seemed to Arminius overly willing to pronounce people damned because of their non-Calvinist theology, all the more strange coming from "a Person who pretends to be an Advocate for Liberty and Toleration in all their Ease and Latitude." Arminius knew that members of Smith's and Colman's evangelical group prided themselves on their latitudinarian spirit, but how could one claim charitableness while damning other Christians to hell? Arminius argued that Smith sympathized with Whitefield not because of his godly character but because Whitefield agreed with Smith's theology, particularly on original sin, which Arminius considered an outdated and irrational doctrine.[12]

Whitefield did not help Smith's portrayal of him as an evangelical moderate with his publication of *Three Letters from the Reverend Mr. G. Whitefield* in February 1740. These made two points that struck Garden and the moderate Anglicans as outrageous. First, Whitefield condemned the popular latitudinarian archbishop John Tillotson, saying he "knew no more about true Christianity than Mahomet." Many of Benjamin Colman's evangelical friends would have found this charge ridiculous as well, as they fancied Tillotson's moderate and essentialist gospel. Whitefield's second charge, in "A Letter to the Inhabitants of Maryland, Virginia, North and South Carolina," was that southern slave owners' treatment of their slaves was too harsh. Reflecting on his January visit, he said he was "touched with a fellow-feeling of the miseries of the poor negroes." Though he knew that the criticism would make many white southerners angry, he asserted "GOD has a quarrel with you, for your abuse of and cruelty to the poor negroes." Given their poor treatment, Whitefield was surprised that the slaves had not more regularly revolted in the southern colonies.[13]

Whitefield reserved a special warning for the South Carolinians. God had been "contending with the people of *South-Carolina*" for two years, with disease, the Stono Rebellion, and the new war against Spain. "A foreign enemy is now threatening to invade you; and nothing will more provoke GOD, to give you up as a prey into their teeth, than impenitence and unbelief." Repentance, however, would mean protection from God, and perhaps also it would mean embracing Whitefield's revivals the next time he visited Charleston.[14]

Supplied with this fuel, the fire of criticism proceeded to burn in the *South-Carolina Gazette* with a response by Garden to Whitefield's denunciation of Tillotson and a mock poem on Whitefield in May, which rhymed, "in style more gross than good or evil, He calls us Children of the Devil." Smith, however, remained committed to painting Whitefield as an evangelical moderate. His most significant promotional work was *The Character, Preaching, &c. of the Reverend Mr. George Whitefield, Impartially Represented and Supported*, which was quickly arranged for publication in Boston by Colman. Benjamin Franklin, well known for his profitable friendship with Whitefield, also printed the sermon in Philadelphia.[15] It later came to serve as a preface for Whitefield's *Fifteen Sermons Preached on Various Important Subjects*. That book misidentified Smith as "Joseph," indicating that Whitefield's fame had already begun outlasting his brokers'.

Colman and William Cooper gave the introduction to Smith's sermon and argued that the revivals promoted no "private and party Cause, but that of primitive Piety and catholic Christianity." As for Whitefield, he was "the Wonder of the Age." Colman and Cooper presented Smith as a "Gentleman of good Sense" and "free from enthusiastic Impressions." Smith was qualified to speak because he was moderate, and he expressed his favorable view of Whitefield "with great Modesty and Caution."[16]

In the sermon, Smith announced his intention to "shew my impartial Opinion of that Son of Thunder, who has lately grac'd and warm'd this Desk; and would have been an Ornament, I think, to the best Pulpit in the Province." Smith only hoped that he could "clinch the Nails, this great Master of Assemblies has already fasten'd." Smith defended Whitefield's doctrines of original sin, justification by faith, spiritual regeneration, and the "Impressions or . . . inward Feelings of THE SPIRIT." Some might scoff at these beliefs as old-fashioned and extreme, but Smith argued that they were signs of biblical and moderate Christianity.

Whitefield's doctrines led him neither to the enthusiastic extremes of the evangelical radicals nor to the dead rationalism of the Anglicans. All his doctrines "are primitive, protestant, puritannick Ones; which our good Fathers, Conformists & Dissenters, have fill'd their Writings with." Smith painted evangelical doctrine as broad-minded, and he insisted that the insinuations that Whitefield's revivals led to immoderate excesses were unwarranted: "our Preacher is orthodox in his Doctrine, which both excludes Licentiousness, establishes the Law, and exalts free Grace." Even in his insistence on the inner impressions of the Spirit, Whitefield took a moderate path: "He renounc'd all Pretensions to the extraordinary Powers & Signs of Apostleship, Gifts of Healing, Speaking with Tongues, the Faith of Miracles; Things peculiar to the Ages of Inspiration, and extinct with them." He still argued, however, that in salvation sinners would feel the work of the Spirit within their souls. "And what is there in all this repugnant to Reason!"[17]

Smith reserved some criticism for Whitefield, however, regarding the itinerant's immoderate accusations against his opponents. All Whitefield's fine preaching and doctrine could not "win my Applause or Approbation of some few harsher Epithets and Expressions (you know what I mean) which dropt from his Lips." We may readily imagine that Smith had in mind Whitefield's attacks on Tillotson and South Carolina slaveholders and his general "inveighing against the clergy," such as his accusations that the Anglican priests had ceased emphasizing the "true nature of regeneration." Smith felt uncomfortable with these public denunciations of other pastors, but he believed Whitefield's improprieties came as an unfortunate side effect of his zeal for orthodoxy. Smith's and Colman's cohort warned Whitefield that even he, despite his celebrity, could be excluded from favor among the moderate evangelicals, as Gilbert Tennent and James Davenport soon would be.[18]

Much more to Smith's liking, however, was Whitefield's attack on the entertainments of Charleston's social elites. "The politest, the most modish of our Vices, he strook at; the most fashionable Entertainments." Specifically, Whitefield railed against "our Balls and Mid-night Assemblies, that Bane of all that is serious and religious." If the socialites took seriously Whitefield's challenge to them, Smith believed that even "our Theatre would soon sink and perish." Smith thought it clear that even if the indulgent would not hear him or Whitefield, they should at least listen to the voice of God in the several judgments that Charleston had faced in the past two years and let "the louder Roarings of Providence, awe and restrain us."[19]

Smith presented Whitefield as a man of great faith and morality, and insisted that Whitefield "affects no Party in Religion." He timed his Sunday sermons to not conflict with the churches' scheduled hours of worship, and "he would not tempt away Hearers from their proper and respective Pastors." Smith's Whitefield had no intention of undermining the authority of the churches. Instead, with a "noble and generous, a catholick and christian Spirit," he embraced devotees of every Protestant denomination. Smith also noted Whitefield's charitable work at the Bethesda orphanage in Georgia, to which his own church made a significant donation. Smith believed this charity would give his congregation much more joy "than what we contribute to the Support of Balls and Assemblies of Musick, to the Pride and Luxuries of Life."[20]

In the end, Smith offered an assessment of why God might have raised Whitefield up for that time. He cautioned that he had no spirit of prophecy, but he thought he knew enough to offer a chastened reading of what God was doing: "Behold! . . . It looks as if some happy Period were opening, to bless the World with another Reformation. Some great Things seem to be upon the Anvil, some big Prophesy at the Birth; God give it Strength to bring forth!" It appeared to him that God might have raised Whitefield up, like Luther and Calvin before him, to accomplish a second Reformation. In Smith's reading, there was no conflict between a second "Reformation" and simple moral reformation; they would go hand in hand.[21] It is clear, however, that Smith viewed the revivals as designed not only to break up the polite culture of the Atlantic world's ports, but also to bring catharsis to corrupt Protestant theology and resurrect dead religion.

With *The Character, Preaching, &c.*, Smith had produced one of the most enduring defenses of Whitefield's character. Whitefield returned to South Carolina on July 1. He continued to cultivate a close relationship with such converts as the planters Hugh and Jonathan Bryan, while giving less attention in his *Journals* to Smith, despite preaching regularly at Smith's meetinghouse. Whitefield also pursued his ongoing battle with Garden, whom Whitefield heard give a sermon that he called "virulent, unorthodox, and inconsistent." In a sermon given a week later, Garden cast Whitefield as the inheritor of the long tradition of rank enthusiasm, which in South Carolina had led most notoriously to the Dutartres family episode of 1724, in which the family, influenced by mystical pietism, fell into incest and murder. Whitefield noted that upon hearing the accusations against him he "felt the Blessed Spirit strengthening me and refreshing my soul."[22]

Despite his feuds with Garden, Whitefield remained optimistic about Charleston and arranged with Smith and other dissenters to set up a weekly lecture for him and other gospel preachers. He was now ready to make a clear break with the Anglicans, if he had not done so already by his inflammatory accusations. "I advised the people, since the Gospel was not preached in the church, to go hear it in the meeting-houses." Whitefield was hopeful, too, about the attack on the vanity of the elites. "On my first coming," he wrote, "the people of Charleston seemed to be wholly devoted to pleasure." But since his revivals had begun, he noticed that many ladies had become convinced that their jewelry-wearing was sin, and dance instructors claimed they were running out of business. Furthermore, he saw progress with the slaves, who came to visit him regularly and whose masters now often taught them to be Christians. Whitefield even dreamed of setting up a "negro school" in South Carolina. His friends the Bryan brothers, who would briefly become the radical leaders in South Carolina's evangelical movement, soon decided to take up that cause.[23] Whitefield, however, left Charleston again in August.

In late 1740 came another particular judgment of God that seemed to vindicate Whitefield's cause, at least in Smith's eyes. On November 18, fire rampaged through Charleston, and while it seems to have killed few or none, it burned a third of the town and much of the merchants' stores of rum and military supplies. Petitions for relief estimated the losses at £250,000. Smith responded with *The Burning of Sodom*, which Colman and Cooper arranged to publish in Boston. The Boston ministers commended Smith again as "a faithful Watchman on the Walls of Charlestown," who with "the zealous Whitefield, had boldly, but in vain, rebuk'd and threatened" the townspeople for their vanity. Colman and Cooper hoped that Whitefield's critics would realize that Whitefield was a "Prophet," and that the townspeople would repent of their ill treatment of God's servants. Jerusalem had burned twice as a judgment for abusing the messengers of God, and "London's PLAGUE and FIRE came soon after the casting out and silencing a Body of . . . faithful ministers." Charlestonians and Bostonians both should pay attention and repent.[24]

Smith blamed the fire on the vanity and corruption of the city. The same communication and transportation technologies integrating the Atlantic world for revival also made Charleston a busy node of Atlantic trades, but Smith loved the one and hated the other. Smith noted that many cities had been destroyed by God in the Bible, including Tyre, which "was a Mart of Nations; like our Charlestown, a Haven for Ships, commodiously scituated in the Center of Trade, and maritime wealth." Like Charleston, God brought Tyre to destruction for the vanity of the tradesmen. Smith's patron Colman had warned Boston's merchants several years earlier about the example of Tyre, but he also argued that increased wealth and mercantile traffic could open up great opportunities for the expansion of the church. Charleston's merchants, according to Smith, had forsaken an opportunity to make their merchandise "holiness to the Lord."[25]

As with Sodom, God destroyed Charleston for its gross sins. Smith was not sure "whether we have any Sodomites in our Town strictly so," but he suspected that there might be. "Such abandon'd Wretches generally curse the Sun, and hate the Light." Smith knew enough, however, to believe that Charleston's sins were as grievous and unabashed as Sodom's. Among the worst offenses were sexual sins: "Let us enquire seriously, Whether our Filthiness be not found in our Skirts?—Whether our Streets, Lanes and Houses did not burn with Lust, before they were consumed with Fire?" There was rampant obscenity and foolish talk: "what Impurities have been belch'd out of the Places of publick Concourse, and defiled our very BAY!"[26]

According to Smith, there was one kind of sin in which Charlestonians might have surpassed the Sodomites, and that was interracial sexual mixing. Smith knew it was impolitic even to speak of sexual engagements between blacks and whites, but God "has seen Heaps of Pollution conceal'd from Man, and in some of those Houses, now lying in Ashes, which requir'd Brimstone it self to purify, and Fire to burn up—That unnatural Practice of some Debauchees, that Mixture and Production, doubly spurious, of WHITE AND BLACK; and taking those to our Bed and Arms, whom at another Time we set with the Dogs of our Flock, ought to stand in red Capitals, among our crying Abominations! I know not, if Sodom had done this!" Anglo-Carolinians' feelings about such mixing were ambivalent, as theories of racial difference and "miscegenation," a term invented during the Civil War, had not yet hardened in 1740 into clear categories. Undoubtedly white men and black women were engaging in sex with some regularity on the plantations and in Charleston's brothels. While South Carolina had a law against white and black cohabitation, as did most of the English colonies, it seems that occasional leeway was offered for public black and white liaisons. In the 1730s the South-Carolina Gazette featured sporadic verses and letters nervously joking about white and black sexual relations. Smith suggested at least two fears that the mixing raised. One was that the production of children from such unions might jeopardize the clear distinctions of race required to maintain slavery. The other was that black and white sex hinted at the unnatural mixing of man and beast. "Slave" was not yet necessarily equated with "black" at this point in Carolina culture, but nevertheless the confusing implications of Anglo elites having sex with people "whom at another Time we set with the Dogs" was unmistakable to Smith. South Carolinians made little public comment about mulatto children during the period, and in law most southern colonies made no distinction between mulattoes and those with pure African ancestry. One article in the South-Carolina Gazette from 1735 made plain that the mulattoes were "seldom well-beloved" by either whites or blacks, with full-blooded Africans thinking them snobbish and full-blooded Anglos seeing them as impudent.[27] To

Smith they seemed "doubly spurious" and reason enough for fire from heaven to descend on the corrupt city.

At root, Smith attributed the liaisons between white men and black women to "greediness," an immoral acquisitiveness connected to the broader consumerism of Charleston polite society. If any consistent condemnation ran through Smith's thought, it was against the effect that the trades had on polite Charleston society. The "PRIDE of Sodom" flourished in the city, Smith believed, and appeared in Charlestonians' "Dress and Address, in our Mien, & High Looks, and supercilious Language." The mimicking of metropolitan Britain had produced their vanity; "our costly Furniture, our Plate, China, Pictures, and our rich Paintings" had swelled the Charlestonians' pride. Some of the women, in particular, had indulged the pride of consumerism, and God had "taken away the Bravery of their tinkling Ornaments; the Chains, the Bracelets, the Ear-Rings, the changeable Suits of Apparel." Smith sharply denounced the consumption of products made possible by the very same processes that had helped facilitate the development of transatlantic evangelicalism and that had helped make his own family wealthy.[28]

For its greediness, God's judgment visited Charleston. "Yes: CHARLES-TOWN is fallen, is fallen." Yet God remained merciful by not allowing the whole city to be consumed or many to die, and all the churches were saved. The warning remained, though, that Charleston must repent. This fire, Smith cautioned, was insignificant next to the threat of the great conflagration in the last days, when "not a Town, a Province, a Nation, but the whole World, shall be burnt up." Whitefield seems only to have echoed Smith's charge when he returned to Charleston in December and received news of the fire.[29]

Whitefield subsequently devoted much of his time to mentoring the Bryan brothers, and he worked with Hugh to produce a letter with a much more radical interpretation of the fire than what Smith had offered. Bryan argued that the judgment of God came against Charleston because of Anglican blind guides, who, "Judas-like, betray our Lord and Master with pretended Kisses of Friendship." Those who criticized Whitefield for not keeping strictly to the expectations of the church establishment cared more for "these Appendages of Religion" than they did for "poor perishing Souls, that are wandering in worse than Egyptian Darkness." The priests had the blood of the lost on their hands. "I doubt not but the Devil triumphs in beholding these Shepherds at the Head of their Flocks," Bryan wrote. Smith had suggested that the fire vindicated Whitefield's denunciations of Charleston's vain excesses, but Bryan raised the prospect that the priests themselves were to blame for the fire.[30] This was a fine point that, again, divided the radical from the moderate awakeners: Smith defended himself in the letters to Arminius and accused Garden publicly of bad faith, but never would he go so far as to blame the fire on the priests' sins. This may have contributed to some private tension between Smith and Whitefield. Smith had already cautioned Whitefield against publicly denouncing pastors of any Protestant communion, and now, with Whitefield's approval, Hugh Bryan had made the most harsh accusations imaginable in the pages of the *South-Carolina Gazette*.

This extravagant behavior, which resulted in the temporary arrest and detention of Whitefield and Bryan, may also help explain the relative silence of Whitefield's *Journals* about Smith, despite the fact that Whitefield continued regularly to use Smith's meetinghouse in his summer and winter visits of 1740–41. Whitefield wrote a letter to Smith in February and seemed indirectly to apologize. "You have been kind to me in many respects; but I have been ungrateful to you, and infinitely more so to my gracious God," Whitefield told Smith, "I have not failed frequently to bemoan my unworthiness."[31] Whether this reflected just a formulaic show of humility or a substantive split between Whitefield and Smith is unclear.

Whatever the case, Smith remained a key player in the evangelical network and the most active manager of Whitefield's revivals in the South Carolina low country. In a postscript to the January 22, 1741, issue of the *Gazette*, Smith convinced the paper to publish Smith's colleagues' accounts of Whitefield's reception in New England. In June, one of Whitefield's critics matched Smith's collection of pro-Whitefield letters with anti-Whitefield and anti-Tennent letters, bemoaning the "sectarian enthusiastick Madness" that came in their wake. As of late 1741, Smith was still feuding with Whitefield's critics and his own.[32]

The year 1742 proved a difficult one across the colonies for the revivalist movement because the taint of enthusiasm seems finally to have jaded popular opinion. In January, Charleston's paper published the *Boston Weekly Post Boy*'s account of radical revivalist James Davenport's ministry, with particular notice given to Davenport's eager denunciations of local pastors as unconverted. The paper's next issue recorded Whitefield's suspension from pastoral duties by Garden, and then in March, as we shall see in a subsequent chapter, Hugh Bryan's true radicalism was exposed when he confessed to being tricked by Satan into claiming prophetic authority and teaching slaves that they might become God's agents of judgment against the colony.[33]

Smith and the recently arrived dissenting pastor James Parker tried gently to spin the Bryan episode as something other than an utter disaster for the evangelical interest with a letter defending the instruction of slaves in Christianity. While not addressing Bryan's case directly, they argued that all Protestants, led by the advice of the bishop of London, should agree to the Christian instruction of the slaves. Obviously, they posited, this should be done with the approval of the planters. If Whitefield encouraged Christianizing the slaves, then he was only doing what all good Anglicans should do, just as Whitefield's doctrine of original sin was faithful to the best Anglican principles. A final blow to the awakeners came in June with the suicide of Anne Le Bresseur, "a prime disciple of Mr. Whitefield's," who shot herself and died claiming full assurance of salvation. She reportedly gave her child over to Garden's care. Not even a letter from Isaac Watts in September recommending Whitefield's character could salvage the revivalist movement in Charleston for the time being.[34]

Smith's efforts continued, however, despite these embarrassments and his colleague James Parker's death in July 1742. Whitefield might come and go, but Smith and his congregation remained the most significant force regularly working for reformation and moderate revival in Charleston. He also continued to promote Whitefield, regardless of what personal reservations he had about the itinerant's excesses. For instance, Smith defended the Bethesda orphanage in the northern colonial presses, most notably in the *Christian History* in 1744. Smith reported that on a visit to Bethesda, he was asked to administer the Lord's Supper, an experience so meaningful that he thought it was like "eating Bread in the Kingdom of Heaven." He continued to dismiss the "Deists, Socinians, Arminians, and Carnalists" who criticized Whitefield and his orphanage. Another of Thomas Prince's correspondents, one of the orphanage's administrators, reported in the same edition that "Religion seems in general to be at a low Ebb in Carolina," but that some remained faithful to the cause of revival. "Mr. Smith labours in his Work, and wishes a happy Revival of Religion."[35]

Whitefield periodically visited Charleston in the mid-1740s. In 1746, the *Boston Gazette* published a letter from Smith commenting on Whitefield's most recent visit, which Smith said was more effective than ever. Smith remained impressed by Whitefield's "genteel Behaviour." Whitefield enjoyed larger audiences at Smith's meetinghouse than before. Once more, there were rumors afoot that Whitefield had associated himself with radicals, but this time, it was the Moravians. Smith assured the Bostonians that this was not the case: "he is far from it, and a judicious Calvinist in Doctrine."[36]

Smith suffered a debilitating stroke in 1749. This affliction severely restricted Smith's public advocacy for Whitefield and the gospel, but his career continued for another quarter century. Before the stroke felled him, Smith apparently contributed to the evangelical wooing of John Newton, the slave trader and eventual leading evangelical and author of the hymn "Amazing Grace, How Sweet the Sound." Newton recalled years later that he came to Charleston, apparently with a cargo of slaves, and happened upon "a dissenting minister, named Smith, who . . . I believe to have been an excellent and powerful preacher of the gospel." During the American Revolution, Josiah Smith was an ardent patriot, as was his son, the plantation agent Josiah Smith Jr. When Charleston was captured, Smith was exiled to Philadelphia despite his old age and poor health, and he died there on October 19, 1781. He was buried next to Gilbert Tennent at the Arch Street Church.[37]

Smith's work as the chief evangelical voice in Charleston during the revivals reveals several distinctive features of early evangelicalism in the southern colonies. First, it was contested—and not just between Whitefield's friends and Whitefield's enemies, but also between moderate and radical supporters of Whitefield. Although Smith rarely made public comments critical of Whitefield, his warning in *The Character, Preaching, &c.* and subsequent management of Whitefield's reputation made it clear that Smith wanted to negotiate a middle way between Garden's rationalist hostility toward revivalism of all kinds and Bryanesque enthusiasm. Smith hoped that Whitefield would help him maintain this moderate course for the revivals. He envisioned an evangelicalism focused on personal salvation and critical of the consumer excesses of Charleston's elites. He would tolerate no damning of orthodox Christian leaders, however, and would countenance no challenge to the racial order. The dominant position in white southern evangelicalism, beginning with Smith and continuing for more than two hundred years, was never socially egalitarian. The radical impulse remained the predilection of the African American churches and a handful of enthusiasts like Hugh Bryan.[38]

Smith's denunciations of Charleston's commercial excesses also illustrate the ambivalent relation of early evangelicalism to Atlantic commerce and communication. Anglicization and the consumer revolution of the eighteenth century depended on improved communication, mercantile, and transportation networks. The Smith family's prosperity and South Carolina's very existence as a colony came from the expansion of the Atlantic trades system.[39] Whitefield's revivalist network depended on these very same trends..Early evangelicals tried hard to purify their movements of excessive and vain consumption, but it was difficult for them to maintain a clear distinction between those changes that allowed Whitefield to become the "Pedlar in Divinity" and those that made it possible for Charleston elites to cultivate a genteel British culture in their provincial capital. Colman's and Smith's evangelicals sanctified commercial pursuits that promoted charity and evangelical activism but hoped that the values of the Kingdom of God could restrain the excesses and abuses of waxing mercantile capitalism. After a generation, southern evangelicalism would take a more agrarian path than its northern evangelical cousin, but in the 1740s, Boston and Charleston still shared many attributes in common as western Atlantic outposts of British commerce and culture.

Smith's work, finally, helps show that Whitefield's ministry, though decisive, was managed by figures such as Smith. Whitefield had the luxury of being able to leave whenever he grew weary of a location's intransigence, but local leaders had to continue promoting the movement after his departure. Sometimes Whitefield left real problems in his wake that men like Smith worked to alleviate. We have known that Whitefield depended on a network of supporters, but we have not done enough to consider these supporters' experiences of revivalism or to show how challenging the promotion of Whitefield's revivals could be. The work certainly tested the moderate Smith, who remained faithful to Whitefield's cause even as he tried to contain the excesses and accusations it elicited.

"This Is No Other Than the Gate of Heaven": George Whitefield in New England

Although Edwards's Northampton awakening had definitely cooled by 1736, New Englanders had hardly given up on the possibility of a larger revival. Sudbury's pastor Israel Loring gave the Massachusetts election day sermon in 1737 and called on New Englanders to ask God for more seasons like Northampton's. Because the Holy Spirit created revival, "let us earnestly seek to God by Prayer, to pour him out upon us for that End." He found special encouragement in the Northampton awakening to think that God might be planning something great. "His People there, have had a marvellous Visit from the Lord of Hosts . . . He has revived Religion marvellously among them, by pouring out his Spirit upon them."[1]

New Englanders began to hear about George Whitefield in 1739, and many hoped that he would soon visit them. Benjamin Colman of Boston's Brattle Street Church wrote to Whitefield in December 1739 after having received a letter from him. Whitefield estimated that he might come to New England by summer 1740.[2] Colman was deeply impressed by what he had learned about Whitefield. He had read Whitefield's *Journals*, as well as some of his sermons. Colman wrote that he had never encountered anything comparable to Whitefield's ministry, although he had witnessed "uncommon Operations of the holy Spirit . . . ; as in our Country of Hampshire of late; the Narrative of which by Mr. Edwards, I suppose you may have seen." If Whitefield would come to New England, he would find the churches' Calvinist doctrine to his liking, "how short soever we may come of your Fervours." Colman told him that the churches had been praying for him publicly, and that when he arrived he could use the commodious Brattle Street Church for meetings. In a letter to Gilbert Tennent, Whitefield wrote that he found Colman's published sermons "acute and pointed, but I think not searching enough by many degrees." If anything, Colman was too polite for

Whitefield. Nevertheless, Whitefield wrote back to Colman and promised that when he came to New England "I shall endeavour to recommend an universal charity amongst all the true members of CHRIST's mystical body." Because of this universal spirit, he suggested that he might stay in the fields to preach, and out of the meetinghouses. He appreciated Colman's latitudinarianism, and they both hoped that the old division of Anglican versus dissenter would become irrelevant in light of the ministry of the new birth.[3]

Jonathan Edwards also received word of Whitefield's revivals, and in November 1739 Whitefield wrote to him, desiring to visit Northampton to see for himself the fruit of the 1734–35 awakening. Edwards wrote back in February 1740, encouraging Whitefield to travel to Northampton but warning him not to expect much. Edwards was heartened by God's raising up Whitefield in the Church of England "to revive the mysterious, spiritual, despised, and exploded doctrines of the gospel." This might be a sign of the coming Kingdom of God, Edwards thought.[4]

The Boston and Philadelphia newspapers began picking up stories about Whitefield's prodigious meetings in England in spring 1739, and Whitefield's fame began to spread into the hinterlands by early 1740. For instance, pastor Nicholas Gilman of Exeter, New Hampshire, on a visit to Boston, began reading Whitefield's *Journals* in mid-January 1740 and commented with admiration on Whitefield's "most Indefatigable labours to Advance the Kingdom of Christ." He borrowed more of Whitefield's sermons from Colman. In June, Gilman noted that "Mr. Whitefield [was] Now much the Subject of Conversations."[5]

In July, Whitefield wrote to Colman to announce that he was coming soon, perhaps within a month, and to ask Colman to spread the word in friendly churches. This advance publicity worked wonderfully, and when Whitefield arrived in Newport, Rhode Island, on September 14, 1740, New England was abuzz with talk of his coming. In Newport, Whitefield was welcomed by Nathaniel Clap, a venerable Congregational minister, and the wandering Jonathan Barber of Oysterponds, Long Island. Whitefield had earlier written the disconsolate Barber, telling him that he did not presume to judge whatever dealings God had with him. As for his visionary experiences, "I rather rejoice in them, having myself been blessed with many experiences of the like nature." He told Barber to expect persecution when God dealt with him in extraordinary ways.[6] These encouraging words led Barber to come to Newport to receive Whitefield. Upon meeting, they agreed that Barber would become part of Whitefield's entourage.

After some successes in preaching, particularly at Clap's meetinghouse, Whitefield traveled north to Boston, where he arrived on September 18. Boston was the largest town in the colonies but still only a small provincial capital with about 17,000 people. In 1740, it was in decline, and it would slowly lose population up through the American Revolution. War with Spain, and later with France, left many widows in Boston, and the city faced high taxes and inflation. The poor in Boston were many, and they responded exuberantly to Whitefield, as they would to the radical piety of James Davenport and others.[7]

As usual, Whitefield met with Anglican authorities in Boston, most notably the Commissary Timothy Cutler, the former Congregationalist rector of Yale turned Anglican "apostate." Cutler was the most formidable proponent of Anglicanism in the colonies, and he and Whitefield did not see eye to eye about Whitefield's relationship with non-Anglicans. Cutler argued that dissenters had no legitimate ordination because they did not follow in the line of apostolic succession. Whitefield thought their ordinations were legitimate, primarily because they preached the new birth: "I saw regenerate souls among the Baptists, among the Presbyterians, among the Independents, and among the Church folks—all children of God, and yet all born again in a different way of worship," he told Cutler. Whitefield was able to leave Cutler on friendly terms, but he would receive a much warmer welcome among the Congregationalists, especially from Benjamin Colman. After visiting Cutler he preached at the Brattle Street Church to about four thousand.[8]

Whitefield spoke from supporters' Boston pulpits as well as on Boston Common. On September 20, he preached at Joseph Sewall's Old South Church to about six thousand, and in the afternoon he addressed a crowd at the common that he estimated at eight thousand, although the papers guessed five thousand. The next day he attended Sunday morning services at the Brattle Street Church and spoke at Thomas Foxcroft's Old Brick Church in the afternoon. The crowd pressing to see him was so large that he went out to the common again and preached to an enormous assembly he totaled at fifteen thousand, close to the whole population of Boston (the newspapers guessed eight thousand). On Monday morning he sermonized at John Webb's New North Church to about six thousand. Then, in the afternoon, tragedy struck the tour. At Samuel Checkley's New South Church, the sound of a breaking board in the gallery triggered a stampede among the overflow crowd. A number of people were severely trampled, and some jumped from the balcony. Five people died. Whitefield decided to go on with the message he planned to deliver, only moving out to the common. No doubt this suggested insensitivity in Whitefield's character, but the crowd wanted him to go on, and one could hardly imagine a better moment for people to contemplate their mortality.[9]

Whitefield visited Harvard and was not impressed with the size of the school or its spirit. He noted that "bad books," such as those by John Tillotson and Samuel

Clarke, defenders of natural religion, were popular there, not the Puritan classics. Whitefield would later regret his harsh assessment of Harvard and Yale and would become a great supporter of the colleges. Whitefield also toured neighboring towns, including Roxbury and Charlestown, in his circuit. On September 27, Whitefield preached to one of his greatest crowds yet, fifteen thousand, on the common. Many were deeply affected, and Whitefield himself wrote that he felt like shouting, "This is no other than the House of God and the Gate of Heaven." Boston Common had become a portal to divine glory.[10]

Whitefield began taking collections for the Bethesda Orphanage, and the number of pounds given was truly remarkable: perhaps £3,000 in local currency. Boston outpaced collections even in London. On September 28 alone, he collected more than £1,000 in services at the Old South and Brattle Street churches. After speaking at Brattle Street in the afternoon, Whitefield held two private meetings that showed the breadth of his appeal. The first was with the governor, Jonathan Belcher, who was an evangelical supporter of Whitefield. The second was with "a great number of negroes," who requested a private session with him. He preached to them on the conversion of the Ethiopian in Acts 8.[11]

Whitefield visited towns up the coast from Boston from September 29 to October 6, finding some successes but also a great deal of passivity. Maine and New Hampshire had a substantial revival tradition, having seen large numbers of conversions and admissions to full communion in the 1727–28 earthquake awakening, and to a lesser extent in 1735–36 as a devastating "throat distemper" (diphtheria) raged there. He preached as far north as York, Maine, at the church of the well-respected Samuel Moody. His northern tour gave Nicholas Gilman of Exeter, who had been reading Whitefield's *Journals* and sermons for almost a year, a chance to meet him. Gilman was perhaps not as adulatory in his initial response to Whitefield as one might expect, noting that "there are Various Conjectures about Mr. Whitefield," but expressing hope that he truly was "a Man of an Excellent Spirit." Whitefield's appearance precipitated a conversion crisis for Gilman, as well, and set him on the path to becoming one of the most radical of New England's evangelicals. Whitefield won some notable converts in Maine, especially John Rogers. The pastor at Kittery, Rogers had been in the ministry for thirty years when he heard Whitefield, but he had never experienced conversion. Whitefield's ministry convinced him of his need for the new birth, and afterwards he became one of Whitefield's foremost proponents in Maine. Rogers's son Daniel, a tutor at Harvard, would soon join Whitefield's entourage and seek his own assurance of salvation. The revivals in Maine and New Hampshire would not begin in force until late 1741, however.[12]

Returning to Boston, Whitefield continued seeing large audiences, but he also gravitated toward Tennent's confrontational style as he spoke against unconverted ministers. "I am persuaded," he wrote in his journal, "[that] the generality of preachers talk of an unknown and unfelt Christ." He felt energized by confronting the unsaved clergy: "Unspeakable freedom God gave me while treating on this head." Although some of the ministers may have grown uneasy at such talk, Whitefield drew ever-larger crowds, until he finally announced a farewell sermon on October 12, which drew a crowd estimated at twenty thousand. If reasonably accurate, this was the largest crowd ever assembled in America up to that time.[13]

From Boston, Whitefield traveled west through New England. Delivering on his promise, Whitefield went slightly out of his way to visit Northampton. It was a poignant occasion for Edwards, who had waited five long years for revival fire to reignite in Northampton. Edwards shed tears during Whitefield's preaching. Whitefield, too, was deeply affected by his visit and impressed with Edwards's wife and children, who seemed to him models of piety and propriety. Whitefield's preaching in Northampton reached a crescendo on the Sabbath, as "Mr. Edwards wept during the whole time of exercise" in the morning. "Mr. Whitefield's sermons were suitable to the circumstances of the town," Edwards wrote later to Thomas Prince, "containing just reproofs of our backslidings." He reported to Whitefield that the revival bore lasting fruit, including the conversion of some of the Edwardses' children. Immediately after Whitefield's departure, however, Edwards did begin a sermon series on the parable of the sower (Matthew 13), including warnings that short-lived episodes of heated preaching and crying did not make for saving religion. He subtly warned that Whitefield's brand of revivalism was ripe for religious hypocrisy. Edwards would continue to support Whitefield, but he insisted that Northampton would experience revival on his terms.[14]

Accompanied by Edwards, Whitefield made his way south to East Windsor, the home of Edwards's parents. Along the way Whitefield kept preaching on unconverted ministers, and at one point Edwards cautioned Whitefield about not judging other ministers too harshly or trying to ascertain whether they were converted. Edwards supported Whitefield overall, but he certainly had doubts about the emotionalism and rash judgments that seemed to characterize the itinerant's ministry. In East Windsor, Whitefield preached to Timothy Edwards's congregation and then visited the elderly pastor and his wife Esther Stoddard Edwards, sharing supper and staying the night in their home.[15]

Out of Whitefield's journey through Connecticut came two remarkable testimonies of conversion. The first was from the East Windsor saddler Samuel

Belcher. Though Belcher grew up in the family of Joseph Belcher, pastor at Ded-ham, Massachusetts, he became "Cold and Dull" in matters of salvation, and though he experienced some concerns for his soul before 1740, they had not lasted. Whitefield's arrival signaled the beginning of a six-month-long conver-sion crisis. When "mr Whitefield p[re]ached here, . . . I was Greatly effected with his preaching both here and att Hartford," Belcher wrote. Belcher grew cold again, but then in April he met a man in Lebanon, Connecticut, who told of the revival there, which deeply impressed him. Then pastors Eleazar Wheelock of Lebanon and Benjamin Pomeroy of Hebron preached at East Windsor, and Belcher fell under deeper convictions than ever before. He felt the terrors of sin and the threat of damnation, "but God was pleased to enable me to Cry mightily unto him in the bitterness of my Soul for mercy in and through Jesus Christ." While he was praying, "I felt my Load Go of and my mouth was Stopt and I Could not utter one word for Some time and I felt as if my heart was Changed." When Belcher could speak again, he began praising God and he knew he had been saved.[16] For Belcher, Whitefield's exhortations began the conversion pro-cess, but Wheelock's and Pomeroy's preaching, and his own prayers, finished the ordeal.

Whitefield's appearance also represented a beginning point for the conver-sion of Nathan Cole, a farmer and carpenter from Kensington, Connecticut. Cole grew up as what he called an "Arminian," likely meaning that he casually assumed that good works would save him. He began to hear reports about White-field's tour, and he "longed to see and hear him, and wished he would come this way." News arrived in October that Whitefield had left Boston for Northamp-ton. Then on October 23, a messenger arrived and told him that Whitefield was coming to nearby Middletown later that morning. Cole ran in from the field to tell his wife that they were leaving immediately, fearing they would not have time to get there. As they neared the road to Middletown, he wrote that

> I saw before me a Cloud or fogg rising; I first thought it came from the great River, but as I came nearer the Road, I heard a noise something like a low rum-bling thunder and presently found it was the noise of Horses feet coming down the Road and this Cloud was a Cloud of dust. . . . I could see men and horses Sliping along in the Cloud like shadows . . . every horse seemed to go with all his might to carry his rider to hear news from heaven for the saving of Souls, it made me tremble to see the Sight, how the world was in a Struggle.

When they arrived at the Middletown meeting house, Cole guessed that perhaps three or four thousand had assembled there, the countryside having emptied of its residents. Then Whitefield came to the scaffold:

He Lookt almost angelical; a young, Slim, slender, youth before some thousands of people with a bold undaunted Countenance . . . he looked as if he was Cloathed with authority from the Great God. . . . And my hearing him preach, gave me a heart wound; By Gods blessing: my old Foundation was broken up, and I saw that my righteousness would not save me; then I was convinced of the doctrine of Election: and went right to quarrelling with God about it; because that all I could do would not save me; and he had decreed from Eternity who should be saved and who not.

Cole's "quarrelling" with God lasted almost two years. Like Jonathan Edwards, he wrestled with the doctrine of predestination, thinking it abhorrent, while at the same time wondering if he himself was damned. "Hell fire was most always in my mind; and I have hundreds of times put my fingers into my pipe when I have been smoking to feel how fire felt." In the midst of his fears of hell's torments, however, God gave him a vision:

God appeared unto me and made me Skringe: before whose face the heavens and the earth fled away; and I was Shrinked into nothing; I knew not whether I was in the body or out, I seemed to hang in open Air before God, and he seemed to Speak to me in an angry and Sovereign way what won't you trust your Soul with God; My heart answered O yes, yes, yes. . . . Now while my Soul was viewing God, my fleshly part was working imaginations and saw many things which I will omitt to tell at this time. . . . When God appeared to me every thing vanished and was gone in the twinkling of an Eye, as quick as A flash of lightning; But when God disappeared or in some measure withdrew, every thing was in its place again and I was on my Bed. My heart was broken; my burden was fallen of[f] my mind; I was set free, my distress was gone.[17]

Cole's long conversion culminated, as it did for many early evangelicals, with a vision of God.

In New Haven, Whitefield visited with Rector Thomas Clap, who would later become one of his most bitter opponents. For now, Whitefield received a universally polite, if not entirely zealous, reception at Yale, despite his speaking to the students about "the dreadful ill consequences of an unconverted ministry." Whitefield then continued toward New York, and when he reached the border, he evaluated New England as impressive because of its godly heritage, but he feared that "Many, nay most that preach . . . do not experimentally know Christ." He loved the excitement his visit generated, though, and he thought New England was pliable enough for true revival. Pastor William Gaylord of Wilton, Connecticut, brother-in-law of James Davenport, wrote that many thought Whitefield "has a Touch of Enthusiasm" but that overheatedness could

be forgiven more easily than lukewarmness. He believed Whitefield's most profound effect might have been "stirring up" the ministers themselves, though he
did have reservations about Whitefield's comments on unconverted ministers.
Much of the power of Whitefield's tours lay in his ability to excite the local ministers to more fervent gospel preaching.[18]

As Whitefield's band crossed into New York, the Harvard tutor Daniel Rogers
came to the spiritual awakening he had sought during weeks of travel. After a
meeting at King's Bridge (now a part of the Bronx), Rogers wrote, "It pleased
God of his free Sovreign Grace to come into my poor Soul with Power and so to
fill me with Peace: yea with Such Joy in the Holy Ghost as I never Experienced
before— I cd not forbear Smiling nay Laughing for Joy and Gladness of Heart."
Rogers shared the news with an elated Whitefield, but soon after Satan was tor-
menting Rogers with "Abominable Horrible Shocking Tho'ts."[19] Assurance was
not always easily gained by the new evangelicals.

In New York, Whitefield met again with James Davenport, "by whose hands
the blessed Jesus has of late done great things." Davenport, Ebenezer Pemberton, and Whitefield took turns preaching at meetings in the city. Whitefield,
however, was stopped short when he received a copy of *The Querists*, which,
along with Alexander Garden's letters, was the first major printed opposition to
his work, produced by members of the New Castle Presbytery. Their peevish
tract against Whitefield scoured his writings to find any incautious theological
remarks and anything smacking of perfectionism, Quakerism, Arminianism, or
Catholicism. The writers of *The Querists* lifted a number of phrases out of context and pounced on Whitefield's occasionally imprecise theological language.
They also suspected that Whitefield's frequent references to the leadings of the
Spirit masked chicanery and asked "Whether or no the strange Fits and Convulsions, and the Noise of Visions and Revelations, that seem to prevail along with
this Scheme, be Matter of Joy and Comfort, or of Grief?"[20]

The extremes of *The Querists* allowed for a relatively easy rebuttal, and Whitefield's published reply did not attempt to defend most of the statements highlighted, noting only that he had written them without enough forethought and
precision and offering appropriate revisions. He questioned the motives of the
authors and wondered whether it was right for them to publicly "censure me
as a Papist or Arminian, because a few unguarded Expressions dropped from
my Pen just as I came out of the University of Oxford?" Samuel Blair of Fagg's
Manor was much less charitable to the authors, blasting his New Castle Presbytery colleagues for painting Whitefield as "a designing Impostor in League with
the Pope." Blair poured out his fury against these "Dead secure Formalists" who
knew they would lose their power if their congregants became born again. When

people are converted, Blair argued, "they can't be satisfied any longer with sap-less, careless Ministers; they can get no suitable Nourishment to their hungring Souls from these dry Breasts." Such blistering counteraccusations obviously did not make for pleasant relations in the New Castle Presbytery or in the Phila-delphia Synod. The controversy over *The Querists* continued for months with printed rebuttals from most of the key parties involved in the Middle Colonies, with the authors of *The Querists* themselves publishing two more pieces, one against Whitefield and another against Gilbert Tennent.[21]

Whitefield continued to preach with considerable success in New York City, then moved on to Staten Island where he rendezvoused with Gilbert Tennent and John Cross. Tennent told him of his recent itineration through south Jersey, Delaware, and northern Maryland, while Cross reported that he had recently "seen great and wonderful things in his congregations." They arrived at Cross's Basking Ridge congregation on November 5, where James Davenport had been preaching in the morning. At an affecting afternoon service, Daniel Rogers re-called that a nine- or ten-year-old boy began speaking loudly, at which time Whitefield called on the crowd "to hear this Lad preaching to them." This led to a "General motion" during which many cried out, some fainted, and some fell into fits. A young man near Rogers was so moved that he had to lean on Rogers during much of the sermon until he finally fell to his knees.[22]

The large crowd then retired to Cross's barn for the evening lecture. Tennent preached first, followed by Whitefield. Whitefield estimated that he had spo-ken for six minutes when one man began to shout, "He is come, He is come!" (Rogers recalled the man as crying "I have found him!") Many others began crying out "for the like favour," and Whitefield stopped to pray over them, which only heightened their fervent emotions. Rogers struggled to adequately describe the meeting, but noted that many were "weeping, Sighing, Groaning, Sobbing, screaching, crying out." The ministers finally retired, but Rogers and Davenport returned at one o'clock in the morning to resume preaching. Many in the con-gregation stayed up all night in the barn, praying and worshipping. "'Tis a night to be remembered," Rogers wrote.[23]

The next morning many penitents approached the departing Whitefield, in-cluding a "poor negro woman," a slave, who asked to join his entourage. Her master actually agreed to this idea (it is unlikely that he had permanent emanci-pation in mind), but Whitefield told her to go home and "serve her present mas-ter." Whitefield and most white evangelicals were unprepared to let the social implications of his gospel run a course to abolitionism.[24]

Whitefield's *Journals* placed his host, Basking Ridge's John Cross, at the cen-ter of the early evangelical movement in America, but Cross would soon bring considerable disruption to the cause. As early as late 1739, Whitefield remarked that Cross's followers "are now looked upon as enthusiasts and madmen." By 1741, the charges of enthusiasm transformed into accusations of sexual abuse. A published letter in Philadelphia "touching the horrid Practice and Delusions of some called NEW-LIGHT-MEN" said that Cross had seduced a virgin in his congregation by telling her that she needed to become a "notorious Sinner" before she could partake of Christ's righteousness. "Whereupon the holy Man, in the Fear of the Lord, deflowr'd her; and for some time repeated the Practice, until he had, by Pregnancy, put her in the Way to receive the Lord Jesus." Cross reportedly arranged for her to marry another man, to whom the woman soon divulged her affair. Cross then "fled from Justice." The writer concluded that Whitefield's word could not be trusted if he recommended such a "Monster."[25]

We do not know how much of this scurrilous account was true, but Cross seems certainly to have committed some serious sexual improprieties: he was removed from the ministry by the New Brunswick Presbytery in 1741 for "unclean speech and carriage." Jonathan Dickinson noted that Cross's scandals badly damaged the revival movement, as Cross's "high Pretensions to extraordinary Piety and Zeal . . . gave the deeper Wound to vital and experimental Godliness." The missionary John Sergeant of Stockbridge, Massachusetts, showed how Cross was perceived by moderate evangelicals in a 1741 letter. "That vile wretch is found to have lived in the Sin of Adultery, at the same time; that he appear'd most zealously set against it." Cross reportedly excused his indiscretion by reference to the biblical case of David, who though a great man of God nevertheless committed adultery and murder. Cross still called his opponents "Pharisees & Hypocrites." His followers had to decide whether "habitual Sin . . . is consistent with a State of Grace" or whether Cross was not converted. Sergeant lamented that Cross's followers claimed that he was being persecuted by the civil authorities. "Good God! What strong Delusions are they under," he wrote. Sergeant also reported suspicions that Cross was actually a Roman Catholic in disguise. Two of Cross's closest friends were Irish Catholics. Others claimed to have seen "a Crucifix hanging in his bosom." Rumors said that Cross never prayed for King George II, and that he held the War of Jenkins' Ear to be unlawful. Despite these terrible reports about Cross, Sergeant still hoped that God might "on this occasion accomplish a glorious Work."[26]

With these problems yet in the future, Whitefield's tour moved on to New Brunswick, where Whitefield began telling Gilbert Tennent and Daniel Rogers to go to New England to follow up on the work there. Tennent initially refused, but after encouragement from Whitefield and an apparent vote by the entourage, Tennent agreed. Whitefield headed south with Davenport while Rogers and Tennent began planning their new tours. In Philadelphia, Whitefield began preaching in the so-called New Building, a structure erected by supporters specifically for his visits. The one-hundred-by-seventy-foot building became Whitefield's usual pulpit in Philadelphia, and though the fervor of his earlier visit had abated, wondrous visitations continued. At one meeting, many reported experiencing the sensation of being pierced by "pointed arrows" as he preached, and a young woman fell down senseless during the meeting and had to be carried home. On another occasion Whitefield reported that he spontaneously spoke against "reasoning unbelievers," and he later found out that "a number of them were present" at his sermon. He attributed his well-timed admonition to the leading of the Holy Ghost.[27]

Through November, Whitefield continued his tour of southern New Jersey, Pennsylvania, Delaware, and Maryland, making stops at friendly congregations in Whiteclay Creek, Fagg's Manor, Nottingham, and Bohemia Manor. Whitefield, as was often the case, fell terribly ill at Fagg's Manor, writing that "straining caused me to vomit much." But he continued preaching and praying, and "soon every person in the room seemed to be under great impressions, sighing and weeping." On December 1, Whitefield departed for South Carolina and Georgia, noting with satisfaction that he had preached perhaps one hundred seventy-five times since he arrived in Rhode Island two-and-a-half months earlier. The presence of God that attended his meetings convinced him that the British American provinces would remain his "chief scene for action."[28] The fall 1740 tour had been a gigantic success for Whitefield. His method of theatrical field preaching rejuvenated New England's substantial revival tradition and captivated tens of thousands of listeners. His incautious remarks about unconverted ministers, however, and his friendship with such figures as Tennent, Davenport, and Cross laid the groundwork for great controversies concerning the awakenings in the years ahead.

"Blowing Up the Divine Fire": Mass Revivalism in New England, 1740–1741

Whitefield left Boston in October 1740, but the town's revivalists hardly let the awakenings wane. Nine days after Whitefield's farewell sermon, Benjamin Colman preached *Souls Flying to Jesus Christ Pleasant and Admirable to Behold*. Whitefield, the "singular servent and holy Youth," had led a revival that touched all quarters of Boston society. Now Colman and his revivalist colleagues hoped to secure the effects of Whitefield's tour, "clinching the Nails driven by the Master of Assemblies." Colman thought that the present revival represented a significant step in the prophesied conversion of the Gentile nations and hinted that it might signal the final days before the return of Christ: "But the Prophecy is daily fulfilling, and at Times in a more remarkable Measure; but more especially it will be so in the latter and more happy Days of the Church when the Calling of the Jews and the Fulness of the Gentiles shall come on. — The LORD hasten the promis'd Day."[1]

Thomas Foxcroft of First Church (a pastoral colleague of antirevivalist Charles Chauncy) likewise wondered whether Bostonians might soon see the time "when the everlasting Gospel shall fly like Lightning . . . with the Holy Ghost sent down from Heaven in a remarkable Manner, and the Kingdom of God be every where diffus'd and establish'd thro' all the Earth." John Webb of the New North Church similarly prayed that "all the Ends of the Earth may see and enjoy the SALVATION of the LORD." Nathaniel Appleton of Cambridge reminded his congregation that "we have glorious Promises of the mighty Success of the Word in the latter Days, and of the flowing in of all People to CHRIST." Appleton, Foxcroft, Webb, and Colman would not pronounce it the inauguration of that promised time but saw the revivals at least as "hopeful Beginnings."[2]

Colman nervously contemplated the possibility, however, that it was only

Whitefield's celebrity that stirred the revival. He called on his congregants to follow the established revivalist ministers and to show that it was not just "vain Curiosity, Novelty, the Fame and Face of a Stranger" that produced a sensation. Colman exhorted all the people, including even servants and slaves, to seek universal awakening, repentance, and conversion. The pastors hoped the continuing awakening would eventually touch rich and poor, young and old, black, white, and red.[3]

Massachusetts authorities had a vested interest in seeing the revivals continue. Beyond their obvious spiritual benefits, they saw in the awakenings a path toward widespread repentance that might alleviate divine judgments on their province. Massachusetts's leaders saw 1740 as the high point of an ongoing economic crisis that had military implications in light of the ongoing War of Jenkins' Ear. Massachusetts faced enormous financial problems, primarily related to rampant inflation and unstable paper currency. Various proposals were suggested to establish a reliable currency for the province, the primary competitors being the Land Bank and the Silver Bank. It appears that the Land Bankers, led by Benjamin Colman's merchant brother John, tended to support the revivals, whereas the Silver Bankers often opposed the revivals. These issues created a firestorm of controversy that persisted through Whitefield's 1740 tour. High grain prices gave the impression that new defenses against Spanish, French, or Native American enemies could hardly be afforded. These troubles bred fears among a cross section of New Englanders, as Nicholas Gilman wrote in his diary: "We are Under Some terrible apprehension of a French and Indian War, May it be Mercifully prevented." Likewise, Isaac Watts in London wrote to Benjamin Colman, "Tis no wonder you are in fear for ye American provinces if a French war should arise . . . yet perhaps it is by the convulsion of nations that Antichrist must be destroy'd, and the glorious kingdom of Christ appear."[4] Jonathan Belcher, the evangelical and increasingly unpopular governor, called for a day of prayer and fasting in December 1740 to ask God for a resolution to these issues.

Joseph Sewall of the Old South Church delivered the official sermon for that day of prayer and fasting, and made clear the connections between the revivals and the financial and military crisis: "Blessed be the Lord, His Spirit has been, we hope, moving on the Hearts of many to convince and awaken them," he said. He hoped that the awakenings would be followed by a "Spirit of saving Conversion and thorow Reformation." God had already sent awful providences against Massachusetts in the "present Difficulties which embarrass our Affairs, . . . the Want of a suitable Medium of Trade," which left "the Country naked and defenceless, in this Day of Calamity and War." Sewall avoided taking a position in the currency debate, but he thought that repentance and reformation, promoted by the ongoing revivals, would alleviate worldly problems. As he wrote several months later, when the revivals had grown more powerful, "So it pleaseth God to send down the Comforter from Heaven into the Hearts of this People, while it is a dark Day with us upon temporal Accounts." Earthly darkness made way for spiritual illumination.[5]

When measured in terms of public religious commitments, especially admissions to full communion, five of the sixteen Boston-area churches showed signs of major revival in the months following Whitefield's fall tour. These included Joseph Sewall's and Thomas Prince's Old South Church, Benjamin Colman's Brattle Street Church, and John Webb's New North Church in Boston, as well as the First Churches in Cambridge and Charlestown. The awakenings produced widespread, but not universal, results in eastern Massachusetts.[6]

As local pastors continued to preach revival in Boston, Gilbert Tennent and Daniel Rogers arrived in a snowy Connecticut in early December, commissioned by Whitefield to follow up on his fall tour. In preparation for their visit to Massachusetts, Whitefield sent a letter commending them to Governor Jonathan Belcher: "This week Mr. G—T—purposes to set out for Boston, in order to blow up the divine fire lately kindled there. I recommend him to your excellency as a solid, judicious, and zealous minister of the LORD JESUS CHRIST . . . Dear Mr. R—grows in grace . . . I hope he will be instrumental in quickening both ministers and people."[7]

Tennent and Rogers came to Boston in mid-December and preached for about three weeks in the area. Tennent continued to deliver fiery sermons, as Rogers noted that on the nineteenth he gave the "most awfull awakening sermon I think I ever heard." Rogers, still a novice preacher, wrote two days later that he preached for the first time without notes. Rogers spent the middle of January ministering to a revived student group at Harvard. Tennent, meanwhile, toured northern New England. He was no master publicist like Whitefield, so the records of his travels are sparse. Nevertheless, he reported to his brother William that he was well pleased with the work in northern New England. He noted "great Appearances in Portsmouth and Charles-town: There were in Time of Sermon such Out-cries that my Voice had like to have been drowned." He also recorded "a great Shock" in Greenland, Ipswich, Hamlet, and Marblehead, and wrote that "many Hundreds in this Eastern Journey have been wounded in one Degree or another." In January 1741, layman Joseph Goodhue and some friends of Newburyport, Massachusetts, made a special visit to York, Maine, "in which place ye work of ye Lord was marvelos to mee." He "went about from hous to house being in Great Destres About ye Salvation of my soul Seecking help." Though he considered himself a "self Ritoues self Runed Wrech . . . who

Deserved hel," Goodhue realized that God would save him, too, and he was born again. The seeds sown by Tennent and Whitefield bore considerable fruit in northern New England in late 1741, when at least ten churches in Maine and New Hampshire showed clear signs of revival.[8]

Returning to Boston in late January, Tennent continued to preach against unconverted ministers. He spent most of his time at the key revivalist Boston congregations: Brattle Street, Old South, and New North. In *The Righteousness of the Scribes and Pharisees Consider'd*, Tennent railed against the pretensions of religious hypocrites and advocated using the "Terrors of the Lord" to shake them out of their duplicity. He particularly worried that the churches admitted unregenerate people to communion, giving them false security. He conceded that many Pharisees were quite moral according to worldly standards, but they still lacked a saving imputation of Christ's righteousness. "Merrily they go on to Damnation," he lamented, "like Fools in Bedlam, they sing and dance in their Shackels." Many Pharisaical (and by implication, unregenerate) leaders also opposed the ministry of the new birth. "If this Work of GOD which is more remarkably begun in New-England of late, be carry'd on, you will see some that profess the greatest Regard to Religion now, stand up and oppose it with implacable Hate. Formalists cannot brook the Power of Religion." He excoriated all those merely religious but not converted as a "prophane Herd of harden'd Mortals" and a "Generation of Vipers." To those convinced of their need for Christ, however, he advised persistence, even in the face of opposition. "Some are so perverse that they will neither enter into the Kingdom themselves, nor suffer those that are entring to enter: Methinks they might be contented with their own Damnation."[9] Tennent's opponents could hardly miss his point: go to hell if you like, but I will not let you take others with you.

Tennent's adversaries disdained his preaching, though few said anything against him publicly yet. The Anglican Timothy Cutler, never shy to attack dissenters and evangelicals, recalled the visiting Tennent as "a monster! impudent and noisy—and told them they were all *damned! damned! damned!* This charmed them; and, in the most dreadful winter I ever saw, people wallowed in snow, night and day, for the benefit of his beastly brayings." Likewise, in 1743, Braintree's pastor, John Hancock, remembered that Tennent's "Visit was full of Extraordinaries . . . entring into other Men's Labours, and devouring their Livings." Hancock thought Tennent despised the established clergy, "cruelly censuring them in general, and raising Jealousies in the Minds of People of their faithful Ministers, even to that Degree as hath ended in a Spirit of dreadful Separation in many Places." Tennent's condemnations led to church splits and Separatism, Hancock believed, and his wildly emotional style had led to "animal

Convulsions into which many of our new Converts have fallen, and upon which great Stress is laid by many in the Work of Conversion."[10] To Cutler and Hancock, Tennent's ministry led the ignorant to question the clergy's authority and to indulge physical and emotional excesses.

Tennent enjoyed considerable popular support, however, as indicated by a 1741 broadside that proclaimed, "I'll hear the Call the lovely Tennent brings, Because I know it's from the King of Kings." The moderate friends of the revival in Boston also remained cautiously positive about Tennent. John Webb wrote that "God has . . . own'd and succeeded" Tennent's ministry. Colman assured Whitefield, "We received [Tennent] just as we did you, as Angels of Christ." He thought that Tennent had generated a powerful revival at Harvard, where "the College is a new Creature." Thomas Prince recalled meeting Tennent during that winter of 1740–41 and was impressed by his learnedness and preaching ability. "He seem'd to have as deep an Acquaintance with the experimental Part of Religion as any I have convers'd with," Prince averred. Prince did have concerns, though, that Tennent's preaching of terror might have kept sincere Christians from approaching the Lord's Table. Ultimately, Prince and others attributed to Tennent a "convicting" ministry, which came through "the searching nature of his ministry," or the way he exposed people's graceless hearts.[11]

In spite of the controversy he generated, Tennent did not back off his provocations. Daniel Rogers wrote that Tennent "boldly exhorted the Ministers to come out for Christ," and that "more of the Pharisees are Shocked." In early March, Tennent delivered his farewell sermon at the Brattle Street Church and began his trip back to New Jersey with a tour through southeastern Massachusetts, Rhode Island, and Connecticut. Daniel Rogers stayed behind in Boston and formally resigned his office as tutor at Harvard in order to preach full time.[12]

After Tennent's departure, Rogers began giving special attention to mixed-race audiences. On March 27, he addressed "a Number of Negroes & Indians. And of Whites in a Hot Room. coming out in the cool Air, took a cold." Similarly, on April 5, he preached to "a Number of Negroes [torn] Indian. & a great Number of White People. God enabled me to preach with Power." A week later he spoke to "the Negroes at the School House." He apparently began holding weekly Sabbath evening meetings with a group of African Americans, for two weeks later he recorded once more that he visited in the evening with "the Negroes." By May, Rogers had apparently begun to struggle with continuing to minister to such a lowly audience, as he wrote that he "was not pleased to be asked so often" to speak to them, but he went ahead with another talk. "One of the Men servants weept," he noted, and "I believe God will call more of the poor negroes to the Knowledge of his Son. . . . Lord make me willing to do any thing for 'em." In June, Rogers still addressed the African Americans regularly, recording at one meeting that he preached extemporaneously "to a gt. Number of Negroes . . . and of white People out of Doors. Some of the poor Negroes were much affected."[13]

Meanwhile, Tennent preached twenty-one times in Newport, Rhode Island, in March 1741. His sermons deeply affected Susanna Anthony and Sarah Osborn, two future evangelical leaders in the town. Anthony "gained light by this worthy minister's preaching and conversation" and soon passed through a deep crisis to conversion. Osborn, who had already been converted but needed assurance, fell under conviction for her frivolous behavior when she heard Tennent preach against "singing songs, dancing, and foolish jesting." Osborn wrote to Tennent asking whether he thought she was truly saved, and Tennent kindly responded that she should be comforted by her struggles because they were a sign of grace. Encouraged, Osborn soon founded a women's meeting at Newport's First Church that served as the most significant source of evangelical devotion in the congregation for decades. Tennent soon appeared at Yale and generated a significant revival after speaking seventeen times in a week. Yale student Samuel Hopkins was so impressed that he contemplated becoming an apprentice to Tennent when he graduated. Later, he decided to study under Jonathan Edwards instead.[14]

Writing to Whitefield from New York in late April, Tennent was well pleased with his tour and with the awakenings generally: in Boston, he estimated that thousands of all ages and races had become concerned for their souls under his preaching. "The Shock was rather more general at Charles-Town. Multitudes were awakened, and several had received great Consolation, especially among the young People, Children and Negroes." He reported that awakenings proceeded elsewhere, as well, and particularly noted that "in and about Mr. Davenport's Place there is a great Commotion; Multitudes are under Soul-Concern: And I hear that he is very warm."[15] The revivals vigorously proceeded in Whitefield's absence.

After Whitefield's and Tennent's tours, local pastors shouldered most of the revival labors in New England. Thomas Prince believed that Whitefield had awakened many and Tennent had convicted many, but that the large numbers of conversions actually began only after Tennent left. Tennent had "excited us to treat more largely of the workings of the Spirit of grace" during the winter, but once he left, "such a time as we never knew" appeared. Colman, Sewall, and Webb opened their churches for weekday revival meetings, and many small private societies began assembling, such as the society of African Americans to whom Rogers regularly spoke. The pastors were overwhelmed with counseling sessions for people "in deep concern about their souls." William Cooper reported that more came in one week than during his previous twenty-four years of ministry, and perhaps six hundred different people visited him in three months. John Webb told Thomas Prince that he had seen more than a thousand in the same period. In March 1741 these private discussions began to bear fruit in the form of new admissions to full communion at the Old South Church, followed by many others at the New North and Brattle Street churches.[16]

Thomas Prince thought that this season profoundly changed Boston. "The very face of the town seemed to be strangely altered. Some who had not been here since the Fall before, have told me their great surprise at the change in the general look and carriage of people." The transformation affected all, including the most unlikely: "Even the negroes and boys in the streets surprisingly left their usual rudeness: I knew many of these had been greatly affected, and now were formed into religious societies." The taverns, too, had emptied, save for visiting out-of-towners.[17]

William Cooper, in his preface to Jonathan Edwards's *The Distinguishing Marks of a Work of the Spirit of God* (1741), claimed that the 1740–41 outpouring had its only historical parallel at Pentecost. "The apostolical times seem to have returned upon us," he wrote. Cooper particularly commented on the general impact of the Spirit on "all ranks and degrees: some of the great and rich, but more of the low and poor. Of other countries and nations: Ethiopia has stretched out her hand; some poor Negroes have, I trust, been vindicated into the glorious liberty of the children of God." How many African Americans were affected is difficult to ascertain, but an anonymous Boston correspondent of Whitefield's wrote that ten were baptized at three different churches on one Sunday in April. To Cooper, it appeared "an extraordinary season wherein God is pleased to carry on a work of his grace in a more observable and glorious manner."[18]

The revivals also extended to the south and west of Boston, into the hinterlands. For instance, at Natick, the site of missionary John Eliot's most successful "praying town" of Christian Native Americans in the seventeenth century, a cautious Oliver Peabody reported that his church, along with others in five neighboring towns, had experienced revival. The work touched "Indians and English, young and old, male and female." In the two years after March 1741 Peabody estimated that "fifty Persons of different Nations" had joined the church. Peabody's account published in the *Christian History* was keen to note, however, that many of the converts dated their convictions prior to Whitefield's arrival, and that he did not approve of the enthusiastic excesses that the revival had generated.[19]

As the example of Peabody's narrative makes clear, Prince's *Christian History* served the interests of moderate evangelicals by downplaying the frequency of bodily exercises and enthusiastic outbursts. Prince himself argued that though many converts had been overcome by joy, "I never saw one either in Town or Country, in what some wrongly call a Vision, Trance or Revelation. And where those few Instances have happened in some Places, appeared but a little while and vanished." Despite Prince's moderation, in the last year of its two-year stint the *Christian History* resorted to publishing many more radical narratives. A lack of sufficiently moderate narratives may, in fact, have helped convince Prince to stop publishing the newspaper.[20]

From Wrentham, moderates Henry Messenger and Elias Haven reported to Prince that revival at Second Church began in February 1741 on a day of prayer and fasting "to implore the blessings of Heaven on our nation in the war with Spain." That fast, paired with an observance of the Lord's Supper, generated considerable concern among the congregation's young people. Similar excitement began at First Church in April. Messenger and Haven also discounted the effect of the itinerants: "this general awakening was not from the influence of travelling ministers (though we are satisfied God has made use of some of them for the revival of religion in many places); for there was but one sermon preached in the town in such a way, and that to a small auditory." They did, however, believe that the news of the Northampton revival, and other more recent revivals, had stirred interest in Wrentham. The awakening had enormous effects on the town's small population: by July, Second Church had almost doubled its communicant members from 63 to 124. In the two years since April 1741, First Church added 136 to its existing 92 communicants. Writing in 1743, the two ministers insisted that the revivals had been moderate in practice: "We have not known trances, visions, revelations, or the like." By that date, the moderates desired to advertise their revivals as serious but controlled, and not tainted by radicalism.[21]

In Bridgewater, Massachusetts, pastor John Porter found himself converted through Whitefield's preaching. "I knew nothing rightly of my sin and danger . . . till I heard that man of God." Soon Porter began to encourage revival in Bridgewater, inviting Tennent to come preach there in March 1741. Tennent's visit convicted many people of sin and led the town to talk of little but religion, Porter reported. The excitement waned during the summer, but in the fall a major awakening came with the arrival of two young Bridgewater men who had been away at Yale. They began holding public meetings and exhorting the youth, which raised some concern about disorder, but Porter thought their ministry was proper, especially because of its fruit. The young people in Bridgewater became deeply concerned with salvation, and at each meeting "God was with us in the convincing & converting and comforting Influences of his Spirit." Unlike Thomas Prince's more moderate correspondents, Porter welcomed bodily exercises. He noted approvingly that some "have their frail Tabernacles overborne" with a sense of God's love. The "Sense of the Perfections of God . . . greatly weakens and overcomes the Body." But these did not evidence "Antinomianism and enthusiastical Frenzies," for the bodily experiences bore the fruit of love and holiness. Porter also assured the readers. "As to Trances, Visions, &c., we have none, and I think have had none from the beginning." Again, by 1743, many pastors wondered how far the revival's emotional and bodily manifestations could go before threatening good order.[22]

Undeterred by such concerns, the radical Daniel Rogers preached tirelessly through the summer of 1741 across Maine and New Hampshire. Soon northern New England witnessed one of the most powerful and radical phases of the awakenings of the 1740s. In October, York, Maine, experienced a startling season of grace. In Cambridge, Massachusetts, evangelical artisan Joseph Bean had already heard about the "wonderful operations of the Spiret of God upon pepels harts doun at York" by October 21, and he prayed for more abundant "out powrings" of the Spirit at York and elsewhere. Physician Edmund Coffin of Kittery wrote that the York revival surpassed even the 1735 Northampton revival. Conversions came quickly, some in a minute or less. The penitents had such "extraordinary concern . . . that the most acute or most sharp pain of body that I ever saw is any way comparable to it." They cried out to God for help and would not eat, drink, or sleep until they found spiritual comfort.[23]

An anonymous diarist arrived at York from Boston on October 10, 1741, to find the congregation in ecstasy. "Such a Sight as I never beheld, Men, Women & Children, some in Raptures of Joy, saying they had Seen Christ." An eight-year-old girl approached him and asked if he loved Jesus, and the diarist said he hoped so. "Upon which she Said, she had seen him twice, & Said he was a lovely Sweet Jesus." The visiting Samuel Willard of Biddeford, Maine, preaching in the meetinghouse, struggled to maintain order. Many began to cry out, "some asking if Christ was come, others if the Day of Judgment was Come." Willard stopped his sermon and asked "them to Compose themselves, for that Satan did what he could, to Disturb this Good Work." After the congregation calmed down, Willard continued, but some people kept talking during his sermon, and afterwards some laypeople exhorted and prayed over others. For Willard, leading such a radical meeting was both gratifying and frightening at the same time.[24]

At Portsmouth, New Hampshire, William Shurtleff recorded that Tennent's and Whitefield's preaching "made instrumental of putting a great many upon shaking off their heavy Slumbers." Area ministers agreed to observe a monthly fast for revival to model the one in York, and at the fast service on November 25, 1741, a great outbreak occurred in Shurtleff's congregation. One person cried out for joy, while others moaned in distress, and many stayed late at the church. Two days later, the church witnessed "the most remarkable Day that was ever known among us." During the commotion many dwelled on "the Appearing of THE SON OF MAN, and of the different Exclamations that shall be heard from the Inhabitants of the World when they shall see Him coming in the Clouds of Heaven, in Power, and great Glory."[25]

That night, a house's chimney near the church caught fire, and when the congregation saw the light of flames through the church windows, some began to scream that "CHRIST was coming to Judgment." Shurtleff considered that response healthy, for people should keep in mind the imminent return and judgment of Christ. Shurtleff argued that the instances of so-called enthusiasm did not make the revival illegitimate, because the people had become much more holy and loving. The work proceeded at all hours of the day and night with visiting preachers speaking and praying. Boston merchant Samuel Savage told Gilbert Tennent that many who had first been "struck of York" now cried out "with an Sudden Beam of divine Joy." Some said that the presence of God "came down . . . like a mighty rushing Wind." An anonymous correspondent wrote that all manner of people had been touched: "young & old, Rich and poor, White & black." He strikingly added that "I believe that 8 or 10 Negroes are made free in our Lord Jesus."[26]

At nearby Durham, Nicholas Gilman wrote excitedly in his diary that revivals were breaking out all over northern New England: "Rec'd a Letter from Mr. Daniel Little giving account of the Glorious Work of God going on at Timberlane in Haverhill—and to day recievd Tidings that it begun Sabbath Evening at Summersworth—and is carried on Marvellously as also at York, Kittery, Berwick etc. Glory to God Most High—thro' Jesus Christ." Gilman hoped he, too, would be used by God to generate revival at Durham. "Gracious God, may I thine Unworthy Servent experience the powerfull converting and comforting Influences of thy Blessed Spirit—and Oh! that thou wouldst begin and carry on Such a glorious Work in Durham; with glorious Efficacy and Success." Soon Gilman's prayers were answered: "December 6, 1741 pr. Durham Acts 17:30— Between Meetings a great crying out, among people in Anguish of Spirits. Many Awakened; All glory to thy Name Most Glorious Lord God." Gilman publicly read from Edwards's *Faithful Narrative* to help promote the work.[27]

The revivals also surged through the Connecticut River valley, which for a generation had been the center of New England revivalism. Stephen Williams (a brother-in-law of James Davenport), pastor of Longmeadow, Massachusetts, just north of the Connecticut border, wrote to Eleazar Wheelock in March 1741 that "Severall are under concern about their Souls—and are Saying, what must we do to be Saved—and there is a greater attention of—and affection of the word than usuall." He associated this concern with what he was hearing about the revivals on Long Island. "I late heard . . . that they were got distracted again at Southhold, about religion." In July, Williams visited a number of other awakened congregations in the valley before his own finally woke up, too. He stopped at Suffield, Connecticut, just across the Massachusetts border, "where I heard of ye remarkable outpouring of ye Spirit of God" and reported that ninety-five people had been added to the church on one recent Sabbath. The visiting Jonathan Edwards, Eleazar Wheelock, and Williams's brother-in-law Joseph Meacham of South Coventry, Connecticut, continued to stoke the fire at Suffield throughout the first week of July. A visitor to the Suffield meetinghouse during one of Edwards's prayer meetings was struck by the "Groans & Screaches as of Women in the Pains of Childbirth," the "Houlings and Yellings," and penitents "so intirely unbraced that you would have thought there bones all broken, or rather that they had no bones." Williams recorded in his diary that there was "considerable crying among ye people . . . & a Screaching in ye streets" of Suffield.[28]

Then, on July 8, Williams witnessed one of the high moments of the revivals: Jonathan Edwards's sermon *Sinners in the Hands of an Angry God*, delivered at nearby Enfield, Connecticut. Edwards had just two days before led a heated, enthusiastic meeting in Suffield. Now, he began to give his sermon, but Williams wrote that "before ye Sermon was done there was a great moaning & crying out throughout ye whole House . . . So yt ye minister was obligd to desist shreiks & crys were piercing & Amazing." The assembled ministers came down and began counseling the people. "Amazing & Astonishing ye powr God was Seen." Edwards designed *Sinners* to be an "awakening sermon" that would shake sinners out of their self-righteous delusions. The topic was not unusual for Edwards or other Calvinist preachers, and Edwards almost certainly did not use any of the performative tactics of Whitefield to generate a reaction. He was reputed to be solemn but intense in his style. So what was it about *Sinners* that led to such a spectacularly emotional response?[29]

First, one should remember that only the day before there had been "Screaching in ye Streets" in Suffield. At this heady stage of the awakenings, even the personally staid Edwards had few reservations about outcries and ecstatic bodily manifestations. We should not imagine, moreover, that Edwards's sermon produced an unusually emotional response in the awakenings' broader context, for surely some of the heated emotions at Suffield spilled over to Enfield, and some of the lay radicals from Suffield and other nearby towns were likely in the audience. Edwards may simply have given these followers what they wanted: an explosive, awakening sermon that generated an enthusiastic response. Scholars, however, agree that much of the sermon's power lay in its rhetoric. *Sinners in the Hands of an Angry God* was brilliant, vivid, and terrifying. Edwards's warnings of judgment made the congregation scream for fear of hell.[30]

Sinners used at least twenty metaphors to picture God's wrath building up against rebellious sinners, including a furnace burning, black storm clouds approaching, flood waters surging against a dam, and most famously, the spider dangling over fire: "The God that holds you over the pit of hell, much as one holds a spider, or some loathsome insect, over the fire, abhors you, and is dreadfully provoked; his wrath towards you burns like fire; he looks upon you as worthy of nothing else, but to be cast into the fire; he is of purer eyes than to bear to have you in his sight; you are ten thousand times so abominable in his eyes as the most hateful venomous serpent is in ours." For the sinner damned to hell, "there will be no end to this exquisite horrible misery. When you look forward, you shall see a long forever . . . you will know certainly that you must wear out long ages, millions of millions of ages, in wrestling and conflicting with this almighty merciless vengeance; and then when you have so done, . . . you will know that all is but a point to what remains." All of Edwards's listeners that day would have affirmed that this judgment awaited unforgiven sinners, but perhaps the doctrine had grown stale with familiarity. Edwards's vivid images may have awakened some previously passive residents, while other visitors may have come expecting to have another emotional encounter with God and got their wish.[31]

Revival also continued in Edwards's Northampton congregation, even among his own children. Earlier, he reported "joyful tidings" to Whitefield in December 1740 that religious interest continued to rise and that several of his children might have been converted. He worried that the excitement would fade away, as it had in 1735, and asked for prayers that God would "pour out his Spirit upon us, and no more depart from us." In March 1741, Edwards wrote to Colman and reported that the revival flourished in his own house, the town generally, and particularly in other Connecticut River valley towns, including Deerfield and Hartford. He implored Colman to keep him apprised of any "more remarkable and glorious things, concerning the city of God in your parts."[32]

The church achieved a new high in May as one of Edwards's private sermons set off great concerns among the young people and produced surprising bodily effects. "Many of the young people and children that were professors appeared to be overcome with a sense of the greatness and glory of divine things . . . the whole room was full of nothing but outcries, faintings and such like." He continued to cultivate the excitement among the young people through the summer, and in August and September the work reached another crescendo. "It was a very frequent thing to see an house full of outcries, faintings, and convulsions and such like, both with distress, and also with admiration and joy." Though late night meetings had formerly been unusual, now some became so overcome that they had to stay at "the house where they were" for the night. Edwards knew that the subject of late night meetings could raise questions of propriety, but he insisted that the young people's emotions were no more heated at night than during the day. Edwards thought that the 1741 awakening was particularly marked by the special work of God among the youth, even more so than in 1735. He also observed that the 1741 conversions were "wrought more sensibly and visibly" than before, making external manifestations more common.[33]

Farther south, at New Haven, Samuel Hopkins (then a student from Waterbury, Connecticut) recalled that Tennent's preaching had awakened thousands in the region. "Many professors of religion received conviction that they were not real christians," he remembered, "and never were born again." He thought Yale was "universally awakened." Hopkins noted that Samuel Buell of Coventry, Connecticut, David Youngs of Southold, Long Island, and David Brainerd of Durham, Connecticut, were particularly zealous in advancing the cause of awakening at the college. Brainerd visited Hopkins, who confessed to Brainerd that he had no "religious affections" regarding Christ. Brainerd suggested that this meant he had not been born again. Hopkins admitted that he "had never gone out of myself and closed with Jesus Christ so as to be united to him by a lively faith." Under deep conviction, Hopkins sought that emotional response to the gospel. One evening, in his prayer closet, he "had a sense of the being and presence of God, as I never had before," and he saw the path of salvation through Christ as "wise, important, and desirable." He walked out of his closet a new creature, born again into a new life with Christ.[34]

In April 1741, Ebenezer Pemberton came to Yale from New York City to preach *The Knowledge of Christ Recommended*, exhorting the students to cultivate experimental knowledge of Christ above all other learning. He insisted that intellectual assent to gospel doctrines was not enough for salvation and encouraged them to discover and preach "a knowlege that is not confined to the head but seated in the heart." Pemberton brought a warning for the students and professors who remained unconverted at Yale: "Every Soul in this Assembly, that has not an experimental knowledge of Christ, is . . . exposed to an infinitely more terrible execution, than any human power can inflict; there remains but a short and uncertain time to fly from the amazing danger and escape the vengeance of eternal fire." He pleaded with them not to neglect the saving experience with Christ in favor of worldly knowledge: "You may be ignorant of many things, and yet wise for salvation." Here one can see the seeds of an anti-intellectualism that has all too often characterized succeeding generations of evangelicals and fundamentalists, but Pemberton hardly meant to denounce learning in general. Speaking to the very few who received a college education during this period, he exhorted them not to let their bookish wisdom distract them from those things that mattered eternally.[35]

George Griswold of Lyme End (Lyme, East Parish), Connecticut, also recalled that his congregation awakened with the visits of Whitefield and Tennent. Tennent preached there on April 1, 1741, and his speaking was "bles'd to a great (if not a general) Awakening." Two weeks later Jonathan Parsons of West Lyme spoke in Lyme End, and the "Word fell with great Power on sundry. . . . Some had Fits, some fainted. . . . Some Hours were spent praying with and counselling the distressed. . . . After this, Cryings out at the preaching of the Word were frequent." Griswold's parishioner, the prominent lawyer John Lee, wrote to Eleazar Wheelock and told him that Parsons's preaching had generated amazing responses: "Such effect of the Word preacht I Never See, two persons while preaching were so overcome with the Sence of the wrath of God ready to fall on them (as they Express it) that they died away with fear and sorrow and were with Difficulty bro't to again, and when Sermon was Ended a great Number Cryed out in such anguish as I never See it." Griswold noted that his was the first parish in the area so affected, and his church began to attract attention: "very few if any at this Time would say that they believed it to be a delusive Spirit." Griswold set up weekly lectures and other special meetings to facilitate the work, and he wrote that "Out-cries, Fainting and Fits were oft in Meetings," though he thought that the majority of the converted never had such experiences. This season lasted from April to June, and he estimated that forty people were converted. Another stir began in late July, prominently featuring people who "had such Discoveries of the Love of GOD and CHRIST, as to be overcome, and to loose their bodily Strength thereby." The revival ebbed considerably in August, but Griswold estimated that perhaps a hundred whites had been converted as a result of the 1741 awakening.[36]

Griswold also noted in a chart that thirteen Neantick (Niantic) Indians had been admitted into church communion, most of them a year or more after August 1741. He considered these especially gratifying converts, as they represented a "poor ignorant People, that for Ages past have lived without God in the World." James Davenport was the catalyst for their awakening, as he came and preached to them in August 1741. Griswold thought perhaps twenty Native Americans converted in the months following Davenport's visit. Most of these showed lasting change, but some slid back into heavy drinking. The combined results of the

Anglo-American and Native-American converts led Griswold to consider the re-vival a "wonderful and remarkable Work of GOD's Grace." This would not be the last time that Davenport helped precipitate Native American revival, a cause in which so many other ministers had failed. As Jonathan Parsons testified, writing in the *Christian History*, Davenport was "made a great Blessing to many Souls; but especially to the Mohegan and Nahauntuc Tribes of Indians. Tho' much Pains had been taken to win them to embrace the Gospel before, yet nothing seem'd to have any considerable Effect 'till Mr. Davenport came among them." Many white evangelicals grieved the lack of effective ministry to Native Ameri-cans in New England. North Haven farm woman Hannah Heaton, who at times saw Christian Native Americans full of the Spirit at revival meetings, wrote, "It affected my heart to think the set time to favour the poor heathen was come. O how wofully have they been neglected by us that had the byble but o what have we been better than christian heathen."[37]

In Lyme, Jonathan Parsons had long been familiar with revivals, as a large ingathering had happened in 1731 within his first year of ministry at West Lyme (Old Lyme). That year he saw fifty-two added to the church and several en-tire families baptized. Parsons confessed, however, that many of these awakened persons may not have been truly saved, and he attributed this shortcoming in part to his dalliance with Arminianism. In fact, Parsons doubted whether he was actually born again himself. He loved John Tillotson's "Notions about the Power of Man to perform the Conditions of the Gospel." Soon, partly through read-ing Solomon Stoddard's works, Parsons became convinced of the sovereignty of God in salvation. He believed his newfound Calvinism made him a much more powerful gospel preacher. Parsons did not receive full assurance of salvation until 1741, when some itinerants questioned whether he was really converted. This led Parsons to a final crisis. He retreated into the fields alone and prayed for two hours, until finally he "could not doubt of the safety of my state."[38]

Whitefield also had a reviving effect on Parsons's ministry: "The News of Mr. Whitefield's rising up with great Zeal for Holiness and Souls, had great In-fluence upon my Mind." Benjamin Colman wrote Parsons personally about Whitefield's tour in Boston, news that Parsons passed among neighboring min-isters. Although Whitefield did not preach in Lyme (the detour to see Edwards took him out of Lyme's way), Parsons did attend his meetings in New Haven and met the itinerant. Parsons considered himself ready to criticize the growing re-vivals should they prove to be wildly enthusiastic, for he had heard many reports that the Whitefield craze only grew from "heated Imagination, or meer Enthusi-asm and Disorder." He concluded that these accusations came mostly from "the looser Sort."[39]

Parsons soon joined the ranks of the revivalist preachers. In late March, he gave a sermon with tremendous, yet controlled, effects: "There were no Out-Cries; but a deep and general Concern upon the Minds of the Assembly discovered itself at that Time in plentiful Weeping, Sighs and Sobs." Tennent appeared in early April, with mixed results, as noted earlier. The Lyme revival continued to grow, and Parsons added a new public lecture and several private meetings. He also preached at Griswold's meetinghouse, where many cried that "fiery Hell [was] just ready to receive them," and congregants stayed almost all night at the church to pray for those in crisis. One wondered, "How shall I escape the Damnation of Hell, who have spent away a golden Opportunity under Gospel Light, in Vanity?" These outcries concerned Parsons, but he thought they "might be reasonably accounted for" as sensible responses to the wrath of God against sinners. Thus, he did not try to stop the outbursts, even though some fell into "Hysterick-Fits." Parsons, strikingly, struggled during these weeks with depressive feelings, reporting to Wheelock on April 21, "Tis a cloudy & dark Day with me: I find my Affections dried up; & if I am easily surprized & overcome: I have reason to walk softly. Pray for me."[40] The intensity of the seasons of grace could lead many of the pastors to emotional highs, sometimes followed quickly by deep lows.

One peak of the Lyme revival came in mid-May, when Parsons spoke to a group of his church's youth, and many cried out, fell down, and had fits. "Those that could not restrain themselves were generally carried out of the Meeting-House," he wrote. Parsons began a month of intense preaching and visiting those troubled about the state of their souls. He tried to moderate the effects of the revival because he feared that the crying out might prevent some from hearing deeper truths that would clinch salvation. He wondered, however, whether he had made a mistake by restricting their emotional outbursts, for he found no scriptural justification for inhibiting whatever reaction sinners might have to the justice and grace of God. He thought that even the apostolic period had seen many noisy disruptions in response to gospel preaching. Parsons decided "If the Lord is pleas'd to make this open Shew of the Victories of his Grace, his Will be done."[41]

Using the heady experiences at Lyme as a springboard, Parsons soon began itinerating in response to requests from ministers in southeastern Connecticut, including Benjamin Lord of Norwich and Andrew Croswell of Groton. He meant to go back to Lyme after this successful tour, but instead he stopped at New London to help Eliphalet Adams manage the growing split in his church. A month before Davenport's July visit to New London, Parsons found "a Number of new Converts with a flaming Zeal" and others "who oppos'd themselves to the

Work going on among them," which led to "mutual rising Jealousies." Parsons attempted to mend the growing rift, but the hostilities would eventually lead to a 1742 church separation in New London.[42]

In mid-October the high point of Parsons's West Lyme revival arrived. Parsons called the day "our Penticost," and it featured a powerfully affecting communion service, reminiscent of the Scots-Irish communion seasons. About three hundred came to receive communion that day, and "God pour'd out his Spirit in a wonderful Measure." Parsons reminded the communicants that the "rich Treasures" of God's grace were abundantly available, reflected in the meal set before them. With this, several began to moan that their sins had pierced Christ, and many began to cry. Some also trembled "as tho' they had heard the Thunderings and seen the Lightnings from the thick Cloud." Parsons considered this a visitation of Christ: "I could not but think that the Lord Jesus was come to his Table, and feasting their Souls with his Love."[43]

With such emotional intensity at this Supper, it was no wonder that some behavior by the communicants became extravagant, eliciting accusations of enthusiasm. In one case, "two Men embraced each other in their Arms before the Blessing was given," but Parsons did not think this was as "indecent, as some would represent it." He was concerned enough, however, to communicate the incident to Benjamin Colman, who thought the embrace "Praise-worthy." Colman did have concerns about overheated religious affections leading to license. "I wou'd not have Joy and Love lead Communicants into too much sensitive Freedoms towards one another; least of all the Brethren and Sisters. Each of those of their own Sex may be allowed and approv'd a great Way, a due Gravity preserv'd." Moderates like Colman thought that the unrestrained emotionalism could easily lead to sexual anarchy if left unchecked, but that believers of the same sex should not refrain from showing their godly affection for one another.[44]

There were also cases of "Persons going about the Meeting-House in the Sacrament Time," but Parsons thought those were insignificant episodes. Overall, "general Reverence and Decency" marked the communicants' behavior, he reported to the *Christian History*. Several older people in the church claimed never to have felt the presence of God so palpably, and some gained an assurance of salvation they had not enjoyed previously. Newer converts found their zeal increased, and some communicants professed to have been converted for the first time at the service. Parsons thought that the revival had waned since that high point in October. Writing in April 1744, Parsons estimated that perhaps 180 people had been converted, and that though the conversions ran primarily among the young people, a number of older people had experienced the new birth as well, including a ninety-three-year-old.[45]

Even more than Parsons's ministry, James Davenport's itinerant preaching in 1741 bore much fruit, and much controversy. The New London farmer and diarist Joshua Hempstead wrote in late July, "Mr Davenport pr att Groton 4 or 5 days & mighty works followed. near 1000 hearers (near ye old meetinghouse) from all Quarters held ye meeting till 2 Clock at night & Some Stayed all night under the oak tree & in the meeting house. about 60 Wounded, many Strong men as well as others." In Stonington, Hempstead went to rake hay but found that it had not yet been cut: "All hands have been hearing Mr. Davenport this week." He heard that at the Stonington meeting Friday, hundreds of people had cried out during Davenport's sermon. That Sunday, he went to hear Davenport "under the trees." Hempstead did not relish what he heard, though. "He was So Severe in Judging & Condemning Mr. [Nathaniel] Eells that many of the People in the Assembly withdrew into the meetinghouse where Mr. Eells preacht to them as he was wont to do & ye Rest Stayed by mr. Davenport until ye Exercise was over."[46]

Not everyone felt the way Hempstead did. Joseph Park, a missionary in nearby Westerly, Rhode Island, dated the beginnings of his greatest ministerial harvest to Davenport's visit to Stonington. The Society for the Propagation of the Gospel in New England had sent Park to Westerly in 1733, but he had seen little success. Tennent preached in Westerly both going and coming on his New England tour but had seemed only to raise the ire of English residents against Tennent and Park, who supported him. Then, "GOD in his Providence sent the Revd. Mr. James Davenport over to NEW-ENGLAND. He preach'd at Stonington adjacent to us." Park went to hear him along with numbers of others from Westerly. He had "heard many strange Things of him, and strange Effects of his preaching." He first encountered the itinerant leading a procession singing a hymn, and Park was deeply impressed: "the dread Majesty of GOD seemed to fill Heaven and Earth." Davenport preached a straightforward presentation of the gospel, and yet it produced remarkable effects, especially "a Cry all over the Meeting-House." Park believed that many were converted through Davenport's work, including a number from Westerly. These began holding regular meetings that eventually resulted in the incorporation of a Westerly church, led by Park. The revival Davenport generated in Westerly was originally limited to English congregants, but it soon affected many local Narragansetts.[47]

Hannah Heaton also wrote approvingly of Davenport's preaching and counsel. At one stretch in 1741 she heard Davenport give eleven sermons, with remarkable effects on the congregation. "Sometimes mr deavenport would cry out with a great voice above the multitude and say come away come away to the lord jesus," and many cried out for mercy, while others exhorted and prayed for sinners. Davenport paid special attention to Heaton and advised her not to marry an unconverted man. Heaton would ignore that advice and later regretted it deeply.[48]

Davenport had many admirers, but he made many others nervous. Solomon Williams of Lebanon noted Davenport's visit to New London in a July 1741 letter to Wheelock and reported on his increasingly strange behavior. He had heard that Davenport "goes singing to Meeting & about the Streets with his Armour bearers & by some other oddities. The People in New London are set into a Mighty Ruffle & disturbance, but especially by his treating Mr. [Eliphalet] Adams as an unconverted Man & praying for him Publickly as such." Williams told Wheelock that many thought Davenport was deluded or distracted and that the growing controversy over Davenport threatened to disrupt the revivals. He asked Wheelock and Benjamin Pomeroy to visit Davenport and plead with him to tone down his antics. "What shall we do," he wrote, "if God Leaves his Ministers to pull down with one hand what they build with the other." Stephen Williams was also concerned, as he noted in his diary on July 31: "I hear Br. J. D. is come out . . . many things in him, are Singular & peculiar."[49]

Up the Thames River from New London, at Norwich, the future Baptist leader Isaac Backus was converted during the summer 1741 revivals, partly through Davenport's preaching. In 1751 Backus recalled that "it pleased the Lord to cause a very general awakening Thro' the Land; especially in Norwich." He traced the operations of the Spirit in his soul to May and June of 1741, when he saw "that now God was Come with the offers of his grace." The arrival of itinerants greatly helped him along the conversion path: "It pleased The Lord to Send many Powerfull Preachers To Norwich," including Wheelock and Jedidiah Mills of Ripton, Connecticut. It was Davenport, however, who most deeply affected Backus: "About the begining of August Mr. Devenport Came to Norwich and preached There three days going in an exceeding Earnest and Powerful manner: and I apprehend that his labours were the most blest For my Conversion of any one mans." Wheelock, Pomeroy, and Davenport cooperated in a number of "powerfull meetings" in Norwich. Backus worried that despite the work of the Spirit, he would miss his opportunity to find grace. But on August 24, 1741, while "mowing in the field alone," Backus finally apprehended the forgiveness available to him in Christ and found that "now my Burden (that was so dreadful Heavey before) was gone."[50]

In the neighboring New Concord parish of Norwich, pastor Benjamin Throop recorded his experiences in the 1741 revivals in a private journal he titled "Secret Interviews." Jedidiah Mills fueled a revival in Norwich in May, and by July, Throop felt that New Concord was fully awakened. "There has been Great workings of heart; not only in my self but in others," he wrote. The young people were especially stirred by regular visits of itinerants. Their preaching produced ecstasies in New Concord. "There has been of late much powerful Preaching amongst us, attended with various Success, and with Strange & unusual Operations: Some Persons falling down as Dead: others put into ye Greatest Distortions & Convulsions. Some fainting & others Screaming . . . These Persons, Many of them, after Some few hours or Days, are Mightily Comforted (and as ye Term now is) have Received Light, or have seen Christ. and by some are pronounced Converted and Renewed Persons." By August, Throop noted that controversy had followed the itinerants, with differing "Sentiments about, Messeurs Devenport, Wheelock, Pumeroy, &c." Throop was not alarmed by the itinerants and the ecstasies they generated, concluding that "without assuming much of a Prophetick Spt; It may be Said yt . . . Providence is pregnant with some very Great things." Many local Connecticut ministers like Throop were prepared to accept the new style of ministry because its spectacular results seemed undeniable and because they were personally touched by the revivals' effects. As Throop confessed in August, "I think I have of late Experienced more of ye Divine presence than Ever before."[51]

Lebanon's Eleazar Wheelock found his preaching in high demand in southeastern New England, just as Parsons had, and in fall 1741 he set out on a preaching tour that took him into Rhode Island and Massachusetts. In late October he visited Plainfield and Voluntown, Connecticut. He met with considerable success, but he worried about the conditions at Voluntown: "There is a great work in this town; but more of the footsteps of Satan than in any place I have yet been in." The demonic presence showed itself, Wheelock thought, in the form of imaginary excesses. "They tell of many visions, revelations, and many strong impressions upon the imagination. . . . Satan is using many artful wiles to put a stop to the work of God in this place." In Scituate, Rhode Island, Wheelock found more opposition to his work. One elderly couple "called me antichrist," he wrote, while a Baptist couple harassed him about the correct mode of baptism. At Providence, Josiah Cotton invited him to preach, but Wheelock struggled to overcome the "dreadful ignorance and wickedness of these parts." In late October, Wheelock found himself confronted by a man who was paid "twenty shillings" to fake a manifestation of the Spirit by falling down and was making a "great disturbance." Later, however, Cotton credited Wheelock with helping his church grow in grace and numbers.[52]

Joseph Steward, *The Reverend Eleazar Wheelock (1711–
1779), 1st President of Dartmouth College (1769–1779).*
Commissioned by the Trustees of Dartmouth College,
Hanover, New Hampshire, Hood Museum of Art,
Dartmouth College.

At Taunton, Massachusetts, Wheelock oversaw a particularly affecting evening meeting at Josiah Crocker's church. "I believe thirty cried out. Almost all
the negroes in town wounded; three or four converted. A great work in the town
. . . I was forced to break off my sermon, before it was done, the outcry was so
great." Crocker remembered that Wheelock used a gentle voice to preach, but
"Power and Authority" accompanied the sermon "too big, awful and majestick,
for any Creature." The next day, Wheelock made a special visit to "Capt. Leonard's negro (a slave)" and "found him under a very clear and genuine conviction."
In Taunton, he happily met up with the itinerating Daniel Rogers, who also had
extensive experience ministering to African Americans in the revivals.[53]

Rogers was deeply impressed with Wheelock. The two rode to Bridgewater,
and Rogers watched as Wheelock preached there for several days with consider-

able effects. Rogers recorded that "Br. Wheelock pr[eached] to a very gt. As-sembly in ye fields, much affected." Wheelock recorded in his journal, "A great multitude. Preached upon a stage." In Easton the two proved a powerful com-bination. Rogers preached first, and "many cryed out in Bitterness of Soul . . . the Cry increas'd—Sang again; and then Br. Wh. pr[eached] wth gt. Power; the out Cry began again and waxed louder & louder. I prayed again and after the Blessing, we came down & discoursed wth the wounded." After preaching at Braintree, their revival contingent moved on to Boston.[54]

In Boston, the itinerants were welcomed by Thomas Prince Sr. and his con-gregant, the Boston merchant Edward Bromfield Jr., who offered his home for lodging and chaise for transportation. While there, Rogers and Wheelock made the standard tour of New North, Brattle Street, and Old South churches. After preaching to a large crowd at New North, Wheelock recorded, "they told me . . . that Mather Byles [pastor of Hollis Street Church] was never so lashed in his life." While the three key revivalist churches warmly received Wheelock and Rogers, elsewhere in Boston opposition to their work was growing. As for Rogers, he was nearly awed by Wheelock's preaching power, as he had been by White-field's. Upon Wheelock's departure, Rogers wrote, "I find by his pr.ing and Con-versation, yt. I am but a Child to Him in Knowledge & Grace."[55]

After a successful five-day visit to Boston, Wheelock set out for Connecticut. Outside Boston he met again with Josiah Cotton of Providence, who tried to convince him to follow up the revival work he had started. but Wheelock in-sisted that he must go home. After visiting Dedham, he preached at Medway and seemed to offend the local minister by telling the people "that Christians generally knew the time of their conversion." This doctrine of palpable conver-sion and immediate assurance was quickly becoming a staple of evangelical the-ology, as opposed to the older Puritan morphology of conversion which empha-sized process. Finally, Wheelock returned to Lebanon. In a little under a month Wheelock preached about forty sermons and gave many personal conferences and consultations. The tireless efforts of evangelists like Wheelock undoubtedly explain a great deal of the widespread impact of these awakenings.[56]

In January 1742, Wheelock wrote to Rogers with a wonderful report of the on-going revivals in Connecticut. Wheelock had been preaching at Wethersfield, south of Hartford, for two weeks, where he saw "Much of ye Great power of God." In one meeting, the "Groans and outcrys of ye Wounded were such yt. my voice cod. not be heard." He also preached to an assembly of African Americans "where also I cod. not go thro with my Sermon their outcry was so great their distress was astonishing their agony Groans &c. Seamed a lively Emblem of ye Damned." He thought that between thirty and forty from this group had been converted. The awakenings also went forward among the Native Americans of Mohegan, Niantic, and Stonington. Again, the "Great instrument" awakening them was James Davenport. All in all, Wheelock was highly optimistic: he believed that the "opposers were out of Credit," and he had more work than he could handle. He meant to go back to Josiah Cotton's Providence church as soon as his schedule would allow, and he hoped to meet Rogers there.[57]

Wheelock's optimistic tone about Davenport and the decreasing opposition gave little hint of the torrent of controversy that would mark the coming years of the revivals. As can be seen in the narratives in the *Christian History* and in the responses to Davenport, the breach between moderate and radical supporters of the revivals was opening wider. As pioneered by Whitefield, among the most controversial issues in the awakenings were unrestrained itinerancy and the subject of unconverted ministers. The year 1741 also saw developing moderate anxiety over the bodily manifestations of revival fervor. Nevertheless, the public image of New England evangelicalism remained relatively unified during 1741. That would hardly remain the case during the next two years.

"Minds Extraordinarily Transported": Testing the Limits of Revivalism, 1741–1742

Even as revivals proceeded in 1741, arguments about them went public. No single moment marked a pivot into controversy. Certainly, Whitefield had always drawn criticism, as seen in his public quarrels with Alexander Garden and the New Castle Presbytery. Gilbert Tennent had generated controversy, too, particularly after delivering *The Danger of an Unconverted Ministry*. But in late summer 1741 a more widespread protest began to rise against two key features of the revivals: the bodily agitations and vocal outbursts of some penitents, and the aggressive tactics of some itinerants, particularly James Davenport.

One can see the controversy emerging in a letter by Jonathan Edwards in August 1741, in which he assessed the "great stir that is in the land." He particularly addressed the ecstasies of the awakened and the methods of the itinerants. As for "persons crying out, and being set into great agonies, with a sense of sin and wrath, and having their strength taken away, and their minds extraordinarily transported with light, love and comfort, I have been abundantly amongst such things." Certainly, he admitted, some of these extremes hid imperfect motives, but "as to the work in general, . . . they have all the clear and incontestable evidences of a true divine work. If this ben't the work of God, I have all my religion to learn over again, and know not what use to make of the Bible." Furthermore, "as to the ministers that go about the country to preach, . . . I believe they are exceedingly misrepresented." He knew Connecticut itinerants Benjamin Pomeroy and Eleazar Wheelock well, and he thought they had never neglected their own flocks or intruded uninvited into other parishes. Ultimately, he recommended that evangelicals "look to God to plead his own cause, and to get himself the victory."[1] For the next several years, Edwards would stake his credibility on his positive assessment of the revivals.

Certainly, James Davenport did not make Edwards's promotion of the revivals easier. Davenport visited New Haven just before Edwards was to give the Yale commencement week sermon, a public defense of the revivals. At Yale, Davenport encouraged student insubordination against staid college officials. A hostile account in the *Boston Weekly Post-Boy* claimed that Davenport and others "held forth every Day of the Commencement Week, and generally continued to 10 or 11 a Clock at Night." The correspondent worried that during a single meeting five or ten people might speak, some at the same time, from different parts of the sanctuary. "So that, some praying, some exhorting & terrifying, some singing, some screaming, some crying, some laughing and some scolding, made the most amazing Confusion that ever was heard." Radical students chafed against pastor Joseph Noyes of New Haven's First Church. Davenport called Noyes a "wolf in sheep's clothing" and exhorted the students to attend new meetings outside of the established church. Daniel Wadsworth of Hartford's First Church was in town for commencement and noted in his diary, "Commencement at New-Haven. Davenport and Bellamy preached and Mills at night, great Confusion." The next day, he wrote, "Much Confusion this day at New-Haven, and at night ye most strange management and a pretence of religion yt ever I saw." A confrontation between Noyes, Yale rector Thomas Clap, and Davenport ended in "great Consternation," as Davenport persisted in calling Noyes unconverted.[2]

On that commencement day of "much confusion" and "strange management," Edwards preached *The Distinguishing Marks of a Work of the Spirit of God*. We do not have the original text, but an expanded version was printed in Boston, Philadelphia, and London. Edwards based his sermon on I John 4:1, which called on believers to "try the spirits whether they are of God." Edwards argued that the apostles had established standards for testing whether religious excitement was legitimate. He believed that the similarities between the apostolic period and the present awakenings made it clear that the apostles' rules would prove highly useful "in this extraordinary day, when that which is so remarkable appears . . . and there is such a variety of opinions concerning it."[3]

Edwards began his examination of the revivals with a list of aspects that "are not signs that we are to judge of a work by." This clever approach allowed him to indirectly dismantle all the objections that conservative critics of the revivals had raised. Were the revivals new and unusual? Surely this was no reason to dismiss them as illegitimate, Edwards argued, for many of God's greatest acts in redemptive history featured effects no one had previously seen. Did penitents demonstrate extraordinary bodily and vocal exercises in the meetings? It was no wonder, since many had gained new insights into the judgment and mercy of God. Edwards may have been thinking of the great outcry at Enfield two months earlier. "If we should suppose," he reasoned, "that a person saw himself hanging over a great pit, full of fierce and glowing flames, by a thread that he knew to be very weak . . . what distress would he be in . . . would not he be ready to cry out in such circumstances?" Those at Enfield certainly had cried out, and Edwards considered their response reasonable.[4]

Likewise, Edwards contended, the presence of "great impressions" on the imagination did not make the revivals bogus. He did worry about the affected giving too much weight to so-called prophetical visions, but overall he considered the mental images a means by which God convicted and comforted. Yes, some of the penitents "have in some extraordinary frames, been in a kind of ecstasy, wherein they have been carried beyond themselves, and have had their minds transported into a . . . kind of visions." He knew that to some opponents these reports signaled reckless enthusiasm. Edwards knew better: "I have been acquainted with some such instances; and I see no manner of need of bringing in the help of the Devil into the account we give of these things." As he had witnessed at Northampton, some visions did follow the authentic work of the Spirit.[5]

He also conceded that the revivals occasionally produced "imprudences and irregularities," "delusions of Satan," and "gross errors or scandalous practices," but so did all great new movements of God. Finally, he insisted that it was no shame to the revival that its leaders sometimes focused "very much on the terrors of God's holy law, and that with a great deal of pathos and earnestness." Hell was real, and many were going there for eternity. Why should ministers not sound the alarm? "If I am in danger of going to hell, I should be glad to know as much as possibly I can of the dreadfulness of it," he noted dryly.[6]

Having concluded that most justifications for dismissing the revivals were unreasonable, he proceeded to "shew positively, what are the sure, distinguishing, Scripture evidences and marks of a work of the Spirit of God." Authentic religious experiences might manifest themselves in various ways, but Edwards argued that they would always produce enduring, godly effects. The work of the Spirit raised the "esteem" of Jesus while working against "the interest of Satan's kingdom." It created a "greater regard" for the Scriptures. It encouraged true love for both God and man. He admitted that Satan could temporarily mimic these signs of the Spirit, but he thought that these lasting features would eventually distinguish true and false works.[7]

Based on these standards, Edwards concluded that the late work "is undoubtedly, in the general, from the Spirit of God." He appealed again to his own experience in the revivals: "I am one that, by the providence of God, have for some months past, been much amongst those that have been the subjects of that work that has of late been carried on in the land." Here he subtly contrasted himself with critics. Had they been there when the outcries began? Had God converted anyone through their preaching? "I look upon myself called on this occasion to give my testimony [that] this work has all those marks" of the Spirit. I know, Edwards implied, because I have been there to see it. He had long been familiar with revivals at Northampton, he reminded them, going back to those during Solomon Stoddard's tenure. There had, of course, been the celebrated revival in his parish in 1735, but the work of God in 1741 was "much purer than that which was wrought there six years before."[8]

Having made such a bold defense of the revivals, Edwards proceeded to threaten the critics of the awakenings. Never one to hold back when he believed himself to be on God's side of an issue, Edwards warned the Yale audience that attempts to slander the late work of God could meet with divine retribution. Specifically, Edwards posited that the critics' carping against the revivals could make them guilty of the "unpardonable sin against the Holy Ghost," that fearsome but mysterious sin that Jesus mentioned in Matthew 12:31–32. The revivals' opponents thought this charge revealed Edwards's "partiality" and "rashness," as the rebuttal tract *The Late Religious Commotions in New-England Considered* put it. Edwards concluded *The Distinguishing Marks* with warnings to the friends of the revival to rein in their enthusiastic excesses and to be particularly wary of preferring "impulses and impressions" to the clear guidance of the Scriptures. To do so would be to "leave the guidance of the pole star to follow a Jackwith-a-lanthorn." In a caution certainly directed at Davenport and his followers, he spoke against "passing censures upon others that are professing Christians, as hypocrites and ignorant of anything of real religion." He further advised the revivals' defenders to avoid "too much heat and appearance of an angry zeal." Having just implied that the revivals' critics had committed the unpardonable sin, one might argue that Edwards needed to take his own advice against angry censuring. *The Distinguishing Marks* did nothing to placate doubters or rein in radicals, but it staked out a moderate evangelical position and forced private naysayers into the open. For the next two years debates would rage over Edwards's points, not only between the Old Lights and New Lights, but between the moderate and radical evangelicals, all trying to define the limits of legitimate revival.[9]

In an important coincidence, on the same day that Edwards preached *The Distinguishing Marks*, Charles Chauncy of Boston's First Church preached *An Unbridled Tongue a Sure Evidence, that our Religion is Hypocritical and Vain.* Although he likely did not intend it to answer Edwards directly, the lecture certainly did so. Chauncy denounced all those who "will presume proudly to take to themselves the sole prerogative of the omniscient God, by looking into the hearts of their neighbours, and judging them carnal, unregenerate men." He was ready, unlike Edwards, to call this censoriousness a clear sign of false religion.[10] Edwards dismissed the radicals' rash judging as unfortunate excesses of a true work of God.

The debate over the revivals between Edwards and Chauncy has been seen as the most significant one of the First Great Awakening with good reason. But their debate was not the only one, and their positions did not define the only options within the larger debates over the awakenings. For instance, one of the earliest public debates over the awakenings matched Alexander Garden, the Anglican commissary of Charleston, South Carolina, against radical pastor Andrew Croswell of Second Church, Groton, Connecticut. In their debate, one can see the intercolonial contest over Whitefield's reputation. In *Six Letters to the Rev. Mr. George Whitefield* (1740), Garden protested Whitefield's assertion that many Anglican clergy were preaching justification by good works instead of grace alone. In a reply to Garden, Croswell made the debate over Whitefield primarily a contest between Calvinism and Arminianism. He agreed with Whitefield that one of the main problems besetting the Anglican church was that the preponderance of the clergy had ceased to preach "the Doctrines of the Reformation." Croswell put the matter bluntly: Garden and most of the Anglican clergy "together with the Papists hold that the way for them to merit, or to be intitled to this merited Justification, are Works of Righteousness." Croswell also bemoaned Garden's persecution of Whitefield in Charleston, concluding that "South Carolina is a Persecuting Country for Religion."[11]

A furious Garden published a rebuttal in South Carolina in 1742, sneering that when he first read Croswell's piece he thought its author must have been "some zealous Lady . . . whose Spirit was . . . greatly stirred within her," not a college-educated minister. After refuting Croswell's points for sixty pages, he ended by wondering, "Shall I conclude with Congratulations on the present Scenes of Religion acting in your Parts? No, Sir! it would be cruel. I greatly pity and bewail them . . . Wilfully abandoning their Reason . . . And throwing themselves into the Arms of strong Delusion!" The evangelicals, not the Anglican Arminians, were courting Romanism, Garden argued: "A Harvest indeed for Romish Missionaries! For who knows not, that this, of laying aside Reason, is a first Doctrine of Popery, the main Foundation of that terrible Fabrick of ROME!" All sides in the debate over the revivals painted their opponents as crypto-Catholics.[12]

John Caldwell, the enigmatic Irish Presbyterian minister of Blanford, Massachusetts, also publicly attacked the revivalists in October 1741. He clearly had Edwards's *Distinguishing Marks* in mind as he preached *An Impartial Trial of the Spirit Operating in this Part of the World* on a visit to the First Church in Londonderry, New Hampshire. He even took I John 4:1 as his main text. Caldwell warned the congregation against "false Prophets . . . , or Men who have alledged they were, and do pretend to be influenced by the Divine Spirit . . . without having any Ground for such Pretences." Caldwell offered a survey of false prophets throughout religious history, mentioning among others "Mahomet," who "pretended to teach nothing but by immediate Influence of the Divine Spirit, and was generally convulsed . . . before he communicated any new Thing." Caldwell insisted that the way to test any prophet was by an unbiased reading of the Scriptures. Edwards had argued that lasting godly effects constituted the ultimate test of the spirit, and now Caldwell put the weight on an impartial searching of the Word. Both, however, assumed that honest examination of the holy text would lead believers to a common apprehension of the truth. This flawed assumption of readers' objectivity would hamstring debates over the revivals, and evangelical theology generally, for years to come.[13]

Caldwell fully agreed with the necessity of repentance and conversion for salvation, but he doubted the authenticity of many recent conversions, especially those featuring bodily exercises and outcries. He characterized the late conversions as "A sudden and terrible Fear of Divine Wrath, or the Miseries of Hell," creating at times intense cold or hot sensations. These caused "People to cry as if distracted; to shed Tears in great Plenty; throwing many into Convulsions." This phase lasted perhaps a few days, and then they became happy, certain "that all their Sins are pardoned, and that they shall be saved." The converts then usually began "bold talking of Experiences." They turned against anyone who questioned their feelings, "calling such carnal, and sentencing them to eternal Misery."[14]

As for the itinerants, they neglected their own congregations as they "travel to and fro upon the Earth, spiriting People against their Pastors . . . by representing them as carnal and dead Men." Anyone who did not respond to their preaching, they reproved, "because they do not shed Tears, fall down into Convulsions [and] scream. . . . [They] declare such as oppose them are guilty of Blasphemy against the Holy Ghost." On that last point he surely had Edwards in mind. Their preaching, moreover, was one-track: they spoke almost exclusively of "Terror, Hell and Damnation, with Pathos and moving Gestures." The itinerants' followers mimicked their style of religion, took "deluded Imaginations for heavenly Visions," and preferred the preaching of the ignorant to any learned pastor who disagreed with them. This enthusiastic religion spread "like an Epidemical Distemper . . . over all Ages and Sexes, but especially the younger Women and Children." Caldwell, like most of the revivals' critics, saw the itinerants as preying on the weak-minded to peddle their false religion. Taking exception to Edwards's characterization of the apostolic period, Caldwell denied that anything like the recent rash of "conversions" had ever been seen before in church history.[15]

Caldwell also believed that the bodily manifestations in the revivals were dangerous. "Are they not the Effect of a sudden Motion of the Blood and Animal Spirits in Persons of abounding Fluids and weak Nerves?" Women and children were particularly given to such behavior, but this spoke only to their weaker physical disposition, not some unusual experience in the Spirit. Caldwell, like Garden, argued that such religion smacked of Catholicism: "Were you to see a Roman Catholick Priest after the Celebration of Mass upon some extraordinary Day, talk in wild enthusiastick Strains, and at proper Periods hold up the Crucifix and Effigies of our Saviour, more crying would happen than at any of the warmest Sermons ever preached in New-England." Caldwell hoped that the eternal destinies of the new "converts" were more secure than those of these weeping Catholics. Edwards claimed that the new converts displayed greater holiness. Caldwell thought their newfound faith seemed mostly to result in "uncharitable and rash judging of others." If this was the chief product of their ecstasies, what good had so-called conversion done them? In conclusion, Caldwell challenged his audience, especially any reticent ministers, "to look upon and plainly declare, that this Work has not the Character of a Work of God." He thought Edwards's sermon had tried to silence dissent, but "Be not afraid of being thought guilty of Blasphemy." Instead, "Let us . . . without Fear oppose Error; especially Antinomianism and Popery, which to me it appears manifest are now blending together, and overspreading the World." Good men had to stand against the irrationality and enthusiasm of these revivals.[16]

Fellow Irish Presbyterian David McGregore of Second Church, Londonderry, soon preached a rebuttal sermon to Caldwell's. Caldwell showed up at this sermon and challenged McGregore to a debate, which McGregore refused. McGregore, however, did receive an invitation to preach at the Brattle Street Church in Boston, and there delivered *The Spirits of the Present Day Tried.* McGregore, too, used I John 4:1 as his main text. He argued that in times of great successes for the kingdom of God, Satan sometimes will "transform himself into an Angel of Light, and to send forth his Ministers; who though inward they are ravening Wolves, yet they come in Sheeps Cloathing; and partly by hellish Lies, partly by aggravating some real Indiscretions . . . they would deceive . . . the very Elect. Thus it is in this glorious Day of Gospel Grace." Clearly, McGregore did not mince words about Caldwell and the other opponents of the revivals. But McGregore made an argument strikingly similar to Caldwell's: a plain reading of the Scriptures will lead honest people to the truth. "Blessed be God, that we have our Bibles," he proclaimed. The key difference between their hermeneutical assumptions was that Caldwell put a great deal of emphasis on reason as the guide to interpretation, whereas McGregore promoted reason enlightened by the Spirit. McGregore conceded that false prophets had always existed in the visible church, but the leaders of the revivals were not "Hereticks and False Teachers."[17]

McGregore believed that only the opponents of the revivals tended toward heresy, particularly Arminianism. McGregore vigorously defended the awakenings as Calvinist in theology, even dismissing the Arminian English Methodist John Wesley as an unfortunate renegade within the revivalists' ranks. Hostility toward God's work in the awakenings was part and parcel of the growing "Error of Arminius in the protestant World," of which "I wish I could say that our Side of the Atlantick were free." Many of the antirevivalists were actually traditional Calvinists, but McGregore was not entirely unfair in associating antirevivalism with Arminian, or free will theology. Becoming more personal in his attack, McGregore also asserted that many of the revivals' opponents were "acted by a lying Spirit," inspired by the "Father of Lies," the devil. "If ever Hell seem'd to be broken loose in horrid Lies and Calumny, now appears to be the Time." Thus, Whitefield was "represented as a base, mercenary, covetous Man" and as an agent of the Pope, "employ'd by the Man of Sin to bring over People to the cursed Errors of the Church of Rome." He also thought that envy lay at the root of some criticisms, as pastors watched thousands convert in other churches with not a stir in their own. He believed some operated in a "profane mocking Spirit," and he singled out Alexander Garden for this charge. Worst of all, as the opponents ridiculed the work of God, people in their own congregations "go smoothly down the Stream to Hell." Agreeing with Edwards, McGregore insisted that this amounted to "sinning against the Holy Ghost."[18]

A second edition of McGregore's sermon was printed in Boston in 1742, with an appendix laying out the details of his clash with Caldwell. Caldwell continued publishing antirevival sermons in 1742, and in 1743 he printed a response to McGregore's second edition. In July, Caldwell spoke at Boston's French meetinghouse on *The Nature, Folly, and Evil of Rash and Uncharitable Judging.* Much of the content of these pieces only expanded his arguments in *An Impartial Trial.* The July sermon came only days after Caldwell had an actual day in court: he sued Boston's Scots-Irish Presbyterian pastor John Moorhead for slander. Moorhead had accused Caldwell of having fraudulent ministerial credentials, and this charge, along with the July award of £250 to Caldwell, began an unraveling of what had seemed a very promising public career. Moorhead appealed the decision, and when the next hearing took place in August 1743, Caldwell did not appear, apparently having left the province. Edinburgh's *Christian Monthly History* claimed in 1743 that Caldwell had been known as "Thompton in Ireland, where he was licensed, and where he committed, for a considerable Time, the most attrocious Thefts." The discovery of his crimes supposedly prompted his flight to New England. Presbyterian Samuel Davies, writing in Virginia in 1748, claimed that Caldwell had escaped to Pennsylvania, where he admitted his wrongdoing publicly. Later, Caldwell supposedly fled to Maryland, where he sought Anglican ordination before finally departing for England.[19]

Even as these arguments boiled, the revivals proceeded apace. Some moderate pastors concerned themselves with regulating the revivals in the face of criticism, while radicals did not. Daniel Rogers continued his tireless preaching schedule and showed continuing comfort with the radical manifestations of the awakenings. He focused most of his efforts on northeastern Massachusetts and his hometown of Ipswich. On December 27, 1741, Rogers recorded in his diary, "God was pleased to begin a Revival of his work in this Town in a most Glorious manner." It originated at a private meeting led by his brother John, and the awakened group sent for Daniel and his brother Nathaniel as well. "When we came," he wrote, they "found some of ye Children of God full of ye Holy Ghost. Some of 'em over come with ye Love of j[esus] even to fainting." Several days later, Rogers saw an explosion of fervor from the Ipswich congregation. He preached on the parable of the Prodigal Son, and "The Spirit of God came down in an astonishing manner—2 or 3 Scream'd out—it Spread like fire—I suppose a Thousand People were present and that some Hundred—3 or 4 at least cryed so gt. weep & Lamentation I never heard before. I extended my Voice as much as possible—but cd. not be heard half over the House." The next day the Spirit came as a "Spirit of Supplication & Intercession & *Prophecy.*" Even in a diary he knew that this last claim needed clarification. By prophecy, he continued, "I here mean a Persons Speaking the Truths of ye *Word* or Gospel by the Immediate Help—or Influence of the Spirit of God, *This is my Faith.*" Among those given this Spirit were several women: "This Spirit was Evidently to me in Lucy Smith. *Her Prayer* was answer'd." Others prayed boldly as well. The group stayed in the meetinghouse all night. The piety of Smith and others deeply affected Rogers, who hit another spiritual high on January 4, when he received a level of assurance "far beyound wt. I ever Experienced before—this Joy is Humbling & Abasing-which I don't remember I perceived so distinctly & plainly in that I had at [his conversion in] New-York. I had now Assurance—was strong in Faith."[20]

On the heels of these intense experiences, Rogers found himself in a showdown with one of the most conservative of the evangelical moderates, Nathaniel Appleton of Cambridge, who arrived in Ipswich to assist and temper the revival there. In effect, Appleton was trying to serve as a conservative itinerant. The artisan Joseph Bean, Appleton's congregant, had written in October 1741 that Appleton warned of great emotional displays masking hypocrisy. Bean remembered that he had cried often in revival meetings, and he feared that he "was the Crieng and weeping hipocrit." Now Appleton exhorted the congregation at Ipswich to be "Jealous & Suspicious" of the ecstatic experiences accompanying their conversions and to look to godliness as a surer sign of salvation. Rogers was deflated. "I saw yt. He threw cold Water upon those who were fired wth ye. Love of God." After the sermon, Rogers stood up and challenged Appleton to tell the converts how they should "judge of yr. Estate now." Appleton told them they should work out their salvation with fear and trembling and tried to close with prayer and a blessing. But again, Rogers stood up and spoke about the woman healed of bleeding in Luke 8. He proposed that people could know that they were "Spiritually healed—when they receive power to touch Xt. by Faith." Conversion had its own signs, he argued, and one did not have to wait to see the results it produced to have assurance of God's favor. The witness of the Holy Spirit was the best evidence of salvation, and "those who have not experienc'd this Witness of the Spirit know nothing of It." Did he mean Appleton was not converted? This was not clear, but surely the tension must have been thick between them. The revival continued that night with some experiencing "an Extacy of Joy," and others came to Rogers and applauded him for standing up to Appleton.[21]

The debate between Rogers and Appleton revealed another fault line between the radicals and moderates: the issue of assurance of salvation. Rogers asserted that real believers would know that they were saved, whereas Appleton argued that lasting godliness offered the best hope, but not total assurance, of salvation. The controversy over assurance had roots in earlier Puritan spirituality, in which radicals trumpeted the liberating possibility of full assurance, while moderate Puritans continued to emphasize obedience to the law through the power of the Spirit as the best means of confirming salvation. Moderate and radical evangelicals split along approximately similar lines. Radical itinerant Andrew Croswell, for instance, argued like Rogers that "a Man can never determine that he hath believ'd, as is passed from Death to Life, without seeing the Fruits of Faith in himself. . . . By his Spirit witnessing with our Spirits, that we are his Children, we can be sure, but no other Way." The Holy Spirit revealed to real believers that they were, indeed, believers. They obtained assurance by "the Spirit of Adoption shining immediately into [their] hearts." Moderate Jonathan Dickinson, by contrast, conceded that the witness of the Spirit might give immediate certainty in very rare circumstances but worried that "some Persons from enthusiastick Heats, from working up their animal Affections and Passions, or else from diabolical Delusions, have pretended to these immediate Influences of the Spirit of God." If lasting holiness did not accompany the supposed feelings from the Spirit, then those experiences were "false and counterfeit."[22]

In spite of Appleton's attempts to moderate the Ipswich revival, its radical features persisted. Rogers paid particular attention to female converts, regularly visiting them or counseling them in the meetings. On January 8, for instance, Rogers recorded that he "went into ye Body of ye Womans seats to one of 'em and pray'd with and for Her." The attention bore considerable fruit. One convert, "Mrs. Whipple," particularly impressed Rogers, and he visited her several times. On January 9 he found her struggling to be saved, afraid that her "proud heart" would keep her from Christ. Two days later she had been delivered through her travail, and he found her "full of Joy, blessing, and praising God." That evening, Mrs. Whipple began exhorting. Rogers wrote that "Mrs. Whipple spoke against Pride Covetousness self Righteousness." That was not all she had to say, however: Rogers wrote that she began "calling herself Mary Magdalene."[23]

What effect did this remarkable moment have on the congregation? As Rogers explained, "about this Time ye Spirit of God was wonderfully pour'd down into many new Converts." He worried about the effects of her exhortation, however: "After Mrs. Whipple went out (whose Discourse didn't seem to be relish'd by some) I was afraid yt. Something Sd to a pticular Person, and ye Manner of her Speaking wasn't right (but I can't tell)." The next day Rogers warned the congregation that he thought "some were too much concern'd abt outwd order" and told them "we must be willing that God sd. carry on his Work in his own Way." He was willing to let women exhort, if God chose to work through them. Later that night one young woman in the meeting "call'd earnestly upon sinners to come to Xt. and so did others."[24]

In the cases of Lucy Smith's prophecies and Mrs. Whipple's exhortations, Rogers approved women converts' authoritative public speaking because he believed that they served as instrumental agents of the Spirit. As the revivalists' arch-opponent Charles Chauncy noted, many ministers (including some moderate evangelicals) believed that the "suffering, much more the encouraging WOMEN, yea, GIRLS to speak in the assemblies" represented a dangerous violation of scriptural standards. Yet in numerous cases, the radicals not only permitted but defended the right of women, and even girls, to exhort and prophesy.[25]

Rogers had approvingly noted uneducated male and female exhorters, and in late January he also began to see children exhorting in the meetings. He wrote that "ye Children began to pray & exhort—pticularly Job Harris's Son had his Soul filled wth. a gt. Concern for perishing Sinners and cry'd to 'em to come to

Xt. in an Extraordinary manner—I desir'd ye People to hear Him." Some visitors from Salem "were struck by ye boys Speaking." The next day one of the boys fell into a "Trance in wch. ye Body is Insensible." When he awoke, he reported having seen "Heaven & Hell, That He had (in Spirit) Seen Xt. That ye Day of Judgement was coming which Exceedingly mov'd ye People." Rogers interviewed the boy further and found that "His *Spirit* had been drawn out & carried up to Heaven where He had a View of Xt. in Glory Sitting at ye right Hand of God—and of Angels & Saints—pticularly his Grand Father. after this yt. He had a View of Hell as a Place of dreadfull Darkness full of Divels—The Angel told Him not to be Afraid." The boy was to tell the people about these things, to warn them to repent, and to reveal that "He sd. die in three mounths." That same day, the Spirit moved remarkably in one woman, leading her to exhort with enormous intensity. "I never saw ye Spirit to this Degree and length before," Rogers wrote. "She continued in this Frame all night—Spoke & pray'd 9 or 10 Hours." Sometimes these exhortations were no brief outbursts, but all-night marathons. They closed the meeting at dawn, praying "for all the world—pticularly for dear Br. Whitefield, Tennent, Wheelock, Pomeroy, Davenport, &c."[26]

The meetings at Ipswich First Church now ran twenty-four hours a day. On February 2, Rogers got some sleep and food and then headed back to the meetinghouse to find William Harris exhorting again. Rogers concluded that he was filled with the "Spirit of Prophecy." He followed the boy and challenged the congregation to believe that Christ "had been speaking to 'em by ye mouth of ys. Child." That night Harris continued to preach, and several in attendance "Recd. ye Dear Ld. Jesus in yr. Hearts." Others fell into trances again.[27]

Rogers had generated significant attention in Chebacco Parish, Ipswich, and in early February some parishioners there helped start a controversy between Rogers and their minister, Theophilus Pickering, who was quite skeptical about the new work. Despite heated disagreements between them, Rogers was still allowed to preach at Chebacco, with remarkable results. Young exhorters generated a "gt. outcry," and almost twenty boys surrounded the pulpit seeking counsel with Rogers. One fell down on his face, while some others began to receive "comfort" and immediately began to exhort. Some African Americans were there, as Rogers noted that "a Negroe Woman recd. Xt. joyfully & 1 or 2 more." Rogers retired at midnight, while others stayed all night. When Pickering received news of these developments, he "made light of 'em."[28]

The next day Rogers woke with an infection in his leg that would keep him confined to bed for weeks. He received many visitors during his illness, particularly women who had responded to his preaching. One gave him concern: a "Mrs. Holiday" seemed to have begun promoting perfectionism. "She sd. She was perfect & She Seem'd to be carry'd beyound her self." The next day Rogers heard that Holiday had taught at a recent meeting that "Xt. was already come by His Spirit—and w[ould] never come in any other manner." Rogers did not seem ready to rebuke her, however.[29]

Rogers, instead, was ready to rebuke people for greed. In fact, when he recovered sufficiently to preach again, his first sermon railed against hoarding and price gouging. New England faced soaring bread prices during the period, making it more difficult in each passing year for the urban poor to feed themselves. It is not clear how many poor people flocked to his ministry, but certainly he pled their case, telling the congregation that he "had heard a Cry among ye Poor in ye Town, for Bread." He warned them that any who withheld grain from those in immediate need of food would be cursed by God. When he finished and descended from the pulpit, the people "shewed gt. and undeserved Love to me." Surely some of these were among those suffering from the bread shortages. But Rogers soon faced criticism from some in Ipswich who "were displeas'd with my Discourse." He prayed that he would fear God alone, not men. Later, during private prayer, he "had some pticular Things put into my Heart wth respect to releiving ye poor," and the next day he visited two suffering families.[30]

Nearby, John White and Benjamin Bradstreet reported on revival in the seaport town of Gloucester. White, pastor at First Church, called for a day of prayer and fasting to promote the revival and invited Nathaniel Rogers (brother of Daniel) to preach. Immediately White began to see "saving Impressions of the Holy Ghost" in the church. Daniel Rogers had also begun to preach in Gloucester in late November 1741, with great effects and much crying out. White and Bradstreet played down Daniel Rogers's role in their narratives, which were printed in the *Christian History*. Perhaps one point of contention between Rogers and the Gloucester ministers was Rogers's encouragement of local lay preacher and baker Richard Elvins, whom Rogers called "a person without a Liberal Education—whom God has furnished wth Extraordinary Gifts & Grace, and employed, owned & Succeeded in the work of ye Ministry."[31]

The Gloucester revival began in force on the last Sunday of January 1742, with many "impressed both with Distress and with Joy, above Measure." As a result of this stir, nine prayer societies had formed. Of specific interest, White pointed out, was a "Society of Negroes, who in their Meetings behave very seriously & decently. . . . Most of them entered into Covenant, and were baptized themselves, and also their Issue." One can hear the white evangelical paternalism here, assuring readers that nonwhite converts behaved "decently." Overall, White worked to moderate the Gloucester revivals. He conceded that there had been visions there, but after White preached against them they mostly ceased.

Likewise, they had outcries, "but I laboured to suppress them." Bradstreet reported that over the course of a year forty people joined Third Church in full communion, and that in a parish of only about eighty families.[32]

In Connecticut, Eleazar Wheelock remained optimistic in early 1742 despite the opposition to the revivals, which he thought "grows much less." In an April letter to Joseph Bellamy, however, he warned, "one thing yt Cloggs Religion among you is Peoples so freely Censuring one another & Beating down Weak [Christians]." Wheelock knew that censoriousness could fracture the revival movement.[33]

In March, Wheelock received a testimony that raised the prospect that the revivals were generating even more mystical incidents. The anonymous correspondent was by his own testimony illiterate, but he reported his experience to an acquaintance of Wheelock's. When the penitent heard itinerant Benjamin Pomeroy preach on Isaiah 40:1–2, he found his "hart in sum measure drawn forth to God" and his "soul whas filld with ravishing transport." There seemed nothing "but a thin paper wall that seperated me from perfect Glory." He fainted and found himself at the foot of a mountain that blocked his "way to the hvenly Canan." A great dove appeared and carried him to the top. There he was confronted by a charging bull, which almost gored him, but he was delivered to safety by an angel. The angel took him to the Gate of Heaven that led into the throne room of God the Father, a sight reminiscent of Revelation 4. Jesus greeted him and showed him his "name reten in Letters of blood," but told him that he must go back to his home on earth. The angel again escorted him past the bull, and the dove took him back down the mountain. There the visionary caught a sight of hell, with some of the damned swearing they would "have me." Again, the voice of God comforted him, and "I told satun I feared him not," upon which the devil crashed back into the flames of hell with his "Ghashly crew." The visionary then returned to his senses.[34]

How common were these mystical experiences in New England's awakenings of the 1740s? Historian Douglas Winiarski has argued compellingly that they were widespread. It seems likely that moderate evangelicals may have covered up some of these experiences in the *Christian History* and other narratives, as they provided exactly the sort of evidence antirevivalists wanted to use to tarnish the whole work.[35] Charles Chauncy, in particular, delighted in exposing any sign of popular mysticism in the revivals, for he believed that these experiences revealed antinomian enthusiasm. Jonathan Edwards argued, to the contrary, that such manifestations might indeed signal the presence of the Spirit, but that wisdom recommended waiting to see what fruit the excitement bore.

Readers may wonder how exotic revival phenomena like trances and visions should be interpreted. Although from such a historical distance it may be difficult to offer any convincing explanations, we should first assume that most of these experiences were not being "faked." People were not acting out or describing experiences they knew were inauthentic. Some reactions, like screaming out for mercy, might be fairly easily explained: people believed in hell, did not want to go there, and became so emotionally overcome at the thought of being condemned to hell that they loudly expressed their fears. The more such outbursts happened, the more likely they were to continue, and radicals no doubt encouraged these verbal responses from the congregation. With regard to shaking, fits, and trances, one might further conjecture that deep emotional distress or elation triggered some kind of physiological response that led to involuntary motions or swooning. Attendees often described going for some time without sleep or food, which may have exacerbated physical reactions. Visions, similarly, may have represented a physiological response to religious excitement, but the content of the visions, as well as dreams, were conditioned by biblical tropes and encouraged by the testimony of others with similar experiences. The extraordinary, and apparently involuntary, character of many phenomena may suggest physiological stimuli, but the timing, performance, and theological content of the phenomena suggest the influence of religious culture and observed precedents in previously attended meetings. As historian Grant Wacker has wisely noted regarding Pentecostal manifestations, religiously enthusiastic experiences may have a "simultaneously physiological and cultural character." This is not at all to comment on whether the occurrences had supernatural or natural origins, however: readers' own convictions will have to guide them on that question. For ministers like Daniel Rogers, these encounters seemed undoubtedly warranted in a new season of grace. To many of the rank-and-file converts, dreams, trances, and visions reflected viscerally the new heights they were reaching in Christ.[36]

Hannah Heaton, converted as a twenty-year-old in the 1741 revivals, made visions and dreams central to her piety, as described in her diary. At her conversion she thought she saw "jesus with the eyes of my soul stand up in heaven. A lovely god man with his arms open ready to receive me his face was full of smiles he lookt white and ruddy and was just such a saviour as my soul wanted." Soon thereafter, as she began to backslide, she hoped for a vision of hell that would scare her into higher devotion. One night she received such a revelation in a dream: "Me thot i see it full of burning flames like a gloing oven." She saw a man who she knew had been wicked, and the "devil in the shape of a great snake all on a flame with his sting out ran violently at the man and seemd to aim at the mans mouth." The devil was never far from Heaton, tempting her to depart from God and appearing in her dreams. Christ, too, was always nearby, filling her dreams with scenes of the approaching Judgment Day.[37]

The artisan Joseph Bean of Cambridge also wrote repeatedly of spiritual visions and "things unutarable" that he saw with his "Eye of faith." Once in 1742 he saw a vision of the future: Christ welcoming him into heaven upon his death. A few weeks later he wrote "by an Eye of fath o methought that I Could see God and Christ at his right hand and the burning throne with millions of shining angels in pos[tures] of adoration . . . indede I did to fly to those blessed mantions and Joyn in Confort with the hole asembly." He noted that he saw none of these with his "bodily" eyes and hoped that the visions did not result from "sudin hete of the brane or pashons" or delusions, but from the presence of the Spirit.[38]

More radical visions, ones seen with bodily eyes, broke out in Nicholas Gilman's Durham, New Hampshire, congregation in early 1742. Of a remarkable Sabbath, January 31, Gilman wrote, "In the Night while I was praying, Stephen Busse Saw a White Dove come down into the Meeting house over head which He stedfastly beheld till prayer was done and then coming to acquaint Me with it, etc. he saw Two Angells." Busse was not the only one who saw these things, but they were "also I am told made known to a Young woman in a vision at the same time More than half a mile off. Hubbard Stevens . . . declard he saw a bright Light like an exceeding bright star about as big as a Mans fist come down out of the Turret and lighted on one of the Beams aloft till after noon time it disappeared—But the circumstances are too many to record." Daniel Rogers reported a vision similar to Busse's in nearby Kittery, but more than a year later. Three men saw "a Bird much larger yn. a Dove White a[s] Snow, hovering at one of ye upper Windows." Rogers seemed to consider this a legitimate sighting of the Holy Spirit.[39]

Busse's and Stevens's visions spread to several others in Durham, and one Mary Reed became particularly affected. Reed sometimes related her visions in the congregation, but it seems that most of the time Gilman wrote her visions down and presented them to the church himself. Reed and Sarah Jonson, another visionary, both spent some nights at Gilman's house discussing their experiences. Soon people began to murmur about their propriety, and the nocturnal sessions ended. Nevertheless, the visions continued and Gilman regularly complied with requests from parishioners that he read Scriptures given to them by direct inspiration. On April 14, 1742, he wrote in his diary, "Visions the Main Subject of Conversation." Several days later he preached on Joel 2:28–29, "And it shall come to pass afterward, that I will pour out my spirit upon all flesh; and your sons and daughters shall prophesy, your old men shall dream dreams, your young men shall see visions: And also upon the servants and upon the handmaids in those days will I pour out my spirit." A month later Gilman had a "Conference" with the visiting Thomas Prentice of Charlestown about visions. In June, Daniel Rogers visited Durham and met Mary Reed, who related another revelation, "a Terrifying View of Hell and the Damned there." Rogers prayed that God would help him "make a Wise Improvement of such Dispensation."[40]

Another kind of mysticism arose at Northampton in early 1742, as seen in the experiences of Jonathan Edwards's wife, Sarah. The regularly itinerating Jonathan Edwards reported in January that religion in the Northampton area was "on the decaying hand," but he remained confident because of ongoing awakenings elsewhere. Edwards also mentioned "some extraordinary affairs at home," apparently referring to an intense season of spiritual ecstasy that his wife had just entered. Edwards made a disguised version of Sarah's testimony central to *Some Thoughts Concerning the Present Revival of Religion* (1742). For hours on end, she felt sensations of God's love, as her "soul dwelt on high, and was lost in God." Her soul seemed almost to separate from her body, but Edwards, growing more moderate, noted that she was *not* in a trance and did not lose her bodily senses. Nevertheless, she sometimes lost her strength and became mute. The joy of Christ even caused her to leap involuntarily. He insisted that these sorts of experiences predated the arrival of the great itinerants: "They arose from no distemper catched from Mr. Whitefield or Mr. Tennent, because they began . . . near three years ago" when she completely dedicated herself to God. Sarah became Jonathan's ideal test case for the fruits of the revival, and she demonstrated love, goodness, and holiness in abundance. "If such things are enthusiasm," he concluded, "and the fruits of a distempered brain, let my brain be evermore possessed of that happy distemper!"[41]

In her own account of these transports, Sarah Edwards emphasized bodily manifestations more than Jonathan did. She repeatedly fainted in response to visions of God's love and power, sometimes requiring others to pick her up and place her in a chair or in bed. During her remarkable time of grace, the recent Yale graduate Samuel Buell arrived in Northampton to substitute for the traveling Edwards. Buell did not initiate Edwards's mystical episode; in fact, Sarah frankly admitted resenting Buell's success during a time when Jonathan's preaching had generated little excitement. She was pleased when she felt herself become resigned to letting God bless Buell's work.[42]

She also became willing to concede higher spiritual experiences to African Americans in Northampton, noting, "I thought I should rejoice to follow the negro servants in the town to heaven." Even while she was asleep, Edwards had visions of God—waking or sleeping seemed to make little difference in her constant spiritual delights. While singing an Isaac Watts hymn, she felt that her "mind was so deeply impressed with the love of Christ, and a sense of his immediate presence, that I could with difficulty refrain from rising from my seat, and leaping for joy." In describing all her revelations, she carefully avoided suggestions that she physically saw anything: "the unspeakable joys of the upper world . . . appeared to my mind in all their reality and certainty, and as it were in actual and distinct vision; so plain and evident were they to the eye of faith."[43] Most evangelical visionaries would exercise less theological caution, but few of them had husbands as precise as Jonathan Edwards.

As for Buell, he had been licensed in 1741 and soon took a place as one of the key New England itinerants. Wheelock was very supportive of the young minister, writing, "The Lord is with Mr. Buell of a truth; hell trembles before him." For about a month, Buell's preaching helped generate a new phase of the Northampton awakening. He preached almost every day in the meetinghouse, and met with enormous successes, particularly among the "professors," or those Edwards thought were already converted. Writing to Thomas Prince, Edwards remembered Buell's revival with some reservations because of radical effects accompanying it. Some had fallen into twenty-four-hour trances and claimed to have had mysterious visions "as though they went to heaven." Edwards believed that these extremes opened a door for Satan, and when Edwards returned "a great deal of caution and pains were necessary to keep the people, many of them, from running wild." In March, soon after Buell's stir, Edwards attempted to secure the fruits of the revival by leading the congregation in signing a covenant promising "with one accord to renew our engagements to seek and serve God."[44]

Edwards had visited Ebenezer Parkman's congregation at Westborough in January and February, and as Buell moved east he visited there as well. Parkman was delighted with the progress of the revivals, but an episode in February gave him pause. A young man, Isaiah Pratt, fell into a trance that lasted more than a day, and when he came to, he claimed to have "seen hell, and seen Christ." Parkman interviewed Pratt about what had happened. Pratt told him that Christ "looked more pleasant than ever he had seen any man, and [he] had a great book before him, and in turning over the leaves of it, told him that his name was there, and showed it to him." Parkman was not entirely pleased with the episode and told Pratt "that these things were not to be depended upon."[45]

In March, Parkman led a fast to pray that the Holy Spirit would continue to flow, but also "that we be not carried away by the many snares, temptations and delusions to which we are greatly exposed." The cautious Parkman then received Buell and three young men accompanying him and asked many pointed questions about Buell's doctrines and behavior. Parkman was impressed by Buell's answers and was particularly pleased to hear that Buell had "made up" with Joseph Noyes of New Haven following the September commencement debacle. He urged Buell to stay and preach at Westborough, but Buell insisted he had to hurry on to Concord. Parkman noted in his journal, "The world full of Mr. Buel's preaching at Concord. In the judgment of some, great success; in the judgment of others, great confusion." In late March, Parkman heard Buell preach at Charlestown, where Andrew Croswell had been itinerating for some time and generating significant controversy. Soon Joseph Bean visited Charlestown and wrote that he had seen "strange things" there, much like Pentecostal scenes from the book of Acts. Some cried out, while others clapped their hands with joy. "I hope it was all in sincerity," the cautious Bean wrote.[46]

In Charlestown, Buell encountered Daniel Rogers, and the two began itinerating together, leaving behind the ailing Croswell. Rogers wrote to Wheelock that Buell "has much of the Presence of ye Lord Assisting and Succeeding Him." In Boston, Rogers noted that Buell preached at the New North Church "to a Vast Assembly—great Numbers cd. not gett into the House." As the opposition to the revivals mounted, New North's John Webb remained one of the only Boston pastors eager to receive the itinerants. Nevertheless, Buell and Rogers continued to find places to preach. For instance, Buell addressed Boston's workhouse for the poor, a large brick building which had opened in 1739. After that meeting, many retired to evangelical merchant Edward Bromfield's home, which was becoming an informal center of Boston revivalism. Rogers glumly noted that "The Devil rages horribly in this Town out of the Mouths of Prophane People; & Formal Professors." Rogers soon met with Charles Chauncy, but he made little comment on their discussion. He continued ministering to African Americans, as well; he "visited a Negroe man, Sick, who gave me good hope that He was Converted." Rogers conversed at length with the man and his family.[47]

Rogers and Buell also visited pastor Daniel Bliss of Concord. Bliss was a Yale graduate who had associated with David Ferris's religious circle there in the 1730s and had become friends with his classmates Davenport, Wheelock, Benjamin Pomeroy, Aaron Burr, and Jonathan Barber. In a letter to Wheelock, Bliss wrote, "Bro. Buel's Labrs. are greatly Blessed here." Bliss also proudly noted that he himself had preached in a "place where the Minister wd. by no means consent thereto." He thought that his preaching had affected even some of the revivals' opponents. "Oh they shrieked they Cryed they Groaned so that I was obliged to cease Speaking." He thought that "All Ministers almost seem agnst. me," but he took this as an identification with the persecutions Christ suffered. He was delighted that the old Yale cohort stood together as revivalists and asked for constant prayers from Pomeroy and Wheelock. He similarly thanked God that "he owns Dr. Bro. Davenport Pumroy Croswell &c." With his utter confidence in the radical revivals, it was perhaps no wonder that his opponents met in church councils on at least two occasions to try and restrain Bliss, whom they called a

"Person so apparently addicted to wrong the Truth." A council in 1743 even recommended that Bliss's opponents in the Concord church withdraw from his
ministry if he failed to moderate his doctrine and tactics. Separation would not
be a tactic used by radical evangelicals alone.[48]

Buell estimated that God had converted more than a hundred through his
preaching in the Boston area. "The Lord Surely is making use of the most Vile
Poluted Lump of Clay, that Could Bee found to open Blind eyes," he exclaimed.
The Lord's blessings also came with opponents' rage, however: "many refuse to
Let me into there Pulpits But my hands are full." Buell preached as much as he
could, but he was humbled by the example of Whitefield, whose progress Buell
monitored through correspondents in Britain. Buell was tempted to boast about
his work in Boston, for he had created more excitement "in Boston than any one
Since Mr. Tennant was here. . . . While thousand admire and flock with Delight
to hear me, and thousands oppose me, may I Bee kept humble." Many of the
itinerants struggled with vanity as the crowds thronged to hear them.[49]

Moderate evangelicals were slowly turning against the ministries of Buell
and Rogers, as evidenced by the closing of Boston's pulpits to them. In late
April, Benjamin Colman gave a lecture in Boston, and while he still affirmed
the "Great and good Work" of God, he nevertheless expressed "Apprehension
and Fear" about the radicals' conduct. New Englanders should not "give Countenance and Encouragement to illiterate and half-learnt Persons to go about
exhorting and drawing Hearers." Such indulgence "tends in Time to run the
Churches into Confusion." Thus, he asked the audience not to "run from your
own Pastors with such open Disrespect after every new Face or fervent Voice,
with far less Furniture for your real spiritual Edification." Surely he had in mind
Rogers and Buell, among others, as Colman explained in a letter to Whitefield.
"Some very young students . . . go about exhorting, and one of them has lately
visited from Northampton down to us. . . . I look upon him to be greatly Spirited to serve Souls but wanting Furniture." Sarah Edwards had struggled with
the issue of Buell's youth as well, but she concluded that it was fitting that God
should use "babes and sucklings to advance his kingdom." Thomas Prince had
allowed him to speak at the Old South Church several times, but Joseph Sewall
and William Cooper complained about Buell's lack of learning. Colman warned
Harvard students not to follow Buell's example.[50]

Buell and Rogers continued their tour north, despite these criticisms. They
visited Lynn and Salem before arriving in Ipswich the last week of April. At Rowley they found the baker Richard Elvins, who took turns preaching with Buell,
Rogers, and Rogers's brother Nathaniel. Moving on to Newbury, they gathered
that John Lowell had forbidden them to preach at the Third Church, but "the

People" invited them to come, unlocked the doors and summoned a large crowd. Lowell was not pleased, and when the entourage went to visit him the next day, he refused to see them.[51]

Rogers and Buell next moved on to Portsmouth, New Hampshire. Buell seems to have finally been overcome by a nagging illness in late April and rested from the tour for several weeks. Rogers led several large and successful meetings, but also "met wth a false Representation of our Conduct at Newberry," almost certainly referring to a May 3 *Boston Evening Post* article describing the incident. The correspondent reported that "N. Rogers of Ipswich, Mr. Daniel Rogers and Mr. Bewell . . . formed a Party, and took Possession of the Rev. Mr. Lowell's Meeting-House. . . . These Itinerants aim very much at dividing the Churches, and disaffecting People to their faithful Pastors, and what wild Scheme they are pursuing next, God only knows." Undeterred, Rogers went to Kittery, Maine, where pastor John Newmarch and his parishioner, the wealthy merchant, timberman, and future military hero William Pepperrell received him. Rogers preached at Newmarch's church and saw remarkable results among Pepperrell's African servants. After he spoke, "a Negroe man sevt. of Col. Pepperell's broke out & spoke in a Wonderfull manner of the Sweet Love of Jesus. . . . He exhorted all to come & taste of ye Love of Xt." Another servant of Pepperell's "cryed out in Distress." That night the African American exhorter spoke again. Rogers spent the next month itinerating all over Maine in most of the existing parishes.[52]

Rogers's and Buell's continuing successes remind us that in spite of the growing controversy about the limits of the revivals in 1742, the revivals themselves continued. Moderates like Jonathan Edwards tried to shape the evangelical movement within ostensibly reasonable boundaries, but the noisy fervor at places like Ipswich proved hard to contain. Moreover, radicals like Daniel Rogers and Nicholas Gilman had no interest whatsoever in placing limits on their followers' mystical experiences. Thus, moderate revivalists, especially those in the Boston area like Nathaniel Appleton and Benjamin Colman, began trying to control the awakenings and exclude the most radical preachers from their pulpits. The summer of 1742 would see a new stage in the controversy. Opponents of the revivals began to take legal actions against itinerants. Public censures of the radicals, both from revival opponents and moderate evangelicals, became more common and strident. Undeterred, radicals like Andrew Croswell and James Davenport vehemently defended and practiced such radical distinctives as the unlimited right to itinerancy, the immediate witness of the Spirit, and the bodily, emotional, and mystical experiences of penitents. Because of these divisive issues, evangelical unity could no longer hold.

"UNDER THE IMPRESSIONS OF A HEATED IMAGINATION": JAMES DAVENPORT, ANDREW CROSWELL, AND THE FRACTURING OF NEW ENGLAND EVANGELICALISM

The winter of 1741–42 saw radical itinerants James Davenport and Andrew Croswell of Groton, Connecticut, busy at their strenuous and vituperative revival work. By then, Croswell had become the chief public advocate for Davenport's ministry. In a September letter attacking Jedidiah Mills of Ripton as unconverted, Croswell told Eleazar Wheelock that he had heard that Mills could not say for sure that he had experienced the new birth, and that "Mr. Mills Spake Slightely of Mr. Davenport, which [is] Suspicious." Similarly, in an October 1741 *Boston Weekly Post-Boy* article, Croswell argued that Davenport might have surpassed Whitefield and Tennent in preaching success. He estimated that at the height of Davenport's summer tour in southern Connecticut, a hundred people had converted in eight days, "among which some were Negroes; and I think about twenty Indians, besides a vast multitude, who . . . were left under hopeful Convictions." He expressed slight uncertainty about the propriety of Davenport's pronouncing ministers unconverted—"I have always declared this to be what I could not as yet perfectly see through"—but he insisted that if a minister was indeed unconverted, they could never lead people to Christ. Croswell promised that fellow ministers Benjamin Pomeroy, Benjamin Lord, and most important, Whitefield and Tennent, would vouch for Davenport's character.[1]

Croswell arrived in Plymouth, Massachusetts, in February 1742 and caused quite a stir there. Pastor Nathaniel Leonard wrote that Croswell visited Plymouth for a fortnight, highlighted by a meeting where "Hundreds of Souls were at one Time in the Meeting-House" crying out for salvation. Many were dramatically converted on the spot. Plymouth's Judge Josiah Cotton, who had originally supported the revivals, now turned against them. The meetings had seen "some Singing, some praying, some exhorting, some shaking of hands, some crying, some laughing for joy, others opposing &c., all at once, & the Pulpit full with Boys & a Negro or two, who were directed to invite others to come to Christ, particularly old Grey headed Sinners," Cotton wrote. He thought it particularly outrageous that Croswell had targeted as unconverted some senior members with a long record of fidelity to the church.[2]

A hostile letter in the *South-Carolina Gazette* (its location of publication reminding us of the intercolonial interest in the revivals) presented an even more radical picture of the Plymouth revival: "The famous C[roswe]ll has been upon promoting the Work . . . not one Stroke of Work was done for three Weeks by Man, Woman or Child. The Fervors and Phrenzies of this Teacher had answerable Effects on the Audience; where you might observe a general Foaming or Fainting, Laughing or Crying." Predictably, the enthusiasm brought out exhorters, including "a big-bellied Woman from an hind Seat [who] straddled into the Pulpit to assist C – – – ll, and was inspired with so much useful Matter, as took her up half an Hour to deliver it . . . extending her Arms every Way, and not a Muscle of her Body but in Action." Hundreds marched in the streets, with "every one delivering the Yell he was particularly inspired with, join'd with all the mad Gestures and Actions that Franticks show, the Rev. Mr. C – – – ll leading the Van." Nathaniel Leonard supposedly joined the frenzy, calling for prayers for his "unconverted Wife," and having his eight-year-old son exhort from a stool.[3]

Croswell moved on to Charlestown by early March. The *Boston Evening-Post* reported that Croswell spoke "every Evening with great Power and Success," but moderate evangelicals began to bristle against what Westborough pastor Ebenezer Parkman called his "irregular zeal." Thomas Prentice of Charlestown recalled the itinerant's "extraordinary former conduct . . . skipping like a ram from pew to pew, and from seat to seat, even from the upper gallery to the floor of the house, . . . when you made your voice to be heard on high in the streets, crying, 'Lo here, a kingdom of God that cometh with observation.'" Croswell fell ill in late March, however, and could not accompany Daniel Rogers and Samuel Buell into Boston.[4]

That same winter James Davenport returned to Long Island and generated significant awakenings in the Easthampton and Bridgehampton churches. He and one of his so-called armor-bearers, Daniel Tuthill, traveled from Southold to Easthampton and began preaching in the stead of the ailing minister Nathaniel Huntting. Soon they began to criticize Huntting publicly, and though the awakening produced perhaps a hundred converts, it also appears to have fractured the church. The story at Bridgehampton was much the same. Davenport also continued his fruitful ministry to Long Island's Native Americans.[5]

Writing about James Davenport's (and to a lesser extent, Andrew Croswell's) ministry in 1742–43 presents significant challenges. Almost all the information we have about Davenport came from his opponents, who had a vested interest in portraying him as negatively as possible. The opponents of the awakenings, especially Charles Chauncy, used Davenport as the ultimate example of the madness the revivals generated. Moderate evangelicals would eventually denounce Davenport in order to preserve what they saw as the godly parts of the awakenings. For example, as the tide began to turn against Davenport in early 1742, suspicious moderate pastor Aaron Burr wrote from Newark, New Jersey, to Joseph Bellamy in Bethlehem, Connecticut, who remained friendly to Davenport. Burr advocated a harsher view of Davenport, whom most evangelicals still regarded as an "eminent man of God." "I dare not justify all his conduct, nor can I see thro' it," Burr wrote. Burr had received a letter from Jonathan Edwards warning that Davenport "does more toward giving Satan & other opposers an advantage against ye work of God than any one person." The moderates were moving to paint Davenport as beyond legitimate evangelical limits. We should receive accounts of Davenport's wild enthusiasm with some caution, realizing that in the increasingly politicized atmosphere of the revivals, a scapegoat like him came in handy.[6]

In 1742, then, a serious rift emerged between the radical itinerants and nearly all the established powers of Connecticut and Massachusetts, including moderate evangelicals. In April, Croswell launched an attack on the moderate Thomas Foxcroft, pastor of Boston's First Church, in the *Boston Weekly Post-Boy*. In his preface to Jonathan Dickinson's *The True Scripture-Doctrine* (1741), Foxcroft had extolled Calvinist doctrine as one of the keys to the revivals' successes, but he had also cautioned that he did not "confine real Christianity" to those who agreed entirely with Calvinism. Croswell argued that Foxcroft was apologizing for the damnable doctrine of free will. Foxcroft's reply two weeks later countered that he only meant to offer Christian charity to those he considered mistaken on a higher point of theology. Foxcroft and many of the Boston ministers had drunk deeply of English latitudinarianism, and though they remained Calvinists, they saw no need to make enemies of all Arminians. Croswell thought friendship with Arminians represented friendship with the hell-bound.[7]

In May, Eleazar Wheelock received a rancorous letter from Croswell that seemed to sever their relationship. Wheelock had apparently sent Croswell a cautionary letter requesting that he not judge prominent men as unconverted. Croswell defended this practice, arguing that it was essential to his ministry. Even if "my Dear Brethren Pomroy and Davenport should forsake me; I Dare not be Dumb, and Muzzle my mouth in this Glorious cause." Croswell also wrote that Jonathan Edwards was "too timerous, or Cowardly in the Cause of Xt.," and that he tried too hard in *Distinguishing Marks* to please "both Sides." Croswell was much more optimistic about Samuel Buell: "The Lord . . . make him to exceed even Mr. Davenport himself." The rambling letter accused Wheelock of trying to become great in the eyes of the world and then expressed hope that all the ministers "be perfectly Joyned together in One Mind." Croswell's tactics in the next year would hardly promote such unity.[8]

Davenport returned to Connecticut in May and immediately ran afoul of a new provincial law that forbade itinerants from preaching in churches without the resident pastor's permission and that outlawed all non-Connecticut itinerants. In passing this law, Connecticut officials had Davenport foremost in their minds, and he became the first quarry caught under the policy. The sheriff of Hartford arrested Davenport and itinerant Benjamin Pomeroy and brought them to the General Court session. Opponents from Stratford, Connecticut, claimed that the itinerants, "together with certain illiterate persons . . . and frequently congregating great numbers of persons, chiefly children and youth . . . put the said town . . . into great confusion and disorder." The *Boston Weekly News-Letter*'s correspondent, "Anti-Enthusiasticus," thought that Davenport represented the perfection of antinomianism: he advised his followers to disobey provincial laws, told children to ignore their parents, and recommended that parishioners abandon their unconverted ministers. He furthermore claimed "some extraordinary discovery and assurance of the very near approach of the end of the world," and made "an indecent and affected imitation of the agony and passion of our blessed SAVIOUR." He pronounced many of his hearers damned, "vehemently crying out, That he saw hell-flames slashing in their faces; and that they were now! now! dropping down to hell." Worse, many of these antics "happened unseasonably and late at night." To Anti-Enthusiasticus, Davenport had become the model rank enthusiast.[9]

The correspondent reported that the scene at the courthouse turned ugly after the court pronounced Davenport banished from Connecticut. Pomeroy and Davenport supposedly began calling for God to rain judgment on the court and the sheriff, which brought a rush of their followers "beginning to sigh, groan, beat their breasts, cry out, and to be put into strange agitations of the body." Davenport seized the moment and began to exhort, pray, and sing, and although he was taken away, the "hubbub" in town continued late into the night. Eventually the authorities summoned the Hartford militia to quell the disturbances, and Davenport was deported to Long Island. Although we cannot be sure how reliable the details of Anti-Enthusiasticus's account were, it must have been a strange day for the Connecticut General Court.[10]

Despite his expulsion, Davenport's radical movement continued in Connecticut, especially with the founding of New London's "Shepherd's Tent" in summer 1742. New London and New Haven had begun to develop reputations as centers for radical evangelicalism by the time of the 1741 Yale commencement. A letter in the *Boston Weekly Post-Boy* expressed critics' fears that enthusiasts in New Haven and New London had cultivated a "Spirit of Censuring, Separation and Contention." The letter claimed that the "new-light-Men" there believed that they could discern whether someone was converted by "immediate Revelation." If true, the radicals and moderates disagreed not only concerning personal assurance by the witness of the Spirit, but also regarding the ability to perceive the presence or absence of the Spirit in others. Also, to "strengthen the Separation at New-Haven two young Women pretended to be in a Trance for a Week, to have been in Heaven and to have seen a Glymps of it: That GOD Revealed to them that Mr. Noyes was Unconverted, and that Multitudes are now Cursing him in Hell for being the Instrument of their Damnation." Daniel Rogers saw this letter and dismissed it as "foolish."[11]

Fueled by such radical behavior, growing antagonism between Yale rector Thomas Clap and his evangelical students, and developing Separate contingents in New Haven and New London, Davenport's followers founded the Shepherd's Tent to help institutionalize the radical wing of the revivalist movement. Similar to the Tennents' Log College, the Shepherd's Tent devoted as much attention to experimental religion as to liberal learning. Some expelled and/or disgruntled Yale undergraduates joined founder Timothy Allen at the school. Allen had known James Davenport since their Yale days, when they both had joined David Ferris's pious club. Allen had been dismissed from his West Haven congregation in 1742 for alleged heterodoxy and overly zealous support for the revivals. Allen became the school's resident instructor, and Davenport served as its chief fundraiser. Connecticut authorities tried to shut down the Tent by imprisoning Allen for violating the General Court's anti-itinerancy measure and passing legislation illegalizing nonsanctioned schools. But Allen got out of jail in November, and by early 1743 the Tent was flourishing. Reports about the Shepherd's Tent, again, came from enemies, but most of the school's activities seemed to involve praying and exhorting, and, according to some accounts, the students included a few African Americans and women.[12]

Perhaps reacting to news emerging from New London, Aaron Burr wrote again to Joseph Bellamy and expressed common moderate concerns about the radicals' perceived excesses. Burr listed them point by point: (1) "Their being led by impulses & impressions," (2) "Their giving heed to visions, trances, & revelations," (3) "Their speaking of divine things with an air of levity & vanity, laughter &c." (4) "Their declaring their Judgt. about others . . . whether they are converted or not," (5) "Their making their own feelings a rule to judge others by," (6) "For laymen to take upon them to exhort in a public assembly," (7) "Their separating from yr minister under a notion of his being unregenerate." Moderate evangelicals were trying to squeeze these mystical, censorious, and populist tendencies out of the movement.[13]

Meanwhile, Davenport, hardly chastened by his expulsion, set out for Boston soon after returning to Long Island. Despite the continuing revivals, Benjamin Colman and other leading moderate ministers in Boston had become increasingly disturbed by the radicals' behavior. Colman wrote to Whitefield in June about the controversies in Connecticut. "The fervent, pious Mr. Devenport, and Mr. Crosswell, have been too much under the Impressions of a heated Imagination, and no doubt often preached under actual Fevers." For some time, observers had suggested that Davenport might suffer from physical and/or mental disorders, and Croswell had only recently been bedridden after his Charlestown itinerancy. We should, however, exercise caution in attributing their radicalism to unspecified medical problems, for this was an accusation moderate opponents used to salvage a reasonable revival. Colman also worriedly noted that the radicals had been "judging and censuring the spiritual State of Ministers and People; who could not go into the Way and Length, of singing thro' the Streets to and from the House of God, and favouring Exhorters of no Gifts, or prudence for publick Speaking." All these practices seriously threatened the stability of the established religious order and took popular evangelicalism into the streets.[14]

Davenport arrived in Charlestown in late June. Stephen Williams of Longmeadow jotted in his diary, "I Pceive my Br J. D—is got to Boston—& his conduct is Such [that] ye ministers there cant invite him, into [their] pulpitts [they] look upon him—Enthusiastick—I pray God to Direct him & keep him [from] dishonouring God." A hostile account in the *Boston Evening-Post* recorded that Davenport and a "Rabble of Men, Women, and Children, began to sing, and walked through the Streets singing." Dismissive reports like this imply a social factor in the disdain for Davenport's ministry, as he seemed to enjoy great successes among the poor and disenfranchised. The correspondent sneered that his sermons were "dull and heavy" and that he "has no Knack at raising the Passions, but by a violent straining of his Lungs." A deluded few responded to him with "great meltings, screamings, crying, swooning and Fits." The newspaper further described Davenport as roaming the streets "with a large Mob at his Heels, singing all the Way thro' the Streets, he with his Hands extended, his Head thrown back, and his Eyes staring up to Heaven, attended with so much Disorder, that they look'd more like a Company of Bacchanalians after a mad Frolick, than sober Christians who had been worshipping God." Upon arrival in Charlestown, Davenport was immediately summoned to appear before the Boston area's ministerial association.[15]

The ministers heard Davenport's testimony, and after offering a polite "hope that God has us'd him as an Instrument of Good unto many Souls," they banned him from speaking in the Boston pulpits. In a printed declaration, they censured him for leaning too much on "sudden Impulses," rashly judging other ministers as unconverted, "going with his Friends singing thro' the Streets and High-Ways," and encouraging "private Brethren to pray and exhort." They pronounced him "deeply tinctur'd with a Spirit of Enthusiasm." The declaration was signed by fourteen Boston area ministers, including moderate evangelicals Benjamin Colman, Joseph Sewall, Thomas Prince, John Webb, William Cooper, Thomas Foxcroft, and Thomas Prentice.[16]

Croswell, the most prolific writer among the radicals (a writer in the *Evening-Post* mocked him and Davenport, asking, "What's the Matter Da[venpor]t don't write? . . . was you pitch'd upon as the Champion of the Party?"), would not let the Boston declaration go unchallenged. He thought the ministers should praise God for Davenport's ministry instead of slandering him. Croswell considered Davenport a model of humility: "Persons of the meanest Rank, Indians and Negroes, have as easy Access to him as the great and honourable." He suggested that the Boston ministers should follow Davenport's example. (Lest we forget, Davenport was a slave owner, so his egalitarianism had definite limits.) Croswell reminded the ministers that Whitefield, Tennent, and all the key supporters of the revivals in Connecticut had affirmed Davenport as an extraordinarily godly man. Croswell portrayed Davenport and Whitefield as receiving the same abuse from opponents but thought that the declaration represented a sad new turn against the revivals. "'Tis no new Thing to [Davenport] (no more than it is to Mr. Whitefield) to be shut out of Pulpits; to be twitted with Impulses; and to be call'd an Enthusiast. However, . . . he never till now received such Treatment from any Ministers, but only those who were look'd upon and known to be Enemies to the glorious Work which God is carrying on in the Land." Croswell suggested that the moderate ministers of Boston were functionally opponents of the revivals, for "the Tendency of the Pamphlet is to give a Wound to the glorious Cause." Croswell left no middle ground for the moderates: they had to be either for or against the work of God. Davenport and Croswell were for it.[17]

Davenport continued preaching in Boston after the declaration of the ministers. The expulsion from Connecticut and the Boston declaration helped make him the hottest topic in town that summer. The visiting Ebenezer Parkman recorded that Davenport was the "subject everywhere." He heard Davenport preach and then retired with a group of ministers to the home of John Webb, who described Davenport as "running out into the street among the crowd, and crying out to them in an indecent voice [and] gesture. . . . In a word, Mr. Webb concludes him to be crazed." Webb had been one of the most eager promoters of the revivals, and running afoul of such a prominent evangelical minister did not bode well for Davenport.[18]

It was less surprising that Davenport would earn the contempt of First Church's Charles Chauncy, who believed that enthusiasm had tainted the whole evangelical movement. In this vein, he published *Enthusiasm Described and Caution'd Against* in July, to which he attached a letter to Davenport. Chauncy considered enthusiasm, with its various strange effects on the body, the result of overwrought imaginations that had become physiologically unbalanced. Davenport was, of course, an ideal case study of this ailment. As he had done with so many ministers, Davenport visited Chauncy and inquired whether Chauncy had been born again. Chauncy was deeply offended by this brash interrogation and was confident that Davenport would judge him unconverted. In his letter in *Enthusiasm Described*, he had warned that Davenport's "enthusiastic wildness" would do more to harm the cause of religion than any so-called unconverted ministers. Chauncy argued that Davenport's "going about, from one part of the country to another, enquiring into the state of the souls, particularly, of ministers, and declaring them, most commonly, unconverted" had no biblical warrant. Davenport's "heated imagination" led him to proclaim the imminence of the final judgment. Davenport operated as if he had special divine authority, but Chauncy thought all his schemes "meer fancy."[19]

Others still supported Davenport, however. For instance, fresh off his July ordination at York, Maine, as an evangelist-at-large, Daniel Rogers came back to Boston to meet with Davenport. Rogers spoke at Webb's New North Church and testified on behalf of Davenport, and in the next two days he heard Davenport preach on Boston Common. Rogers met with Thomas Prince and tried to convince him that the declaration of the ministers had unfairly represented Davenport, but he "recd. no Satisfaction." Rogers found that none of the Boston ministers, except for Webb and John Moorhead, would invite him into their pulpits any more. Webb conceded to him that the ban came because he publicly defended Davenport. Now Davenport and Rogers found themselves mostly limited to preaching at supporters' homes and on the common.[20]

In early August, Rogers and Davenport set out for the friendlier climes of Ipswich. They had a successful week of ministry there, after which Davenport and his armor-bearer, Daniel Tuthill, returned to Boston. Davenport continued to receive negative coverage, especially in the antirevivalist *Boston Evening-Post*.

One report scoffed at Davenport's followers as "chiefly made up of idle or igno-rant Persons, and those of the lowest Rank." The correspondent noted that in a late July meeting on the common, Davenport held a collection for the Shepherd's Tent, and continued, the "wiser and better Sort of People, will, I think, scarce be wheedled a second Time into Collections for building Castles or Colleges in the Air." The report accused Davenport of calling the Boston ministers "carnal unconverted Men" and claimed that in a sermon preached on the common he had said, the "Ministers of Boston were going to Hell themselves, and drawing multitudes after them." On August 19, Ebenezer Parkman wrote that Davenport had begun naming names, announcing that Benjamin Colman, Joseph Sewall, and Charles Chauncy were unconverted. The next day he named nine others as belonging to this group.[21]

On August 21, in Ipswich, Rogers wrote in the margin of his diary, "Br. Dav-enpt. was confin'd at Boston." The ministers had become fed up with the itin-erant and had him arrested and charged with slander. Davenport's follower Michael Hill wrote to evangelical pastor Philemon Robbins of Branford, Con-necticut, calling Boston "ye place where Satans Seat is" because "the Ministers In Boston seem to Be Bound in one Bundle & will Doutless here after Keep out all True Lovers of Jesus." He admitted that Davenport had prayed "for ye Con-vertion of 3 Docts: Colman Sewel & Chancy & then the Divel Could Bair it no Longer" and he was arrested. Hill was apparently staying with Davenport in the jail. He warned Robbins that the "Rage of ye Clargy is beyond wt you ever saw, Dont think it strang if you are soon Called to blood." Davenport added a brief note and asked for prayer that he would bear up under suffering. "Ye Lord makes a prison Sweet—Oh ye Cross is precious." Davenport saw himself as one of the last remaining true followers of Christ.[22]

The government produced a number of witnesses who testified to hearing Davenport call prominent ministers carnal and unconverted. A jury voted twenty-one to two to convict him (the *Post* reported that the two dissenting votes came from "an ignorant Exhorter" and a Quaker). On further consideration, however, the court declared Davenport non compos mentis and released him on September 2.[23]

In New Brunswick, New Jersey, the increasingly moderate Gilbert Tennent de-nounced his colleague Davenport in a letter printed in the *Pennsylvania Gazette* and the *Boston Weekly News-Letter*. Although he did not question Davenport's "Piety and Integrity," Tennent enumerated several of Davenport's tactics that he could no longer countenance. Among them were calling out unconverted min-isters by name (apparently Tennent believed that *naming* unconverted ministers distinguished Davenport's methods from his own), setting up separate meetings, sending unlearned men into the ministry, singing in the streets, and claiming "immediate Inspiration or objective Revelation, all following of immediate Impulses without Consulting the Word of God." This latter practice "may lead its deluded Votaries into the strangest Absurdities in Opinion, and most enormous Evils in Practice." Already cooling his zeal by 1742, Tennent had become involved in a pamphlet war with the radical perfectionist Moravians and their leader, Nicholas Ludwig von Zinzendorf. Whereas Tennent had once led the radical evangelical critique of antirevivalist pastors, he now began to see danger on both sides, believing that both cold rationalism and overheated emotionalism worked against a proper balance of heart and head in religion. He became thoroughly moderate when in 1744 he accepted a more socially prestigious pastorate at Philadelphia's "New Building." There he finally abandoned his radicalism in favor of a more learned, polite style of ministry. He gave up his former attire, reminiscent of John the Baptist's clothing, and started wearing ministerial robes and a wig. He even began preaching from manuscripts instead of speaking extemporaneously. Becoming a fashionable moderate evangelical required all these changes, plus distancing himself from Davenport.[24]

Following Davenport's departure from Boston, Sarah Moorhead, spouse of John Moorhead, attempted to aid the unity of the evangelical movement through the publication of a poem, *To the Reverend Mr. James Davenport*. Moorhead tried to establish a mediating position between the radicals and moderates, confessing "I love the Zeal that fires good DAVENPORT's Breast, But his harsh Censures give my Soul no rest." Moorhead thought that the radicals had gone too far, but she also thought that the evangelicals' real enemy was Arminianism, which she called "deadly Poison." Much of her poem reflected on the prospect of damnation for those who believed in free will. She concluded with a postscript to Croswell, whom she also rebuked for his harsh denunciations. "You have the Art to win with melting Words; You need not use Granadoes, Darts, and Swords," she chastised. She offered an expansive vision of the different roles pastors could play in the movement:

> Each faithful Shepard does perform his Part;
> Some rouse the Conscience, others chear the Heart:
> Some from mount Sinai throw the awful Flame;
> While some sweet Peace in Jesus do proclaim.

For the time being, few embraced Moorhead's vision of a united evangelical front.[25]

Rogers was reunited with Davenport, "lately released frm his Bonds," in Concord. Davenport was not dissuaded in the least from his preaching, as he, Rogers, and Samuel Buell took turns speaking. They stayed at pastor Daniel Bliss's house, taking "Sweet Council together." Davenport received another collection for the Shepherd's Tent and then left to go back to Long Island. Rogers remained steadfast in his support of Davenport, whom he called "a wonderful man of God a beloved Disciple leaning on Xts Bosom." Davenport returned to his neglected Southold congregation, which called a ministerial council to censure him in October.[26]

Moderate revivalists and opponents of the awakenings both made a concerted effort during the second half of 1742 to discredit Davenport, Croswell, and the radicals in transatlantic evangelical circles. American evangelicals routinely appealed to British friends, and the broader British religious audience, to legitimate their view of the revivals and influence the parallel development of the movement across the ocean. American leaders, then, were always keenly aware of their international context. Benjamin Colman and Yale's Thomas Clap regularly complained about Davenport in their correspondence to the leading London dissenter Isaac Watts. In November, Watts replied to a letter from Colman, writing, "As for Mr. Davenport I take him to be distracted. . . . Such warm spirits as Davenport and Crosswell are not fit for manageing so important a work as God has begun and carrys on amongst you." Obviously, Watts believed that Colman and Clap were fit to manage the work, as he told Colman earlier that the "great work of God" needed "guards" like Colman in Boston and Clap in New Haven.[27]

Perhaps the most significant moderate effort to define the movement was Jonathan Dickinson's *A Display of God's Special Grace*, to which seven Boston ministers, led by Colman, signed their attestation in August 1742. Dickinson wrote this treatise in the form of a dialogue between a skeptical congregant, "Epinetus," and his moderate evangelical minister, "Theophilus." Much like Edwards's *Distinguishing Marks*, *A Display* addressed the problems of the revivals' excesses and found them neither necessary nor damning to the awakenings. Dickinson defended both the preaching of terror and the ecstatic joys of the converts as potentially authentic parts of the conversion process. Theophilus readily acknowledged that some in the revivals had suffered "from animal Impressions, or from diabolical Delusions," but he believed that a moderate path could deliver Epinetus from these excesses and from outright rejection of the work of God. Moreover, he conceded that there were occasions to doubt another person's salvation, but he objected to the hasty condemnation of those who appeared to be serious Christians, especially established ministers. Epinetus, having received good answers to all his questions, prayed for mercy from God and was saved. Then a radical evangelical named "Libertinus" joined the conversation. The radical denounced all moderates like Theophilus as carnal and unconverted and insisted that gospel preachers should call on people to come to Christ immediately for salvation. Theophilus protested that conversion was a process. Preparation was essential to true repentance and conversion. Libertinus insisted that people could be saved instantly and would know exactly the moment it happened. The inner witness of the Spirit would confirm salvation, argued Libertinus. Theophilus warned that impressions were deceiving, but that a holy life was the best proof of true conversion. Again, Dickinson showed that differing views of assurance provided among the sharpest contrasts between moderate and radical evangelicals.[28]

Andrew Croswell and the leaders of the Shepherd's Tent thought A *Display*'s dialogue between Libertinus and Theophilus was outrageous, primarily because of Dickinson's endorsement of the moderate view of assurance. In a letter to the Rogers brothers, Croswell called it "the most Dangerous book that ever was, or Indeed can be printed." He published a rebuttal in November. Croswell argued that the caricature of the radicals resembled no actual person, including Davenport. But he commended Libertinus for "calling Sinners to come to Christ immediately" and for teaching instant assurance of salvation. These were not antinomian but "Anti-Arminian Tenets." Calling people immediately to come to Christ was "highly recommended by Dr. Franck [and] Mr. Whitefield" and was the normal invitation for Calvinists to give, for they understood that God's grace flooded a sinner's soul in a flash. As for assurance, it would seem "the greatest Absurdity in the World to suppose that the Soul should trust Jesus Christ for Salvation, and love him, and not be sensible of it." Dickinson's emphasis on good works amounted to soul-destroying Arminianism, and by approving that doctrine Colman and the other moderates had "done what will be a Means of Damning many Thousands of Souls unless the infinite Mercy of God prevent." The Spirit drew men to be saved, and the inner witness of the Spirit confirmed the work of Christ. Morality had nothing to offer but pride and deceit. Holiness would only follow the recognizable work of the Spirit. In sum, Dickinson's book was "more adapted to destroy the Power of Godliness than the worst Arminian Performance that ever was written." Croswell, as usual, painted only in black and white: ministers were Arminian or Calvinist, deceitful or faithful.[29]

In a letter to Benjamin Pomeroy, Croswell wrote that he meant his pamphlet to expose Dickinson's "Deadly poyson," but he did not intend to carry on a sustained argument with the Boston ministers about it. Instead, "the next step will bee for a number that are *like minded* to warn the people in Boston, and every where in the countrey, to Separate from Ministers that hold Such Christ despising and Soul murdering Tenets." Croswell was not able to get Pomeroy,

Wheelock, or the Rogers brothers to sign the endorsement of his book, however, noting only that "The Rev. Mr. Wheelock and the Rev. Mr. Pomeroy have also in Conversation highly condemned the above-mentioned Book." He upbraided Pomeroy and Wheelock in his letter for seeking the esteem of men rather than God. Perhaps Croswell knew that if he publicly lost the support of Wheelock and Pomeroy, he would become the leader of an uncomfortably small faction. Croswell soon began encouraging his proposed next step of separation, and in 1746 he permanently relocated from Groton to Boston to begin working full time with Boston's Separate church.[30]

Radical Separates had begun establishing private meetings in 1741–42 across New England, most notably in New London, New Haven, and Boston. In New London, Davenport's supporters began to withdraw from Eliphalet Adams's church in late 1741. In Boston, Daniel Rogers encountered Separates from both the Congregationalist and Baptist churches during his fall 1742 preaching tour. He disapproved of the Congregationalists who had separated, but he affirmed the Baptists' separation, perhaps because theirs was more clearly an anti-Arminian separation than that of the Congregationalists. Of the Baptists he wrote, "They have made a Noble Stand for the Truth *The Doctrines of Grace* & ought to be Encourag'd." He declined to speak at the Congregational Separates' meeting, but he did preach for the Baptists. Rogers felt that the revival had dulled significantly in Boston as of November, which he sullenly attributed to "the Conduct of the Ministers, particularly with Respect to Mr. Davenport."[31]

By contrast, in Grafton, Massachusetts, the revival was only getting started in Solomon Prentice's congregation. The Grafton church had installed Prentice as their first minister in 1731, and he had clearly fallen in with the radicals by 1742. Samuel Buell had preached at Grafton on the way to Boston in March, and Prentice worked closely with such ministers as Daniel Bliss of Concord to generate revival the rest of the year. In December 1742, Grafton observed a day of prayer and fasting for revival that bore amazing results. Within two weeks, "there was as great or greater Manifestations of Gods Power and Grace in the Conviction of Siners and Consolation of His Dear Children as ever had been among us." Prentice also received an invitation to speak from members of Israel Loring's Sudbury church. Prentice wrote to Loring and asked his permission to do so, but Loring declined. Prentice decided to hold a week of revival meetings at the Grafton meetinghouse instead.[32]

From January 4 to 11, 1743, the Grafton meetinghouse hosted meetings around the clock, and people came from Sudbury and other towns to hear preaching by Prentice, Bliss, David Hall of Sutton, and others. The assemblies saw many emotional outbursts, and the "Crying out . . . was very great and peircing," yet Prentice and others were "Rationaly Convinced" it was the work of God. Even radical revivalists accepted the standard of rationality to assess emotional responses because they believed it was sensible for unconverted sinners to cry out in fear of damnation. Ebenezer Parkman noted in his diary that the revival week had generated considerable debate: "Much has been said of these Exercises—some Number being very dissatisfy'd with them. Others much applauding and praising God for the great Grace appearing in them." Even after a week of nonstop meetings, many people wanted more, so Prentice began regularly preaching at private homes, including that of one local Native American family. Many of these engagements lasted into the early morning, though Prentice attributed this lateness mostly to penitents "so overcome they could not get away of Some hours Somtimes: by which Means . . . Some times Persons were Not at home, till 12 or One Clock at Night." Critics grumbled about these "Night-Frolicks."[33]

In late February, Prentice and Daniel Bliss also led an extraordinary three-day revival at Mendon, Massachusetts, at which many "fell down Slain. . . . Great and awfull were the Crys of Such as apeared wounded in Spirit, while they Said with Anguish of Soul, Srs. *what must we do to be Saved!* while Others rejoyced greatly in the Lord . . . yea they did Shout aloud for Joy, when the Spirit of God witnessed with their Spirits that they were the Children of God." All these meetings took place in a barn. Prentice defended the revival as a true work of God, full of converting grace and the witness of the Spirit for assurance. A critic of the revivals offered a very different interpretation of the Mendon awakening in the *Boston Evening-Post.* The correspondent attended one of the meetings, at the end of which Bliss "began to raise his Voice, and to use many extravagant Gestures, and then began a considerable groaning amongst the Auditors, which as soon as he perceiv'd, he raised his Voice still higher, and then the Congregation were in the utmost Confusion, some crying out in the most doleful Accents, some howling, some laughing, and others huging, and Bliss still roaring to them to come to Christ, they answering, I will, I will, I'm coming, I'm coming."[34]

These commotions led to trouble at the established church meeting the following Sunday, where pastor Samuel Barrett's sermon was interrupted by a yelling boy. The pastor instructed the boy to compose himself, upon which the boy "hallowed out, it is not I, but you, Mr. Barret, that makes the Disturbance." A constable was present and started to remove the boy, but other congregants moved to protect him and supposedly threatened "that if he touch'd him, he should have his Brains knock'd out: And several more of the Congregation cry'd out, and a Woman jump'd up on the top of a Pew and began to Exhort, and scream'd out, that she saw the devil. A little Girl (who has lately been in a Trance) says to her, Aunt, you are mistaken, it is Jesus Christ! And then in several Parts of the House they cry'd out, The Glory of the Lord is come down, and Christ is come amongst us." Barrett fled the meetinghouse with a number of his alarmed congregants. The correspondent also noted that the little girl had, in her trance, been carried to hell, but then "a Person whom she supposes was CHRIST, took her by the Hand, led her out, and carried her up to Heaven, and shewed her the Book of Life, where she saw a great many Names, among which were her Mistress's, and that the Book wanted but two Inches to be fill'd up, and that CHRIST told her, that if the good Work which was carrying on upon Earth succeeded, he should come to Judgment in a short Time." The critic ended the account by exclaiming "Oh! Wretched Delusion!"[35]

Despite his critics, Prentice affirmed itinerant ministers, ecstatic responses, and extended meetings. He had "Seen So much of the blessed Fruits of frequent Preaching, Yea Day after day, that I can'nt but heartyly Recommend the Practice to all who are true Friends to the Cause of Ct." Moreover, "Exchanging Pulpits, and frequently Preaching for One Another on Occasional Lecture Days has been greatly owned and blessed by God in this remarkable Day of Grace." He thought that the greatest revivals had happened through the preaching of visiting ministers and added, "It has been So in Grafton." He believed that the excitement at Grafton had touched "all Sorts; Old and Young, Male and Female, Sober and Prophane, Indians Blacks and whites." Again, the radicals emphasized that their ministries cut across social divisions.[36]

Daniel Rogers continued to see considerable results from his preaching in Ipswich during the winter of 1742–43, revealing that the controversy over Davenport and the awakenings had not shut down revival activity, particularly among the radicals. On December 18, for instance, Rogers noted, "in Prayer a Woman was So filled with ye Spirit of God, that She fell on her Knees, and blessed & praised God — in Sermon another Spake out: the Power of ye Ld. was Present." He visited Newburyport regularly, where baker Richard Elvins continued to minister without degree or ordination. Rogers also maintained his focus on African American penitents, as in late December at Ipswich he recorded that "a negroe man was wonderfully fill'd wth. ye Love of Xt. and some others felt some Concern for formal Professors & Spake to 'em Several Times." In early January, Rogers and the visiting Nicholas Gilman devoted attention to the spiritual travails of one slave, Cato. At one meeting, Rogers noted, "poor Cato almost Distracted wth. ye Terrors of ye Lord. yt. were forced to bind Him." Apparently, the overwrought Cato had become deranged or even suicidal, which required him to be restrained. A week and a half later, "poor Cato, was in a gt. Agony, Br. Gilman pray'd over Him." Two days later came Cato's breakthrough: "In the Evening Cato Man Servt. of my Deceas'd Bro. who had been undr. deap

Convictions a fortnight past had a Discovery of the mercy of God in Xt. and recd. Comfort, had his mouth wonderfully open'd to Praise the Lord and exhort others to come." Rogers paid close, sustained attention to Cato's experiences and delighted in his exhortations, even as he failed to criticize or acknowledge the gross inequalities of social power that separated the two of them.[37]

Meanwhile, James Davenport stewed on Long Island during the winter. A pastoral commission including Jonathan Dickinson and Ebenezer Pemberton arrived in Southold during the fall to investigate his behavior. Dickinson told Thomas Foxcroft, "We found the several Congregations in that Town in utmost Confusion, Antinomianism in its worst Form." He was not sure whether Davenport had "patronized" the chaos. The commission advised patience but conceded that if Davenport did not soon repent, his church could seek a new minister. For the time being, the church stood by Davenport. In late February, Joshua Hempstead visited Southold and heard Davenport preach. As usual, he did not like what he heard. He called the whole service a "Meer Confused medley." Davenport kept repeating the same phrases, like "the hand of the Lord is upon me," over and over. He also reported that Davenport and others had received "Revelation . . . Concerning the Shepherds Tent & other Such things." This revelation led Davenport and Daniel Tuthill to return over Long Island Sound to New London, where he would stage the defining event of his career.[38]

Ignoring the warnings from the Connecticut General Assembly not to return, Davenport made his final grand assault on New London in the first week of March 1743. He apparently meant to organize a church there among students at the radical Shepherd's Tent. Suffering from an ailment in his leg, Davenport was carried about in a chair. On the Sabbath, Davenport called on his followers to begin burning books of popular authors opposed to him, or Reformed classics he perceived as Arminian. Among the authors deemed fit for the flames were John Flavel, Increase Mather, Benjamin Colman, Joseph Sewall, Charles Chauncy, Jonathan Dickinson, and New London's own Eliphalet Adams. They also reportedly burned the works of Jonathan Parsons and Solomon Williams, who once might have been embraced in the radical camp. On the town wharf Davenport's devotees built a bonfire and sang "Hallelujahs and Gloria Patri over the Pile." They cried, "That the Smoak of the Torments of such of the Authors of the abovesaid Books as died in the same Belief as when they set them out, was now ascending in Hell in like Manner as they saw the Smoak of them Books rise." The next day Davenport called on his followers to burn vain clothing. Some apparently began to comply, casting down such items as "Scarlet Cloaks, Velvet Hoods, fine Laces, and every Thing that had two Colours." Others had second thoughts about these extremes. Davenport himself reportedly contributed a pair of plush breeches to the growing pile, but a young woman thought all this crossed the line of propriety and she snatched out his pants, cried, "The calf you have made is too big," and "flung D – – – t's Plush Breeches into his Face." This act of defiance broke Davenport's spell over the radical crowd, which quickly turned against him. It does not appear that the Monday fire ever was set, an eventuality that one observer counted fortunate because "had fire been put to the pile, [Davenport] would have been obliged to strutt about bare-arsed."[39]

Even Davenport's most devoted followers began immediately to repent of their frenzy and called themselves "Judases" to the awakenings. One of the armor-bearers, perhaps Tuthill, lamented that he had become a "Spectacle" and that he deserved to be hanged. All the radicals apparently agreed that their actions represented the "Fruit of a Delusion." Most significantly, "even the Ringleader himself declared the same." The authorities in New London arrested the leaders of the bonfire incident, but in the end they were fined lightly for Sabbath-breaking. The Shepherd's Tent quickly closed, and its leader, Timothy Allen, left town. Davenport fell into a repentant despondency; as one friend noted in May, "he lyes in ye dust before God for his conduct at N. London." He found himself "very much alone in ye world his friends forsake him he rides from town to town without any attendance." But he reportedly had a comforting sense of God's grace. Davenport's ministry was not over, but his days as a radical were.[40]

In late March a ministerial council of leading Connecticut evangelicals assembled in New London "to Settle the disorders that are Subsisting among those Called New Lights." Among those attending were Benjamin Lord, Solomon Williams, Benjamin Pomeroy, Joseph Bellamy, "young Buel," and their leader, Jonathan Edwards. Edwards wrote to his wife that he reluctantly agreed to make the trip to New London "to reclaim the people there from their errors." Edwards preached a sermon that diarist Joshua Hempstead described as "very Suitable for the times to bear Wittness against ye prevailing disorders & destractions." Edwards denounced Davenport's behavior as beyond the pale of legitimate evangelicalism, but the two would resume friendly correspondence after Davenport found pastoral work in New Jersey. Within a few years of the New London conflagration, Davenport was back in the good graces of the moderates and served the cause of revivalism in New Jersey, Maryland, and Virginia. In 1747 Davenport's brother-in-law William Gaylord remarked approvingly to Eleazar Wheelock that Davenport had told him about a revival in Maryland, and by early 1750 Davenport was denouncing Separatism and praying that "false Religion might come to an End." He invited Wheelock and Benjamin Pomeroy to itinerate with him in Virginia. Wheelock reported Davenport's and Jonathan

Edwards's death in the same letter to George Whitefield in 1758, lamenting the passing of "those eminent Men of God."[41]

By March 1743, the evangelical movement in New England and the Middle Colonies had publicly split between radicals and moderates, due in large part to the exacerbating effects of Croswell's and Davenport's tactics. Nevertheless, the personalities of Croswell and Davenport alone did not explain the growing rift within the movement. The initial excitement of the awakenings and Whitefield's ministry failed ultimately to contain real disagreements between evangelicals over the role of exhorters and itinerants, the doctrine of assurance, the witness of the Spirit, ecstatic responses among laypeople, and the leveling effects of the revivals. Croswell and Davenport, then, should not be dismissed as fanatics. Instead, they were key early leaders of the radical wing of the movement. Even though Davenport would become a moderate, just as Tennent did, the radicals remained a serious alternative presence in the long First Great Awakening. Many in New England came to believe that their only option to fulfill the radical awakening was to start illegal Separate congregations. Out of the embers of Davenport's bonfire, however, moderate evangelicals would work to salvage a reasonable awakening. Critics of the revivals would exult that Davenport's fire had illuminated evangelicals' true colors, while moderates and radicals alike would try to narrate the memory of a legitimate awakening.

"Beyond Any Former Outpouring of the Spirit": Debating the Legitimacy of the Awakenings

Israel Loring of Sudbury, Massachusetts, a moderate opponent of the revivals, wrote in his diary in late March 1743: "It is Certainly an exceeding Difficult time with us. Such an Enthusiastick, factious, Censorious Spirit was perhaps never more predominant in the Land." Loring and skeptics like him had grown weary of enthusiastic excesses and intrusions on their ministries. In June, Loring recorded with exasperation that as he preached in Bedford, Massachusetts, he perceived "a Stir among the Women" and found out afterwards that "a Woman . . . was (as it is Called) Struck." He thought the display was distasteful. The affected woman was brought to a nearby home, and there she continued to cry that "she was bound, She was bound, and Cou'd not Speak." Loring and others tried to calm her down, but they were interrupted by "a proud, Impudent, boisterous exhorter" who tried to encourage the woman's spiritual torments. The woman was carried home, but Loring found the next day that she had not slept and she continued in her agonies. He prayed that God would restore the "free Exercise of her reason."[1]

In light of such episodes, and especially following James Davenport's conflagration, many believed that the time had come to debate publicly the legitimacy of the revivals. These arguments had begun earlier, and revivals continued after the book burning in New London. The year 1743 saw the high point of a series of arguments about the awakenings, most prominently represented by the debate between Charles Chauncy and Jonathan Edwards. The printed contributions did not represent all views, however. After the New London debacle, radicals had fewer opportunities to defend themselves in print, and even Croswell began to back off his strident support of the radical awakening. Davenport also issued half-hearted retractions, with an eye toward salvaging his pastoral career. Despite the limitations of these debates, they helped define the acceptable limits of the movement, at least in the view of the moderate evangelicals.

One debate was centered in Scotland, where the massive Cambuslang revival occurred in 1742. British Americans were always deeply concerned with their reputations across the Atlantic, and colonists frequently sought allies in Britain by publicizing the wild enthusiasm, or glorious effects, of the North American revivals. In 1742, the pamphlet *The State of Religion in New-England* was published in Glasgow by "A.M.," likely Charles Chauncy or another Boston opponent of the revivals. This pamphlet described all the revivalists, including Whitefield and Tennent, in the worst terms, arguing that they generated a "superstitious Pannick" in New England. It called Whitefield a "bold and importunate Beggar" for the Georgia orphan house, and of the "clownish" Tennent it claimed, "Every one that was not exactly of his Mind, he damned without Mercy." As for Boston's Presbyterian minister John Moorhead, he was "as ignorant, stupid, conceited, impudent, ill-natured and turbulent a Man as ever you knew," who ministered to the "poor Irish" and "common Sailors." It described how Davenport "in a hot Day . . . strips to his Shirt, mounts a Cart, or any Eminence upon the Street, and roars and bellows, and flings about his Arms, till he is ready to drop down with the Violence of the Action." Finally, the "strolling Preacher" Samuel Buell preached sermons that were "the most stupid Stuff that ever came from a Man's Mouth." George Whitefield, then in Scotland, replied to the pamphlet and argued that the "base and wicked" tract really should be titled *The State of Religion Falsly Stated.* His reply was printed in Glasgow and Boston.[2]

Pastor Jonathan Ashley of Deerfield, Massachusetts, generated another debate when he denounced the revivals' censoriousness in *The Great Duty of Charity*, a sermon he preached at the Brattle Street Church in November 1742. He conceded that God had "remarkably shower'd" the New England churches with the Spirit but contended that the awakenings had been tainted by factionalism. Ashley was particularly concerned about growing hostility toward the established ministers and the way that the itinerants' charismatic personalities substituted for godly characters. Some at the Brattle meetinghouse walked out during his sermon, but Ashley's defenders characterized them as lower-class parishioners, including a "Maid" and a "Barber." William Cooper, one of the ministers at the Brattle Street Church, tried unsuccessfully to get Ashley not to publish the sermon. Cooper responded with dismay in the *Boston Gazette*, arguing that Ashley's sermon "hid the Glory of the illustrious Work of God's Power and Grace under a Cloud of Disorders." Cooper acknowledged that some had separated from Boston's established churches, but that this group amounted to no more than fifty people. He was concerned that Boston's pastors should speak up in the face of rising criticism and "rejoice in that extraordinary Manifestation of the divine Presence, with which our Land has been favoured." An anonymous friend of Ashley's replied that Cooper falsely represented Ashley's sermon and that "Whatsoever Work stands in need of false Representations to support it, cannot be a good Work." Critics also pointed out that Cooper himself had appeared at a Separate meeting in Boston, where he supposedly prayed and gave them his blessing.[3]

One can see, then, that Edwards and Chauncy were not without company in the contest to characterize the revivals. Nevertheless, their contributions came to define the positions of moderate evangelicals and antirevivalist skeptics, respectively. In March 1743, Edwards produced *Some Thoughts Concerning the Present Revival of Religion in New-England*. Edwards was confident in his ability to show that what had lately occurred in the churches was, in general, a "wonderful work of God." He expanded significantly (to 378 pages) his previous arguments in *The Distinguishing Marks* and devoted most of the treatise to affirming the revivals while characterizing the radicals' tactics as illegitimate. Edwards's *Some Thoughts* represented the finest articulation of the moderate evangelical position.[4]

Edwards argued that the intemperance of the zealots and the deadness of some ministers both presented terrible problems. The latter tendency was the more "abominable to God; vastly more hateful in his sight than all the imprudence and intemperate heats, wildness and distraction (as some call it) of these zealous preachers. A supine carelessness and a vain, carnal, worldly spirit in a minister of the Gospel, is the worst madness and distraction in the sight of God." He even believed that God might use the overheated zeal of the radicals to awaken some of the worldly clerics.[5]

Edwards insisted that, according to scriptural standards, the revivals had produced an unprecedented bounty of good fruit. In its extent and power, he thought the awakening was "vastly beyond any former outpouring of the Spirit that ever was known in New England." Edwards posited that the revivals might have global eschatological significance. "'Tis not unlikely that this work of God's Spirit . . . is the dawning, or at least a prelude, of that glorious work of God, so often foretold in Scripture." Perhaps this awakening would inaugurate, or at least portend, the millennium. Edwards's geographical speculations became breathtakingly specific: "the beginning of this great work of God must be near," he wrote. "And there are many things that make it probable that this work will begin in America." Moreover, if it was to begin in America, New England "must needs appear the most likely of all American colonies, to be the place whence the work shall principally take its rise." New Englanders conventionally believed that the millennium would be preceded by massive revivals. Edwards was not exactly arguing that the millennium was at hand, but he certainly believed that the revivals might help usher it in.[6]

Edwards devoted the fourth section of *Some Thoughts* to drawing the boundaries between warranted zeal and unwarranted enthusiasm. Although Edwards exhibited a relative patience for the radicals, he fundamentally preferred an orderly, hierarchical, and socially conservative awakening. He did not, however, criticize itinerant preaching, which he had done so often. Edwards denounced the radicals' "censuring others that are professing Christians, in good standing in the visible church, as unconverted." He lamented this practice as "the worst disease that has attended this work." He also rebuked "common people" who "clothe themselves with the like authority with that which is proper for ministers." He conceded that laymen, and even women and children, might speak to groups under "extraordinary circumstances" but insisted that official church preaching was reserved for ordained ministers. Moreover, he believed that no layperson should speak out during a church service, and when one did informally address any group, he or she should use a moderate tone of voice. Edwards also advised against irregular singing, such as impromptu choruses in the streets, because it led to "uproar and confusion." The mixing of these disruptive practices with the true work of God revealed how the "Devil has driven the pendulum far beyond its proper point of rest" and tried to prevent religion from "settling in a proper medium." Edwards believed that he had apprehended that moderate path between the revivals' opponents and the radicals.[7]

Other ministers in New England disagreed with Edwards and were ready to dismiss the whole awakening as irredeemable. In May 1743, the lightly attended annual convention of ministers at Boston issued the deceptively titled *The Testimony of the Pastors of the Churches in the Province of the Massachusetts-Bay in New-England.* The label made it sound as if this document won universal acceptance, but it did not: the antirevivalists saw the convention as a chance to seize a bare majority and issue the statement in the absence of many prorevivalist ministers. *The Testimony* spoke against "Errors in Doctrine," such as spiritual impulses, and the belief that true converts would know the time of their conversion. More broadly, however, *The Testimony*'s authors denounced the "Disorders in Practice" of the revivals. Unlike Edwards, they considered itinerancy, even by ordained ministers, a "Breach of Order," particularly when itinerants did not seek the approval of the resident minister. Furthermore, they excoriated unlearned exhorters as "an heinous Invasion of the ministerial Office, offensive to GOD, and destructive of these Churches." They also denounced the ordination

of evangelists-at-large (such as Samuel Buell and Daniel Rogers), church separations, and the "ungoverned Passions of People" crying out in meetings. The only
grudgingly positive note struck in *The Testimony* ambiguously gave God glory
"where there is any special Revival of pure Religion in any Parts of our Land."[8]

Joshua Gee, minister at Boston's Second Church, would not let *The Testimony*
go unchallenged and soon printed a rebuttal. Gee was troubled about the title's
implications and especially about the way "those at a great Distance" might read
it (again, one sees the colonists' concern for their reputation in Britain). Gee
lamented the publication of various antirevivalist tracts in Scotland, such as *The
State of Religion in New-England*, and thought that *The Testimony* would only
increase the misapprehensions of the North American revivals among Britons.
Moreover, he worried that by denouncing the whole revival, the pastors would
tempt recent converts to doubt the sincerity of all the colony's ministers. Gee
wanted it publicly noted that only about one-third of Massachusetts' pastors had
attended the convention, and that only a small majority of those present (thirty-
eight out of seventy) had voted to approve *The Testimony*. Thus, he estimated
that only a fifth of all Massachusetts pastors subscribed to *The Testimony*'s negative assessment of the whole work.[9]

Gee called for a meeting of pastors supporting the revivals, summoning
"Brethren as are persuaded there has of late been a happy Revival of Religion"
to meet in Boston after Harvard's commencement. Daniel Rogers came down
from Ipswich for the meeting, which he estimated eighty or ninety pastors attended. He was pleased to note the great "Unanimity" among them, which was
to be affirmed by issuing a statement to counter the May convention's *Testimony*. A committee, including Joseph Sewall, Thomas Prince, and Nathaniel
Rogers of Ipswich, was chosen to draft an affirmation of the revivals.[10]

The result, *The Testimony and Advice of an Assembly of Pastors*, asserted that
"there has been a happy and remarkable Revival of Religion in many Parts of this
Land" and that the work was "extraordinary" in its effects. Much of the rest of
the statement became defensive. It argued that the revivals had, on the whole,
proceeded in a rational manner. Those with "outward Distresses" could usually
give a "rational Account of what so affected their Minds." Penitents usually cited
holy terrors or specific passages of Scripture that led them to heightened emotions. The convention characterized as insignificant those whose "Affections
were produced by visionary or sensible Representations, or by any other Images
than such as the Scripture it self presents." *The Testimony and Advice* readily
conceded that some places had seen "Extravagancies," but the pastors thought it
indefensible for anyone to send accounts "abroad, representing this Work as all
Enthusiasm, Delusion and Disorder."[11]

The Testimony and Advice concluded with warnings to the radicals to contain their excesses. It particularly cautioned against anyone making "secret Impulses . . . the Rule of their Duty," itinerating without the approval of local ministers, and permitting "raw and indiscreet young Candidates" to take prominent preaching roles. The assembly did affirm the benefits of regulated itinerancy, noting that "GOD has in this Day remarkably bles'd the Labours of some of his Servants who have travelled in preaching the Gospel." It also warned against separations and censoriousness. Not all their cautions concerned the radicals, however, as they did warn "all Sorts of Persons not to despise these Out-pourings of the Spirit, lest a holy GOD be provok'd to withhold them."[12]

The Testimony and Advice defended the revivals against opponents who painted the evangelical movement as entirely compromised by radical enthusiasm. Sixty-eight ministers from Massachusetts, New Hampshire, and Maine signed the document, and forty-three others who could not attend sent letters attesting to the work of God. Nevertheless, disagreements within the moderate camp were evident, as fifteen signers added a stronger statement against itinerancy. Among these most moderate of the evangelicals were Ebenezer Turell of Medford, Ebenezer Parkman of Westborough, and most notably, Boston's Benjamin Colman. Daniel Rogers was apparently not asked to sign, likely because of his lack of a permanent parish assignment. Those signing with no reservations were the stalwarts of the moderate camp, as well as some who leaned toward radicalism. Among them were Joshua Gee, John Webb, and John Moorhead of Boston, Solomon Prentice of Grafton, and Josiah Crocker of Taunton. Isaac Watts arranged for the statement's reprinting in London in 1744.[13]

Some lay critics of the revivals were not satisfied with *The Testimony and Advice*, however, and joined the debate with *The Testimony and Advice of a Number of Laymen* in September. This sneering pamphlet dismissed Whitefield as a "Man but of weak Mind, little Learning, and no Argument" who whipped up the masses with his theatrics, designing only to empty their pockets. Tennent was even worse: "he was no Orator, had neither Sense, Argument, nor good Stile." The authors believed that Boston's revivalist pastors embraced Whitefield only because they saw him as a way to buttress the tottering intellectual façade of Calvinism. The revivals were essentially an attack on reason, manifested in the lay exhorters' howlings. The pamphlet advised the evangelical ministers to return to reason as the basis for their preaching and never again to invite touring strangers like Whitefield and Tennent into their pulpits.[14]

September also saw the publication of Charles Chauncy's magisterial antirevivalist book, *Seasonable Thoughts on the State of Religion in New-England*. Designed to answer Edwards's *Some Thoughts*, Chauncy's 424 pages marshaled all the relevant historical and theological arguments against enthusiastic and antinomian excesses. In typical antirevivalist fashion, he denounced the revivalists' censoriousness, the itinerants' lack of respect for the established ministers, and the meetings' bodily exercises. He worriedly noted how many revival meetings had seen "strange effects upon the Body such as swooning away and falling to the Ground, where Persons have lain, for a Time, speechless and motionless; bitter Shriekings and Screamings; Convulsion-like Tremblings and Agitations, Strugglings and Tumblings, which, in some Instances, have been attended with Indecencies I shan't mention." Moderates tried to argue that these excesses happened at few meetings. Chauncy thought they were widespread. These hysterics made the current revivals fatally flawed, in Chauncy's estimation. All the errors and extravagancies of the awakenings, Chauncy believed, were exemplified in James Davenport, and he provided exhaustive details of Davenport's strange career as an itinerant.[15]

It would be easy to forget that as these debates over the awakenings proceeded, revivals continued as well. Historian Edwin Gaustad has described New England's awakenings as moving like a flood that surged "in, all over, and out," disappearing as quickly as they had sprung up.[16] There can be no doubt that 1740–42 saw massive numbers of revivals and conversions across New England, but American evangelicalism was also becoming a movement that would not cease to exist when public attention waned. May 1743 actually saw one of the most remarkable events of these revivals, the instantaneous healing of Mercy Wheeler of Plainfield, Connecticut.

Wheeler had become unable to walk because of a wasting fever in 1726 and had published a pietistic account of her illness in 1733 in *An Address to Young People*. As of May 1743, Wheeler could move about a bit with crutches, but it had been sixteen years since she had taken an unaided step. At Wheeler's request, a special lecture was appointed at her family's home, at which pastor Hezekiah Lord of Preston would preach. A few days before the lecture, she began feeling a rising confidence that God might do something wonderful at that meeting. She was particularly affected by John 11:40, "If thou wouldst believe, thou shouldst see the Glory of God." The verse "led her to view the Help there was for her in God, in the Way of believing." Soon she developed a "strong Perswasion, that she should be healed."[17]

The morning of the appointed meeting, Wheeler's faith increased as she prayed for healing and meditated on Christ's curing of the invalid in John chapter 5. Hezekiah Lord believed that God had directed her to the many healing narratives in the Gospels to build faith for her own healing. These gave her a "Soul-reviving View of the Power of Christ." At the meeting, Hezekiah Lord preached from Isaiah 57:15 ("to revive the Spirit of the Humble") and promised that God would "revive and bring you out of a Furnace." Wheeler believed that this promise was meant for her, and she began to tremble.[18]

She shook involuntarily but quietly. Afterward Samuel Newell, a recent Yale graduate who was working in Plainfield while looking for a permanent position, asked how she felt. When she first tried to speak the words came out as gibberish. She was laid upon her bed, and Hezekiah Lord began counseling her. She informed him that God would soon heal her. Soon she became so "overpowered with the Sense of God" that she felt like an "Atom drowned in the Sea." Lord thought she just needed to rest, so he stepped away from her room. Wheeler had a fleeting moment of doubt, thinking perhaps the time for the healing had passed. Then "those Words were repeated to her,—*If thou wilt believe, thou shalt see the Glory of God.*" With this assurance, she was "wholly taken out of her self, into the Hands of God; and enabled her to believe that he could and would heal her. Immediately upon which, she felt a strange irresistible Motion and Shaking, which began first with her Hands; and quickly spreading over her whole Frame. . . . And as she had this Sensation of new Strength and Freedom, she felt as if she was a raising up, and must rise; and immediately rose up and walked away among the People, with evident Sprightliness and Vigour, to the Astonishment of her self and those about her. She went this Time near 16 Feet, crying out, 'Bless the Lord Jesus, who has healed me!'" The shocked Hezekiah Lord told her that she was in a "Frenzy" and forced her to sit down on the bed, but Wheeler would not remain there; she walked across the room several more times. Wheeler's healing caused a minor sensation in New England in 1743–44, generating a debate over the legitimacy of miracles after the apostolic period. Radicals seized on Wheeler's healing as evidence of the continuation, or perhaps resumption, of miracles. Moderate evangelicals worried about the episode jeopardizing the long-held Reformed belief in cessationism, or the doctrine that miracles had ceased after the time of the apostles. Skeptics jeered that such bogus miracles smacked of Catholic piety.[19]

The radical Daniel Rogers also did not mean to give up on the revivals in 1743. In August, he fanned the flames of revival in the Separate congregation at Exeter, New Hampshire, along with the former baker Richard Elvins and a blind exhorter named Joseph Prince. In early August, he woke up to find that he "had Faith given that the Lord wd. be with us Remarkably to Day." His faith was rewarded. When he arrived he found the congregation in "holy Joy," and "Prayer was made in ye holy Ghost." Rogers began to preach with great power, and the "King of Glory came down and manifested his Glory in the Hearts of his People." The congregation erupted in a chorus of extemporaneous praise. But even Rogers had to admit in October that there had been a "Suspension of ye late Remarkable work of Conviction and Conversion." That day he preached in Exeter on Psalm 85:6, "Wilt thou not revive us again?"[20]

While radicals continued to promote revival, other subjects commanded public debate, such as James Davenport's status as a gospel minister. The New London debacle scattered his supporters, and Davenport began working to salvage his career. So did Andrew Croswell, who printed a repudiation of Davenport's ministry in May 1743. Croswell admitted that denouncing ministers as unconverted, and that permitting unlearned exhorters to preach led to unnecessary troubles in the churches. He remained committed to separation from established churches when warranted, however. One antirevivalist critic found Croswell's repudiation unconvincing, to say the least. He thought the "Insincerity of this pretended Recantation" was obvious, as Croswell hardly accepted any of the blame he deserved for the disastrous consequences of "Whitefieldism." "I hope it will be for his Humiliation all his Days, that he has been so much the Occasion of sowing dreadful Errors thick in the Country." Croswell, never one to be humiliated, soon became pastor to a Separate congregation in Boston.[21]

Davenport had scaled more radical heights than Croswell, however, and received the brunt of antirevivalist ridicule. For Davenport to be accepted again by the moderate evangelicals, he would have to show a great deal of public contrition. This process began with visits to offended ministers, such as Joseph Fish of Stonington, Connecticut, who wrote that Davenport "came with such a mild, meek, pleasant and humble spirit, broken and contrite, as I scarce ever saw excelled or equalled." Davenport privately sought forgiveness from the ministers and publicly retracted his errors. Davenport also had an apologetic letter printed, written to his old Long Island colleague Jonathan Barber at the Bethesda orphanage. He explained that the "awful Affair of Books and Cloaths at New-London, which affords Grounds of deep and lasting Humiliation" was the result of a "false Spirit" that controlled him for several days. The devil had used the "Cancry Humour" in his leg to gain a foothold and deceive him. The humiliating experience and the festering sore nearly killed him. His dreadful scourging brought a new apprehension of God's grace. It almost seemed as if the near-death experience led to his being born again. "What heavenly Light and ravishing Joys broke in then upon my Soul!" he told Barber. Chastened by these experiences, Davenport warned Barber against "Extremes on both Sides the Path of Duty." He knew that recovering his credibility required him to strike a new moderate pose.[22]

Davenport also courted the help of former friends, most notably Solomon Williams and Eleazar Wheelock, who composed and published formal letters to Davenport in 1744. It is not evident that these letters actually played a role in convincing Davenport to repent. They seem more likely to have been designed to provide a context in which Davenport could issue his formal retraction of errors. Williams defended ordained ministers against rash judging, arguing that any minister who had been properly ordained was "lawful" and deserved respect. Some surely got through the process of ordination without having actually experienced conversion, but they remained official ministers nonetheless and should not have to answer public questions about their salvation. The external call of ordination gave a minister of the gospel his authority, not inner conversion. Similarly, Wheelock argued against the authority of "private Christians" to act as ministers and exhorters. He saw the public ministry as a special calling given only to "such as are called and commissioned thereto by [God]." Wheelock did not mean to suppress "mutual, zealous, Christian Conversation upon all proper Occasions," which God had used powerfully in the revivals. He specifically prohibited the "ministerial Kind of exhorting" in which laypeople assumed to speak with the clout of their ministers.[23]

Finally, in late summer 1744 Davenport issued his *Confession and Retractions*, printed with an introductory letter by Solomon Williams testifying to its sincerity. The confession was carefully crafted to suit the moderate evangelicals' positions. Davenport began by asserting that there had indeed been a "glorious and wonderful Work" in New England. Moreover, he believed that God had granted him and several other ministers "special Assistance and Success." Davenport confessed, however, that "several Appendages to this glorious Work are no essential Parts thereof, but of a different and contrary Nature." He admitted that his "misguided Zeal" and the influence of a false spirit had tainted his ministry. This corruption led many to question and oppose the work of God.[24]

Davenport repudiated his former practices of publicly calling ministers unconverted, advising congregations to separate from those ministers, following after spiritual impressions, encouraging private Christians toward ministerial exhorting, and singing in the streets. He further apologized for his "great Stiffness" against criticism. He cited the influence of the false spirit and the ailment in his leg as his primary excuses for his rash behavior. On the whole, it was a sincere but limited confession. Davenport specifically repudiated his most offensive practices, but he blamed them on an affliction for which he could not be faulted, and he insisted that most of the late work had been from God.[25]

Antirevivalist critics were not satisfied with the confession's limitations, as demonstrated by the anonymous *Impartial Examination of Mr. Davenport's Retractions*. The author lamented that "this Confession is neither so full nor so early as might have expected" and argued that all the confession meant to do

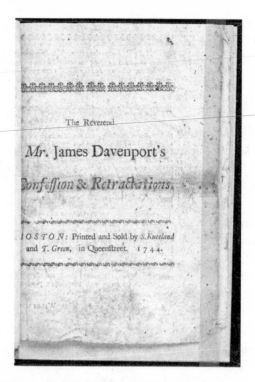

James Davenport, *Confession and Retractions*
(Boston, 1744). Beinecke Rare Book and
Manuscript Library, Yale University.

was "to recover the Reputation, and make his Court to some few real Friends of the late Work, who had suffered by his Indiscretion." The *Impartial Examination* contended that Davenport's ministry (and that of all the itinerants) was illegitimate from first to last, as was the revival itself. "The Work is plainly proved to be not of GOD but of Men, because 'tis come to Nothing, and overthrown by themselves and the remarkable Providence of GOD."[26]

Benjamin Colman cautiously welcomed Davenport's confession, but he remained concerned enough to print a letter about it. He noted that Davenport called his errors "appendages to the work," but Colman insisted they were no appendages "but the Working of Satan . . . to blemish defame and destroy the Work of GOD." Colman hoped that the Separates and the exhorters who continued to pop up in New England "like Mushrooms in a Night" would repent as Davenport had. He also hoped that "whoever of us [perhaps including himself] went early and too suddenly into a good Opinion of the Transports of weak

People and Children" would be ready to confess their imprudence. Colman still asserted that the late revivals were a "Work of God," despite all their excesses. Colman encouraged Davenport to return to Long Island to try to repair the spiritually damaged churches there. Colman remained an evangelical, but in light of the revivals' errors, he had become a very reluctant one. Davenport apparently was sincerely concerned about responding to Colman's criticisms, as he wrote to Solomon Williams and asked that any future editions include passages that comported with Colman's characterization of Davenport's revival ministry. His *Confession and Retractions* saw only one edition, however.[27]

The only "mushroom in a night" that Colman mentioned by name was Richard Woodberry of Rowley, an exhorter of "Infatuations and impious Extravagances" that one historian has described as "apparently psychopathic." Woodberry had come under Nicholas Gilman's tutelage by 1742, and though he proved himself to be incendiary and confrontational, Gilman generally approved of his ministry. In June 1743, Gilman recorded in his diary that "Mr. Woodbury exhorted. gave Some great uneasiness, occasiond an Uproar and Tummult—Overrule it, O! Father of Mercies for the good of Thy Chosen." Woodberry was precisely the kind of untutored exhorter that the moderates loathed. But beginning in May 1744, Woodberry, Gilman, and Daniel Rogers helped generate another powerful revival in northeastern Massachusetts.[28]

Rogers had been struggling for months to restore the spiritual highs he and his followers had reached in the earlier awakenings, and it seemed that Woodberry became the catalyst for Rogers's own revival. At a private meeting in Newbury in late May, Rogers recorded that "Br. Woodberry & Br. Gilman fell prostrate upon the Ground floor & the Holy Gh. came upon Almost Every One in the Room, near 20. . . . Some Rejoycing with Trembling Body's." That evening, Gilman "publickly acknowledged [Woodberry] as a fellow Labourer in the Lords Vineyard; & told ye People He had given him ye right Hand of Fellowship and recommended Him as Such to ye People." Apparently Gilman now believed that such acknowledgment sufficed for the ordination of exhorters.[29]

Gilman and Rogers both referred in their diaries to Woodberry's "motions" as generating controversy. Perhaps he, like Whitefield, made liberal use of gestures and other bodily effects during his exhortations. Whatever Woodberry's "motions" were, Rogers found himself struggling to approve of the tactics. "People Gen[era]lly Offended at Br. Woodberry's Motions—I find Pride & Shame working in me upon the Acco[unt] of Him & his Ways." But Rogers soon repented of his ill will toward Woodberry.[30]

A team of moderate evangelical pastors, led by Joshua Gee and John Webb, came to Ipswich in July to investigate Woodberry's activities. John Rogers,

Daniel's elderly father and pastor of Ipswich's First Church, told them that Woodberry "acted in such a strange and unaccountable Manner" that he was afraid it might hurt Ipswich's ongoing revival. The commission found that Woodberry was "an illiterate Person, generally apprehended of a disordered Brain." They noted with concern how Gilman had given Woodberry a private ordination, and with Gilman's encouragement he began to promote "the Revelation of secret Things, by pretended Predictions and Denunciation of temporal and eternal Curses upon particular Persons." He claimed the power to work miracles and cast out demons. He may have even claimed to be immortal. A critic once supposedly challenged Woodberry's tactics, upon which the exhorter "did with strange Emotion and violent Agitation throw himself upon and rowl over the Floor, crying out, *You have crucified Christ in what you have said.*"[31]

In a statement printed in the *Boston Evening-Post* and the *Boston Gazette*, the ministers reprimanded Gilman and any others who encouraged Woodberry. They thought that such extremists threatened the revivals as a whole and believed that the episode should provide another warning "against any Persons intruding themselves into the sacred Ministry without proper Qualifications and regular Call; much more proudly and falsely pretending to extraordinary and immediate Mission from Christ . . . and accomplishing God's Prophesies and Purposes." A writer for the *Boston Evening-Post* thought that the pastors handled those involved with the Woodberry affair too gently, particularly those unnamed supporters, "by which 'tis more than probable that they intend the two R[oger]s's." The pastors had "artfully and jesuitically" concealed their identities despite their having been as intimately involved with Woodberry as Gilman had been. The writer suggested that the reason they did not reveal Nathaniel and Daniel Rogers as Woodberry's supporters was because they had been "great Promoters of their imaginary REVIVAL."[32]

There was no doubt that the moderate evangelicals were in a difficult position: they could not countenance the radicals' openness to unlettered exhorters, but they also knew that radicals like the Rogers brothers and Gilman, and even exhorters like Woodberry, had done as much or more than most moderates to preach up revival. How could they continue to promote an exclusively moderate revival if it seemed that the radicals were the only ones seeing awakenings by 1743–44? Another anonymous critic in the *Boston Evening-Post* argued that the commission's statement meant to hide the fact that the whole revival was tainted by radical enthusiasm, and that what pastors like Gee and Webb called "a gracious Revival of Religion, was in all Respects . . . more like such Torments of Delusion, as the Begging Fryars, the Mistical Divines, and the French Prophets, than like any really religious Reformations." Despite the denunciations, Woodberry apparently continued his ministry in Durham for many more years. In 1751, he attracted the disapproving notice of Isaac Backus, who on a visit worried about Woodberry's "awful wild extreams."[33]

These debates over the revivals' legitimacy came full circle with George Whitefield's long-awaited return to America in October 1744. Landing at York, Maine, Whitefield was greeted personally by friends, mostly those with radical leanings, including Samuel Buell, Jonathan Parsons, Benjamin Pomeroy, and the Rogers family. Daniel Rogers wrote that they "found him in Bed very Ill of a nervous Cholick," but Whitefield was delighted to see them. A letter writer in the *Boston Evening-Post* immediately used this party of greeters to tar Whitefield as an unrepentant enthusiast: "P – – – y, P – – – ns, B – – – l, &c., furious Zealots, moulded into his very Temper, were the Men . . . who first met him at his coming," along with some Maine Separates. The writer called on Whitefield to apologize to all those he had offended on his earlier visit before being admitted to their pulpits. Whitefield's return precipitated the most intense storm of printed arguments over the revivals. Dozens of writers debated whether Whitefield should be welcomed back as an honored man of God or shunned as a troublemaker.[34]

Charles Chauncy again led the public attacks on Whitefield. He advised against welcoming Whitefield in an installation sermon for Thomas Frink, pastor at Plymouth's Third Church. He warned Frink and other pastors to "mark this Man who has caused Divisions and Offences . . . and to avoid him." Chauncy pointed to the confusion, disorder, and censoriousness reigning in many of New England's churches and declared Whitefield the "true Source of most of this Mischief." Even if Whitefield moderated his accusations against the established ministers, he still was chief among the itinerants and therefore had no place in a good church order.[35]

In Boston, Whitefield was able to convince Colman, Sewall, Foxcroft, and Prince that he did not intend to promote separations, and the moderates welcomed him into their pulpits again. During December, Whitefield toured eastern Massachusetts and upon returning to Boston proclaimed that he had "scarce had a pleasanter circuit since I have been a Preacher." Nevertheless, controversy followed Whitefield during his visit.[36]

Although some moderate New England ministers remained friendly to Whitefield, opposition became very vocal against him, and some moderates were not sure what position to take. Andrew Eliot of the New North Church in Boston expressed the moderates' concerns about Whitefield in a 1745 letter when he conceded that, despite the revivalist's good intentions, he had too often "Mistaken Nature for Grace & Imagination for Revelation." Eliot's correspondent, Richard Salter of Mansfield, Connecticut, had called Whitefield a "rank Enthusiast," but

Eliot thought this went "too far." For his part, Whitefield wrote that in Boston the "common people" received him happily, but "many of the ministers how shy?" The moderating Whitefield conceded that "some occasions of offence" had accompanied his last visit, but he thought overall "nothing . . . appeared but a pure, divine power . . . without any extraordinary phenomena attending it." Still, "wild-fire will necessarily blend itself with the pure fire" and some honest Christians became "guilty of great imprudence." Whitefield thought these extremes were precisely what his opponents had been waiting for.[37]

The antirevivalist mood created by Davenport's debacle emboldened Whitefield's opponents to speak out. The faculty of Harvard College remembered all too well Whitefield's unkind remarks about them, and in a published letter they warned that his ministry tended "very much to the Detriment of Religion, and the entire Destruction of the Order of these Churches." They singled out Whitefield's itinerancy and enthusiasm as harmful to the peace of the churches. The faculty used Whitefield's published journals against him, citing every instance of Whitefield giving credence to a dream or impression, or making rash judgments of ministers, to brand him as "an Enthusiast, a censorious, uncharitable Person, and a Deluder of the People." They concluded that it was "high Time to make a stand against the Mischiefs" wrought by Whitefield.[38]

Not to be outdone, rector Thomas Clap and the tutors of Yale College published a February 1745 letter against Whitefield. They agreed substantially with the points made by the Harvard faculty but added that they believed that Whitefield and the itinerants "have laid a Scheme to turn the generality of Ministers out of their Places" and replace them with pro-Whitefield ministers. Again, they cited his journals to show that Whitefield believed that the "generality of Ministers are unconverted," from which naturally followed the belief that the people should remove or separate from them. They acknowledged that Whitefield had publicly spoken against church separations, but they thought that, in practice, his principles could only support them. They suggested that Whitefield and the Tennents intended to bring over suitable candidates from Scotland and Ireland as replacements, just as the Tennents' Presbytery had been sending ministers to help Connecticut's separating churches. They even hinted that students at the Shepherd's Tent had been told that the leadership of the college, and even that of the colony, would soon be overthrown and replaced with prorevivalists, so that there was no point in obeying the antirevivalist authorities. The Yale faculty recommended that the ministers "be fully upon their Watch against all divisive Plots and Designs" carried on by Whitefield and his followers.[39]

More than half a dozen ministerial associations across New England printed public resolutions against Whitefield and itinerancy in 1744–45. Whitefield's defenders tended to be more circumspect. A group of New Hampshire and Maine pastors, led by Portsmouth's William Shurtleff, offered an endorsement of Whitefield and thanked God that he "has rais'd up Mr. Whitefield, and evidently owned and honoured him with so much Success in preaching the everlasting Gospel of JESUS CHRIST in this Land." They also asserted that Whitefield was not the "culpable Cause" of any separations. A group of ministers in Bristol County, Massachusetts, including Josiah Crocker of Taunton and Nathaniel Leonard of Plymouth, agreed that though Whitefield had his "Mistakes & Foibles, as well as other Men," he and Tennent had been the "chief Instruments" used by God to create an authentic revival in New England. Unlike the critics, they saw the itinerant's work as biblically supported. Thus, they invited Whitefield back to their pulpits.[40]

Some individuals also rose to defend Whitefield in print, including Thomas Foxcroft, who wrote the most extensive defense of Whitefield in 1745, *An Apology in Behalf of the Revd. Mr. Whitefield*, which was published with letters of endorsement from London's Isaac Watts. Perhaps the most radical defense of Whitefield came in the anonymous *A Vindication of the Reverend Mr. George Whitefield*, which argued that Whitefield's relative silence in the press indicated that he did not have time to engage in controversy on behalf "of the people nick named *new-lights*," for he was working to save souls and revive religion again. The author dismissed Whitefield's critics, writing, "it may be expected, in a time of great revival of religion, that men's corruptions should vent themselves . . . PHARISEES, tho' friends to the outside of religion, yet can't bear to see it flourish in its power." The critics were only "half-way christians" and no fair judges of the itinerant's character. The author went so far as to defend Whitefield's earlier denunciations of Harvard and Yale by positing that if the colleges were not in an "evil state," then Davenport's fundraising for the Shepherd's Tent would not have raised such large sums of money. Whitefield had backed off his earlier suggestions that many New England ministers might not know Christ personally, but this author thought no apology was necessary: "Is there not reason for such a fear? Don't many, nay, the most of our ministers oppose the good work?" A *Vindication* showed that the radicals' public voices had not fallen entirely silent.[41]

Whitefield spent much of February 1745 in northeastern New England, among friendly pastors like the Rogers family, Samuel Buell, and Nicholas Gilman. On February 8, for instance, Whitefield preached at Ipswich in the morning and afternoon, and Buell preached in the evening. Daniel Rogers noted that "the Power of God came down Remarkably upon Some." Two weeks later Whitefield and his entourage went to New Hampshire and Maine. His attention shifted to the campaign against the French citadel at Louisbourg on Cape Breton Island, led by Whitefield's supporter William Pepperrell of Kittery. Whitefield visited with Pepperrell and preached to "the Officers and Soldiers engaged in the Expedition." He reported that "many of them were stirred up to God." On February 28 a public fast was held for the expedition, and Whitefield prayed for God to "give us Cape Briton. Lord prepare us either for Victory or defeat. But if it be thy will grant it may be a Garrison for Protestants and thy dear Children who will worship thee in spirit and in truth!" Whitefield gave the expedition a motto for its flag, *Nil desperandum Christo duce* (No need to fear with Christ as our leader). This blending of religion and politics evidenced what historian Nathan Hatch has called "civil millennialism," but it was nothing new to New Englanders. They had viewed the French with an apocalyptic hatred for decades, especially since the beginning of the imperial wars between Britain and France in 1689. Evangelical religion helped perpetuate the tendency to read imperial military developments through apocalyptic lenses, while fears of wartime depredations also helped fuel evangelicals' sense of urgency about fostering revivals.[42]

Evangelicals and nonevangelicals responded to imperial developments in essentially the same way: when news arrived of Louisbourg's surrender in the summer, all New Englanders took the victory as a sign of God's favor on Protestant Britain against the antichristian French Catholics. Thomas Prince rejoiced that "hereby a great support of Antichristian Power is taken away, and the visible Kingdom of CHRIST enlarged." He prayed that the defeat of the French might "be the dawning Earnest of our DIVINE REDEEMER's carrying on his Triumphs thro' the Northern Regions; 'till He extends his Empire from the Eastern to the Western Sea, and from the River of Canada to the Ends of America." Charles Chauncy, who had agreed with Prince on few matters in the past five years, concurred with his reading of the victory, hoping "that the pure gospel of Christ be preached in this part of the Dominion of Antichrist. May the Man of Sin, that Son of Perdition, be no longer acknowledged as Christ's Viceregent." New England's pastors could not unite around the revivals, but they could all celebrate the defeat of French Catholics.[43]

In August, Whitefield set out for an overland journey to Georgia. In Connecticut, Joshua Hempstead still found Whitefield arresting. The itinerant spoke before great crowds at New London, "p'haps twice So many as could possibly Sitt in ye meetinghouse." Hempstead thought he was "an Excellent preacher." Whitefield moved on to Long Island and then to Philadelphia, where he found Gilbert Tennent preaching in the new building erected at the beginning of the awakenings. Whitefield noted with great pleasure that conversions had begun among some Native Americans, especially through the ministry of the missionary David Brainerd. His supporters tried to get him to take a semi-permanent preaching position in Philadelphia. He declined and moved on to Bethesda. He spent the early months of 1746 there, trying to put the orphanage's finances in order.[44]

The debates over the legitimacy of the awakenings settled nothing, but they did define more clearly the positions of the antirevivalists and moderate evangelicals. The antirevivalists tried to highlight the role of enthusiasm in order to denounce the revivals generally, while the moderate evangelicals denied that the radical impulse was an integral part of the movement. Nevertheless, radical manifestations of revivalism continued to appear, and in the later stages of the revivals of the 1740s, it seemed that only the radicals had much success in continuing to promote awakenings. Although the radicals were harmed by the retractions of Davenport and Croswell, radical ministries and mystical experiences continued to fuel aspects of the movement, including especially Separatism. For many radicals, separation from the established churches proved the only palatable alternative once evangelical unity became irredeemably fractured.

"The Gospel Is Not Preached Here":
The Crisis of New England Separatism

The passions of the revivals led not only to heated arguments and noisy exhortations, but to something even more threatening to religious establishments: church separations. Today, Protestant church splits occur frequently and can happen over seemingly any issue. Although they often deeply wound the people and churches involved, almost no one would claim that such splits subvert the social order. Instead, they reflect America's individualized approach to religious matters: if a church does not suit someone, he or she can easily leave it or start a new church. In the mid-eighteenth century, however, rejection of the church establishment's authority was viewed as a profoundly threatening act, jeopardizing the Christian order of society. Connecticut, in particular, passed a host of new laws designed to stop radical itinerants and the congregations they spawned. But the momentum of the awakenings was difficult to contain, and many enthusiasts seemed to thrive amidst persecution. Liberty of conscience became one of the rallying points of radical evangelicalism, especially as the movement entered the revolutionary period.

New England set the pace in church separations, seeing hundreds of Separate or Separate Baptist congregations founded during the eighteenth century.[1] The case of Chebacco Parish in Ipswich, Massachusetts, is a good example of how these separations often occurred. During Daniel Rogers's massive Ipswich revival of 1741–42, he received a letter from members of pastor Theophilus Pickering's Chebacco parish, pleading with the itinerant to visit them. Pickering, it seemed to them, refused to cooperate with the great move of God that was going on. The petitioners had asked Pickering "to join in Calling upon the Holy God to extend his mercy to us in these Extraordinary Times, of ye Holy Ghosts moving." If he would not do that, they asked that he at least call in a revivalist minister to stoke the flames. Pickering refused. Eight members of the church invited Rogers to preach anyway.

At the same time, Rogers received a letter from Pickering expressing doubts about the special nature of the work proceeding in Ipswich and elsewhere. Pickering conceded that God's initiative was necessary to convert sinners, but he saw no precedent for an extraordinary work of God or that "which you emphatically call This Work." He asked the Rogers brothers to explain this distinction to him, but Pickering was hardly in a mood to be convinced. Daniel Rogers visited him, but Pickering would not agree to hold a revival meeting or to sanction one among his people. Rogers left and went to Pickering's meetinghouse (apparently without clear permission from Pickering) and began preaching, precipitating a response like he had seen so often in Ipswich. The emotional gathering continued until early morning, but Pickering only scoffed at the results.[2]

The Rogers brothers formally responded to Pickering by arguing that though there was no fundamental difference between the present work of God and others in the past, they believed that the "Holy Spirit has of late remarkably descended upon many Places in this Land," perhaps more powerfully than at any time since the apostolic period. Pickering replied and still objected to their "Terms of Distinction" in speaking of the revivals. He also objected to Rogers preaching from his pulpit without his consent. He accused Rogers of having "too great a Dependance upon the remarkable Effects or Occurrences so often seen in your Night-meetings," which Rogers would try to whip up if they did not naturally occur.[3]

By midsummer 1742, the situation at Chebacco had not improved. In another published letter, Pickering accused the Rogers brothers of holding assemblies at his church and praying for him publicly "that God would open mine Eyes— and that the Scales might fall from 'em." Rogers privately told Pickering he was spiritually blind. Then, in the midst of a fervent meeting, Rogers indeed seems to have publicly described Pickering as spiritually lost, saying that he "desired some of 'em to go and call yt. blind minister the Shepherd to come & take care of ye Sheep." Some of the deacons went and pled with Pickering to come to the meeting, but he again refused. Soon he banned the brothers from his church, but Nathaniel continued to hold private conferences in the parish. In August, some in Pickering's congregation invited James Davenport to visit only days after he was banned from the Boston pulpits.[4]

Andrew Croswell wrote a letter in September 1742 to the Rogers brothers that makes clear why the crisis of separatism became so strident and bitter. He congratulated them for preaching where "your company is not Desired by the Ministers." He told them that he suspected more than three-quarters of New

England's ministers "would not let one Soul of their hearers go to heaven if they could help it." He encouraged them to keep warning people against opponents of the revivals like Pickering. When the antirevivalists fought against the "Work of God, they take Arms against the Great God himself." The Rogerses may not have wholly agreed with Croswell's stark characterizations, for when Croswell asked them to sign the endorsement of his tract excoriating Jonathan Dickinson's *A Display of God's Special Grace*, they apparently refused.[5]

The troubles in Chebacco's church continued to stew, and in March 1744, Pickering claimed in a sermon that "none knew the Actings of Faith, but God only." The evangelical faction in his congregation received this assertion as an insult and drew up articles of grievance against him for surly behavior and poor preaching. Pickering escalated the crisis by suing the complainants for defamation of character, a charge of which they were acquitted. The Chebacco evangelicals attempted to hold hearings regarding their complaints against Pickering, but the pastor blocked their attempts. As the church sunk into utter dysfunctionality, Pickering tentatively offered to resign if that might solve the problem. Apparently, he overestimated his support in the congregation, for a majority quickly agreed to his departure. Surprised by the result, Pickering refused to leave, and the majority proved unwilling to vote for his dismissal. As if his position with regard to the revivals was not yet clear, when some in his church invited George Whitefield to preach on his return visit to New England in early 1745, Pickering published a letter denouncing Whitefield and denying him access to his pulpit. Whitefield, of course, got a warm reception from the Rogers family. The Chebacco evangelicals continued to invite Daniel Rogers to speak at the church, requests that Pickering denied because Rogers would not condemn the "People in his Parish yt. have Separated."[6]

In early 1746, aggrieved members decided formally to withdraw from Pickering's church and covenant together as a congregation committed to revivalism. Soon they began to look for a pastor and found an ideal candidate in John Cleaveland of Canterbury, Connecticut. Cleaveland's radical credentials were impeccable. Cleaveland had studied at Yale during the awakenings' height in the early 1740s, but in 1744 he and his younger brother Ebenezer ran afoul of Yale's rector Thomas Clap because they had attended revivalist meetings in Canterbury led by their uncles Solomon and Elisha Paine. The Canterbury church had been without a pastor and the church split over the question of a replacement, with the Paines and Cleavelands opposing the proposed replacement candidate as antirevivalist. Clap caught wind of the Canterbury controversy, summoned the students upon their return, and summarily expelled them. Clap judged that they had "imbibed and practiced sundry of those Principles and Errors, by their withdrawing from the publick Worship of God in the Congregation in Canterbury and attending upon the Meeting of those Paines."[7]

Because of the strict Connecticut laws against itinerancy and unlicensed preaching, Cleaveland's expulsion put him in a bind. He continued his studies with Philemon Robbins of Branford and contemplated a move to New Jersey. He also received an invitation to preach on probation at Canterbury, but he declined, perhaps worrying that working as an unlicensed preacher in Connecticut would prove to be professionally limiting. In summer 1745, the Separate church in Boston called on him to serve temporarily, which he did. In February 1746, the congregation asked him to settle permanently, but he hesitated again. Soon he began visiting the Separate congregation in Chebacco, which he found much more to his liking than the Canterbury or Boston jobs. He preached in Chebacco periodically during 1746, and in early 1747 he accepted an invitation to settle there and was ordained as their new minister. Andrew Croswell eventually became the minister of the Boston Separate congregation.[8]

Theophilus Pickering, predictably, fumed at Cleaveland's settlement. He was particularly irritated by Nathaniel Rogers's participation in Cleaveland's ordination. He thought Rogers's action was "encouraging of unwarrantable Separations, a disparaging of ecclesiastical Councils, a Breach upon the Fellowship of the Churches and destructive of their Peace and Order, and highly injurious to the Second Church of Ipswich." Pickering denied the legitimacy of Cleaveland's ordination. Cleaveland and the Separates argued that they had every right to separate from Pickering's church, for Pickering failed to preach "the Doctrines of Grace" and refused to promote the "Operations of the Holy Spirit upon the Hearts of Men." Moreover, Pickering took no positive actions to address their grievances. The Separates understood the value of vital church community, but they did not believe such community could be sustained under a lifeless, neglectful pastor. They could no longer countenance being "held down under spiritual Tyranny," and the separation was justified in the eyes of God, if not man. Pickering died soon after Cleaveland's ordination, as did the controversy over the Separate congregation. In the long run, Cleaveland's Separates would win out, as the Chebacco church dwindled after Pickering's death, and in 1766 the old church invited Cleaveland to preach to them in joint services. This move followed Yale's granting Cleaveland a degree in 1763, the death of Pickering's successor, and a major revival in Cleaveland's church in 1763–64. In 1775, the two churches reunited under Cleaveland's evangelical principles.[9]

Although it is difficult to make universal generalizations about the founding motives of hundreds of Separate congregations, the most common reasons for separations were a perceived lack of purity in the churches and opposition to pastors either tepidly committed, or opposed, to the revivals. Unlike in Chebacco, many churches that suffered separations experienced significant revivals before the separation occurred. Often the zeal of the revivals generated a new concern for church purity that fed into separation. Sometimes the Separates might also reject infant baptism and become Baptists, the next logical step in the pursuit of a pure church of converted believers.[10]

The Separates also often supported the right of laypeople to serve as ministers. This was perhaps best exemplified in the case of Solomon and Elisha Paine's Canterbury, Connecticut, church. The brothers were both converted during the 1721 revival at Windham and were prominent in law and politics. Elisha began itinerating in 1742, probably with the encouragement of such local pastors as Eleazar Wheelock. The Windham County Ministerial Association even agreed to license him if he would subscribe to the Saybrook Platform, the 1708 system of church discipline for Connecticut's churches. Paine resisted, not liking Saybrook's intermingling of church and state. He continued to itinerate, and in early 1743 he ran afoul of the authorities in Woodstock, Massachusetts (now in Connecticut), was arrested and confined in "the dirtiest prison [he] ever saw." Supporters offered to bail him out, but he refused to have his bail paid because he was unjustly imprisoned. Ministers, including Eleazar Wheelock and Benjamin Pomeroy, wrote from Connecticut to vouch for his good character and doctrine, which helped secure his release. The ministers would come to regret their support for the radical Paine.[11]

Paine itinerated in Massachusetts and Rhode Island for five months in late 1743, and in summer 1744 he toured Cape Cod, including his hometown of Eastham, seeing more successes that by 1744 seemed increasingly limited to radical evangelicals alone. He reported to his family that the "Lord is doing wonders in this sandy land; but as Christ triumphs, Satan rages." Paine helped generate a particularly powerful revival at Chatham in late June. As he exhorted, "there was a screeching and groaning all over the multitude, and hath ever since been very powerful." During this period, the Canterbury church lacked a pastor and hosted itinerants like Buell, Parsons, Pomeroy, and Wheelock, as well as the Paines. Soon the church began to attract negative attention from the revivals' opponents. In the *Boston Gazette*, a skeptical correspondent noted in December 1742, "Canterbury is in worse confusion than ever . . . and they grow more noisy and boisterous so that they can get no minister to preach to them yet." Exhorters, including the Paine brothers, preached regularly at the church. "Lawyer [Elisha] Paine," the correspondent reported, "has set up for a preacher" and recruited followers from house to house.[12]

When a probationary pastor, James Cogswell, was found to be unsympathetic to the revivals, the Paine faction tried to have him removed. A majority of the townspeople and the Windham County Ministerial Association backed Cogswell against the opposition of a majority of church members, and because of the dictates of the presbyterian-leaning Saybrook Platform of 1708, Cogswell won out and was ordained as the new minister. The Paines argued that only church members could properly call a minister, but they had no legal backing in Connecticut. Elisha Paine wrote a letter sharply rebuking the Windham Association, which again landed him in jail. This time he faced opposition from his previous supporters, men like Wheelock and Joseph Meacham, both members of the association. Paine cheerfully took the opportunity to preach in the jail yard, and after about a month he was released. The Canterbury radicals continued trying to bring in Separate-friendly speakers, such as Andrew Croswell, who was barred from the meetinghouse. Paine continued to feud with the Windham Association, which released a public statement against him in December 1744.[13]

Showing ever more clearly the growing rift between radical and moderate evangelicals, the Windham Association firmly asserted that there had been a "very great and merciful Revival of Religion" of late. Its members believed, however, that Satan had used the outpouring of the Holy Spirit as an opportunity to imitate the work of the Spirit, "to excite and keep up a blind and furious Zeal" and "to puff them up with Pride and vain Notions of immediate Impulses on their Minds." They also cautioned against the antirevivalists, who condemned the whole work as Satanic because of these excesses. They believed that a moderate course between opposition and enthusiasm was the most prudent. The Separates, who "vented diverse erroneous and dangerous Principles, calculated to overthrow the Institution of the Gospel Ministry," had to be exposed.[14]

The Association assembled testimonies against Elisha Paine. James Cogswell, who had as much reason as anyone to dislike Paine, testified that Paine had cornered him after one of Cogswell's sermons and told him, "I had rather have been burnt at the Stake than to have heard such a Sermon." Paine accused Cogswell of neglecting the role of the Holy Spirit in conversion. When Cogswell explained that he thought saving faith involved "Receiving and Embracing CHRIST in all his Offices," Paine said that he "talked like the Papists, or that this was Popish Doctrine." Others testified that Paine promoted separation as a means to achieve a pure church. The association doubted whether anyone could perfectly discern the elect from the damned in the visible church, suggesting again the evangelical split over the witness of the Spirit and the sure knowledge of those who were saved.[15]

The members of the Windham Association began to receive sharp criticism from area Separates, some of whom questioned the moderate evangelicals' salvation. Lest we think that only Old Lights had their conversions questioned, consider the letter Eleazar Wheelock received from a Plainfield, Connecticut, radical in 1744. Wheelock had begun preaching against Separatism in his itinerant tours, prompting Nathaniel French to ask him, "Do you think you are out of danger of committing the unpardonable sin against the holy ghost: itt would not surprise mee much to hear that God had opened the flood gates of his wrath and lett out the horrors of conscience on you: and many more of your party who deny the truth." French recalled that he had confronted Wheelock publicly at the Plainfield church, challenging him to prove from Scripture that untutored exhorters were not permissible. French cited I Corinthians 14, where Paul permitted prophets to speak in church meetings, but Wheelock argued that "these Scriptures were not meant for these days wherein the Extraordinary gifts of the holy ghost were ceased from the church." French called Wheelock a "secret opposer" of God's work, worse than the open opponents, and "most like the devil." Wheelock called him deluded, but French said, "if this bee delusion lett mee have more of it: and if you have none of this you are no Christian." French regretted Wheelock's opposition, noting that he seemed "strangely fallen" from his zealous support for the revivals a couple years earlier. With the encouragement of the Canterbury radicals, the Plainfield Separates would start a new church, ordaining their first pastor in 1746.[16]

In spite of the Windham Association's attempts to prevent it, in January 1745 fifty-seven Canterbury Separates signed a new church covenant that repudiated the Saybrook Platform and denied magisterial control over the churches. Those who separated at Canterbury had dense family connections and may have also had common political allegiances represented by the Paine brothers. The group's first choice as pastor, understandably, was Elisha Paine, but he declined the position, perhaps growing fearful of prosecution. He soon left for Long Island, where in friendlier climes he settled as pastor of a Separate church in Bridgehampton.[17] John Cleaveland refused the Canterbury pastorate for the reasons described above. Finally, the church agreed to call Solomon Paine, who proved an articulate leader of the Separate movement in Connecticut until his death in 1754.

Paine accepted the church's call, but not before a significant struggle over the meaning of baptism. Believing that he had the right "to do all Christian offices &c. as the Lord should call," Paine studied all the responsibilities of a pastor until he was confident he could fulfill his duties. He "found plain Scripture for all [requirements] but the Baptizing of Infants," but in a dream God showed him that infant baptism was the correct method. Paine led the early fight in Connecticut for liberty of conscience for Separates, who suffered from all manner of persecution, penalties, and abuse from the government and church establishment. In 1748, Solomon Paine and North Stonington minister Matthew Smith presented a petition with 330 signatures to the Connecticut General Assembly, pleading for the right of religious dissent.[18]

The petition presented the history of the British colonies as a great quest for liberty of conscience, that "unalienable Right" given to man by God. "Our Fore-Fathers . . . left their Native Country for an howling Wilderness, full of savage Men and Beasts, that they might have Liberty of Conscience." Paine also noted William and Mary's respect for religious dissenters. Liberty of conscience, then, was at the heart of British constitutionalism, but it was not honored in Connecticut. The Separates "are all exposed, either to make Shipwreck of a good Conscience, or to suffer by Fines or Imprisonment . . . for preaching the Gospel." The petition warned that the judgment of God was coming against the colony should it continue to oppress the Separates. The Assembly, predictably, refused to grant legal relief to them.[19]

The Canterbury church became a mother church for Separates across the region, standing up to the province's persecution. A Separate group in Peekskill, New York, wrote to Solomon Paine in 1747 and expressed a common view of the troubles that the Canterbury Separates faced. A good number of Separates immigrated to eastern New York during this period, perhaps seeking a freer environment. The Peekskill Separates directly associated the Connecticut establishment with Antichrist, "ye Be[a]ste with two Horns Li[ke] a Lam but Speack Li[ke] a Dragon" (referring to Revelation 13:11). Their persecutors set "Latin & greek and Hebrew over Christ" in their requirement of college education for minsters. The Peekskill group encouraged the Canterbury brethren not to fashion themselves "acording to ye traditions of ye pope of Romes Invention" but according to those of the "primitive Church." The Peekskill radicals invited the Paine brothers to visit them soon.[20]

In Norwich, Connecticut, disputes over the Saybrook Platform also precipitated a church schism and launched the career of the most influential Separate Baptist leader of the eighteenth century, Isaac Backus. Backus was converted in Norwich in 1741. The revivals continued in Norwich for two more years, and in June 1743 Norwich's pastor, Benjamin Lord, wrote of "a great and glorious work of divine grace, and a great reformation of religion" transpiring in the area. Lord's church saw ninety-one new full members added between 1741 and 1744, including the church's first Native American and African American full members. Lord feared the excesses of lay exhorters, however, who seem to have sprung up in or visited Norwich and were "so Infatuated by [a] Strange kind of Spirit as to think (Many would think) there was much of the Spirit of God" in them.[21]

REV·ISAAC BACKUS·A͟

Unidentified artist. *Isaac Backus*. Franklin Trask
Library, Andover Newton Theological School.

In late 1744, the church began to squabble over the Saybrook Platform, and its
standards of full membership. It is not clear whether the separation preceded or
followed a relaxing of membership standards, but it does seem that Lord wanted
both to deemphasize personal conversion testimonies for full membership and
to continue an informal compliance with the Saybrook standards through his
involvement with the New London County Ministerial Association. By summer 1745, thirteen members, including Isaac Backus, had withdrawn from the
church. Lord summoned them to explain their absence, and in August 1745, Lord
recorded some of their reasons. Many expressed objections to Lord himself, saying that he denied "the power of godliness" and was not sufficiently supportive
of the late revivals. Some complained that the church had lax membership standards, and that the church did not make "conversion a term of Communion."
Others protested that the church body was committed to the congregational
model of church government, but that Lord had swayed toward Saybrook's pres-

byterian model. One mentioned that Lord was no "friend to Lowly Preaching and Preachers" and that he had banned Andrew Croswell from preaching there. Mary Lathrop may have spoken for most Separates when she stated simply, "By Covenant I am not held here any longer than I am edified." The Separates established a new congregation in the western part of Norwich. The church appears to have benefited both from the radicals' zeal and ongoing frustrations on the west side of town concerning the relatively distant location of Lord's meetinghouse. In any case, the church ordained one of the Separates, Jedidiah Hide, as its first pastor in October 1747. Hide and Backus frequently itinerated together during this period. Hide testified that he separated from Lord's church because "the Gospel [is] not preached here."[22]

Backus later gave his reasons justifying church separations: (1) when "manifest unbelievers are indulged in the Church," (2) when corrupt doctrine is preached, (3) when the true gospel and its messengers are shut out of the church, and (4) when the church admits to membership those who "have the form of Godliness but [deny] the power thereof." Backus cultivated a network of Separates that opponents would call the "Eastern Exhorters." Among these were the Paines, Cleavelands, and Joseph Snow Jr., a Separate pastor in Providence, Rhode Island. In December 1747, Backus and Snow visited Titicut, a new parish in southeastern Massachusetts. Little did Backus know that this would be the place where he would minister for the rest of his life, nor did he anticipate the controversies over baptism and church-state relations that he would soon generate. But as he sat down for dinner at his host family's home, "'em words in John 4.35 to 38, were brought in With great clearness and power upon my Soul, and Thro' 'em Truths I was Led to View a Large field all white to harvest here . . . my hart was so drawn forth towards God, and in love to his People here that I felt willing to Impart not only the gospel to them But my own soul also, because they were made dear unto me; tho' I knew none of 'em personally. Thus the Lord bound me to this People ere I was aware of it." Without seeking the approval of local ministers or officials, the evangelical inhabitants of Titicut asked Backus to help them form a new church. Backus drew up a church covenant, which the new members signed in February 1748.[23]

Backus had no college education, but those who joined the church believed that his spiritual call to the ministry far outweighed his unfamiliarity with classical learning and languages. He later noted that the Separates' and Baptists' ordination of pastors with no college education brought together antirevivalists and moderate evangelicals, who "united their power and endeavored to stop all such proceedings." The Titicut church arranged for his ordination by inviting pastors and delegates from nearby Separate churches. To Solomon Paine they wrote, "The Lord hath appear'd Gloriously for us here . . . & he hath united our hearts in the Choice of our brother Isaac Backus to be our pastor." Paine attended Backus's ordination along with Ebenezer Cleaveland, Jedidiah Hide, and Joseph Snow, among other key Separates. As the ceremony began, a town official and several local ministers arrived and asked them to stop, but the Separates took no heed of them and proceeded to ordain Backus. The twenty-four-year-old threw himself into the work of the church, and the original sixteen members became sixty-one by the end of 1748. Members had to give convincing evidence of their conversion and practiced strict congregational rule. No halfway members were allowed.[24]

Backus and the Titicut Separates faced fines and occasional imprisonment for resisting tax payments to support the established churches in the area. Persecution would not remain as consuming an issue for Backus, however, in light of internal dissent in his church over the mode of baptism. In summer 1749, two church members began to proselytize for believer's baptism, against the time-honored practice of infant baptism. Originally, Backus was stridently opposed to this innovation, as were most ministers across New England, whether Anglican, Presbyterian, or Congregational. Nevertheless, the question of scriptural warrant for infant baptism began to haunt Backus and led him into the most profound spiritual crisis of his life after his conversion.[25]

To most Reformed Christians, rejecting infant baptism seemed both subversive and callous. It struck at the fabric of the social order, which required the passing on of the faith to each successive generation, and it seemed to abandon infant children to fend for themselves outside the church. Baptists, of course, saw the matter much differently. They saw no clear command for infant baptism in Scripture but noticed plenty of evidence, particularly in the book of Acts, to suggest that baptism was for those who had put their faith in Christ for salvation. To them, the ritual was not a mark of entrance into the covenanted community, parallel to the Old Testament practice of circumcision. Instead, baptism was a symbol of the spiritual death and resurrection experienced in conversion.

Baptists had been present in the colonies from their beginnings. Massachusetts had outlawed Baptists in the 1640s as dangerous incendiaries. The Baptists achieved informal toleration in New England by the late seventeenth century, and in the freer climes of the Middle Colonies, they prospered in the early eighteenth century, particularly under the auspices of the Philadelphia Baptist Association, founded in 1707. Before the revivals of the 1740s, however, Baptists in America had little connection to the developing evangelical movement, with the exceptions of the German Baptist communities of Pennsylvania that were deeply affected by Pietism and the occasional Baptist congregation that welcomed Whitefield.

All this changed when radical evangelicalism began to promote a new primitivism and concern for the absolute purity of the church. Most Separate churches, as well as established evangelical ministers like Jonathan Edwards, rejected New England's Halfway Covenant, which allowed baptized but unconverted parents to baptize their children. Separates and some other evangelicals saw this practice as a corrupt concession, allowing the unregenerate to share in one of the two most sacred privileges of church members (the other was the Lord's Supper). Some Separates, however, took the abandonment of the Halfway Covenant one logical step further, to the conviction that baptizing unregenerate children meant that the church would necessarily have unregenerate pseudo-members. Some began to wonder whether baptizing infants was just a remaining corrupt practice not remedied by the Reformation. When they returned to Scripture, they realized that a plain reading gave little direct justification for baptizing infants. Some Separates, therefore, began to see baptism simply as a public recognition of conversion. Baptizing only converted believers would clear up all confusion regarding the status of infants: though believing parents would raise them in the church, children could not in any sense join the church until they showed hopeful signs that they had been born again.[26]

Backus must have wondered about these matters even before they became an open controversy in his church in August 1749. Otherwise, one could hardly conceive of his decision late in that month to come out—temporarily—against infant baptism. He spent a great deal of time in prayer seeking direction about the matter, until suddenly he came to the conclusion that Baptist principles must be right precisely "because I felt Such a Strugling against it." Backus assumed that if tradition strongly supported some theological notion, it was likely to be proved wrong by a plain reading of Scripture. Thus, in August 1749 he told his congregation "that none had any right to baptism but Believers, and that plunging, Seemed the only right mode." Even as he preached, however, Backus had second thoughts, and within a month his mind was "turned back to infant baptism."[27]

Backus could not dismiss believer's baptism, however, and struggled with the question for the next two years. Finally, in July 1751 Backus announced to his church that he could find no grounding in Scripture for infant baptism. This was no easy decision, not only because of pressure against it from outside the church, but also because a majority of his church members were opposed to believer's baptism. In August, Backus took a final step in his personal journey to Baptist convictions by receiving believer's baptism himself. Benjamin Pierce, a visiting

Baptist pastor from Rhode Island, held a service in Titicut at which Backus gave his conversion testimony and "went down Into the Water with him And was Baptized." This move put many in his congregation into a "jumble," he wrote.[28]

The "jumble" at Titicut persisted for months and a church council was called to address the "Unhappy Divisions" caused by "Isaac Backus his Travail in Baptism." The church had almost ceased to function because of divisions over baptism, and Backus had stopped trying to enforce church discipline, even in flagrant cases. Backus could not agree to a proposed covenant renewal, and for a time he left to go back to Norwich. He was recalled to pastor the Titicut church under a mixed-communion plan, which accepted either infant or believer's baptism for membership. This never worked very well, and the church staggered along in debilitating disagreement for five more years.[29]

The Separates and Baptists were very close to one another theologically, but their split over baptism allowed no ultimate reconciliation. For instance, although he once entertained the idea of becoming a Baptist, Wethersfield's Separate pastor Ebenezer Frothingham was calling believer's baptism the "mystery of iniquity" by 1752. After many tumults in local congregations, the Baptists and Separates held a synod in Stonington, Connecticut, on May 29, 1754, to decide whether they could continue in mixed communion. The Paines argued that either the paedobaptist "sins in making infants the subject of baptism" or the antipaedobaptist sins "in cutting them off" from baptism. They recognized, probably correctly, that there was no point in trying to hold the two groups together, despite their common origins. In a key vote, the Separates at the synod carried a bare majority to close communion against Baptists. Backus continued to try and salvage a Separate-Baptist union, but to little avail. In 1756 Backus decided to make a final break and start a Baptist church that would only accept believer's baptism for membership. Once at Norwich and twice at Titicut, Backus helped to engineer separations in the name of church purity.[30]

Rhode Island also witnessed church separations, though in its freer religious atmosphere potential schismatics did not have to fear civil penalties. Backus's friend Joseph Snow led a separation from Providence's Congregational church in 1744. The Separate congregation originally invited Elisha Paine to become its pastor. Upon receiving his refusal they offered the position to Snow, who turned the congregation into one of Providence's strongest, while the Congregational church slowly faded away.[31]

The most interesting church separation in Rhode Island was among the Narragansetts of Westerly. Joseph Park had seen a significant revival in his church among British Americans and Indians. No doubt influenced by radical supporters of James Davenport, who itinerated in the area with success, many of the

Narragansett evangelicals became enthusiastic and fractious. They followed the preaching of the Narragansett exhorter Samuel Niles, whom some of the English regarded with disdain. The skeptical pastor Joseph Fish many years later recorded that Niles was illiterate and thus was "in imminent danger of leaving The Word, for the Guidence of Feelings, Impressions, Visions, Appearances and Directions of Angels and of Christ himself in a Visionary Way." Around 1745, a group of about a hundred Narragansetts withdrew from Park's church, set up their own congregation, and ordained Niles themselves, since no other Separates would do it. The church accepted both infant and believer's baptism. The congregation seems eventually to have dissolved, though a Narragansett church in nearby Charlestown may have had connections to the Westerly Separates.[32]

One might wonder about the lasting significance of New England Separatism, since only a few of the hundreds of new congregations endured, and many turned Baptist. Perhaps their most important lasting effect was the exporting of the Separate Baptist movement to the Middle Colonies, and especially to the South. The new Baptist churches heavily influenced the northern colonies, but in the South the movement exploded and, along with the Methodists and Presbyterians, later helped turn the South into the Bible Belt.

The critical early figures in carrying the Separate Baptist movement to the South were Shubal Stearns and his brother-in-law Daniel Marshall. Stearns was one of the most important figures in early American religious history, but a lack of primary sources blocks a surer account of his career. He was converted during Whitefield's awakening and helped organize a Separate congregation at Tolland in northeastern Connecticut, where he worked as an exhorter and pastor. Stearns participated in the Separates' largely futile efforts in the late 1740s to win toleration in Connecticut. Like many other New England Separates, he was also lured by the consistency of Baptist theology. In 1751, Stonington's Baptist minister, Wait Palmer, converted Stearns and much of his extended family to Baptist principles, baptized them by immersion, and helped them organize a Baptist church in Tolland. Soon Stearns was ordained as minister over the new congregation.[33]

Daniel Marshall was married to Stearns's younger sister Martha, and the couple relocated in the late 1740s to Onnaquaggy, a mission village among the Mohawks on the Susquehanna River in Pennsylvania. After about a year and a half, the Marshalls left the mission and drifted south, eventually arriving in Winchester, Virginia. Probably through the influence of Stearns and local Separate Baptists, Marshall and his family accepted baptism by immersion around 1753. Near the same time, Stearns began to contemplate leaving Connecticut for the South, where he had heard that thousands lived without access to Baptist minis-

ters. Stearns and his family left Tolland in 1754 and were reunited with the Marshalls in Virginia. They settled briefly north of Winchester but soon decided to
travel farther south, arriving at Sandy Creek, North Carolina, in 1755. Stearns's
family and companions constituted a new Baptist church there in November
1755. Marshall settled to the southwest at Abbot's Creek, North Carolina, where
he was also ordained as a Baptist minister. Stearns and Marshall would help lead
the enormous growth of Separate Baptist churches in the southern backcountry that in the early nineteenth century would help make the South profoundly
evangelical.[34]

In a sense, the split between the Separates and the established churches insti-
tutionalized the rift between moderate and radical evangelicals. Not all radicals
became Separates, and not all Separates became Baptists, but in New England
many of the most notable long-term radicals, men like John Cleaveland, Daniel
Rogers, the Paine brothers, and Andrew Croswell, did indeed find a home
within the Separate movement. The Separates united around commitments to
immediate, discernible conversions and the right of uneducated laypeople to exhort, itinerate, and even to become ordained ministers. In the case of the Westerly Separates, Native American radicals promoted the independent leadership
and ordination of one of their own, a move that even white radicals rarely countenanced. The Baptists rejected not only halfway membership, but infant baptism itself, in the radical quest for a fully converted church membership. The
Separates and Baptists, then, formalized the radical impulse and helped to break
down the legal hegemony of the established Congregational churches of New
England. In the 1750s, they began to export their noisy, populist religious style
to the largely unchurched reaches of the southern backcountry.

"Bringing Them to a Subjection to the Religion of Jesus": Native American Missions

Many Anglo-American colonists had long expressed interest in proselytizing among the Indians, and the new revival movement spurred evangelicals to send more missionaries to Native Americans. White evangelical ministers used the spectacle of Native American conversions as a way to generate interest in and promote the legitimacy of the revivals. Stories about Christianizing the Indians had always served to confirm the validity of the colonists' endeavors in British eyes. Benjamin Colman reported to George Whitefield in 1742, in a letter subsequently printed in the *Glasgow-Weekly-History*, that "among the Mokeag, Pequot, Niantick, and other Tribes of the obstinate infidel Indians, a general Concern hath come upon them for their Souls Instruction and Salvation." Before 1742, European relations with the Indians were characterized by violence, imperial expansion, and sporadic attempts at evangelization by most Christian denominations. Although most Native American tribes faced grievous social disorder brought on by epidemic disease and war, many maintained their existence in the Atlantic coast colonies, even as the frontier moved west. Mission agencies, drawing financial support from British sources, never lost interest in bringing the gospel to the "poor Indians." Colonists saw Indian missions as both spiritually and politically beneficial, as reflected in Ebenezer Pemberton's 1758 note to Eleazar Wheelock: "Nothing can be more Agreable to our Christian Character tha[n to] send the Gospel to the benighted Pagans; Nothing mor[e] Conducive to our Civil Interests than to bring them to a Subjection to the Religion of Jesus." Not only would missions presumably save Native Americans from an eternity in hell, but they might also secure the Indian nations' vital support in the wars between Catholic and Protestant imperial powers that overshadowed America during the mid-eighteenth century.[1]

During the 1740s, white evangelicals made some inroads among Native Americans and began to entertain the possibility of an interracial evangelical movement. Young, earnest Anglo-American missionaries believed that willingness to serve in these missions was a mark of true spirituality. The missions often ended in disappointment, as workers regularly complained of poor supplies, tenuous health, and uninterested Indians. Hundreds of Anglican, dissenting, and Moravian missionaries went to the Native Americans of New England and New York between 1700 and 1775, and the majority spent only a few years or less in the field. Nevertheless, some stalwarts like John Brainerd and Gideon Hawley spent decades of their adult lives on mission. Soon the evangelical movement saw the emergence of key Native American pastors and missionaries, too. These Native Americans rarely enjoyed fair treatment within the movement, leading some to separate from white evangelicals and start their own independent churches. Some even decided to establish an independent Christian Indian settlement at Brothertown, New York. Christian Native Americans' efforts proved among the most effective in preserving a distinct Indian identity in the swelling sea of British-American culture. Leaders of Brothertown and other Christian Native Americans sometimes resisted assimilation into dominant English society, ironically, by creating their own distinct forms of evangelical Christianity.[2]

Given its central place in the history of early American evangelicalism, it is no surprise that Long Island saw the first sustained missionary effort emerging directly from the revivals of the early 1740s. This mission was undertaken by Azariah Horton, a native of Southold, Long Island, the home of James Davenport. Horton, a 1735 Yale graduate, was fired with evangelistic zeal but also ran afoul of radical exhorters on Long Island. Horton preached in New Providence, New Jersey, during 1740–41, where he won the confidence of Ebenezer Pemberton of New York, who led the moderate evangelical New York Presbytery. The Presbytery, with funding from the Society in Scotland for Propagating Christian Knowledge (SSPCK), ordained Horton in 1741 and sent him as a missionary to the Montauks and Shinnecocks on the southern shore of Long Island.[3]

James Robe of Kilsyth, Scotland, with encouragement from Pemberton, arranged for Horton's letters and missionary journals to be published in his *Christian Monthly History* (Edinburgh), so we must understand Horton's accounts of his Long Island ministry as written with a transatlantic evangelical audience in mind. Robe thought that readers would be "pleasantly entertained" by these journals and that the conversions of Native Americans would lead antirevivalist skeptics to "see God's wondrous Works, declaring his Name to be near." Robe bluntly expressed hope that "Christian rich People" would read the accounts and give more money to spread the gospel "among the Heathen."[4]

Horton's journal opened with a note that the Indians among whom he worked had initially been evangelized by James Davenport and others. He wanted to place himself in the context of Connecticut and Long Island evangelicalism, and his insistence on mentioning Davenport reminds us of Davenport's early centrality to the evangelical movement. Horton then described how in his own mission to the Indians he worked up and down the island, visiting "from Wigwaam to Wigwaam." His goal was to "make them sensible, that there was a God . . . , that he was holy, and would punish the Wicked." Once he had convinced them of their sin, he hoped to point the Indians to "the Way of Reconciliation by Jesus Christ." Soon there appeared considerable concern among the Montauks and Shinnecocks, some of whom were "awakened to a very lively Sense of their Desert of Hell and Damnation." To reassure his audience of the Indians' gratefulness for his coming, he noted the "repeated Thanks" and joyful reception they gave him.[5]

Horton seemed to enjoy particular success among Montauk and Shinnecock women, and the vast majority of individual references in his journals were to "Squaws." One woman related how she felt a desperate need for salvation. She told him that she found Christ "exceedingly lovely." While she spoke, she choked back tears and spontaneously praised God "in such the Expressions, 'Good God! blessed Lord Jesus!'" During an exhortation by Horton at Montauk, one woman began trembling, and she "cried out in such like Expressions and Importunity, 'Lord Jesus, take away my stony Heart' dear Lord Jesus save 'or I perish.'" He regularly noted that girls and women were "ravished with a Sense of the Love of Christ." Though he tended toward moderation, Horton was pleased with these emotional responses to his ministry.[6]

Some Indians applied Horton's exhortations in ways that he may not have expected. In early 1742, he commented on an Indian exhorter at Montauk who spoke in the Montauks' language about the gospel of Christ. Horton was always hampered by his need for translators, but this man faced no such barriers. Horton checked with English speakers to see what the man was saying and was satisfied that the exhorter sought "the best Good of his Fellow Indians." Another man, near death, claimed that he "saw Christ, and hoped that he should go to a good Place." Horton was happy to hear of his assurance but warned, "Now I don't suppose that he saw Christ with his bodily Eyes, by reason the Indians often use the Expression of seeing, when, upon further Enquiry, they say they see with their Hearts." Most evangelical leaders balked at any suggestion that someone had actually seen Christ, but we cannot know what this dying man meant by stating that he "saw Christ."[7]

The height of the Indian revival on Long Island came in September 1742, when many at Montauk experienced "astonishing Views of the glorious Fullness and Excellency of Christ." Horton remarked that he had never seen "so much of Heaven in the short Course of my Ministry, as at this astonishing Season!" The next February he welcomed the visiting missionary David Brainerd. Brainerd preached for a couple days at Montauk to some success. Soon thereafter, however, Horton began to complain about the arrival of meddling exhorters. On March 6, the same day that James Davenport held his book burning in New London across the Long Island Sound, Horton wrote that his prospects were no longer as encouraging as the previous fall because the exhorters' "Manner of Procedure create Jars and Disagreements among [the Indians], and hence are the Occasion of strengthening the Interest of Satan." Surely some of these exhorters were among Davenport's followers, as Davenport had spent the winter of 1742–43 in Southold fighting to keep his pastorate. Horton began to cast his lot with the moderate evangelicals and against the radicals and Separates. In November 1743, Horton lamented that in his periodic absences from the Indians, some apparent converts fell away, owing "partly to the Prejudice some endeavor to fill their Minds with against me and my Instructions." Soon Horton would have to contend with the presence of the Separate Elisha Paine, who settled at Hay Ground, Long Island, after fleeing Connecticut around 1745. Horton may have grown weary of the arduous mission work, made more complicated by the Separates, and in the late 1740s, Horton endorsed the Mohegan Samson Occom as his successor in the missions to Long Island's Indians. Horton settled as pastor at South Hanover, New Jersey, in 1751 and died in 1777 of smallpox, contracted while ministering to the Continental Army.[8]

Unlike Horton, most new evangelical missionaries after the awakenings of the 1740s focused on reaching Native Americans on the frontier of Anglo-American settlement, with an aim of extending Protestant influence into the backcountry. Beyond the purpose of saving "heathen" souls, Samuel Hopkins (the elder) of West Springfield, Massachusetts, believed such missions would spare the frontier Indians from the "enticing Insinuations of Romish Emissaries" of the "French Interest." The model for these missions was John Sergeant's work among the Housatonics of Stockbridge, Massachusetts. The New England Company, a leading missionary society, had appointed Sergeant in 1734 to go to the Housatonics after their leaders agreed to receive a missionary. Other Mahican Indians scorned the Housatonics for accepting Sergeant, but they apparently saw in the British Christians' overtures a possible new source of spiritual power and a means of preserving cultural integrity. Mission Indians rarely seemed to view conversion as a wholesale abandonment of their traditions in favor of British ways.[9]

Sergeant enjoyed early success among the Housatonics, and by the end of 1735 he had baptized nearly forty of them. Benjamin Colman, one of the commissioners of the SSPCK, was delighted with Sergeant's successes, particularly in light of other recent disappointments among the Indians of Maine, who preferred French Catholicism. Earlier missionaries had failed among the "Papisted Indians," but now Colman saw "an open and effectual Door at Housatunnuk." The New England Company arranged for Sergeant to be ordained in August 1735. Sergeant was joined by schoolmaster Timothy Woodbridge, and plans developed for a new Indian town, Stockbridge, which Massachusetts chartered in 1739. Sergeant anticipated that soon hundreds of Housatonics would be delivered from their "gross Darkness." God had wrought a "remarkable Reformation" among them.[10]

Despite the successful establishment of Stockbridge, Sergeant became more pessimistic about the mission's prospects by the early 1740s. Even as revivals commenced among British settlers, he wondered if he would ever see real transformation among the Housatonics. Even some originally promising proselytes were falling back into drunkenness. He guardedly expressed his fears to Stephen Williams when he asked "whether the rejecting the grace & salvation of the Gospel will not be an aggravating circumstance in the punishment of Reprobates?" If most Mahicans ultimately refused to embrace the Christian gospel, was he making their judgment that much worse? To a top SSPCK official, Sergeant wrote that the "Indians are a very difficult People to deal with" and that "obstinate Patience" was required of any missionary among them. In 1741, Sergeant took a generally unsuccessful missionary trip, along with some of his Housatonic converts, into the backcountry. He visited a Shawnee village along the Susquehanna River, but those Shawnees who would stay to listen to him disputed his message, demonstrating "strong and invincible Prejudices against Christianity, at least the Protestant Religion; deriv'd, it shou'd seem, from the French." The French had supposedly told the Shawnees that the British meant only to enslave them. Sergeant returned to Stockbridge discouraged. Focusing on his Indian missions, Sergeant kept his distance from the new evangelical movement and seems to have wavered between a moderate evangelical and antirevivalist position.[11]

In the later years of his mission, Sergeant and his supporters began to contemplate a new strategy for transforming the Indians of Stockbridge. In a published letter to Benjamin Colman, Sergeant proposed building a boarding school for the Indian youths, where the English missionaries could "change their whole Way of Living" before they became recalcitrant as adults. But the outbreak of new war with France and continued lack of interest, especially by potential benefactors in New England, stalled the project indefinitely. Sergeant became even more pessimistic about the Indians' "great national and fundamental Vices . . . , Idleness and Drunkenness." In his final years, Sergeant remained conflicted about Native Americans' potential for change: "unless this People are . . . under a Curse from Heaven," they could change through conversion and cultivation. "Except their Complection, I see nothing, in this People, but that they may be cultivated into as agreable as any other." At his death from fever and a throat canker in 1749, Sergeant suspected that he had made little progress in cultivating them.[12]

Sergeant's death presented an opportunity for Jonathan Edwards, who was dismissed from his congregation in 1750. In Northampton, he had argued that only parents who were full communicant members of the church should be allowed to have their children baptized. This was a decidedly unpopular repudiation of his grandfather Stoddard's more inclusive policy, and it led to his removal. Although it would be a mistake to equate Edwards's repudiation with widespread weakness in New England's evangelical movement, he was one of the most visible evangelical leaders, and his congregation had experienced the best-known revival in the Anglo-American world. His dismissal, then, at least signaled his own church's bitter repudiation of his evangelical ideal of a pure church of converted saints. Edwards's and his colleagues' attention to Native American missions, moreover, proceeded during a decade of relative quiet with regard to revivals in New England.[13]

Edwards and his family moved to Stockbridge in 1751. In general, Edwards appears to have become sympathetic to the Indians' spiritual potential as he worked at Stockbridge. He, like almost all of his British contemporaries, had no appreciation for Indian religions or traditions. Nevertheless, Edwards saw the Indians as less blameworthy than Europeans who had access to the true gospel and denied it. Because of Edwards's consistent application of the doctrine of original sin, he saw Indians and Europeans as equal in their depravity and their potential for redemption. If anything, the Stockbridge Indians seemed to Edwards more inclined to receive the gospel than did his fellow British colonists.[14]

Edwards and his family generally liked Stockbridge, especially given the roiling controversies they left behind in Northampton. Edwards's daughter Esther loved the skating and sledding offered in the winters and recorded how Indian boys pulled her sled through the hills. Edwards was there on serious business, however. He was intensely aware of the French Catholic menace to the north and feared Catholic missionaries' influence among the Indians. Not only did the Catholics lead them astray spiritually, but the Indians' political and military allegiance lay in the balance as well. Like many Britons at the time, Edwards took an apocalyptic view of the ongoing conflict between the world's Catholic and Protestant powers. Indian missions were a critical front in that war. The French were trying to "establish their interest among all the Indian nations in North America, and to alienate them from the British interest." The only hope for the British was "instructing [the Indians] thoroughly in the Protestant religion, and educating their children," he wrote. Edwards pushed hard to see Sergeant's planned boarding school succeed and insisted that Indian children be taught "things, as well as words." Moreover, they needed to learn English, for "Indian languages are extremely barbarous and barren, and very ill-fitted for communicating things moral and divine."[15]

Edwards's aspirations seemed relatively simple, but his continuing feud with the wealthy Williams clan of the Connecticut River valley threw a wrench into his plans. Edwards especially disliked John Sergeant's widow, the former Abigail Williams, who secured an appointment as mistress of the girls' boarding school at Stockbridge. He also disapproved of the Williamses' instructor at the boys' school, Captain Martin Kellogg. Edwards thought there was enough nepotism and mismanagement at the mission "to make one sick." In 1752 Edwards secured the melancholic Gideon Hawley, a recent Yale graduate, as the new instructor at the boarding school. Edwards's former ally, Brigadier General Joseph Dwight, proposed marriage to Abigail Sergeant in 1752, and soon Dwight turned against Edwards and Hawley. Hawley, perhaps an easier target than the intimidating Edwards, received a tongue-lashing from an irate Dwight, who told Hawley that he was "of no judgment, of no prudence . . . [and] a mischief-maker." Months later, under suspicious circumstances, the boarding school, along with Hawley's property and library, burned in February 1753. That was enough for Hawley, who soon departed for a mission among the Oneidas. But the bitter squabbling continued, and the mission and schools declined precipitously over the next couple years. The controversy was not settled until 1754, when Isaac Hollis, the chief British benefactor of the mission, stepped in and appointed Edwards as the director of the boarding school. By the next spring, however, a paltry six Indian students were left, their families having grown weary of the British feuding.[16]

During Edwards's tenure at Stockbridge he spent much of his time composing theological treatises, including two of his greatest, *Freedom of the Will* and *Original Sin*. Thus his contributions to Native American missions were limited. But Edwards's legacy in the historiography of Native American proselytization, and Christian missions generally, was foundational because of his sponsorship of David Brainerd. In fact, Edwards's *The Life of David Brainerd* became his most popular and often-reprinted work. Brainerd entered Yale in 1739, and the sickly student was inspired by Whitefield, Tennent, and Ebenezer Pemberton to become "abundantly engaged" in the evangelical cause. Brainerd befriended fellow evangelical students Samuel Buell and Samuel Hopkins, and in 1741 he came under the influence of James Davenport, who openly challenged Yale rector Thomas Clap during the 1741 commencement. Brainerd listened approvingly to Edwards's commencement address *The Distinguishing Marks*, which argued that enthusiastic excesses did not negate the overwhelming good in the revivals.[17]

Testy Yale officials voted in 1741 to punish any students who suggested that they were unconverted. Soon thereafter, Brainerd was overheard commenting that tutor Chauncey Whittelsey had "no more grace than a chair," and when Brainerd refused to confess to the statement, he was expelled. He found support from key evangelical ministers Joseph Bellamy and Jonathan Dickinson and was licensed to preach in July 1742 by a clerical association in Connecticut. Brainerd began to contemplate the possibility of a mission to Native Americans, and by late 1742 he received an appointment as a missionary through the Correspondents of the SSPCK, who had also commissioned Azariah Horton. In Brainerd's diary, his own emotions were on display as much or more than his ministry, and he reflected that he "scarce ever felt myself so unfit to exist, as now: I saw I was not worthy of a place among the Indians." Evangelical missionaries and itinerants regularly expressed self-debasing sentiments, but it is often difficult to discern whether they reflected an exaggerated humility or darker self-loathing. In March 1743, Brainerd visited Sergeant's Stockbridge mission, during which time his "mind was overwhelmed with an exceeding gloominess and melancholy," as Edwards noted. To Bellamy, Brainerd wrote that he often felt as if he was "placed alone in the midst of an immense vacuum or empty space," and that the "Eternal God methinks (if indeed there be any such Being, which indeed I cannot conceive to be oftentimes,) is not sufficient to make my poor immortal soul happy. . . . I'm ready to wish to be annihilated." The roller coaster of alternating intense commitment and near skepticism marked Brainerd's meteoric career.[18]

West of Stockbridge, Brainerd began ministering to a group of Mahicans at Kaunaumeek, New York, where Sergeant had periodically preached since 1737. Brainerd, then twenty-five years old, was assaulted with feelings of loneliness and worthlessness. He did not seem to like his intended proselytes very much. His journal, even with Edwards's editing, became a showcase for Brainerd's morbid emotions. On balance, Edwards seems not to have been troubled by Brainerd's extreme melancholy, recognizing that a desperate sense of powerlessness and sin often turned one's heart toward God. "It seemed to me I deserved to be kicked out of the world," Brainerd wrote, but "'tis good for me to be afflicted . . . , that

I may die wholly to this world." He seemed particularly troubled by his earlier zealous behavior at Yale, and by 1743 he had repudiated the radical spirit that he had embraced only a year earlier. In a letter to Joseph Bellamy, he particularly worried about the effects of James Davenport's New London book burning, reporting that he had heard that Davenport even burnt the Old Testament. When he went to New Haven for commencement in September 1743, Brainerd tried to regulate radical behavior he encountered along the way. In Horseneck, Connecticut, he sought to "moderate some noisy sort of persons that appeared to me to be [actuated] by unseen spiritual pride." He worked against "wildfire party zeal" and privately counseled some to avoid "some confusions that I perceived were among the people." At Yale, Brainerd unsuccessfully tried to reconcile with the college officials and wrote a letter of apology for his comment about Whittelsey's lack of grace.[19]

After a year at Kaunaumeek, Brainerd and the Correspondents of the SSPCK decided it would be best to merge his mission with Sergeant's and to reassign Brainerd to another Indian mission. Brainerd received an offer to settle as a pastor at Easthampton, Long Island, the position Samuel Buell would eventually accept. But Brainerd was determined to continue evangelizing Native Americans, despite the meager success he encountered at Kaunaumeek. He struggled to find the right place, however, as a proposed mission at the "Forks of the Delaware" fell through. Brainerd prayed for a spiritual breakthrough among the Indians, but admitted that he saw "nothing *special* among them." The absence of revival proved an opportunity for the devil to tempt him with the thought that "there is no God . . . , or if there be, he is not able to convert the Indians."[20]

From the Forks of the Delaware, Brainerd wrote to Ebenezer Pemberton and the Correspondents of the SSPCK, assessing his mission work over the past year. He hoped that some of his labors had born fruit, but overall he found the "Christianizing of these poor pagans" very difficult. Among the chief obstacles to his mission, he thought, was the profane, corrupt behavior of European settlers. Also, the Indians were "extremely attached to the customs, traditions, and fabulous notions of their fathers." The "foundation" of all their beliefs was separate creation, or the idea that a different God had created them than the one who created white people. This belief led many Delawares to reject the Europeans' offers of salvation, for only Indian traditions offered hope for their race. Finally, their nomadic ways made consistent instruction difficult to sustain. Only prayer could break down the spiritual barriers that stood between white missionaries and these tribes, Brainerd thought.[21]

Not until late summer 1745 did Brainerd settle on a focused mission, this time among a group of Delaware Indians at Crossweeksung and Cranberry, New Jersey. The Delawares of central New Jersey proved much more receptive than those at the Forks, in part because of the enormous cultural and economic dislocations they had suffered at the hands of European colonists. In New Jersey, Brainerd finally broke through to substantial numbers of Delawares and led a considerable awakening. His perseverance was no doubt assisted by a number of local Log College pastors, most notably William Tennent Jr. of Freehold. He was also surely encouraged by the assistance of his Native American translator, Moses Tattamy, whom Brainerd baptized in 1745. The height of the conversions came in early August. At one meeting, Brainerd reported, "most were much affected . . . and some few could neither go nor stand, but lay flat on the ground, as if pierced at heart, crying incessantly for mercy." The next day, at a meeting of about sixty-five Delawares, the Spirit came like "the irresistible force of a mighty torrent." Persons of all ages were affected. One of the "principal" leaders among them was brought to tears because of his sins against God, while another old man, whom Brainerd characterized as a murderer, conjurer, and drunkard, pleaded with God for mercy. Soon Brainerd baptized twenty-five converts.[22]

He noted with satisfaction that despite the intensity of the revival, "There has here been no appearance of those Convulsions, bodily Agonies, frightful Screamings, Swoonings . . . Visions, Trances, [or] Imaginations of being under prophetick Inspiration." Once during a private meeting at his house, a convert began to cry "Oh, blessed Lord, do come, do come!" She remained enraptured and kept shouting similar phrases. Brainerd thought this outburst was acceptable, because it sprang from "a true spiritual discovery of the glory, ravishing beauty, and excellency of Christ." It did not feature "any gross imaginary notions of his human nature; such as that of seeing him in such a place or posture, as hanging on a cross, as bleeding, dying, as gently smiling . . . ; which delusions some have been carried away with." Brainerd had come to deliver the Indians from their pagan enthusiasm and would not allow them to substitute pseudo-Christian ecstasies. Edwards commended Brainerd for his opposition to visionary experiences, writing that the diary featured "no one instance of a strong impression on his imagination through his whole life . . . no imaginary sight of Christ . . . no sight of heaven . . . no sight of the Book of Life . . . no hearing God or Christ immediately speaking to him . . . no new objective revelations, no sudden strong suggestions of secret facts." To Edwards, any immediate sensory perception of God in this life was almost certainly a delusion. Brainerd showed that one could be intensely pious while eschewing such extremes.[23]

Rambling soothed Brainerd's melancholy, so even after the great successes in central New Jersey he quickly departed to seek out more Indians to whom he had not yet preached. He visited the large Indian town of Shamokin, on the Susquehanna River, where he discoursed with the "Delaware king" about Christianity. Brainerd concluded that "the devil now reigns in the most eminent manner" in the town. He also visited the Delawares of Juniata Island, where Brainerd sunk into deeper despair as "they now seemed resolved to retain their pagan notions and persist in their idolatrous practices." He witnessed a ceremonial dance around a bonfire during which the Indians sacrificed ten deer. The next day conjurers sought to discern the reasons for epidemic fever and dysentery, which had visited the island. Brainerd distastefully noted how they made "all the wild, ridiculous, and distracted motions imaginable; sometimes singing, sometimes howling . . . grunting, puffing, etc." He no doubt saw these actions as reminiscent of the radical Christian enthusiasts' extremes and found it all thoroughly depressing.[24]

Brainerd considered one encounter on Juniata Island particularly troubling and yet intriguing: he met a Delaware prophet, a "restorer, of what he supposed was the ancient religion of the Indians." His ceremonial garb was "pontifical," and he wore a large wooden mask. At first the prophet danced in front of Brainerd and shook a tortoise-shell rattle at him, but soon the two began to discuss religion. "Some of my discourse he seemed to like; but some of it he disliked entirely," Brainerd wrote. The prophet told Brainerd that he opposed the Indians' corruptions, such as abusing alcohol. The racial image of the drunken Indian resonated as a serious problem in Brainerd's mind, and he welcomed the prophet's stance against intemperance. Brainerd thought that the prophet had a serious, well-considered religion. As Brainerd told him about Christian doctrine the prophet would "sometimes say, 'Now that I like: so God has taught me.'" But the prophet disagreed with Brainerd on key points: he denied the existence of the devil, and he argued that good people gained admission in death to "a beautiful town with spiritual walls," while bad people had to hover outside the town forever. No doubt Brainerd saw in the Delaware prophet a man not unlike himself, as other Indians derided the prophet as a "precise zealot that made a needless noise about religious matters." Indeed, Brainerd concluded that "there was something in his temper and disposition that looked more like true religion than anything I ever observed amongst other heathens." This prophet was part of a larger nativist revival among the Delawares that called for a return to traditional practices and a rejection of European culture. It was a movement with which Brainerd found a strange, fleeting sympathy.[25]

By November 1745 Brainerd had baptized forty-seven Delawares, half of them adults and half children, and most of them at Crossweeksung. Despite his successes, Brainerd had his detractors among local whites, some of whom stirred up the preposterous rumor that Brainerd was an agent of the Catholic Pretender to Britain's throne, Bonnie Prince Charlie. This rumor reveals the continuing cultural utility of anti-Catholicism and fear of Jacobites (those who supported the restoration of the Catholic Stuart line to the British throne) in the colonies. In January 1746, the colonies received word of Bonnie Prince Charlie's attempted overthrow of King George II. Now Brainerd's opponents suggested that he, backed by a Scottish missions agency, was working for the Jacobites. In particular, locals whispered that Brainerd meant to "draw the Indians into an insurrection against the English." The insinuations appalled Brainerd, who wondered how anyone could mistake a work of God's grace for a "Popish Plot." He thought that his defense of the Indians' rights had stirred up the trouble, as he had criticized European colonists for "making the Indians drunk, and then cheating them out of their lands and other properties." Brainerd suffered opposition from all sides, even as the revival progressed among the Delawares at Crossweeksung.[26]

In late summer 1746, Brainerd took yet another missionary journey up the Susquehanna, but it became clear that his health was in grievous condition. He was regularly coughing up blood, signaling the progress of tuberculosis in his lungs. Upon his return Brainerd convalesced among evangelical friends. To the end, Edwards noted, Brainerd spoke against the radical evangelicalism that had once led him astray. In particular, he railed against the Separates in Connecticut and "a disposition in persons to much noise and show in religion, and affecting to be abundant in proclaiming and publishing their own experiences." Brainerd and Edwards's seventeen-year-old daughter Jerusha apparently fell in love in the last months of both of their lives. She "chiefly tended" the dying Brainerd, who asked her in his last days, "Dear Jerusha, are you willing to part with me? I am quite willing to part with you. . . . Though, if I thought I should not see you and be happy with you in another world, I could not bear to part with you. But we shall spend an happy eternity together!" Jonathan Edwards approved of their spiritual bond. Brainerd soon died, and when Jerusha was taken by an acute fever four months later, Edwards arranged for the two to be buried side-by-side in the Northampton cemetery.[27]

Before he passed away, Brainerd wrote to his brother John, who he expected would take up his missions work in New Jersey. David was concerned that John, too, might be deceived by radical Christianity: "I fear you are not sufficiently aware how much false religion there is in the world: . . . 'tis a brat of hell that always springs up with every revival of religion and stabs and murders the cause of God. . . . Set yourself, my brother, to crush all appearances of this nature among the Indians." John Brainerd had seen his brother expelled from Yale for intemperate zeal, but John himself graduated in 1746, and in April 1747 he was licensed by the New York Presbytery to carry on David's work in New Jersey.[28]

Before he left Crossweeksung, David Brainerd had begun to relocate the Christian Delawares to a more permanent settlement near Cranberry, a place he called Bethel. This was to become the temporary headquarters of John Brainerd's mission. In mid-1747 he estimated that 160 Delawares lived there. John described Bethel as "far better for cultivation and more commodious for such a number as were now collected into one body." Like many white missionaries during the colonial period, the Brainerds agonized over the Indians' nomadic ways. When John arrived at Bethel, he found that the revival was cooling. A "mortal sickness" ravaged the Christian Indians, and skeptics began to argue that the Indians had become sick because they "had forsaken the old Indian ways." Despite the diseases, Bethel grew modestly, and Brainerd maintained an English school there.[29]

John, like David, was comforted by the presence of leading evangelical ministers nearby, whom he regularly visited. Among these were William Tennent Jr., Aaron Burr, and the recovered James Davenport, who had been ministering occasionally in New Jersey. In 1749 Brainerd noted in his diary that he came home from a visit to Tennent to find a sickly Davenport resting at his home. That Sunday, Davenport mustered the energy to preach at Brainerd's church, and Brainerd thought his address generated considerable solemnity among the whites and Indians in attendance. Davenport commended Brainerd's ministry to Jonathan Edwards in a 1751 letter, reporting that Brainerd had enjoyed "some special success lately through mercy," including convictions among both Indians and whites. Davenport would continue to supply pulpits in New Jersey and Virginia until he finally received a permanent appointment at Hopewell and Maidenhead, New Jersey, in 1754. By 1751, Bethel seems to have grown slightly; Brainerd reported to Ezra Stiles that 200 Indians lived there. He still hoped it was "the Beginning of a more glorious Work among the poor benighted Pagans."[30]

John worried, however, that Moravian missionaries might win over prospective Indian converts. On a trip into the Susquehanna Valley, Brainerd found that a number of Indians once influenced by his brother had now settled at Gnadenhütten, the key Moravian mission town in Pennsylvania in the 1740s and 1750s. He found them "entirely brought into their scheme of religion," and "erroneous and enthusiastic" in their new doctrines. Brainerd was particularly concerned that the Moravians did not seem to call for a dramatic conversion experience but instead simply asked proselytes if they loved Jesus because he died for them. If they said they did love him, they were baptized and admitted to the Lord's Supper. Brainerd also worried about the Moravians' doctrine of communion, as they believed in the "Real Presence" of Christ in the sacrament. He took this to mean that they thought they "did absolutely eat and drink Christ's body and blood," which, he told the Indians, was absurd and impossible. Brainerd appealed to the Moravians' Indian proselytes to reject this heterodoxy, but to little avail.[31]

John Brainerd made repeated visits to Indian communities in the Susquehanna region. In 1751 he gave a remarkable description of surging militant spirituality in the town of Wyoming. A council had been called there to deliberate the meaning of a divine communication given to a young Indian woman. He gathered that the message confirmed earlier revelations, and that "it was the mind of the Great Power that they should soon destroy the poison from among them." This "poison" may have been a "witch bundle" used by authorities to curse enemies with sickness and death. John, like David, may have noted discomforting similarities between radical evangelical and Native American revelations.[32]

More disturbingly, the Indians at Wyoming also had a racial theory on which they based their rejection of Brainerd's gospel. "They told me that the great God first made three men and three women, viz.: the Indian, the negro, and the white man." The white man was born last, so whites should not think of themselves as better than Indians. "God gave the white man a book," they argued, and told him that he must worship him by that; but gave none either to the Indian or the negro, and therefore it could not be right for them to have a book." They accused whites of "contriving a method to deprive them of their country in those parts, as they had done by the sea-side, and to make slaves of them and their children as they did of the negroes." Brainerd became afraid that they might kill him, and they instructed him to leave and not come back. Brainerd later expressed hope to government officials that they could work to allay the Indians' fears of enslavement, which might open the door for the gospel and bring more Indians under British, instead of French, influence. The threat of French Catholic missions was never far from these missionaries' minds. Brainerd unsuccessfully pled with the correspondents to give more money to help his mission to the Susquehanna.[33]

Indeed, Brainerd struggled through much of his ministry to secure the necessary funds for the kind of traveling missions and poor relief that he envisioned. He believed that the correspondents simply did not understand the mission's vast needs. Brainerd's high costs escalated because of repeated trips into the backcountry, and he may have received some sharp questions from the correspondents about the propriety of these journeys. Brainerd was unapologetic. The Delawares at Bethel, he knew, represented only a tiny fraction of the Indians to whom he might preach if he could itinerate in the Susquehanna region. He bitterly noted that the Anglican Society for the Propagation of the Gospel did little to help the Indians but instead focused on ministering to American Anglicans and fishing for converts among dissenters. Thus, the backcountry Indians represented a nearly untapped mission field for evangelicals. Brainerd continued to struggle mightily with his lack of support, however, as he confided to novice missionary Gideon Hawley in 1753 that he had been "miserably faltered & pinioned" in his work.[34]

Although John Brainerd enjoyed modest success in New Jersey, the turmoil of war nearly ended his missionary career. In 1755, with the French and Indian War having begun, the SSPCK decided to terminate their relationship with Brainerd. Jonathan Edwards wrote to Scottish pastor William McCulloch in April 1756 and expressed concern that the society had done this "hastily." William Tennent was given modest funds to visit Brainerd's mission, and Brainerd found work at Newark supplying Aaron Burr's pulpit after Burr became the president of Princeton. The dismissal sent Brainerd into a "great plunge," as he told Wheelock. The next several years would be dark ones for Brainerd, as the death of his wife and of two of his children added to the pain of his dismissal.[35]

Brainerd served as a chaplain during the French and Indian War, as did many evangelical ministers who believed deeply in the war's defense of British Protestantism. In 1759 Brainerd ministered alongside Connecticut's Benjamin Pomeroy in the Lake Champlain corridor of New York. In August 1759, Brainerd wrote to Wheelock and rejoiced in the British victories at Niagara, Crown Point, and Ticonderoga: "God has done wonderful things for us! 'Tis his own right hand and his holy arm that has gotten the victory!" While in New York, Brainerd and Pomeroy also recruited Mohawk boys for Wheelock's Indian school. When Brainerd returned from the war, he received a little funding to resume his Indian mission, this time at a new reservation in New Jersey called Brotherton. New Jersey proprietors had expropriated Bethel and other Indian lands but had provided Brotherton as a substitute residence, and Brainerd found it an adequate place for the Christian Delawares, though almost entirely undeveloped. He built a meetinghouse there mostly at his own expense. Brainerd remained aware of the course of the war, as he led a fast at Brotherton in June 1762 "especially on Acct. of the Spanish War," presumably referring to the siege of Havana, to which New Jersey and other colonies were sending reinforcements.[36]

Brainerd now found himself with as many responsibilities to white settlers as to Christian Indians. South-central New Jersey had few Presbyterian pastors, and Brainerd supplied for or regularly visited about twenty small congregations, where many of the white people stayed "but one Remove from a State of Heathenism." Brainerd routinely offered consecutive services for Indians and whites. On one Sabbath in June 1762, he noted in his journal that he "Prayed once in Indian & twice in English, and had two short Discourses, one for the Indians, the other for the White People." The scarcity of ministers forced Brainerd into multiracial and bilingual ministry.[37]

Though the needs of New Jersey were many, Brainerd had not given up hope for missions deeper into the backcountry, as he attended the Lancaster treaty meeting of August 1762 to gauge the Ohio Indians' receptivity to the gospel, "hoping there by to lay a Foundation for the Introduction of Christianity among those poor Salvages." He left disappointed, however, as the assembled chiefs would not listen to his preaching. Similarly, in late 1762 city officials from Phila-delphia requested that the Synod of Philadelphia and New York send missionar-ies into the Pennsylvania frontier in order "to preach to the distressed frontier in-habitants, and to report their distresses," and to assess the possibilities for Indian missions. Brainerd and Charles Beatty were appointed to go on the mission, and they planned to venture as far west as Pittsburgh. They were "entirely prostrated" by the outbreak of Pontiac's Revolt, however. In fact, Brainerd was forced to de-fend the loyalty of his own mission Indians in the *Pennsylvania Gazette* in Sep-tember 1763. He denied that his proselytes had gone back "to join the murdering Indians on the Frontiers" and assured the readers that the Christian Indians de-plored the activities of their "remote savage Brethren." War seems universally to have hampered evangelical missions, especially since it often raised anti-Indian prejudice among white settlers. The "melancholy prospect" of war between whites and Indians seemed only to increase during the 1760s, and Brainerd saw his hopes for expansive backcountry missions dashed.[38]

Discouragement and declining health led Brainerd to focus more on cul-tivating churches for New Jersey's white settlers. Increasingly he complained about the apostasy of once-hopeful Indian converts. Visiting Methodist itinerant Thomas Rankin noted in 1774 that Brainerd's mission was struggling to survive and had fallen far from the ostensibly thriving state under David Brainerd in the 1740s. John explained that many had died, while others had gone apostate, sinking into alcoholism and returning to local villages. Rankin doubted whether John Brainerd had really been called by God to minister to the hard-hearted Indians. Maybe Brainerd wondered about this too, as he finally settled at a white congregation in Deerfield, New Jersey, in 1777, and preached there until his death in 1781.[39]

Gideon Hawley suffered similar difficulties in his Indian missions, despite the patronage of Jonathan Edwards. Edwards actively promoted Hawley to the Bos-ton Board of Commissioners for Indian Affairs, calling the fellow Yale graduate a "young man of uncommon prudence and steadiness of mind, spirit of government, and faculty of teaching . . . his qualifications appear beyond my expectation." Edwards also seemed to read Hawley's melancholy as a sign of spiritual seriousness, just as he had with David Brainerd. Hawley told Joseph Bellamy, "I am afraid of living too long tho I am unfit to die as I am; I am good for nothing . . . melancholy has too much power over me." At times, Edwards might have said the same about himself.[40]

After the 1753 fire that consumed most of his possessions, Hawley reluctantly left Stockbridge for Onohquaga, New York. He wrote to his close friend Joseph Bellamy that he was "going to a barbarous ignorant uncultivated Nation" and suggested that he was not sure whether he could survive the mission. He asked Bellamy to prepare Edwards's "mind . . . to have me decline ye service." He remembered what missions work did to David Brainerd, and he feared that his constitution was even weaker than Brainerd's. Decades later he recalled that he wanted to establish "christianity at a distance from any white people, and where the Indians were not in so much danger of having their minds poisoned by them." Hawley thought that John Brainerd might come with him, but he was only accompanied on his initial mission by Timothy Woodbridge, the Stockbridge schoolmaster; Rebecca Kellogg Ashley, a renowned interpreter; Ashley's husband Benjamin, whom Hawley called a "fanatick" (referring to his radical evangelical views); and "three or four blacks," probably slaves. For books, Hawley brought only a copy of the Bible and *The Life of David Brainerd*. Along the way the party met increasing hostility, particularly from drunken Indians, and one of the Indian guides nearly shot Hawley, save for a timely turn of the missionary's head.[41]

At Onohquaga, Hawley was confronted immediately with mystical experiences of the Native Americans, as he recorded how an ill boy took a visionary journey to hell. In the vision, he "saw ye people Squorming like worms in ye fire." One tormented Native American came out of the fire and cried to God for mercy, but the devil appeared "in an awful Shape with Horns looking dreadfully." The devil forced the damned man to drink from a cup, said "why do you cry for mercy this is what you used to love, you used to love rum," and then "kicked Him into Hell again." Hawley found himself in a contest for spiritual power, as one promising Indian disappointed Hawley because he "went to a Wizzard or Conjuror to cure his Wife." The conjurer rattled a "gourd shell" and made "all Sorts of Noise," and he put her in a hot house to sweat. Periodically he would "put his mouth to ye place where she was most ailing & suck," by which he intended to draw out the sickness from her body. Hawley wanted to convince them that Jesus alone provided a true source of spiritual power. A month later, after a sermon through an interpreter on John 3:3 ("except a man be born again he cannot see the Kingdom of God"), the same woman approached Hawley and repented for "having any thing to do with the Conjuror." Hawley was delighted and prayed for the Indians to be turned from the "power of Satan to God."[42]

Hawley returned to Boston in mid-1754 for his ordination as a missionary. By early 1755 Hawley was more optimistic than before about the mission's prospects. Over the past five months there had been "more evidence of the strivings & operations of God's Spirit than ever before from the time of my first coming among them." The moderate Hawley, however, feared the incursions of Separates. If they heard of religious interest among the Indians, they would "flock" to Onohquaga to proselytize them. Hawley thought he had "more influence here than a million of them," but even having to engage radicals in argument could result in an "unhappy effect" on the Oneidas' minds.[43]

If the Onohquaga mission was developing well, it could not continue during the Seven Years' War, which disrupted Hawley's mission, just as it did John Brainerd's. In January 1756 Hawley fled the mission, and he believed that it was too dangerous to go back. Also like John Brainerd, he joined the war as a chaplain. Hawley agonized over whether to return permanently to Onohquaga, fearing that Jonathan Edwards might doubt his commitment if he chose to avoid the obvious dangers there. Edwards seemed to needle Hawley, who wrote in his journal that Edwards was "a very good man but capible of being biased." After a year of service in the army, the New England Company arranged for Hawley to begin ministering among the Mashpee Indians in southeastern Massachusetts, a position he initially received as a "hiding place & cover from ye storm" after the disappointments and dangers at Onohquaga. He settled at Mashpee in 1758 and spent the rest of his life there. Hawley became co-pastor with the independent-minded Wampanoag minister Solomon Briant, whom the New England Company had been trying unsuccessfully to dislodge for years.[44]

Evangelical missions to Native Americans found halting success often disrupted by war and backsliding converts, but they did raise up some successful Native American pastors and missionaries. Undoubtedly the most celebrated Native American missionary was Samson Occom. The Mohegan Occom was converted in 1740 through James Davenport's preaching. "When I was 16 years of age," Occom recalled, "we heard a Strange Rumor among the English, that there were Extraordinary Ministers Preaching from Place to Place. . . . Some Ministers began to visit us and Preach the Word of God; and the Common People also came frequently, and exhorted us to the things of God." Occom attended numerous revival meetings, and he also began to learn English. Finally, he was "enabld to put my trust in [Christ] alone for Life & Salvation." Occom

The Reverend Mr. SAMSON OCCOM,

Jonathan Pilsbury after Mason Chamberlin,
The Reverend Samson Occom (1723–1792). Hood
Museum of Art, Dartmouth College, Hanover,
New Hampshire, Gift of Mrs. Robert W. Birch.

became a student at Moor's Charity School, run by Eleazar Wheelock in Lebanon, Connecticut. Wheelock came to call Occom his "black Son."[45]

Occom's promising character helped convince Wheelock to make Indian education the school's primary mission. Like Sergeant's planned boarding school in Stockbridge, Wheelock took Indian boys and girls from their families and tribes and instructed them in Christian theology, the liberal arts, and English domesticity. As Wheelock explained to George Whitefield, separating Indian children from tribal culture and educating them would be the most expedient way to train Indian missionaries. Native missionaries could most effectively and inexpensively reach fellow Indians with the gospel. In addition to turning them to Christ, Native evangelization would help "remove their Prejudices, attach them to the English; & to the Crown of great Brittain," and save them from "the subtle Insinuations of great Numbers of Jesuits" trying to convert them to Catholicism and the French national interest.[46]

After struggling through his education because of health and vision problems, in 1749 Occom began tutoring and preaching among the Montauks of Long Island, where Azariah Horton labored. Solomon Williams reported that Horton was very pleased with Occom's work, especially because Occom had "very much help'd them against some wild enthusiastical Notions they had been led into by some foolish Indian Exhorters." Horton sensed that he was losing many of the Montauks to the radical Native preachers, but Occom helped draw them back. Occom won the support of Wheelock, Williams, Horton, and Samuel Buell (then pastoring at Easthampton, Long Island), and he soon began to receive a small salary from the SSPCK.[47]

During the 1750s, Occom met with numerous requests to leave Long Island for other missions, including among the Cherokees of Virginia and the Carolinas, the Mohawks and Oneidas of New York, and John Brainerd's Delawares. Long Island pastors Samuel Buell and James Brown recommended him as a Christian of model character, hard work, and moderation, noting that he had been instrumental in "preventing the Increase of divisive and seperating Principles" among the Montauks. Despite his popularity, the region's presbyteries and associations dragged their feet regarding Occom's ordination. Their hesitation was no doubt influenced by their concerns about Occom's race and his presumed inclination toward backsliding and alcohol abuse. After an examination, Wheelock and the Windham Association in Connecticut finally licensed him in 1757, with Occom commenting that "they were so far satisfied, as to Conclude to proceed, to an ordination hereafter." "Hereafter" turned into two years. Nevertheless, Occom saw a considerable awakening among the Long Island Indians in 1758. Perhaps in response to these successes, Occom was ordained in 1759 by the Long Island Presbytery at Samuel Buell's Easthampton meetinghouse.[48]

In Occom's ordination sermon, Buell enthusiastically juxtaposed Occom's ordination with the British successes in the Seven Years' War as signs of prophecies being fulfilled. Occom had been called "in a Day in which we have Reason to believe from Scripture Prophecy, and the present Aspect of Divine Providence, that the Latter-Day Glory is dawning." Because of the successes of British forces in the war, "a joyous Prospect opens to View, far beyond all that ever appear'd before, for evangelizing the Heathen." George Whitefield agreed, telling Eleazar Wheelock in 1759 that victories in the war signaled that the "womb of Providence is big with something Uncommon." Wheelock replied that through the war God was preparing to call "the poor Creatures into his Family." Like the seventeenth-century Puritan missionary John Eliot, Wheelock and others still entertained the idea that Native Americans might be remnants of the Ten Lost Tribes of Israel, which gave their evangelization added eschatological appeal.

The missions to Native Americans, paired with British military successes, appeared to have apocalyptic significance.[49]

Despite these high hopes, Occom's meager support left him struggling in poverty and debt. He contemplated returning to Mohegan and resuming his labors as a cooper and bookbinder. Finally, New York's David Bostwick, president of the Correspondents of the SSPCK, and Wheelock arranged for Occom and his brother-in-law David Fowler to go on a mission to the Oneidas of upstate New York in 1761. Fowler and Occom stopped through New York City on their way, where Occom was appalled at the behavior of the town's whites. He heard "all Sorts of Evil Noises Caried on by 'em Drunkards." They "Spoke Hells Language" and were "English Heathen," he concluded. He received celebrity treatment in the city's churches, however. In Albany, Occom secured a pass from General Jeffery Amherst, who promised assistance from British officers and troops in the backcountry.[50]

Wheelock continued to see Occom's moderation as one of the chief characteristics recommending him as a missionary to Native Americans. He feared that the "uncommon Concern" for religion among the Indians would be exploited by the Separates. Wheelock told Thomas Foxcroft of Boston that he believed a plot was afoot "to introduce a Number of our wild Separates & lay Exhorters among them." He already worried about the Separate inclinations of Samuel Ashpo, a sometime Wheelock protégé who had once received a Separate ordination, and who in 1760 had gone to Onohquaga to help fill the gap left by Gideon Hawley's departure. Wheelock feared radicals "more dangerous" than Ashpo, however, as "[Benjamin] Ashley is very busie among them from one end of the Government to the other." Before Hawley left, he had worriedly noted that Ashley possessed "wild enthusiastic Notions," including that he must "go thro' all N. England this Winter to warn ye Inhabitants of approaching Judgments." Hawley's departure left the mission vulnerable to the radicals, and Occom's presence might temper the enthusiastic spirit toward which the Indians inclined. But Wheelock still doubted Occom's own perseverance, as he told him that "the Adversary will ruin you if possible."[51]

Occom struggled badly with his health and supplies at the Oneida mission. He wrote a lugubrious letter to Wheelock saying that he had lost his horse and that he had been unable to read or write for a month. Gideon Hawley paid a visit to Onohquaga in 1761 and reported that Occom insisted too strenuously that the Oneidas give up their native traditions. Hawley judged him deficient in prudence. Wheelock painted a much more positive picture for George Whitefield, writing that Occom had been warmly received by the Oneida and Tuscarora chiefs, who built a house for him and Fowler. When they left, the chiefs presented Occom with a wampum belt and requested that a school be built among them. They further requested that English traders bring no more rum into their lands and that their territory be protected from British encroachments. Again, Native Americans often saw missionaries as possible advocates for their protection as well as sources of spiritual power. Occom returned to Oneida in 1762 and 1763, but poor provisions and the outbreak of Pontiac's War in 1763 prevented extended stays. Wheelock tried yet again to send Occom into New York in 1764, but an obvious lack of funding led George Whitefield, who visited America from 1763 to 1765, to rebuke Wheelock for the "imprudent scheme." Occom was growing tired of his lack of funding, complaining to Wheelock that "no white Missionary wou'd go in such Circumstances." Whitefield refused to help raise funds for the mission this time and sent Occom back to Connecticut, an intervention that Wheelock deeply resented, telling John Brainerd that it represented the worst "Blow" that his school had ever received.[52]

Wheelock continued to solicit funds for his Indian school as Occom returned to Mohegan. Partly inspired by a suggestion from Whitefield, Wheelock arranged for Occom and Nathaniel Whitaker of Norwich, Connecticut, to go to England on a fundraising tour for the academy. All realized that the novelty of Occom's presence in England might "get a Bushel of Money for the School," as missionary Charles-Jeffrey Smith put it. There was, however, growing hostility toward Occom among white New Englanders, which was apparently related to Occom's involvement in a land dispute with Connecticut. Whitaker and Occom received a cool welcome in Boston, from which they were to depart. Only John Moorhead, the longtime ardent evangelical, asked Occom to preach in his church. In December 1765, Whitaker and Occom sailed for London, where they encountered a totally different welcome. Whitefield himself introduced them to London society. Occom preached at Whitefield's tabernacle and met a number of luminaries, including the Earl of Dartmouth (later Wheelock's key benefactor) and King George III, who donated £200 to the school. Occom received celebrity treatment everywhere he went and was unsuccessfully invited by Anglican bishops to receive episcopal orders. The campaign, lasting more than two years, was a brilliant success, eventually raising more than £12,000.[53]

Occom enjoyed no triumphal return to Connecticut, however. Upon his arrival in 1768, he found his family languishing in near-starvation conditions, neglected by Wheelock, who had promised to look after Occom's wife, Mary, and his children. On at least one occasion following his return, Occom was "shamefully overtaken with strong Drink," but Samuel Buell and the Suffolk Presbytery acquitted him of intemperance. Occom wrote to Wheelock denying that he had been drinking heavily, complaining that "many White People . . . call me a Drunkard . . . a liar a Rogue & what not." He confessed that he did "take some Strong Drink some Times but I don't use a quarter so much as I use to do, yea I don't keep any in my House." Occom pitifully noted, "I never was so discourag'd as I am now." Wheelock continued reporting to correspondents that Occom was sinking into persistent drunkenness. To make matters worse, Wheelock decided to relocate the "Indian" school to New Hampshire, where he would begin to focus exclusively on white students. In a 1771 letter to Wheelock, Occom concluded that "instead of your Institutions becoming Alma Mater to my Brethren, she will be too Alba Mater to Suckle the Tawnies, for She is already adorn'd up too much like the Popish Virgin Mary." He bitterly remembered how he had served as a "Gazing Stocke" in England to raise thousands of pounds for the school, but now Wheelock had abandoned him and the promise of Native education. After years of neglect and manipulation by Wheelock, Occom finally "broke of[f] from him" and gave up hope of an interracial evangelical movement. He believed that white leaders like Wheelock saw him more as a useful "Gazing Stocke" than as a fully competent brother in Christ.[54]

Occom soon joined with other Native American leaders in New England in an effort to resettle many of New England's Christian Indian communities among the Oneidas in New York. As with John Brainerd's Brotherton settlement and the old Puritan "praying towns," Occom and his associates hoped separation from English culture would encourage greater piety and viability for the Native Christians. This time, however, they envisioned an Indian town with no white leadership. Occom's son-in-law Joseph Johnson was the key organizer for the migration, though Occom lent his considerable credibility to the effort and hoped that "the Lord is about opening a Door for the gospel among the Western Tribes of Indians by their Eastern Brethren." The American Revolution stalled the plans for resettlement, but in 1784 Occom led a group to Brothertown (surely named in part for Brainerd's mission), west of Albany. Occom itinerated in the area for the rest of his life, ministering to Natives and scattered whites in the area. He died in 1792. In the end, Occom and the Brothertown settlers remained committed to the Christian gospel, but they doubted whether they could maintain their cultural, or Christian integrity, in the midst of white Christians.[55]

Despite financial problems, wartime disruptions, and white passivity, evangelical missions to Native Americans after 1740 led small numbers of Indians to make lasting commitments to Protestant Christianity. Political and military concerns indelibly colored the missionaries' agendas, as the colonists longed for Native proselytes as security against the dreaded French, ever more so as the Seven Years' War engulfed the American backcountry starting in 1754. Moderate missions agencies seemed consumed with countering Catholic missions and radical evangelicals, concerns that undoubtedly conveyed a certain lack of interest in the proselytes' own spiritual lives. When it came to empowering Native American missionaries or pastors, white evangelicals moved very hesitantly, as demonstrated abundantly in Eleazar Wheelock's dismal treatment of Samson Occom. Ultimately, white missionary agencies' neglectful policies and patronizing attitudes led Indians like Occom and his Brothertown colleagues to abandon their white evangelical sponsors altogether. Nevertheless, some white evangelicals seemed unable to escape the spiritually inclusive mandate of their gospel, and some like John Brainerd and Gideon Hawley worked long and hard to bring Native Americans into the fold of the church. Similarly, despite the mixed motives of white missionaries, a handful of Native Americans accepted Christianity as intellectually viable, culturally beneficial, and spiritually satisfying.

"Ethiopia Shall Stretch Out Her Hands unto God": Slavery, African Americans, and Evangelicalism

The itinerant Daniel Rogers recorded an April 1743 conversation with a woman in York, Maine, who "told me she had a View of ye Coming of ye King-dome of God, and p[ar]ticularly of ye Negroes being brot into It." They agreed that Psalm 68:31 ("Ethiopia shall soon stretch out her hands unto God.") had been "fulfilled in the Conversion of many poor Negroe slaves in N. Eng[lan]d." He hoped these conversions would represent the "first Fruits" of a general awakening among Africans extending to the "West Indies and East." But other whites feared the power of evangelical blacks, as exemplified in a bizarre story in the *Boston Weekly Post-Boy* in 1742. A report from Colchester, Connecticut, told that after a revival meeting, "a Negro Man, who, 'tis said, was Converted, endeavour'd to exhort in the Congregation; but being oppos'd by some, he with-drew into an Orchard near the Meeting-House, where many of the Congrega-tion follow'd him; and as he was exhorting the People, two large monstrous black Snakes crept up on his Back, and look'd over each of his Shoulders to the great Surprize both of himself and his Audience: They kill'd the Snakes, and dismiss'd the Exhorter for that Night." The conversion of African Americans could signal the coming of the kingdom of God or the rise of malevolent spirits, depending upon one's perspective. According to antirevivalist Charles Chauncy, however, one of the most disconcerting features of the revivals was that "Women and Girls; yea, Negroes, have taken upon them to do the Business of Preachers."[1]

Like many early white evangelicals, Rogers and the unnamed Maine woman embraced a certain kind of spiritual egalitarianism. They believed strongly that the gospel of the new birth should be preached to all, including America's Afri-can peoples. But Anglo-American evangelical leaders usually did not think that the egalitarian implications of their gospel would have substantial social rami-

fications for African or Native Americans. But early American white evangelicals' commitment to evangelization set in motion perhaps the most remarkable
change in American religious history: the nearly wholesale conversion of African
Americans to some form of evangelical Christianity. That great transformation
began in force in the mid-1780s, and by the early nineteenth century African
Americans were converting at almost unparalleled rates. Evangelical thought
among whites and blacks would help fuel the antislavery movement before the
American Civil War, even as many southern white evangelicals helped develop
a new proslavery theology. From the 1740s to the 1780s, a foundation was set by
new evangelicals, both black and white, upon which to build a new black evangelical church in North America and the Caribbean.[2]

The Africans unwillingly transported to the Americas in the seventeenth and
eighteenth centuries practiced their own religions, usually indigenous faiths of
West Africa. They sometimes embraced forms of Islam or Roman Catholicism
as well. Sketchy but significant evidence shows that many Africans maintained
modified versions of their religions in the Americas, despite the trauma of forced
migration and enslavement. Understandably, many Africans were reluctant to
accept the evangelistic overtures of the Anglican Society for the Propagation of
the Gospel in Foreign Parts. Anglican priests had to contend with planters' resistance to the evangelization of their slaves, and so the Anglicans' gospel heavily
emphasized obedience for servants. Anglicans also often associated Christianity
with literacy, making the recruitment and full inclusion of illiterate slave converts difficult.[3]

The new evangelicals slowly began to breach the gap between European and
African American religion. Evangelical Christianity reminded African Americans more of their preexisting religions than did traditional Anglicanism. Some
evangelicals welcomed greater emphases on the Spirit's operations and accepted lay and clerical expressions of religious emotion. Some evangelicals in
the South, particularly early Baptists, were themselves marginalized from dominant planter culture, so building bridges with other lowly groups may have come
naturally. Evangelical Christianity also held the message of liberation and equality at its core, even if many white evangelicals saw only spiritual implications for
those tenets. Soon after the revivals began in the southern colonies, powerful
black preachers and lay African American women and men began to spread
evangelical Christianity to fellow African Americans in ways that white leaders
could not.[4]

German Moravians took the lead in evangelical efforts to proselytize Africans
in the New World. In Denmark in 1731, Count Nicholas Zinzendorf met a teenage slave named Anthony, who told him of the slaves' sufferings on the island

of St. Thomas. Zinzendorf became convinced that the Caribbean slave populations were ripe for conversion and recruited two of his Herrnhut followers to
start a mission on St. Thomas. In 1732, the Moravians founded their mission on
the estate of a friendly planter, but they soon encountered resistance from other
planters on the island who feared the subversion implicit in the evangelical message of salvation. One Moravian Brethren slave on St. Thomas reportedly proclaimed "that black men were no less creatures of God and beneficiaries of the
promise of eternal salvation, bought by the blood of Jesus Christ, than were the
Whites." The Danish West Indies planters regarded the slaves with deep fear,
and a 1733 slave uprising on St. John confirmed their worst suspicions. As on the
North American mainland, the planters often saw evangelical missionaries as a
social threat, and on St. Thomas many began agitating to have the Moravians
expelled.[5]

The Moravians remained on St. Thomas, however, and spread their mission
throughout the West Indies, part of a remarkable effort of global evangelization
by the Unity of Brethren that saw stations established from South Africa to Rus-
sia to America. In the Caribbean, the Moravians' substantial appeal to the African populations resulted from their dogged determination to stay in the face of
persecution, their willingness to learn and preach in Dutch creole, their efforts
to teach slaves to read, and soon, the empowerment of black converts to help
spread the gospel. But like many other European evangelicals, white Moravian
leaders made significant concessions to the slave regimes, and some even bought
slaves themselves. Partly due to the pressure from local planters, the Moravians
emphasized the slaves' duty to obey their masters. White Moravians' attitudes
toward black proselytes were quite complicated: a potentially subversive message of spiritual equality was preached by whites who at least cooperated with, if
not shared in, the institution of slavery. Despite this compromise, the Moravians
enjoyed continuing successes on several Caribbean islands, especially on Anti-
gua, where by the end of the eighteenth century the Moravians counted 11,000
followers in their mission stations.[6]

On the mainland, no similarly intentional plans to evangelize African Americans appeared until the late eighteenth century, at the earliest. The evangelical
pastors promoting the revivals of the 1740s, however, routinely expressed happiness to see African Americans and Native Americans in the attentive crowds.
Successes among these groups, who had historically displayed little interest in
other Protestant overtures, helped validate the revivals. In the heady days of the
early 1740s, some ministers expressed a socially subversive view of the awakenings. In *Souls Flying to Jesus Christ*, for instance, Benjamin Colman invited
"You that are Servants, and the meanest of our Household Servants, even our

poor Negroes, chuse you the Service of CHRIST; He will make you his Freemen; The SON OF GOD, shall make you free, and you shall be free indeed. Why should you be Men's Slaves and Satan's too. CHRIST calls you, mean as you are, into the glorious Liberty of the Sons of GOD. . . . It is in my Sight, I can truly say, a Beauty to our Communion, to see a Number of the poor Blacks with us." William Cooper concurred, reminding an audience at the Old South Church in 1741 that God would choose "SOME of all Countries and Climates, Complexions and Colours; some of the black as well as the white: For GOD has made of one Blood all Nations of Men. . . . Some of the Slaves in our Families are taken, and made the LORD's Free-men, brought into the glorious Liberty of the Children of GOD, while others are left in spiritual as well as temporal Servitude, and continue the Devil's Slaves; or it may be while the Master or Mistress is left." The social implications of these sermons seem inescapable to us, and perhaps they did to African American hearers then, too. But early white evangelicals rarely attacked slavery directly.[7]

White evangelical tailor Joseph Bean of Cambridge, Massachusetts, wrote a brief but fascinating meditation on a slave in his neighborhood that also suggested a limited spiritual egalitarianism and sympathy. He heard that this slave was "so Ignorant that thay Cannot lern him to reade nor anny thing else Concerning Religion." Bean prayed for the slave's "dark Soul" to be saved. Bean also thanked God that he had been born "in a land of light" with godly parents and exposure to the gospel, while the slave "was brought up in a dark and Ignorant part of the woorld whare he was holly deprived of those glorious Seasons and opertunitys of grace." Only God's pleasure had made this "difarance" between their origins, and Bean regretted his "hard hartedness to Such objects of Pitty." While he appreciated nothing about this unnamed slave's culture or religious beliefs, Bean's own Calvinism led to a certain kind of humility, knowing that he could have just as easily been chosen to be born as an African. He did not doubt his common humanity with the slave or their shared need for salvation through Christ. Later, after discoursing with a pious African American man, Bean wrote, "Lord I perseve thou art a God unto all that Call upon the[e] in dede and in truth wether bou[n]d or free white or black it is all the same." He prayed for God to send the gospel "amoung the black."[8]

Jonathan Edwards and George Whitefield also illustrated common Anglo-American evangelical attitudes toward African Americans: both ministers were very pleased with blacks' interest in the gospel, and both not only approved of slavery but were slave owners themselves. Edwards made a point of separately mentioning that "several Negroes . . . appear to have been truly born again" in *A Faithful Narrative*, and Edwards's Northampton church admitted nine blacks into membership during his tenure, including one of his own slaves. He believed that during the millennium, "many of the Negroes and Indians will be divines, and that excellent books will be published in Africa, in Ethiopia, [and] in Turkey." Edwards lived in a white-dominated world comfortable with profound social inequality, but he believed that blacks and Native Americans would gain full equality with Europeans in the millennial church. Edwards also privately criticized the slave trade because it seemed to block the way for Africa to be Christianized, but he did not apply that analysis to American domestic slavery.[9]

Whitefield's 1740 "A Letter to the Inhabitants of Maryland, Virginia, North and South Carolina" chastised slave owners for abusing their slaves and for failing to evangelize them. Whitefield suspected that the masters had withheld Christianity from the slaves for fear that it would make them subversive. The evangelist thought, to the contrary, that Christianity taught people to accept their station in life, so that a Christian African would make a good slave. Whitefield showed particular attention to blacks on his tours and demonstrated at least a fleeting interest in educating African Americans. But he also came to own a South Carolina plantation worked by slaves, which would provision the Bethesda orphanage. In the 1750s the itinerant pushed for the legalization of slavery in Georgia.[10]

Whitefield's preaching could have unpredictable social consequences, however, and in South Carolina several of his disciples veered toward revolutionary egalitarianism. This penchant was most obviously displayed in the excesses of the planter and slaveholder Hugh Bryan. The brothers Hugh and Jonathan Bryan were converted under Whitefield's preaching in 1740. Hugh recalled that after he heard Whitefield preach on the new birth, he entered a season of crisis, but after receiving impressions of Scripture passages in his mind, he became confident of his salvation. "Since that time the affections of my soul are changed," he wrote. "I delight no more in worldly goods, but in a life of faith in Jesus Christ." Sometimes he was even "transported with raptures of joy from the rays of divine light and love darted into my soul, which fill my mouth with thanks." Whitefield encouraged the Bryan brothers to open a school for slaves.[11]

Bryan blamed the Charleston fire of November 1740 on the sins of the Anglican priests, and this event marked Bryan's entrance into subversive radicalism. In early 1742, South Carolina's House of Commons received reports that Bryan and other evangelicals were promoting "frequent and great Assemblies of Negroes." Bryan began to believe that God had raised him up as a prophet against Charleston. Nineteen-year-old Eliza Lucas, on a plantation near Charleston, wrote, "He came to working miracles and lived for several days in the woods barefooted and alone and with his pen and Ink to write down his prophecies."

Charleston's whites feared "the consiquence of his prophecys coming to the ears of the African Hosts," she noted. Fully embracing his prophetic office, Bryan decided to send his book of prophecies to the legislature. Among his reported forecasts was, "Charles Town . . . should be destroyed by fire and sword, to be executed by the Negroes before the first day of next month." The worst fears of Whitefield's opponents were coming true.[12]

Hugh Bryan's prophetic career abruptly ended in an episode reminiscent of Davenport's book-burning. The Assembly ordered Bryan's arrest, but when officers arrived they found him repentant, admitting that his inspirations had been "a Delusion of Satan." Bryan had been sobered by a failed attempt to part the waters of a river. A letter sent to Boston, reputedly from his brother Jonathan, told how an "invisible Spirit" led Hugh to take a rod and "smite the Waters of the River, which should thereby be divided, so as he might go over, on dry Ground." Hugh went "full Tilt" flailing into the water until he nearly drowned. The skeptical correspondent chalked this episode up to the "Workings of Whitefieldism in its native Tendency." The Assembly apparently fined the Bryans and a number of other white evangelicals for promoting assemblies of blacks, but soon the brothers regained the favor of white South Carolina elite society. They did not free their slaves. To the contrary, later they were chiefly responsible for helping Whitefield acquire his own plantation and slaves. The Bryan brothers eschewed radicalism in favor of a moderate evangelicalism that promoted the Christianization of slaves and the moral reform of slavery, but not the questioning of slavery itself.[13]

Despite Bryan's collapse, Jonathan Barber, the director of Whitefield's Bethesda orphanage, remained optimistic about the results of the brothers' overtures to the slave community. He wrote to Daniel Rogers in October 1742 about the "work among ye poor Negroes in Carolina." Barber had fled Georgia during the War of Jenkins' Ear and saw the revival in South Carolina firsthand. He thought "many poor Souls were savingly converted" there. Though Hugh Bryan's excesses had given ammunition to critics, Barber thought the African Americans' conversions were generally as convincing as those of British Americans. Bryan "was in some Things decieved by ye Devil," but Barber regarded the repentant planter as an "honest, humble Man . . . much engaged in promoting ye best Interest of ye poor Negroes. Who have been shamefully neglected, and I fear much abused by ye White People." The real problem, according to Barber, lay not in Bryan's radicalism, but in religious "pretenders [who] may oppose ye Religion of Jesus." The radical-leaning Barber did not consider Bryan's extremes a debilitating failure for the southern evangelical movement.[14]

Following Bryan's exposure, moderate Charleston pastors Josiah Smith and

James Parker tried to salvage the reputation of the movement in an April letter to the *South-Carolina Gazette* that defended the Christianization of the slaves. The Anglican authorities would not let Smith's argument stand and countered in the paper's next issue with a letter stating that the awakeners really meant to gather "cabals of Negro's, . . . filling their Heads with a Parcel of Cant-Phrases, Trances, Dreams, Visions, and Revilations." To the Anglicans, the enthusiasm of Whitefield, which Josiah Smith had long tried to deny, would lead to slave insurrection if allowed to proceed unchecked. To the revivalists' opponents, radical evangelicalism truly represented a social threat.[15]

Evangelical ideas about equality and impending judgment against oppressors seem to have motivated some later slave revolts, most notably Nat Turner's 1831 rebellion in Southampton County, Virginia. But most Africans and African Americans who converted to evangelical Christianity appear to have found in it both spiritual solace and a means to assert individual and collective identity in the face of slavery and white America's increasingly racist onslaught. Not surprisingly, there are comparatively few autobiographical accounts from African Americans in the eighteenth century, yet a high percentage of the records that do exist come from African American evangelicals. Although these accounts are usually heavily edited, if not written, by white evangelical amanuenses, one can assume that they reflect in some measure blacks' own experiences in the evangelical movement. Many of these women and men helped spread evangelicalism to North America's black population, fully embracing the gospel of salvation yet also seeing the faith from a distinctively African American perspective.[16]

Among the best-documented lives of early African American evangelicals are those of James Albert Ukawsaw Gronniosaw, Jupiter Hammon, Phillis Wheatley, David George, and John Marrant. For most of them, accepting evangelical Christianity was both a spiritual and a social move, as conversion typically led, over time, to improved social status or even freedom. Gronniosaw, Wheatley, and Marrant attracted the attention of Selina Hastings, the countess of Huntingdon, an English evangelical philanthropist (and slaveholder) who sponsored major publications by all three writers and who arranged for Marrant's ordination in her Calvinist "connection." According to his 1770 *A Narrative of the Most Remarkable Particulars in the Life of James Albert Ukawsaw Gronniosaw, An African Prince*, Gronniosaw was born a prince in "Baurnou," or Borno, in present-day northeastern Nigeria. On a trip to the Gold Coast he was seized by a local king and sold into slavery to a Dutch captain. The captain took Gronniosaw to Barbados, where he was sold to a gentleman from New York. In New York he worked as a house slave. Although Gronniosaw claimed to have believed in God's existence all along, he came into direct contact with the new evangelical movement when the New Jersey minister Theodorus Frelinghuysen purchased him from his New York master.[17]

Frelinghuysen immediately began to proselytize his slave and prayed with Gronniosaw night and day. He also sent Gronniosaw to school so he could learn to read, and he made him attend church meetings. Under Frelinghusen's preaching, Gronniosaw began to learn about Christian doctrine and fell under conviction of sin. The family began to supply Gronniosaw with favorite Puritan texts, including John Bunyan's *The Holy War* and Richard Baxter's *A Call to the Unconverted*. These only added to his growing distress, and once he attempted suicide but failed when his knife bent instead of piercing his skin. Soon Gronniosaw began to emerge from his despair as God impressed texts of Scripture on his mind. He also began to "relish" Baxter's *Call to the Unconverted*. Finally, he experienced a breakthrough and was born again: "I was so drawn out of myself, and so fill'd and awed by the presence of God, that I saw (or thought I saw) light inexpressible dart down from heaven upon me . . . and joy unspeakable took possession of my soul." Although twenty-five years passed before he wrote about the event (his conversion likely happened around 1747–48), one can sense through his words the mystical power of his conversion experience. He received assurance of salvation and happily reported the news to Frelinghuysen. Frelinghuysen soon died of a fever, but he granted Gronniosaw his freedom. For years Gronniosaw struggled to find stable employment, and eventually he was forced to serve on a privateer and a navy ship during the Seven Years' War. In 1762 he arrived in England where he received assistance from George White-field, whom he claimed to know well from hearing the evangelist preach in New York.[18]

Jupiter Hammon and Phillis Wheatley, atypically, both had masters who urged them to become educated. Both also found opportunity for religious expression in poetry. Hammon, a slave born in 1711 to the prominent Lloyd family of Long Island, became the first published African American poet with the broadside *An Evening Thought* (1760). This poem defended orthodox Calvinism, proclaiming that "Salvation comes by Jesus Christ alone" and that salvation was given to both "high and low." Hammon's next published poem was an admiring 1778 tribute to Phillis Wheatley, by then the most famous African in America. Hammon apparently had not met Wheatley, but he delighted in her literary fame. *An Address to Miss Phillis Wheatly* saw the hand of God in bringing Wheatley "from distant shore, To learn His holy word." Despite the difficulties of slavery, Hammon believed, "Thou hast left the heathen shore; Thro' mercy of the Lord." Some might see this justification of the slave trade as a sort of false consciousness or even white brainwashing of Hammon, but we should at least recognize that he assumed there was nothing as important as eternal salvation. The temporal sufferings of the slaves were ephemeral compared to God's great gift in Christ, "worth all the gold of Spain."[19]

Although we know little about Hammon's life on Long Island or in Hartford, Connecticut, where he and the Lloyds lived during the American Revolution, it seems likely that Hammon received Christian instruction by attending Anglican services with the Lloyds and perhaps by attending a nearby school run by Harvard graduate Nehemiah Bull. By early adulthood he probably became a lay preacher for local African Americans. His published prose and sermons featured common evangelical themes as well as an understated appeal to a collective black American identity. In *A Winter Piece* (1782), Hammon expressed a desire to "enlighten the minds of my brethren; for we are a poor despised nation, whom God in his wise providence has permitted to be brought from their native place to a christian land." As before, Hammon emphasized the primacy of salvation, not earthly freedom, but here he also nodded toward the desirability of emancipation. "Many of us are seeking a temporal freedom, and I wish you may obtain it; remember that all power in heaven and on earth belongs to God; if we are slaves it is by permission of God." But Hammon also turned to biblical images of deliverance from bondage that would become central to the black evangelical tradition: "Cannot that same power that divided the waters from the waters for the children of Israel to pass through, make way for your freedom . . . and ye shall know the truth and the truth shall make you free. . . . If the Son shall make you free you shall be free indeed."[20]

Hammon displayed only limited aspirations for temporal freedom for slaves and no such concern for himself. As he wrote in *An Address to the Negroes in the State of New-York* (1787), "for my own part I do not wish to be free, yet I should be glad if others, especially the young Negroes, were to be free. . . . But this, my dear brethren, is by no means the greatest thing we have to be concerned about. Getting our liberty in this world is nothing to our having the liberty of the children of God." Hammon may have entertained sharper views on emancipation, but he would have had to muffle them for the purposes of publication. In any case, Hammon tended to spiritualize the liberating effects of Christ's gospel, just as most white evangelicals did. How grievous a shortcoming this was probably depends on whether Hammon was right about the believers' future in heaven, where "we shall find nobody to reproach us for being black, or for being slaves."[21]

Although they shared much in common, Phillis Wheatley became much better known and connected in the early evangelical movement than her admirer Jupiter Hammon. In 1761, John Wheatley, a Boston merchant and tailor, bought the seven- or eight-year-old Phillis, who had recently arrived in a shipment of slaves from Africa, to serve his wife Susanna. Susanna became the greatest influence on Phillis's life and her patron in the wider world of Anglo-American evangelicalism. The Wheatleys soon began to recognize Phillis's aptitude for reading and writing, which they encouraged. In 1770, the teenage Wheatley published her first poem, an elegy to George Whitefield, who had recently died in Newburyport, Massachusetts. Wheatley recommended Whitefield's Christ to her fellow Africans:

> Take him, ye Africans, he longs for you,
> Impartial Saviour is his title due:
> Wash'd in the fountain of redeeming blood,
> You shall be sons, and kings, and priests to God.[22]

Wheatley's poem was widely published in American newspapers, and in 1773 a volume of her poetry was printed in London under the sponsorship of her evangelical patroness, the countess of Huntingdon. Wheatley corresponded with the countess and other British evangelical luminaries, and she bolstered her connections by a visit to England during 1773. Liberal Boston pastor John Lathrop considered Wheatley a "singular genius" but worried that she might return home from London a "flaming Methodist." Wheatley's poems and visit caused a stir in London, where she visited a number of admiring elites, including Benjamin Franklin. Wheatley's poetry was learned and evangelical, and at times it displayed the same passive acceptance of slavery and the slave trade as had Hammon's writings. For instance, her "On being brought from AFRICA to AMERICA" asserted:

> 'Twas mercy brought me from my Pagan land,
> Taught my benighted soul to understand
> That there's a God, that there's a Saviour too:
> Once I redemption neither sought nor knew.
> Some view our sable race with scornful eye,
> "Their colour is a diabolic die."
> Remember, Christians, Negroes, black as Cain,
> May be refin'd, and join th' angelic train.[23]

Like Hammon, Wheatley saw the value of the Christian gospel as outweighing the suffering of Africans in the slave trade. Wheatley may have become insensitive to the plight of slaves in hard labor elsewhere in the Americas, as her relatively benign enslavement concluded with her emancipation by the Wheatleys in late 1773, just before Susanna Wheatley's death. But the very act of an

Phillis Wheatley, *Poems on Various Subjects*
(London, 1773). Beinecke Rare Book and
Manuscript Library, Yale University.

evangelical black woman publishing poetry posed a potential threat to the racial categories of white revolutionary America. Thomas Jefferson, for one, dismissed her poetry with a sneer, writing in *Notes on the State of Virginia* (1787), "Religion, indeed, has produced a Phyllis Whately; but it could not produce a poet. The compositions published under her name are below the dignity of criticism." Jefferson needed Wheatley's poetry to be religious pap, or it might jeopardize his assumptions about African Americans' intellectual inferiority to European Americans.[24]

Despite Wheatley's apparent acceptance of slavery, in one notable instance she publicly protested against the institution. In a letter to Native American pastor Samson Occom that was subsequently published in two Boston newspapers, Wheatley argued that blacks possessed "natural Rights," which slavery contradicted. She still expressed gratitude that "the divine Light is chasing away the thick Darkness which broods over the Land of Africa," but she also averred that "in every human Breast, God has implanted a Principle, which we call Love of

Freedom; it is impatient of Oppression, and pants for Deliverance." Though she knew many whites in New England did not acknowledge African Americans' desire for freedom, "by the Leave of our Modern Egyptians I will assert, that the same Principle lives in us." In light of the spiraling revolutionary crisis, Wheatley puzzled at the Anglo-Americans' devotion to slavery: "How well the Cry for Liberty, and the reverse Disposition for the Exercise of oppressive Power over others agree,—I humbly think it does not require the Penetration of a Philosopher to determine." The newly freed Wheatley had come to see the gospel and American republicanism as both implicitly calling for freedom for the slaves.[25]

Wheatley also shared the growing sense of many New England evangelicals that slavery could be attacked at its roots by sending Christian Africans back to Africa. She corresponded with Samuel Hopkins and the evangelical London merchant John Thornton about the prospects of African missions. They agreed, as Wheatley expressed in a 1774 letter to Hopkins, that "this is the beginning of that happy period foretold by the Prophets, when all shall know the Lord from the least to the greatest. . . . I hope that which the divine royal Psalmist says by inspiration is now on the point of being accomplished, namely, Ethiopia shall soon stretch forth her hands unto God." Accordingly, she endorsed Hopkins's and Ezra Stiles's circular proposal to train and send Guinea natives John Quamine and Bristol Yamma, both members of Hopkins's church in Newport, Rhode Island, as missionaries to "their poor, ignorant, perishing, heathen brethren."[26]

For this venture, Hopkins hoped to solicit the help of the Philip Quaque, an African missionary working for the Anglican Society for the Propagation of the Gospel in Foreign Parts. Quaque seems to have conducted significant work on Quamine's behalf, tracking down his surviving family members, but Quaque also cautioned Hopkins against sending any missionaries, especially those not under the auspices of the Society for the Propagation of the Gospel. Wheatley apparently heard from Hopkins that Quaque's mission was a failure, and she wrote to Hopkins, "Let us not be discouraged, but still hope, that God will bring about his great work, tho' Philip may not be the instrument in the Divine Hand, to perform this work of wonder, turning the African 'from darkness to light.'" John Thornton forwardly suggested that Wheatley herself return to Africa as the wife of Quamine or Yamma, but she kindly informed him that she did not know either of them personally, and that her long residence in America made her unfamiliar with the African language and culture, which the missionaries would need. The arrival of the Revolutionary War made planning for the African mission difficult, but Hopkins continued to support the project through the 1790s, when he promoted African American colonization in Sierra Leone.[27]

Wheatley and her evangelical patrons believed that the enslavement and re-location of Africans to America would, ironically, help bring about the millen-nial proclamation of the gospel to all corners of the globe, including Africa. The first generation of American evangelicals, however, saw little progress in their designs to send black missionaries to Africa. Probably the most significant pas-tor and missionary who did fulfill this hope was the former slave David George, who was born in Virginia of African parents. In the early 1770s, at Silver Bluff, South Carolina, George fell under the influence of two itinerating black preach-ers, one of them George Liele, soon to be a missionary in Kingston, Jamaica. George was baptized at Silver Bluff by "Brother Palmer," almost certainly Wait Palmer, the Baptist minister who had baptized Shubal Stearns in 1751. If this was Wait Palmer, one can hardly imagine one American pastor baptizing two more significant converts than Stearns and George, both great pioneers of the Baptist faith. George soon began preaching and became the pastor of the Silver Bluff Church, which claims to have been the first continuously operating black church in America, founded around 1773.[28]

George and his family suffered several displacements during the American Revolution, eventually finding transport to the British-controlled Halifax, Nova Scotia, where he arrived in 1782. He found no preaching opportunities in Hali-fax, so he moved southwest to Shelburne, where he found that "numbers of my own color were here, but I found the White people were against me." George successfully founded a quickly growing church in the Loyalist haven of Shel-burne, but local unemployed white soldiers, angry because the Loyalist blacks were taking jobs at cheap pay, threatened his life. Nevertheless, George itiner-ated regularly and helped start a number of Baptist congregations in Nova Sco-tia.[29]

George soon met John Clarkson, a British agent who encouraged him and his church to consider a missionary resettlement venture in Sierra Leone, West Africa. George, his family, and much of his church agreed to go, sensing a new missionary opportunity along with the promise of relief from white persecution. The party arrived at Freetown, Sierra Leone, in 1792, and George's congregation erected a grass-roof pole-barn as their new meetinghouse there. Although the community of free blacks was desperately hampered by disease and occasional insurrections, George remained optimistic that, as he wrote to evangelical cor-respondents in London in the mid-1790s, "the work of God revives here among our people, and I hope it will begin among the NATIVES OF AFRICA." In the expansion of the gospel, the former slave saw the possibility of the redemption of his ancestral continent. George would go on to become a key defender of the

Particular (Calvinist) Baptist faith in Africa. He was one of many African Americans who went to West Africa in the eighteenth and nineteenth centuries with the hope of spreading the gospel and assaulting the slave trade at its roots.[30]

John Marrant also journeyed from South Carolina to Nova Scotia, but he took a longer path than David George. Marrant was a free black from New York who moved to Charleston with his family in the late 1760s. Marrant bound himself as an apprentice there, became a popular musician, and started "drinking in iniquity like water." One evening, apparently in early 1770, Marrant and a companion happened upon a revival meeting headlined by George Whitefield. Marrant resolved to disrupt the meeting by blowing his French horn, but he did not count on the power of Whitefield to convict sinners. As the great preacher looked around, "as I thought, directly upon me," he pointed at Marrant and named his text, "PREPARE TO MEET THY GOD, O ISRAEL." The power of the words literally knocked Marrant to the ground, and he passed out for half an hour. People roused him, but he remained terrified: "I thought I saw the devil on every side of me. I was constrained in the bitterness of my spirit to halloo out in the midst of the congregation." Other congregants dragged his limp body from the meetinghouse, but Whitefield visited him afterwards, and told him "JESUS CHRIST HAS GOT THEE AT LAST."[31]

Whitefield arranged for Oliver Hart, pastor of Charleston's First Baptist Church, to visit Marrant, who days later was still debilitated and under deep conviction. At first he resisted Hart's offer to pray with him, but soon Hart brought Marrant through the crisis. As Hart prayed for him, Marrant wrote, "the Lord was pleased to set my soul at perfect liberty," and he was born again. Marrant soon became ostracized from his family and friends and retreated to the woods where he prayed and read Scripture for days at a time. He befriended a Cherokee hunter who brought him to his fort, where the tribal authorities imprisoned Marrant and sentenced him to death. At his planned execution, Marrant prayed earnestly, first in English and then in Cherokee, which he seemed miraculously able to speak fluently despite his relative unfamiliarity with the tongue. This instance helped secure his pardon and release. After traveling among a number of tribes, Marrant returned to his family, who received him as one brought back from the dead.[32]

Marrant then began working as a contractor on the Jenkins plantation at "Cumbee," probably on the Combahee River southwest of Charleston. He wrote that he became known as the "free Carpenter," perhaps casting himself as a Christ figure. On the plantation, he instructed the slave children and some of their parents in reading and Christian doctrine. Soon he had about thirty blacks in his "society," and "the Lord was pleased often to refresh us with a sense of his love and presence amongst us." Mr. Jenkins knew of the meetings and did not disrupt them, but when Mrs. Jenkins found out about them, she insisted that her husband put a stop to them, saying that Marrant's teaching "was the ready way to have all his negroes ruin'd." Mr. Jenkins agreed, raised a group to raid one of the meetings, arrested the slaves and viciously flogged them. Because Marrant was free, he did not receive a whipping, but Mr. Jenkins confronted him and accused him of trying to make the slaves seditious. Marrant argued that his instruction had made the slaves more responsible and hard-working and told Jenkins that "the blood of those poor negroes which he had spilt that morning would be required by God at his hands." Marrant left the plantation, but the meetings reportedly continued in secret. Mrs. Jenkins soon died, struck by what Marrant regarded as a providential fever. Marrant's account of the violence on the Cumbee plantation did not appear in later editions of his *Narrative*, for its antislavery implications were too obvious. Shorn of this controversial section, Marrant's partially allegorical *Narrative* went through at least fifteen editions in Britain.[33]

Marrant was impressed into the British navy during the American Revolution, and after the war he landed in London. He became increasingly confident of his call to preach to his "countrymen" and was ordained as a minister in the countess of Huntingdon's Calvinist "connection" in 1785. As with Wheatley, the countess saw Marrant as a possible agent for the evangelization of Africans in the Atlantic world. Marrant soon sailed back across the Atlantic to Nova Scotia, to minister among the black Loyalist community there. Marrant made his home in Birchtown, close to David George's at Shelburne. By the mid-1780s, Nova Scotia had witnessed the preaching of diverse powerful evangelical ministers, and amidst their displacements and persecutions, Nova Scotia's black Loyalist community proved one of the most welcoming to evangelicalism in revolutionary North America.[34]

In Birchtown, Marrant met a warm response to his preaching, despite regular harassment from Freeborn Garrettson and other local Wesleyan Methodists, who objected to his Calvinism. At one of his first meetings, he preached to an audience of whites, blacks, and Indians, and "groans and sighings were heard through the congregation, and many were not able to contain." That night Marrant preached again, and the power of the Spirit was so great that he was rendered mute for five minutes. Five days later, on Christmas 1785, he had ten people to baptize and four marriages to perform. Marrant itinerated in the tiny towns and villages of southeastern Nova Scotia, preaching to blacks, poor whites, and Micmac Indians. In a January 1786 meeting at Green's Harbour, Marrant preached to a large mixed-race audience that had trudged through deep snows to get to the meetinghouse. Again Marrant was struck dumb by the Spirit, but he continued with his planned baptism service. After he had baptized five people, "the rest were fallen to the ground; however I baptised them on the floor [Marrant was baptizing by sprinkling], while the rest were crying out, and saying, 'Lord Jesus have mercy upon us.'"[35]

Marrant founded a Connection congregation and school in Birchtown before returning to London in 1790, discouraged because of continual illness, persecution, and lack of sufficient funds. The Birchtown congregation, under the leadership of Cato Perkins, emigrated to Sierra Leone, just as David George's Baptist congregation and about half of all black Nova Scotians did. George and Marrant, though from different denominations, found many African Americans ready to embrace the gospel, but even the relatively free climate of Nova Scotia proved too oppressive for them to remain there.[36]

The evangelical movement held an ambiguous message for African Americans. Even the evangelicalism of Jupiter Hammon and Phillis Wheatley had uncertain social implications for blacks. We must remember that although the early evangelical movement always blurred racial boundaries through its acceptance of African American and Native American converts, individual evangelicals always came to Christ for salvation first, not for social or political change. Many also came because they sought a clearer purpose in life and a nurturing community. Most early white evangelical leaders preached that Christ had come to set people free, but not to set them free in this world. Black evangelicals, and a few white evangelicals, would accept that contradiction only for so long.

For at least a hundred years, a handful of Anglo-American Protestants, led by Quakers such as George Fox, had protested against the immorality of slavery. Some white evangelicals in all denominations—Congregational, Presbyterian, Baptist, and Methodist—made at least theoretical stands against slavery during the revolutionary period. We may assume that black evangelicals agreed with them and privately wished for more white pressure against slave owners and traders. Although new black evangelicals like Phillis Wheatley did occasionally speak out against slavery, they barely cracked open the door to the almost all-white public sphere. Zealous agitation against slavery by blacks was not likely to get a publisher, even if African American writers had been so inclined. In most cases, fleeting early signs of antislavery sentiments among white evangelicals failed to flourish in the postrevolutionary period. In the first generation of American evangelicalism, however, the New Divinity movement in New England did produce some serious antislavery thinking and activism.[37]

Among the New Divinity pastors, Samuel Hopkins became the most outspoken antislavery advocate. Hopkins was one of a cadre of evangelical ministers converted at Yale in the early 1740s, and he became one of Jonathan Edwards's

Attributed to Joseph Badger, *Samuel Hopkins*, c. 1755.
Massachusetts Historical Society.

chief protégés. The New Divinity movement, led by Hopkins and Joseph Bellamy, sought to elaborate and extend Edwards's formidable theological influence. Hopkins agreed with Edwards's Calvinism on most points, but he came to
see Edwards's concept of virtue as deficient. In *The Nature of True Virtue* (1757),
Edwards had emphasized virtue as "benevolence to Being in general," a view
that Hopkins saw as potentially self-indulgent and impractical. Hopkins, instead,
defined true virtue as "love to God and our neighbour, including ourselves . . . or
friendly affection to all intelligent beings." Hopkins's ideal morality was rooted
in "disinterested benevolence," or a willingness to sacrifice self for the good of
others, especially the good of those most in need of benevolence.[38]
    Hopkins's ideas about disinterested benevolence began to flower just as he
left Great Barrington, Massachusetts, to take the pastorate at First Church, Newport, Rhode Island. In the Massachusetts backcountry Hopkins dealt little with
the grim realities of the Atlantic slave trade, in which Newport was a critical
hub. Hopkins wrote that Newport might "have more concern in the slave trade

. . . than in all North America besides," and that the slave traders "are much opposed to an attempt to carry the gospel to the negroes." Newport merchants traded sugar, rum, whale oil, and humans with great skill and few qualms. Hopkins's congregant and good friend Sarah Osborn introduced Hopkins to some Newport slaves whom she sometimes hosted in her home. As the revolutionary crisis grew, Hopkins began to see slavery as sin, a symptom of the greed and acquisitiveness of American society, and a profound contradiction of the expressed ideals of American republicanism. Despite the importance of slavery in Rhode Island's economy, and proslavery sentiments even within Hopkins's own congregation, a majority of white Rhode Islanders found antislavery arguments like Hopkins's convincing enough to pass a modest 1774 law banning further slave importations.[39]

Hopkins began to criticize slavery and the slave trade in his church by the early 1770s. Some of his congregants never accepted him because of his "opposition to the slavery of Africans," he wrote to a friend. He was soon joined in a small choir of protest by fellow New Divinity ministers Levi Hart and Jonathan Edwards Jr. Hart, minister of Preston, Connecticut, and a student and son-in-law of Joseph Bellamy, circulated a 1774 proposal for an emancipation plan in Connecticut. It suggested compensation for owners and the possibility of some freed slaves returning to Africa. Hart then published *Liberty Described and Recommended* in 1775, in which he publicly advocated emancipation. Hart appealed equally to republicanism and Christianity to make his case against chattel slavery, which he called "a most attrocious violation of one of the first laws of nature." He refused to see Christian liberty as only spiritual, but argued that liberty in Christ included this-worldly freedom. He longed for the day when "Americans shall be consistently engaged in the cause of liberty, and a final end be put to the cruel slavery of our fellow men." Hart deftly blended the principles of Christian freedom and Anglo-American republicanism to argue that the "sacred cause of liberty" included the goal of freeing the slaves.[40]

Hopkins similarly linked the cause of American independence to abolition in his *Dialogue Concerning the Slavery of the Africans*, dedicated to the members of the Continental Congress. To Hopkins, slavery represented the height of human selfishness and a direct contradiction of the republican values expressed by the Congress. He was "deeply sensible of the inconsistence of promoting the slavery of the Africans, at the same time we are asserting our own civil liberty." Hopkins published the tract in early 1776, around the same time as Tom Paine's *Common Sense* but before the Declaration of Independence. He hoped that the logic of American freedom would lead the Congress to push for total abolition in the colonies.[41]

Hopkins denounced the cruelties of the slave trade and dismissed the idea that the passage to the Americas would ultimately benefit Africans by introducing them to Christianity. The brutality of slavery turned Africans away from the Christianity of their masters, he believed, and it was a wonder "that any of them should think favorably of Christianity and cordially embrace it." Even if they did Christianize, that would not justify the evil of slavery. Hopkins argued that God had providentially caused the crisis with Britain in order to reveal Americans' hypocrisy. "God has raised up men to attempt to deprive us of liberty, and the evil we are threatened with is slavery." While the patriots protested against the threat of economic dependence and "slavery" to Britain, they made "slaves of many thousands of our brethren, who have as good a right to liberty as ourselves." White Americans should expect no deliverance from their oppressors as long as they persisted in this hypocrisy, Hopkins predicted. Later in 1776, Hopkins indicated in an unpublished sermon that he was well pleased with the Declaration of Independence's egalitarian language, but Hopkins believed that men's self-evident equality should lead to the abolition of slavery. That institution was "equally against the Law of Nature and the Law of Christ."[42]

Hart and Hopkins were joined in their New Divinity antislavery activism by Lemuel Haynes, who also used the Declaration's language to push for abolition. Haynes was a mulatto orphan who grew up as an indentured servant in an evangelical household in Middle Granville, Massachusetts. He served in both the Massachusetts militia and the Continental Army during the Revolution, after which he began studying for the ministry. His race seemed to pose less of a professional obstacle than one might imagine, though Haynes had to face many taunts and insults regarding his parentage. In 1788 he accepted a call to pastor in Rutland, Vermont, where he enjoyed considerable success for three decades. He was dismissed in 1818, however, and his advancing age and race both played roles in his removal. Early in his career, perhaps in 1776, Haynes penned "Liberty Further Extended: Or Free thoughts on the illegality of Slave-keeping," a treatise he probably hoped to publish but never did. Nevertheless, it is likely that this powerful tract was widely known in New England's New Divinity circles.[43]

The title page of "Liberty Further Extended" pointedly quoted the slaveholder Jefferson's assertion that "all men are created Equal." Haynes argued that liberty was the natural right of all men, but that sin led men to become tyrants and to deprive others of their liberty. "Liberty is a Jewel which was handed Down to man from the cabinet of heaven," and "even an affrican, has Equally as good a right to his Liberty in common with Englishmen." Jefferson and the founders might have imagined "all men" as including only white male property owners, but the language of liberty was easily turned into a case for African American

Tray (depicting Rev. Lemuel Haynes in the pulpit), English, early nineteenth century.
Museum of Art, Rhode Island School of Design, Gift of Lucy Truman Aldrich.
Photograph by Erik Gould.

freedom by pastors like Haynes. Citing what was becoming a favorite passage of antislavery activists, Haynes noted that Acts 17:26 showed that "It hath pleased god to make of one Blood all nations of men," and thus "Liberty is Equally as pre[c]ious to a Black man, as it is to a white one." Borrowing from the Quaker Anthony Benezet's *Some Historical Account of Guinea* (1771), Haynes detailed the cruelties of the slave trade and thundered against the complacent "Christian Land" that tolerated such enormities. "What will you Do in that Day when God shall make inquisision for Blood? he will make you Drink the phials of his indignation which Like a potable Stream shall Be poured out without the Least mixture of mercy." God would not forget the hypocrisy of "Christian" America.[44]

Limitations on slavery went forward, step by step, in the northern states during the revolutionary era, aided significantly by such evangelicals as Wheatley, Hopkins, Hart, and Haynes. The new Methodist movement, led in America by Francis Asbury, also agitated against slavery after the Revolution. But American slavery would hardly take the path to extinction that some founders might have hoped for in 1776 or 1787. The rise of the South's "cotton kingdom" ensured that slavery could only be destroyed by the sword. Anglo-American churchmen, particularly in the South, often remained passive in the face of slavery, and some even began to develop a theology of slavery as a positive, God-ordained good. The first generation of evangelicalism had seen the sprouting of antislavery arguments that would continue to flourish and expand in the early nineteenth-century North. These new evangelicals, along with more liberal Christians, would help turn immediate abolition into a national moral crusade, even as other evangelicals in the North and South regarded their abolitionist brethren as dangerous incendiaries. Many whites worried about evangelical preachers contributing to the threat of slave insurrection "when they fill their discourses with a *ranting cant* about equality." The white fear of African American evangelicalism became particularly acute following the 1831 Virginia revolt led by the black preacher and visionary Nat Turner.[45]

The eighteenth century ended with the number of black evangelical church members still very low: perhaps less than 5 percent of the South's black population belonged to a Baptist, Methodist, or Presbyterian church. A great many more African Americans had been touched by the gospel, however, and momentum was building toward the massive conversions of the nineteenth century that would ultimately place evangelical Christianity at the heart of black American culture. Despite the evangelical movement's failings and limitations with regard to race, many African Americans still ultimately found hope in the offer of freedom in Christ for the afterlife, if not in this life.[46]

"Do the Holy Scriptures Countenance Such Wild Disorder?": Evangelicalism in Virginia

A pious bricklayer named Samuel Morris helped initiate the evangelical movement in Virginia. Some time before the revivals there began, the Anglican Morris received salvation. He struggled, however, to find like-minded believers in the Anglican church. He tried to evangelize many of his neighbors by publicly reading works by Martin Luther and John Bunyan. Morris learned of George Whitefield's visit to Williamsburg in late 1739, and though he could not go there to hear him, a recent Scottish immigrant to Hanover County brought with him a book of Whitefield's sermons, which Morris included in his public orations. A group of his followers began to meet frequently and sometimes skipped church to hear Morris. The gatherings became quite emotional, as the sermons caused some to begin "crying out, weeping bitterly." Some of the manifestations became so "strange and ridiculous" that Morris thought they must be authentic. Soon Morris's assemblies grew so large that his followers built a meetinghouse "meerly for Reading." Morris also began to itinerate, delivering Whitefield's sermons. The Anglican establishment summoned Morris and his associates before a Virginia court to explain their separation from the church. Anglican authorities saw these meetings as "convened sometimes by merely Lay Enthusiasts, who, in those meetings, read sundry fanatical Books & used long extempore prayers, and Discourses; sometimes by strolling pretended Ministers." When asked what denomination they were, Morris and his friends declared themselves "Lutherans," not knowing what else to say.[1]

Evangelicals in Virginia had to deal with two main challenges. First, like the Separates in New England, they faced an unfriendly established church. Baptists and Presbyterians in Virginia struggled to avoid legal penalties as they became increasingly visible threats to the Anglican establishment. Second, evangelicals had to confront the reality of Virginia's slave society and make decisions about the social implications of the movement. In general, early white evangelicals in Virginia chose to evangelize African Americans, but they rarely empowered them with freedom or leadership responsibilities.

Evangelicals in the Middle Colonies and New England had for some time contemplated sending missionaries to the southern colonies, and the revivals of the 1740 gave new momentum to that cause. In 1743 the Presbytery of New Castle commissioned Log College graduate William Robinson to preach in Virginia and the Carolinas. Morris's Hanover evangelicals caught wind of his tour and persuaded him to visit. Robinson's sermons precipitated such enthusiastic fervor that he was forced to correct some "Antinomian Mistakes." His preaching bred "an agreable Confusion of various Passions . . . some could not refrain from publickly declaring their Transport." Robinson soon departed, but he was followed by John Blair, brother of Samuel Blair of Fagg's Manor, Pennsylvania, who had also graduated from the Log College and been licensed by the New Castle Presbytery. One of his meetings also created a frenzy, as people could "hardly sit or stand, or keep their Passions under any proper Restraints." Morris, tutored to become a moderate, confessed later that they did not realize such enthusiasm could breed "Apostacy." Another Log College graduate, John Roan, arrived in the winter of 1744–45. His work expanded the reach of the revivals, and he also began publicly denouncing the Anglican clergy.[2]

Under Roan's preaching, the Hanover awakeners ran afoul of the Virginia authorities. Governor William Gooch called for the suppression of "ministers under the pretended infatuation of new light, extraordinary impulse, and such like fanatical and enthusiastic knowledge." Charges were brought against Roan and several of the evangelical leaders, but the arrival of Samuel Finley and Gilbert Tennent to plead for the Hanover dissenters' liberty helped ease the tension. Still, Samuel Morris was fined on several occasions for not attending church and for holding unlawful meetings. William Tennent and Samuel Blair also visited Hanover and introduced the traditional Scots-Irish communion service. Morris recalled that the large celebration appeared as "one of the Days of Heaven." Finally, Whitefield made a visit to the area, which generated surprisingly little comment from Morris, who noted only that the itinerant gave them "farther Encouragement" and more recruits among the Anglicans.[3]

Patrick Henry, Anglican rector of St. Paul's Parish, Hanover, and uncle of the famous Patriot leader of the same name, led the countercharge against the surging evangelicals. In a lengthy letter to William Dawson, Virginia's Anglican Commissary, he delineated the threats posed by the evangelicals' doctrines, which he closely associated with Separatism. Following information he had received from

John Thomson, one of the key antirevivalists of the Philadelphia Synod, Henry characterized the Hanover evangelicals and the northern itinerants as incendiaries. Henry and the Anglicans did not believe that the principle of freedom of conscience (which everyone accepted in theory) meant that the dissenters could hold unauthorized public meetings. He noted with concern that Gilbert Tennent's faction had sent poorly qualified itinerants into "all parts of America, to disturb the established Churches," and that their preachers needed no qualification other than "experiences of a work of grace in their hearts." Henry heard that John Roan had taught that sinners needed not only to be willing to be damned, but to "disbelieve the very being of a God!" before they could be saved.[4]

Affirming the evangelicals' new belief in the witness of the Spirit, Henry noted that they taught that converts would know exactly when their conversion happened because the Spirit would be perceived by the "outward Senses." Moreover, believers had the "Spirit of discerning," whereby they could perceive true Christians from hypocrites. Henry himself had been identified as a hypocrite by some of the Hanover revivalists. The evangelicals called on people to abandon the graceless Anglican ministers and to seek churches where they would be fed. Their behavior in the meetings was outrageous to Henry: they called "old people, Grey headed Devils, and all promiscuously, Damn'd double damn'd, whose [souls] are in hell, though they are alive on earth, Lumps of hellfire, incarnate Devils, 1000 times worse than Devils &c and all the while the Preacher exalts his voice puts himself into a violent agitation, stamping & beating his Desk unmercifully, until the weaker sort of his hearers being scar'd, cry out, fall down & work like people in convulsion fits." The noisy preachers supposedly regarded the convulsionaries as the only legitimate converts. Henry recommended continued vigilance against these "wild & wicked men."[5]

The Log College men had given Hanover a great deal of attention since 1743, but Morris and his followers longed for a permanent pastor, which they received in 1748 when Presbyterian pastor Samuel Davies came to stay among them. Davies was a graduate of Samuel Blair's academy at Fagg's Manor. He finished his studies in 1746 and received ordination from the New Castle Presbytery in 1747. He began visiting Hanover in 1747, settled there in 1748, and immediately incurred the wrath of the Anglican establishment. Patrick Henry raged against Davies's popularity. Itinerants like Davies, he believed, tried to "Screw up the People to the greatest heights of religious Phrenzy, and then leave them in that state." The established ministers were left to clean up the mess.[6]

Samuel Davies vigorously denied the accusation of "Phrenzy," and during his time in Virginia he became the consummate evangelical moderate. He regulated any hint of enthusiasm in his congregations and routinely repudiated the

Samuel Davies. Union Theological Seminary and
Presbyterian School of Christian Education.

radical awakeners. Henry, like most prominent antirevivalists, tried to conflate
the moderate and radical evangelicals, but Davies would have none of it. Davies, going by the letter of the law, secured licenses to preach from the governor's
office and began ministering to dissenting meetings in several Virginia counties.
Despite his deference to the government, Davies's Anglican opponents arranged
for the reprinting of John Caldwell's *An Impartial Trial of the Spirit*, which railed
against the enthusiasm and "Quack Methods" of Whitefield and his followers.
Davies, recognizing this as a "Design to render us odious in this Colony," responded in 1748 with *The Impartial Trial Impartially Tried and Convicted of
Partiality.*[7]

Davies defended the Presbyterians' doctrine and practice of itinerancy. He
claimed that he preached only the essentials of Reformed Christianity, which
the Church of England traditionally had shared. He repudiated open proselytizing of other churches' members, and accused the Church of England priests of
"exclamatory Harangues . . . against New-Lights, Methodists, Enthusiasts, De-

ceivers, Itinerants, Pretenders, &c." The Church of England men were driven by party zeal, not the Presbyterians. Davies claimed only the right to "faithful peaceable preaching of the Gospel, and necessary Self-Defence, when unjustly aggressed." Davies explicitly repudiated enthusiasm, suggesting "that sundry Irregularities have attended the Work of God [in New England], which did not attend it in Pennsylvania. — Speculative Antinomianism has infected a few; and Lay-Exhorters were too much tolerated by some." He singled out James Davenport as having been "governed by enthusiastic impulses." But Davenport's evangelicalism was not the same as that of the Presbyterians, whose moderation deserved a respected place within Virginia's religious order.[8]

Davies also claimed the rights of Protestant dissenters in Virginia under the 1689 Act of Toleration, passed shortly after the Glorious Revolution in England. Some in the Virginia government argued that the act did not apply to the colonies, but Davies insisted that it had previously been invoked for the Quakers and that it applied to the Presbyterians. Davies expanded on this argument in a letter to the bishop of London in 1752. He asked "whether, if those that were formerly conformists, follow their own judgments, and dissent, they are cut off from the privileges granted by law to those that are dissenters by birth and education? If not, had not these people a legal right to separate from the established church, and invite any legally qualified minister they thought fit to preach among them?" By law, and by conscience, Virginia's evangelicals had the right to dissent from the Anglican church. Davies's initial appeal for toleration would, in time, flower into the case for disestablishment in Virginia, led by Thomas Jefferson and others.[9]

As Davies defended moderate evangelicals' rights in Virginia, his influence continued to grow. Although most of his dissenting churches had only fifteen or twenty families in full communion, he reported preaching to crowds of five hundred to a thousand on a regular basis, with many Anglicans attending his meetings. All told, he estimated in 1751 that he had about three hundred communicant members under his care. Davies tried to recruit more pastors to come to Virginia to help him with the work, including the recently dismissed Jonathan Edwards, whom he considered a model of sober moderation. Whomever the northern churches might send, Davies wrote, they should make sure that they were free of "enthusiastical freaks of ardent zeal." Revealing his redeemed reputation among moderates, James Davenport itinerated in 1750 in Virginia with Davies's approval. Eventually the New York Synod sent several other ministers, including John Todd and John Wright, to pastor new congregations. Davenport wrote excitedly in 1753 that the "interests of religion are perceivably advancing since Mr. Todd's settlement near [Davies]." Since there were more preachers in Virginia, the effects of the Word preached had less time to "wear off."[10]

Davies and his pastoral friends considered African Americans central to the revivals in their congregations. "Ethiopia has also stretched forth her Hands unto God," Davies told Joseph Bellamy, referring to the oft-cited Psalm 68:31. He baptized about forty adult African Americans in his first three years at Hanover. He judged most of them sincere converts, with "their artless Simplicity [and] their passionate Aspirations after Christ." The Virginia Presbyterians regularly reported their successes among African Americans in Anglo-American evangelical circles. Davies particularly hoped that the prospect of African American conversions would help fundraising efforts for charity and education in Virginia. Davies's and other white Virginians' accounts of African American piety provide among the best (albeit slanted) views of the early inroads of moderate evangelicalism among the southern slave population.[11]

Davies wrote often to correspondents associated with the Society in London for Promoting Religious Knowledge among the Poor, many of whose members he had met on a fundraising tour in England from 1753 to 1755. Davies and Gilbert Tennent successfully promoted the College of New Jersey on that visit, but Davies also sold his vision of evangelizing Native Americans and African Americans in Virginia. In 1755, Davies wrote that the slaves had no opportunity for education and were often neglected by their masters. They were "originally African savages, and never heard of Jesus or his gospel, till they arrived at the land of their slavery in America." Davies called the slaves "objects of my compassion." By 1755 he had baptized about one hundred slaves and perhaps three hundred attended his meetings regularly. Most apparently belonged to white members of his congregation. He thought John Todd had about the same number of slaves in his church. Colonel James Gordon, an Irish Presbyterian who attended Todd's meetings, noted with pleasure that "our negroes" had attended all four days of a sacramental festival led by Todd.[12]

Davies was impressed with some slaves' ability to read and asked for the society and other benefactors to send Bibles and Watts's *Psalms and Hymns*. On at least one occasion, Methodist leader John Wesley sent him books from England to distribute among poor blacks and whites. Davies thought African Americans were particularly given to "music, and a kind of extatic delight in Psalmody." The books sent by English benefactors reportedly had a great effect on the pious slaves, who spent much of their spare time at Davies's house. They especially loved Watts's hymns, and Davies found that "sundry of them have lodged all night in my kitchen; and sometimes, when I have awaked about two or three a-clock in the morning, a torrent of sacred harmony poured into my chamber, and carried my mind away to Heaven. In this seraphic exercise, some of them spend almost the whole night." Davies contrasted this idyllic scene with the slaves' prospects should they languish in pagan darkness. Not only did Davies appeal to the spiritual reasons for converting the slaves, but he also shrewdly noted to prospective donors the threat of French influence. The French, with whom the British were at war in America starting in 1754, might be able to stir the slaves into rebellion with promises of freedom, he suggested. Making the slaves educated Protestants would help them understand the "Impostures, Superstitions and Cruelties of POPERY," and keep them pacified. Despite the revivals' successes, much work remained to be done, as thousands of Virginia's African Americans continued "as rank Pagans, as when they left the wilds of Africa." Davies similarly worried about the allegiances of the Cherokees, "because their situation exposes them . . . to the intrigues of the French." He tried unsuccessfully to recruit missionary Gideon Hawley to work among the unevangelized Indians.[13]

Davies adhered to George Whitefield's ideas regarding slavery. He did not oppose the institution itself, and he owned slaves. He did, however, criticize Anglican slave masters for not evangelizing their slaves, and he included slaves in the everyday life of his church, believing that they were as fit for salvation as any other humans. Davies, who practiced the traditional Scots-Irish Presbyterian communion seasons, was pleased to report "seeing forty . . . black faces around the Table of the Lord, who all make a credible profession of Christianity." Davies continued to baptize black converts regularly and interviewed one who told him (in Davies's words), "I am a poor slave, brought into a strange country, where I never expect to enjoy my liberty. While I lived in my own country, I knew nothing of that JESUS I have heard you speak so much about." Now he did, and he resolved to follow Christ. White evangelical readers might feel some vague sympathy for this black Christian bound in perpetuity, but they would also be glad that the man had found Christ in slavery. By 1757, Davies estimated that he had baptized 150 African American adults in all, and 60 participated in one communion service. He confessed some difficulty in communicating basic doctrines to them, such as the meaning of baptism, but in "experimental Religion," some blacks had progressed further than many "Christians of a fairer colour." An anonymous correspondent expressed thanks for the converts in Virginia, whether white or black, for "in Christ Jesus they are all one." Whether spiritual equality would lead to social equality was another question.[14]

In 1758, Davies published *The Duty of Christians to Propagate their Religion among Heathens* in London, which furthered his argument that Christ was "a common Saviour for Britons, Africans, and Americans." Davies's pamphlet, and his continued evangelization of slaves, made some Anglican slave owners nervous. Colonel Edwin Conway of Lancaster charged Davies with circulating a pamphlet (probably the appendix to Benjamin Fawcett's 1756 *A Compassionate Address to the Christian Negroes in Virginia*) in which he "much Reproached Virginia. And informs the Negroes they are Stronger than the Whites, being Equal in Number then & having an Annual addition of thousands." This, by any fair reading, was an exaggeration, as the appendix merely noted that the numbers of blacks and whites were roughly equal in Virginia, and that many slaves came to the Americas every year in the slave trade. For Conway to consider such information reproachful suggests just how anxious the slave masters were. Regardless of Davies's passivity toward slavery itself, some whites could hardly avoid viewing his attention to African Americans as subversive.[15]

Like Davies, the Presbyterian John Wright also made African Americans a chief concern of his ministry. Wright settled in Cumberland County, Virginia, in 1754, and in 1755 he saw a significant revival spawned by fears over the Seven Years' War. British General Edward Braddock's calamitous defeat in July 1755 woke Virginians up to the real threat posed by the French and their Native American allies. Samuel Davies told a military company raised in Hanover County in 1755, "If you would save yourselves . . . from all the infernal Horrors of Popery, and the savage Tyranny of a mongrel Race of French and Indian Conquerors, . . . REPENT, and turn to the Lord." Wright saw many people convinced by this sort of warning, as thousands "acknowledge their wickedness and ignorance, and believe that the new light clergy and adherents are right." Two thousand people came to a July 1755 communion season, listening to Wright preach and watching 180 take the sacrament.[16]

Wright's church continued to grow for several years, and he too received books from the Society in London for Promoting Religious Knowledge among the Poor, which he distributed among poor whites and blacks. Wright saw his greatest revival yet in 1761. This stir began among African Americans. "When ye revival began, it spread more powerfully among ye Blacks than ye Whites, in so much yt they crowded to me in great numbers . . . to know what they should do to be saved." In two months he received more than a hundred new communicant members, with African Americans comprising half the total. As of 1761, he had "about 300 *Ethiopians* solicitously engaged after ye great salvation. Thus the prophecy in Psalm 68. 31 seems in some measure to have its accomplishment." Wright saw in the slaves' conversions a direct fulfillment of prophecy.[17]

After Davies's return from England, evangelical Presbyterianism continued to spread in Virginia. In particular, Davies and John Todd began preaching in the Northern Neck, south of the Potomac River, in 1757. Priests there registered the same complaints against the dissenters' threat to the establishment. In Northumberland County, Davies preached "in an Orchard," and in Lancaster County "he had a Desk erected for him in the Woods." These "Conventicles & Field preachings" raised the prospect of disorderly extrainstitutional religion. Finally a sixty-by-thirty-foot meetinghouse was built for the itinerants in Lancaster County, but the priests continued to fear that the dissenters might give a "mortal wound to the purest and most edifying Worship of the Church of England." It may have come as a relief to the Anglicans when Davies reluctantly accepted a call to become president of the College of New Jersey in 1759. Like Edwards before him, Davies's tenure at Princeton would be brief; he died in 1761 at the age of thirty-eight.[18]

Although the established churchmen led the charge against the new evangelicals in Virginia, revivalism did have a few friends among the Anglicans. Key among these supporters was Devereux Jarratt. Though Jarratt was subsequently ordained as an Anglican priest, he was converted under the ministry of evangelical Presbyterians in the early 1750s. Before he experienced the new birth, Jarratt, a nominal Anglican schoolmaster in Albemarle County, chanced to board with a family where "the lady of the house was a New-Light." She introduced Jarratt to evangelical piety and Puritan devotional texts. Then Jarratt began to attend a Presbyterian itinerant's meetings. He experienced sharp doubts about his eternal fate until in private devotion Isaiah 62:12 ("Thou shalt be called, sought out, a city not forsaken") impressed him. Finally, he was "blessed with faith to believe, not one promise only, but all the promises of the gospel with joy unspeakable and full of glory . . . it was a little heaven upon earth — so sweet, so ravishing, so delightful."[19]

Jarratt initially thought he would become a Presbyterian minister because he was prejudiced against the "loose lives of the [Anglican] Clergy, and their cold and unedifying manner of preaching." As he studied for ordination, however, he warmed to the evangelical tradition within the Anglican communion and noted that both George Whitefield and John Wesley had remained Anglicans. After a trip to England to receive ordination, Jarratt became the minister of Bath parish in Virginia in 1763. There "ignorance of the things of God, Prophaneness, and Irreligion then prevailed." He believed that the people of Bath had never heard anything about conversion, and he wrote that in response to his preaching they said to themselves, "This new man of ours brings strange things to our ears." His evangelical style brought the contempt of fellow priests, who called him "an enthusiast, fanatic, visionary, dissenter, Presbyterian, madman, and what not." Jarratt's insistence on the necessity of the new birth stirred an awakening among his parishioners, which slowly spread through the surrounding region. Jarratt soon began itinerating, and his circuit took him though much of central Virginia and North Carolina.[20]

In 1773, Jarratt encountered Wesleyan Methodist preachers for the first time in neighboring Virginia counties. In particular, he met with Robert Williams, who pioneered the Methodist work in Virginia and who helped establish the first Methodist preaching circuits around Petersburg. Soon Jarratt and Williams began to see remarkable numbers of conversions throughout south-central Virginia. Many private, or class, meetings were organized in the churches, and it was in these smaller groups that conversions often transpired. At a May 1776 meeting in his parish, Jarratt noted that "the windows of heaven were opened, and the rain of Divine Influence poured down." At a love feast during this meeting, "the power of the Lord came down on the Assembly, like a rushing, mighty Wind." A number of people fell on the floor and cried out for mercy, and the whole meetinghouse seemed to fill with God's presence. The "multitudes" that attended returned to homes throughout the region and related their incredible experiences. Jarratt estimated that "several hundreds" were converted within weeks of this meeting.[21]

The moderate Jarratt worried that some enthusiasm had mixed with authentic religious experiences in the revival, but, explicitly following Jonathan Edwards, he conceded that these extremes always accompanied true awakenings. Nevertheless, he wrote, "there were some circumstances . . . which I disliked: such as loud outcries, tremblings, fallings, convulsions." He also worried about exhorters and laypersons speaking simultaneously during meetings, "so that the Assembly appeared to be all in confusion, and must seem . . . like a drunken rabble." One of Jarratt's correspondents, Thomas Saunders, reported that sometimes as many as twenty men and women would "fall down as dead" in meetings. Those who exhibited the most dramatic physical manifestations often converted quickly: one woman went from total spiritual passivity to assurance of salvation in fifteen minutes. Among the Methodists, an even greater rapidity of conversion and assurance became the norm.[22]

Jarratt merged his efforts with those of Methodist itinerants Thomas Rankin and George Shadford, who helped generate a widespread Methodist-Anglican revival in south-central Virginia in 1775 and 1776, at the beginning of the American Revolution. Rankin wrote of meetings in the summer of 1776 where "hundreds fell to the ground, and the house seemed to shake with the presence of God." These meetings were commonly filled with both white and black Virginians. At a meeting at White's Chapel, near Jarratt's home, the moderate Rankin preached before a packed assembly and had to stop repeatedly to ask the congregation to "compose themselves." Many fell on their knees or faces, crying out to God. "Hundreds of Negroes were among them," he noted, "with the tears streaming down their black faces." Although their inclusion of African Americans in the revival meetings was not unique, a number of these early white Methodist preachers, including Rankin, soon came out against chattel slavery, following the example set by John Wesley in England. In the course of one year, the Methodists' numbers in Virginia had swelled from about twenty-six hundred to about forty-four hundred. Although the revival slowed as the Methodists increasingly labored under suspicions of their loyalty in the war to King George III, this progress augured well for their future in the South.[23]

Devereux Jarratt and Samuel Davies both promoted a faith that made inroads in Virginia by emphasizing doctrinal commonalities with the Anglican church and also by offering attention to Virginians who had found the church wanting or inaccessible to them. The second phase of early Virginia evangelicalism featured the rise of the Separate Baptists, who entertained no illusions that they had any similarities to the Anglicans. Jarratt, for one, fancied himself a very ecumenically minded Christian, but he could not countenance the Baptists and their "notion of going into the water, and its evil train of consequences." Evangelicals like Davies and Jarratt might once have appeared enthusiastic to staid Anglicans, but in comparison to the Baptists, they seemed to be exemplars of moderation. The Baptists appealed to the common people's desire for spiritual power and community in a highly unequal society, and their raging popularity and resistance against vicious persecution seriously challenged the Anglican establishment and transformed Virginia society.[24]

Shubal Stearns and Daniel Marshall led the Separate Baptist incursion into the South in the 1750s, but there were some Regular Baptists working in Virginia before the Separates' appearance. In the colonies, "Regular" Baptists typically referred to Calvinist Baptists associated in some way with the Philadelphia Association of Baptists, whereas "Separates" were those, mostly Calvinists, who emerged from the sectarian ferment of the Great Awakening, primarily in New England. The Arminian, or "General" Baptists, suffered during the mid-eighteenth century, overwhelmed by the surging evangelical Calvinistic Baptist churches. The most influential of the Regular Baptist pastors in Virginia was David Thomas of the Broad Run Baptist Church in Fauquier County. Though Thomas tried to present Baptists also as sober and theologically sound, he encountered persecution and harassment from Anglicans, Presbyterians, and angry mobs. Some perceived the Baptists as threats to Virginia's traditional social order of male independence, social dominance, and public leisure. Among various episodes of violence and insults against him, Thomas was once "pulled down" and dragged out as he preached at a tobacco house. Another time an outraged man tried to shoot Thomas but was stopped by one of Thomas's followers, whereupon "a battle followed wherein many were hurt." On another occasion a "parcel of Virginia bucks" interrupted Thomas's service with this conversation: "That is he, (quote one) yeas, (said a second) it is he that stole my neighbour Johnson's bull, did he eat it, (said a third). No (replied a fourth) for I saw him ride the bull about the country to preach. Yeas (added a fifth) and I saw him ride the bull last night to Moll Heerly's baudy-house." Thomas was accused of criminality and illicit sexuality, both of which would have betrayed the high standards of masculine purity expected in Baptist congregations.[25]

Despite the threats against him, Thomas tried publicly to paint the Baptists as mainstream Protestants. In *The Virginian Baptist* (1774), he swore off Baptist radicalism. He did not accept immediate inspiration of the Holy Spirit but asserted that one could not be a true Christian without the Spirit's indwelling presence. Thomas noted that critics charged the Baptists with having "noisy meetings." Where in the Bible could he find justification for "loud crying? What jumping up? What falling down? What roaring, schreeching, screaming? Does the Holy Scriptures countenance such wild disorder?" The moderate Thomas said he could not justify such "horrid vociferations and obstreperous commotions" and that they "never were the effects of my preaching." Thomas drew a clear line between the practices of the Regular and the Separate Baptists, as the latter countenanced the more exotic bodily effects of the Spirit. Nevertheless, he meant to proselytize those who "depend on an outward form of religion, without possessing the power of it." No doubt he had in mind northern Virginia's nominal Anglicans.[26]

While the Regulars defended moderate evangelicalism, the Separates embraced a hearty radicalism that eventually jeopardized the dominant religious order in Virginia. The Separates moved out of North Carolina into Virginia, flowing from Shubal Stearns's epicenter at Sandy Creek. Daniel Marshall, Stearns's brother-in-law, began preaching in the border region between North Carolina and Virginia in 1758–59. A Separate Baptist church led by Marshall's disciple Dutton Lane was constituted in 1760 at the Dan River. Lane was a former Anglican who was converted following a reported encounter with the devil, who chased Lane home after a hunting trip. The terrified Lane was then ready to accept the Baptists' gospel. Though Lane's church met with many threats, early Baptist historian Morgan Edwards believed that God intervened on behalf of its members. A party coming to arrest the church's leaders was struck temporarily blind in the night by a flash of light followed by thick darkness. The persecutors "agreed that this strange event was a warning to them; . . . which procured quietness to the poor baptists."[27]

The Separate Baptists regularly reported signs, wonders, and divine communications in their early years in the South. North Carolina Baptist minister James Read reported receiving "frequent teachings from God" and dreams calling him into Virginia. Both waking and sleeping, "he felt his soul earnestly impressed" with the desire to preach there. In his dreams he saw large congregations assembled to hear him, and his family heard him crying out, "O Virginia, Virginia, Virginia!" in his sleep. Just as he was preparing to set out, messengers arrived from Virginia pleading with him to come. Read toured Virginia several times in the mid-1760s, baptizing hundreds of converts. Meetings typically ran late into the night, and "sometimes the floor would be covered with persons struck down under conviction of sin."[28]

Through the late 1760s, Separate Baptist churches grew slowly in southern Virginia. Afterwards, however, the Separates swarmed throughout the rest of the colony. They publicized conversions of former opponents, such as the lawyer John "Swearing Jack" Waller of Spotsylvania County. Waller had actively persecuted the Baptists, until the fortitude of a persecuted Baptist pastor convicted Waller of the truth of their beliefs. Drawn out of the hierarchical, rough-and-tumble world of gentry manliness, Waller himself began to encounter sharp persecution for his criticism of the traditional world he once enjoyed. In 1768, Waller was fined and imprisoned for holding illegal assemblies, but he continued preaching from the jail windows. A mocking crowd tried to drive Waller's supporters away by "singing obscene songs, breeding riots, beating drums, pelting the minister through the bars, etc., but all in vain."[29]

In another remarkable episode, Waller was confronted in 1771 in Caroline County, not only by the sheriff but also by the local Anglican priest. At the outdoor meeting, the priest supposedly jammed the butt end of a whip in Waller's mouth, and the men dragged Waller from the stage and horsewhipped him, so that "poor Waller was presently in a gore of blood and will carry the scars to his grave." Waller, undeterred, went back to the stage and preached freely. Waller was reported to have remarkable preaching gifts, and at least once he administered a miraculous healing. The wife of the Baptist minister in Buckingham, Virginia, was healed of "deplorable violent spasms" by Waller's prayers and an anointing of oil. Although we may doubt the precise details of such extraordinary stories (supplied, of course, by Baptists), there can be no doubt that many Virginians, often clergy, gentry, and/or militia leaders, regarded the Baptists' religion and style as grievously subversive.[30]

Waller helped precipitate the conversion of the Trabue family, a group of Anglican Huguenots who lived in Chesterfield County. Daniel Trabue, in an 1827 memoir, remembered that Separate Baptists began to arrive in Piedmont Virginia in 1770, when Daniel was ten years old. His uncle fell in with the Baptists and asked Trabue's father to let John Waller speak at his house. Trabue's father reluctantly agreed to let Waller conduct an informal service, at which Waller "gave his views" on John 3 and the new birth. The service convinced young Daniel that Waller was a man of God, and most of his family members were soon baptized as believers.[31]

Chesterfield County began crawling with Baptist itinerants, many of whom were imprisoned. Crowds came to hear the preachers speak at the jail, prompting the authorities to build a brick wall around the prison to discourage the meetings. Trabue himself lingered in doubts and sinfulness until 1785, when he began to receive words of Scripture impressed on his mind. After attending a Baptist revival meeting, Trabue retired to the woods, where "these words came into my mind, 'Stand still and see the salvation of god.' These words came with power, and in my emagination I saw the great salvation of Jesus christ to save a lost world. . . . I was so Delighted to view this great and mighty sight." At his next revival meeting, Trabue was overcome with a belief that he was truly saved and began to cry aloud "Free grace!" He recalled that he "did not intentinally hollow it out a loud but was constrain to Do so. I hollowd it out, 'Free grace'; etc. 'Glory, glory'; etc. I called on the people to praise the lord." Soon he too received believer's baptism. Trabue, who worked as a miller and farmer, went on to become a key Baptist organizer in Kentucky.[32]

Baptist leaders like Trabue faced considerable cultural resistance to their message. Masculinity in genteel colonial southern society was defined in large part by the performance of public leisure entertainments like horse racing, drinking, dancing, and cockfighting, all activities that the Baptists rejected. Former friends of Baptist converts sometimes tried to drag them back into the traditional gentlemanly style they had forsaken. James Ireland, a Scottish schoolmaster who once had delighted in the gaiety of balls and dances, was confronted by an old friend who tried to "convert me, and that to the dance, on Monday." But his friend was not prepared for Ireland's gloomy, emaciated appearance, and he was so stunned upon seeing Ireland that he could only gasp, "In the name of the Lord, what is the matter with you?" Ireland would not go to the dance, but soon sunk into a spiritual crisis during which the devil confronted him with doubts about divine election. Just as he began to fear that he was damned, "a voice from Heaven reached my soul with these words. 'But I will have mercy upon whom I will have mercy.'" Though he knew some might read it as "wild enthusiasm," he "possessed a certainty of satan's presence with me, in that temptation, and that he now withdrew from me." He began to cry, and his "hard heart was thawed to contrition." The old world of genteel society had now become Satan's domain from which God's grace delivered him.[33]

Further confirming his belief in God's favor on him, Ireland experienced a dream at the outset of his ministry in which he was taken prisoner by a man on a red horse, whom he took to be the symbol of persecution from Revelation 6:4. The rider showed him the course of his future travels and the place where he would soon be imprisoned. The dream gave Ireland a framework for understanding the cruel persecution he would face for his itinerant preaching. He was soon arrested and jailed in Culpepper. His followers came to the jail and listened to him preach through the grate, but his opponents tried to break up the crowds. Some of his African American followers were immediately stripped and whipped. Some "miscreants" went so far as to urinate on him as he tried to speak. Others made a failed attempt to blow up his cell, and some attempted to "smoke me with brimstone and Indian pepper." Ireland would not be dissuaded, however, as he saw a divine purpose in his persecution.[34]

Not only did Baptists reject the masculine norms of the gentry, but they seemed also to threaten the Anglican establishment. Anglicans perceived that the Baptists insulted them mercilessly, as the churchman William Green wrote to a Baptist pastor in 1767, "Worse could not be said of the Pagans & Idolators, who sacrificed their Children to Moloch, than has been said by some of your Society, concerning the Church and its Members." Because of this behavior, the Baptists could not "reasonably expect to be Treated with common decency or respect," according to Green. Others noted that the Baptists flaunted the Act of Toleration entirely, whereas the Presbyterians had tried to operate within its strictures. A mocking "recipe to make an ANABAPTIST PREACHER" printed in the *Virginia Gazette* reflected the establishment's fears:

> Take the Herbs of Hypocrisy and Ambition, of each one Handful, of the Spirit of Pride two Drams, of the Seed of Dissention and Discord one Ounce, of the Flower Of Formality three Scruples, of the Roots of Stubbornness and Obstinacy four Pounds. . . . This will make the Schismatick endeavour to maintain his Doctrine, wound the Church, delude the People, justify their Proceedings of Illusion, foment Rebellion, and call it by the Name of Liberty of Conscience.

The countercultural ways of the Baptists made them appear as offensive, delusive revolutionaries to their opponents.[35]

No wonder, then, a number of Baptist itinerants were imprisoned in Virginia in the 1760s and 1770s, perhaps about thirty-four. In Orange County, authorities jailed four Baptists in July 1768, charging them as "Vagrant and Itinerant Persons and for Assembling themselves unlawfully at Sundry Times and Places Under the Denomination of Anabaptists and for Teaching & preaching Schismatick Doctrines." Also in Orange County, Baptist preacher Nathaniel Saunders was arrested and warned to preach only in the limited sphere where he had been licensed by the authorities. Saunders continued to itinerate widely, eliciting a rebuke from the Anglican William Bradley, who chastised Saunders for trampling the "Laws that is the Support of our Holy Church" and for coming "in at a Back Door to Delude her Dissiples." Bradley considered the Baptists' religion an enthusiastic mess, "Ba[w]ling as you Do to be heard for half a mile Round." In Chesterfield County, Joseph Antony and William Webber were arrested and fined in 1771 "for misbehaviour by Itinerant preaching in this County, being of that Sect of dissenters from the Church of England commonly called ana baptists."[36]

No doubt one of the most disturbing aspects of the Separate Baptists' work was their disregard for the colony's conventional hierarchies of race and gender. As Baptist preacher Henry Toler exclaimed in his journal, having just baptized several slaves, "The Lord is good and converts People of different Coulers and Ranks." The 1772 "Address to the Anabaptists Imprisoned in Caroline County," printed in the *Virginia Gazette*, worried that the Baptists' ministry loosened all kinds of social bonds: "Wives are drawn from their Husbands, Children from their Parents, and Slaves from the Obedience of their Masters. Thus the very Heartstrings of those little Societies which form the greater are torn in sunder, and all their Peace destroyed." From the beginning, Separate Baptist churches in Virginia included both black and white members, although black membership remained low overall until after 1780. White Baptist missionaries often gave serious attention to slaves, many of whom surely felt neglected by the Anglican establishment. African American Baptists received as much or more persecution as did whites, as a 1771 report to the Philadelphia Association of Baptists noted: "there is an unusual outpouring of the Spirit on all ranks of men in [Virginia, and] that many negroes endure scourgings for religion's sake." As early as 1758, Sandy Creek missionaries helped organize a slave congregation, the Bluestone Church, on the plantation of William Byrd III, which may have been the first independently functioning African American church in North America. The church did not last long, but it reflected the Baptists' commitment to evangelizing African Americans.[37]

Baptists had high behavioral standards for all members, and blacks' names appeared periodically as individuals in church records and cases of discipline. Theoretically, African American Baptists could bring complaints against white members in church discipline cases, but they rarely did. Baptists did not usually try to persuade their white members to free their slaves, but conversion to Baptist principles did influence a few slave masters to do so. In the most notable case of such emancipation, Robert Carter III, of the great Virginia family of planters, freed more than four hundred fifty slaves beginning in 1791. He had been baptized as a believer in 1778, after experiencing a long spiritual struggle and growing fascination with the enthusiastic religion of poor whites and slaves. But by 1791, the mercurial Carter had left the Baptist church, perhaps partly because of the church's growing conservatism on race, and would soon embrace the more exotic faith of Swedish visionary Emanuel Swedenborg.[38]

Carter's experience was unusual; relatively few elites became Baptists or liberated their slaves out of evangelical conviction. The Baptists did sometimes require masters to treat slaves without cruelty, however. For instance, the Meherrin Baptist Church in Lunenberg County admonished master Charles Cook in 1772 for burning one of his slaves. Lest we rush to commend the church for its vigilance, we should also note that Cook was forgiven and restored a month later after repenting before the congregation, presumably including the black members. Cook was soon appointed as an exhorter, and in 1775 he became a teaching elder in one of Meherrin's branch churches.[39]

There is considerable evidence to show that women (both black and white) and African American and Native American men did find integral roles and spiritual empowerment in Separate Baptist churches. Several Virginia churches had "deaconnesses," giving women official leadership positions. Regular Baptist churches reportedly refused fellowship with the Separates because they allowed women to pray in public and allowed any man to preach. At least one Pamunkey Indian, Robert Marsh, worked as a Baptist itinerant in Virginia in the 1780s. This "Indian preacher" shared pulpits with white pastors. Black men certainly itinerated and served as deacons, and some may have held office as elders in mixed congregations. The perceived empowerment of African Americans by the Presbyterians and Baptists frightened many white Virginians. A bill in the House of Burgesses threatened dissenters with imprisonment should they encourage slaves to disobey their masters, agitate against slavery, or "baptize or admit any Slave . . . a Member . . . of any Congregation, or religious Society, without the Permission of the Owner of such Slave." Some feared that slaves would pose as evangelical itinerants in order to run away, as the *Virginia Gazette* advertised a reward for capturing "a likely Negro fellow named ADAM," who "pretends to be a Newlight." Slowly, Baptist churches also began to limit African Americans' ability to preach freely. Ironically, as more blacks flocked to Separate Baptist churches, white church leaders increasingly consolidated their power over slaves. Some evidence indicates that evangelical white men, who ran the Baptist church courts, disciplined and expelled African Americans and women far more zealously than they did white men.[40]

By the 1790s, white Baptists in Virginia had deeply conflicted views of slavery. John Waller and John Ireland both owned slaves at the time of their deaths, and Ireland even had one of his slaves, a woman named Luck, tried for trying to poison his family. Remarkably, she was acquitted. In contrast, a number of white Baptist ministers still saw slavery as a grievous sin. John Poindexter of Louisa County wrote to Isaac Backus and asked that he pray for the slaves, "who are groaning under grievous oppression in this part of the Lord's Vineyard, I have been an advocate for Slavery, but thanks be to God, My Eyes have been Opened to see the impropriety of it, and I long for the Happy time to Come, when the Church of Christ shall loose the Bands of Wickedness, undo the Heavy burdens, and let the oppressed go free." Similarly, Benjamin Watkins of Powhatan County called slavery the "greatest evil in our land or Church." The "evangelical revolt" against the Anglican establishment, as the Baptists' emergence in Virginia has been styled, certainly held egalitarian potential, but often that potential went unrealized for African Americans and women.[41]

Nevertheless, the Separate Baptists in Virginia did offer a richly emotional community life to their adherents. The rituals of Baptist revivalism were physically intimate and emotionally vulnerable in ways that would have been ridiculed in traditional male-dominated gentry society. The 1771 diary of twenty-four-year-old preacher John Williams, soon to become pastor at the Meherrin Baptist Church, gives us a glimpse of the fervency of the early Baptists in the South. At Cub Creek in southern Virginia, Williams participated in the Separate Baptist ritual of feet washing, which lasted late into the night and early morning: it "continued till abt. 2 hours before day, & I believe the blessed Jesus blessed his ordinance, tho' deny'd by the greates part of the world." Feet washing was a way for Separate Baptists to distinguish themselves, even from other evangelicals, who rarely practiced the ritual.[42]

Williams, of course, relished no exercise more than the baptism of converts, the distinguishing mark of the Baptist churches. After another all-day meeting of preaching and testimonies, the congregation "proceeded to baptizm, & oh, such a baptizm I never saw, not only with water, but in a great measure by the Holy Ghost. The Christians [fell] to shouting, sinners trembling & falling down convulsed, the Devil a raging & blaspheming." In Faquier County, preacher Daniel Fristoe wrote in 1771 about a baptismal service with two thousand people in attendance. Observers climbed trees to get a better look at those being immersed. Afterward, the converted gathered in a field to lay hands on the newly baptized.

"The multitude stood round weeping, but when we sang *Come we that love the lord* & they were so affected that they lifted up their hands and faces towards heaven and discovered such chearful countenances in the midst of flowing tears as I had never seen before. In going away I looked back and saw multitudes, some roaring on the ground, some wringing their hands, some in extacies . . . and other so outragious cursing & swearing that it was thought they were really possessed of the devil. I saw strange things today." The physical experiences of baptism by immersion and laying on hands led some participants and observers to heights of spiritual joy, and others to despair of their standing before God. Baptism was the outward sign of inner conversion and of deliverance out of old Virginia society into a new redeemed community of saints.[43]

By the Revolution, evangelical Presbyterians and Baptists in Virginia had successfully broken the near-monopoly of Anglican religious adherence. A minority of Virginians, both black and white, perceived in evangelicalism a new, satisfying source of spiritual expression and comfort. While persecution made the evangelicals' task difficult in obvious ways, it also gave their movement a solidarity that might otherwise have been missing. Finally, in Virginia white evangelicals grappled with the realities of multiracial ministry and the inclusion of African Americans. Most white evangelicals took a moderate path on questions of race, but their serious attention to the spiritual needs of African Americans heralded the massive shift of southern blacks into the evangelical fold during the nineteenth century. Evangelicals in the Carolinas, though in a relatively freer context, would have to contend with the issues of establishment, traditional culture, and race as well.

"A Happy Revival of Religion in the Interior Parts": Evangelicalism in the Carolinas

In 1767, the irritable Anglican itinerant Charles Woodmason visited Lynch's Creek, South Carolina, where his fellow churchmen complained they had been "eaten up by Itinerant Teachers, Preachers, and Imposters from New England and Pensylvania—Baptists, New Lights, Presbyterians, Independants, and an hundred other Sects." By the time of the revolutionary crisis, evangelical churches and itinerants had spread through the Carolinas. Similar to the Presbyterians' and Baptists' experiences in Virginia, though under a lighter burden of establishment, evangelicals in the Carolinas rapidly expanded their reach. The Deep South had once worried New Englanders because of its apparent godlessness. Now evangelicals had broken into the backcountry of the future Bible Belt.[1]

We have seen how the moderate Josiah Smith and the radical Hugh Bryan responded to George Whitefield's itinerant preaching in South Carolina. But Whitefield's work hardly suffices to account for the development of evangelicalism in North and South Carolina. Indeed, the case of the Carolinas reveals even more clearly that the concept of the "First Great Awakening," when confined to the 1740s, limits our understanding of the early evangelical movement. Whitefield's ministry bore fruit, especially in the Charleston area, but the most explosive growth of evangelicalism came in the backcountry from the 1750s to the 1770s, through the agency of the Separate Baptists. Over time, evangelical Presbyterians and Baptists started to break the Anglican hold on South Carolina religious life and to make inroads among the black population of the Carolinas.

In the low country of South Carolina, Hugh Bryan and his brother Jonathan helped found the Stoney Creek Independent Presbyterian Church, following Hugh's prophetic embarrassment when he failed to part the waters of a river. The minister at Stoney Creek was another of Whitefield's converts, William Hutson, an English immigrant and a former stage actor like Whitefield. After his conversion, Whitefield and the Bryans arranged for Hutson to work as a tutor to slaves on the Bryans' plantation. In 1743 Hutson was ordained by local dissenting ministers, including Josiah Smith. The Stoney Creek Church was organized near the Pocotaligo River, with Hugh and Jonathan Bryan serving as deacons. Hutson and the Bryans included slaves in the life of the church, admitting "George a Negroe & Sarah his Wife" to full membership in 1745. Hutson frequently baptized slaves belonging to the Bryans or himself. While Hutson perpetuated Whitefield's desire that slaves be given serious attention in the church, he and Jonathan Bryan also helped turn Hugh Bryan into a moderate on slavery again. They also encouraged Whitefield to introduce slavery at his Bethesda orphanage in Georgia, where slavery was initially illegal. Whitefield told Hutson, "If you think propr as you once sd. to give me a Negroe, I will venture to keep him, & if he shod. be seized it is but for me to buy him again." But later he wrote, "Upon 2d thots. you may Deferr sendg ye Negroe till I talk furthr abot. it." Leaders like Hutson helped sharpen the distinction between spiritual and social equality for African Americans.[2]

Despite Stoney Creek's success, evangelical Presbyterian churches grew modestly in South and North Carolina before the Revolution. Northern presbyteries, having earlier sent itinerants like William Robinson to preach in Virginia and North Carolina, continued periodically to commission itinerants' journeys into the region, hoping to establish churches among the burgeoning Scottish and Scots-Irish populations there. They also remained hopeful that they could proselytize the Native American populations in the South.

Probably the most influential Presbyterian minister in the Carolina backcountry before the Revolution was William Richardson of the Waxhaw church, in upper South Carolina. Richardson, a student of Samuel Davies, was licensed in 1758 to serve as a missionary among the Cherokees. By late 1758 he arrived at Fort Loudon in east Tennessee, where rumors of Cherokee violence were rampant. He found the local Cherokees resistant to his gospel. "They show the greatest Indifferency. How blind to their best Interests," he wrote in his diary. Still, he thought that by "conversing familiarly with them, giving them small Presents inviting them to eat with me, smoking with them, [and] going to their Town House," he might yet convince some to accept Christianity. As he came to know some leaders among the Cherokees, he found that "they are very much given to conjuring & the Conjurers have great Power over ym." One conjurer circled the town day and night "hollowing & crying" for a blessing on a "Physick" he had prepared to drive sickness away. Richardson repeatedly requested opportunities to preach to the Cherokees, but was denied. He also feared the imminent arrival of war, so he left east Tennessee in February 1759 after staying only a few months. Though Richardson did not display much resolve, he was probably right to leave, as the vicious Cherokee War (1759–61) broke out later in the year, precipitated by British land encroachments and unresolved killings on both sides. Fort Loudon fell to the Cherokees in 1760.[3]

Having fled the Cherokees' lands, in 1759 Richardson settled at the Waxhaw church. Even there he found "very distressing conditions," and "almost every night we expect to be awakened with the Indian hollow." In 1760 he lamented that his "success in the ministry is very small" and noted that he remained one of two Presbyterian pastors on the frontier of the lower South. A year later, however, he wrote that he "must not complain" about his lack of success, for he had received almost a hundred communicant members in less than two years. Richardson appealed to Davies's supporters in Britain for books to help educate his Scots-Irish parishioners, who he feared "will soon turn Heathens, and be as savage as the Indians themselves" should they not receive proper instruction.[4]

Richardson's promising life and ministerial career ended under suspicious circumstances. Charles Woodmason, who liked almost no dissenters, respected Richardson ("a good Sort of Man," he called him). In a strange "memorandum," Woodmason memorialized Richardson, whom he believed fell prey to sectarian madness. Richardson apparently married the daughter of the Pennsylvania revivalist and Scottish Covenanter Alexander Craighead, who had arrived in North Carolina in 1755. Woodmason considered Richardson's wife a fanatic for the Scottish Presbyterian church and implicated her in Richardson's mysterious death. In 1771, Richardson was found, in Woodmason's words, "dead on his Knees in his Study, with a Bridle round his Neck, reaching to the Ceiling." Pastor John Zubly of Savannah less suggestively noted that Richardson was found "hold[in]g to a chair with one hand stretched out, in an ordinary posture—stiff dead." On first glance, it appeared that Richardson had hung himself, and he was quickly buried. But after suspicions arose, his body was exhumed and an examination revealed strangulation marks and bruising on the chest. Woodmason confidently concluded that he fell a "Martyr to the persecuting Spirit that Distinguishes Superstition and Enthusiasm, from Reason and Religion." Whether Richardson was murdered or not, he lived and died aware of the dangers of evangelizing the southern colonial frontier.[5]

While the Presbyterians enjoyed a growing presence in the Carolinas before the Revolution, the Baptists outpaced them and saw perhaps their most spectacular early successes in the Carolina backcountry. Regular Baptists had a strong presence in the South Carolina low country even before the 1740s. Isaac Chanler of the Ashley River Baptist Church had avidly supported George Whitefield since the revivalist had preached to overflow crowds at his church in July 1740. Chanler played a key role in spreading the Calvinistic Baptist tradition through the low country, helping found the Welsh Neck and Euhaw churches, among others. Chanler baptized and mentored the Swiss Calvinist immigrant Francis Pelot, who became a Baptist in 1744. Pelot soon became the pastor at the Euhaw Baptist Church. Clearly establishing its connection to the Anglo-American evangelical network, Whitefield preached the opening sermon at that church's new meetinghouse on March 5, 1752.[6]

By the late 1740s, Regular Baptist churches were well established in the low country, but no one did more to help make the Baptist churches respectable in South Carolina than Oliver Hart, who became pastor at Charleston's First Baptist Church in 1749. Hart grew up in a Baptist family in Southampton, Pennsylvania. He was converted early in life was baptized in 1741, and warmly responded to Whitefield's preaching in the Philadelphia area. Though lacking a college education, Hart was ordained in 1749, and responded to a call from the Charleston church. In 1751 Hart arranged for the establishment of the Charleston Baptist Association, which was composed originally of the Charleston, Ashley River, and Welsh Neck churches. Hart's irenic temperament and organizing skills helped make the association an increasingly powerful force for Regular Baptist growth in the low country.[7]

Hart promoted revival in the Baptist churches, remembering fondly the awakenings under Whitefield and Tennent in Philadelphia. The greatest single awakening Hart saw in the low country came in 1754, when "the power of divine grace was eminently displayed" in several churches. By late August he had witnessed a great deal of concern among the young people of his church, and he thought "that the Revival may prove to be more Extensive than at first I expected." One of the young people converted in the revival was Samuel Stillman, who later became pastor of First Baptist Church, Boston.[8]

During 1754, Hart's home filled with anxious young people hoping to find assurance of salvation. He took a particular interest in a young woman, Margaret, who had lived in his home for two years, probably working as a servant. He found her confident that God had visited her powerfully, as "she had these Words; *I have Loved thee with an Everlasting Love* [Jeremiah 31:3], set home with so much Light, and Evidence, that she could not avoid taking Comfort from them." She began to testify to the other young women about her salvation: "Oh Miss Betsy! Said she, Jesus Christ is Sweet, he is precious; had I known his sweetness said she; I would not have lived so long without him." To another Margaret said, "Oh! Miss Nancy, Christ is Sweet! and since he hath had mercy upon such a Vile Wretched Sinner as me; I am sure none need ever to Despair, Oh! Come to Christ; Come to Christ!" Betsy and Nancy both began crying and went outside to "vent their Grief." Many of the young men and women then began crying out, "Oh give me Christ! give me Christ!" Hart was stunned, and wrote, "is all this possible! is it Really So! Lord, why me!" For pastors like Hart, the experience of leading a revival could be emotionally overwhelming.[9]

Like Whitefield, Hart was remarkably ecumenical in his work, sharing pulpits with other pastors, such as Stoney Creek Church's William Hutson, Anglican rector Richard Clarke (the successor to the acerbic Alexander Garden in Charleston) and the Swiss Presbyterian John Zubly. Hart was less a precisionist Baptist than a revivalist and moral reformer, preaching regularly against "stage plays" and dancing. He expected new converts to receive baptism by immersion, of course, and he prepared the young converts for baptism with doctrinal instructions and questions about their experiences with Jesus. In October 1754 he recorded a service he conducted on nearby James Island, where he baptized ten people "according to the primitave Mode" of immersion.[10]

Along with Hart's Charleston and Chanler's Ashley River churches, the turbulent Welsh Neck Baptist Church on the Pee Dee River was one of the three most influential early Baptist churches in the coastal region of South Carolina. Welsh Baptists from Pennsylvania settled the area in the 1730s, but after the successful pastorate of Philip James from 1743 to 1754, the church struggled to maintain a permanent pastor. John Brown, ordained in 1750, presumably with the intention of replacing the aging James, did not stay long at the church. He seems to have entertained strange beliefs regarding the resurrection and the last days. Joshua Edwards soon became minister at Welsh Neck, but he was suspended for drunkenness at least once. His colleague Robert Williams fell out with the church and began to teach that Welsh Neck was "not a Church of Christ." In 1759, following Edwards's death and Williams's dismissal, Nicholas Bedgegood became pastor, but he left in 1764, apparently in an attempt to dislodge Oliver Hart from the pastorate of the Charleston church. Evan Pugh then became pastor, but he stayed only for a year because of the "general dislike" of him in the church. Remarkably, Bedgegood returned to Welsh Neck in 1767. In 1774, the deceased Bedgegood was replaced by the soon-to-be-notorious Elhanan Winchester, who left for Philadelphia in 1779, where he began preaching universal salvation. Welsh Neck's sort of troubles plagued many of the new, unsettled, and individualistic evangelical churches in rural America.[11]

We can gather a good sense of the Welsh Neck Baptist Church's practices, since the early church records have survived. Many entries concerned church discipline cases. Under Bedgegood, the church adopted a covenant in August

1760, promising "to walk in all holiness & humility with brotherly love." Members regularly fell short of that standard. Jane Poland, for instance, was called before the church in 1761 and charged with failing to attend services regularly and with "selling liquor at a horse race." She did not appear sufficiently repentant and was suspended. The church struggled with how to treat converts who would not accept believers' baptism: within two months in 1761 the church proclaimed open communion, then rescinded the policy, declaring that it resulted in "dreadful consequences."[12]

The Welsh Neck church seems always to have accepted African American members, but its policy became contested in the transition between future universalist Elhanan Winchester and his successor, Edmund Botsford. In his last year at the church, Winchester led a revival and baptized a remarkable 240 converts. Oliver Hart described it to Isaac Backus as a "glorious display of ye Power & Goodness of God" that gave him hope for the "final result of our national troubles" in the Revolutionary War. Winchester, however, admitted that his developing universalism expanded the numbers who responded. Many of these new members were slaves. Winchester also helped the African American members establish a "Church by themselves" in August 1779. Botsford, a traditional Calvinist, interviewed and then excommunicated many of Winchester's converts, "both white and black, but the greater number of blacks; many of the latter upon examination appeared to be very ignorant of the nature of true religion." Botsford also broke up the separate African American church and interviewed all its members who desired readmission to Welsh Neck. Forty-six passed the test, but we do not know how many refused or failed the interview.[13]

The ongoing support of the Philadelphia Association was critical for the development of these Carolina Regular Baptist churches. In the minutes of their 1755 meeting, the association resolved that they should send two "ministering brethren" to North Carolina, and through the 1760s, the Philadelphia Association kept commissioning itinerants to visit the Carolinas. For instance, John Gano repeatedly visited there, and in the late 1750s he served briefly as pastor of a Baptist church at Jersey Settlement, North Carolina. Gano had been baptized in his hometown, Hopewell, New Jersey. In 1754 he made his first tour of the Carolinas. In early 1755, he visited Oliver Hart's Charleston congregation and preached before a "numerous and brilliant" audience that included George Whitefield. At Ashley River Baptist Church, he preached to "a large congregation of negroes," and their intelligent responses to his questions led him to believe that "they had been touched by the Spirit of the Lord." On a second visit to the Carolinas, he preached at Jersey Settlement on the Yadkin River in North Carolina, where the Baptists pleaded with him to stay as their minister. Even after he returned to

New Jersey, the North Carolina congregation sent messengers asking for him to come back, and he finally agreed. He ministered to a diverse group of Christians who eventually united as a Baptist congregation. While at Jersey Settlement, Gano also occasionally supplied the pulpit at Cashaway Baptist Church, a hundred and ten miles away in South Carolina, where the minister, Joshua Edwards, had been suspended for drunkenness. In 1760, Gano decided to leave North Carolina because of fears related to the Cherokee War, and in 1762 he became the pastor at the First Baptist Church of New York City. He continued to itinerate, however, and contributed significantly to Baptist revivals in New England in 1764. Isaac Backus wrote that Gano's preaching "seems to be as much admired as Mr. Whitefields."[14]

Hezekiah Smith, who apparently experienced the new birth under Gano's preaching, also witnessed firsthand the impressive growth of the Baptists in coastal South Carolina in 1762–64. Smith had been converted and baptized in Morristown, New Jersey, in the mid-1750s. He graduated from the College of New Jersey in 1762 and soon journeyed through the South. There he met most of the South's key Baptist leaders. At Sandy Creek, North Carolina, he met Shubal Stearns and "tarried with Him all Night, to my Satisfaction." He then made his way to Nicholas Bedgegood's home at Welsh Neck. Smith would spend most of his time at Welsh Neck and the nearby Cashaway Baptist Church. He reported to a Pennsylvania minister that "many Thousands are in ye back Parts, without any one, to break unto ym ye Bread of Life." In September 1763, Smith was ordained in Charleston, probably at the request of the Cashaway church, which hoped to make him their permanent minister. He estimated that by the end of September, he had traveled "4235 Miles and preached 173 Sermons" in a year. In January, however, Smith inexplicably left the Cashaway church "in a Flood of Tears" and went back to New Jersey. Oliver Hart was disappointed, as he noted that two churches were now "entirely destitute on [the Pee Dee] River; and the People are vastly numerous." Smith would later become the longtime pastor of the First Baptist Church in Haverhill, Massachusetts. Pastors like Gano and Smith found the demands of long-term ministry in the rural Carolinas too demanding to tarry for long, but their departures represented only minor difficulties in the general trend of rapid Baptist expansion in the South.[15]

Through friendships with ministers like Gano and Smith, the Baptist churches of the Carolinas maintained deep connections with the Baptists of the Philadelphia Association. Oliver Hart and Evan Pugh both maintained a regular correspondence with the influential pastor Samuel Jones of the Pennepack Baptist Church near Philadelphia. The bookish Pugh, raised a Quaker in Pennsylvania, was converted to Baptist principles and immersed in Virginia in 1754. In 1760–

61 he lived in the Charleston area, studying for the ministry with Hart, and then in early 1762 he relocated to the Welsh Neck church to study with Nicholas Bedgegood. Pugh was pessimistic about the state of religion in South Carolina and told Jones that there was a pressing need for gospel ministers in the province, where hundreds were "perishing for lack of Knowledge." Finally, Pugh moved to the Euhaw Baptist Church and was ordained by Francis Pelot in 1763.[16]

In 1763–64, Pugh traveled to and from Philadelphia, itinerating in Virginia and North Carolina along the way. He was afraid that he preached "to little purpose. Some time I was afraid ye Indians would catch me." But he pressed on, preaching at Gano's former congregation on the Yadkin River for a month then returning to Welsh Neck to find that Bedgegood had departed for Charleston to become Hart's assistant. Hart wanted Hezekiah Smith to take over for Bedgegood but expressed reservations about Pugh's candidacy. Pugh did become pastor at Welsh Neck, but he was dismissed after a year. Hart came to believe that bringing Bedgegood to Charleston had been a disaster, and that God had chastised them for "bringing Mr. Bedgegood from a numerous, well-affected People, where he was greatly useful, to serve us, who were not in so much Need of Help." Despite their struggles with keeping ministers in place, Hart's network of Regular Baptists continued to grow, particularly because of the strength they drew from their Philadelphia Association connections.[17]

In 1769, Hart wrote another letter to Samuel Jones, deploring the religious conditions in Charleston, where "Religion is grown extremely unfashionable," and the "God Mammon is much more rever'd." Hart had exciting news to report from the backcountry, however. "There is a happy Revival of Religion in the interior Parts of this Province, among the separate Baptists." Hart had visited the Separate churches twice recently, once with Evan Pugh, and they found the awakenings among the Separates remarkable to behold. Although the Regular Baptists enjoyed more institutional strength in South Carolina than in Virginia, the Separate Baptists' rapid growth outpaced all others in the Carolinas. The Separates' successes began to turn the southern backcountry toward the more radical style of evangelicalism emerging from the awakenings of the 1740s.[18]

The Separates' rise, again, was keyed by the activism of the Sandy Creek churches in North Carolina and by the powerful efforts of itinerants like Shubal Stearns. Within several years of Stearns's and Daniel Marshall's move to North Carolina, Separate Baptists had established churches in numerous settlements along the rivers of the Piedmont region. One convert on the Yadkin River, Tiden Lane, recalled that he attended a Baptist meeting where he found Stearns teaching under a peach tree. "He fixed his eyes upon me immediately," and Stearns's disconcerting gaze made Lane think the preacher might have mystical powers or

Sandy Creek meetinghouse, built circa 1801. Randolph County
Public Library Historical Photograph Collection.

perhaps "an evil eye." Once Stearns began to exhort, Lane could take no more and he fell, immobile, to the ground.[19]

Lane was not the only person to ascribe mystical powers to Stearns. Elnathan Davis went with "8 or 10 of his companions in wickedness" to see Stearns lead a baptismal service. Davis was the only one of his friends who went close enough to hear Stearns preach, and he began to notice that others in the crowd "tremble[d] as if in a fit of the ague." One penitent leaned on the incredulous Davis and wept profusely on the shoulder of his "white new coat." Davis ran back to his friends, telling them that "there is a trembling and crying spirit among them: but whether it be the spirit of God or the devil I don't know." Davis resolved not to go back, "but the enchantment of Shubal Stearn[s's] voice drew him to the crowd once more." Soon "trembling seized him also," and he fell to the ground. When he woke up he felt intense dread, fearing the wrath of God, but after several days Davis broke through to conversion. Immediately he was baptized by Stearns and began to preach, "raw as he was." Soon Davis was ordained and became the pastor of the Haw River Baptist Church, near present-day Bynum, North Carolina.[20]

Stearns itinerated through much of North Carolina in the 1760s, reporting in 1765 that "the Lord carries on his work gloriously in sundry places in this province." He preached for six days at Davis's Haw River church, where about seven hundred people attended, and eighteen were baptized. The Sandy Creek Baptists' efforts bore considerable fruit by the mid-1760s. Charles Woodmason reported that by 1765 "the Baptists are now the most numerous and formidable Body of People which the [Anglican] Church has to encounter with, in the Interior and Back Parts of [North Carolina]."[21]

The radicalism of the Sandy Creek Baptists was reflected in their roles for women, not only as deaconesses, but also eldresses, an apparently unique practice among eighteenth-century evangelicals. According to Morgan Edwards, eldresses served a pastoral role among the women of the Baptist congregations. They baptized and taught women, and they related the women's views on church matters to the elders. They were to be elected by "choice of the church." Edwards entertained the possibility that the eldresses might sometimes teach mixed audiences of men and women, for he insisted that they must "be veiled when they preach or pray, especially if men be sent to their assemblies." These offices represented some of the most far-reaching formal recognitions of women's authority in the church in eighteenth-century American Christianity. Predictably, this radical innovation was abandoned among the moderating Separate Baptists of the late eighteenth century.[22]

Some Baptist women seem also to have exhorted publicly in the early years of the movement. Shubal Stearns's sister (and Daniel Marshall's wife) Martha Marshall "in countless instances melted a whole concourse into tears by her prayers and exhortations," according to one account. Daniel Marshall's sister, Eunice, reportedly took it "upon herself to exhort and preach Baptist doctrines; was ordered to desist, but not obeying, was (although pregnant at the time) thrown into jail." Charles Woodmason scoffed at one of the Baptists' "She Saints" who "was highly celebrated for her extraordinary Illuminations, Visions and Communications." He claimed that she had a vision of an angel coming to her in flames, but the angel turned out only to be her Baptist minister and lover, and the flames only "the Fire of Lust." Again, by the early nineteenth century, the Separate Baptists had largely forbidden women from publicly exhorting or sharing mystical revelations.[23]

The Separate Baptists took their socially radical gospel not only into Virginia, but also into South Carolina and Georgia. Philip Mulkey and a small group of Baptists founded the first Separate church in South Carolina in 1760. Mulkey, a native North Carolinian and Anglican, had a dramatic conversion to Baptist principles in 1756. Mulkey was a fiddle player, and after a dance one night he was met at the door by a "hideous specter" of the "Devil grinning at him with fiery eyes." The sight knocked him unconscious for ten minutes. He became desperately afraid that he would be damned, and he could not eat or sleep for days. Mulkey would occasionally "roar out, 'I am damned! I shall soon be in hell!'" He believed that God had created him for no other reason than to burn eternally. Soon, however, a Baptist minister visited his home and assured him of the forgiveness available through Christ, and he was converted.[24]

Mulkey immediately began to preach, first to his perplexed wife, and then to a neighbor named Campbell. He showed Campbell John 3:3 and told him he needed to be born again. Campbell began to curse at Mulkey and shouted, "What devilish project are you now upon with the word of God in your hand?" With this, Campbell stripped off his shirt and challenged Mulkey to a brawl, "spitting on his hands and clenching his fists." Mulkey began to cry, and Campbell put his shirt back on and began to cry, too. Again, Baptists' conversions often meant repudiating the rowdy ways of southern masculine culture, including fistfights. Mulkey was soon baptized at the Sandy Creek church, and in 1760 he and a small group of Separates founded a church on Broad River in South Carolina. Two years later the growing church relocated to Fairforest, South Carolina. Charles Woodmason was not impressed with "the infamous Mulchey, who came here lately in Rags, hungry, and bare foot." By 1772, Mulkey's church and its branches served about three hundred families. Mulkey also itinerated in the Congaree region of central South Carolina, successfully recruiting a number of Woodmason's former communicants.[25]

Daniel Marshall and some members of the Abbot's Creek church in North Carolina also relocated to South Carolina in 1762. The group settled near Stephens Creek in far western South Carolina, near the Savannah River. Marshall also continued to itinerate in the province, and along with Mulkey he helped establish a Separate Baptist church on the Congaree River. The minister there was Joseph Reese, who was converted under Mulkey's preaching. Predictably, Charles Woodmason also disparaged Reese, suggesting that he exercised improper authority over the women of the Congaree church. "What Man amongst all the Beaus and fine Gentlemen of the Land has such Influence over the Women as Joseph Reez?" he asked. Woodmason claimed that one Sunday Reese forced the women strip to their shifts "and made them all walk home bare footed and bare legged. And had He only said it, they would have stript off their Smocks, and gone home stark Naked." Whether this account was true or not, it suggested critics' fears of overweening power, overheated emotions, and sexual immorality among the evangelicals. Significantly, Reese was ordained by

Oliver Hart and Evan Pugh, which signaled growing friendship between the Separates and Regulars in South Carolina. Reese was soon censured, however, by the Sandy Creek Association for his cooperation with the Regulars.[26]

The distinction between moderate and radical evangelicals blurred in the South Carolina backcountry, partly because the Congaree Association (1771), which was originally connected with the Sandy Creek Association, drifted toward moderation and affiliation with the Philadelphia Association. The backcountry's radicalism also may have been obviated because race and slavery were much less immediate issues in the mostly white prerevolutionary upstate. No person did more to bridge the divide between the Separate and Regular Baptists in South Carolina than Richard Furman. Furman was converted to Baptist principles under Joseph Reese's itinerant preaching at the High Hills of Santee, where a Baptist church had been gathered in 1770.[27]

When Furman began to hear Reese's preaching, he became afraid of "instant destruction" and even considered a lightning storm "the messenger of vengeance." Finally, he attended a baptismal service, but his doubts led him to flee into the woods, where he prostrated himself. There he received "manifestations of divine love" that inspired him to return and receive baptism by immersion, repudiating his Anglican infant baptism. Furman was quickly licensed to preach, and in 1774 he was ordained by Evan Pugh and Joseph Reese as the minister of the High Hills church. In 1774, Oliver Hart preached at a revival meeting at the High Hills church along with Furman and Reese. Despite Furman's conversion under Separate principles, Furman and Hart would become friends and frequent correspondents. Furman succeeded Hart as the pastor of Charleston's First Baptist church in 1787 and became the most important leader in the second generation of South Carolina Baptists.[28]

Before the American Revolution, the Baptists also made some progress across the Savannah River into Georgia. Edmund Botsford, who would replace Elhanan Winchester at the Welsh Neck Baptist church, spent several years in the early 1770s preaching in east Georgia. He ministered to a group of Baptists at Tuckaseeking, Georgia, and itinerated in the Savannah River area from Augusta to Savannah. The ever-rambling Daniel Marshall and his son Abraham also itinerated in that area after relocating to Kiokee Creek, Georgia, in the early 1770s. The moderate Presbyterian John Zubly of Savannah encountered Marshall near Augusta, Georgia, in 1772 and disgustedly noted that Marshall "insisted on washing of feet & the holy kiss as necessary Practices." Soon thereafter Zubly heard more about "Marshals Crazy Behav[io]r & his intruding himself every where to hold forth."[29]

Botsford had to flee Georgia in 1779 because of the American Revolution, but he wrote in 1790 that he was impressed with the progress of the gospel there, especially among slaves. He noted, "There is in Georgia, a Baptist Church composed wholly of blacks, and a great number of negroes in other churches in that state." Revealing his proslavery ideology, Botsford wrote, "God hath done great things for them, and their owners begin to discover that their slaves are of increasing value to them if they become religious." This was the fulfillment of George Whitefield's hope that slaves would be converted and become better slaves in the process.[30]

Despite the lack of a rigorous white evangelical critique of slavery, some African Americans in the prerevolutionary South also became Baptists. George Liele founded an African American church in Savannah in 1775. Liele was a slave from Virginia whose master took him to Georgia, where Liele was converted, baptized, and licensed to preach in Burke County. Liele then began itinerating among the slaves of the Savannah River area. He helped convert David George to Baptist principles before George became the pastor of the Silver Bluff Church in western South Carolina around 1773. Liele was freed in 1777 and fled Savannah when it was evacuated by the British at the end of the war. He went to Jamaica, where he founded the first Baptist church in Kingston, which ministered to poor blacks and whites. Liele's convert Andrew Bryan became the key black Baptist minister in Savannah.[31]

Andrew Bryan was owned by the evangelical planter Jonathan Bryan, who encouraged Andrew's preaching to slaves, but local whites became frightened of the black Baptists because so many slaves had run away during the Revolution. Around fifty of these African American evangelicals were rounded up by authorities and whipped. Andrew bled profusely but "held up his hands, and told his persecutors that he rejoiced not only to be whipped, but would freely suffer death for the cause of Jesus Christ." Jonathan Bryan intervened and helped Andrew and his followers, who were released and told to meet only during daylight hours. Jonathan also allowed Andrew's church to begin meeting at his barn in Brampton, outside Savannah. In 1788 Daniel Marshall's son Abraham visited Andrew Bryan's congregation, baptized forty-five new converts, and ordained Bryan to the ministry. Marshall admired Bryan and the church for their "repeated proofs, by their sufferings, of their zeal for the cause of God." Whatever antislavery potential southern evangelicalism once possessed was now fading, however, as planters such as Jonathan Bryan allowed their slaves to worship as Christians but believed that the evangelical faith bolstered the institution of slavery. Remarkably, even Andrew Bryan went on to own slaves after he gained his freedom.[32]

Taking advantage of the institutional weakness of the Anglican church, and a scattered and spiritually hungry population, evangelicalism quickly spread through the Carolinas and eastern Georgia before the Revolution. By 1770, for instance, Presbyterians and Baptists may have claimed as much as 14 percent of the white and 35 percent of the total population of South Carolina as adherents. (Counting the numbers of evangelicals in eighteenth-century America is quite difficult, as many church records do not survive, and many more people may have been influenced by evangelical religion than appear on evangelical church rolls. Also, it is difficult to interpret the reasons that many in colonial America attended but did not join churches, and that disparity could dramatically skew downward church membership rates.) The evangelicals' numbers would continue to rise, especially with the coming of the Methodists to the lower South after the Revolution. What once had been viewed by northerners as a godless mission field was now beginning to turn into an evangelical stronghold. The radicalism of white southern evangelicalism faded as the movement matured, however, and never presented a serious challenge to the institution of slavery. But by 1776 evangelicalism had secured a significant foothold among African American people on the plantations and in the towns of the lower South. To the new African American converts, evangelicalism brought spiritual comfort, personal dignity, racial solidarity, and assurance that in God's eyes all people were sinners in need of grace.[33]

"There Is Really a Great Awakening in Those Parts": The Evangelical Revivals of the 1760s

In 1767 John Cleaveland, minister of Ipswich, Massachusetts, published *A Short and Plain Narrative of the Late Work of God's Spirit*, detailing a new work of God in his parish and defending it from critics who complained about his followers' violations of parish boundaries. Cleaveland argued that he and other ministers had the right as "Part of the visible Spouse of Jesus Christ" to shepherd those God gave them. Some opponents tried to deny communion to congregants led away by the revivalist churches, which Cleaveland considered an outrageous violation of liberty of conscience. He specifically compared the revivalists' cause to that of the Sons of Liberty who opposed the abuses of the British government. "Pray, what has roused up the Spirits of the SONS OF LIBERTY at this Time, but an apprehended, or supposed unreasonable Encroachment upon their civil Rights and Liberty! And ought we not esteem our sacred Right and Liberty as dearly?" Christians should defend their "sacred Right and Liberty of private Judgment as to their spiritual Edification," just as the Sons of Liberty had defended their civil rights and liberties.[1]

Cleaveland and a number of other previously radical pastors had long waited for new revivals to appear. Many moderates, wearied from squabbles over the awakenings, turned their attention after 1745 from mass conversions to renewed wartime concerns. During the excitement of the early 1740s, some New Englanders imagined that the revivals might signal the imminent coming of the kingdom of God. With the coming of King George's War (1744–48) and the attack on Louisbourg in 1745, millennial readings of current events shifted back to the fortunes of the British Empire at war with French and Spanish Catholicism. New England saw comparatively few revivals during the 1750s, and the colonial South became the chief scene of revivalist activity.[2] Starting in 1762, however, a number of New England's formerly radical evangelical churches witnessed another round of awakenings. Personal correspondence networks, especially those coordinated by Isaac Backus and Eleazar Wheelock, distributed news of revival with the hope that the work of God would spread. Former radical leaders like Cleaveland and Samuel Buell used printed narratives to paint these new revivals as the successors to the triumphs of the 1740s, even as they continued to promote enthusiastic manifestations and separation from corrupt churches as reasonable responses to the Spirit. These leaders saw the revivals of the 1760s as recurrences of the Spirit's outpourings in the 1740s.

In their narratives, the leaders transformed the local practice of revivals into public appeals for the rights of individual conscience and reasonable enthusiasm. Narrating revivals became a tool for legitimizing radical evangelicalism. In their printed accounts of the 1760s revivals, one sees the maturation of radicals who tried to establish their definition of the evangelical movement in the Anglo-American public sphere. The practical experiences of the 1760s revivals helped the former radicals articulate two key tenets of the revolutionary age: the freedom of private judgment, and the liberty to separate from established powers. The revivals of 1762–65 were historically crucial, therefore, in mainstreaming the radical tendencies of the evangelical movement, in building a foundation for evangelical populism and democratization in America, and in helping align the movement with the incipient Patriot cause.[3]

Although significantly obscured by the "First" and "Second" Great Awakenings framework, the revivals of 1762–65 have not gone unnoticed. Historian Erik Seeman has shown that the 1760s awakenings demonstrate "the continuity of revivalism." He saw these revivals as the fourth of four major seasons of revival in colonial New England and coined the term "the Seacoast Revival of 1763–64" to describe them. This is as good a description as any, though the revivals seem to have lasted from 1762 to 1765 and to have flared in places away from the coast, such as Bennington, Vermont.[4] Contemporaries also connected the New England revivals to others happening in New Jersey, Virginia, South Carolina, and abroad.

The 1760s revivals spawned no intercolonial celebrity and marketing genius like George Whitefield. They saw no resurgence of the earlier evangelical magazines, and what news of evangelical religion the newspapers carried nearly exclusively concerned the aging Whitefield and his travels. Whitefield remained the darling of the media, and it seems that the newspapers were disinclined to give coverage to revivals that did not involve the Grand Itinerant. By contrast, Buell's and Cleaveland's revival narratives ignored Whitefield's role.[5]

After 1742, moderate evangelicals tended to deemphasize the cause of revival.

Though he continued to preach on the new birth, Whitefield became less confrontational and increasingly active in ecumenical charitable activities, and he became a favorite again at Yale and Harvard. Gilbert Tennent took a Philadelphia pastorate and became moderate and stylistically refined. Edwards, removed by his own congregation, was exiled to the Massachusetts frontier and then died shortly after his arrival at Princeton. Edwards's theological successor Samuel Hopkins and the "New Divinity" theologians engaged in a long-standing paper war with Arminians and liberals over the viability of Calvinism.[6] In 1762, however, revivals began again among inheritors of the radical tradition. The former radicals' continued advocacy of the right of private judgment and the freedom to separate from established authorities allowed them to articulate religious versions of salient principles in the growing American resistance movement against imperial rule.

In February 1764, the Baptist leader Isaac Backus had much of interest to record in his diary. On a visit to Norwich, Connecticut, he witnessed a revival that had touched a number of his family members with "unspeakable wonders of divine grace." The itinerating but ill George Whitefield came through Norwich at the same time. Many came to hear Whitefield, but Backus only commented that Whitefield was "very infirm in body." The next day's entry carried news of revival in Ipswich, Massachusetts. "By letters in town from Mr. Cleaveland and Col. Choate of Ipswitch there is an account of a great revival there in Decr. past and 'twas thought that more than 30 were converted among 'em in that month." John Cleaveland's Ipswich congregation had begun a season of awakenings in December 1763, which he now sought to publicize by circulating letters for the possible awakening of other churches in New England, and for the normalization of Separate Congregationalist ideology.[7]

In 1763, John Cleaveland was a twenty-year veteran of Separate evangelicalism. While a teenager he saw a great revival in his hometown of Canterbury, Connecticut, and he began attending Yale in 1741 just as the crisis of evangelical radicalism shook the campus. Cleaveland eventually ran afoul of rector Thomas Clap and was expelled. Cleaveland surely knew fellow revivalist Samuel Buell from those Yale days. The Yale radicals, so critical to the emergence of New England evangelicalism in the 1740s, continued their revival work as a cohort in the 1760s. In April 1763, Cleaveland wrote to Eleazar Wheelock, New England's key disseminator of revival information, and a onetime Connecticut itinerant whom Cleaveland had also known since the revivals in Canterbury and at Yale.[8]

Cleaveland told Wheelock: "Religion in general with us, is at a low Ebb; but at Holles [Hollis, New Hampshire] about Fifty [miles] to the Westward of Ipswich, there has been a remarkable Effusion of the Divine Influences of late,

chiefly upon the younger sort. . . . The Rev. Mr. Daniel Emerson is the Minister
there, a very pious man and greatly engaged, ready to spend and be spent, his
Study is crouded He says with persons under pressing Soul-concern: I pray God
it may become unaversal! and that the Glory of Christ may fill the whole Earth."
Cleaveland was referring to Hollis's evangelical minister Daniel Emerson, who
twenty-two years earlier as a Harvard student had joined George Whitefield's
revival entourage. Now one of Emerson's many late eighteenth-century revivals
had begun in Hollis. With this note, Cleaveland broke into verse:

> Gird on thy Sword, Sov'reign victor'ous Lord
> And Spread the Conquests of thy holy word,
> Make Jew & Greek, make ev'ry Tribe and Land
> Thy Glory See, and bow to thy command . . .
> Thy Rod of Strength shall break Old Satan's yoke:
> Thy willing Converts shall by far excell
> The Drops of Dew that e'er on Hermon fell.

Cleaveland imagined that the expansion of Christ's kingdom would touch not
only British colonists, but also Native Americans, newly accessible because of
the British victory in the Seven Years' War. Cleaveland even proposed a new
colony in the Ohio River valley "to propagate the Gospel, and spread the Savor
of the Knowledge of Christ among the Indian Tribes."[9]

With such high ambitions, Cleaveland continued to look for revival in his
own congregation, and influenced by news of awakenings in nearby towns such
as Hollis, the Ipswich stir began in late 1763. The 1760s revivals were notable in
part for their leaders' attempts to continue promoting awakenings through print,
despite the absence of an evangelical magazine like the *Christian History*. In
their accounts, Cleaveland and Buell tried to show that their revivals were not
irrationally enthusiastic, even though they continued to promote radical distinctives, such as the believer's right to separate from antirevivalist churches and the
dramatic manifestations of the Holy Spirit.[10]

In his narrative, Cleaveland lamented the "groundless Prejudices" against the
awakenings. Among these prejudices was the continuing problem of Separates
drawing congregants away from established churches. Cleaveland and his Ipswich rival Theophilus Pickering had publicly quarreled over the issue in the
1740s, when evangelicals had separated from Pickering's congregation, covenanted as a new church in 1746, and made Cleaveland their new pastor in 1747.
The conflict reemerged in 1763 as Cleaveland cultivated and then publicized
the revival. Just like in the 1740s, he again saw people from area churches wanting to attend or join Cleaveland's awakened congregation. This threatened the

crucial structure of the parish boundary and drew a vicious response from critics.[11]

The anonymous *An Answer to a Letter of December 26, 1763* was published in Boston in 1764, apparently written by an antirevivalist to whom a friend of Cleaveland's had written to report the goings-on in Ipswich. The initial letter favorably commented on the work of Francis Worcester, a sometime itinerant who stirred Cleaveland's congregation in late 1763. *An Answer* attacked the revivals and Worcester in particular, associating these so-called revivals with the spirit of Antichrist. The revival's leaders were "enemies to the gospel you profess in words, (and in words only) to believe." Nothing good was coming from the late enthusiasm, but instead "you have gotten there among you a goodly number of deluded followers of the Beast." Clearly, this respondent felt that the revivals' threat to the establishment represented the most destructive kind of false religion. The revivalists' opponents tarred them with accusations of fanatical enthusiasm and secret malevolent agendas.[12]

The revivalists knew printed public accounts would most effectively make the case for legitimacy, necessitating Cleaveland's 1767 narrative. He recorded how the church had joined the Scottish-led Concert of Prayer in 1761, and then began holding regular "private religious Conferences" in 1763, both of which contributed to the "late Effusion." Religious interest percolated among young people of the congregation who had heard of recent conversions at Concord of some "who had been (as was said) extreamly addicted to Frolicking and Vanity, if not Prophaneness." In October, Francis Worcester arrived, his sermons struck a number of the young people deeply, and they began to pursue conversion.[13]

Converts in the Ipswich revival expressed fears of being left out of the revival and being cast into hell. Mercy Holmes recounted that "seeing others under concern brot me to think of my lost and perishing estate," while Isaac Procter and Thomas Choate both told of their worry that, despite the conversions happening all around them, "I shod be left." Erik Seeman has analyzed other conversion narratives that the Ipswich church elders recorded and discovered that penitents routinely assigned great importance to Worcester's preaching, the private gatherings in homes of elders and deacons, and the leaders' preaching against the sins of the youths. At least one man came from another parish, claiming that his pastor taught that there was no original sin. "'Do you think you have any?" asked Cleaveland. "O yes, (said he) enough to damn me to all Eternity!" Other conversion accounts from Chebacco parish recorded people hearing the voice of God in the night and being struck with temporary speechlessness. A slave named Phillis, converted in April during the Ipswich revival, communicated her anxiety that "I should be left while others were saved." She came under deep conviction of her sin and pled with God for mercy. Finally, the verse "come unto me all ye that labour and are heavy laden and I will give you rest" gave her assurance of God's favor, and she finally believed that Christ could save her. She concluded by giving thanks for "this blessed Time of the outpouring of God's Spirit."[14]

Cleaveland defended all his converts, including those who came from other parishes. He argued that their right to private judgment freed them to attend churches friendly to the revival. In order to encourage the regional aspects of the awakening, Cleaveland opened his pulpit to such ministers as Worcester and Jonathan Parsons of Newburyport, whom Cleaveland had also known since the heady 1740s Yale revivals. Parsons, formerly of Lyme, Connecticut, became the pastor of the Separate church in Newburyport in 1746. Cleaveland offered his meetinghouse as a regional revival center, listing fourteen area ministers who visited and preached in Ipswich, and noted that each one's efforts were "attended with the Blessing of God." During the winter of 1763–64, the church hosted two public lectures a week from Cleaveland and the visiting ministers. Attracted to news of the ongoing awakenings, George Whitefield preached in Ipswich between late March and early April. Whitefield, who had electrified Ipswich and the surrounding area in September 1740, wrote in April 1764 to Eleazar Wheelock, "We had sweet seasons at Newbury, Ipswich, and Portsmouth—There is really a great awakening in those parts."[15] Yet Cleaveland did not find this visit significant enough to mention in *A Short and Plain Narrative*. Whitefield had always built on the long-term work of local evangelical pastors, but in the 1760s the sickly Whitefield's preaching was at best a sidelight to the revival. His fading importance was one of the few key differences that American evangelicals seemed to perceive in the nature of the 1760s revivals compared to the pioneering events of the 1740s.

Cleaveland contended that the Separate evangelicals' revival was vindicated by its very success. People followed their consciences and hurried to those churches where God was at work. Breaking down traditional structures of power, either in politics or religion, was justified when conscience called for it. Spiritual edification of individuals was a great responsibility of churches, and any person has a "right to seek his Edification where he thinks he can best obtain it. . . . His using his Right can be no Injury to any Man, because it is his unalienable Right." Citing John Locke on toleration, Cleaveland argued that any church that tried to prevent individuals from pursuing their spiritual happiness was "a Prison, in which the Rights, Liberties and Consciences of their Members are fast bound in Chains." The pursuit of happiness, according to Cleaveland, was an inalienable *religious* privilege.[16]

None of the other revivalists would link the cause of the Separates to Lockean rights as explicitly as Cleaveland did. Nevertheless, one can see a common thread in their accounts of the revivals: the desire to promote the pursuit of religious edification, even in the form of reasonable enthusiasm or an outwardly emotional or ecstatic response to the movement of the Spirit. The former radicals found that their style of evangelicalism was prospering throughout New England and elsewhere. For example, simultaneous to Ipswich's revivals, Isaac Backus recorded a great number of conversions in the Baptist churches of New England, beginning with the Third Baptist Church in Middleborough, Massachusetts, which in summer 1762 saw a great new concern for piety. Backus thought these revivals were both more fruitful and more orderly than those of the 1740s. The Congregational church at Woodstock, Connecticut, saw its revival begin at almost exactly the same time as the ones in Ipswich. As in Ipswich, a traveling Baptist pastor's sermons set off a wave of concern among Woodstock's youths. The leader of the young people, one Biel Ledoyt, was converted and began exhorting his former partners in frivolity to surrender to Christ. About forty of them eventually received salvation, and Ledoyt led a secession from the church and constituted a new Separate Baptist church in Woodstock in 1766.[17]

Similarly, the Baptist church at Norwich, Connecticut (Backus's hometown), reported to Backus that "50 or more have been converted there since Decr. Great and marvelous are Gods works sought out of all that have pleasure in them." Backus and Norwich's Benjamin Lord developed a running argument in the 1760s over Separate and Baptist principles. In 1764, Backus replied to Lord's charges that the Baptists were apostate. Backus noted that churches like Lord's had been declining in the early 1740s. Although the revivals reenergized the moderate evangelical churches for a time, their corrupt admission practices and hostility to popular manifestations of revival required honest Christians to separate. The "liberty for christians to improve their gifts, was allowed for a while," but soon the moderates "joined with others that had called [the work of God] a delusion of the Devil" and attacked the lay exhorters, among whom Backus became one of the most prominent. The moderates called the exhorters "disturbers, [and] deluded pretenders to an extraordinary call," and had some of them arrested and fined.[18]

Lord predicted that the Separates' pursuit of individual edification would produce declension and apostasy, but Backus concluded with delight that as of 1764, it seemed that only the Separates' churches were flourishing. He saw the Separate Baptists as the authentic bearers of 1740s-style revivalism. "Instead of apostacy, there has been a great revival of religion within these two or three years, among these people that you bear so hard against." To Backus, the revivals vindicated the Separates' ideology. "There has been a glorious reformation, and several hundred souls turned from sin to GOD, in many parts of New-England, within these two or three years; and a very great part of it among those which you represent as going the way of apostacy."[19] The Separates and Baptists argued that they were simply carrying the Great Awakening forward into the 1760s, a claim they thought the new awakenings clearly confirmed.

Backus eagerly welcomed evidence that the revivals extended beyond New England into the Middle Colonies, and even to the Carolinas. He met Baptist minister Hezekiah Smith in June 1764, who had recently returned from a preaching tour in the South. Smith and Nicholas Bedgegood of Welsh Neck, South Carolina, had baptized by immersion several of the key leaders of George Whitefield's Bethesda orphanage in Georgia. Smith told Backus that "a great reformation has apeared in several other places that way, particularly at a place called Pee-dee an 140 miles from Charlstown in South Coralina, and in some parts of North Coralina; and that a great awakning is now in New-York etc. [presumably referring to Buell's revival]." Smith routinely met with very large, receptive audiences despite the scattered settlements and estimated that in about eleven months he gave 164 sermons and traveled four thousand miles. The South Carolina Baptists were cognizant of the northern revivals, too, as Oliver Hart of Charleston inquired in early 1766 how the work continued in the North, "where it has lately appeared so glorious."[20] It seemed to Backus and other Baptist leaders that God was blessing their revival work, even though defenders of the Anglican and Congregational establishments viewed them as subversives.

Even though many churches saw significant awakenings across the colonies during 1764, none became as celebrated or influential as Samuel Buell's revival in Easthampton, Long Island. Buell's revival narratives demonstrate most clearly how the former radicals helped make reasonable enthusiasm the norm for the continuing evangelical movement. Buell, a onetime radical Congregationalist itinerant, settled at Easthampton in 1746. Easthampton and the surrounding area had experienced awakening by James Davenport's preaching in 1741. Now Buell led a revival that Isaac Backus called "the most astonishing of all," as he received a letter from Buell in June 1764.[21]

Others, including Eliphalet Williams and Levi Hart, also received accounts from Buell in 1764. Buell exulted that the revival "has all the Marks & Signitures of the most glorious and excellent Work of Divine Power & Grace that ever I had knowledge off." Coming from one of the key itinerants of the 1740s, Buell's hope was clear: the new revivals would both continue and surpass the earlier ones. Buell also wrote to Jonathan Barber of Groton, Connecticut, who

Rev. SAMUEL BUELL, D.D.

Samuel Buell, *Connecticut Evangelical Magazine and Religious Intelligencer* 2, no. 1 (Jan. 1809), o_1. Mudd Library, Yale University.

in the 1730s served as a pastor on Long Island, where he was a close associate of James Davenport. Buell's letter to Barber was soon published, apparently without his explicit approval, in Boston, New London, New York, and London. He later expressed reservations about the letter, no doubt because it spoke in rather unrestrained terms about the revival's importance. The power of the awakening, Buell reported, exceeded "all I ever before saw, and all I have read or heard of, since the primitive Times of Christianity." Wheelock confirmed this characterization in a 1764 letter to Whitefield, in which he claimed that "it exceeds what he ever saw, read or heard of since the Apostles days. Scores converted in a few days, &c." Thousands flocked to the Easthampton meetinghouse and came under deep influences of the Spirit. The results, as Buell described them, were reminiscent of Pentecost: "from Time to Time, Day after Day, the Holy Ghost evidently came down as a mighty rushing Wind; sometimes almost as sudden as a Flash of Lightning; bowing our Assembly, and producing the most amazing Agonies of Soul, & Cries, that ever you heard."[22] Buell would interpret these enthusiastic manifestations as evidence of the awakening's legitimacy.

Buell knew that his spectacular stories would invite criticism, but he was utterly convinced that, on the whole, "the Work of God now in East-Hampton, is far the most God-like, Christ-like, excellent and glorious, that I ever knew." Buell reflexively referenced all revivals that he "ever knew," implying continuity with, and progress beyond, the 1740s awakenings. He further speculated that the revival would not be limited to Long Island, and "if this Work of God should spread, & be diffused over New-England, as I pray God it may be, I believe that much more of God and Christ . . . will be there known, than was ever known before!" Printing accounts of his revival, Buell and his publishers hoped, might generate similar local events and more reports of revivals, which then could exponentially multiply converts and evidences for the legitimacy of moderately enthusiastic awakenings. The former radicals knew that print not only promoted new revivals but subtly redefined the evangelical movement by advocating continuing episodes of revivalist enthusiasm in the print domains of Britain and America.[23]

English printer Thomas Luckman of Coventry, an agent in one such print domain, obtained a letter roughly equivalent to Buell's letter to Barber and published it in 1765 along with letters from others familiar with the revival as *An Account of the Late Success of the Gospel, in the Province of New-York, North America*. Luckman heartily affirmed the work of God on Long Island, writing, "It goes forward with great Solidity, and is free from Mixtures of enthusiastic Folly." He called on evangelical readers in England to "glorify God for this eminent Revival of a Work of Religion in our Colonies. . . . May it spread its happy Influence over the vast American World. May our God again visit Britain, and pour down his Spirit from on high upon us." Luckman believed that the new work of God in the western Atlantic might flow to its eastern shores as well. He hoped that through print English readers could appropriate the depiction of the Long Island revival to envision and promote their own revivals.[24]

Despite this good publicity, Buell wanted to exercise more editorial control over his presentation of the awakening and to paint it in more moderate colors. If he could market the revivals as moderate *and* enthusiastic, he could change the public image of the evangelical movement itself. Accordingly, he published an authorized account of the revival in 1766 as *A Faithful Narrative of the Remarkable Revival of Religion, in the Congregation of East-Hampton, on Long-Island*. Obviously modeled after his mentor Jonathan Edwards's 1737 *A Faithful Narrative of the Surprising Work of God*, Buell's treatise was printed in Glasgow in 1768, and again in Sag Harbor on Long Island in 1808. He hoped that the Easthampton revival would spark a global fire. He optimistically posited that the "Lord's Work will not stop thus," and that in answer to prayers "the heavenly Influences will still be descending in immense Plenty: The Name and Fame of Jesus, and his Salvation, shall be defused [*sic*] thro' all Tribes and Ranks of Mankind, and whole Nations shall be new born in one glorious Day of Divine Influence."[25]

Buell consciously sought to rank his revival, along with Edwards's in Northampton and the one in Cambuslang, Scotland, in 1742, as a monument in the coherent narrative of redemptive history. He thought that "a copious Effusion of the Holy Spirit upon a People, is such an Event, as tends to confirm the Divinity of the glorious Gospel of our Lord," and it appeared to him that God willed "that such an Event in the divine Economy, should be recorded; not only for the present Benefit of some; but also for the future Good of others." Buell followed Edwards's example by giving details concerning the location, history, and demographics of the church, thereby setting the context in which revival appeared.[26] He recalled revivals of the 1740s that continued to influence the church in 1764. Buell described his own pastorate as generally successful and sometimes marked by minor outbursts of conversions. He noted one revival that happened in the early 1750s, but he thought the church had mostly been like a dry land, which sometimes saw promising, but ultimately rainless, clouds pass above. He estimated that between 1746 and 1764 he received about eighty persons into full communion.

In 1764, however, he began to observe more hopeful signs of "a gracious Visitation," including larger crowds and more fervent devotion to prayer. Strangely, like Cleaveland, Buell failed to mention that Whitefield passed through Easthampton in late January or early February 1764. Perhaps these omissions reflected an unspoken resentment or disdain toward the Grand Itinerant, who reported to a correspondent that "a sweet influence hath attended the word at East-hampton, Bridgehampton, and South-hold upon Long-Island." In any case, Buell recorded that on the weekend of March 18, the torrent of the Spirit began with great concern among the unconverted about their sins. He conversed with youths whose consciences had been troubled by his preaching. At a home meeting that week, Buell observed that many young people had become convinced that they would be damned for their sins, and "30 or 40 Persons went Home from this Meeting under most powerful Conviction of Sin and Misery."[27]

Buell saw the revival in distinctly Calvinist terms. At one meeting, he insisted that the people must be "dependent upon a sovereign GOD, for such Effusions of the Holy Spirit." He doubted the efficacy of any particular revival tactic, but instead he told the penitents "we must look beyond Means, and have our Expectations upon God only." He told the congregants "again and again, to give God the Glory, all the Glory, if He should now condescend to grant a marvelous Out-pouring of the Spirit." Immediately "there appeared to be a most surprising Effusion of the Holy Spirit" across the church. "An Almighty Energy seem'd to accompany the same Words."[28] This episode subtly revealed Buell's conflicted attitude toward "means." He, like Edwards, tried to put all the causal weight of revival on God, but Buell's exhortation seemed to function as a summons: insistence on the sovereignty and glory of God brought the remarkable effusion of the Spirit.

The Spirit had wondrous effects on the people. Some had vivid "Views of divine Things, seeing Truth and the awful and glorious Realities of the eternal World." Penitents fell "upon their Knees, with Hands extended toward Heaven, and in flowing Tears, begging and crying for the Exercise of sovereign Mercy . . . , with as much Earnestness and Importunity, to all Appearance, as tho' the Lord Jesus Christ was then coming in flaming Fire to the final Judgment." The comforts of the assured and distresses of the convicted ran so deep that the contrast gave them "a Sort of Resemblance of the Day of final Judgment, and it appeared as if Persons were now entering upon their eternal States of Heaven and Hell." His account suggested a new level of pure spiritual transport beyond anything seen in his previous experiences, even in the early 1740s. Unlike more moderate evangelicals, he did not try to restrain these enthusiastic outbursts because he considered them reasonable responses to penitents' apprehension of divine realities.[29]

Buell hoped the awakening would not be limited to Easthampton, and he promoted it as a regional event and also a model for the Anglo-American evangelical movement. He widely advertised the revival, which brought travelers to the church. "The Report of these Doings and mighty Acts . . . hath awakened and engaged the Attention of Multitudes in other Places," Buell rejoiced, and he estimated that "thousands have been brought to think more seriously about the Salvation of their Souls." He suspected that the revival began so "that it might be taken the more Notice of in the World." The divine event would only receive more notice, however, if Buell narrated it in the public sphere.[30]

Later in his account, he began specifically to map the course of the revival, constructing an image of a burgeoning Atlantic awakening. On Long Island, he estimated that the revival had touched twelve to fourteen congregations. He thought that it had reached down into "the Jerseys," where he had itinerated in fall 1764. It is possible that Buell may have known about the Hopewell, New Jersey, Baptist revival in 1764, where Isaac Eaton, a native of Southampton, Long

Island, saw 123 persons added to his church. Buell had also received reports from New York City that "very many of the Inhabitants of that Metropolis . . . hopefully share largely in the special Blessings of this Day, of the Out-pouring of the Holy Spirit." Buell noted itinerant Charles-Jeffery Smith's reports of revival in Virginia and Maryland, which Smith explicitly connected with the revivals on Long Island.[31]

Smith, present on Long Island during June and July 1764, assessed the revivals in his diary as "free from that bitter Censorious Spirit which prevailed in the Land in yt Work of God twenty four years ago." Smith also wrote in August 1764 to Eleazar Wheelock, "Its likely you may have heard by this Time that the Glorious Work at Long Island has reached some Parts of the Jerseys." Smith even saw possible eschatological significance in the new revival that might herald the end of British and Native American hostilities, which currently raged on the frontier in the form of Pontiac's Revolt. He thought that the widespread successes might indicate a "general Revival of Religion," perhaps presaging "that glorious Day . . . when the Wilderness shall blossom as a Rose, & the Tawny Inhabitants thereof bow to the Scepter of King Jesus." By November, however, Smith described the revival at Long Island as in "status quo" but still reported that "it spreads in the Jerseys."[32]

Buell also noted that "this Work" had progressed further in New England. Verifying the revivalists' success at publicizing the new revivals as an important next stage in redemptive history, farm woman Hannah Heaton of North Haven, Connecticut, wrote in her diary in May 1764: "I hear gods work agoing on at long island wonderfully in many places. O arise here sun of righteousness lord come quickly." Sarah Rogers of Boston, an avid evangelical correspondent, had heard of the revival by July 1764, when she wrote to Nathaniel Whitaker of Chelsea parish in Norwich, Connecticut, who led his own Congregational revival in the 1760s, and who may have also visited Easthampton. She told Whitaker that she could not help "congratulating you on account of the glorious news from Longisland and other places." She sadly noted that the revival had produced no results in spiritually slumbering Boston. Indian missionary John Brainerd wrote to Eleazar Wheelock concerning the "good news we have from Long Island and some other parts." Buell remarked on a letter received in New York of an ongoing revival in Amsterdam, making the revival Atlantic-wide. He took from all this news that the Easthampton revival was only "one Branch of the Glory of the Lord's Work at this Day, that 'tis so extensive."[33]

Buell knew that some critics would grow uneasy at his talk of the Holy Spirit, raising the prospect of enthusiastic excesses. He would not relent, though, and countered that no one observing the revival could imagine that "the Influences of the Holy Spirit were confin'd and restricted to the Apostolick Age, and are not now to be expected." He hoped that the "Days are not very far off, when such Outpourings of the Spirit will become more frequent and general among the Lord's People: And in Process of Time the World over." Here Buell again connected his local revival to the global eschatological awakening. He reminded his readers that a day was coming, and perhaps soon, "when an immence Plenty of the Lord's spiritual Waters, will be pour'd out upon thirsty Souls." This would signal "the coming of our Lord Christ in his Kingdom."[34]

This speculation inevitably raised questions concerning the time of Christ's coming. Buell did not propose exact dates, but he did think there were good reasons to believe that the last days were imminent. Referencing Daniel 2, he proposed "with all humility and modesty" that "the papistical antichristian Power in the West, and the Mehometan antichristian Power in the East, will be smitten, by the Stone cut out of the Mountain." From that presumption he inferred that "as the 5th Vial [of Revelation] is pouring out upon the antichristian Power in the West; the 6th Vial will more especially be poured out upon the Mehomitan [*sic*] antichristian Power in the East." He thought that Rome was slowly falling even at the time of his writing and that the Ottoman Empire would fall suddenly, "whereupon, the Way will be prepared for the Grand eastern Kingdoms, to become Christian." Buell speculated that though it would take some time for "the Millenium or latter Day-Glory" to appear "in its full Meridian, Splender and Brightness," most of the prophetic events preceding the millennium had been fulfilled, so that it was not unreasonable to expect "approaching terrible Things in Righteousness; amazing Changes hastening on the Earth; marvellous Out-pourings of the Holy Spirit; and following Glories."[35]

Despite Buell's zeal for the revival's manifestations and eschatological potential, he used a moderating tone, assuring readers that frenzied excesses had not generated the awakening. "This Work hath been uncommonly free from meer imagination, and Satanical Delusion." Likewise, he told Eliphalet Williams that the revival was "free from enthusiastick Heats—Imaginary Views, a Spirit of Censure & bitterness." He could not say that no one in the revivals had become delusional, but he believed that overall, the emotions he witnessed were legitimate. He accepted "strong and pleasing Imaginations, and a kind of delightful Visions," but he cautioned that these should never become the focus of the revival. If anyone made them the focus, "such Persons will likely be led a woful Jaunt by the Devil." Buell reserved the more ecstatic visions for the lowly, reporting that he had spoken to only a few who had mentioned visions that he thought dangerously imaginary, and "them mostly Servants, that I suppose could not read." Although not as moderate as his patron Edwards, Buell disavowed the most radical manifestations of revival. He may also have specifically desired to separate himself from Jacob Johnson of Groton, Connecticut, who claimed that his daughter received a visit from Christ during the revival.[36]

Johnson's revival account pointed to greater wonders, the sort that only the unabashedly radical could countenance. Cleaveland, Backus, and Buell believed the liberty of individual conscience could sanction separations or reasonable enthusiasm, but they also knew that chaos could masquerade as true religion. Antinomian spiritual experiences appeared regularly from the 1730s and 1740s onward, despite the moderates' best efforts to deny or regulate them and the antirevivalists' disgust with them. In the 1762–65 revival narratives, the most radical manifestations were detailed by Johnson. Johnson came under the influence of radicals by the time of his 1740 graduation from Yale. In 1743 he nearly became pastor of a Separate congregation in Milford under the ordination of the revivalist New Brunswick Presbytery, but the Presbytery balked at threatening the Congregational establishment of Connecticut and advised the congregation to reconcile with its parent church. Johnson then began missions work among Native American groups in New York until he was called to pastor at Groton, Connecticut, in 1749. There he led the church's 1760s awakenings. Levi Hart of nearby Preston recorded in May 1764 that he "heard joyfull News of a great Work of God begun at Groton, as I had before heard of it at Long Island & some other places." Hart visited Groton in June and preached at Johnson's church. He "had some special evidences that God was at work on ye Minds of great Numbers of people, while I had Reason to fear that some were led astray." Perhaps Johnson himself gave the moderate Hart reason to pause.[37]

Among the revival narratives, Johnson's was the most mystical, yet he associated the work at his church with the ongoing general revival that he called "the late out-pouring of the holy Spirit (Anno 1764) in this and some other towns, near and farther off." His stated motivations for publishing *Zion's Memorial* (1765) were similar to Buell's. In light of the "conspicuous" work of grace, he set down a narrative with the hope that "by a collection of the repeated openings and dawns of the morning of the glorious latter-day, the day itself may at length shine forth." Johnson sought a voice in the public sphere to justify his own antinomian revivalism.[38] He described the awakening through the experiences of two people in his congregation, the second of whom appears to have been his daughter. The first convert's experience was radical enough with its reported visions and dreams, but the second witness recorded a physical appearance of Christ. This apparently was a matter of some significant controversy, which Johnson blamed for a delay in the manuscript's publication and which drew criticism in Wheelock's correspondence network.

Johnson set the 1760s revivals in the context of redemptive and revival history, noting that God had often given "remarkable seasons of the visitations of divine grace." He viewed the "protestation against popery" as one of the chief moments of divine visitation, but he thought that the Protestant churches were struggling to complete the Reformation and that some had "sunk into the darkness of popery again." But he believed that there had been "many glorious displays of divine power and grace among our puritan fathers, and others, before and since the settlement of New-England." The "last reformation," the awakenings of the 1740s, had been very significant but had not led to general sanctification, and a great decline in religion had followed it. Johnson thought that some authentic conversions had taken place since he had come to Groton, but "now of late there has been a great, remarkably great shaking, like that of an earthquake; or the voice of thunder!"[39]

Johnson knew that the "earthquake" had rumbled not only in Groton but also across the British colonies. He cited the revivals on Long Island and "especially at East-Hampton, (with the towns round about) where the holy Spirit was said to come down as a mighty rushing wind, almost as glorious as on the day of pentecost." He further mentioned revival activity in New Jersey, Rhode Island, Massachusetts, New Hampshire, and specifically at Norwich, Preston, Stonington, and Voluntown, Connecticut. Johnson's primary interest, however, was the revival at Groton, where the "very remarkable shaking" had been like that in "the valley of dry-bones in Ezekiel's vision." Like Buell, Johnson insisted that the Holy Spirit had stirred the revival, but he did comment that the preaching of George Whitefield had influenced the revivals "in sundry places east and west. Among American contemporaries, Johnson's mention of Whitefield's influence on the 1760s revivals appears unique.[40]

Like Buell, Johnson defended the revivals as legitimate, but Johnson pushed the bounds of legitimacy much further than had Buell. "As far as I am able to judge," said Johnson, "it is a genuine work of the holy SPIRIT, brought on by a conviction of sin and danger." In fact, Johnson thought that "no minister, or christian, not to say jew, papist, turk, or pagan," would deny that it was a true work of the Spirit had they honestly observed the happenings at Groton. As evidence, Johnson presented his "two witnesses," in the style of Revelation 11:3.[41]

The first witness, "Philo Christos," grew up in a devout New England family and began wrestling with sin and salvation early in life. He confessed that his travails took him down a mystical path, to dreams and visions of God. In one dream he witnessed the final judgment of Christ, in which the "book of life" lay open before the throne of judgment, and Philo Christos could not find his own name there. In another, he dreamed that an angel took him to hell to witness the torments of the damned. Neither of these dreams led him to repentance, however, and in his teen years he gave himself up to sin and wasteful pursuits.[42]

After the death of a close relative, Philo Christos began a new season of struggle with his faith and determined to follow Christ but found that all his striving led only to external appearances of righteousness, not to inward conversion. One day in his private meditation, however, a voice spoke to him, in the style of Saint Augustine's *Confessions,* saying, "Hast thou enquired at the ORACLE?" He took this to mean that he should seek the truth in Scripture, and opening the Bible, he read, "as it were by chance," the account of Jesus feeding the multitude. What struck him in particular was Christ's access to bread that the apostles did not know about. Finally, one Sunday morning, a sermon (presumably by Johnson) led Philo Christos into a vision of light. "In this astonishing, and amazing light, I saw the glory of God shining in the face of Jesus Christ." The afternoon sermon revived the vision, and it stayed with him for about two days, "all which time, I was as it were overshadowed by the Holy-Ghost," after which he discovered that he had been born again. With Johnson's encouragement, he made these visions public and called them "a work of God's grace."[43]

As enticing as Philo Christos's narrative was, that of the second witness was even more so, as Johnson solicited a testimony from his own daughter about her bodily visit from Christ. In his writings about the incident, he identified this witness only as Lydia J., but Johnson's successor at Groton revealed her as Johnson's daughter. Johnson described the eight-year-old girl as under deep conviction of sin and recorded that on September 2, 1764, she spent most of the day in her room alone. Around the same time, the Johnsons' baby daughter Zipporah became very sick and eventually died, and Lydia seemed to her father unusually capable of articulating her hope in the afterlife. He pursued this increased sophistication and asked her a great number of theological questions, which she seemed much more adept at answering than before that Sunday spent in her room. When he pressed her about what had happened that day, she finally confessed that she saw Christ "with my eyes." Johnson, incredulous, asked whether she had not just envisioned him in her mind. "No, sir," replied Lydia, "I [saw] him with my eyes as much as ever I [saw] any body in my life."[44]

Johnson knew that he had to narrate this claim delicately, and he professed to be skeptical at first. He further cautioned his readers that he did not "give it as a witness to the present work of grace; or essential to any work of grace, (as such) but a thing of an extraordinary nature." It is not clear how Johnson meant to use the testimony if not as a "witness to the present work of grace," but perhaps he thought putting too much weight on his daughter's sighting of Christ could jeopardize the credibility of the revival's more conventional features. He gingerly noted that extraordinary divine visitations did not necessarily accompany saving works of the Spirit. Johnson, however, quickly moved to a description of the vision, followed by a broader essay on the legitimacy of some visions as authentic works of God. He recorded that as Lydia sat on her bed reading the Bible, a light visible to the eye filled the chamber. When she looked up, she saw "the appearance of a man in bright, shining apparel." She described him as wearing a white priestly garment, but Johnson recorded that Christ did not wear a mitre or crown. He accounted for this absence by arguing that the "Pope, and antichristian powers, have stolen the Saviour's crown, and mitre from his head, and put it on their own, . . . No wonder Christ appears, as stript of these, in a great measure, at the present time." Johnson here appealed to a broadly shared anti-Catholicism among New Englanders. Lydia described the man as very beautiful, pleasant, and majestic. Johnson quizzed Lydia as to how Christ could be both in heaven and with her personally, and she replied "can't Christ come to be seen here when he will?" After some time, she looked down at her Bible, and when she looked back up, Jesus had left.[45]

Johnson continued to question his daughter about the episode, and she gave him the same account over and over, never doubting that she had really seen Jesus. He revisited the subject seven months later, and she was as confident as ever that it had happened and she had not just imagined it. Johnson took this to mean that the vision was likely a real sighting of Jesus, and he proceeded to defend the idea that God could communicate in such extraordinary ways as he apparently had to Philo Christos and Lydia. He noted that though God normally spoke through the Bible, he also used extraordinary means like miracles, signs, prodigies, apparitions, and audible voices. He did not believe that miracles had ceased with the apostolic period, citing "Father Austin" [Augustine] hearing the voice in the garden that told him to "TAKE UP AND READ." Johnson thought that all great outpourings of the Holy Spirit would be accompanied by extraordinary communications by God, the first such moment being the day of Pentecost. He believed that the church was at the edge of the last days during which God would pour out the Holy Spirit on his people, likely accompanied by new signs and wonders. He anticipated further that those days would see the conversion of the "whole nation of the Jews, with the fullness of the Gentiles."[46]

He saw no evidence of "fiction, imagination, or enthusiasm" in Lydia's claims, nor did he see any "satanical" influences at work. He thought it not unusual that God would send such appearances: "Because some great revolution is near; 'tis reasonable to expect something extraordinary to preceed it—Because the latter-day glory is dawning: it is reasonable to expect some extraordinaries to introduce it." He recognized that some could be visited with visions and still not be converted, or even run away with extraordinaries as the main point of religious devotion. But Johnson believed it an equally bad mistake to rule out visions in general, especially since they would become more common as the millennium approached.[47]

Many moderate evangelicals must have found Johnson's claims troubling. The freedom to pursue individual religious experiences had to be limited in some fashion, especially in the matter of physical visions. Scottish minister James Robe had warned of visionary excesses in his narrative of the revival at Cambuslang, Scotland: "Jesus Christ in the body cannot be seen by any with their bodily eyes in this life," he insisted. Most evangelical visions of Christ were through the "eyes of faith" alone, such as Jonathan Edwards's Northampton congregants who saw mental visions of Christ suffering on the cross. Similarly, one "young Lad" in Ipswich, Massachusetts, "had (in Spirit) seen Christ" during a trance, according to Daniel Rogers's 1741 diary.[48]

One surviving expression of dismay about the sighting of Jesus described in *Zion's Memorial* came from Princeton tutor Jeremiah Halsey, who wrote at some length to Eleazar Wheelock about the imminent publication of the account. He noted that Johnson had sent a proposal to New Jersey concerning the book. Halsey worried that a "pretended Vision" like this would tarnish the evangelical movement's reputation. "Things of this Nature had need to be well attested before they will gain any Credit with considerate Men, and then to be published with the greatest Caution." He thought that the "Separatists and other Enthusiasts" would make a great deal of the episode, while it would lead the "profaner Sort" to ridicule religion generally. He believed that such visions were probably "imaginary" and that they would "never work any rational Convictions."[49] Many evangelicals believed that these sorts of physical visions could never be defended against charges of fakery. Despite Halsey's concern, the expanding public sphere had begun to make room for all manner of enthusiasts and visionaries like Johnson. Like Cleaveland, Backus, and Buell, they could use the experiences of local revivals to narrate their own ideology of evangelicalism.

In spite of the wonders seen in Ipswich, Easthampton, Groton, and elsewhere, by the end of 1765, the revivals were clearly waning. Isaac Backus recorded a small awakening in Wrentham, Massachusetts, in December and noted that "some other places in the Country have had like visitations in the year that is now closed, tho' not near so many as in the year preceeding." He also reflected on the controversy over the Stamp Act, which he interpreted as a chastisement from God because "we have as a Nation grown wanton under our enjoyments."[50] Another important revival had come and gone, and certainly these did not match the revivals of the early 1740s in numbers of conversions or in media excitement.

They did, however, reflect the continuity of the evangelical movement, which still longed for revival and vigorously promoted evidence of it. Twenty years after the excitement of the 1740s, many of the former radicals remained in key places of revivalist leadership.

American evangelicalism continued to develop, too, even in the absence of massive revivals. On Buell's Long Island, for instance, radical piety continued to stew, as seen in the diary of farm woman Mary Cooper of Oyster Bay. In 1769 she joined a Separate congregation where her sister, Sarah Townshend, was a key leader. A critical historian called Townshend "a zealous advocate for that unrestrained freedom which destroys all decorum in divine worship." In the church, African Americans, Native Americans, and Anglo-Americans mixed freely. Cooper occasionally attended a Quaker meeting, where in June 1769 she heard "a most [amiable] woman" preach. Three days later she heard a Native American preacher speak at the Separate church. Finally, in August, she "went to the New Light meeten to here a Black man preach." Long Island's radical evangelicals inverted the social order by their acceptance of nonwhite male preachers. It is important to remember that evangelicalism, as a movement, did not disappear with the end of revivals in the 1740s and 1760s. From the perspective of someone like Mary Cooper, the movement seemed quite strong as of 1769.[51]

The former radical revivalists had seen the awakenings of the 1760s as potentially becoming larger than those of the 1740s, but they did not. The reason why the 1760s revivals mattered is because they demonstrated that the First Great Awakening, as a movement, persisted long after the early 1740s and under much of the same leadership. The 1760s revivals emerged because Buell, Cleaveland, and the other leaders confidently expected revivals to come again. They knew the signs of revival from the morphology established in the 1740s, and they eagerly seized upon any growing interest to try and stoke up a major conflagration. But the 1760s revivals departed significantly from the earlier revivals, most obviously because of the marginalization of Whitefield. More important, the 1760s revivals differed from those twenty years earlier because of the way that the former radicals now sought to become mainstream. Cleaveland and Backus argued that the liberty of conscience justified separation from established churches, while Buell tried to seize a position of great influence and present the new revivals to Anglo-American readers as reasonable *and* enthusiastic. Buell's narratives found a welcoming audience on both sides of the Atlantic, but Jacob Johnson's essay on visions seems, if anything, to have caused only embarrassment to the new evangelical mainstream.

These revivals reveal two important characteristics of the evangelical movement during the 1760s. First, the center of the movement shifted in a more radical direction. Many of the older moderate evangelicals did not experience new revivals in their churches, and the former radicals used their awakenings to narrate a new middle way between radical enthusiasm and antirevivalism. By the early nineteenth century, American evangelicalism was devoted to the individual's right to pursue religious happiness, and the churches usually took ordinary people's "deepest spiritual impulses at face value rather than subjecting them to the scrutiny of orthodox doctrine." As one can see in the worried response to Jesus's physical appearance to Jacob Johnson's daughter, orthodoxy and order remained serious concerns to many evangelicals in the 1760s. The democratization of American Christianity was slow in coming, as it ran against old hierarchical habits in Anglo-American religion. Signs of the democratic impulse within radical evangelicalism had already appeared in the 1740s, especially with the Separates' rejection of the established ministers' authority. To the extent that mainstream evangelicalism became populist and egalitarian by the Second Great Awakening, however, the revivals of the 1760s also represented a key moment of transition, when Buell's, Cleaveland's, and Backus's reasonable enthusiasm and advocacy of the right of individual conscience began to move from radical to normal.[52]

Second, this transition indirectly helped align many former radicals with the developing Patriot movement. Separating from corrupt established powers was a cause Cleaveland and the former radicals had long embraced. Backus, in particular, would soon become one of the revolutionary era's foremost advocates of liberty of conscience, the rights of religious dissenters, and abolishing religious establishments. As seen especially in Cleaveland's appeal, the revivals of the 1760s helped identify the maturing evangelical movement with the new rights-based American ideology and foreshadowed the development of the populist evangelicalism that dominated American Protestantism in the nineteenth century. Although some would not support the Patriot cause, most white evangelicals did, spurred in part by a conviction that the republican ideals of the Revolution reflected the evangelicals' belief in the individual right of conscience.

18

"The God of Glory Is on Our Side":
Evangelicals and the
American Revolution

On September 17, 1775, Continental Army volunteers in Newburyport, Massachusetts, preparing for a campaign against Quebec, attended Sunday services at the town's First Presbyterian Church. The church was led by Jonathan Parsons, a Separate evangelical and ardent Patriot. First Presbyterian held the final resting place of the Grand Itinerant, George Whitefield, who had died in Newburyport on his last visit to America in 1770. After a military procession, the troops' chaplain preached to the assembly. Then some of the officers went down to the crypt and opened Whitefield's tomb. From his decaying body, the men took pieces of his clothes, including his clerical collar and wristbands. They hoped that these relics from an evangelical saint would help them win the battle before them, but the mission to Quebec led to a grievous defeat. In this memorable way, the Continental officers made a connection between evangelicalism and the American Revolution.[1]

Many have attempted to link the evangelical movement to the American Revolution, suggesting that early evangelicalism mattered because it helped birth the American nation. Alan Heimert famously argued in *Religion and the American Mind* (1966) that Protestant liberalism made its devotees reluctant revolutionaries, while evangelical Calvinism lay at the heart of the "radical, even democratic, social and political ideology" that powered the Revolution. Many have rejected his point about liberalism (liberals crossed the revolutionary spectrum, and many of the most visible Patriot leaders were theological liberals), but others have agreed that there was a remarkable affinity among evangelicals for the Revolution. Yet a direct connection between the two movements remains elusive. Certainly many Patriots embraced an evangelical faith. But many did not, as seen most obviously in the case of "founding fathers" like Washington,

288

Madison, Franklin, and Jefferson. Evangelicals that became Patriots did not necessarily become Patriots because they were evangelicals. One cannot even identify a common evangelical response to the Revolution, although it appears that
the majority of evangelicals from Maine to Georgia (but not in Canada) were
Patriots. Nevertheless, evangelicalism bred an egalitarian spirit that fed a deep
social transformation, that revolution in "hearts and minds" accompanying the
military and political rebellion. The American Revolution made evangelicalism more democratic, but evangelicalism did not need the Revolution to create
within it a powerful egalitarian impulse. That tendency existed within evangelicalism from its beginnings.[2]

Some historians have argued that evangelicalism gave the Revolution one of
its most potent ideological resources, and that "evangelical piety and temperament shaped the political practices of those who were the most ardent republi-
cans." Evangelicalism taught the common people who embraced it that sometimes they must "take matters into their own hands," a subversive tendency that
exploded during the imperial crisis. The church separations and disruptions of
the revivals have been identified as "a 'practice model' which enabled the pro-
vincials to 'rehearse'—though unwittingly—. . . the arguments . . . that would
reappear with the political crisis of the 1760s and 1770s." Although I am sympathetic to such arguments, it remains difficult to demonstrate them except by
inference. Early evangelicalism, especially in its radical manifestations, was both
spiritually and socially subversive. The evangelical revivals caused the greatest
social upheaval of any movement in the colonies prior to the Revolution. This
"massive defiance of traditional authority" must have exercised some shaping
influence on the Revolution.[3]

Evangelical faith clearly influenced many Patriots' views, giving them a framing vocabulary through which to discuss the imperial crisis. Patriots routinely
called Americans back to moral virtuousness and implied that the Revolution
had quasi-millennial significance. Evangelicals also lent widespread credibility
to republican ideology, the ideas that propelled the Revolution. Evangelicals
elsewhere in the world largely rejected republicanism, but American evangelicals embraced its "fear of abuses from illegitimate power and . . . nearly messi-
anic belief in the benefits of liberty." Although republicanism had often joined
historically with humanism and religious skepticism, evangelicals in America
found republican ideals utterly congenial. Some Patriots directly linked Christianity and republicanism, as did Philadelphia physician Benjamin Rush, who
wrote to Baptist minister Elhanan Winchester in 1791 that "republican forms of
government are the best repositories of the Gospel." Since the 1960s, a generation of historians have conclusively demonstrated that these republican ideals

fueled the Revolution. Evangelicals championed republicanism as eagerly as their more liberal or skeptical Patriot friends.[4]

My purpose in this chapter is to assess the various evangelical responses to, and influences on, the Revolution. First, as historian Harry Stout has shown, some notable nonevangelical Patriots were shaped by evangelical rhetoric and ideals. Although this book's analysis has focused primarily on written sources, much of evangelicalism's power lay in its rhetoric. Itinerants, led by George Whitefield, gathered audiences of people they did not know and spoke in everyday language filled with biblical allusions. Many of the leading Patriots also mobilized the people-at-large in the revolutionary cause by giving simple speeches in every-day language. The informality and anonymity of these sermons and speeches rejected older norms of hierarchy by implicitly endorsing the right of common people to hear, evaluate, and respond to unregulated discourses. Certainly the Patriot assemblies were less participatory, democratic, and inclusive than were many evangelical meetings, but one still sees similarities between them, espe-cially in public tactics used by such Patriot leaders as Virginia's Patrick Henry.[5]

The power behind Patrick Henry's famous speaking ability lay in his popular, homespun style that was often peppered with biblical references. Henry, an An-glican, successfully used the evangelical rhetorical mode in revolutionary poli-tics. As a teenager, Henry had often listened to Samuel Davies and sermons by other Virginia Presbyterians. Henry's uncle and namesake, the Anglican priest Patrick Henry, feuded incessantly with Presbyterians in Hanover County. On Patrick Henry the nephew, however, the Presbyterians' style made a more fa-vorable impression. Henry reportedly called Davies "the greatest orator he ever heard." Some acquaintances reckoned that Henry spoke like an evangeli-cal minister, and that "his figures of speech . . . were often borrowed from the Scriptures." A close examination of Henry's 1775 "Liberty or Death" speech has shown that it is full of biblical phrases, particularly from the prophet Jeremiah. Calling resistance against the British government the "holy cause of liberty," Henry insisted that "Gentlemen may cry, peace, peace—but there is no peace" (Jeremiah 6:14). Henry thundered, "Is life so dear, or peace so sweet, as to be purchased at the price of chains and slavery? Forbid it, Almighty God!" An early biographer remembered that at the famous final line of the speech, Henry lifted his arms and bellowed, like the patriarch Joshua, "I know not what course others may take; but as for me, give me liberty, or give me death!" This was Henry, the evangelist for independence, at his finest rhetorical moment.[6]

Evangelicalism influenced some founding founders, then, but our primary question is how evangelicals themselves responded to the American Revolution. Evangelical faith tended to feed into the Patriot cause, but neither moderate nor radical evangelicalism determined people's views of the Revolution. Modifying a model constructed by historian Mark Noll, in this chapter I organize evangelicals into four categories of opinion regarding the Revolution. First are the Patriot evangelicals, who embraced the Revolution and republicanism with little hesitation and framed the cause in evangelical and anti-Catholic language. Second are the reformist evangelicals, who more-or-less eagerly supported the Revolution but expected social change to emerge from it, particularly regarding religious establishments and chattel slavery. Third, and apparently least common, were the Loyalist evangelicals, who publicly advocated remaining faithful to the empire. Perhaps most distinctive, however, was the fourth group, the sojourning evangelicals, who tried to remain aloof from the war. These evangelicals believed that the affairs of the Kingdom of God demanded detachment from the wars of nations. Although no religious explanation may fully account for individual reasons to choose these positions, the sojourning evangelicals came disproportionately from the ranks of the socially marginalized or spiritually radical evangelicals, who did not easily identify America's cause with that of Christ's kingdom. Ironically, then, moderate evangelicalism tended to feed into violent revolution, while radical evangelicalism led many into neutrality. These diverse responses continue to demonstrate the dangers of viewing early evangelicals as a monolith.[7]

The patriotic evangelical ministers, whom Tory historian Peter Oliver called the "black regiment," played a prominent role in recruiting the people at large for the Patriot cause. Nowhere was this proselytizing work more salient than in South Carolina, where the provincial congress in 1775 sent Presbyterian William Tennent III and Baptist Oliver Hart into the backcountry to encourage settlers to join the Patriot side. Hart was the most influential Baptist pastor in the low country, but he also maintained friendly relations with Separate Baptists in the backcountry. Tennent, the son of William Tennent Jr. of Freehold, New Jersey, and the nephew of Gilbert Tennent, had deep roots in the evangelical movement. He graduated from the College of New Jersey in 1758 and itinerated on behalf of the New Brunswick Presbytery for several years before accepting a pastorate at Norwalk, Connecticut in 1764. Then, in 1772, Tennent took a position at the Independent Presbyterian church in Charleston, South Carolina, Josiah Smith's congregation.[8]

Tennent became so popular at the outset of the revolutionary crisis that Charlestonians elected him as a member of the provincial congress. He prophesied against the British threat in a jeremiad titled *An Address, Occasioned by the Late Invasion of the Liberties of the American Colonists by the British Parliament* (1774). Tennent noted that the prophet Jeremiah's "patriotic Soul glowed with an enthusiastic Love for his Country." Like Jeremiah, Tennent agonized over the impending doom of his country and the national sins that provoked God's judgment. Following the widespread opinion of those influenced by republican ideology, Tennent argued that the key question in 1774 was "whether we shall continue to enjoy the Privileges of Men and Britons, or whether we shall be reduced to a State of the most abject Slavery." Tennent added that the colonists' troubles had come because of their rampant sins. To avert the crisis, they needed to repent and turn back to God.[9]

These views helped make Tennent one of the most admired leaders in low country South Carolina. The backcountry settlers' allegiances remained up for grabs, however, so the assembly sent Tennent and Hart to convince the people there to support the province, not the empire. Some prominent backcountry evangelicals, like Philip Mulkey of the Fairforest Baptist Church, had come out in favor of the British government. Hart spent several days at Fairforest, and, along with Separate Baptist Joseph Reese of Congaree, tried to convince Mulkey and his congregants to support the Patriot side. They had little success, finding the people "obstinate and irritated to an extreme." Two weeks later, Hart, Tennent, and William Henry Drayton of the provincial assembly held a joint meeting in the upcountry, where despite heckling from Loyalists they persuaded sixty men to sign a pledge of fidelity to the Patriot cause.[10]

Tennent and Hart split up during much of the tour, and Tennent seemed to enjoy more success, perhaps because he labored among more moderate Presbyterians. While Hart was failing to convince Mulkey at Fairforest, Tennent spoke before a large audience at Jackson's Creek meetinghouse. He gave a sermon and then "harangued the crowd an hour on the state of the country." He won over several leaders, and an entire militia company agreed to support the province's cause against Britain. At the muster of another company on King Creek, however, Tennent was interrupted by "two gainsaying Baptist preachers" who convinced most of the men to oppose Tennent. Near Little River, Tennent spoke for two and a half hours before a hostile audience and "conjured them by all that was sacred that they would not give themselves up to be the dupes of ministerial artifice, or the instruments of opposition and slavery." Tennent used his evangelical preaching skills to convince the people that British officials were plotting against their liberty. Soon the resistance broke and many gathered around him, asking him to keep going. Tennent's assembly at the Bull Town meetinghouse became very much like a revival meeting, as he spoke extemporaneously for three hours to an overflow crowd. Although many initially opposed him, he found them "very affectionate." His speech's "effect was very visible," and the people remained dead silent for more than a minute after he finished. Many who had formerly committed themselves to loyalty now converted to the Patriot side. Carolina Loyalists remained determined, however, to "frustrate the wicked schemes of these political Enthusiasts," as they called the Patriot commission.[11]

Although Tennent was thoroughly committed to independence, he also saw in the Revolution a great opportunity for disestablishment, a development that would benefit South Carolina's Baptists and Presbyterians alike. Thus, the "fiery patriot," as some had begun calling Tennent, drafted a petition calling for disestablishment of the Anglican church and presented it to the Assembly in early 1777. The petition argued that establishment resulted in "odious discrimination" against dissenters, whose numbers were by then much larger than those of South Carolina's Anglicans. With the onset of the colonists' rebellion, he argued, "government has returned to its just and natural source and a constitution is framing with a view to perpetuate the freedom and quiet of the good people of this state." Since religious freedom was "the most valuable of all liberty," the new state constitution would surely guarantee it. Tennent cried that "EQUALITY OR NOTHING! ought to be our motto. In short, every plan of establishment must operate as a plan of injustice and oppression; and therefore, Sir, I am utterly against all establishments in this state." He called on the assembly to "yield to the mighty current of American freedom and glory." They did so, as the legislature passed the petition and disestablished the Anglican church, briefly putting a general "Protestant" establishment in its place before total disestablishment came in 1790.[12]

Hart's and Tennent's mission was not unique; the Continental Congress also sent pastors Elihu Spencer and Alexander McWhorter into the North Carolina backcountry to gather support for independence. The Regulator movement had rocked North Carolina in the early 1770s, and this tide of popular resistance against the provincial government garnered much support from radical evangelicals, especially Presbyterians and Separate Baptists. In 1775, North Carolina officials wanted to convince former Regulators and cantankerous evangelicals to support the Revolution, and they sent Spencer and McWhorter to make the appeal. Spencer was part of the radical Yale network of the early 1740s, and he had gone with his cousin John Brainerd to the Shepherd's Tent in New London. Like Brainerd, he also served for a time as a missionary to Native Americans. In 1750, however, Spencer accepted a call to replace the deceased Jonathan Dickinson in Elizabethtown, New Jersey. McWhorter, who lived in North Carolina as a teenager, graduated from the College of New Jersey in 1757, and in 1759 he became Aaron Burr's replacement at Newark, New Jersey.[13]

In 1764, the Synod of New York and Philadelphia sent McWhorter and Spencer on a missionary journey into backcountry North Carolina. They organized congregations in western North Carolina near Sugar Creek. Eleven years later, the North Carolina delegates to the Continental Congress wrote to Spencer asking him to appeal to former Regulators and disaffected Highland Scots. Though the backcountry settlers did not trust the provincial officials, "they look to their Spiritual pastors with great respect," the Congress noted. Like Tennent and Hart, these New Jersey Presbyterians faced strong resistance from other evangelicals in the southern backcountry, and the several-month mission seems largely to have failed.[14]

The leaders of the evangelical movement who supported the Revolution also helped mobilize their congregations and towns, and some served as chaplains in the army. Nonevangelical ministers did the same sort of work, and they often used essentially the same religious language to promote the cause. Nevertheless, evangelical ministers, especially in New England, played a critical role in generating popular support for independence. One of the best examples of evangelical Patriot advocacy came from Ipswich's John Cleaveland, the former Yale radical and key leader of the revivals of the mid-1760s. Cleaveland wrote a series of editorials in Salem's *Essex Gazette* from 1768 to 1775 that trace his journey from resistance to revolution. In his 1768 protest against the Townshend duties, Cleaveland made an utterly typical republican case, asserting the "Birth-Right of Englishmen to be free." He wondered "wherein . . . we differ from mere Slaves" if Parliament could tax without the Americans' consent? He cautioned, however, that the colonists would never rebel against George III.[15]

By 1774, Cleaveland's rhetoric had become more strident, and he called for both a boycott of British goods and a rigorous commitment to holiness. He summoned New Englanders to pray for God "to maintain our Rights and Privileges, civil and religious; and above all Things to make us a holy, a truly virtuous People." He threatened that any merchants not participating in the boycott "will discover themselves to be Enemies of their Country, wholly destitute of all public Virtue." He called for their names to be published so Patriots could boycott their businesses.[16]

The battles at Lexington and Concord finally broke Cleaveland's remaining ties to Britain, and he proclaimed, "Great Britain adieu! no longer shall we honour you as our mother . . . King George the third adieu! no more shall we cry to you for protection! no more shall we bleed in defence of your person, — your breach of covenant!" To General Thomas Gage, that "profane, wicked — monster of falsehood and perfidy," he declared, "The God of glory is on our side and will fight for us." Cleaveland had been entirely confident in the rectitude of his earlier church separation, and he did not intend to hang back from a separation from Britain, either.[17]

Some evangelical ministers framed the crisis with Britain in the language of biblical millennialism, which helped give the Patriot cause transcendent meaning. Some have argued that this kind of "civil millennialism" drove the Revolution as much or more than republican ideology, although the two were often wedded in the same sermons. Among the most articulate of the evangelical millennialists was Samuel Sherwood of Fairfield, Connecticut. Sherwood published a sermon in 1774 that warned the people, in republican fashion, about the conspiracy against their liberties. An "infamous herd of vile miscreants," led by the American supporters of the crown, were carrying out "clandestine, mischievous operations" against the colonists in order to deprive them of their basic liberties. The colonists should remain vigilant against corrupt rulers, repent of their own sins, and God would deliver them from their enemies, Sherwood assured his audience.[18]

Two years later, the crisis and Sherwood's rhetoric had both escalated considerably. Sherwood, preaching on Revelation 12:14–17, argued that God had raised up the leaders of the Revolution "to fulfil scripture-prophecies, in favour of his church, and American liberty." Sherwood described the revolutionary crisis as the next great event in the earthly struggle between God's true church and Antichrist, or the Roman Catholic Church. By presenting the controversy in this fashion, Sherwood drew on the deep wells of anti-Catholicism in New England's culture. Sherwood acknowledged that the pope did not directly control England, but he suggested that all nations were threatened by "the popish mysterious leaven of iniquity and absurdity." That influence, which viciously opposed the true church, had "infected and corrupted" the British government and accounted for the recent conspiracies against British Americans. The "leaven" appeared especially in the 1774 Quebec Act, which gave Catholics in Canada freedom to worship. These "attempts to propagate and establish popery, that exotic plant, in these northern regions" showed just "how fond they are of the kind embraces of this old filthy harlot."[19]

Sherwood associated the church in America with the woman who fled to the wilderness in Revelation 12. "God has, in this American quarter of the globe, provided for the woman and her seed, a fixed and lasting settlement and habitation," he said. The "dragon" pursued her there, and tried throughout colonial history to deprive her of her liberties and enslave her. Britain's evil conspirators could not win, however, as "God Almighty, with all the powers of heaven, are on our side. Great numbers of angels, no doubt, are encamping round our coast, for our defence and protection. Michael stands ready; with all the artillery of heaven, to encounter the dragon, and to vanquish this black host." Though it is difficult to assess the reception of Sherwood's sermon, such apocalyptic framings offered a possible source of motivation to those who in early 1776 might have wavered on the question of independence.[20]

A few conservative Christians commanded audiences at the highest levels of political power during the Revolution. The two key Presbyterians in the Middle Colonies, George Duffield and John Witherspoon, deeply influenced the Continental Congress. A 1752 College of New Jersey graduate, Duffield promoted revivalism in his first pastorate at Carlisle, Pennsylvania. In 1772, Duffield was called by the evangelical congregation at Philadelphia's Third Presbyterian Church. Antirevivalist leaders at First Presbyterian bitterly opposed his installation and actually tried to lock Duffield out of his new church, obliging him to crawl in through a window to give his first sermon. Despite this difficult beginning, by the Revolution Duffield had become the most influential Presbyterian minister in Pennsylvania. He served as a chaplain to the Continental Congress and the Continental Army, and John Adams expressed great admiration for Duffield's preaching.[21]

Shortly after the 1776 publication of Tom Paine's *Common Sense*, and months before the Declaration of Independence, Duffield preached a remarkable patriotic sermon at Third Presbyterian that adopted Paine's arguments and made them more explicitly Christian and eschatological. In words strongly reminiscent of Paine's, Duffield declared, "This western world appears to have been retained . . . by an ordinance of heaven as an ASYLUM for LIBERTY, civil and religious." The Americans' forefathers left Europe to find sanctuary in the "howling wilderness, where they might rear the banner of liberty . . . , esteeming this more than all the treasures of a British Egypt, from whence they were driven forth." God ordained the settlement of the colonies, and he would not "deliver up this asylum to slavery and bondage."[22]

Duffield, like Sherwood, placed the conflict in the context of eschatological history, arguing that "there is great reason to believe that the Church of Christ is yet to have a glorious day in America." Also like Sherwood, Duffield hinted that America might become a key player in the last days, proposing that "AMERICA seems to have been prepared as the wilderness to which the woman should fly from the face of the dragon, and be nourished for a long series of time. Rev. xii. 6." Duffield, who had gone on a backcountry mission in 1766, thought that God had blessed the churches in America partly to ensure the conversion of Native Americans. "Yonder to-day are the praises of God singing . . . , where but a few years back, his name was not known, nor anything heard but the yells of savage beasts, or poor indarkened Indian tribes." Through revivals and missions, "the king of glory has here indeed gone forth, with his sword on his thigh, riding prosperously in state, conquering and to conquer!" Duffield remained confident that the gospel would continue to march westward in America: "The church shall flourish here and hold on her way triumphant, in spite of Kings, Lord, Commons, and Devils, until yonder vast unexplored western regions shall all resound the praises of God, and the unenlightened tribes of this wilderness shall know and adore our Immanuel." God would ensure the triumphs of America and the gospel.[23]

Once the war concluded, Duffield was no less optimistic about the millennial significance of the conflict. Preaching on Isaiah 66:8 ("Shall a nation be born at once?"), he proclaimed that indeed, a nation had been born at once in the late war. Since Isaiah's forecasts spoke to "that happy period, generally termed the latter day glory," America's victory might possess the greatest eschatological import. Duffield reiterated his claims that America had been set aside as an "asylum for the poor and oppressed," and that "here also, shall our Jesus go forth conquering and to conquer; and the heathen be given him for an inheritance." He became more ambitious in his predictions regarding America's future, however, asserting that "justice and truth shall here yet meet together, and righteousness and peace embrace each other: And the wilderness blossom as the rose, and the desert rejoice and sing." Duffield even speculated that the millennium would begin in America, or perhaps was already starting: "Here shall the various ancient promises of rich and glorious grace begin their compleat divine fulfillment; and the light of divine revelation diffuse it's beneficent rays, till the gospel of Jesus have accomplished it's day, from east to west, around our world." The refugees in the asylum for liberty would see the establishment of the global kingdom of God.[24]

No minister played as prominent a role in the political rebellion as Duffield's friend John Witherspoon, president of the College of New Jersey. Witherspoon was an active member of the Continental Congress and a signer of the Declaration of Independence. Whether we should call Witherspoon an "evangelical" is debatable, for he had little sympathy for revivalism or the devotees of Jonathan Edwards. Nevertheless, the classically Reformed Witherspoon did contribute a Scottish Presbyterian strain to American republicanism. Witherspoon believed that only sincere Christianity could sustain the purity of the republic. In *The Dominion of Providence over the Passions of Men* (1776), Witherspoon argued that "the public interest of religion, or . . . zeal for the glory of God and the good of others," would elicit God's blessing on America. "A general profligacy and corruption of manners make a people ripe for destruction," but "when the manners of a nation are pure, when true religion and internal principles maintain their vigour, the attempts of the most powerful enemies to oppress them are commonly baffled and disappointed." While more secular revolutionaries held that independence and liberty bred virtuous men, Witherspoon and many Christian revolutionaries could not extricate personal faith from public virtue.[25]

The pastors of the "black regiment" not only provided intellectual support for the Revolution, but many also served as chaplains in the army, just as they had during the Seven Years' War. Ammi Robbins, the son of Connecticut revivalist Philemon Robbins and a minister in Norfolk, Connecticut, served as chaplain to a Litchfield County regiment in 1776. Ministers like Robbins sought to instill discipline and moral behavior, and to exhort the soldiers to contemplate their fragile mortality. One desperately ill soldier asked Robbins to "save him if possible; said he was not fit to die." Robbins "endeavored to point him to the only source of peace." The chaplain felt troubled by the immorality he encountered in the army, writing, "'Tis impossible to describe the profaneness and wickedness of some of these men. It would be a dreadful hell to live with such creatures forever." Despite such musings, Robbins seems to have been a popular chaplain. He responded sensitively to the troops' needs and regularly visited sick soldiers in the hospital.[26]

As Robbins's regiment entered Canada with an invading Continental force, he reflected on the apocalyptic significance of the Americans' cause, noting that he "had pleasing views of the glorious day of universal peace and spread of the gospel through this vast extended country, which has been for ages the dwelling of Satan, and reign of Antichrist." Upon viewing a Catholic church in Chambly, Quebec, Robbins wondered, "When shall Satan be bound and Antichrist meet a final overthrow?" He hoped the American defeat of British Canada might hasten such triumphs. Sailing toward Quebec City, a seasick Robbins mustered his strength and "discoursed to the people in our boat, on the millenium." The British, aided by ravaging smallpox, repulsed the Americans at Quebec, but Robbins remained convinced that "our cause is just, and we shall prosper." During the retreat he noted a conversation with other chaplains "about the accomplishment of the promises, differ a little about the millenium." Robbins dutifully served the troops and the new American cause all with the possible imminence of the last days in mind.[27]

A number of Baptists also worked as chaplains in the Continental Army, continuing to solidify their formerly tenuous place in mainstream American society. Hezekiah Smith proved one of the most successful Baptist itinerants of the 1760s in both the southern and northern colonies, and he settled in 1765 as pastor of a new church in Haverhill, Massachusetts. Early in the Revolution he began serving in Washington's army, telling his wife that "the prospect of usefulness in the glorious cause of our country, joined with that of usefulness to souls," compelled him to go with the Continentals. Smith participated in the great Continental victory at Saratoga in October 1777, and in his next Sabbath sermon he preached to the troops on God's miraculous destruction of the Pharaoh's army in the Red Sea. Two years later, Smith delivered an anniversary sermon extolling Saratoga as "the grandest conquest ever gained since the creation of the world" and suggesting that it was the earthly parallel to Christ's victory over Satan. "We may with the utmost propriety cordially unite in celebrating the two grand events . . . ; the one affording the happy prospect of earthly felicity, the other the most pleasing hope of celestial happiness." In a time of war, the Patriots' willingness to insert America's successes into the history of redemption knew no limits. Smith returned to the army several times. He continued to promote revival wherever he went; he wrote to his wife from Peekskill, New York, in 1780 that he thought several in town had come under conviction of sin since his arrival. He hoped that his preaching in camp, too, "may be attended with power."[28]

Many other evangelical ministers served as chaplains in the Revolution. The missionary Samuel Kirkland worked in the Continental Army and as an Indian agent for Congress, trying to convince the Indians of the Iroquois League not to fight against the Americans, with mixed success. Baptist pastor John Gano fled New York City with Washington's army in 1776, and since the British invasion had scattered his church, he became a chaplain to a Connecticut regiment. Even Benjamin Pomeroy, one of the most radical of Connecticut's itinerants in the 1740s, served briefly as a chaplain at age seventy-one. These Patriot evangelicals reminded men of the righteous cause they served, scolded them about their vices, warned them of dying without Christ, and assured them that the God of armies held the future in his hands.[29]

Clearly, large numbers of evangelicals supported the Revolution without a second thought. For the patriotic evangelicals, religious views sacralized political opinions. Other evangelicals, however, gave more tentative support to the cause, hoping that the war would lead to critical reforms. Religion strongly shaped, or constrained, the reformist evangelicals' politics. The two most important initiatives promoted by the reformist evangelicals were religious disestablishment and abolition of slavery. We have already seen how William Tennent promoted disestablishment in South Carolina after his backcountry tour. Unlike in New England, the outbreak of Revolution in Virginia seems to have obscured differences between dissenters and Anglicans, as the Anglicans wisely began to concede more liberty to the dissenters in 1776 in order to hold together the diverse Patriot cohort. That wave of disestablishment crested with the adoption in 1786 of Jefferson's "Act for Establishing the Freedom of Religion." The most celebrated case for disestablishment, however, came from the New England Baptists, led by Isaac Backus.[30]

Many Baptists in New England seem to have contemplated remaining loyal to the British, for the British government seemed perhaps more likely than the provincial legislatures to protect their religious liberty. In a dispute concerning Ashfield, Massachusetts, in 1771, the king revoked a Massachusetts General Court law that forced the town's Baptist majority to pay taxes to support the town's Congregational minister. This led Ashfield's Baptist minister Ebenezer Smith to tell a group of Boston Patriots that "they were calling themselves the sons of liberty and were erecting liberty poles about the country, but they did not deserve the name, for it was evident all they wanted was liberty from oppression that they might have liberty to oppress!" Many of Ashfield's Baptists became Loyalists.[31]

Critically, Isaac Backus and many other New England Baptists believed that supporting the Patriot side, not the British, would best serve the interest of their liberty. Backus began his campaign for the rights of religious dissenters in 1749 when he and other Separates protested against a local tax requiring Separates to help pay for a new Congregational meetinghouse. Their petition was rejected by the Massachusetts General Court. Backus suffered quietly under this kind of taxation until the late 1760s, when he began publishing tracts advocating the termination of the state-supported establishment. His key text on the subject was *An Appeal to the Public for Religious Liberty, against the Oppressions of the Present Day* (1773). In it, Backus argued that God clearly intended to separate civil and ecclesiastical governments, in contrast to the frame of Massachusetts's government. "Who can hear Christ declare, that his kingdom is, NOT OF THIS WORLD, and yet believe that this blending of church and state together can be pleasing to him?" Backus wondered. He cleverly linked the Baptists' cause to that of the Patriots, arguing that to deny the one while supporting the other was hypocritical. No American should expect that God "will turn the heart of our earthly sovereign to hear the pleas for liberty, of those who will not hear the cries of their fellow-subjects, under their oppressions." The colonists complained of taxation without representation, yet "is it not really so with us?" Did not the Baptists have to support ecclesiastical governments in which they had no voice? The Baptists of Massachusetts arranged for a copy of *An Appeal to the Public* to be distributed to every member of the First Continental Congress.[32]

Backus decided to take his case directly to Congress, as little help seemed to be forthcoming from the Massachusetts legislature. Arriving in Philadelphia, Backus and his colleagues found themselves in over their heads in the city's political waters. The Philadelphia Baptists were developing a reputation for Loyalism, keyed by pastor and historian Morgan Edwards's fidelity to the British side. Backus immediately met several Quaker leaders who opposed the Continental

Congress. "These friends manifested a willingness to be helpful in our case," but their assistance ultimately proved damaging. The Quakers advised Backus not to meet with the whole Congress, but with the Massachusetts delegates and others friendly to religious liberty. The meeting assembled on October 14, 1774, and included Samuel Adams, John Adams, and a number of other skeptical delegates. James Manning, president of the College of Rhode Island (Brown University), opened the session by reading a memorial of the Baptists' grievances. John and Samuel Adams both responded with long speeches in which they argued that "there is indeed an ecclesiastical establishment in our province but a very slender one, hardly to be called an establishment." The meeting went downhill from there, with Samuel Adams suggesting that the outlandish complaints "came from enthuseasts who made a merit of suffering persecution, and also that enemies to these colonies had a hand therein." The Massachusetts delegates pointed out that Baptists needed only to file certificates of tax exemption for dissenters, but Backus insisted that the often-abused certificates also represented a violation of conscience. The Massachusetts delegates ended the session by offering to bring the grievances to the Massachusetts assembly, but John Adams still cautioned that "we might as well expect a change in the solar systim, as to expect they would give up their establishment."[33]

Backus was not the only Separate in New England to realize that the revolutionary crisis represented an opportunity to seek the dissenting churches' liberty. Eleven Separate Congregational churches of Connecticut, led by Suffield's Israel Holly, petitioned the legislature in 1777 for relief from taxes that supported the Congregational establishment. "We thought it a good time now . . . when all are earnestly contending for what they call their Rights and Privileges, for us under this oppression, to make . . . a bold claim for our just Rights and Privileges," Holly explained. Citing the rights language of John Locke, the petitioners argued that they "have an unalienable right, by the two grand characters, of nature, and scripture, to choose our religion." The petition suggested that, at its root, British tyranny represented the judgment of God against sinful America, "which doubtless is a loud call . . . to reform, and break off all our own oppression." The Separates insisted they were true Patriots, with not one Tory among them. Was it not "discouraging to your Memorialists," however, "when they are held under oppression themselves" by their fellow revolutionaries? What hypocrisy, Holly concluded, to "judge and condemn tyranny and oppression in the court of great Britain, and uphold and maintain it in the court of Connecticut." To Holly and the Connecticut Separates, the Patriot cause did not equal God's. Though they supported independence, they believed that New Englanders could not succeed without first reforming their own evils.[34]

While some reformist Patriots clamored for an end to religious establishments, others, such as Lemuel Haynes, Samuel Hopkins, and many "New Divinity" theologians, called for an end to chattel slavery. Another instructive example of revolutionary abolitionism came from New Jersey Presbyterian Jacob Green. Green had converted under Gilbert Tennent's preaching in 1741 while he was a student at Harvard. In 1745, he began a long pastorate at Hanover, New Jersey. When the revolutionary crisis started, Green joined the ranks of the radical Patriots in New Jersey, along with John Witherspoon. Green heartily commended the resistance against Britain as a "just" and "glorious" cause "on which we may hope for a divine blessing." He also saw the Revolution as an occasion for American repentance from slaveholding. Green's republican views were typical, but his Calvinist ethics led him to criticize American slavery even as he supported the Patriot cause.[35]

Green told his congregation that he did not mean to discourage them from supporting independence, even though he was "obliged to point out many crying sins among us." The fight against Britain, and the sins of American society, required separate ethical judgments. Green, like Backus and Holly, saw massive hypocrisy in America's calls for freedom. "Can it be believed that a people contending for liberty should, at the same time, be promoting and supporting slavery?" Citing the Declaration of Independence, just as Lemuel Haynes had, Green argued that African Americans shared the same fundamental rights as all other peoples: "Is not the hard yoke of slavery felt by negroes as well as by white people? Are they not fond of liberty as well as others of the human race? Is not freedom the natural inalienable right of all?" Green believed that the British oppression of Americans represented the chastisement of God, and that Americans might lose the war if they did not abolish slavery. If they did win, he still thought Americans would see "convulsions, contentions, oppressions, and various calamities, so that our liberty will be uncomfortable, till we wash our hands from the guilt of negro slavery." Green, like the other reformist evangelicals, reserved the right to speak prophetically against American hypocrisy, even in time of war.[36]

While a majority of American evangelicals probably supported the Revolution, with or without ethical reservations, some explicitly opposed independence. Like many Loyalists, the evangelicals who remained faithful to Britain often paid a heavy price for their position. The most articulate evangelical Loyalist was John Zubly of Savannah's Independent Presbyterian Church, a friend of leading South Carolina evangelicals who routinely preached in William Tennent's and Oliver Hart's pulpits. One would not have guessed that Zubly would become a Loyalist, since before independence he emerged as Georgia's chief pamphleteer criticizing British imperial policy toward the colonies. He insisted that Parliament did not have total sovereignty over the colonies, but rather shared its authority with colonial legislatures. As late as 1775, Zubly wrote a widely circulated pamphlet, *The Law of Liberty*, in which he warned the British government, "The Americans are no ideots, and they appear determined not to be slaves. Oppression will make wise men mad."[37]

So respected was Zubly among Georgia Patriots that in 1775 they chose him to represent the colony in the Second Continental Congress. Zubly agreed, but soon after his arrival in Philadelphia he recognized that the Congress had begun to slide toward radicalism and possible independence. This Zubly could not countenance. As he wrote in his journal in September 1775, he "made a point of it in every Company to contradict & oppose every hint of a desire of Independency." He began to irritate some of the radicals in Philadelphia by his conservatism, and soon he was exposed for having carried on a secret correspondence with Georgia's royal governor. He quickly returned to Georgia, where he refused to sign an oath of allegiance to the Continental Congress. He fled Georgia in 1778 for South Carolina's Black Swamp but returned to Savannah in 1779 after the British captured the town.[38]

Zubly's Loyalism distinguished between resistance and rebellion. The former was justified by Britain's inept bureaucratic policies, but the latter was not. When the crisis came to a head, Zubly's evangelical faith birthed a principled conservatism that led to his humiliation and exile. Once he returned to Savannah, Zubly penned a series of essays in the *Royal Georgia Gazette* excoriating his countrymen for starting an unjustifiable civil war. "There cannot be worse beings in hell," Zubly wailed, "than those who begin and keep up a war in the nation of which they are a part without cause, and they (without previous repentance) must appear conspicuous and next in rank, on the last day, to Lucifer and the fallen angels, who without any cause introduced rebellion in the creation." Zubly cited Romans 13:2 as a warning against those who fought against the powers established by God. Political and economic resistance Zubly could accept and even promote, but at bloody rebellion he drew a line that could almost never be crossed. Most of his evangelical colleagues did not make such a distinction. The bitter Zubly died in Savannah in 1781, several months before Cornwallis surrendered at Yorktown.[39]

The newest evangelical force in America, the Wesleyan Methodists, also became closely associated with Loyalism. British Methodist leader John Wesley famously defended the Tory position in the Revolution, even as he advised his itinerants to remain silent on political issues. Wesley's Tory sentiments tarred his American preachers, sometimes unfairly, with a reputation for Loyalism. On the Delmarva Peninsula (containing Delaware and the Eastern Shore of Maryland and Virginia), where the Methodists made some of their earliest American converts, Methodist Loyalism became common. Wesley's superintendent in America, Thomas Rankin, privately promoted Loyalism in Maryland, and in 1778 he and a number of other Methodist itinerants departed for Britain to ride out the war. Among the licensed Methodist itinerants, only Francis Asbury remained in Patriot territory through the conflict. Largely because of its reputation for Loyalism, the Methodist connection nearly ceased to function in America during the Revolution.[40]

Often the line between Loyalism and neutrality was blurred, but at least among evangelicals, there remained a distinction between the two positions. Loyalists stayed committed, for a variety of reasons, to the British government itself. Neutrals preferred to remain aloof from the war. Sojourning evangelicals decided that the business of the Kingdom of God precluded their engagement with the wars of nations. Historians have generally accepted the idea that rank-and-file Loyalists "represented conscious minorities, people who felt weak and threatened." This thesis may indeed work for the many evangelical Loyalists and also neutrals. The Loyalist Baptists, such as those in Ashfield, Massachusetts, clearly felt threatened by the Congregationalist-dominated government. There are obvious exceptions to the rule: John Zubly, for instance, would seem to have had little reason to feel threatened by Patriot authorities prior to his Loyalist commitment. Yet radical evangelical faith not only helped its neutral or Loyalist adherents express political or social anxiety, it also seems to have provided a doctrinal justification for the skepticism many in its ranks felt regarding the Patriots' cause.[41]

The Carolinas became a hotbed of sojourning and Loyalist evangelical sentiment, much to the dismay of Patriot authorities. The Patriot missions of Tennent, Hart, Spencer, and McWhorter all reflected the American politicians' sense that the Baptists and Presbyterians of the southern backcountry were not committed to resistance against Britain, and that those groups might in time decide to fight on behalf of the empire. Many radical evangelicals had supported the Regulators' fight against the North Carolina provincial government, and many determined that they would not join the Patriot cause, either. Evangelical minister James Miles of Cross Roads meetinghouse near North Carolina's Haw River reportedly threatened to excommunicate anyone who took up arms on either side of the war. A witness claimed that Miles exhorted his congregation to "show him a great man with a half moone in his hat with Liberty writ upon it and his hat full of feathers . . . and he would show you a Devil and that Poore men was bowing and scraping to them and they a Leading them to hell as soon as they had a Come from the Congress." Those men "were Blow'd up as bigg as a Blather," and "he did not value the Congress nor the Committee no more than as percel of Rackoon Dogs for he got his Com[mands] from the King and the feild officers Got thar Com[mands] from hell or the Devil." James Childs, a pacifist Separate Baptist minister from Anson County renowned for his visionary experiences, was summoned to testify before a Patriot committee in 1776. He declared that as a Baptist, "one of the tenets of his church was not to bear arms . . . and that he had inculcated [that doctrine] by the terrors of excommunication." While many southern evangelicals did support the Patriot side, others distrusted their provincial governments and saw no reason for their church bodies to serve one side or the other in war.[42]

Many African Americans saw the American Revolution as a war for liberty, but that liberty, they hoped, would come by way of the British army. The British made halting efforts to recruit slaves with offers of freedom in exchange for service in the military. Loyalist blacks could not realistically expect better treatment should the Patriots succeed. A number of African American evangelicals eventually became Loyalists, too, and filled refugee settlements in Nova Scotia. David George, the Baptist pastor of the Silver Bluff Church in South Carolina, fled with his family to British-occupied Savannah when his "Antiloyalist" master abandoned his plantation. Some Loyalists suspected that George was a Patriot spy, and they briefly imprisoned him. George's family later moved to Charleston, but when the British evacuated the city late in the war, authorities advised him to go to Nova Scotia. The British gave "the few Black people . . . their passage for nothing." It is not clear how many of the Loyalist African Americans in Nova Scotia were evangelicals, but hard-working pastors like David George helped convert many refugees to the faith.[43]

Forced to make their own difficult choices, some Native American evangelicals also attempted to remain neutral. Samson Occom made the most powerful case for Native American sojourning neutrality. In a 1775 letter to the Oneidas, he strongly encouraged them to remain at peace, despite his sympathy for the Patriot cause. In a poignant defense of Christian pacifism, Occom recommended that they not "meddle with the Family Contentions of the English, but will be at peace and quietness, Peace never does any hurt, Peace is from the God of Peace and Love. . . . Jesus Christ is the Prince of Peace." The devil commissioned the wars of men, not Jesus. Occom explained that "the English Quarrils over the great Waters" came because "the present King of England wants to make [the colonists] Slaves." Occom assured the Oneidas that God would help the oppressed, but they should not "intermeddle in these Quarrils among the White People."[44]

By its end, Occom's view of the war had grown darker, as the conflict proved devastating to many Native Americans and especially to missionary efforts among them. In 1783, Occom lamented that all the Indian missions and schools had shut down because of the war. He particularly regretted missionary and Indian agent Samuel Kirkland's decision to serve as a chaplain in the army, which jeopardized Kirkland's credibility among many Native Americans. "Mr. Kirkland went with an Army against the poor Indians, & he has prejudiced the minds of Indians against all Missionaries, especially against White Missionaries; seven Times more than any thing, that ever was done by the White People." From Occom's perspective, the war had borne bitter fruit and hampered the business of the Kingdom of God. What most white evangelicals saw as a patriotic cause, Occom saw as a vicious distraction, or in Kirkland's case, a sell-out of the gospel. In time, Kirkland would become a wealthy land speculator among the vulnerable native people he once hoped to evangelize, acquiring thousands of acres of Iroquoian territory made ripe for the picking by the outcome of the Revolution.[45]

Along with Occom, Nova Scotian evangelist Henry Alline made the most compelling case for sojourning neutrality during the war. Alline was born in 1748 in Newport, Rhode Island, but moved with his family to Nova Scotia in 1760. After a powerful conversion in 1775, Alline began a meteoric preaching career in Nova Scotia and northern New England that flamed out with his death in 1784. Although Alline's gospel of the new birth replicated the message preached by colleagues to the south, he came to view the Revolution as fatally corrupt. Shortly after the onset of the war, the pacifist Alline was offered an enlistment in Nova Scotia's militia, but he "utterly refused," seeing it as a temptation from the devil. He resolved to forsake "all commissions but a commission from heaven to go forth, and enlist my fellow-mortals to fight under the banners of King Jesus."[46]

Just as the war began, a massive series of revivals shook Nova Scotia's British and African American communities, a sign to Alline that Nova Scotia had become a godly refuge in a degenerating, violent world. In 1782, Alline marveled at how the Nova Scotians had been "screened from the trials of our (once happy) Nation in the convulsions of the present day." While other Britons "were involved in the dreadful calamity, we have been blest with that unparalleled blessing the moving work of the Spirit of God." Other American evangelicals saw God's hand moving in the war, but Alline saw the war as a scourge rooted in human evil. For him, God's hand was lately visible only in outpourings of the Holy Spirit which flowed even as the war rampaged.[47]

Occom's and Alline's responses reveal, again, that there was no one evangelical response to the American Revolution. Though the revivals aided in the creation of an American culture ready for revolution, and though a seeming majority of evangelicals supported the Patriot side, many other evangelicals remained loyal to Britain or tried to stay neutral. Besides those already mentioned, other minority evangelical groups—German Pietists, Mennonites, Moravians, and Shakers among them—all inclined toward neutrality. For most American evangelicals, however, faith provided a framework through which to interpret the crisis. Perhaps many responded like Connecticut farm woman and evangelical Hannah Heaton, who needed courage when her two sons enlisted. In February 1777 she dreamed that she "was talking to jonathan and calvin. I thot i told them to pray to god that they might live threw this deluge of war for when it was over i believed there would be greater glory seen in new england than ever was before. And while i was speaking i thot my soul was raised with a vew of the glory and so i awaked. O lord i hope to see thy word fulfilled on which i have hoped. Pray come quickly and send down a rain of righteousness." Heaton's belief in God gave her hope for her sons' safety and confidence that God would give New England, and America, "greater glory" once the war was over. Evangelical Christianity supplied a means by which many colonists could fathom what was happening in the revolutionary crisis, but it neither caused the rebellion nor conditioned a unidirectional response to the war. If anything, the more radical or socially marginalized evangelicals seem often to have leaned toward neutrality or Loyalism, while moderate evangelicals tended toward Patriotism, or at least reformism. Patriots seemed to let religion support their political opinions, while reformists' theological views constrained their ability to support the Revolution unreservedly. These conclusions further highlight the problems with interpreting early American evangelicalism as a unified cohort.[48]

"Many Thought the Day of Judgment Was Come": The New Light Stir
of 1776–1783

On May 19, 1780, much of New England fell under a thick, smoky veil of darkness. In a time of war and millennial expectations, many evangelicals read this "Dark Day" as an ominous portent. A broadside rhymed

> Nineteenth of May, a gloomy day,
> When darkness veil'd the sky;
> The sun's decline may be a sign,
> Some great event is nigh.

The poem's author declared that the phenomenon signaled America's need for repentance and awakening:

> Awake, awake, your sins forsake,
> And that immediately;
> If we don't turn, his wrath will burn,
> To all eternity.[1]

Polite observers considered the event an unusual meteorological phenomenon. Yale College president Ezra Stiles averred that it could be explained "without having recourse to any Thing miraculous or ominous" and identified forest fires as the darkness's primary cause. Isaac Backus, however, noted that "many in town and countery thought the day of judgment was come." Hannah Heaton considered the phenomenon "no eclips but a forerunner of some great thing coming on the world" and cited prophecies of Acts 2:20 and Joel 3:15, "the sun shall be darkned and the moon turned into blood." Samuel Gatchel of Marblehead, Massachusetts, made explicit Heaton's implication that the Dark Day had fulfilled the prophecy of Joel 3:15. Gatchel believed that the American church was the woman in the wilderness of Revelation 12:6, so that when Joel prophesied in 3:16 that "The LORD shall roar out of Zion, and utter his voice from Jerusalem," "Zion" and "Jerusalem" referred specifically to New England. The Lord's voice spoke in the Dark Day, which covered New England alone, marking its special identity. The apocalyptically minded would remember the Dark Day for decades, as the Millerite Josiah Litch asked in 1842: "Has the sun been darkened in these days, as predicted by Joel and the Saviour? It has; and that within the memory of many now living. I refer to the dark day of A. D. 1780, May 19th."[2]

The Dark Day marked the moment of greatest eschatological anticipation in the midst of another series of North American revivals, the "New Light Stir," which ran from about 1776 to 1783. Although this period was marked by vigorous Baptist growth in the South, Baptists and other evangelicals also saw great successes in New England and Nova Scotia. The revivals of 1776–83 show that though American church growth had generally slowed during the third quarter of the eighteenth century, the inheritors of the radical evangelical movement still thrived, setting the stage for the fractious triumphs of evangelical churches in the early nineteenth century. As the first generation of American evangelical Christianity drew to a close, the movement continued to expand and develop, despite the challenges associated with the revolutionary crisis. Some former radicals, like the Separate Baptists, consolidated into more rationalized denominations during this period, whereas new, even more radical groups like the Shakers continued to appear on the borders of evangelicalism. These sects' intensely emotional spirituality contributed to their bending of social conventions related to race, class, and gender. The tensions between radical and moderate evangelicalism persisted.[3]

In Nova Scotia, the radical Henry Alline was the indispensable leader of the revivals during the Revolution. He was a pacifist neutral during the war, and his piety continued and extended the legacy of evangelical radicalism from New England in the 1740s. Alline left a vivid description of his conversion, showing the agonizing process he endured before breaking through to salvation. After moving to Nova Scotia with his family in 1760, the teenaged Alline became obsessed with hell and damnation, and he despaired to the point of becoming suicidal. His morbid thoughts were distracted by youthful frolicking, and in time he became "very wild and rude." Carnal living did not satisfy his soul, however. One evening, as he walked through the woods, God sent him a vision of hell. "An uncommon light" surrounded him, "it seemed like a blaze of fire . . . I thought I saw thousands of devils and damed spirits, by whom I expected to be tormented. . . . Thus God shewed me in some degree for about three quarters of a minute" what the Judgment Day would be like for him. He looked behind him to "see how far the burning flood and sweeping deluge . . . was from me, that I might know how long I should be out of hell." But the flames were not there. He was alone and soon saw another burst of light that revealed that he had only seen "a common phenomena of nature," but one "designed by God as an alarming means."[4]

But the day's ordeal had hardly finished. Alline returned to his parents' house only to be confronted by a vision of a "beautiful woman (one whom I had seen before, but had no great acquaintance with)." He thought of how happy he might be with her, and the "devil told me that I need not commit any sin for to enjoy her; that I might marry her, which was lawful: yea, so I acquiesced in the temptation, that my affections were after her, and she appeared the most beautiful object that ever I beheld." His "passions were so inflamed" that he thought he would take the first opportunity to propose marriage to her. Soon, however, God broke through his fantasy and "shewed me that I was on the devil's ground." He resolved not to seek marriage or any other pleasure until he was converted.[5]

Alline found himself torn between the enticements of a frolicking youth culture and his impending conversion. Some of Alline's young friends ridiculed radical evangelicals, and "made a game of what they had seen of the New-Lights in New-England . . . and in derision cried out, they were converted, they were converted, and a young woman fell down on the floor and frothed out of her mouth, and cried, &c." Alline felt very uncomfortable with this mocking behavior and reckoned that "it was the work of God" they parodied.[6]

Finally, Alline came to the end of his struggles on March 26, 1775. He concluded that he could not do anything to win God's favor and surrendered himself to God's mercy. "At that instant of time . . . redeeming love broke into my soul with repeated scriptures with such power, that my whole soul seemed to be melted down with love." Hardly reflecting mere intellectual assent to theological propositions, the bachelor Alline described his conversion as a deeply emotional, almost sexual experience: "attracted by the love and beauty I saw in his divine perfections, my whole soul was inexpressibly ravished with the blessed Redeemer." Alline repeatedly described this spiritual "ravishing," with its explicitly sexual overtones, as essential to the experience of the new birth.[7]

Almost immediately, Alline sensed a call to preach. With no college education, he knew that many would not accept his calling. The learned class's monopoly of the pastorate only supported "the ministry of antichrist," Alline believed. After struggling for a year over his lack of education, he finally began preaching publicly on April 19, 1776, the anniversary of the battles of Lexington and Concord. Soon great crowds, "even whole boat-loads," came from the surrounding towns to hear him preach on Sundays. He also began to itinerate through Nova Scotia, where few established churches existed. Some Congregational ministers did oppose him, leading Alline to lament the damage wrought by "unconverted ministers." He considered "the power of God's Spirit far more important than the . . . bare traditions of men." He began setting up Separate meetings composed of Congregationalists and Baptists who had experienced the new birth. So focused was Alline on individual conversion that he considered the method of baptism a nonessential matter that should be left up to the individual's private judgment.[8]

Alline embraced the antiauthoritarian, egalitarian spirit of James Davenport and other radicals before him. He endorsed common people's spiritual experiences, for instance. He regularly noted the presence of Africans at his meetings. At a March 1781 meeting in Falmouth, he recorded seeing a "poor negro-man get up and tell what God has done for his soul." Alline delighted in the public testimony of such African saints, writing, "blessed be God, that he chooses the weak things of the world, and things despised of men. I have often seen in the compass of my travels, poor servants and slaves shouting forth the Redeemer's praise." By contrast, "their masters stood in open rebellion, and rejected the simplicity of the gospel."[9]

Alline approved public exhortations by common men, women, and children. At one meeting he recorded with pleasure how "some of the brethren exhorted and prayed. Some of them were almost ready to leave their bodies with raptures." At Windsor, he once observed a woman so "overjoyed, that she could not contain, but cried out in divine raptures, with shouts of praise to God, and exhorting souls to come and share with her." At Liverpool he saw a child "take his father by the hand, and cry out, O father, you have been a great sinner, and now are an old man: an old sinner, with grey hairs upon your head, going right down to destruction. O turn, turn dear father, return and fly to Jesus Christ." Some scoffed at Alline's indulgence of such public speeches, and one man at Liverpool shouted during Alline's sermon that he was preaching "damned foolishness."[10]

Alline also anticipated one of the distinctives of the Second Great Awakening in his rejection of Calvinist theology. Forging an individualistic approach to theology, he recalled struggling with the implications of Calvinism before his conversion. He wondered why "all the world must be sent to hell and be punished with all that could be inflicted on them for [Adam's] sin, excepting here and there one, that God had picked out, and the rest, though they were invited to come to Christ, and a sort of sham-offer of salvation made them, yet there was none for them, neither did God intend to save them, when he made them the offer." That old Reformed theology led Alline to conceive God as cruel and capricious, but after his conversion he came to believe that God lovingly allowed all to choose or reject salvation. God did not cause people to be saved. "The very Nature of GOD," he wrote, "is a Freedom of Choice, and therefore GOD cannot redeem those, that will not be redeemed, or save them without their Consent." Many Maritime evangelicals rejected his anti-Calvinism, and Alline lost the support of some key churches because of his Arminian views. Alline's beliefs about predestination, however, reflected the emerging anti-Calvinism of many second-generation North American evangelicals like the Methodists.[11]

American evangelicalism did not often produce Arminianism in its early decades, but by the Revolution one began to see cracks in the Calvinist evangelical edifice. Rising antiauthoritarianism made a rejection of Calvinism possible, signaling the centrifugal theological impulses coming in the next generation of American evangelicalism. Alline served as a critical precursor to anti-Calvinist, doctrinally individualist evangelicalism, but he died of consumption in January 1784 at the beginning of a tour in northern New England. His gravestone read, "He was a burning and shining Light, and was justly esteemed the apostle of Nova Scotia." Alline's sojourning neutrality should not obscure his critical place in the first generation of American evangelicalism. His ministry set the tone for evangelical development in Nova Scotia and New Brunswick for the next twenty-five years. While some Calvinist Baptists tried to rein in radical enthusiastic tendencies, others among Alline's successors reached unprecedented heights of spiritual ecstasy. From the Saint John River valley in the 1790s came reports of prophecies, miracles, and speaking in tongues. In Yarmouth, the radical itinerant Harris Harding preached against idolatry and hosted a clothes-burning, successfully compelling his followers to burn their affected finery, a request on which James Davenport floundered fifty years earlier. Harding's followers reportedly walked the streets of Yarmouth late at night crying, "Behold, the Bridegroom cometh!"[12]

Alline's ill-fated journey to New England reflected that region's continuing receptiveness to radical revivalism which flourished in the 1770s and 80s. Many evangelical groups, especially in backcountry New England, grew during the period. Continental Army chaplain David Avery wrote in 1779 that "in the midst of Judgment God has remembered Mercy, & appeared for our land," both through military successes and local revivals in Congregational churches at New Preston, Connecticut, and Northampton and Amherst, Massachusetts. From far western Massachusetts, in the Berkshire Hills, Avery heard from Daniel Collins of Lanesborough that "nigh 200 have lately received a saving conversion." A year later, however, Avery reported to New Jersey's John Witherspoon that he had become concerned about the revivals in western Massachusetts, where "a most surprising Spirit of fanaticism prevails." Moderate Congregationalists struggled to keep the radical spirit out of the revivals.[13]

Despite other evangelicals' successes in New England, the Baptists took the lead in the New Light Stir. For them, revivals from 1778 to 1782 resumed and surpassed those of 1762–65. Because of their rapid growth across New England, and America generally, by the mid-1780s the Baptists had become poised to emerge as one of the two (along with the Methodists) dominant denominations of American evangelicalism. In New England, the number of Baptist churches went from fifty-three to eighty-nine between 1778 and 1782. Moreover, Isaac Backus estimated that about two thousand New Englanders received believer's baptism in 1780 alone. By his judgment, the outpouring of the Spirit "spread the most extensively and powerfully through New England, that any revival had done for near forty years," and it "was undoubtedly a great means of saving this land from foreign invasion, and from ruin by internal corruption." Not only had the New England Baptists supported the Revolution, but their revivals may have saved America from the British army and its own sin, Backus suggested.[14]

Baptist itinerants spurred the new revivals. Jonathan Jeffers, a young preacher who had fled British-occupied Newport, Rhode Island, in 1776, reported to Backus in 1778 that "for Weeks Together These Words 'Go Preach to the Lost Sheep of the House of Israel' has Been in my Thoughts." He and Asa Hunt of Middleborough, Massachusetts, preached at meetings across Cape Cod. Jeffers witnessed a number of conversions and baptisms at Hyannis. Two teenage sisters there, despite their parents' opposition, had begun zealously "speaking of what Jesus Christ has done for them." Hunt also led a major revival in his Middleborough church in 1780. Shortly after the Dark Day in May, Hunt held a remarkable meeting in his home where "the Divine power was like pentecoste." By sunset six people had been converted, and "such Rejoicing of Saints and crys of Sinners as I Never heard among the rest." A nine-year-old boy "who appear'd to have been deliv'd in ye [time?] of the darkness more than a week ago" now exhorted "Sinners to come to Christ." Between May and August, Hunt baptized 83 converts, and the Middleborough church's membership nearly doubled from 78 to 150.[15]

From Woodstock, Connecticut, Biel Ledoyt, a veteran of the revivals of the 1760s, reported to Backus that the Dark Day helped precipitate a new revival in his church as well. "The Sabbath after the late uncommon Darkness I observed uncommon attention and solemnity among the people," and the following Sundays saw overflow crowds and many baptisms at the church. Ledoyt hoped that the new revival would not only lead to conversions, but to the final destruction of Connecticut's establishment. He anticipated that soon "Religious Establishments by humane Laws" would face "a final over Through in our Land." He signed the letter as a "fellow Labourer in the gospel against the power of the Beast which God knows my Soul abhors." To the Baptists, revivals not only energized the churches but vindicated their efforts to break the power of the establishments.[16]

The Baptist revivals also proceeded in New Hampshire, fed by the itinerant ministry of the medical doctor Samuel Shepard. Shepard had received believer's baptism from Hezekiah Smith in 1770 and became pastor of several small Baptist churches in New Hampshire. In 1781 he wrote to Backus with news that "some hundreds of souls are hopefully converted in the counties of Rockingham, Strafford, and Grafton, in New Hampshire, within a year past." He had baptized seventy-two people on a recent itinerant journey and had seen the formation of at least eight new Baptist meetings in New Hampshire. He assured Backus of the "general increase of the Baptist principles through all the eastern parts of New England."[17]

These revivals demonstrated again the tension between radical and moderate tendencies in evangelicalism, as well as the tendency of radicals like the Baptists to become moderate over time. In New England the revivals produced more sober Baptists as well as a host of new radical sects. A number of Backus's Baptist associates sought cultural legitimacy in their conduct of the revivals and newly tried to restrict itinerancy to properly ordained ministers. Though Asa Hunt did note with some concern that young men and women stayed up late at Middleborough singing and exhorting, overall he thought that their zeal was "so tempered with knowledge that we have been remarkably free from disorders." Critics found little to complain about in the converts' behavior. Baptist minister Elkanah Ingalls of Raynham, Massachusetts, worried about "doors Being opened to persons to preach that are not in Good Standing." He particularly feared that the "old cruel Crooked Serpent will make his appearance under the notion of a very Large Liberty in the Impo[ve]ments of Gifts which works Under Ground and is as Cruel as the Grave towards the Dear ministers of Christ." The Separate Baptists of New England now worked to restrain the popular exercise of spiritual gifts and enthusiastic experiences, signaling their emergence as a more respectable denomination.[18]

The Separate Baptists also spun off more radical sects during this period, however. All these groups shared a common commitment to revivals but fractured over old issues like lay preaching and antinomian, emotional spiritual experiences. Increasingly, the Baptists and their progeny, including the Freewill Baptist movement, feuded over theological differences, especially between Calvinism and Arminianism. The key organizer of Freewill Baptists was Benjamin

Randel, a tailor who had grown up in an antirevivalist congregation in New Hampshire. Randel became one of George Whitefield's very last converts; he heard the aged itinerant preach in Portsmouth, New Hampshire, in September 1770. At that time, Randel stood "opposed to all travelling preachers, who in those days, by way of derision, were called Newlights." He thought evangelical preachers only wanted "to make the people cry out, and make a noise." Likewise, he found Whitefield to be a "worthless, noisy fellow." But Whitefield soon died in Newburyport, Massachusetts, and Randel became gravely concerned, thinking, "Whitefield is now in heaven, while I am in the road to hell." He was soon converted, and he separated from his Congregational church in 1775. In 1776, Randel converted to Baptist principles and received believer's baptism from William Hooper, pastor of the Baptist meeting at Madbury, New Hampshire.[19]

Randel itinerated through New Hampshire and fell under suspicion of Loyalism during the Revolutionary War because of his radical pacifism. He also ran afoul of Separate Baptist leaders because of his Arminian theology, a holdover from his antirevivalist Congregational background. The troubled Randel sought God out in a cornfield, asking for the way to truth. God told him that he must give up all tradition and rely only on the leading of the Spirit and the Word. Randel yielded to the Spirit and wrote, "O! the flaming power, which instantly passed through my soul. . . . I had no feeling of any thing, but the great and awful, terrible and dreadful majesty of God, which sunk me, as it were, into nothing." He seemed to separate from his own body, and he saw a white robe descend and cover him. "A bible was then presented before the eyes of [his] mind," which he realized "ran in perfect connection with the universal love of God to men — the universal atonement in the work of redemption, by Jesus Christ, who tasted death for every man — the universal appearance of grace to all men, and with the universal call of the gospel." Unlike earlier radical evangelicals, but similar to his contemporary Henry Alline, Randel's mystical experiences sealed his anti-Calvinist, free will convictions.[20]

Randel went on to organize many Freewill Baptist congregations during the New Light Stir, even as the moderating Calvinist Baptists had their own revivals in the same areas. By the end of 1781, Randel had helped start fourteen Freewill Baptist churches in New Hampshire and Maine. William Hooper of Madbury, New Hampshire, who had baptized Randel, reported to Isaac Backus in 1780 that Calvinist Baptist revivals proceeded in Loudon, Barrington, Gilmanton, and Madbury. He worried about "the Brethren that hold to Free will Plan" who were causing divisions in the churches, however. Revival vindicated the Calvinist side's legitimacy, as the Freewill Baptists "find to thir grat mortification that the work of the Lord goes on wounderfully under the preaching of those that hold to the Doctrine of Sovereign Grace." Conditions during the Revolution allowed revival, theological innovation, and conflict among evangelicals to develop simultaneously. The Freewill Baptists would become one of the most vigorous evangelical denominations in backcountry New England, with about three hundred churches by 1827.[21]

Some groups in the 1770s and 1780s far surpassed the Freewill Baptists' theological radicalism and leapfrogged over Arminianism, out of evangelicalism, and into universalism. Baptist itinerant Elhanan Winchester led a major revival in Welsh Neck, South Carolina, before returning to Massachusetts in 1779. Yet even as Winchester dabbled in literature regarding the "universal restoration" of all people, he preached in churches touched by the New Light Stir. Isaac Backus admired Winchester and his account of the Welsh Neck revival, and he invited Winchester to preach at his church. Winchester itinerated in Baptist and Congregational meetings across New England, precipitating more revivals and leading Backus to comment, "his success is wonderful." Winchester baptized 109 converts between December 1779 and May 1780. Winchester left Massachusetts in September 1780 with the intention of returning to South Carolina. He unexpectedly received an invitation to pastor the First Baptist Church of Philadelphia, however, and led a considerable revival there before he came out publicly for universalism in 1781. Although he was quickly dismissed from the Philadelphia church, Winchester continued to use revival techniques to convince people of universal salvation.[22]

Caleb Rich, like Winchester, came over to universalism by way of evangelicalism. In contrast to Winchester's more learned path, Rich's extreme radicalism and visionary experiences fueled his theological innovations. Rich grew up in Separate Baptist churches and was converted in 1771 in Warwick, Massachusetts. But he doubted the doctrine of eternal torment for the damned and through a series of mystical spiritual experiences came to believe in universal restoration. In one vision, a "celestial guide" told him that he "was placed by unerring wisdom into God's building before the foundation of the world." Armed with this assurance, Rich met another "celestial friend" in a night vision who warned him against slavishly believing the Baptists: "you must follow no man any further . . . tho' they follow Christ." Ascending Mount Zion in his vision, Rich finally arrived at a bright shining light, "the house of God and the Gate of Heaven." Rich believed that he had begun to receive these visions in fulfillment of Joel 2:28 and "in consequence of the out pouring of the spirit upon me." Soon he "ceased to believe in endless misery," for which he was denied membership in the Warwick Baptist Church.[23]

In the mid-1770s, Rich organized several universalist meetings in Massachusetts and New Hampshire. In 1778 he experienced two more mystical episodes. In the first, "a person, or the likeness of one" entered his home and preached to him. The angelic figure confirmed to him "the restoration and salvation of every man made in the image of God, as in any one of the human race." Moreover, the mysterious visitor told him, in a warning reminiscent of that given to Mormon leader Joseph Smith three decades later, "that there was not one formal church among them that stood in the Apostolic rectitude or that contended for the Faith once delivered to the saints—i.e. to Abraham, Isaac and Jacob." He also "spoke of the consumption of Anti-christ by the second coming of Christ." Then the figure vanished. Soon afterward Rich became overwhelmed with the magnitude of the new revelation and "felt as it were a shock of electricity, my lips quivered, my flesh trembled, and felt a tremour throughout my whole frame for several days."[24]

Rich's visions concluded with a visit from Jesus himself. "With the sociability of an equal . . . did he converse with me," Rich recalled. The experience convinced Rich that Christ had commissioned him to preach the gospel of universal restoration. Christ's humility also gave him "the greatest aversion to any thing that savours in the least degree of pomposity or worldly grandeur in a professed gospel minister." He anticipated that "all formal church establishments, all the prejudices of education, [and] all the superstitions of the age" would oppose him. But he confidently asserted that he had received his ministry "by the revelation of Jesus christ, through the medium of the holy spirit in opening my understanding." Rich's theological individualism, and his success in promoting universalism in the New England backcountry, shows how spiritual radicalism in the revolutionary era continued to grow and diversify, even in some heterodox directions.[25]

The revivals also spun off some radical sects that endorsed female leadership and public authority. Among the most ecstatic of these were the so-called Come-Outers of Gorham, Maine. Dissatisfaction began growing in 1773 against Gorham's antirevivalist pastor Josiah Thacher. Some disaffected radicals denounced the learned ministry and held late-night private meetings where laypeople preached instead. A local historian recalled that young returning veterans from the Revolutionary War brought back with them "looser ideas of religious liberty, and liberal religion." These veterans fueled the Separate movement in Gorham. Led by female worshippers, the Come-Outers would work "themselves up to complete frenzy, even to frothing at the mouth, dancing, stamping, and whirling around." Then they would fall to the floor in "a trance, or spiritual state, and as they said, holding communion with God." When they emerged from the trance, the Come-Outers would often approach some person for whom they had a "special message, assailing them with a torrent of invectives, such as calling them devils, children of the devil, sinful, lustful, artful devils, men of sin, anti-Christs." The Come-Outers harassed Thacher incessantly, spoke out against him during his own sermons, and once tried to bar him from the meetinghouse. Ultimately, their antagonism contributed to Thacher's dismissal. The Gorham radicals also embraced the ideals of perfectionism, sinlessness, and pacifism. Their intensity flagged in 1781, however, and a number of them joined either the Freewill Baptists or the Shakers.[26]

The heterodox Shakers drew many of their American followers from the ranks of the revivalist churches. Early leader Joseph Meacham provides an instructive example of the journey from radical evangelicalism to the Shaker church. Meacham grew up in a Baptist church in Enfield, Connecticut, and became a Baptist exhorter by the mid-1770s. He grew dissatisfied with the "standing orders, . . . for he saw that they were all lacking of salvation." He began a quest "to find the work of full salvation." Meacham found the violence between Christians in the Revolutionary War disconcerting and sought a new pure community of believers. He thought he found it at New Lebanon, New York, where he helped lead a heated revival in 1779. His Shaker biographer noted that "he had many powerful gifts; many prophesies and bright views of the Second coming of Christ; the setting up of his everlasting kingdom &c."[27]

The millennial expectations cooled with some disappointment that Christ had not yet returned. Some called on Meacham to "come forth and lead them into the kingdom; but this he confessed with the rest, he was not able to do." In spring 1780, some of Meacham's followers encountered the Shaker community at Niskeyuna, New York. The Shakers had originated in Manchester, England, as a fusion of Quaker and radical evangelical piety. Their key leader, Mother Ann Lee, became convinced that she was Christ's successor on earth, and that she should preach that sexual intercourse was the cause of evil and the original sin. Lee never downplayed her female gender but styled herself the bride of Christ and mother of the true church. Lee and her followers encountered vicious persecution in England, and in 1774 they decided to depart for America, arriving in New York. In 1775 they relocated to Niskeyuna, outside of Albany. Their meetings featured fervent worship that produced extraordinary bodily shaking. Mother Ann reportedly spoke in tongues, which a male leader would interpret. For several years the sect remained fairly isolated, but to Mother Ann the Dark Day of 1780 seemed to herald the "first opening of the gospel in America." Meacham, whom Lee called "the first man in America," became "convinced that these strange people professed the spirit, kingdom, & work for which he had so earnestly prayed, & sought, & of which he had prophesied." It remained only for him to accept a woman as the leader of the true church, but through her instruction he came to realize that "Mother Ann was the Bride, *the lambs wife.*" He and many of his New Lebanon church joined the Shakers.[28]

A combination of radical evangelicalism and Quakerism also helped produce the ministry of the "Public Universal Friend," Jemima Wilkinson. As with Ann Lee and her followers, Wilkinson's radicalism emerged partly from evangelical influences, but it ultimately took her beyond and out of the limits of the evangelical movement. Wilkinson had been born into a Quaker family in Cumberland, Rhode Island, a town that became a hotbed of radical evangelical piety. Following a near-death experience in 1776, Wilkinson reportedly announced that her body had died and been "re-animated by the power and spirit of Jesus Christ, that this was the second coming of the Lord." Wilkinson soon began calling herself the "Public Universal Friend" and preaching an apocalyptic, Arminian message of salvation and holiness. She began to win converts and founded several churches of Universal Friends. In 1788 the sect moved to a settlement they called New Jerusalem, near Seneca Lake in New York, but the community floundered after Wilkinson's death in 1819.[29]

Radical, visionary evangelical piety helped produce Wilkinson's public ministry as a woman, but the limits of radical egalitarianism surely helped foster the most intriguing aspect of Wilkinson's persona: the negation of her gendered characteristics. Applying the claim of Galatians 3:28 ("there is neither male nor female" in Christ) to an extreme, the Public Universal Friend argued that she herself was neither male nor female. Her long, loose gowns and cloaks obscured the lines of her body. Although she explicitly claimed a nongendered identity, unlike Ann Lee, she attempted publicly to downplay her female characteristics. She even cultivated a more masculine appearance. Her attempt to transcend her female gender ironically reinforced the principle that women, as women, still should not preach in revolutionary America.[30]

The revivals of the New Light Stir further nuance our understanding of evangelical development during the revolutionary era. The tensions between moderate and radical evangelicals that had emerged in the 1740s persisted into the 1780s, but the Separate Baptists had begun to assume a moderate position, in opposition to radical groups that had often emerged from their midst. Among the greatest innovations of the New Light Stir, suggesting the beginning of a new generation of evangelical development, was the radicals' frequent abandonment of Calvinism, which would become even more common by the early nineteenth century. It seems clear that, with some exceptions, Congregationalism had begun to lag by the early 1780s, but moderate Baptist and radical sectarian growth had not. The Methodist onslaught, delayed by the Revolution, was just on the horizon. Congregational evangelicalism had laid very deep roots in the north, however, and would continue as a powerful force in northern religious culture and reform movements through the Civil War, producing such leaders as Timothy Dwight, Asahel Nettleton, and the Beecher family. Growth among the inheritors of the radical tradition, including Separate Baptists and other more radical groups, built a foundation for their massive expansion that began in the mid-1780s. Although Mark Noll and others have viewed the late eighteenth century as a period of "evangelical decline," the patterns of evangelical growth in parts of the North (especially frontier New England and Nova Scotia) and the South (especially the backcountry) during that period show that this was a time of reorganization, not of general decline. The Baptist and sectarian churches began building the groundwork for their ascendancy even before disestablishment had been fully accomplished, as a prelude to the new evangelical explosion soon to come.[31]

Epilogue

The end of the American Revolution may be an arbitrary point at which to end this book, given the enduring characteristics of the evangelical movement. The push for revival did not wane after 1783, nor did the conflicts over the nature of evangelicalism. There was simply no clear break between the First and Second Great Awakenings. Although it is outside the scope of this book, I might note that the term "Second Great Awakening" is misleading in many of the same ways that "First Great Awakening" is. There was, really, no Second Great Awakening, but rather a long-term turn toward Baptist and Methodist piety from the American Revolution to the Civil War, punctuated by new revivals like the one at Cane Ridge, Kentucky, in 1801. The end of the Revolution did seem to signal new opportunities, however, and decades of even more dramatic evangelical growth. Disestablishment created more potential for religious innovation, and many more early nineteenth-century evangelicals became Arminian in theology. Another book (at least) would be required to establish that the awakenings of America's early republic represented a further elaboration of a movement that began in the 1740s. But from the perspective of the eighteenth century, the Second Great Awakening looks like a story of continuity as much as change.

Anticipating this new period of growth, Baptist leaders James Manning and Isaac Backus wrote in 1784 that the "American Revolution . . . doubtless, stands closely connected with many other [events], which will take place in their order, and unite in one glorious end, even the advancement and completion of the Redeemer's kingdom." The Revolution, they believed, was "design'd by the Lord to advance the cause of Christ in the world; or as one important step towards bringing in the glory of the latter day." As the "principles of liberty" spread, so also would true religion. "As light or sacred knowledge shall be diffused, Antichrist will be destroyed." The gospel would spread throughout the whole earth, but they thought it not "at all improbable, that America is reserved in the mind of JEHOVAH, to be the grand theatre on which the divine Redeemer will accomplish glorious things." They noted with pleasure that some revivals had recently appeared as signs of those "glorious things." They called on the Baptist churches to pray for "a more universal effusion of the Holy Ghost." Backus and Manning would have been delighted to know just how quickly the Baptist churches would grow in America over the next seven decades. As part of the stunning evangelical Protestant boom during that period, the total number of Baptist churches in America rose from about 150 in 1770 to just more than 12,000 in 1860.[1]

The war's end afforded not only the Baptists but also the fledgling Methodist movement great new opportunities in America. In 1784, John Wesley reluctantly conceded to American Methodists the right to ordain their own ministers who could administer the sacraments. This breakthrough led to the creation of the separate American Methodist Episcopal Church, which allowed the American Methodists to jettison their identification with British Anglicanism. The brilliance of Wesley's organizing system, the energy of Methodist itinerants, and the power of their gospel message could now be applied unfettered in American culture, and the results were astounding. Having been largely absent from the first generation of American evangelicalism, the Wesleyan Methodists flooded the American religious landscape, and by the Civil War they became the largest American Protestant denomination. In 1770, Methodists had a paltry 20 churches in America. By 1860, that number had swelled to just under 20,000.[2]

Many other Protestant denominations would see similar growth, while the once-dominant Congregational and Episcopalian (Anglican) churches would fall behind in numbers, although not in cultural and political influence. By the mid-nineteenth century, evangelical piety had become dominant in American Protestantism. Yet evangelicals remained deeply conflicted concerning the gospel's social implications, particularly with regard to slavery. Hamstrung by their inability to realize that cultural locations and political agendas deeply colored their hermeneutics, white evangelicals split over whether the Scriptures did or did not sanction slavery. Evangelical leaders offered little theological wisdom to mitigate the coming storm of the Civil War. Nevertheless, African Americans became evangelicals in greater numbers in the years between 1770 and 1830, helping swell the growth of Baptist, Methodist, and other Protestant churches.[3]

This book has shown that there was, indeed, a First Great Awakening, but it was a long Great Awakening and produced a new variation of Protestant Christianity: evangelicalism. Although revivals were an essential part of the new movement, their frequent absence between 1735 and 1785 did not signal the termination of the movement. As Mark Noll has insightfully explained, "for evangelicalism to take root, the longing for revival was more important than revival itself."[4] Evangelicals primarily sought revivals, conversions, and outpourings of the Spirit, but successes came in fits and starts, punctuated by the massive excitement of the early 1740s and the slow but dramatic emergence of evangelical faith in the American backcountry. Above all, this book has shown that the evangelical movement was deeply divided between moderates and radicals, especially over the manifestations of the Spirit. Those divisions did not prevent evangelicalism from growing, however, and they hinted toward the contemporary global evangelical expansion that remains split between Pentecostal and noncharismatic believers. Much more, no doubt, can and will be done to show how evangelicalism shaped, and was influenced by, social, economic, and political developments in colonial and revolutionary America. In the meantime, the Great Awakening can be acknowledged as "great" because it produced the evangelical movement.

Although the movement's most explosive growth remained in the future, eighteenth-century evangelicals had successfully established the religion of the new birth as a permanent fixture on the American cultural scene. The new evangelicals successfully convinced thousands of Americans that their conversion by the grace of Christ was the single most important goal of their lives. Lest we forget, the conversion experience was, and is, the raison d'être of the evangelical movement, whether in its radical or moderate forms. There remains an irreducible spiritual significance to an individual's acceptance of forgiveness from God. The myriad conversion experiences described in this book all point, in some way, to that human longing.

The convictions, however, that Jesus died to save women and men of all ethnicities and classes, and that the Holy Spirit empowers each believer equally, produced mixed social consequences in the first generation of American evangelical Christianity. Evangelical beliefs worked at times to erode traditional barriers of race, class, and gender. Radical evangelicals of the eighteenth century opened up unprecedented, if ultimately limited, opportunities for African Americans, Native Americans, women, the uneducated, and the poor to assert individual religious, and even social authority. Early American evangelicalism also helped pioneer the American abolitionist movement that emerged more fully in the nineteenth-century North.

Other evangelicals used their beliefs to buttress the historic barriers of race, class, and gender. The moderate evangelicals of the eighteenth century repressed enthusiastic radicals partly because of their modest empowerment of the disenfranchised. Far from opposing slavery, the moderates insisted that Christianizing the slaves would make them better slaves. These contradictory uses of evangelicalism may imply to some that there is no essential truth to this faith, but instead that it only justifies believers' worldly purposes. To others, however, the contradictions may suggest that in a broken world where the faithful are deeply flawed, fleeting hints of a coming egalitarian kingdom appear in the most surprising places, even in the church.

NOTES

KEY TO ABBREVIATIONS

Newspapers

Boston Gazette — BG
Boston Evening-Post — BEP
Boston Weekly Post-Boy — BWPB
South-Carolina Gazette — SCG

Diaries, Papers

Diary of Daniel Rogers, New-York Historical Society — DDR
William Kidder, ed., "The Diary of Nicholas Gilman" (master's thesis, University of New Hampshire, 1972) — DNG
Microfilm edition of the Papers of Eleazar Wheelock, Hanover, N.H., 1971 — PEW
Microfilm edition of the Papers of Isaac Backus, Ann Arbor, Mich., 2003 — PIB

Archives

Connecticut Historical Society, Hartford — CHS
Historical Society of Pennsylvania, Philadelphia — HSP
Massachusetts Historical Society, Boston — MHS
Presbyterian Historical Society, Philadelphia — PHS

INTRODUCTION

1. The Barna Group, "Born Again Christians," at http://www.barna.org/FlexPage.aspx?Page=Topic&TopicID=8, accessed 8/24/05; Tony Carnes, "A Presidential Hopeful's Progress," *Christianity Today*, Nov. 2000, at http://www.christianitytoday.com/ct/2000/011/8.62.html, accessed 8/24/05.

2. David Bebbington, *Evangelicalism in Modern Britain: A History from the 1730s to the 1980s* (Grand Rapids, Mich., 1992), 3; Jerald C. Brauer, "Conversion: From Puritanism to Revivalism," *Journal of Religion* 58, no. 3 (July 1978): 238–43; D. Bruce Hindmarsh, *The Evangelical Conversion Narrative: Spiritual Autobiography in Early Modern England* (New York, 2005), 53–54, 61–62.

3. J. M. Bumsted and John Van de Wetering, *What Must I Do to Be Saved? The Great Awakening in Colonial America* (Hinsdale, Ill., 1976), 96–126; G. A. Rawlyk, *The Canada Fire: Radical Evangelicalism in British North America* (Kingston, Ont., 1994), xvi. David Harlan proposed the categories of "New Lights," "Old Lights," and "Regular Lights" as the Awakening's three parties, David Harlan, *The Clergy and the Great Awakening in New England* (Ann Arbor, Mich., 1979), 4. Puritanism is also described as a movement with porous boundaries and internal tensions in Geoffrey F. Nuttall, *The Holy Spirit in Puritan Faith and Experience* (Oxford, Eng., 1947), 28; David Como, *Blown by the Spirit: Puritanism and the Emergence of an Antinomian Underground in Pre-Civil War England* (Stanford, Calif., 2004), 172.

4. Gordon S. Wood, *The Radicalism of the American Revolution* (New York, 1991), 43–56.

5. Philip F. Gura, *Jonathan Edwards: America's Evangelical* (New York, 2005), 232; James E. Block, *A Nation of Agents: The American Path to a Modern Self and Society* (Cambridge, Mass., 2002), 202–32.

6. Nathan O. Hatch, *The Democratization of American Christianity* (New Haven, Conn., 1989), 5–9; Christine Heyrman, *Southern Cross: The Beginnings of the Bible Belt* (New York, 1997), 254; Michael J. McClymond, "Issues and Explanations in the Study of North American Revivalism," in Michael J. McClymond, ed., *Embodying the Spirit: New Perspectives on North American Revivalism* (Baltimore, 2004), 24–31.

7. See, for example, Catherine A. Brekus, *Strangers and Pilgrims: Female Preaching in America, 1740–1845* (Chapel Hill, N.C., 1998), 1–113; Susan Juster, *Disorderly Women: Sexual Politics and Evangelicalism in Revolutionary New England* (Ithaca, N.Y., 1994), and *Doomsayers: Anglo-American Prophecy in the Age of Revolution* (Philadelphia, 2003); and Douglas Winiarski, "Jonathan Edwards, Enthusiast? Radical Revivalism and the Great Awakening in the Connecticut Valley," *Church History* 74, no. 4 (Dec. 2005): 683–739; "Souls Filled with Ravishing Transport: Heavenly Visions and the Radical Awakening in New England," *William and Mary Quarterly*, 3d ser., 61, no. 1 (Jan. 2004): 3–46.

8. Wesley Gewehr, *The Great Awakening in Virginia, 1740–1790* (Durham, N.C., 1930); Charles H. Maxson, *The Great Awakening in the Middle Colonies* (Chicago, 1920); Edwin S. Gaustad, *The Great Awakening in New England* (New York, 1957); Harry S. Stout, *The Divine Dramatist: George Whitefield and the Rise of Modern Evangelicalism* (Grand Rapids, Mich., 1991); Frank Lambert, *"Pedlar in Divinity": George Whitefield and the Transatlantic Revivals* (Princeton, N.J., 1994); George M. Marsden, *Jonathan Edwards: A Life* (New Haven, Conn., 2003); Gura, *Jonathan Edwards.*

9. Mark A. Noll, *The Rise of Evangelicalism: The Age of Edwards, Whitefield, and the Wesleys* (Downers Grove, Ill., 2003), 136–45.

10. Jon Butler, "Enthusiasm Described and Decried: The Great Awakening as Interpretative Fiction," *Journal of American History* 69, no. 2 (Sept. 1982): 309.

11. Ibid., 323.

12. Ibid., 324.

CHAPTER 1. "PRAYER FOR A SAVING ISSUE"

1. Michael Wigglesworth, "God's Controversy with New England" (1662), in Alan Heimert and Andrew Delbanco, eds., *The Puritans in America: A Narrative Anthology* (Cambridge, Mass., 1985), 234.

2. William Torrey, *A Brief Discourse Concerning Futurities* (Boston, 1757), i–ii; John Sibley, ed., *Biographical Sketches of Graduates of Harvard University*, vol. 1 (Cambridge, Mass., 1873), 564–67; Kenneth Murdock, *Handkerchiefs from Paul* (Cambridge, Mass., 1927), xxxix.

3. Samuel Torrey, *An Exhortation unto Reformation* (Cambridge, Mass., 1674), 10, 34; Michael Crawford, *Seasons of Grace: Colonial New England's Revival Tradition in Its British Context* (New York, 1991), 19.

4. William Adams, *The Necessity of the Pouring Out of the Spirit* (Boston, 1679), A2–A5.

5. Samuel Torrey, *A Plea for the Life of Dying Religion* (Boston, 1683), 25; Samuel Torrey, *Mans Extremity, Gods Opportunity* (Boston, 1695), 10, 36, 59; Crawford, *Seasons of Grace*, 34–35; Stephen Foster, *The Long Argument: English Puritanism and the Shaping of New England Culture, 1570–1700* (Chapel Hill, N.C., 1991), 271–72.

6. Perry Miller, "Jonathan Edwards and the Great Awakening," in *Errand into the Wilderness* (Cambridge, Mass., 1956), 160.

7. Thomas Prince, *Christian History*, June 4, 1743, 1:106–7. On covenant renewals, see Foster, *Long Argument*, 223–30, 239; Mark Peterson, *The Price of Redemption: The Spiritual Economy of Puritan New England* (Stanford, Calif., 1997), 48; Mark Peterson, "The Plymouth Church and the Evolution of Puritan Religious Culture," *New England Quarterly* 66, no. 4 (Dec. 1993): 581–82, 587–88; Charles Hambrick-Stowe, *The Practice of Piety: Puritan Devotional Disciplines in Seventeenth-Century New England* (Chapel Hill, N.C., 1982), 130–32, 248–53; Harry S. Stout, *The New England Soul: Preaching and Religious Culture in Colonial New England* (New York, 1986), 96–99; Richard Gildrie, *The Profane, the Civil, and the Godly: The Reformation of Manners in Orthodox New England, 1679–1749* (University Park, Pa., 1994), 26–27, 38.

8. Peterson, "Plymouth Church," 587–88.

9. Foster, *Long Argument*, 229; *A Copy of the Church-Covenants Which Have Been Used in the Church of Salem* (Boston, 1680), 5–7.

10. Peterson, *Price of Redemption*, 48; Seymour Van Dyken, *Samuel Willard, 1640–1707: Preacher of Orthodoxy in an Era of Change* (Grand Rapids, Mich., 1972), 39–40; Prince, *Christian History*, June 4, 1743, 1:108.

11. Cotton Mather, *Methods and Motives for Societies to Suppress Disorders* (Boston, 1703), *Private Meetings Animated and Regulated* (Boston, 1706); Gildrie, *Profane, the Civil, and the Godly*, 202–8; Prince, *Christian History*, June 4, 1743, 1:108–9; Crawford, *Seasons of Grace*, 46–47.

12. Prince, *Christian History*, June 4, 1743, 1:109–12; Danforth, *Piety Encouraged*, A2, A5; Cotton Mather, *The Diary of Cotton Mather* (New York, n.d.), 513.

13. Among the New England revivals noted by contemporaries, beyond those I will discuss here, were in Lynn, Mass., 1712, Jeremiah Shepard, pastor; East Windsor, Conn., 1712–13, 1715–16, Timothy Edwards, pastor; Preston, Conn., 1716, Salmon Treat, pastor; Norwich, Conn., 1718, Benjamin Lord, pastor; Woodbury, Conn., 1726–27, Anthony Stoddard, pastor. List mainly derived from Crawford, *Seasons of Grace*, 108.

14. John E. Smith, Harry S. Stout, and Kenneth Minkema, eds., *A Jonathan Edwards Reader* (New Haven, Conn., 1995), 58; Solomon Stoddard, *The Safety of Appearing* (Boston, 1687), A4; Thomas A. Schafer, "Solomon Stoddard and the Theology of the Revival," in Stuart C. Henry, ed., *A Miscellany of American Christianity: Essays in Honor of H. Shelton Smith* (Durham, N.C., 1963), 332–40. On Stoddard, and his influence on Jonathan Edwards and evangelicalism generally, see also Ralph J. Coffman, *Solomon Stoddard* (Boston, 1978); Paul R. Lucas, "'The Death of the Prophet Lamented': The Legacy of Solomon Stoddard," in Stephen J. Stein, ed., *Jonathan Edwards's Writings: Text, Context, Interpretation* (Bloomington, Ind., 1996), 69–84; Lucas, "An Appeal to the Learned: The Mind of Solomon Stoddard," *William and Mary Quarterly*, 3d ser., 30, no. 2 (Apr. 1973): 257–92; Perry Miller, "Solomon Stoddard, 1643–1729," *Harvard Theological Review* 34 (1941): 277–320; E. Brooks Holifield, "The Intellectual Sources of Stoddardeanism," *New England Quarterly* 45, no. 3 (Sept. 1972): 373–92; James Walsh, "Solomon Stoddard's Open Communion: A Reexamination," *New England Quarterly* 43, no. 1 (Mar. 1970): 97–114; Patricia J. Tracy, *Jonathan Edwards, Pastor: Religion and Society in Eighteenth-Century Northampton* (New York, 1980), 13–50; Norman Pettit, *The Heart Prepared: Grace and Conversion in Puritan Spiritual Life*, 2d ed. (Middletown, Conn., 1989), 200–207; Crawford, *Seasons of Grace*, 47–50, 71–76; George M. Marsden, *Jonathan Edwards: A Life* (New Haven, Conn., 2003), 11–14, 114–27.

15. Solomon Stoddard, *An Appeal to the Learned* (Boston, 1709), A3; Smith, *Jonathan Edwards Reader*, 58.

16. Schafer, "Stoddard and the Revival," 335–46; Lucas, "The Death of the Prophet Lamented," 79; Jill Lepore, *The Name of War: King Philip's War and the Origins of American Identity* (New York, 1998); John Demos, *The Unredeemed Captive: A Family Story from Early America* (New York, 1994).

17. Solomon Stoddard, *The Efficacy of the Fear of Hell, to Restrain Men from Sin* (Boston, 1713), 34, 40.

18. Ibid., 190, 197; George Whitefield, *George Whitefield's Journals* (Carlisle, Pa., 1962), 462, 476. *Guide to Christ* saw these American editions: Boston (1714), Boston (1735), Boston (1742), New York (1751), Newburyport, Mass. (1801), New York (1813), Northampton, Mass. (1816); and these British editions: Yarmouth (1819), London (1825), Edinburgh (1848).

19. Solomon Stoddard, *An Answer to Some Cases of Conscience Respecting the Country* (Boston, 1722), 10–13, 16; Stoddard, *Question Whether God Is Not Angry* (Boston, 1723), 9–12; Thomas S. Kidd, *The Protestant Interest: New England after Puritanism* (New Haven, Conn., 2004), 104–6, 160–61; Lucas, "Death of the Prophet," 75–76. On Stoddard's relationship to Timothy and Jonathan Edwards, see Marsden, *Jonathan Edwards*, 23, 29–33, 112–25.

20. Increase Mather, *A Discourse Concerning Faith and Fervency* (Boston, 1710), 65, 84. This book, which seems to have been sold by at least five Boston booksellers in the 1710s, was also printed in London in 1713 and Ireland in 1820. Michael Hall, *The Last American Puritan: The Life of Increase Mather* (Middletown, Conn., 1988), 325.

21. Lucas, "Appeal to the Learned," 290n83.

22. Kenneth Minkema, "The East Windsor Relations, 1700–1725," *Connecticut Historical Society Bulletin* 51 (1986): 3–63; Marsden, *Jonathan Edwards*, 25–26, 33.

23. Eliphalet Adams, *A Sermon Preached at Windham, July 12th, 1721* (New London, 1721), ii–vi, 39–40.

24. Crawford, *Seasons of Grace*, 108–10.

25. Ibid., 114–17; Erik Seeman, *Pious Persuasions: Laity and Clergy in Eighteenth-Century New England* (Baltimore, 1999), 149–54; Stout, *New England Soul*, 177–79.

26. Kenneth Minkema, "The Lynn End 'Earthquake' Relations of 1727," *New England Quarterly* 69, no. 3 (Sept. 1996): 490; *On a Day of Public Fasting and Prayer* (Boston, [1727?]); Samuel Phillips, *Three Plain Practical Discourses, Preach'd at Andover* (Boston, 1728).

27. John Cotton, *A Holy Fear of God* (Boston, 1727), appendix, 5–7.

28. Ibid., 6.

29. Thomas Foxcroft, *The Voice of the Lord* (Boston, 1727), 37–38, 41–44.

30. Thomas Prince, *Earthquakes the Works of God*, 2d ed. (Boston, 1727), appendix; Prince, *Christian History*, June 11, 1743, 1:114; Stout, *New England Soul*, 179.

CHAPTER 2. "A SHOWER OF DIVINE BLESSING"

1. Jonathan Edwards, letter to Benjamin Colman, May 30, 1735, in Jonathan Edwards, *The Great Awakening*, ed. C. C. Goen, vol. 4 of *The Works of Jonathan Edwards* (New Haven, Conn., 1972), 101.

2. Jonathan Edwards, "Personal Narrative," in John Smith, Harry Stout, and Kenneth Minkema, eds., *A Jonathan Edwards Reader* (New Haven, Conn., 1995), 281–82.

3. George M. Marsden, *Jonathan Edwards: A Life* (New Haven, Conn., 2003), 28, 519n11. This chapter is deeply indebted to Marsden.

4. Ibid., 283.

5. Ibid., 284–85; Marsden, *Jonathan Edwards*, 39–43.

6. Jonathan Edwards, *A Faithful Narrative of the Surprizing Work of God*, in Edwards, *Great Awakening*, 146.

7. Marsden, *Jonathan Edwards*, 121–32.

8. Jonathan Edwards, *God Glorified in the Work of Redemption*, in Wilson Kimnach, Kenneth Minkema, and Douglas Sweeney, eds., *The Sermons of Jonathan Edwards: A Reader* (New Haven, Conn., 1999), 71. Marsden, *Jonathan Edwards*, 140–41.

9. Edwards, *Faithful Narrative*, 147. On the Northampton revival, see among others Marsden, *Jonathan Edwards*, 152–69; Frank Lambert, *Inventing the "Great Awakening"* (Princeton, N.J., 1999), 62–69; Patricia Tracy, *Jonathan Edwards, Pastor: Religion and Society in Eighteenth-Century Northampton* (New York, 1980), 78–89; Goen, "Editor's Introduction," in Edwards, *Great Awakening*, 19–25.

10. Edwards, *Faithful Narrative*, 147–48.

11. Ibid., 149.

12. Michael Crawford, *Seasons of Grace: Colonial New England's Revival Tradition in Its British Context* (New York, 1991), 125.

13. Edwards, *Faithful Narrative*, 153–56.

14. Ibid., 157–59. On Edwards and slavery, see Marsden, *Jonathan Edwards*, 255–58; Kenneth Minkema, "Jonathan Edwards on Slavery and the Slave Trade," *William and Mary Quarterly*, 3d ser., 54, no. 4 (Oct. 1997): 823–34.

15. Leigh Eric Schmidt, *Holy Fairs: Scotland and the Making of American Revivalism*, 2d ed. (Grand Rapids, Mich., 2001), xvii; Marsden, *Jonathan Edwards*, 161; Jonathan Edwards, *The Distinguishing Marks of a Work of the Spirit of God*, in Edwards, *Great Awakening*, 270.

16. Edwards, *Faithful Narrative*, 188–89; Ann Taves, *Fits, Trances, and Visions: Experiencing Religion and Explaining Experience from Wesley to James* (Princeton, N.J., 1999), 34–41.

17. Douglas C. Stenerson, ed., "An Anglican Critique of the Early Phase of the Great Awakening in New England: A Letter by Timothy Cutler," *William and Mary Quarterly*, 3d ser., 30, no. 3 (July 1973): 482–83.

18. Edwards, *Faithful Narrative*, 205; Gail Thain Parker, "Jonathan Edwards and Melancholy," *New England Quarterly* 41, no. 2 (June 1968): 199–203.

19. Edwards, *Faithful Narrative*, 206–7. On Hawley's suicide, see Marsden, *Jonathan Edwards*, 163–69; James R. Trumbull, *History of Northampton, Massachusetts, From Its Settlement in 1654*, vol. 2 (Northampton, Mass., 1902), 79–81.

20. Marsden, *Jonathan Edwards*, 170–73; Lambert, *Inventing the "Great Awakening*," 69–81; Goen, "Editor's Introduction," in Edwards, *Great Awakening*, 32–46. On the continuing publishing history of *A Faithful Narrative*, see Joseph Conforti, *Jonathan Edwards, Religious Tradition, and American Culture* (Chapel Hill, N.C., 1995), 44–45.

21. William Williams, *The Duty and Interest of a People* (Boston, 1736); Isaac Watts to Benjamin Colman, Feb. 28, 1737, in *Proceedings of the Massachusetts Historical Society*, 2d ser., 9 (1895): 353.

22. Edwards, *Faithful Narrative*, 130–37.

23. DNG, 230, 232; Philip F. Gura, *Jonathan Edwards: America's Evangelical* (New York, 2005), 109.

24. Crawford, *Seasons of Grace*, 156–63, 183–90; Arthur Fawcett, *The Cambuslang Revival: The Scottish Evangelical Revival of the Eighteenth Century* (London, 1971); W. R. Ward, *The Protestant Evangelical Awakening* (New York, 1992), 335–39; David W. Bebbington, "Remembered around the World: The International Scope of Edwards's Legacy," in David W. Kling and Douglas A. Sweeney, eds., *Jonathan Edwards at Home and Abroad: Historical Memories, Cultural Movements, Global Horizons* (Columbia, S.C., 2003), 178–80.

25. Conforti, *Edwards, Religious Tradition*, 105; *Nol-La-Woon Hoe-Shim Iya-Kee* (Seoul, 1997); Guy Chevreau, *Catch the Fire: The Toronto Blessing an Experience of Renewal and Revival* (New York, 1995); Bebbington, "Remembered around the World," 193; M. X. Lesser, "An Honor Too Great: Jonathan Edwards in Print Abroad," in Kling and Sweeney, eds., *Edwards at Home and Abroad*, 304.

CHAPTER 3. "SOUL-SATISFYING SEALINGS OF GOD'S EVERLASTING LOVE"

1. Randall H. Balmer, *A Perfect Babel of Confusion: Dutch Religion and English Culture in the Middle Colonies* (New York, 1989), 109; James Tanis, *Dutch Calvinistic Pietism in the Middle Colonies: A Study in the Life and Theology of Theodorus Jacobus Frelinghuysen* (The Hague, 1967), 43, 100.

2. Ted Campbell, *The Religion of the Heart: A Study of European Religious Life in the Seventeenth and Eighteenth Centuries* (Columbia, S.C., 1991), 65–68, 71–73; F. Ernest Stoeffler, *The Rise of Evangelical Pietism* (Leiden, The Netherlands, 1965), 127–41; Richard Lovelace, *The American Pietism of Cotton Mather: Origins of American Evangelicalism* (Washington, D.C., 1979), 38–40.

3. Stoeffler, *Evangelical Pietism*, 161–69; Tanis, *Dutch Calvinistic Pietism*, 44, 142–45; Campbell, *Religion of the Heart*, 82–84.

4. Campbell, *Religion of the Heart*, 84; W. R. Ward, *The Protestant Evangelical Awakening* (New York, 1992), 57–60; W. R. Ward, *Christianity under the Ancien Régime, 1648–1789* (New York, 1999), 75; Lovelace, *American Pietism*, 216.

5. Philip Jacob Spener, *Pia Desideria*, trans. Theodore Tappert (Philadelphia, 1964), 78; Campbell, *Religion of the Heart*, 84–85; Ward, *Christianity under the Ancien Régime*, 76; Elizabeth W. Fisher, "Prophecies and Revelations: German Cabbalists in Early Pennsylvania," *Pennsylvania Magazine of History and Biography* 109 (1985): 302–5.

6. Increase Mather, *A Dissertation, Wherein the Strange Doctrine* (Boston, 1708), 106; Campbell, *Religion of the Heart*, 87–88; A. G. Roeber, *Palatines, Liberty, and Property: German Lutherans in Colonial British America* (Baltimore, 1993), 62–75; Renate Wilson, *Pious Traders in Medicine: A German Pharmaceutical Network in Eighteenth-Century North America* (University Park, Pa., 2000), 15–48; Ward, *Christianity under the Ancien Régime*, 76–82, and *The Protestant Evangelical Awakening*, 61–63; Jon Butler, "The Spiritual Importance of the Eighteenth Century," in Harmut Lehmann, Hermann Wellenreuther, and Renate Wilson, eds., *In Search of Peace and Prosperity: New German Settlements in Eighteenth-Century Europe and America* (University Park, Pa., 2000), 102–3.

7. Cotton Mather, *Nuncia Bona e Terra Longingua* (Boston, 1715), 2, cited in Lovelace, *American Pietism*, 248–49; Thomas Prince, *Christian History*, Oct. 13–Nov. 3, 1744, 2:262–83; Michael Crawford, *Seasons of Grace: New England's Revival Tradition in Its British Context* (New York, 1991), 82.

8. Tanis, "Reformed Pietism," 34–35; Tanis, *Dutch Calvinistic Pietism*, 11–12, 28–29; Ward, *Christianity under the Ancien Régime*, 84–85; Ward, *Protestant Evangelical Awakening*, 224–30.

9. Tanis, *Dutch Calvinistic Pietism*, 30–41.

10. Ibid., 46–49.

11. Hugh Hastings, ed., *Ecclesiastical Records, State of New York*, vol. 4 (Albany, 1902), 2318.

12. Balmer, *Perfect Babel of Confusion*, 115; Tanis, *Dutch Calvinistic Pietism*, 62–63.

13. Joel E. Beeke, ed., *Forerunner of the Great Awakening: Sermons by Theodorus Jacobus Frelinghuysen, 1691–1747* (Grand Rapids, Mich., 2000), 107.

14. Tanis, *Dutch Calvinistic Pietism*, 68–69; Milton J. Coalter, *Gilbert Tennent, Son of Thunder: A Case Study of Continental Pietism's Impact on the First Great Awakening in the Middle Colonies* (Westport, Conn., 1986), 12.

15. Prince, *Christian History*, Nov. 10, 1744, 2:292–93; Tanis, *Dutch Calvinistic Pietism*, 69; Coalter, *Gilbert Tennent*, 16–18.

16. Hastings, *Ecclesiastical Records*, 2587; Tanis, *Dutch Calvinistic Pietism*, 70; Balmer, *Perfect Babel of Confusion*, 119–20.

17. Prince, *Christian History*, Nov. 10, 1744, 2:294.

18. Patrick Griffin, *The People with No Name: Ireland's Ulster Scots, America's Scots Irish, and the Creation of a British Atlantic World, 1689–1764* (Princeton, N.J., 2001), 1; Leigh Eric Schmidt, *Holy Fairs: Scotland and the Making of American Revivalism*, 2d ed. (Grand Rapids, Mich., 2001), 3; Ward, *Protestant Evangelical Awakening*, 265–69.

19. Westerkamp, *Triumph of the Laity*, 142.

20. Leonard Trinterud thought Tennent might have been born in Scotland, not Ireland, but the standard position is still Ireland. Trinterud, *The Forming of an American Tradition: A Re-Examination of Colonial Presbyterianism* (Philadelphia, 1949), 35.

21. Richard Warch, *School of the Prophets: Yale College, 1701–1740* (New Haven, Conn., 1973), 130–31; Westerkamp, *Triumph of the Laity*, 167; Coalter, *Gilbert Tennent*, 1–5; Ward, *Protestant Evangelical Awakening*, 269–73.

22. Elizabeth Nybakken, "In the Irish Tradition: Pre-Revolutionary Academies in America," *History of Education Quarterly* 37, no. 2 (summer 1997): 163–83; Thomas J. Wertenbaker, *Princeton, 1746–1896* (Princeton, N.J., 1946), 11, 14–25; George Pilcher, *Samuel Davies: Apostle of Dissent in Colonial Virginia* (Knoxville, Tenn., 1971), 7–12; Keith Hardman, *Seasons of Refreshing: Evangelism and Revivals in America* (Grand Rapids, Mich., 1994), 98.

23. Prince, *Christian History*, Nov. 10, 1744, 2:294–95; Coalter, *Gilbert Tennent*, 40.

24. Gilbert Tennent, "Preface," in John Tennent, *The Nature of Regeneration Opened*, appended to Gilbert Tennent, *A Solemn Warning to the Secure World* (Boston, 1735), ii–iv.

25. Tennent, *Solemn Warning*, v–vi; Charles Maxson, *The Great Awakening in the Middle Colonies* (Chicago, 1920, repr. 1958), 31; Ned Landsman, *Scotland and Its First American Colony, 1683–1765* (Princeton, N.J., 1985), 180–82.

26. Prince, *Christian History*, Nov. 17, 1744, 2:300.

27. Susan Juster, *Doomsayers: Anglo-American Prophecy in the Age of Revolution* (Philadelphia, 2003), 65.

28. Archibald Alexander, *Biographical Sketches of the Founder, and Principal Alumni of the Log College* (Princeton, 1845), 168–71; Jon Butler, "Coercion, Miracle, Reason: Rethinking the American Revolutionary Experience in the Revolutionary Age," in Ronald Hoffman and Peter Albert, eds., *Religion in a Revolutionary Age* (Charlottesville, Va., 1994), 15.

29. Alexander, *Biographical Sketches*, 182–86.

30. Ibid., 182–84.

31. Prince, *Christian History*, Nov. 17, 1744, 2:302.

32. Ibid., Nov. 24, 1744, 2:307–8.

33. Ibid., Nov. 24, 177, 2:309–10; Janet Fishburn, "Gilbert Tennent, Established Dissenter," *Church History* 63 (Mar. 1994): 31–49; Schmidt, *Holy Fairs*, 54.

34. Coalter, *Gilbert Tennent*, 41–42, 48.

35. Maxson, *Great Awakening*, 33; Westerkamp, *Triumph of the Laity*, 169; Whitefield, *Journals*, 354.

36. Coalter, *Gilbert Tennent*, 48–49.

37. George Ingram, "The Erection of the Presbytery of New Brunswick," *Journal of Presbyterian History* 6 (1911–12): 230, 329, 336, 346; Coalter, *Gilbert Tennent*, 50–51, 57; Trinterud, *Forming of an American Tradition*, 81–83; Griffin, *People with No Name*, 147–48; Westerkamp, *Triumph of the Laity*, 171.

38. Westerkamp, *Triumph of the Laity*, 192–93; Griffin, *People with No Name*, 147–48.

39. John Rowland, *A Narrative of the Revival and Progress of Religion*, appended to Gilbert Tennent, *A Funeral Sermon Occasion'd by the Death of the Reverend Mr. John Rowland* (Philadelphia, 1745), 52–53.

40. Ibid., 54–55; Landsman, *Scotland and Its First American Colony*, 183–88; Fishburn, "Gilbert Tennent," 39–41.

41. Rowland, *Narrative of the Revival*, 56–59; Whitefield, *Journals*, 353.

42. Rowland, *Narrative of the Revival*, 62–68.

CHAPTER 4. "PLENTIFUL EFFUSIONS
OF GOD'S SPIRIT IN THESE PARTS"

1. Frank Lambert, *"Pedlar in Divinity": George Whitefield and the Transatlantic Revivals, 1737–1770* (Princeton, N.J., 1994), 8; Harry Stout, *The Divine Dramatist: George Whitefield and the Rise of Modern Evangelicalism* (Grand Rapids, Mich., 1991), xvi.

2. Stout, *Divine Dramatist*, 1–15.

3. George Whitefield, *The Journals of George Whitefield* (Carlisle, Pa., 1960), 41–42.

4. Ibid., 44; Mechal Sobel, *Teach Me Dreams: The Search for Self in the Revolutionary Era* (Princeton, N.J., 2000), 6–9.

5. Whitefield, *Journals*, 45–47; George Whitefield, *Letters of George Whitefield for the Period 1734–1742* (Carlisle, Pa., 1976), 6.

6. Whitefield, *Journals*, 52–58.

7. Geoffrey Holmes, "The Sacheverell Riots: The Crowd and the Church in Early Eighteenth-Century London," *Past and Present* 72 (Aug. 1976): 55–85.

8. Whitefield, *Journals*, 159–60.

9. Ibid., 201.

10. Whitefield, *Letters*, 47; Whitefield, *Journals*, 219; W. R. Ward, *Christianity under the Ancien Régime, 1648–1789* (New York, 1999), 137–38; Lambert, *"Pedlar in Divinity,"* 62–63.

11. Gary Nash, *The Urban Crucible: The Northern Seaports and the Origins of the American Revolution*, abr. ed. (Cambridge, Mass., 1986), 109–11; Carl Bridenbaugh, *Cities in the Wilderness: Urban Life in America, 1625–1742* (New York, 1938), 303–467.

12. Lambert, *"Pedlar in Divinity,"* 52–55; Frank Lambert, *Inventing the "Great Awakening"* (Princeton, N.J., 1999), 111; Lambert, "'Pedlar in Divinity': George Whitefield and the Great Awakening," *Journal of American History* 77, no. 3 (Dec. 1990): 836.

13. Whitefield, *Journals*, 341–42.

14. Ibid., 343.

15. Ibid., 344–45.

16. Ibid., 345–46.

17. Ibid., 347.

18. Ibid., 347–50.

19. Quoted in Arnold Dallimore, *George Whitefield: The Life and Times of the Great Evangelist of the Eighteenth-Century Revival*, vol. 1 (Carlisle, Pa., 1970), 435.

20. Jon Butler, *Awash in a Sea of Faith: Christianizing the American People* (Cambridge, Mass., 1990), 187–88.

21. Bryan Le Beau, *Jonathan Dickinson and the Formative Years of American Presbyterianism* (Lexington, Ky., 1997), 110–11.

22. Whitefield, *Journals*, 352–53.

23. Ibid., 354–55; Lambert, *Inventing the "Great Awakening,"* 88.

24. Whitefield, *Journals*, 355, 357–58; John Frantz, "The Awakening of Religion among the German Settlers in the Middle Colonies," *William and Mary Quarterly*, 3d ser., 33, no. 2 (Apr. 1976): 283.

25. Whitefield, *Journals*, 362–64; Archibald Alexander, *Biographical Sketches of the Founder, and Principal Alumni of the Log College* (Princeton, N.J., 1845), 249–50.

26. Timothy Feist, "'A Stirring among the Dry Bones': George Whitefield and the Great Awakening in Maryland," *Maryland Historical Magazine* 95, no. 4 (2000): 395.

27. Richard Cox, ed., "Stephen Bordley, George Whitefield, and the Great Awakening in Maryland," *Historical Magazine of the Protestant Episcopal Church* 46 (1977): 303–7.

28. Whitefield, *Journals*, 371–72.

29. Ibid., 376–77.

30. Ibid., 377–78; David Morgan, "The Great Awakening in North Carolina, 1740–1775: The Baptist Phase," *North Carolina Historical Review* 45, no. 3 (July 1968): 265–70.

31. Whitefield, *Journals*, 379. On Whitefield and slavery, see Alan Gallay, "The Origins of Slaveholders' Paternalism: George Whitefield, the Bryan Family, and the Great Awakening in the South," *Journal of Southern History* 53, no. 3 (Aug. 1987): 369–94; Stephen Stein, "George Whitefield on Slavery: Some New Evidence," *Church History* 42, no. 2 (June 1973): 243–56.

32. Whitefield, *Journals*, 382–83.

CHAPTER 5. THE DANGER OF AN UNCONVERTED MINISTRY

1. Thomas Prince, *Christian History*, Oct. 8, 1743, 1:252; Sept. 29, 1744, 2:243–44; Archibald Alexander, *Biographical Sketches of the Founder, and Principal Alumni of the Log College* (Princeton, N.J., 1845), 267.

2. Prince, *Christian History*, Sept. 29, 1744, 2:244–46.

3. Ibid., 246–48.

4. Ibid., Oct. 6, 1744, 2:250; Susan Juster, *Disorderly Women: Sexual Politics and Evangelicalism in Revolutionary New England* (Ithaca, N.Y., 1994), 37.

5. Prince, *Christian History*, Oct. 6, 1744, 2:251.

6. Ibid., 252; Leigh Schmidt, *Holy Fairs: Scotland and the Making of American Revivalism*, 2d ed. (Grand Rapids, Mich., 2001), 54.

7. Prince, *Christian History*, Oct. 6, 1744, 2:254.

8. Ibid., 254; Juster, *Disorderly Women*, 64–65; George Rawlyk, *Ravished by the Spirit: Religious Revivals, Baptists, and Henry Alline* (Kingston, Ont., 1984), 15 and passim.

9. Prince, *Christian History*, Oct. 6, 1744, 2:256; Schmidt, *Holy Fairs*, 115–17.

10. Charles Chauncy, *Seasonable Thoughts on the State of Religion in New-England* (Boston, 1743), 249–50; Gilbert Tennent, *The Danger of an Unconverted Ministry* (Philadelphia, 1740), 2, 8, 11, 13, 17.

11. Tennent, *Danger of an Unconverted Ministry*, 16, 18–19, 21–22; Timothy Hall, *Contested Boundaries: Itinerancy and the Reshaping of the Colonial American Religious World* (Durham, N.C., 1994), 49–50; Milton J. Coalter, *Gilbert Tennent, Son of Thunder: A Case Study of Continental Pietism's Impact on the First Great Awakening in the Middle Colonies* (Westport, Conn., 1986), 64–67; on breast imagery, see Susan M. Stabile, "A 'Doctrine of Signatures': The Epistolary Physicks of Esther Burr's Journal," in Janet Moore Lindman and Michelle Lise Tarter, eds., *A Centre of Wonders: The Body in Early America* (Ithaca, N.Y., 2001), 109.

12. Whitefield, *Journals*, 406–8.

13. Ibid., 411; John Weinlick, "The Whitefield Tract," *Transactions of the Moravian Historical Society* 23, no. 2 (1979): 54–57.

14. Whitefield, *Journals*, 412; Sally Schwartz, *"A Mixed Multitude": The Struggle for Toleration in Colonial Pennsylvania* (New York, 1987), 127–28; John Weinlick, "Moravianism in the American Colonies," in F. Ernest Stoeffler, ed., *Continental Pietism and Early American Christianity* (Grand Rapids, Mich., 1976), 136.

15. Whitefield, *Journals*, 412–13, 415; James Tanis, *Dutch Calvinistic Pietism in the Middle Colonies: A Study in the Life and Theology of Theodorus Jacobus Frelinghuysen* (The Hague, 1967), 81–82.

16. Whitefield, *Journals*, 416; Charles Chauncy, *Seasonable Thoughts on the State of Religion in New-England* (Boston, 1743), 213; quoted in Richard Warch, *School of the Prophets: Yale College, 1701–1740* (New Haven, Conn., 1973), 169; see also Robert Cray, Jr., "More Light on a New Light: James Davenport's Religious Legacy, Eastern Long Island, 1740–1840," *New York History* 73, no. 1 (1992): 8–10.

17. Joseph Tracy, *The Great Awakening: A History of the Revival of Religion in the Time of Edwards and Whitefield* (Carlisle, Pa., 1976, orig. pub. 1842), 232–33; Cray, "More Light," 10–11.

18. Eleazar Wheelock to [Sarah Wheelock], Apr. 26, 1740, PEW, no. 740276; Samuel Buell to Eleazar Wheelock, Mar. 2, 1740, quoted in Richard Warch, *School of the Prophets: Yale College, 1701–1740* (New Haven, Conn., 1973), 313; Eleazar Wheelock to Stephen Williams, May 22, 1740, PEW, no. 740322; Eleazar Wheelock to Stephen Williams, June 6, 1740, PEW, no. 740356; John Fea, "Wheelock's World: Letters and the Communication of Revival in Great Awakening New England," *Proceedings of the American Antiquarian Society* 109, no. 1 (1999): 120–21; Tracy, *Great Awakening*, 233; Whitefield, *Journals*, 416–17; Cray, "More Light," 12.

19. James Davenport to Eleazar Wheelock, July 9, 1740, Gratz American Colonial Clergy, 8/22, HSP.

20. Whitefield, *Journals*, 419–21.

21. Ibid., 421–23.

22. Ibid., 424–25; Nancy Ruttenberg, "George Whitefield, Spectacular Conversion, and the Rise of Democratic Personality," *American Literary History* 5, no. 3 (autumn 1993): 442.

23. Whitefield, *Journals*, 425–27; Coalter, *Gilbert Tennent*, 67.

24. Samuel Blair, "A Vindication of the Brethren," in *The Works of the Reverend Mr. Samuel Blair* (Philadelphia, 1754), 224–25; Coalter, *Gilbert Tennent*, 68–71; Charles Maxson, *The Great Awakening in the Middle Colonies* (Chicago, 1920), 60–61.

25. *Pennsylvania Gazette*, June 12, 1740; Prince, *Christian History*, Oct. 8, 1743, 1:255–58; Bryan Le Beau, *Jonathan Dickinson and the Formative Years of American Presbyterianism* (Lexington, Ky., 1997), 122–23; Leigh Schmidt, "Jonathan Dickinson and the Moderate Awakening," *American Presbyterians* 63, no. 4 (1985): 346; Maxson, *Great Awakening*, 63.

26. *Pennsylvania Gazette*, July 24, 1740, postscript; Aug. 14, 1740.

27. Coalter, *Gilbert Tennent*, 71–72; Maxson, *Great Awakening*, 64.

CHAPTER 6. "A FAITHFUL WATCHMAN ON
THE WALLS OF CHARLESTOWN"

1. Jack Greene, *Pursuits of Happiness: The Social Development of Early Modern British Colonies and the Formation of American Culture* (Chapel Hill, N.C., 1988), 141–51, 166–69; Robert Olwell,

Masters, Slaves, and Subjects: The Culture of Power in the South Carolina Low Country, 1740–1790 (Ithaca, N.Y., 1998), 40–42. On Anglicization, see John Murrin, "Anglicizing an American Colony: The Transformation of Provincial Massachusetts" (Ph.D. diss., Yale University, 1966).

2. Olwell, *Masters, Slaves, and Subjects*, 21–27, 62–64; Erskine Clarke, *Our Southern Zion: A History of Calvinism in the South Carolina Low Country, 1690–1990* (Tuscaloosa, Ala., 1996), 77; Peter Wood, *Black Majority: Negroes in Colonial South Carolina from 1670 through the Stono Rebellion* (New York, 1974), 308–26; Robert Weir, *Colonial South Carolina: A History* (Millwood, N.Y., 1983), 193–94; David T. Morgan, Jr., "George Whitefield and the Great Awakening in the Carolinas and Georgia, 1739–1740," *Georgia Historical Quarterly* 54, no. 4 (1970): 524.

3. George Whitefield, *George Whitefield's Journals* (Carlisle, Pa., 1960), 384.

4. Ibid., 384–85.

5. Ibid., 400–401.

6. Ibid., 401–3.

7. Josiah Smith, *A Discourse Delivered at Boston, on July 11, 1726* (Boston, 1726), i; Clifford Shipton, ed., *Sibley's Harvard Graduates*, vol. 7, 1722–25 (Boston, 1945), 569; M. Eugene Sirmans, *Colonial South Carolina: A Political History, 1663–1763* (Chapel Hill, N.C., 1966), 53–54; D. W. Meinig, *The Shaping of America*, vol. 1: *Atlantic America, 1492–1800* (New Haven, Conn., 1986), 162, 185; Greene, *Pursuits of Happiness*, 152–54; Boyd Stanley Schlenther, "Religious Faith and Commercial Empire," in P. J. Marshall, ed., *The Oxford History of the British Empire*, vol. 2: *The Eighteenth Century* (New York, 1998), 130; Henry Wilkinson, *Bermuda in the Old Empire* (New York, 1950), 262.

8. Smith, *Boston, July 11, 1726*, iii, 16–17, 20; John Corrigan, *The Prism of Piety: Catholick Congregational Clergy at the Beginning of the Enlightenment* (New York, 1991), 32–64.

9. Josiah Smith, *A Sermon Preached in Boston, July 10th, 1726* (Boston, 1727), 25–26.

10. Isaac Watts, letter to Benjamin Colman, Oct. 12, 1739, in *Proceedings of the Massachusetts Historical Society*, 2d ser., 9:370; *Sibley's Harvard Graduates*, 7:571.

11. SCG, Jan. 12, 1740.

12. SCG, Jan. 26 and Feb. 2, 1740.

13. Luke Tyerman, *The Life of the Rev. George Whitefield*, 2 vols. (London, 1876), 1:360; Harry S. Stout, *The Divine Dramatist: George Whitefield and the Rise of Modern Evangelicalism* (Grand Rapids, Mich., 1991), 101–2; Corrigan, *Prism of Piety*, 15–16. For Colman's view of Tillotson, see Charles Chauncy, *Seasonable Thoughts on the State of Religion in New-England* (Boston, 1743), 146–47. George Whitefield, "A Letter to the Inhabitants of Maryland, Virginia, North and South Carolina," in *The Works of the Reverend George Whitefield*, vol. 4 (London, 1771), 37–38; Alan Gallay, *The Formation of a Planter Elite: Jonathan Bryan and the Southern Colonial Frontier* (Athens, Ga., 1989), 38–39.

14. Whitefield, "Letter to the Inhabitants," 41.

15. SCG, Apr. 26 and May 24, 1740; Prince, *Christian History*, Jan. 12 and 19, 1745, 2:366–74; Frank Lambert, "Subscribing for Profits and Piety: The Friendship of Benjamin Franklin and George Whitefield," *William and Mary Quarterly*, 3d ser., 50, no. 3 (July 1993): 529–54.

16. Josiah Smith, *The Character, Preaching, &c.* (Boston, 1740), i–ii.

17. Ibid., 1–10; Calhoon, *Evangelicals and Conservatives*, 33.

18. George Whitefield, *Letters of George Whitefield for the Period 1734–1742* (Carlisle, Pa., 1976), 500;

Whitefield, *Journals*, 400; Smith, *Character, Preaching*, 10; Edwin S. Gaustad, *The Great Awakening in New England* (repr. Gloucester, Mass., 1965), 69.

19. Smith, *Character, Preaching*, 12–13.

20. Ibid., 14–16.

21. Smith, *Character, Preaching*, 19–20; Clarke, *Our Southern Zion*, 83; Leigh Eric Schmidt, "'A Second and Glorious Reformation': The New Light Extremism of Andrew Croswell," *William and Mary Quarterly*, 3d ser., 43, no. 2 (Apr. 1986): 228–30; Michael Crawford, *Seasons of Grace: Colonial New England's Revival Tradition in Its British Context* (New York, 1991), 129.

22. Whitefield, *Journals*, 439, 442. On the Dutartres episode, see David T. Morgan, Jr., "The Consequences of George Whitefield's Ministry in the Carolinas and Georgia, 1739–1740," *Georgia Historical Quarterly* 55, no. 1 (1971): 66–67; Jon Butler, *The Huguenots in America: A Refugee People in New World Society* (Cambridge, Mass., 1983), 119–20.

23. Whitefield, *Journals*, 444.

24. Josiah Smith, *The Burning of Sodom* (Boston, 1741), ii–v; Weir, *Colonial South Carolina*, 118.

25. Ibid., 9; Benjamin Colman, *The Merchandise of a People Holiness to the Lord* (Boston, 1736), 1–6; Christine Heyrman, "The Fashion among More Superior People: Charity and Social Change in Provincial New England, 1700–1740," *American Quarterly* 34, no. 2 (summer 1982): 116–17.

26. Smith, *Burning of Sodom*, 10–11.

27. Martha Hodes, *White Women, Black Men: Illicit Sex in the Nineteenth-Century South* (New Haven, Conn., 1997), 9, 199; Peter S. Onuf, "Every Generation Is an 'Independant Nation': Colonization, Miscegenation, and the Fate of Jefferson's Children," *William and Mary Quarterly*, 3d ser., 57, no. 1 (Jan. 2000): 158–60; Kathleen M. Brown, *Good Wives, Nasty Wenches, and Anxious Patriarchs: Gender, Race, and Power in Colonial Virginia* (Chapel Hill, N.C., 1996), 194–201, 332–33, 355–56; Ira Berlin, *Many Thousands Gone: The First Two Centuries of Slavery in North America* (Cambridge, Mass., 1998), 158; Winthrop Jordan, "American Chiaroscuro: The Status and Definition of Mulattoes in the British Colonies," *William and Mary Quarterly*, 3d ser., 19, no. 2 (Apr. 1962): 187, 196–200; Winthrop Jordan, *White over Black: American Attitudes toward the Negro, 1550–1812* (Chapel Hill, N.C., 1968), 144–50; Wood, *Black Majority*, 98–99.

28. Smith, *Burning of Sodom*, 11–12; T. H. Breen, "'Baubles of Britain': The American and Consumer Revolutions of the Eighteenth Century," *Past and Present* 119 (May 1988): 73–104.

29. Smith, *Burning of Sodom*, 16–23; Whitefield, *Journals*, 499.

30. Whitefield, *Journals*, 499, 502; SCG, postscript, Jan. 15, 1741; Harvey H. Jackson, "Hugh Bryan and the Evangelical Movement in Colonial South Carolina," *William and Mary Quarterly*, 3d ser., 43, no. 4 (Oct. 1986): 601–3.

31. Whitefield, *Letters*, 246.

32. SCG, Jan. 22, June 18, Oct. 10, 1741.

33. SCG, postscript, Jan. 9, Feb. 27, 1742.

34. SCG, Apr. 10, June 21, Sept. 13, 1742; Jackson, "Hugh Bryan," 611.

35. Prince, *Christian History*, May 26, 1744, 2:103–4.

36. BG, June 17, 1746.

37. George Howe, *History of the Presbyterian Church in South Carolina* (Columbia, S.C., 1870), 1:260–61; Shipton, *Sibley's Harvard Graduates*, 7:582–83.

38. Leland Bellot, "Evangelicals and the Defense of Slavery in Britain's Old Colonial Empire," *Jour-*

nal of Southern History 37, no. 1 (Feb. 1971): 22; Donald Mathews, *Religion in the Old South* (Chicago, 1977), 66–80; Bernard Bailyn, *The Ideological Origins of the American Revolution*, rev. ed. (Cambridge, Mass., 1992), 230–46; Nathan O. Hatch, *The Democratization of American Christianity* (New Haven, Conn., 1989), 106–7.

39. Olwell, *Masters, Slaves, and Subjects*, 143.

CHAPTER 7. "THIS IS NO OTHER THAN
THE GATE OF HEAVEN"

1. Israel Loring, *The Duty of an Apostasizing People* (Boston, 1737), 44–46.

2. George Whitefield to Benjamin Colman, Nov. 16, 1739, *Letters of George Whitefield for the Period 1734–1742* (Carlisle, Pa., 1976), 120–21.

3. Benjamin Colman to George Whitefield, Dec. 3, 1739, in *Three Letters to the Reverend Mr. George Whitefield* (Philadelphia, [1739]), 5–6; [George Whitefield to Gilbert Tennent], Jan. 22, 1740, George Whitefield to Benjamin Colman, Jan. 24, 1740, *Letters of George Whitefield*, 142. On Colman as promoter of Whitefield, see Frank Lambert, *Inventing the "Great Awakening"* (Princeton, N.J., 1999), 121–23.

4. Whitefield to Jonathan Edwards, Nov. 16, 1739, *Letters of George Whitefield*, 12; George M. Marsden, *Jonathan Edwards: A Life* (New Haven, Conn., 2003), 204.

5. Lambert, *Inventing the "Great Awakening,"* 105; DNG, 69, 121.

6. George Whitefield to Jonathan Barber, June 13, 1740, *Letters of George Whitefield*, 188; Harry S. Stout, *The Divine Dramatist: George Whitefield and the Rise of Modern Evangelicalism* (Grand Rapids, Mich., 1991), 117–18.

7. Carl Bridenbaugh, *Cities in the Wilderness: The First Century of Urban Life in America, 1625–1742* (New York, 1938), 303; Gary Nash, *The Urban Crucible: The Northern Seaports and the Origins of the American Revolution*, abr. ed. (Cambridge, Mass., 1986), 101–8, 128–37.

8. George Whitefield, *Journals of George Whitefield* (Carlisle, Pa., 1960), 457–59.

9. Ibid., 460–61.

10. Ibid., 462–64.

11. Ibid., 464; Stout, *Divine Dramatist*, 122–23.

12. Whitefield, *Journals*, 465–68, 526; DNG, 142; Michael Shute, "A Little Great Awakening: An Episode in the American Enlightenment," *Journal of the History of Ideas* 37, no. 4 (Oct.-Dec. 1976): 589–602; Charles Clark, *The Eastern Frontier: The Settlement of Northern New England, 1610–1763* (New York, 1970), 272–77; Charles Clark, "Nicholas Gilman: He Set a Frontier Town to Dancing," *New Hampshire Profiles* (May 1976): 48; Alexander Gillman, *Searches into the History of the Gillman or Gilman Family* (London, 1895), 240–41; Elizabeth Nordbeck, "Almost Awakened: The Great Revival in New Hampshire and Maine, 1727–1748," *Historical New Hampshire* 35 (spring 1980): 34–37; Douglas Fidler, "John Odlin of Exeter and the Threat to Congregational Peace and Order in Northern New England," *Historical New Hampshire* 55 (2000): 9–10.

13. Whitefield, *Journals*, 470–72; Stout, *Divine Dramatist*, 125.

14. Whitefield, *Journals*, 476–77; Jonathan Edwards to Thomas Prince, Dec. 12, 1743, in Jonathan Edwards, *Letters and Personal Writings*, ed. George Claghorn, vol. 16 of *The Works of Jonathan Edwards* (New Haven, Conn., 1998), 116; Marsden, *Jonathan Edwards*, 206–8; Ava Chamber-

lain, "The Grand Sower of the Seed: Jonathan Edwards's Critique of George Whitefield," *New England Quarterly* 70, no. 3 (Sept. 1997): 368–85.

15. Whitefield, *Journals*, 479; Marsden, *Jonathan Edwards*, 211.

16. Kenneth Minkema, "A Great Awakening Conversion: The Relation of Samuel Belcher," *William and Mary Quarterly*, 3d ser., 44, no. 1 (Jan. 1987): 125–26.

17. Michael Crawford, ed., "The Spiritual Travels of Nathan Cole," *William and Mary Quarterly*, 3d ser., 33 no. 1 (Jan. 1976): 92–96.

18. Whitefield, *Journals*, 480, 482–83; William Gaylord to Eleazar Wheelock, Nov. 24, 1740, PEW; Harry Stout and Peter Onuf, "James Davenport and the Great Awakening in New London," *Journal of American History* 70, no. 3 (Dec. 1983): 565. On Gaylord, Franklin B. Dexter, *Biographical Sketches of the Graduates of Yale College* (New York, 1885), 414.

19. DDR, Oct. 30, 1740.

20. Whitefield, *Journals*, 484; *The Querists, or an Extract of Sundry Passages* (Philadelphia, 1740), 31–32.

21. George Whitefield, *A Letter from the Reverend Mr. George Whitefield to Some Church Members* (Boston, 1740), 13; Samuel Blair, *A Particular Consideration of a Piece, Entitled, The Querists* (Philadelphia, 1741), 4, 7–8; Charles Maxson, *The Great Awakening in the Middle Colonies* (Chicago, 1920), 66–67; Leonard J. Trinterud, *The Forming of an American Tradition: A Reexamination of Colonial Presbyterianism* (Philadelphia, 1949), 100–101.

22. DDR, Nov. 2, 5, 1740; Whitefield, *Journals*, 486–87.

23. Whitefield, *Journals*, 486–87; DDR, Nov. 5, 1740.

24. Whitefield, *Journals*, 488.

25. Ibid., 352; *An Abstract of a Letter* [Philadelphia? 1741?]. Thanks to the Harry Ransom Humanities Center at the University of Texas for providing a photocopy of this unique imprint.

26. Prince, *Christian History*, Oct. 8, 1743, 1:254; John Sergeant to unknown correspondent, June 23, 1741, Gratz American Colonial Clergy, 8/24, HSP; Trinterud, *Forming of an American Tradition*, 112.

27. DDR, Nov. 6, 1740; Whitefield, *Journals*, 491–92.

28. Whitefield, *Journals*, 497–99.

CHAPTER 8. "BLOWING UP THE DIVINE FIRE"

1. Benjamin Colman, *Souls Flying to Jesus Christ Pleasant and Admirable to Behold* (Boston, 1740), 6–7, 9. See also J. Richard Olivas, "Partial Revival: The Limits of the Great Awakening in Boston, Massachusetts, 1740–1742," in Carla Pestana and Sharon Salinger, eds., *Inequality in Early America* (Hanover, N.H., 1999), 71–72; Edwin S. Gaustad, *The Great Awakening in New England* (New York, 1957), 50–51.

2. Thomas Foxcroft, *Some Seasonable Thoughts* (Boston, 1740), 17, 41; John Webb, *Some Plain and Necessary Directions to Obtain Eternal Salvation*, 2d ed. (Boston, 1741), preface; Nathaniel Appleton, *God, and Not Ministers to Have the Glory* (Boston, 1741), 20.

3. Colman, *Souls Flying*, 22.

4. DNG, 89, see also May 14 entry, 111–12; Isaac Watts to Benjamin Colman, Mar. 18, 1741, in *Proceedings of the Massachusetts Historical Society*, 2d ser., 9 (1894–95): 382; Gary Nash, *The Urban*

Crucible: The Northern Seaports and the Origins of the American Revolution abr. ed. (Cambridge, Mass., 1986), 132–34; Rosalind Remer, "Old Lights and New Money: A Note on Religion, Economics, and the Social Order in 1740 Boston," *William and Mary Quarterly*, 3d ser., 47, no. 4 (Oct. 1990): 566–73; Elizabeth E. Dunn, "'Grasping at the Shadow': The Massachusetts Currency Debate, 1690–1751," *New England Quarterly* 71, no. 1 (Mar. 1998): 54–76; T. H. Breen and Timothy Hall, "Structuring Provincial Imagination: The Rhetoric and Experience of Social Change in Eighteenth-Century New England," *American Historical Review* 103, no. 5 (Dec. 1998): 1411–39; Frank Lambert, *Inventing the "Great Awakening"* (Princeton, N.J., 1999), 134–36.

5. Joseph Sewall, *Nineveh's Repentance* (Boston, 1740), 26, 29–30; Joseph Sewall, *The Holy Spirit Convincing the World of Sin, of Righteousness, and of Judgment* (Boston, 1741), v.

6. J. Richard Olivas, "Great Awakenings: Time, Space, and the Varieties of Religious Revivalism in Massachusetts and Northern New England, 1740–1748," (Ph.D. diss., University of California, Los Angeles, 1997), 21.

7. George Whitefield, *Letters of George Whitefield for the Period 1734–1742* (Carlisle, Pa., 1976), 221.

8. DDR, Dec. 19–20, 28, 1740, Jan. 12–17, 1741; Gilbert Tennent to William Tennent, Jan. 24, 1741, in the *Weekly History* (London), 9:1; Joseph Goodhue diary, Phillips Library, Peabody-Essex Museum, Salem, Mass.; Milton J. Coalter, *Gilbert Tennent, Son of Thunder: A Case Study of Continental Pietism's Impact on the First Great Awakening in the Middle Colonies* (Westport, Conn., 1986), 74; Erik Seeman, *Pious Persuasions: Laity and Clergy in Eighteenth-Century New England* (Baltimore, 1999), 161; Olivas, "Great Awakenings," 243–44, 261.

9. Gilbert Tennent, *The Righteousness of the Scribes and Pharisees Consider'd* (Boston, 1741), 3, 10–12, 15, 17, 19; Olivas, "Great Awakenings," 324–25.

10. Timothy Cutler to Zachary Grey, Sept. 24, 1743, quoted in Luke Tyerman, *The Life of the Rev. George Whitefield* (London: Hodder and Stoughton, 1877), 2:125; [John Hancock], *The Examiner, or Gilbert against Tennent* (Boston, 1743), 8–9.

11. *On the Reverend Mr. Gilbert Tennent's Powerful and Successful Preaching in Boston* (Boston, 1741), 1; Webb, *Plain and Necessary Directions*, preface; Benjamin Colman to George Whitefield, n.d., in the *Weekly History* (London), 17:1-2; Thomas Prince, *Christian History*, Jan. 26, Feb. 9, 1745, 2:384, 396; Thomas Prince, *An Account of the Revival of Religion in Boston in the Years 1740-1-2-3* (Boston, 1823), 17; Olivas, "Great Awakenings," 324, 330.

12. DDR, Feb. 12–14, Mar. 11, 1741; Prince, *Account*, 18; Daniel Rogers to George Whitefield, May 1, 1741, in the *Weekly History* (London), 16:4; C. C. Goen, *Revivalism and Separatism in New England, 1740–1800: Strict Congregationalists and Separate Baptists in the Great Awakening* (repr. Middletown, Conn., 1987), 12.

13. DDR, Mar. 27, Apr. 5, 12, 26, May 17, June [16?], 1741.

14. Samuel Hopkins, *The Life and Character of Miss Susanna Anthony* (Worcester, Mass., [1796]), 22; Samuel Hopkins, *Memoirs of the Life of Mrs. Sarah Osborn* (Worcester, Mass., 1799), 45–48; Charles Hambrick-Stowe, "The Spiritual Pilgrimage of Sarah Osborn, 1714–1796," *Church History* 61, no. 4 (1992): 409–10; Coalter, *Gilbert Tennent*, 74–75, 185 n.60; Richard Warch, *School of the Prophets: Yale College, 1701–1740* (New Haven, Conn., 1973), 314.

15. Gilbert Tennent to George Whitefield, Apr. 25, 1741, in the *Weekly History* (London), 11:2-3.

16. Prince, *Account*, 18–21; Olivas, "Partial Revival," 68–69, 75.

17. Prince, *Account*, 24.

18. William Cooper, "Preface," in Jonathan Edwards, *The Distinguishing Marks of a Work of the Spirit of God*, in Jonathan Edwards, *The Great Awakening*, ed. C. C. Goen, vol. 4 of *The Works of Jonathan Edwards* (New Haven, Conn., 1972), 217–21; Anonymous Boston writer to George Whitefield, in the *Weekly History* (London), 17:4.

19. Prince, *Christian History*, Aug. 6, 1743, 1:182–84.

20. Ibid., Feb. 16, 1745, 2:403; Timothy Gloege, "For 'the Glory of our Redeemer' and 'the Increase of his Triumphs': *The Christian History* and the Boston Revivalists" (unpub. seminar paper, University of Notre Dame, 2002).

21. Prince, *Christian History*, Oct. 1 and 8, 1743, 1:238–50.

22. Ibid., Feb. 11 and 18, 1744, 1:396–408.

23. Edmund Coffin to Nathaniel Coffin, Oct. 14, 1741, in Joshua Coffin, *A Sketch of the History of Newbury* (Boston, 1845), 210–11; Diary of Joseph Bean, Oct. 21, 1741, Bryn Mawr College Library, Special Collections; Douglas Winiarski, ed., "'A Jornal of a Fue Days at York': The Great Awakening on the Northern New England Frontier," *Maine History* 42 (2004): 47–60; Charles E. Clark, *The Eastern Frontier: The Settlement of Northern New England, 1610–1763* (New York, 1970), 280; Elizabeth C. Nordbeck, "Almost Awakened: The Great Revival in New Hampshire and Maine, 1727–1748," *Historical New Hampshire* 35 (Spring 1980): 35–36.

24. Winiarski, ed., "Jornal," 62–63.

25. William Shurtleff to William Cooper, June 1, 1743, in Prince, *Christian History*, Jan. 28, 1744, 1:384.

26. William Shurtleff to William Cooper, June 1, 1743, in Prince, *Christian History*, Feb. 4, 1744, 1:385; William Parker to Richard Waldron, Nov. 28, 1741, Misc. Bound MSS, MHS; [Samuel P. Savage] to Gilbert Tennent, Feb. 2, 1741/2, in Samuel P. Savage Papers, MHS; "Extract of a Letter from Piscataqua," Samuel P. Savage Papers, MHS; Winiarski, ed., "Jornal," 58–59.

27. DNG, 226, 232; Clark, *Eastern Frontier*, 284–85; Douglas K. Fidler, "Preparing the Way of the Lord: Three Case Studies of Ministerial Preconditioning in Congregations before the Great Awakening, 1675–1750," (Ph.D. diss., Univ. of New Hampshire, 1997), 155–58.

28. Stephen Williams to Eleazar Wheelock, Mar. 16, 1741, no. 741216, PEW; Stephen Williams Diary, Storrs Library, Longmeadow, Mass., typescript copy, 3:374–75; "Extract from a Letter; Suffield, July 6, 1741," in the Samuel P. Savage papers, MHS, transcribed in Douglas L. Winiarski, "Jonathan Edwards, Enthusiast? Radical Revivalism and the Great Awakening in the Connecticut Valley," *Church History* 74, no. 4 (Dec. 2005): 738–39; John Demos, *The Unredeemed Captive: A Family Story from Early America* (New York, 1994), 198–200.

29. Stephen Williams Diary, 375–76; George M. Marsden, *Jonathan Edwards: A Life* (New Haven, Conn., 2003), 220–21; Gaustad, *Great Awakening in New England*, 48.

30. On Suffield's connection to Enfield, see Winiarski, "Jonathan Edwards, Enthusiast?" 711.

31. Jonathan Edwards, *Sinners in the Hands of an Angry God*, in Jonathan Edwards, *Sermons and Discourses, 1739–1742*, ed. Harry Stout and Nathan Hatch with Kyle Farley, vol. 22 of *The Works of Jonathan Edwards* (New Haven, Conn., 2003), 401, 411, 415; Marsden, *Edwards*, 221–24.

32. Jonathan Edwards to George Whitefield, Dec. 14, 1740, in Jonathan Edwards, *Letters and Personal Writings*, ed. George Claghorn, vol. 16 of *The Works of Jonathan Edwards* (New Haven, Conn., 1998), 87; Jonathan Edwards to Benjamin Colman, Mar. 9, 1741, in Edwards, *Letters and Personal Writings*, 88–89. See also Marsden, *Edwards*, 214–16.

33. Jonathan Edwards to Thomas Prince, Dec. 12, 1743, in Edwards, *Letters and Personal Writings*,

117–20; Marsden, *Jonathan Edwards*, 217–18; *Boston Weekly News-Letter*, July 1, 1742, quoted in Richard Bushman, ed., *The Great Awakening: Documents on the Revival of Religion, 1740–1745* (repr. Chapel Hill, N.C., 1989), 48.

34. Samuel Hopkins, *Sketches of the Life of the Late, Rev. Samuel Hopkins*, in Stephen Nissenbaum, ed., *The Great Awakening at Yale College* (Belmont, Calif., 1972), 17–19; Samuel Hopkins diary, Nov. 13, 1741, Gratz Sermon Collection, Box 6, HSP.

35. Ebenezer Pemberton, *The Knowlege of Christ Recommended* (New London, 1741), 6, 11, 19.

36. Prince, *Christian History*, June 2, 9, 1744, 2:105–14; John Lee to Eleazar Wheelock, Apr. 20, 1741, no. 741270, PEW.

37. Prince, *Christian History*, June 2, 9, July 14, 1744, 2:105–14, 154; John Lee to Eleazar Wheelock, Apr. 20, 1741, no. 741270, PEW; Barbara Lacey, ed., *The World of Hannah Heaton: The Diary of an Eighteenth-Century Farm Woman* (DeKalb, Ill., 2003), 13; William Simmons, "Red Yankees: Narragansett Conversion in the Great Awakening," *American Ethnologist* 10, no. 2 (May 1983): 261.

38. Prince, *Christian History*, June 16, 1744, 2:122–24; Goen, *Revivalism and Separatism*, 6; Jonathan Greenleaf, *Memoir of Jonathan Parsons* (Boston, 1841), 4–5.

39. Prince, *Christian History*, June 16, 1744, 2:125–26; Franklin B. Dexter, *Biographical Sketches of the Graduates of Yale College* (New York, 1885), 343; Christopher Grasso, *A Speaking Aristocracy: Transforming Public Discourse in Eighteenth-Century Connecticut* (Chapel Hill, N.C., 1999), 90–93; Bruce P. Stark, *Lyme, Connecticut: From Founding to Independence* (Lyme, Conn., 1976), 22.

40. Prince, *Christian History*, June 23, 1744, 2:133–35; J[ohn] L[ee] to Gilbert Tennent, in *Glasgow-Weekly-History* (1743), in *Proceedings of the Massachusetts Historical Society* 53 (1920): 201; Jonathan Parsons to Eleazar Wheelock, Apr. 21, 1741, no. 741271, PEW.

41. Prince, *Christian History*, June 23, 30, 1744, 2:136–39.

42. Ibid., June 30, 1744, 2:140–43; Goen, *Revivalism and Separatism*, 68–69.

43. Prince, *Christian History*, July 7, 1744, 2:146–47.

44. Ibid., 148; Susan Juster, *Disorderly Women: Sexual Politics and Evangelicalism in Revolutionary New England* (Ithaca, N.Y., 1994), 35.

45. Prince, *Christian History*, July 7, 1744, 2:148–51.

46. Joshua Hempstead, *Diary of Joshua Hempstead* (New London, Conn., 1901), 380; Goen, *Revivalism and Separatism*, 21–22.

47. Prince, *Christian History*, Aug. 27, 1743, 1:201–5, quotes 205; Simmons, "Red Yankees," 261–62.

48. Lacey, *World of Hannah Heaton*, 12–13.

49. Solomon Williams to Eleazar Wheelock, July 17, 1741, no. 741417, PEW; Stephen Williams Diary, 3:384; John Fea, "Wheelock's World: Letters and the Communication of Revival in Great Awakening New England," *Proceedings of the American Antiquarian Society* 109, no. 1 (1999): 138–39.

50. William McLoughlin, ed., *The Diary of Isaac Backus*, vol. 3: *1786–1806* (Providence, R.I., 1979), appendix 1, 1523–26; William McLoughlin, *Isaac Backus and the American Pietistic Tradition* (Boston, 1967), 12–15.

51. Benjamin Throop, "Secret Interviews," May 29, July 19, and August 23, 1741, CHS.

52. William Allen, "Memoir of Rev. Eleazar Wheelock," *American Quarterly Register* 10, no. 1 (August 1837): 12–13; Gaustad, *Great Awakening in New England*, 45–46; Josiah Cotton to Eleazar Wheelock, Dec. 16, 1742, Gratz American Colonial Clergy, 8/22, HSP.

53. Allen, "Wheelock," 14; Prince, *Christian History*, Dec. 15, 1744, 2:335.

54. Allen, "Wheelock," 14–15; DDR, November 2, 3, and 4, 1741.

55. Allen, "Wheelock," 15; DDR, Nov. 6, 7, 8, 9, and 10, 1741. On Bromfield, see Thomas Prince's funeral sermon *The Case of Heman Considered* (Boston, 1756); Mark Peterson, *The Price of Redemption: The Spiritual Economy of Puritan New England* (Stanford, Calif., 1997), 80; Olivas, "Great Awakenings," 405–6.

56. Allen, "Wheelock," 16.

57. Eleazar Wheelock to Daniel Rogers, Jan. 18, 1742, no. 742118, PEW.

CHAPTER 9. "MINDS EXTRAORDINARILY TRANSPORTED"

1. Jonathan Edwards to Deacon Lyman, August 31, 1741, in Jonathan Edwards, *The Great Awakening*, ed. C.C. Goen, vol. 4 of *The Works of Jonathan Edwards* (New Haven, Conn., 1972), 533–34.

2. *BWPB*, Sept. 28, 1741, Oct. 5, 1741; George M. Marsden, *Jonathan Edwards: A Life* (New Haven, Conn., 2003), 232–33; Norman Pettit, "Prelude to Mission: David Brainerd's Expulsion from Yale," *New England Quarterly* 59, no. 1 (Mar. 1986): 34–35; Wadsworth diary, *Post-Boy* of Oct. 5, 1741, in Stephen Nissenbaum, ed., *The Great Awakening at Yale College* (Belmont, Calif., 1972), 55, 113–15; Louis L. Tucker, *Puritan Protagonist: President Thomas Clap of Yale College* (Chapel Hill, N.C., 1962), 126–28.

3. Jonathan Edwards, *The Distinguishing Marks of a Work of the Spirit of God*, in Edwards, *Great Awakening*, 226.

4. Ibid., 228–31, quotes 228, 231.

5. Ibid., 235–37.

6. Ibid., 241–48, "If I am," 247.

7. Ibid., 248–60, "Shew positively," 248.

8. Ibid., 260–64, 268–70, quotes 260, 263–64, 270.

9. Ibid., 275, 282–83, 287; [William Rand], *The Late Religious Commotions in New-England Considered* (Boston, 1743), 38, 40; C. C. Goen, "Editor's Introduction," in Edwards, *The Great Awakening*, 64n6; Marsden, *Edwards*, 234–38.

10. Charles Chauncy, *An Unbridled Tongue a Sure Evidence, That Our Religion Is Hypocritical and Vain* (Boston, 1741), 19.

11. Alexander Garden, *Six Letters to the Rev. Mr. George Whitefield*, 2d ed. (Boston, 1740); Andrew Croswell, *An Answer to the Rev. Garden's Three First Letters to the Rev. Mr. Whitefield* (Boston, 1741), 6, 9, 60; Leigh Schmidt, "'A Second and Glorious Reformation': The New Light Extremism of Andrew Croswell," *William and Mary Quarterly*, 3d ser., 43, no. 2 (Apr. 1986): 217–18.

12. Alexander Garden, *The Doctrine of Justification According to the Scriptures* (Charleston, S.C., 1742), 3, 66.

13. John Caldwell, *An Impartial Trial of the Spirit* (Boston, 1742), 7, 11; on a Reformed, literal reading of Scripture, see Mark Noll, *America's God, From Jonathan Edwards to Abraham Lincoln* (New York, 2002), 367–85.

14. Caldwell, *Impartial Trial*, 20–21.

15. Ibid., 21–23.

16. Ibid., 26–27, 37, 47–48. On "animal spirits" in revival, see Ann Taves, *Fits, Trances, and Visions:*

Experiencing Religion and Explaining Experience from Wesley to James (Princeton, N.J., 1999), 27–41.

17. David McGregore, *The Spirits of the Present Day Tried*, 2d ed. (Boston, 1742), 2, 8; Barney L. Jones, "John Caldwell, Critic of the Great Awakening in New England," in Stuart C. Henry, ed., *A Miscellany of American Christianity: Essays in Honor of H. Shelton Smith* (Durham, N.C., 1963), 173.

18. McGregore, *Spirits of the Present Day*, 11, 19–20, 22–23, 25, 27.

19. Journal of Ebenezer Parkman in Joseph Tracy, *The Great Awakening: A History of the Revival of Religion in the Time of Edwards and Whitefield* (1842; repr. Carlisle, Pa., 1976), 208; Jones, "John Caldwell," 175–77; *Christian Monthly History* 1 (Nov. 1743): 24; Samuel Davies, *The Impartial Trial, Impartially Tried* (Williamsburg, Va., 1748), cited in Jones, "John Caldwell," 168–69.

20. DDR, Dec. 27–31, 1741, Jan. 1, 4, 1742.

21. Diary of Joseph Bean, Oct. 11, 1741, Bryn Mawr College Library, Special Collections; DDR, Jan. 5, 1742.

22. Andrew Croswell, *What Is Christ to Me, If He Is Not Mine?* (Boston, 1745), 31–32, cited in Ava Chamberlain, "Self-Deception as a Theological Problem in Jonathan Edwards's 'Treatise Concerning Religious Affections,'" *Church History* 63, no. 4 (Dec. 1994): 547; Jonathan Dickinson, *The Witness of the Spirit* (Boston, 1740), 20–21; Schmidt, "Second and Glorious Reformation," 240; Geoffrey F. Nuttall, *The Holy Spirit in Puritan Faith and Experience* (Oxford, Eng., 1947), 135–37; David R. Como, *Blown by the Spirit: Puritanism and the Emergence of an Antinomian Underground in Pre-Civil-War England* (Stanford, Calif., 2004), 36.

23. DDR, Jan. 9, 11, 1742.

24. DDR, Jan. 11, 12, 1742.

25. Charles Chauncy, *Enthusiasm Described and Caution'd Against* (Boston, 1742), 13, quoted in Susan Juster, *Disorderly Women: Sexual Politics and Evangelicalism in Revolutionary New England* (Ithaca, N.Y., 1994), 30–31; see also Catherine Brekus, *Strangers and Pilgrims: Female Preaching in America, 1740–1845* (Chapel Hill, 1998), 51–67; Mary Keller, *The Hammer and the Flute: Women, Power, and Spirit Possession* (Baltimore, 2002), 74–75.

26. DDR, Jan. 31, Feb. 1, 1742.

27. DDR, Feb. 2, 1742.

28. DDR, Feb. 3, 1742.

29. DDR, Feb. 6–7, 1742.

30. DDR, Feb. 23–26, 1742; Gary Nash, *The Urban Crucible: The Northern Seaports and the Origins of the American Revolution*, abr. ed. (Cambridge, Mass., 1986), 107, 135–36.

31. John White, "Epistle to the Reader," in Benjamin Bradstreet, *Godly Sorrow Described* (Boston, 1742), ii; DDR, Nov. 23–24, 1741; C. C. Goen, *Revivalism and Separatism*, 107–8.

32. White, "Epistle to the Reader," in Bradstreet, *Godly Sorrow*, ii; Prince, *Christian History*, Aug. 13, 1743, 1:188; Apr. 7, 1744, 2:44–45; on Gloucester revivals, Christine Heyrman, *Commerce and Culture: The Maritime Communities of Colonial Massachusetts, 1690–1750* (New York, 1984), 182–88.

33. Eleazar Wheelock to Stephen Williams, Feb. 3, 1742, no. 742153, PEW; Eleazar Wheelock to Joseph Bellamy, Apr. 11, 1742, bound with Stephen Williams, *Two Letters from the Reverend Mr. Williams & Wheelock* (Boston, 1744), Beinecke Rare Book and Manuscript Library, Yale University.

34. Account transcribed in Douglas Winiarski, "Souls Filled with Ravishing Transport: Heavenly Visions and the Radical Awakening in New England, 1742," *William and Mary Quarterly*, 3d ser., 61, no. 1 (Jan. 2004): 43–46.

35. Douglas Winiarski, "All Manner of Error and Delusion: Josiah Cotton and the Religious Transformation of Southeastern New England, 1700–1770," (Ph.D. diss., Indiana University, 2001), 214.

36. Grant Wacker, *Heaven Below: Early Pentecostals and American Culture* (Cambridge, Mass., 2001), 51–57.

37. Barbara Lacey, ed., *The World of Hannah Heaton: The Diary of an Eighteenth-Century New England Farm Woman* (DeKalb, Ill., 2003), xiii–xvii, 9, 12.

38. Diary of Joseph Bean, May 17, June 10–11, 1742.

39. DNG, 242–43; DDR, June 5, 1742.

40. DNG, 253–58, 261–65, 268; DDR, Apr. 19, 1743; Winiarski, "Souls Filled," 14–17; Charles Clark, "Nicholas Gilman: He Set a Frontier Town to Dancing," *New Hampshire Profiles* (May 1976), 51–52; Catherine A. Brekus, *Strangers and Pilgrims: Female Preaching in America, 1740–1845* (Chapel Hill, N.C., 1998), 55.

41. Jonathan Edwards to Joseph Bellamy, Jan. 21, 1742, in Edwards, *Letters and Personal Writings*, 98–99; Jonathan Edwards, *Some Thoughts Concerning the Present Revival of Religion* (1742), in Edwards, *Great Awakening*, 331–32, 341; Marsden, *Jonathan Edwards*, 239–41.

42. Sereno Dwight, *The Works of President Edwards: With a Memoir of His Life* (New York, 1829–30), 171–75, quote from 175.

43. Dwight, *Works of President Edwards*, 176–86, quotes from 176, 178, 185; Marsden, *Jonathan Edwards*, 240–47; Philip F. Gura, *Jonathan Edwards: America's Evangelical* (New York, 2005), 105–7.

44. Eleazar Wheelock to Joseph Bellamy, Dec. 27, 1741, Richard Webster transcription, Joseph Bellamy Papers, PHS; Jonathan Edwards to Thomas Prince, Dec. 12, 1743, in Edwards, *Great Awakening*, 549–51; Samuel Buell, *The Import of the Saint's Confession* (New London, Conn., [1792]), 41–42; Marsden, *Jonathan Edwards*, 244–47, 260–63; Patricia Tracy, *Jonathan Edwards, Pastor: Religion and Society in Eighteenth-Century Northampton* (New York, 1980), 137, 154; Douglas L. Winiarski, "Jonathan Edwards, Enthusiast? Radical Revivalism and the Great Awakening in the Connecticut Valley," *Church History* 74, no. 4 (Dec. 2005): 731–33.

45. Parkman Journal, Feb. 9, 11, in Tracy, *Great Awakening*, 204–5; Winiarski, "Souls Filled with Ravishing Transport," 13–14.

46. Parkman Journal, Mar. 11, 20, 29–30, in Tracy, *Great Awakening*, 205–6; Schmidt, "Second and Glorious Reformation," 220–21; Diary of Joseph Bean, Apr. 4, 1742. On Buell and Croswell's preaching schedule during March and April, see J. Richard Olivas, "Great Awakenings: Time, Space, and the Varieties of Religious Revivalism in Massachusetts and Northern New England, 1740–1748" (Ph.D. diss., University of California, Los Angeles, 1997), 403.

47. DDR, Apr. 6, 15–16, 21, 1742; Daniel Rogers to Eleazar Wheelock, Apr. 21, 1742, no. 742271, PEW; Nash, *Urban Crucible*, 117; Olivas, "Great Awakenings," 404–5.

48. Daniel Bliss to Eleazar Wheelock, Mar. 22, 1742, no. 7422222, PEW; *A Result of a Council of Churches at Concord, June 21, 1743* ([Boston, 1743]), 5–6; Robert A. Gross, *The Minutemen and Their World*, rev. ed. (New York, 2001), 18–20; C. C. Goen, *Revivalism and Separatism in New England, 1740–1800: Strict Congregationalists and Separate Baptists in the Great Awakening* (repr.

Middletown, Conn., 1987), 20; Franklin B. Dexter, *Biographical Sketches of the Graduates of Yale College* (New York, 1885), 439–40.

49. Samuel Buell to Eleazar Wheelock, Apr. 20, 1742, no. 742270, PEW.

50. Benjamin Colman, *The Great GOD* (Boston, 1742), 31–32; Benjamin Colman to George White-field, June 3, 1742, in *Glasgow-Weekly-History*, reprinted in *Proceedings of the Massachusetts Historical Society* 53 (1920): 214–15; Dwight, *Works of President Edwards*, 175; Olivas, "Great Awakenings," 408–12.

51. DDR, Apr. 27–28, 1742; Goen, *Revivalism and Separatism*, 100.

52. DDR, Apr. 29, May 5–6, 1742; *BEP*, May 3, 1742; Goen, *Revivalism and Separatism*, 100; Charles Clark, *The Eastern Frontier: The Settlement of Northern New England, 1610–1763* (New York, 1970), 288–89; Usher Parsons, *The Life of Sir William Pepperrell* (Boston, 1855), 29.

CHAPTER 10. "UNDER THE IMPRESSIONS OF A HEATED IMAGINATION"

1. Andrew Croswell to Eleazar Wheelock, Sept. 30, 1741, no. 741530, PEW; *BWPB*, Oct. 5, 1741, no. 352.

2. Prince, *Christian History*, Dec. 1, 1744, 2:314–15; Josiah Cotton, "Memoirs," MHS, quoted in Leigh Eric Schmidt, "'A Second and Glorious Reformation': The New Light Extremism of Andrew Croswell," *William and Mary Quarterly*, 3d ser., 43, no. 2 (Apr. 1986): 220; Douglas Winiarski, "All Manner of Error and Delusion: Josiah Cotton and the Religious Transformation of Southeastern New England, 1700–1770," (Ph.D. diss., Indiana University, 2000), 186–88.

3. SCG, June 21, 1742, letter dated Mar. 15; Timothy Hall, *Contested Boundaries: Itinerancy and the Reshaping of the Colonial American Religious World* (Durham, N.C., 1994), 58.

4. BEP, Mar. 8, 1742; Journal of Ebenezer Parkman, quoted in Joseph Tracy, *The Great Awakening* (1842; repr. Carlisle, Pa., 1976), 205; [Thomas Prentice], *A Letter to the Reverend Andrew Croswell* (Boston, [1771]), 20; *Sibley's Harvard Graduates*, 8:390–91; Schmidt, "Second and Glorious Reformation," 220–21.

5. Robert Cray, Jr., "More Light on a New Light: James Davenport's Religious Legacy, Eastern Long Island, 1740–1800," *New York History* 73, no. 1 (1992): 13–16; Nathaniel Prime, *A History of Long Island* (New York, 1845), 181–82, 203; Robert Brockway, *A Wonderful Work of God: Puritanism and the Great Awakening* (Bethlehem, Pa., 2003), 124.

6. Aaron Burr to Joseph Bellamy, Jan. 13, 1742, Richard Webster transcription, Joseph Bellamy Papers, PHS; J. Richard Olivas, "Great Awakenings: Time, Space, and the Varieties of Religious Revivalism in Massachusetts and Northern New England, 1740–1748," (Ph.D. diss., University of California, Los Angeles, 1997), 423–26. Olivas interpreted Davenport as a radical advocate for the poor and dispossessed. Harry S. Stout and Peter Onuf, "James Davenport and the Great Awakening in New London," *Journal of American History* 70, no. 3 (Dec., 1983): 557–58 advocated seeing Davenport's ministry in the context of social upheaval in southern New England.

7. Thomas Foxcroft, preface, in Jonathan Dickinson, *The True Scripture-Doctrine* (Boston, 1741), v; *BEP*, Apr. 12, 26, 1742; Schmidt, "Second and Glorious Reformation," 222. On the Boston area ministers and latitudinarianism, see John Corrigan, *The Prism of Piety: Catholick Congregational Clergy at the Beginning of the Enlightenment* (New York, 1991), 3–5.

8. Andrew Croswell to Eleazar Wheelock, May 3, 1742, no. 742303, PEW; Schmidt, "Second and Glorious Reformation," 221.

9. *Boston Weekly News-Letter*, July 1, 1742, reprinted in Richard Bushman, ed., *The Great Awakening: Documents on the Revival of Religion, 1740–1745* (repr. Chapel Hill, N.C., 1989), 45–48.

10. *Boston Weekly News-Letter*, July 1, 1742, reprinted in Bushman, *Great Awakening*, 45–49; Brockway, *Wonderful Work of God*, 129–31.

11. *BWPB*, Mar. 1, 1742; DDR, Mar. 6, 1742.

12. Richard Warch, "The Shepherd's Tent: Education and Enthusiasm in the Great Awakening," *American Quarterly* 30, no. 2 (summer 1978): 181–89; Stout and Onuf, "Davenport," 570–72; Brockway, *Wonderful Work of God*, 133–36.

13. Aaron Burr to Joseph Bellamy, June 28, 1742, Richard Webster transcription, Joseph Bellamy Papers, PHS.

14. Benjamin Colman to George Whitefield, June 3, 1742, in *Glasgow-Weekly-History*, no. 45, in *Proceedings of the Massachusetts Historical Society* 53 (June 1920): 214.

15. Stephen Williams Diary, transcription, July 9, 1742, Pocumtuck Valley Memorial Association Library, Deerfield, Mass., 4:30; *BEP*, July 5, 1742; Olivas, "Great Awakenings," 428; Gary Nash, *The Urban Crucible: The Northern Seaports and the Origins of the American Revolution*, abr. ed. (Cambridge, Mass., 1986), 130–36.

16. *The Declaration of a Number of the Associated Pastors* (Boston, 1742), 4–7; also *BEP*, July 5, 1742.

17. *BEP*, Aug. 30, 1742; Andrew Croswell, *Mr. Croswell's Reply to the Declaration* (Boston, 1742), 4–5, 8–9, 16–17; Jon Butler, "Enthusiasm Described and Decried: The Great Awakening as Interpretative Fiction," *Journal of American History* 69, no. 2 (Sept. 1982): 319.

18. Journal of Ebenezer Parkman, July 8, 1742, in Tracy, *Great Awakening*, 209.

19. Charles Chauncy, *Enthusiasm Described and Caution'd Against* (Boston, 1742), iii–vi; Ann Taves, *Fits, Trances, and Visions: Experiencing Religion and Explaining Experience from Wesley to James* (Princeton, N.J., 1999), 21–33; Edward Griffin, *Old Brick: Charles Chauncy of Boston, 1705–1787* (Minneapolis, 1980), 67–70.

20. DDR, July 28–Aug. 5, 1742; C. C. Goen, *Revivalism and Separatism in New England, 1740–1800* (repr. Middletown, Conn., 1987), 12.

21. *BEP*, Aug. 2, 1742; Journal of Ebenezer Parkman, Aug. 19–20, 1742, in Tracy, *Great Awakening*, 209; Olivas, "Great Awakenings," 458.

22. DDR, Aug. 21, 1742; Michael Hill and James Davenport to [Philemon Robbins], Aug. 30, 1742, Philemon and A. R. Robbins papers, CHS.

23. *BEP*, September 6, 1742; Brockway, *Wonderful Work of God*, 143–44; Olivas, "Great Awakenings," 452.

24. *Boston Weekly News-Letter*, Sept. 23, 1742; Milton J. Coalter, *Gilbert Tennent, Son of Thunder: A Case Study of Continental Pietism's Impact on the First Great Awakening in the Middle Colonies* (Westport, Conn., 1986), 96–108, 118–23.

25. [Sarah Parsons Moorhead], *To the Reverend Mr. James Davenport* (Boston, 1742), 1, 4, 7–8.

26. DDR, Sept. 7–10, 1742; Cray, "More Light," 16.

27. Isaac Watts to Benjamin Colman, Oct. 22, Nov. 15, 1742, in *Proceedings of the Massachusetts Historical Society*, 2d ser., 9 (1894–95): 396–98, see also Watts to Colman, Feb. 24, 1742, 391.

28. [Jonathan Dickinson], A *Display of God's Special Grace* (Boston, 1742), 46, 69–70, 89–90, 107–8; Bryan Le Beau, *Jonathan Dickinson and the Formative Years of American Presbyterianism* (Lexington, Ky., 1997), 141–43; David Harlan, "A World of Double Visions and Second Thoughts: Jonathan Dickinson's *Display of God's Special Grace,*" *Early American Literature* 21 (fall 1986): 118–30; Leigh Eric Schmidt, "Jonathan Dickinson and the Moderate Awakening," *American Presbyterians* 63, no. 4 (1985): 344, 350.

29. Andrew Croswell to Nathaniel and Daniel Rogers, Sept. 23, 1742, Gratz American Colonial Clergy Manuscripts, 8/22, HSP; Andrew Croswell, *Mr. Croswell's Reply to a Book* (Boston, 1742), 5–6, 8, 12, 18, 23; Schmidt, "Second and Glorious Reformation," 223.

30. Andrew Croswell to Benjamin Pomeroy, Nov. 13, 1742, no. 742613, PEW; Croswell, *Mr. Croswell's Reply,* 3; Schmidt, "Second and Glorious Reformation," 223, 225.

31. DDR, Nov. 6–9, 1742; Goen, *Revivalism and Separatism,* 68–69, 86–87, 97, 237–39; Stout and Onuf, "Davenport," 570; Peter Onuf, "New Lights in New London: A Group Portrait of the Separatists," *William and Mary Quarterly,* 3d ser., 37, no. 4 (Oct. 1980): 629–30.

32. Ross Beales, ed., "Solomon Prentice's Narrative of the Great Awakening," *Proceedings of the Massachusetts Historical Society* 83 (1971): 137–38; Journal of Israel Loring, Sudbury Archives, transcription, www.sudbury.ma.us/archives (Apr. 28, 1742, to Nov. 11, 1743), 25.

33. Beales, "Solomon Prentice's Narrative," 138–39; Francis G. Walett, ed., *The Diary of Ebenezer Parkman, 1703–1782* (Worcester, Mass., 1974), Jan. 7, 1743, p. 89.

34. Beales, "Solomon Prentice's Narrative," 140; *BEP,* Mar. 14, 1743.

35. *BEP,* Mar. 14, 1743; Douglas L. Winiarski, "Souls Filled with Ravishing Transport: Heavenly Visions and the Radical Awakening in New England," *William and Mary Quarterly,* 3d ser., 61, no. 1 (Jan. 2004); 39.

36. Beales, "Solomon Prentice's Narrative," 140–41.

37. DDR, Dec. 18, 22, 28, 1742, Jan. 4, 12, 14, 1743.

38. Jonathan Dickinson to Thomas Foxcroft, Feb. 1743, Jonathan Dickinson Collection, Princeton University Library, quoted in Keith Hardman, "Jonathan Dickinson and the Course of American Presbyterianism, 1717–1747," (Ph.D. diss., University of Pennsylvania, 1971), 287–88; Le Beau, *Jonathan Dickinson,* 160; *The Diary of Joshua Hempstead* (New London, Conn., 1901), 406–7.

39. *BEP,* Mar. 14, Apr. 11, 1743; *BWPB,* Mar. 28, 1743; Thomas Clap to Jonathan Dickinson, Mar. 14, 1743, in Richard Webster, *A History of the Presbyterian Church in America* (Philadelphia, 1857), 204; Stout and Onuf, "James Davenport," 556–57; Brockway, *Wonderful Work of God,* 147–49; "bare-arsed" quote from Dr. Alexander Hamilton, in Brockway, *Wonderful Work of God,* 149.

40. *BEP,* Apr. 11, 1743; Brockway, *Wonderful Work of God,* 149–50; Stout and Onuf, "James Davenport," 576; Sarah Pierpont to Eleazar Wheelock, May 30, 1743, no. 743330, PEW.

41. *Diary of Joshua Hempstead,* 407; Jonathan Edwards to Sarah Edwards, Mar. 25, 1743, in Jonathan Edwards, *Letters and Personal Writings,* ed. George Claghorn, vol. 16 of *The Works of Jonathan Edwards* (New Haven, Conn., 1998), 104; Stout and Onuf, "James Davenport," 576; Brockway, *Wonderful Work of God,* 150; on Edwards's future correspondence with Davenport, see Edwards, *Letters and Personal Writings,* 275–76, 376–79; William Gaylord to Eleazar Wheelock, Nov. 24, 1747, no. 747624, PEW; James Davenport to Eleazar Wheelock, Jan. 25, 1750, no. 749125, PEW; Eleazar Wheelock to George Whitefield, July 30, 1758, no. 758430, PEW.

CHAPTER 11. "BEYOND ANY FORMER
OUTPOURING OF THE SPIRIT"

1. Journal of the Rev. Israel Loring, Mar. 24, 1743, Sudbury Archives, transcription, www.sudbury. ma.us/archives (Apr. 28, 1742, to Nov. 11, 1743), 35, 45.

2. A.M., *The State of Religion in New-England* (Glasgow, 1742), 3–5, 11, 13, 16; George Whitefield, *Some Remarks on a Late Pamphlet*, 2d ed. (Boston, 1743), 3.

3. Jonathan Ashley, *The Great Duty of Charity* (Boston, 1742), 2; *BG*, Jan. 11, 1743; Jonathan Ashley, *A Letter from the Reverend Mr. Jonathan Ashley* (Boston, 1743), 3 (letter also printed in *BEP*, Feb. 7, 1743]; J.F., *Remarks on the Rev. Mr. Cooper's Objections* ([Boston, 1743]), 8; *BEP*, Jan. 17, 24 1743.

4. Jonathan Edwards, *Some Thoughts Concerning the Present Revival of Religion in New-England* (Boston, [1743]), in Jonathan Edwards, *The Great Awakening*, ed. C. C. Goen, vol. 4 of *The Works of Jonathan Edwards* (New Haven, Conn., 1972), 291. On the context of *Some Thoughts* see Goen, "Editor's Introduction," in Edwards, *Great Awakening*, 65–78; Edwin S. Gaustad, *The Great Awakening in New England* (New York, 1957), 89–92; George M. Marsden, *Jonathan Edwards: A Life* (New Haven, Conn., 2003), 263–67.

5. Edwards, *Some Thoughts*, 296.

6. Ibid, 345, 353, 358; Thomas S. Kidd, *The Protestant Interest: New England after Puritanism* (New Haven, Conn., 2004), 164–66.

7. Edwards, *Some Thoughts*, 474, 484–86, 488–90, 495.

8. *The Testimony of the Pastors of the Churches* (Boston, 1743), 6–13; Gaustad, *Great Awakening in New England*, 63; Frank Lambert, *Inventing the "Great Awakening"* (Princeton, N.J., 1999), 229.

9. Joshua Gee, *A Letter to the Reverend Mr. Nathanael Eells*, 2d ed. (Boston, 1743), 4, 8–11, 14.

10. *BG*, May 31, 1743; Prince, *Christian History*, July 16, 1743, 1:157; Gaustad, *Great Awakening in New England*, 65; DDR, July 6–7, 1743.

11. *The Testimony and Advice of an Assembly of Pastors* (Boston, 1743), 7–8, 10.

12. Ibid, 11–12.

13. Ibid, 12–15; Prince, *Christian History*, July 16–Aug. 20, 1743, 1:155–201.

14. *The Testimony and Advice of a Number of Laymen* (Boston, 1743), 3–9, quotes on 3, 5.

15. Charles Chauncy, *Seasonable Thoughts on the State of Religion in New-England* (Boston, 1743), 77; partially quoted in Gaustad, *Great Awakening in New England*, 94. On *Seasonable Thoughts*, see Gaustad, *Great Awakening in New England*, 93–97; Charles Lippy, *Seasonable Revolutionary: The Mind of Charles Chauncy* (Chicago, 1981), 36–37; Edward Griffin, *Old Brick: Charles Chauncy of Boston, 1705–1787* (Minneapolis, 1980), 81–88; Ann Taves, *Fits, Trances, and Visions: Experiencing Religion and Explaining Experience from Wesley to James* (Princeton, N.J., 1999), 21–33; Marsden, *Jonathan Edwards*, 280–83.

16. Gaustad, *Great Awakening in New England*, 61.

17. Benjamin Lord, *GOD Glorified in His Works, of Providence and Grace* (Boston, 1743), 29–31.

18. Ibid., 31–33.

19. Ibid., 34–36. For a fuller discussion of Wheeler's healing and others like it, see Thomas S. Kidd, "The Healing of Mercy Wheeler: Illness and Miracles among Early American Evangelicals," *William and Mary Quarterly*, 3d ser., 63, no. 1 (Jan. 2006): 149–70.

20. DDR, Aug. 7, 1743. On Prince, see also DNG, 330; *Sibley's Harvard Graduates*, 7:343.

21. *BEP*, May 30, June 13, 1743; *Boston Weekly News-Letter*, May 26, 1743; Leigh Eric Schmidt, "'A Second and Glorious Reformation': The New Light Extremism of Andrew Croswell," *William and Mary Quarterly*, 3d ser., 43, no. 2 (Apr. 1986): 224.

22. Fish quoted in William B. Sprague, ed., *Annals of the American Pulpit*, vol. 3 (New York, 1868), 88; cited in Robert Brockway, *A Wonderful Work of God: Puritanism and the Great Awakening* (Bethlehem, Pa., 2003), 152–53; James Davenport, *A Letter from the Rev. Mr. Davenport* ([Philadelphia, 1744]), 3–4, 7–8, 11.

23. *Two Letters from the Reverend Mr. Williams and Wheelock* (Boston, 1744), 6, 23, 27. 29.

24. James Davenport, *The Reverend Mr. Davenport's Confession and Retractions* (Boston, 1744), 3.

25. Ibid., 4–7; Timothy Hall, *Contested Boundaries: Itinerancy and the Reshaping of the Colonial American Religious World* (Durham, N.C., 1994), 96.

26. *An Impartial Examination of Mr. Davenport's Retractions* ([Boston, 1744]), 1–2, 8.

27. Benjamin Colman, *A Letter from the Reverend Dr. Colman of Boston* (Boston, 1744), 3–5, 7; James Davenport to [Solomon Williams], Aug. 30, 1744, Mss. 71042, CHS.

28. Colman, *Letter*, 4; see also *An Impartial Examination*, 3; Eugene White, "Decline of the Great Awakening in New England: 1741 to 1746," *New England Quarterly* 24, no. 1 (Mar. 1951): 46; DNG, 326.

29. DDR, May 25, 1744.

30. DNG, 299; DDR, June 14, 1744.

31. *BEP*, July 30, 1744, Aug. 6, 1744; *BG*, July 24, 1744; Erik Seeman, *Pious Persuasions: Laity and Clergy in Eighteenth-Century New England* (Baltimore, 1999), 133–38.

32. *BEP*, July 30, 1744, Aug. 6, 1744; *BG*, July 24, 1744.

33. *BEP*, July 30, 1744, Aug. 6, 1744; *BG*, July 24, 1744. Backus quote in Seeman, *Pious Persuasions*, 138.

34. DDR, Oct. 27, 1744; *BEP*, Nov. 19, 1744. On Whitefield's return, see *George Whitefield's Journals* (Carlisle, Pa., 1960), 516–18.

35. Charles Chauncy, *Ministers Exhorted and Encouraged* (Boston, 1744), 37–38; also in *BEP*, Dec. 3, 1744.

36. *Whitefield's Journals*, 542.

37. Andrew Eliot to Richard Salter, Apr. 15, 1745, Gratz American Colonial Clergy, 8/22, HSP; George Whitefield to Mr.——, Jan. 18, 1745, in George Whitefield, *The Works of George Whitefield*, 6 vols. (London, 1771–72), 2:72–73.

38. Harvard College, *The Testimony* (Boston, 1744), 3–4, 15.

39. Yale College, *The Declaration of the Rector and Tutors* (Boston, 1745), 4, 10, 12, 14.

40. William Shurtleff, *A Letter to Those of His Brethren* (Boston, 1745), 22; *The Testimony of a Number of Ministers Conven'd at Taunton, in the County of Bristol* (Boston, 1745), 3, 10. Anti-Whitefield resolutions included *Some Reasons Given by the Western Association upon Merrimack River* (Boston, 1745); *The Sentiments and Resolutions of an Association of Ministers* (Boston, 1745); *The Declaration of Ministers in Barnstable County* (Boston, 1745); *A Letter from Two Neighboring Associations of Ministers in the Country, to the Associated Ministers of Boston and Charlestown* (Boston, 1745); *The Testimony of an Association of Ministers Convened at Marlborough* (Boston, 1745); *The Testimony of the North Association in the County of Hartford* (Boston, 1745); *The Declaration of the Association of the County of New-Haven* (Boston, 1745).

41. A *Vindication of the Reverend Mr. Whitefield* (Boston, 1745), 3–4, 13–14.

42. DDR, Feb. 8, 1745; *Whitefield's Journals*, 551; George Whitefield, letter, July 29, 1745, in Luke Tyerman, *The Life of the Rev. George Whitefield* (London, 1877), 2:150–51.On the Louisbourg campaign, see Robert E. Wall, Jr., "Louisbourg, 1745," *New England Quarterly* 37, no. 1 (Mar. 1964): 64–83; Nathan O. Hatch, "The Origins of Civil Millennialism in America: New England Clergymen, the War with France, and the Revolution," *William and Mary Quarterly*, 3d ser., 31, no. 3 (July 1974): 417; Marsden, *Jonathan Edwards*, 310–14; Kidd, *Protestant Interest*, 138.

43. Thomas Prince, *Extraordinary Events the Doings of God* (Boston, 1745), 34–35; Charles Chauncy, *Marvellous Things Done by the Right Hand and Holy Arm of God* (Boston, 1745), 22.

44. Joshua Hempstead, *Diary of Joshua Hempstead* (New London, Conn., 1901), 447; Tyerman, *Life of the Rev. George Whitefield*, 2:152–53.

CHAPTER 12. "THE GOSPEL
IS NOT PREACHED HERE"

1. C. C. Goen, *Revivalism and Separatism in New England, 1740–1800: Strict Congregationalists and Separate Baptists in the Great Awakening* (repr. Middletown, Conn., 1987), 302–27.

2. DDR, Feb. 3, 1742. Pickering's letter also published in *The Rev. Mr. Pickering's Letters to the Rev. N. Rogers and Mr. D. Rogers* (Boston, 1742).

3. Pickering, *Rev. Mr. Pickering's Letters*, 4, 6.

4. DDR, Mar. 15–16, 1742; Pickering, *Rev. Mr. Pickering's Letters*, 8–9, 18.

5. Andrew Croswell to Nathaniel and Daniel Rogers, Sept. 23, 1742, Gratz American Colonial Clergy, 8/22, HSP.

6. A *Plain Narrative of the Proceedings Which Caused the Separation* (Boston, 1747), 5–7, 11–12; Theophilus Pickering, *Mr. Pickering's Letter to Mr. Whitefield* (Boston, 1745); DDR, May 9, 1746; Christopher Jedrey, *The World of John Cleaveland: Family and Community in Eighteenth-Century New England* (New York, 1979), 49–50.

7. Thomas Clap, et al., *The Judgment of the Rector and Tutors of Yale College* (New London, Conn., 1745), in Stephen Nissenbaum, ed., *The Great Awakening at Yale College* (Belmont, Calif., 1972), 226.

8. Jedrey, *World of John Cleaveland*, 40–46, 50–51; Leigh Eric Schmidt, "'A Second and Glorious Reformation': The New Light Extremism of Andrew Croswell," *William and Mary Quarterly*, 3d ser., 43, no. 2 (Apr. 1986): 226.

9. Theophilus Pickering, *A Bad Omen to the Churches of New-England* (Boston, 1747), 3; *Plain Narrative*, 13–15; Anne S. Brown, "Visions of Community in Eighteenth-Century Essex County: Chebacco Parish and the Great Awakening," *Essex Institute Historical Collections* 125, no. 3 (1989): 260–62; Jedrey, *John Cleaveland*, 55.

10. Goen, *Revivalism and Separatism*, 36–67; James F. Cooper, *Tenacious of their Liberties: The Congregationalists in Colonial Massachusetts* (New York, 1999), 201–5.

11. Isaac Backus, *A History of New England with Particular Reference to the Denomination of Christians Called Baptists* (repr. Paris, Ark., 2001), 2:64–66; Goen, *Revivalism and Separatism*, 116–18.

12. Backus, *History of New England*, 2:66–68; Goen, *Revivalism and Separatism*, 117–18; BG, Dec. 16, 1742, quoted in Goen, *Revivalism and Separatism*, 71.

13. Goen, *Revivalism and Separatism*, 72–75, 119; Joseph Bacon and Benjamin Smith deposition, Dec. 26, 1744, James Terry Collection, CHS.

14. Windham County Ministerial Association, *A Letter from the Associated Ministers* (Boston, 1745), 3–5.

15. Windham Association, *Letter*, 7–14; Goen, *Revivalism and Separatism*, 119–21.

16. Nathaniel French to Eleazar Wheelock, Aug. 13, 1744, no. 744463, PEW; Douglas L. Winiarski, "Souls Filled with Ravishing Transport: Heavenly Visions and the Radical Awakening in New England," *William and Mary Quarterly*, 3d ser., 61, no. 1 (Jan. 2004): 38.

17. John W. Jeffries, "The Separation in the Canterbury Congregational Church: Religion, Family, and Politics in a Connecticut Town," *New England Quarterly* 52, no. 4 (Dec. 1979): 549; Earnest E. Eells, "Indian Missions on Long Island," in Gaynell Stone, ed., *The History and Archaeology of the Montauk* (Stony Brook, N.Y., 1993), 182–83.

18. Solomon Paine to the Canterbury Separate Church, July 7, 1746, in James Terry Collection, CHS.

19. Solomon Paine, *A Short View of the Difference* (Newport, R.I., 1752), 9–11.

20. Simon Dakin et al. to Solomon Paine, Mar. 22, 1747, James Terry Collection, CHS; Goen, *Revivalism and Separatism*, 109–10.

21. Lord quoted in J. M. Bumsted, "Revivalism and Separatism in New England: The First Society of Norwich, Connecticut, as a Case Study," *William and Mary Quarterly*, 3d ser., 24, no. 4 (Oct. 1967): 600.

22. Bumsted, "Revivalism and Separatism," 602–4, 607–8; Norwich Separates' reasons for separation, in Frederic Denison, *Notes of the Baptists, and Their Principles, in Norwich, Conn.* (Norwich, 1857), 21–22, 24–26, reprinted in Richard Bushman, ed., *The Great Awakening: Documents on the Revival of Religion, 1740–1745* (repr. Chapel Hill, N.C., 1989), 102–3. There is confusion as to whether Hide was ordained in 1746 or 1747, but there seems to be no reason why they would have waited until 1747. William McLoughlin, ed., *The Diary of Isaac Backus* (Providence, R.I., 1979), 1:7 n12.

23. Isaac Backus, "Reasons of Separation" [1756?], in McLoughlin, ed., *Diary of Isaac Backus*, 3:1528; Samuel Finley to Joseph Bellamy, Sept. 20, 1745, Richard Webster transcription, Joseph Bellamy Papers, PHS; McLoughlin, ed., *Diary of Isaac Backus*, 1:12; Goen, *Revivalism and Separatism*, 217–28.

24. Bridgewater and Middleborough Church to Canterbury Church, Apr. 1, 1748, James Terry Collection, CHS; Isaac Backus to Benjamin Wallin, Nov. 16, 1764, no. 2695, PIB; McLoughlin, ed., *Diary of Isaac Backus*, 1:37–39; William McLoughlin, *Isaac Backus and the American Pietistic Tradition* (Boston, 1967), 42–43.

25. McLoughlin, ed., *Diary of Isaac Backus*, 1:67 n1.

26. Goen, *Revivalism and Separatism*, 208–9; Stanley Grenz, *Isaac Backus—Puritan and Baptist* (Macon, Ga., 1983), 70–71.

27. McLoughlin, ed., *Diary of Isaac Backus*, 1:68.

28. Ibid., 1:143, 147–48.

29. Council at Bridgewater and Middleborough, Oct. 2, 1751, James Terry Collection, CHS; McLoughlin, *Isaac Backus*, 82; Goen, *Revivalism and Separatism*, 219–21.

30. Council at Bridgewater and Middleborough, Oct. 2, 1751, James Terry Collection, CHS; Ebene-

zer Frothingham to Solomon Paine, Nov. 23, 1752, James Terry Collection, CHS; Goen, *Revivalism and Separatism*, 127–28, 219–21, 262–64; McLoughlin, *Isaac Backus*, 82–84; Backus, *History of New England*, 2:113–15.

31. Goen, *Revivalism and Separatism*, 92–93.

32. Joseph Fish to Joseph Sewall, [after Sept. 18, 1765], in William S. and Cheryl L. Simmons, eds., *Old Light on Separate Ways: The Narragansett Diary of Joseph Fish, 1765–1776* (Hanover, N.H., 1982), 5; William S. Simmons, "Red Yankees: Narragansett Conversion in the Great Awakening," *American Ethnologist* 10, no. 2 (May 1983): 262–63; Goen, *Revivalism and Separatism*, 90–91.

33. John Sparks, *The Roots of Appalachian Christianity: The Life and Legacy of Elder Shubal Stearns* (Lexington, Ky., 2001), 29–30, 43.

34. Sparks, *Shubal Stearns*, 50–51, 63; William B. Sprague, ed., *Annals of the American Pulpit*, vol. 6 (New York, 1865), 59–60.

CHAPTER 13. "BRINGING THEM TO A SUBJECTION TO THE RELIGION OF JESUS"

1. Benjamin Colman to George Whitefield, June 3, 1742, in *Glasgow-Weekly-History* (1743), in *Proceedings of the Massachusetts Historical Society* 53 (1920): 215; Ebenezer Pemberton to Eleazar Wheelock, Nov. 18, 1758, no. 758618, PEW; Kristina Bross, *Dry Bones and Indian Sermons: Praying Indians in Colonial America* (Ithaca, N.Y., 2004), 27; Daniel R. Mandell, *Behind the Frontier: Indians in Eighteenth-Century Eastern Massachusetts* (Lincoln, Neb., 1996), 2–3, 5–6; Laura Stevens, *The Poor Indians: British Missionaries, Native Americans, and Colonial Sensibility* (Philadelphia, 2004), 16–18, 141–42.

2. Joanna Brooks, *American Lazarus: Religion and the Rise of African-American and Native American Literatures* (New York, 2003), 22–25, 57–59; Jean F. Hankins, "Bringing the Good News: Protestant Missionaries to the Indians of New England and New York, 1700–1775," (Ph.D. diss., University of Connecticut, 1993), 1:167–69.

3. Franklin B. Dexter, *Biographical Sketches of the Graduates of Yale College* (New York, 1885), 536–37; John Strong and Zsuzsanna Török, "Taking the Middle Way: Algonquian Responses to the Reverend Azariah Horton's Mission on Long Island, 1741–1744," *Long Island Historical Journal* 12, no. 2 (1999): 147.

4. *Christian Monthly History* (1744) 5:6–7.

5. "Journal of Azariah Horton," reprinted in Gaynell Stone, ed., *The History and Archaeology of the Montauk*, 2d ed. (Stony Brook, N.Y., 1993), 195–96, 198–99.

6. Strong and Török, "Taking the Middle Way," 153; "Journal of Azariah Horton," 195–96.

7. "Journal of Azariah Horton," 202–3.

8. Ibid., 209, 213; Azariah Horton to the President of the SSPCK, Nov. 19, 1743, in Stone, ed., *History and Archaeology*, 216; Earnest E. Eells, "Indian Missions on Long Island," in Stone, ed., *History and Archaeology*, 174; Jonathan Edwards, *The Life of David Brainerd*, ed. Norman Pettit, vol. 7 of *The Works of Jonathan Edwards* (New Haven, Conn., 1985), 59.

9. Samuel Hopkins, *Historical Memoirs, relating to the Housatunnuk Indians* (Boston, 1753), 4, 166; Patrick Frazier, *The Mohicans of Stockbridge* (Lincoln, Neb., 1992), 17–19; Rachel M. Wheeler, "Living upon Hope: Mahicans and Missionaries, 1730–1760," (Ph.D. dissertation, Yale University,

1998), 47–59; David J. Silverman, "Indians, Missionaries, and Religious Translation: Creating Wampanoag Christianity in Seventeenth-Century Martha's Vineyard," *William and Mary Quarterly*, 3d ser., 62, no. 2 (Apr. 2005): 172–73.

10. Benjamin Colman to John Sergeant, June 18, 1735, in Hopkins, *Historical Memoirs*, 30, also 32–33, 39, 54; Frazier, *Mohicans*, 29–31, 36; Wheeler, "Mahicans and Missionaries," 59; Thomas S. Kidd, *The Protestant Interest: New England after Puritanism* (New Haven, Conn., 2004), 42–50.

11. John Sergeant to Stephen Williams, Nov. 24, 1741, in Gratz American Colonial Clergy, 8/24, HSP; John Sergeant to George Drummond, Apr. 29, 1741, John Sergeant to George Drummond, June 23, 1741, in Hopkins, *Historical Memoirs*, 88–91; John Sergeant, *The Causes and Danger of Delusions* (Boston, 1743); Wheeler, "Mahicans and Missionaries," 70–71; Frazier, *Mohicans*, 49–51; George M. Marsden, *Jonathan Edwards: A Life* (New Haven, Conn., 2003), 379.

12. John Sergeant, *A Letter from the Revd Mr. Sergeant of Stockbridge, to Dr. Colman of Boston* (Boston, 1743), 5, 7; Hopkins, *Historical Memoirs*, 107–8, 115, 121–23, 129–30; Wheeler, "Mahicans and Missionaries," 71–72.

13. Marsden, *Jonathan Edwards*, 341–74.

14. Ibid., 375–94; Gerald McDermott, "Jonathan Edwards and American Indians: The Devil Sucks Their Blood," *New England Quarterly* 72, no. 4 (Dec. 1999): 539–57; Rachel Wheeler, "'Friends to Your Souls': Jonathan Edwards' Indian Pastorate and the Doctrine of Original Sin," *Church History* 72, no. 4: (Dec. 2003): 736–65.

15. Jonathan Edwards to Thomas Hubbard, Aug. 31, 1751, Edwards to William Pepperrell, Nov. 28, 1751, in Jonathan Edwards, *Letters and Personal Writings* ed. George Claghorn, vol. 16 of *The Works of Jonathan Edwards* (New Haven, Conn., 1998), 400–401, 408, 413; Frazier, *Mohicans*, 94–95; Marsden, *Jonathan Edwards*, 389.

16. Frazier, *Mohicans*, 99–102; Marsden, *Jonathan Edwards*, 395–405; Jonathan Edwards to Andrew Oliver, Feb. 18, 1752, Jonathan Edwards to Andrew Oliver, May 1752, in Edwards, *Letters and Personal Writings*, 425, 472; William B. Sprague, ed., *Annals of the American Pulpit*, vol. 1 (New York, 1969), 498.

17. Joseph Conforti, *Jonathan Edwards, Religious Tradition, and American Culture* (Chapel Hill, N.C., 1995), 63; Edwards, *Life of David Brainerd*, 38–42, 153.

18. Edwards, *Life of David Brainerd*, 41–42, 51–52, 195; David Brainerd to Joseph Bellamy, Feb. 4, 1743, in Joseph Bellamy Papers, Richard Webster transcription, PHS; Henry W. Bowden, *American Indians and Christian Missions: Studies in Cultural Conflict* (Chicago, 1981), 152.

19. Hopkins, *Historical Memoirs*, 61; Edwards, *Life of David Brainerd*, 211, 217–20; David Brainerd to Joseph Bellamy, Mar. 26, 1743, Richard Webster transcription, Joseph Bellamy Papers, PHS.

20. Edwards, *Life of David Brainerd*, 245, 262–63.

21. Ibid., 338; David Brainerd to Ebenezer Pemberton, Nov. 5, 1743, in Edwards, *Life of David Brainerd*, 579–80; Gregory E. Dowd, *A Spirited Resistance: The North American Indian Struggle for Unity, 1745–1815* (Baltimore, 1992), 30.

22. Edwards, *Life of David Brainerd*, 307–8, 318; Bowden, *American Indians and Christian Missions*, 154–55; Richard W. Pointer, "'Poor Indians' and the 'Poor in Spirit': The Indian Impact on David Brainerd," *New England Quarterly* 67, no. 3 (Sept. 1994): 417; James Merrell, *Into the American Woods: Negotiators on the Pennsylvania Frontier* (New York, 1999), 86–87; Jane T. Merritt, *At the Crossroads: Indians and Empires on a Mid-Atlantic Frontier, 1700–1763* (Chapel Hill, N.C., 2003), 94.

23. David Brainerd, *Mirabilia Dei inter Indicos* (Philadelphia, [1746]), 75; Pointer, "Poor Indians," 423; Edwards, *Life of David Brainerd*, 369–71, 503–4.

24. Edwards, *Life of David Brainerd*, 324, 326–27.

25. Ibid., 329–30; Peter Mancall, *Deadly Medicine: Indians and Alcohol in Early America* (Ithaca, N.Y., 1995), 115–16; Ava Chamberlain, "The Execution of Moses Paul: A Story of Crime and Contact in Eighteenth-Century Connecticut," *New England Quarterly* 77, no. 3 (Sept. 2004): 420–21; Dowd, *Spirited Resistance*, 27, 29.

26. Edwards, *Life of David Brainerd*, 338, 360–61.

27. Ibid., 430n3, 474; Marsden, *Jonathan Edwards*, 326–29.

28. David Brainerd to John Brainerd, [1747], in Edwards, *Life of David Brainerd*, 498; Edwards, *Life of David Brainerd*, 442.

29. John Brainerd to Elizabeth Smith, Aug. 24, 1761, in William Sprague, ed., *Annals of the American Pulpit*, vol. 3 (New York, 1868), 150, cited in Thomas Brainerd, *The Life of John Brainerd* (Philadelphia, [1865]), 107–8; John Brainerd to Ebenezer Pemberton, June 23, 1747, in Brainerd, *Life of John Brainerd*, 116.

30. John Brainerd, diary, Sept. 10, Oct. 27, 1749, in Brainerd, *Life of John Brainerd*, 179, 212; James Davenport to Jonathan Edwards, Apr. 26, 1751, copied in Jonathan Edwards to John Erskine, June 28, 1751, in Jonathan Edwards, *Letters and Personal Writings*, ed. George Claghorn, vol. 16 of *The Works of Jonathan Edwards* (New Haven, Conn., 1998), 378; John Brainerd to Ezra Stiles, July 19, 1751, in the Papers of Ezra Stiles, Beinecke Library, Yale University; Robert E. Cray, Jr., "James Davenport's Post-Bonfire Ministry, 1743–1757," *Historian* 59, no. 1 (Fall 1996): 69–71.

31. John Brainerd, diary, Oct. 12, 1749, in Brainerd, *Life of John Brainerd*, 196–98, 207; on Moravians' conversion theology, Jon Sensbach, *A Separate Canaan: The Making of an Afro-Moravian World in North Carolina, 1763–1840* (Chapel Hill, N.C., 1998), 110–12; Craig Atwood, *Community of the Cross: Moravian Piety in Colonial Bethlehem* (University Park, Pa., 2004), 48–50, also 110, 164–67 on communion theology.

32. John Brainerd to Ebenezer Pemberton, Aug. 30, 1751, in Brainerd, *Life of John Brainerd*, 233–34; Dowd, *Spirited Resistance*, 30.

33. John Brainerd to Ebenezer Pemberton, Aug. 30, 1751, in Brainerd, *Life of John Brainerd*, 235, 239–40, 242; Dowd, *Spirited Resistance*, 30.

34. John Brainerd to Ebenezer Pemberton, Aug. 30, 1751, in Brainerd, *Life of John Brainerd*, 246–47; John Brainerd, *A Genuine Letter from Mr. John Brainerd* (London, 1753), in Brainerd, *Life of John Brainerd*, 262; John Brainerd to Gideon Hawley, Apr. 19, 1753, in Joseph Bellamy Papers, Richard Webster transcription, PHS.

35. Jonathan Edwards to William McCulloch, Apr. 10, 1756, in Edwards, *Letters and Personal Writings*, 685; John Brainerd to Eleazar Wheelock, May 17, 1755, in Brainerd, *Life of John Brainerd*, 289; also 300, 307.

36. John Brainerd to Eleazar Wheelock, August 9, 1759, in Brainerd, *Life of John Brainerd*, 312; John Brainerd to Elizabeth Smith, Aug. 24, 1761, in Brainerd, *Life of John Brainerd*, 317; Eleazar Wheelock to George Whitefield, Nov. 3, 1759, no. 759603, PEW; John Brainerd to Eleazar Wheelock, Aug. 26, 1760, no. 760476, PEW; John Brainerd, *John Brainerd's Journal, 1761–1762* (Newark, N.J., 1941), 24; Fred Anderson, *Crucible of War: The Seven Years' War and the Fate of Empire in British North America* (New York, 2000), 500–501.

37. John Brainerd to Eleazar Wheelock, Sept. 14, 1761, in Brainerd, *Life of John Brainerd*, 334; Brain-

erd, *Brainerd's Journal*, 10, 17, 23; John Brainerd to Mrs. Smith, Aug. 24, 1761, Gratz American Clergy, 9/4, HSP.

38. Brainerd, *Brainerd's Journal*, 25–26; Brainerd, *Life of John Brainerd*, 339–40; John Brainerd to Eleazar Wheelock, June 6, 1763, in Brainerd, *Life of John Brainerd*, 341; John Brainerd to Eleazar Wheelock, Feb. 12, 1768, in Brainerd, *Life of John Brainerd*, 377; *Pennsylvania Gazette*, Sept. 15, 1763, cited in Gregory Dowd, *War under Heaven: Pontiac, the Indian Nations, and the British Empire* (Baltimore, 2002), 191; Merrell, *Into the American Woods*, 283.

39. John Brainerd to Eleazar Wheelock, June 22, 1769, Aug. 25, 1769, Dec. 25, 1772, in Brainerd, *Life of John Brainerd*, 383–84, 395; Thomas Rankin diary, in Brainerd, *Life of John Brainerd*, 404–5.

40. Jonathan Edwards to the Commissioners, Feb. 19, 1752, in Edwards, *Letters and Personal Writings*, 431; Gideon Hawley to Joseph Bellamy, Feb. 23, 1751, Joseph Bellamy Papers, Richard Webster transcription, PHS.

41. Gideon Hawley to Joseph Bellamy, Apr. 14, 1753, Feb. 14, 1757, in Joseph Bellamy Papers, Richard Webster transcription, PHS; Gideon Hawley, "A Letter from Rev. Gideon Hawley of Marshpee," *Collections of the Massachusetts Historical Society* 4 (1795): 55–57, 61–64; Gideon Hawley to [?], June 13, 1753, Hawley Papers, Congregational Library, Boston (microfilm).

42. Journal of Gideon Hawley, 1754, Hawley Papers, Congregational Library. First entry is after Jan. 23, 1754 but poor page quality prevents precise citation. Also Mar. 9, 1754, Apr. 7, 1754.

43. Gideon Hawley to Joseph Bellamy, Feb. 3, 1755, in Joseph Bellamy Papers, Richard Webster transcription, PHS; Sprague, ed., *Annals*, vol. 1, 498.

44. Gideon Hawley to Joseph Bellamy, Jan. 8, 1756, Feb. 14, 1757, Jan. 13, 1758, in Joseph Bellamy Papers, Richard Webster transcription, PHS; Journal of Gideon Hawley, Feb. 17, 1757, Hawley Papers, Congregational Library; Sprague, ed., *Annals*, vol. 1, 499; Jean Hankins, "Solomon Briant and Joseph Johnson: Indian Teachers and Preachers in Colonial New England," *Connecticut History* 33 (1992): 45–47.

45. Samson Occom, autobiography, in Stone, ed., *History and Archaeology*, 238; Eleazar Wheelock to George Whitefield, Nov. 25, 1761, no. 761625.1, PEW; Love, *Samson Occom*, 34; Brooks, *American Lazarus*, 56–57.

46. Eleazar Wheelock to George Whitefield, Mar. 11, 1756, no. 756201, PEW; Brooks, *American Lazarus*, 57; Bowden, *American Indians and Christian Missions*, 139–40.

47. Solomon Williams to Andrew Oliver, Apr. 16, 1750, no. 750266, PEW; Eleazar Wheelock, *A Plain and Faithful Narrative of the Original Design, Rise, Progress and Present State of the Indian Charity-School* (Boston, [1763]), 29; Love, *Samson Occom*, 42–44.

48. Samuel Buell and James Brown, letter of recommendation for Samson Occom, Mar. 21, 1758, no. 758221, PEW; Eleazar Wheelock to George Whitefield, July 30, 1758, no. 758430, PEW; Samuel Buell to David Bostwick, May 9, 1761, in Samuel Buell, *The Excellence and Importance of the Saving Knowledge* (New York, [1761]), vii–viii, xiii; Occom diary, in Stone, ed., *History and Archaeology*, 229; Love, *Samson Occom*, 51–52.

49. Buell, *Excellence and Importance*, 31; George Whitefield to Eleazar Wheelock, Mar. 7, 1759, no. 759207, PEW; Eleazar Wheelock to George Whitefield, Nov. 3, 1759, no. 759603, PEW; Eleazar Wheelock to John Smith, Sept. 15, 1761, no. 761515, PEW; Bross, *Dry Bones*, 13.

50. Eleazar Wheelock to Andrew Oliver, May 29, 1760, no. 760329, PEW; Occom diary, in Stone, *History and Archaeology*, 235; Samson Occom to Eleazar Wheelock, June 24, 1761, no. 761374, PEW; Love, *Samson Occom*, 85–86.

51. Eleazar Wheelock to Thomas Foxcroft, June 18, 1761, no. 761368.1, PEW; Eleazar Wheelock to Gideon Hawley, June 10, 1761, no. 761360.2, PEW; Journal of Gideon Hawley, Dec. 10, 1756, Hawley Papers, Congregational Library; Eleazar Wheelock to Samson Occom, May 27, 1761, Occom Papers, CHS; Love, *Samson Occom*, 74–76 .

52. Samson Occom to Eleazar Wheelock, Sept. 25, 1761, no. 761525, PEW; Gideon Hawley quoted in Samuel Hopkins to Eleazar Wheelock, Sept. 30, 1761, no. 761530, PEW; Eleazar Wheelock to George Whitefield, Nov. 25, 1761, no. 761625.1, PEW; George Whitefield to Eleazar Wheelock, Sept. 5, 1764, no. 764505, PEW; Samson Occom to Eleazar Wheelock, Sept. 8, 1764, no. 764508.3, PEW; Eleazar Wheelock to John Brainerd, Jan. 14, 1765, no. 765114.3, PEW; Love, *Samson Occom*, 92–98, 103–4.

53. Charles-Jeffrey Smith to Eleazar Wheelock, Mar. 30, 1764, no. 764230, PEW; Nathaniel Whitaker to Eleazar Wheelock, Dec. 18, 1765, no. 765668, PEW; Love, *Samson Occom*, 119, 130–51.

54. Brooks, *American Lazarus*, 51–52; Samson Occom confession, [1769?], Samson Occom letter [1784?], Occom Papers, CHS; Samson Occom to Eleazar Wheelock, Mar. 17, 1769, Gratz American Colonial Clergy, 8/24, HSP; "Gazing Stocke," Samson Occom to Eleazar Wheelock, July 24, 1771, PEW, no. 771424; Love, *Samson Occom*, 162–66.

55. Samson Occom to Eleazar Wheelock, Jan. 6, 1774, in Laura J. Murray, *"To Do Good to My Indian Brethren": The Writings of Joseph Johnson, 1751–1776* (Amherst, Mass., 1998), 205; Bowden, *American Indians*, 144–45.

CHAPTER 14. "ETHIOPIA SHALL STRETCH OUT HER HANDS UNTO GOD"

1. DDR, Apr. 30, 1743; BWPB, May 17, 1742, also in *American Weekly Mercury*, May 27, 1742; Charles Chauncy, *Seasonable Thoughts on the State of Religion in New-England* (Boston, 1743), 226.

2. Sylvia Frey and Betty Wood, *Come Shouting to Zion: African American Protestantism in the American South and British Caribbean to 1830* (Chapel Hill, N.C., 1998), xi.

3. Ibid., 35, 76–79.

4. Ibid., 82–83; Mechal Sobel, *Trabelin' On: The Slave Journey to an Afro-Baptist Faith* (Princeton, N.J., 1988), 100–101.

5. Quote from Johann J. Bossard, ed., *C. G. A. Oldendorp's History of the Mission of the Evangelical Brethren on the Caribbean Islands of St. Thomas, St. Croix, and St. John* (Ann Arbor, Mich., 1987, orig. pub., 1770), 322; cited in Jon F. Sensbach, *A Separate Canaan: The Making of an Afro-Moravian World in North Carolina, 1763–1840* (Chapel Hill, N.C., 1998), 33. On the founding of the Moravian missions, see Bossard, ed., *Oldendorp's History*, 269–396; Jon F. Sensbach, *Rebecca's Revival: Creating Black Christianity in the Atlantic World* (Cambridge, Mass., 2005), 45–68; Sensbach, *Separate Canaan*, 29–34.

6. Sensbach, *Separate Canaan*, 36–43; Frey and Wood, *Come Shouting to Zion*, 85–87.

7. Colman, *Souls Flying*, 24–25; William Cooper, *One Shall Be Taken, and Another Left* (Boston, 1741), 13. On white evangelicals' inclusion of blacks, Donald Mathews, *Religion in the Old South* (Chicago, 1977), 66–67; Christine L. Heyrman, *Southern Cross: The Beginnings of the Bible Belt* (New York, 1997), 46–52.

8. Diary of Joseph Bean, Bryn Mawr College Library, Special Collections, Dec. 2, 1741, Mar. 17,

1742; J. Richard Olivas, "Great Awakenings: Time, Space, and the Varieties of Religious Revivalism in Massachusetts and Northern New England, 1740–1748," (Ph.D. dissertation, University of California, Los Angeles, 1997), 395.

9. Jonathan Edwards, *A Faithful Narrative of the Surprizing Work of God* (London, 1737), in Edwards, *The Great Awakening*, ed. C. C. Goen, vol. 4 of *The Works of Jonathan Edwards* (New Haven, Conn., 1972), 159; Joanna Brooks, *American Lazarus: Religion and the Rise of African American and Native American Literatures* (New York, 2003), 24; George M. Marsden, *Jonathan Edwards: A Life* (New Haven, Conn., 2003), 257–58; Kenneth Minkema, "Jonathan Edwards's Defense of Slavery," *Massachusetts Historical Review* 4 (2002): 23–59; Kenneth Minkema and Harry S. Stout, "The Edwardsean Tradition and the Antislavery Debate, 1740–1865," *Journal of American History* 92, no. 1 (June 2005): 49–50.

10. Olwell, *Masters, Slaves, and Subjects*, 124; Calhoon, *Evangelicals and Conservatives*, 23–24; Alan Gallay, *The Formation of a Planter Elite: Jonathan Bryan and the Southern Colonial Frontier* (Athens, Ga., 1989), 49–50; Stephen Stein, "George Whitefield on Slavery: Some New Evidence," *Church History* 42, no. 2 (June 1973): 243–56.

11. Hugh Bryan to his sister, Feb. 5, 1741, in Hugh Bryan, *Living Christianity Delineated* (London, 1760), 14–15; Thomas Little, "The Rise of Evangelical Religion in South Carolina during the Eighteenth Century," (Ph.D. diss., Rice University, 1995), 211; Harvey Jackson, "Hugh Bryan and the Evangelical Movement in Colonial South Carolina," *William and Mary Quarterly*, 3d ser., 43, no. 4 (Oct. 1986): 605.

12. Eliza Lucas, letter to Miss Bartlett, [Mar. 1742], and "Memdam," Mar. 11, 1742, in Elise Pinckney, ed., *The Letterbook of Eliza Lucas Pinckney, 1739–1762* (Columbia, S.C., 1997), 29–30. Also Jackson, "Hugh Bryan," 607–8; Leigh Eric Schmidt, "The Grand Prophet, Hugh Bryan: Early Evangelicalism's Challenge to the Establishment and Slavery in the Colonial South," in Stanley Katz et al., eds., *Colonial America: Essays in Politics and Social Development*, 4th ed. (New York, 1993), 608–10.

13. *BWPB*, May 3, 1742; Schmidt, "Grand Prophet," 610; Gallay, *Formation of a Planter Elite*, 46–48; Jackson, "Hugh Bryan," 609–10.

14. Jonathan Barber to Daniel Rogers, Oct. 5, 1742, Gratz American Clergy, 9/3, HSP.

15. *SCG*, Apr. 17, 1742; Jackson, "Hugh Bryan," 611–12. Thomas Little has argued that the April 17 article was speaking more directly to the case of Joseph Moody, another Whitefield disciple who had been arrested for preaching to assemblies of slaves. Little, "Evangelical Religion in South Carolina," 216.

16. Kenneth S. Greenberg, ed., *The Confessions of Nat Turner and Related Documents* (Boston, 1996), 16–17. On the problem of finding authentic black voices in slave narratives, see Robert E. Desrochers, Jr., "'Not Fade Away': The Narrative of Venture Smith, an African American in the Early Republic," *Journal of American History* 84, no. 1 (June 1997): 43–44.

17. Ira Berlin, *Many Thousands Gone: The First Two Centuries of Slavery in North America* (Cambridge, Mass., 1998), 139–40; James Albert, *A Narrative of the Most Remarkable Particulars*, in Adam Potkay and Sandra Burr, eds., *Black Atlantic Writers of the Eighteenth Century: Living the New Exodus in England and the Americas* (New York, 1995), 28–35. There are reasons to doubt whether the minister that Gronniosaw called "Freelandhouse" was, in fact, Frelinghuysen. Gronniosaw indicated, for instance, that he was required to speak English to the minister, despite the

fact that Gronniosaw almost certainly spoke Dutch better than English. Potkay and Burr, as well as Frank Lambert, "'I Saw the Book Talk': Slave Readings of the First Great Awakening," *Journal of Negro History* 77, no. 4 (autumn 1992): 187, agree that it was Frelinghuysen.

18. Albert, *Narrative*, 35–45, quotes on 39.

19. Jupiter Hammon, *An Evening Thought* (n.p., 1760); Hammon, *An Address to Miss Phillis Wheatly* (Hartford, 1778); Sondra A. O'Neale, *Jupiter Hammon and the Biblical Beginnings of African American Literature* (Metuchen, N.J., 1993), 66–69. On the New Divinity's views of the providential purposes behind the slave trade see, John Saillant, "Slavery and Divine Providence in New England Calvinism: The New Divinity and a Black Protest, 1775–1805," *New England Quarterly* 68, no. 4 (Dec. 1995): 584–608.

20. Jupiter Hammon, *A Winter Piece* (Hartford, 1782), in Stanley A. Ransom, Jr., ed., *America's First Negro Poet: The Complete Works of Jupiter Hammon of Long Island* (Port Washington, N.Y., 1970), 69, 73; Phillip Richards, "Nationalist Themes in the Preaching of Jupiter Hammon," *Early American Literature* 25, no. 2 (1990): 125–28; O'Neale, *Jupiter Hammon*, 85–86; Charles Vertanes, "Jupiter Hammon: Early Negro Poet of Long Island," *Nassau County Historical Journal* 18, no. 1 (winter 1957): 2–5; Leslie Harris, *In the Shadow of Slavery: African Americans in New York City, 1626–1863* (Chicago, 2003), 66–67.

21. Jupiter Hammon, *An Address to the Negroes in the State of New-York* (New York, 1787), in Ransom, *America's First Negro Poet*, 112–13, 117.

22. Phillis Wheatley, "On the Death of the Rev. Mr. GEORGE WHITEFIELD. 1770," in Phillis Wheatley, *Poems on Various Subjects, Religious and Moral* (London, 1773), in John C. Shields, ed., *The Collected Works of Phillis Wheatley* (New York, 1988), 23; Charles W. Akers, "'Our Modern Egyptians': Phillis Wheatley and the Whig Campaign against Slavery in Revolutionary Boston," *Journal of Negro History* 60, no. 3 (July 1975): 397–98; James Rawley, "The World of Phillis Wheatley," *New England Quarterly* 50, no. 4 (Dec. 1977): 668.

23. Wheatley, "On being brought from AFRICA to AMERICA," in Shields, ed., *Collected Works*, 18; John Lathrop to ——, Aug. 14, 1773, Gratz American Clergy, 9/11, HSP; Akers, "Our Modern Egyptians," 400; Henry Louis Gates, Jr., *The Trials of Phillis Wheatley: America's First Black Poet and Her Encounters with the Founding Fathers* (New York, 2003), 34.

24. Thomas Jefferson, *Notes on the State of Virginia* (London, 1787), in David Waldstreicher, ed., *Notes on the State of Virginia* (Boston, 2002), 178; Rawley, "World of Phillis Wheatley," 673–74; Betsy Erkkila, "Phillis Wheatley and the Black American Revolution," in Frank Shuffelton, ed., *A Mixed Race: Ethnicity in Early America* (New York, 1993), 229; Gates, *Trials of Phillis Wheatley*, 42–44; Brooks, *American Lazarus*, 3–5.

25. Phillis Wheatley to Samson Occum, [Feb. 11, 1774], in Shields, ed., *Collected Works*, 176–77; Akers, "Our Modern Egyptians," 406–7.

26. Phillis Wheatley to Samuel Hopkins, Feb. 9, 1774, in Shields, ed., *Collected Works*, 175–76; Samuel Hopkins and Ezra Stiles, circular letter, Aug. 31, 1773, Joseph Bellamy Papers, CHS; also published in Hopkins and Stiles, *To the Public* (Newport, R.I., 1776); Rawley, "World of Phillis Wheatley," 674; Joseph Conforti, *Samuel Hopkins and the New Divinity Movement* (Washington, D.C., 1981), 143–46.

27. Philip Quaque to Samuel Hopkins, Aug. 30, 1773, extract, Joseph Bellamy Papers, CHS; Phillis Wheatley to Samuel Hopkins, May 6, 1774, Phillis Wheatley to John Thornton, Oct. 30, 1774, in

Shields, ed., *Collected Works*, 181–82, 182–84; Rawley, "World of Phillis Wheatley," 674; Conforti, *Samuel Hopkins*, 145–46; Lamin Sanneh, *Abolitionists Abroad: American Blacks and the Making of Modern West Africa* (Cambridge, Mass., 1999), 46.

28. John Rippon, "An Account of the Life of Mr. David George," *Baptist Annual Register for 1790, 1791, 1792, and part of 1793*, 473–76; Sanneh, *Abolitionists Abroad*, 74–75; Simon Schama, *Rough Crossings: Britain, the Slaves and the American Revolution* (New York, 2006), 94–98; Wood and Frey, *Come Shouting to Zion*, 116–17. On the case for "Brother" Palmer as Wait Palmer, see Grant Gordon, *From Slavery to Freedom: The Life of David George, Pioneer Black Baptist Minister* (Hantsport, Nova Scotia, 1992), 24–27.

There is considerable debate, especially among local church historians along the Savannah River, about which was the first, or the first continually operating, African American church. Historians of the Storm Branch Baptist Church of Clearwater, South Carolina, for instance, claim that it was founded before Silver Bluff, on July 9, 1772, though its early pastors were white Baptists. Thanks to Oscar L. Kemp, Deacon, Storm Branch Baptist Church, personal conversation with author, December 2002. See also Frank G. Roberson, Oscar L. Kemp et al., *Go Yonder and Pray: A Historical Account of the Storm Branch Baptist Church from 1772 to the Present* (Clearwater, S.C., 1994), 6–7. For the broader debate, see Frank G. Roberson and George H. Mosley, *Where a Few Gather in My Name: The History of the Oldest Black Church in America — The Silver Bluff Church* (North Augusta, S.C., 2002), ix–xi.

29. Rippon, "David George," 476–80; Sanneh, *Abolitionists Abroad*, 75–76; Schama, *Rough Crossings*, 239–43; Ellen G. Wilson, *The Loyal Blacks* (New York, 1976), 121–23; Gordon, *From Slavery to Freedom*, 60–62.

30. Rippon, "David George," 480–83; Sanneh, *Abolitionists Abroad*, 76–80; Mark Noll, "Evangelical Identity, Power, and Culture in the "Great" Nineteenth Century," in Donald Lewis, ed., *Christianity Reborn: The Global Expansion of Evangelicalism in the Twentieth Century* (Grand Rapids, Mich., 2004), 37–38.

31. John Marrant, *A Narrative of the Lord's Wonderful Dealings with John Marrant, A Black*, 4th ed. (London, 1785), in Joanna Brooks and John Saillant, eds., *"Face Zion Forward": First Writers of the Black Atlantic, 1785–1798* (Boston, 2002), 50–52; John Saillant, "'Wipe Away All Tears from Their Eyes': John Marrant's Theology in the Black Atlantic, 1785–1808," *Journal of Millennial Studies* 1, no. 2 (winter 1999): 2, at http://www.mille.org/publications/journal.html; Peter Wood, "'Jesus Christ Has Got Thee at Last': Afro-American Conversion as a Forgotten Chapter in Eighteenth-Century Southern Intellectual History," *Bulletin of the Center for the Study of Southern Culture and Religion* 3, no. 3 (Nov. 1979): 1–2.

32. Marrant, *Narrative*, 52–67, quote 53.

33. Ibid., 68–70; Brooks and Saillant, "A Note on the Texts," in *"Face Zion Forward,"* 39; Saillant, "John Marrant's Theology," 3–4; Benilde Montgomery, "Recapturing John Marrant," in Shuffelton, ed., *Mixed Race*, 107–8; Joanna Brooks, "John Marrant's Journal: Providence and Prophecy in the Eighteenth Century Atlantic," *North Star: A Journal of African American Religious History* 3, no. 1 (fall 1999): 1.

34. Brooks, "John Marrant's Journal," 6; George Rawlyk, *Ravished by the Spirit: Religious Revivals, Baptists, and Henry Alline* (Kingston, Ont., 1984), 80–81.

35. John Marrant, *A Journal of the Rev. John Marrant* (London, 1790), in Brooks and Saillant, eds., *"Face Zion Forward,"* 104, 109; Brooks, "John Marrant's Journal," 1.

36. Saillant, "John Marrant's Theology," 15–16.

37. Mathews, *Religion in the Old South*, 68–69; David Brion Davis, *The Problem of Slavery in the Age of Revolution, 1770–1823*, rev. ed. (New York, 1999), 203–12; Jon Butler, *Awash in a Sea of Faith: Christianizing the American People* (Cambridge, Mass., 1990), 150–51; Philippe Rosenberg, "Thomas Tryon and the Seventeenth-Century Dimensions of Antislavery," *William and Mary Quarterly*, 3d ser., 61, no. 4 (Oct. 2004): 620–22.

38. Samuel Hopkins, *An Inquiry into the Nature of True Holiness* (Newport, R.I., 1773), 11; cited in Conforti, *Samuel Hopkins*, 117; David S. Lovejoy, "Samuel Hopkins: Religion, Slavery, and the Revolution," *New England Quarterly* 40, no. 2 (June 1967): 233–34. On Edwards and virtue, see Marsden, *Jonathan Edwards*, 467–71.

39. Samuel Hopkins to John Erskine, Dec. 28, 1774, Gratz American Colonial Clergy, 8/23, HSP; Conforti, *Samuel Hopkins*, 126–27; William G. McLoughlin, *Rhode Island: A History* (New York, 1986), 63–65, 106; Jonathan Sassi, ed., "'This whole country have their hands full of Blood this day': Transcription and Introduction of an Antislavery Sermon Manuscript Attributed to the Reverend Samuel Hopkins," *Proceedings of the American Antiquarian Society* 112, part 1 (2004): 49; Minkema and Stout, "Edwardsean Tradition," 50–61.

40. Samuel Hopkins to Stephen West, June 23, 1780, Gratz American Clergy, 9/10, HSP; Levi Hart, *Liberty Described and Recommended* (Hartford, Conn., 1775), 8, 16, 20; Hart's emancipation proposal is printed in John Saillant, ed., "'Some Thoughts on the Subject of Freeing the Negro Slaves in the Colony of Connecticut, Humbly Offered to the Consideration of all Friends to Liberty & Justice,' by Levi Hart, with a Response from Samuel Hopkins," *New England Quarterly* 75, no. 1 (2002): 107–28.

41. Samuel Hopkins, *Dialogue Concerning the Slavery of the Africans*, 2d ed. (New York, 1785), in *The Works of Samuel Hopkins* (repr. New York, 1987), 2:549–50; Conforti, *Samuel Hopkins*, 128–29.

42. Hopkins, *Dialogue*, 556–57, 585; Sassi, ed., "Antislavery Sermon Manuscript," 71.

43. Ruth Bogin, ed., "'Liberty Further Extended': A 1776 Antislavery Manuscript by Lemuel Haynes," *William and Mary Quarterly*, 3d ser., 40, no. 1 (Jan. 1983): 85–87, 90; John Saillant, *Black Puritan, Black Republican: The Life and Thought of Lemuel Haynes, 1753–1833* (New York, 2003), 9–15; Richard D. Brown, "'Not Only Extreme Poverty, but the Worst Kind of Orphanage': Lemuel Haynes and the Boundaries of Racial Tolerance on the Yankee Frontier, 1770–1820," *New England Quarterly* 61, no. 4 (Dec. 1988): 505–8, 515–16.

44. Bogin, ed., "Liberty Further Extended," 94–95, 98; Saillant, *Black Puritan*, 17.

45. *The Constitutional Whig*, Sept. 26, 1831, in Greenberg, *Confessions of Nat Turner*, 80.

46. Black church membership number from Heyrman, *Southern Cross*, 46.

CHAPTER 15. "DO THE HOLY SCRIPTURES
COUNTENANCE SUCH WILD DISORDER?"

1. Samuel Davies, *State of Religion among the Protestant Dissenters in Virginia* (Boston, 1751), 8–11; Petition of Some of the Clergy to the House of Burgesses, n.d., in William S. Perry, ed., *Historical Collections Relating to the American Colonial Church* (Hartford, Conn., 1870), 381; Wesley Gewehr, *The Great Awakening in Virginia, 1740–1790* (Durham, N.C., 1930), 47–50.

2. Davies, *State of Religion*, 12–14; Gewehr, *Great Awakening in Virginia*, 50–54.

3. Davies, *State of Religion*, 14–17; Gewehr, *Great Awakening in Virginia*, 53–58; Leigh Eric

Schmidt, *Holy Fairs: Scotland and the Making of American Revivalism*, 2d ed. (Grand Rapids, Mich., 2001), 56–57.

4. Patrick Henry to William Dawson, Feb. 13, 1745, in William Dawson Papers, Library of Congress.

5. Patrick Henry to William Dawson, Feb. 13, 1745, in William Dawson Papers, Library of Congress; also cited in Dan Hockman, "Hellish and Malicious Incendiaries": Commisary William Dawson and Dissent in Colonial Virginia, 1743–1752," *Anglican and Episcopal History* 59, no. 2 (June 1990): 158; Rhys Isaac, *The Transformation of Virginia, 1740–1790* (Chapel Hill, N.C., 1982), 150.

6. George W. Pilcher, *Samuel Davies: Apostle of Dissent in Colonial Virginia* (Knoxville, Tenn., 1971), 11–13; Patrick Henry to [William Dawson], June 8, 1747, William Dawson Papers, Library of Congress.

7. John Caldwell, *An Impartial Trial of the Spirit* (Williamsburg, Va., 1747), vii; Samuel Davies, *The Impartial Trial Impartially Tried* (Williamsburg, Va., 1748), 4; Gewehr, *Great Awakening in Virginia*, 71.

8. Davies, *Impartial Trial*, 26, 34, 36; Gewehr, *Great Awakening in Virginia*, 82–85.

9. Davies, *Impartial Trial*, "Appendix," 4; Samuel Davies to the Bishop of London, Jan. 10, 1752, in William H. Foote, *Sketches of Virginia, Historical and Biographical*, vol. 1 (Philadelphia, 1850), 191.

10. Davies, *State of Religion*, 22, 28; Samuel Davies to Joseph Bellamy, July 4, 1751, Samuel Davies to Joseph Bellamy, July 13, 1751, James Davenport to Joseph Bellamy, May 29, 1753, Joseph Bellamy Papers, PHS; Gewehr, *Great Awakening in Virginia*, 89–90.

11. Davies, *State of Religion*, 23–24.

12. Samuel Davies to R.C. [Robert Crutenden], Mar. 1755, in "Attempts to Evangelize the Negroe-slaves in Virginia and Carolina, from 1747 to 1755," *Evangelical and Literary Magazine and Missionary Chronicle* (Oct. 1821): 540–41; "Journal of Col. James Gordon, of Lancaster County, Va.," *William and Mary College Quarterly Historical Magazine* 11, no. 2 (Oct. 1902): 109; Mechal Sobel, *The World They Made Together: Black and White Values in Eighteenth-Century Virginia* (Princeton, N.J., 1987), 184–86.

13. Samuel Davies to John Wesley, Jan. 28, 1757, in *The Journal of the Rev. John Wesley* (London, 1938), 194–95; Samuel Davies to R. C., Mar. 1755, in "Attempts to Evangelize the Negroe-slaves," 541; Samuel Davies to J. F., Mar. 2, 1756, in *Letters from the Rev. Samuel Davies*, 2d ed. (London, 1757), 16, 18; Samuel Davies to Joseph Bellamy, Feb. 23, 1757, in *Evangelical and Literary Magazine* (Nov. 1823): 568–69; Sobel, *World They Made Together*, 183–87.

14. Samuel Davies to J.F., Mar. 2, 1756, Samuel Davies to the Rev. Mr. F——, Feb. 7, 1757, "Extract of a Letter from a Gentleman in Town," in *Letters of Samuel Davies*, 19, 28, 30–31, 43; Pilcher, *Samuel Davies*, 110–11; Schmidt, *Holy Fairs*, 57.

15. Samuel Davies, *The Duty of Christians to Propagate Their Religion among Heathens* (London, 1758), 13; Edwin Conway to [William Dawson], Mar. 3, 1758, in William Dawson Papers, Library of Congress; Benjamin Fawcett, *A Compassionate Address to the Christian Negroes in Virginia* (Salop, Eng., 1756), 31, 35; Gewehr, *Great Awakening in Virginia*, 96.

16. Samuel Davies, *Religion and Patriotism the Constituents of a Good Soldier* (Philadelphia, 1755), 22; John Wright to the Publisher, Aug. 18, 1755, in "Attempts to Evangelize the Negroe-slaves," 551.

17. John Wright to Joseph Bellamy, Nov. 7, 1761, Joseph Bellamy Papers, PHS.

18. David Currie and John Leland to [William Dawson], Apr. 12, 1758, William Dawson Papers, Library of Congress; Gewehr, *Great Awakening in Virginia*, 93–95.

19. Devereux Jarratt, *The Life of the Reverend Devereux Jarratt* (repr. New York, 1969, orig. pub., 1806), 31, 49.

20. Ibid., 56, 85–86, 96–97; Devereux Jarratt, *A Brief Narrative of the Revival of Religion in Virginia* (London, 1778), 3.

21. Jarratt, *Brief Narrative*, 8–11; Gewehr, *Great Awakening in Virginia*, 143–52.

22. Jarratt, *Brief Narrative*, 12, 15, 17–18; Gewehr, *Great Awakening in Virginia*, 152–55; David Bebbington, *Evangelicalism in Modern Britain: A History from the 1730s to the 1980s* (Grand Rapdis, Mich., 1992), 45–50.

23. Thomas Rankin diary excerpted in Jarratt, *Brief Narrative*, 30–32; Gewehr, *Great Awakening in Virginia*, 151; John H. Wigger, *Taking Heaven by Storm: Methodism and the Rise of Popular Christianity in America* (New York, 1998), 114; Sylvia R. Frey and Betty Wood, *Come Shouting to Zion: African American Protestantism in the American South and British Caribbean to 1830* (Chapel Hill, N.C., 1998), 107–12.

24. Jarratt, *Life*, 107; Richard R. Beeman, "Social Change and Cultural Conflict in Virginia: Lunenberg County, 1746 to 1774, *William and Mary Quarterly*, 3d ser., 35, no. 3 (July 1978): 468.

25. Morgan Edwards, *Materials Towards a History of the Baptists*, ed. Eva Weeks and Mary Warren (Danielsville, Ga., 1984), 2:36–37; William L. Lumpkin, *Baptist Foundations in the South: Tracing through the Separates the Influence of the Great Awakening, 1754–1787* (Nashville, Tenn., 1961), 62–68; Janet Moore Lindman, "Acting the Manly Christian: Evangelical Masculinity in Revolutionary Virginia," *William and Mary Quarterly*, 3d ser. 57, no. 2 (Apr. 2000): 401–2.

26. David Thomas, *The Virginian Baptist* (Baltimore, [1774]), 56, 63, 66; Gewehr, *Great Awakening in Virginia*, 115; C. Douglas Weaver, "David Thomas and the Regular Baptists in Colonial Virginia," *Baptist History and Heritage* 18, no. 4 (Oct. 1983): 7–8, 11.

27. Edwards, *Materials*, 2:44–46.

28. Robert B. Semple, *A History of the Rise and Progress of the Baptists in Virginia* (Richmond, Va., 1894), 21–24.

29. Edwards, *Materials*, 2:54–55; Rhys Isaac, *The Transformation of Virginia, 1740–1790* (Chapel Hill, N.C., 1982), 162–63.

30. Edwards, *Materials*, 2:54–56, 61; Isaac, *Transformation of Virginia*, 162–63.

31. Chester R. Young, ed., *Westward into Kentucky: The Narrative of Daniel Trabue* (Lexington, Ky., 1981), 128–29.

32. Young, *Westward into Kentucky*, 129–33.

33. James Ireland, *The Life of the Rev. James Ireland* (Winchester, Va., 1819), 84–85, 94–95; Lindman, "Acting the Manly Christian," 393–96; Isaac, *Transformation of Virginia*, 161–62; Christine L. Heyrman, *Southern Cross: The Beginnings of the Bible Belt* (New York, 1997), 211–17.

34. Ireland, *Life of the Rev. James Ireland*, 123–25, 164–66.

35. William Green to Nathaniel Saunders, Feb. 7, 1767, in Lewis Peyton Little, *Imprisoned Preachers and Religious Liberty in Virginia* (Lynchburg, Va., 1938), 80–81; *Virginia Gazette*, Oct. 31, 1771; Gewehr, *Great Awakening in Virginia*, 128–33; Sandra Rennie, "Virginia's Baptist Persecution, 1765–1778," *Journal of Religious History* 12, no. 1 (June 1982): 50–53.

36. Orange County Order Book, July 28, 1768, in Little, *Imprisoned Preachers*, 135–36; William Bradley to Nathaniel Saunders, n.d., in Little, *Imprisoned Preachers*, 206–7; Gewehr, *Great Awakening*

in Virginia, 122; "Prosecution of Baptist Ministers," in *Virginia Magazine of History and Biography* 11 (1903): 416.

37. "An Address to the Anabaptists Imprisoned in Caroline County, August 8, 1771," *Virginia Gazette*, Feb. 20, 1772, in Little, *Imprisoned Preachers*, 259; William S. Simpson, Jr., ed., "The Journal of Henry Toler, Part II, 1783–1786," *Virginia Baptist Register* 32 (1993): 1643; Mechal Sobel, *Trabelin' On: The Slave Journey to an Afro-Baptist Faith* (Princeton, N.J., 1988), 102; Jewel L. Spangler, "Salvation Was Not Liberty: Baptists and Slavery in Revolutionary Virginia," *American Baptist Quarterly* 13, no. 3 (Sept. 1994): 223; A. D. Gillette, ed., *Minutes of the Philadelphia Baptist Association 1707 to 1807* (Springfield, Mo., 2002), 120.

38. Andrew Levy, *The First Emancipator: The Forgotten Story of Robert Carter, the Founding Father Who Freed His Slaves* (New York, 2005), xi, 67, 140; Spangler, "Salvation Was Not Liberty," 225.

39. Meherrin Church Book, June, July, and September, 1772, Virginia Baptist Historical Society, Richmond, Va.; Sobel, *World They Made Together*, 194; Spangler, "Salvation Was Not Liberty," 225.

40. Edwards, *Materials*, 2:46, 50–51, 54, 56, 59–61; *Virginia Gazette* (Rind), Mar. 26, 1772; *Virginia Gazette* (Rind), Apr. 23, 1772; Simpson, "Journal of Henry Toler," 1630, 1653n179; Semple, *Rise and Progress of the Baptists*, 16; Elder John Sparks, *The Roots of Appalachian Christianity: The Life and Legacy of Elder Shubal Stearns* (Lexington, Ky., 2001), 44; W. Harrison Daniel, "Virginia Baptists and the Negro in the Early Republic," *Virginia Magazine of History and Biography* 80 (1972): 61–62; Spangler, "Salvation Was Not Liberty," 222; Jewel Spangler, "Becoming Baptists: Conversion in Colonial and Early National Virginia," *Journal of Southern History* 67, no. 2 (May 2001): 258–67; Isaac, *Transformation of Virginia*, 201; Lindman, "Acting the Manly Christian," 411–13; Rhys Isaac, "Evangelical Revolt: The Nature of the Baptists' Challenge to the Traditional Order in Virginia, 1765 to 1775," *William and Mary Quarterly*, 3d ser., 31, no. 3 (1974): 345–68.

41. Transcription of court record of Luck's trial, Court of Oyer and Terminer, Frederick Co., Virginia, May 26, 1792, Virginia Baptist Historical Society; John Poindexter, Jr., to Isaac Backus, Apr. 3, 1797, Louisa County, Va., photocopy, Virginia Baptist Historical Society; Benjamin Watkins to Isaac Backus, May 22, 1795, Powhatan County, Va., photocopy, Virginia Baptist Historical Society.

42. John S. Moore, ed., "John Williams' Journal," *Virginia Baptist Register* 17 (Richmond, Va., 1978), 803; Isaac, *Transformation of Virginia*, 165–67; Lindman, "Acting the Manly Christian," 398; Sparks, *Roots of Appalachian Christianity*, 44–45; Heyrman, *Southern Cross*, 20–21; Spangler, "Becoming Baptists," 274, 280–81; Richard R. Beeman, "The Political Response to Social Conflict in the Southern Backcountry: A Comparative View of Virginia and the Carolinas during the Revolution," in Ronald Hoffman, Thad W. Tate, and Peter J. Albert, eds., *An Uncivil War: The Southern Backcountry during the American Revolution* (Charlottesville, Va., 1985), 225.

43. "John Williams' Journal," 803; Daniel Fristoe's journal, 1771, in Little, *Imprisoned Preachers*, 242–43; Isaac, "Evangelical Revolt," 355–56.

CHAPTER 16. "A HAPPY REVIVAL OF RELIGION IN THE INTERIOR PARTS"

1. Richard Hooker, ed., *The Carolina Backcountry on the Eve of the Revolution: The Journal and Other Writings of Charles Woodmason, Anglican Itinerant* (Chapel Hill, N.C. 1953), 13.

2. George Howe, *History of the Presbyterian Church in South Carolina* (Columbia, S.C., 1870), 248–50; Harvey Jackson, "Prophecy and Community: Hugh Bryan, George Whitefield, and the Stoney Creek Independent Presbyterian Church," *American Presbyterians* 69, no. 1 (1991): 15–18; R. W. Huston, ed., "Register Kept by the Rev. Wm. Hutson, of Stoney Creek Independent Congregational Church and (Circular) Congregational Church in Charles Town, S.C., 1743–1760," *South Carolina Historical and Genealogical Magazine* 38 (1937): 22, 27; Alan Gallay, *The Formation of a Planter Elite: Jonathan Bryan and the Southern Colonial Frontier* (Athens, Ga., 1989), 49; Thomas Little, "'Adding to the Church Such as Shall Be Saved': The Growth in Influence of Evangelicalism in Colonial South Carolina, 1740–1775," in Jack Greene, Rosemary Brana-Shute, and Randy Sparks, eds., *Money, Trade, and Power: The Evolution of Colonial South Carolina's Plantation Society* (Columbia, S.C., 2001), 365–66; George Whitefield to William Hutson, Dec. 16, 1745, in John Christie, ed., "Newly Discovered Letters of George Whitefield, 1745–46," *Journal of the Presbyterian Historical Society* 32, no. 2 (June 1954): 77.

3. William Richardson, Diary, Dec. 5, 1758, Jan. 14, 1759, New York Public Library; Ian K. Steele, *Warpaths: Invasions of North America* (New York, 1994), 228–32.

4. William Richardson to J. F., May 6, 1760, William Richardson to J. F., May 21, 1761, in Samuel Davies, *Letters from the Rev. Samuel Davies, and Others* (London, 1761), 20–22, 30–31; Ernest T. Thompson, *Presbyterians in the South*, vol. 1: *1607–1861* (Richmond, Va., 1963), 65; Frederick V. Mills, Sr., "The Society in Scotland for Propagating Christian Knowledge in British North America, 1730–1775," *Church History* 63, no. 1 (Mar. 1994): 25.

5. Woodmason, *Journal*, 14, 132–34; Lilla Mills Hawes, ed., *The Journal of the Reverend John Joachim Zubly* (Savannah, Ga., 1989), 14. On Craighead, see Alice M. Baldwin, "Sowers of Sedition: The Political Theories of Some of the New Light Presbyterian Clergy of Virginia and North Carolina," *William and Mary Quarterly*, 3d ser., 5, no. 1 (Jan. 1948): 64–71.

6. George Whitefield, *George Whitefield's Journals* (Carlisle, Pa., 1960), 440–41; Morgan Edwards, *Materials Towards a History of the Baptists*, ed. Eve Weeks and Mary Warren, vol. 2 (Danielsville, Ga., 1984), 130; Little "Adding to the Church," 370.

7. Oliver Hart, "Extracts from the Diary of Rev. Oliver Hart," *Year Book* [Charleston, S.C.] (1896): 378; Richard Furman, *Rewards of Grace Conferred on Christ's Faithful People* (Charleston, S.C., [1796]), 21–23; Loulie L. Owens, *Oliver Hart, 1723–1795: A Biography* (Greenville, S.C., 1966), 7; Little, "Adding to the Church," 371.

8. Furman, *Rewards of Grace*, 24–26; Oliver Hart, Diary, Aug. 23, 26, 1754, South Carolina Baptist Historical Society, Furman University, Greenville, S.C. (hereafter Hart, Furman Diary); Little, "Adding to the Church," 371–72.

9. Hart, Furman Diary, Aug. 26, 1754.

10. Ibid., Sept. 15, 18, 23, Oct. 10, 16, 27, 1754; Little, "Adding to the Church," 371; Randall Miller, ed., "A Warm and Zealous Spirit": John J. Zubly and the American Revolution, A Selection of His Writings* (Macon, Ga., 1982), 8; Leah Townsend, *South Carolina Baptists, 1670–1805* (Florence, S.C., 1935), 21–22.

11. Townsend, *South Carolina Baptists*, 61–69.

12. Welsh Neck Baptist Church minutes, transcription, 6–10, South Caroliniana Library, University of South Carolina, Columbia.

13. Townsend, *South Carolina Baptists*, 69; Welsh Neck Baptist Church minutes, 29–32; Oliver Hart

to the Warren Baptist Association, Nov. 12, 1779, PIB; *Reverend Elhanan Winchester: Biography and Letters* (New York, 1972), 27.

14. A. D. Gillette, ed., *Minutes of the Philadelphia Baptist Association, 1707 to 1807* (Springfield, Mo., 2002), 72; Terry Wolever, ed., *The Life and Ministry of John Gano, 1727–1804* (Springfield, Mo., 1998), 60–61, 71–73, 78–79; William B. Sprague, ed., *Annals of the American Pulpit*, vol. 6 (New York, 1969), 63–64; William McLoughlin, ed., *The Diary of Isaac Backus*, vol. 1 (Providence, R.I., 1979), 583.

15. John D. Broome, ed., *The Life, Ministry, and Journals of Hezekiah Smith* (Springfield, Mo., 2004), 8, 15–16, 220, 222–23, 234–35, 239; Hezekiah Smith to Samuel Jones, Feb. 23, 1763, Oliver Hart to Samuel Jones, Feb. 7, 1764, McKisson Collection, HSP.

16. Evan Pugh to Samuel Jones, Apr. 23, Nov. 16, 1761, May 14, 1762, McKisson Collection, HSP.

17. Oliver Hart to Samuel Jones, Dec. 1, 1763, July 15, 1765, Evan Pugh to Samuel Jones, June 21, 1764, McKisson Collection, HSP.

18. Oliver Hart to Samuel Jones, June 30, 1769, McKisson Collection, HSP.

19. Edwards, *Materials*, 2:93.

20. Ibid., 2:96–97; George W. Paschal, *History of North Carolina Baptists*, vol. 1 (Raleigh, N.C., 1930), 296–97; Robert Calhoon, "The Evangelical Persuasion," in Ronald Hoffman and Peter Albert, eds., *Religion in a Revolutionary Age* (Charlottesville, Va., 1994), 156–57.

21. Shubal Stearns to correspondent in Connecticut, Oct. 16, 1765, in Isaac Backus, *Church History of New England from 1620 to 1804* (Philadelphia, 1844), 228; Paschal, *North Carolina Baptists*, 297; Woodmason, *Journal*, 80.

22. Edwards, *Materials*, 2:91; Morgan Edwards, *The Customs of Primitive Churches* (Philadelphia, 1768), 41; Catherine A. Brekus, *Strangers and Pilgrims: Female Preaching in America, 1740–1845* (Chapel Hill, N.C., 1998), 63–66.

23. Woodmason, *Journal*, 104; Kars, *Breaking Loose Together*, 105; Paschal, *North Carolina Baptists*, 289; Brekus, *Strangers and Pilgrims*, 61–67; Gary Nash, *The Unknown American Revolution: The Unruly Birth of Democracy and the Struggle to Create America* (New York, 2005), 77.

24. Edwards, *Materials*, 2:140–42.

25. Ibid., 2:139–43; Woodmason, *Journal*, 112–13.

26. Edwards, *Materials*, 2:143–46; Woodmason, *Journal*, 113; Little, "Adding to the Church," 374–75.

27. Edwards, *Materials*, 2:149–50; James Rogers, *Richard Furman: Life and Legacy* (Macon, Ga., 1985), 17–18.

28. Unsigned manuscript on Richard Furman, South Carolina Baptist Historical Society; Townshend, *South Carolina Baptists*, 152; Rogers, *Richard Furman*, 17–22; Hart, "Extracts," 386.

29. Charles Mallary, *Memoirs of Elder Edmund Botsford* (Charleston, S.C., 1832), 38–51; Hawes, *Journal of John Zubly*, 21, 24; William L. Lumpkin, *Baptist Foundations in the South: Tracing through the Separates the Influence of the Great Awakening, 1754–1787* (Nashville, Tenn., 1961), 55.

30. Edmund Botsford to John Rippon, 1790, quoted in Townshend, *South Carolina Baptists*, 256.

31. John Rippon, *The Baptist Annual Register* (London, 1793), 332–33; Sylvia Frey and Betty Wood, *Come Shouting to Zion: African American Protestantism in the American South and British Caribbean to 1830* (Chapel Hill, N.C., 1998), 115–17, 131.

32. Rippon, *Baptist Annual Register,* 339–41; Albert Raboteau, *Slave Religion: The "Invisible Institution" in the Antebellum South* (New York, 1978), 141; Gallay, *Formation of a Planter Elite,* 52–53.

33. Little, "Adding to the Church," 377; John B. Boles, *The Great Revival: Beginnings of the Bible Belt,* rev. ed. (Lexington, Ky., 1996), 6–7.

CHAPTER 17. "THERE IS REALLY A GREAT AWAKENING IN THOSE PARTS"

1. John Cleaveland, *A Short and Plain Narrative of the Late Work of God's Spirit at Chebacco in Ipswich* (Boston, 1767), 64, 71; Timothy D. Hall, *Contested Boundaries: Itinerancy and the Reshaping of the Colonial American Religious World* (Durham, N.C., 1994), 114–15.

2. Nathan O. Hatch, "The Origins of Civil Millennialism in America: New England Clergymen, War with France, and the Revolution," *William and Mary Quarterly,* 3d ser., 31, no. 3 (July 1974): 417.

3. David Lovejoy, *Religious Enthusiasm in the New World: Heresy to Revolution* (Cambridge, Mass., 1985), 222; Susan Juster, *Disorderly Women: Sexual Politics and Evangelicalism in Revolutionary New England* (Ithaca, N.Y., 1994), 108–11; James E. Block, *A Nation of Agents: The American Path to a Modern Self and Society* (Cambridge, Mass., 2002), 219–22; Patricia Bonomi, *Under the Cope of Heaven: Religion, Society, and Politics in Colonial America* (New York, 1986), 152–53. On evangelicalism and the public sphere, see Susan Juster, *Doomsayers: Anglo-American Prophecy in the Age of Revolution* (Philadelphia, 2003), 15–16; Christopher Grasso, *A Speaking Aristocracy: Transforming Public Discourse in Eighteenth-Century Connecticut* (Chapel Hill, N.C., 1999), 99. On the use of local events and practices for ideological purposes in the public sphere, see David Waldstreicher, "Rites of Rebellion, Rites of Assent: Celebrations, Print Culture, and the Origins of American Nationalism," *Journal of American History* 82, no. 1 (June 1995): 37–61.

4. Erik Seeman, *Pious Persuasions: Laity and Clergy in Eighteenth-Century New England* (Baltimore, 1999), 174–77. Alan Heimert argued that this revival was "far more extensive than historians of the colonial church generally allow," *Religion and the American Mind: From the Great Awakening to the Revolution* (Cambridge, Mass., 1966), 97. Isaac Jennings, *Memorials of a Century: Embracing a Record of Individuals and Events Chiefly in the Early History of Bennington, Vt., and Its First Church* (Boston, 1869), 37–38, 72; C. C. Goen, *Revivalism and Separatism in New England, 1740–1800: Strict Congregationalists and Separate Baptists in the Great Awakening* (repr. Middletown, Conn., 1987), 84, 184–85.

5. This characterization of the newspaper coverage is based on readings from 1763–65 in the *Boston Gazette, Boston News-Letter, New-London Gazette,* and the *Pennsylvania Gazette.*

6. Harry S. Stout, *The Divine Dramatist: George Whitefield and the Rise of Modern Evangelicalism* (Grand Rapids, Mich., 1991), 250–55; Arnold Dallimore, *George Whitefield: The Life and Times of the Great Evangelist of the Eighteenth-Century Revival,* vol. 2 (Westchester, Ill., 1979), 437–38; Milton Coalter, *Gilbert Tennent, Son of Thunder: A Case Study of Continental Pietism's Impact on the First Great Awakening in the Middle Colonies* (Westport, Conn., 1986), 118–25; Joseph Conforti, *Samuel Hopkins and the New Divinity Movement: Calvinism, the Congregational Ministry, and Reform in New England between the Awakenings* (Washington, D.C., 1981), 59–75.

7. William McLoughlin, ed., *The Diary of Isaac Backus,* vol. 1: 1741–1764 (Providence, R.I., 1979),

549–53. The 1763–64 revival is briefly described in Christopher Jedrey, *The World of John Cleaveland: Family and Community in Eighteenth-Century New England* (New York, 1979), 116–19.

8. On Cleaveland in the 1740s and the founding of the Ipswich Fourth Church, see Jedrey, *World of John Cleaveland*, 17–58; Anne S. Brown, "Visions of Community in Eighteenth-Century Essex County: Chebacco Parish and the Great Awakening," *Essex Institute Historical Collections* 125, no. 3 (1989): 256–62; Ross Beales, ed., "The Diary of John Cleaveland, Jan. 15–May 11, 1742," *Essex Institute Historical Collections* 107, no. 2 (1971): 143–72. On Buell and Brainerd's friendship, "Sketches of the Character, Life, and Death of the Rev. Samuel Buell," *Connecticut Evangelical Magazine* 2, no. 1 (1801): 147; Jonathan Edwards, *The Life of David Brainerd*, ed. Norman Pettit, vol. 7 of *The Works of Jonathan Edwards* (New Haven, Conn., 1985), 39; John Fea, "Wheelock's World: Letters and the Communication of Revival in Great Awakening New England," *Proceedings of the American Antiquarian Society* 109, no. 1 (1999): 99–144.

9. John Cleaveland to Eleazar Wheelock, Apr. 5, 1763, no. 763255, PEW. Emerson apparently led revivals in 1766, 1772, 1781, and 1788–89. Samuel Gerould, *A Brief History of the Congregational Church in Hollis, N.H.* (Bristol, N.H., 1893), 21; Clifford K. Shipton, *Sibley's Harvard Graduates*, vol. 10 (Boston, 1958), 359–61; Samuel T. Worcester, *History of the Town of Hollis, New Hampshire* (Boston, 1879), 236–38.

10. Michael Crawford, *Seasons of Grace: New England's Revival Tradition in Its British Context* (New York, 1991), 234–37.

11. Cleaveland, *Short and Plain Narrative*, 3; Goen, *Revivalism and Separatism*, 99; Hall, *Contested Boundaries*, 112–15; Heimert, *Religion and the American Mind*, 334.

12. *An Answer to a Letter of December 26, 1763* (Boston, 1764), 3–5.

13. Cleaveland, *Short and Plain Narrative*, 4–5.

14. Mercy Holmes, Isaac Procter, and Thomas Choate relations, [1764?], John Cleaveland Papers, microfilm, Phillips Library, Peabody-Essex Museum, Salem, Mass.; Cleaveland, *Short and Plain Narrative*, 15; Seeman, *Pious Persuasions*, 174–75; Juster, *Disorderly Women*, 69; Erik Seeman, "'Justice Must Take Plase': Three African Americans Speak of Religion in Eighteenth-Century New England," *William and Mary Quarterly*, 3d ser., 56, no. 2 (Apr. 1999): 413.

15. Cleaveland, *Short and Plain Narrative*, 13; John Cleaveland, *A Reply to Dr. Mayhew's Letter of Reproof* (Boston, [1765]), 95–96; George Whitefield to Eleazar Wheelock, Apr. 19, 1764, no. 764269, PEW. Whitefield preached in Newburyport on Mar. 22, 1764. Whitefield to Charles Hardy, Mar. 23, 1764, in Luke Tyerman, *The Life of the Rev. George Whitefield*, vol. 2 (London: Houghton and Stoughton, 1877), 475; Goen, *Revivalism and Separatism*, 11, 100–101.

16. Cleaveland, *Short and Plain Narrative*, 38–40; Hall, *Contested Boundaries*, 114–15; Patricia Bonomi, *Under the Cope of Heaven: Religion, Society, and Politics in Colonial America* (New York, 1986), 154–57.

17. Isaac Backus, *A History of New England with Particular Reference to the Denomination of Christians Called Baptists* (Newton, Mass.: Backus Historical Society, 1871), 2:135–36; Goen, *Revivalism and Separatism*, 228–29.

18. McLoughlin, ed., *Diary of Isaac Backus*, 1:558–59; Isaac Backus, *A Letter to the Reverend Mr. Benjamin Lord* (Providence, R.I., 1764), 32–34.

19. Backus, *Letter*, 39–40.

20. McLoughlin, ed., *Diary of Isaac Backus*, 1:564; John David Broome, ed., *The Life, Ministry, and Journals of Hezekiah Smith* (Springfield, Mo., 2004), 226, 235; Hezekiah Smith to Samuel Jones,

Feb. 23, 1763, McKisson Collection, HSP; Oliver Hart to Samuel Jones, Mar. 7, 1766, McKisson Collection, HSP. On Baptists in the Pee Dee region, Morgan Edwards, *Materials Towards a History of the Baptists*, ed. Eve Weeks and Mary Warren, vol. 2 (Danielsville, Ga.: Heritage Papers, 1984), 126–29; Thomas Little, "'Adding to the Church Such as Shall Be Saved,' The Growth in Influence of Evangelicalism in Colonial South Carolina, 1740–1775," in Jack Greene, Rosemary Brana-Shute, and Randy Sparks, eds., *Money, Trade, and Power: The Evolution of Colonial South Carolina's Plantation Society* (Columbia, S.C., 2001), 376.

21. McLoughlin, ed., *Diary of Isaac Backus*, 1:566. On Buell's ministry in the Great Awakening, see Hall, *Contested Boundaries*, 53; Edwin Gaustad, *The Great Awakening in New England* (New York, 1957), 44–45; Franklin B. Dexter, *Biographical Sketches of the Graduates of Yale College* (New York, 1885), 665; William B. Sprague, ed., *Annals of the American Pulpit* (repr. New York, 1969), 3:102–3; Nathaniel Prime, *A History of Long Island* (New York, 1845), 176–83.

22. Samuel Buell to Eliphalet Williams, June 12, 1764 [Buell marked 1763 in the heading, but the letter is clearly from 1764], CHS; Levi Hart diary, Gratz Sermon Collection, Box 6, HSP, June 24, 1764; Samuel Buell, *A Copy of a Letter from the Rev. Mr. Buell* ([New London, Conn., 1764]), 1–3; Eleazar Wheelock to George Whitefield, Apr. 18, 1764, no. 764268.1, PEW. On Barber and Davenport, Robert Cray, Jr., "More Light on a New Light: James Davenport's Religious Legacy, Eastern Long Island, 1740–1840," *New York History* 73, no. 1 (1992): 10–11.

23. Buell, *Copy of a Letter*, 5–7; Waldstreicher, "Rites of Rebellion," 49; Lambert, *Inventing the "Great Awakening,"* 80–81.

24. *An Account of the Late Success of the Gospel, in the Province of New-York, North-America* (Coventry, Eng., 1765), iii–iv. Thanks to the Amherst College library for providing a copy of this rare imprint. Bibliographic references to this piece seem universally to misidentify the place of publication as Coventry, New York. On Luckman, see John Money, "Taverns, Coffee Houses, and Clubs: Local Politics and Popular Articulacy in the Birmingham Area, in the Age of the American Revolution," *Historical Journal* 14, no. 1 (Mar. 1971): 27–28n47.

25. Samuel Buell, *A Faithful Narrative of the Remarkable Revival of Religion* (New York, 1766), viii–ix, xii–xiii.

26. Ibid., 2–3. Compare Jonathan Edwards, *A Faithful Narrative of the Surprizing Work of God*, in Jonathan Edwards, *The Great Awakening*, ed. C.C. Goen, vol. 4 of *The Works of Jonathan Edwards* (New Haven, Conn., 1972), 144–47.

27. Prime, *History of Long Island*, 167–70; George Whitefield to Mr. R – – – K – – – n, Mar. 3, 1764, in Whitefield, *The Works of the Reverend George Whitefield*, 6 vols. (London, 1771–72), 3:305; Buell, *Faithful Narrative*, 6–9.

28. Buell, *Faithful Narrative*, 12.

29. Ibid., 15, 17.

30. Ibid., 21–22.

31. Ibid., 49–50; Charles Maxson, *The Great Awakening in the Middle Colonies* (Chicago, 1920), 133; David Benedict, *A General History of the Baptist Denomination in America* (Boston, 1813), 572–73.

32. Charles-Jeffery Smith, Diary No. 3, July 1, 1764, Yale University Manuscripts and Archives, Sterling Memorial Library, MS 1372; Charles-Jeffery Smith to Eleazar Wheelock, August 6, 1764, no. 764457, PEW; Charles-Jeffery Smith to Eleazar Wheelock, November 2, 1764, no. 764602, PEW; see also Charles-Jeffery Smith to Eleazar Wheelock, September 7, 1764, no. 764507.2, PEW. On

Smith, see Dexter, *Biographical Sketches*, 2:495–96; David McClure, *Memoirs of the Rev. Elea- zar Wheelock* (repr. New York, 1972), 28.

33. Barbara Lacey, ed., *The World of Hannah Heaton: The Diary of an Eighteenth-Century New En- gland Farm Woman* (DeKalb, Ill., 2003), 97; Sarah Rogers to Nathaniel Whitaker, July 26, 1764, no. 764426, PEW; John Brainerd to Eleazar Wheelock, June 17, 1764, in Thomas Brainerd, ed., *The Life of John Brainerd* (Philadelphia, [1865]), 345; Buell, *Faithful Narrative*, 49–50.

34. Buell, *Faithful Narrative*, 22–23, 48, 77.

35. Ibid., 23–25.

36. Ibid., 54–55; Buell to Williams, June 12, 1764, Williams Family Papers, CHS.

37. Levi Hart diary, May 5, June 18, 1764, CHS; Franklin Bowditch Dexter, *Biographical Sketches of the Graduates of Yale College, 1701–1745* (New York, 1885), 649–50; Trinterud, *Forming of an American Tradition*, 118–19.

38. Jacob Johnson, *Zion's Memorial* (New London, Conn., 1765), 3; Jacob Johnson, *Honours Due to the Memory* (New London, Conn., 1768), 28, quoted in Heimert, *Religion and the American Mind*, 97.

39. Johnson, *Zion's Memorial*, 5–6.

40. Ibid., 7–8.

41. Ibid., 9–10, 12.

42. Ibid., 13–14.

43. Ibid., 17–18, 26.

44. Johnson, *Zion's Memorial*, 27–32; Dexter, *Biographical Sketches*, 651.

45. Johnson, *Zion's Memorial*, 32, 34–35.

46. Ibid., 35–39, 44.

47. Ibid., 45, 47–49. Compare Jonathan Edwards, *Religious Affections*, 162–64.

48. James Robe, *Narratives of the Extraordinary Works of the Spirit of God at Cambuslang* (Glasgow, 1790), 200–201, quoted in Juster, *Doomsayers*, 115; Jonathan Edwards, *Faithful Narrative*, 188–89; DDR, Feb. 1, 1741. See also Leigh Eric Schmidt, *Holy Fairs: Scotland and the Making of American Revivalism*, 2d ed. (Grand Rapids, Mich., 2001), 148; Terryl Givens, *By the Hand of Mormon: The American Scripture that Launched a New World Religion* (New York, 2002), 41–42.

49. Jeremiah Halsey to Eleazar Wheelock, Apr. 2, 1765, no. 765254, PEW.

50. McLoughlin, ed., *Diary of Isaac Backus*, 2:622.

51. Field Horne, ed., *The Diary of Mary Cooper: Life on a Long Island Farm, 1768–1773* (Oyster Bay, New York, 1981), 13, 18; Nathaniel Prime, *A History of Long Island* (New York, 1845), 266–68.

52. Nathan O. Hatch, *The Democratization of American Christianity* (New Haven, Conn., 1989), 10.

CHAPTER 18. "THE GOD OF GLORY IS ON OUR SIDE"

1. Charles Royster, *A Revolutionary People at War: The Continental Army and American Character, 1775–1783* (Chapel Hill, N.C., 1979), 23–24; Alan Heimert, *Religion and the American Mind: From the Great Awakening to the Revolution* (Cambridge, Mass., 1966), 483.

2. Christopher Grasso, *A Speaking Aristocracy: Transforming Public Discourse in Eighteenth-Century Connecticut* (Chapel Hill, N.C., 1999), 497; Harry S. Stout, "Religion, Communications, and the Ideological Origins of the American Revolution," *William and Mary Quarterly*, 3d ser., 34, no. 4

(Oct. 1977): 524–25; Heimert, *Religion and the American Mind*, viii; John Murrin, "No Awakening, No Revolution? More Counterfactual Speculations," *Reviews in American History* 11, no. 2 (June 1983): 161–71; Gary Nash, *The Urban Crucible: The Northern Seaports and the Origins of the American Revolution*, abr. ed. (Cambridge, Mass., 1986), 127–38, 247; Nathan Hatch, "New Lights and the Revolution in Rural New England," *Reviews in American History* 8, no. 3 (Sept. 1980): 323–28.

3. Philip Greven, *The Protestant Temperament: Patterns of Child-Rearing, Religious Experience, and the Self in Early America* (Chicago, 1977), 354; Nash, *Urban Crucible*, 135–36; Patricia Bonomi, *Under the Cope of Heaven: Religion, Society, and Politics in Colonial America* (New York, 1986), 153; Heimert, *Religion and the American Mind*, viii; Hatch, "New Lights," 327; William McLoughlin, "'Enthusiasm for Liberty': The Great Awakening as the Key to the Revolution," *Proceedings of the American Antiquarian Society* 87 (1978): 69–95; Philip Goff, "Revivals and Revolution: Historiographic Turns since Alan Heimert's *Religion and the American Mind*," *Church History* 67, no. 4 (Dec. 1998): 695–721; Philip Gura, "The Role of the 'Black Regiment': Religion and the American Revolution," *New England Quarterly* 61, no. 3 (Sept. 1988): 439–54; Gordon Wood, "Religion and the American Revolution," in *New Directions in American Religious History* (New York, 1997), 182; Cedric Cowing, *The Great Awakening and the American Revolution: Colonial Thought in the 18th Century* (Chicago, 1971), 224–25.

4. Benjamin Rush to Elhanan Winchester, Nov. 12, 1791, quoted in Mark Noll, *America's God: From Jonathan Edwards to Abraham Lincoln* (New York, 2002), 65, "fear of abuses" quote from p. 56. Bailyn's and Wood's classic histories of republicanism include Bernard Bailyn, *The Ideological Origins of the American Revolution* (Cambridge, Mass., 1967); Gordon Wood, *The Creation of the American Republic, 1776–1787* (Chapel Hill, N.C., 1967); Wood, *The Radicalism of the American Revolution* (New York, 1992).

5. Stout, "Religion, Communications, and the Ideological Origins," 519–41; Rhys Isaac, *The Transformation of Virginia, 1740–1800* (Chapel Hill, N.C., 1982), 265–67. For an opposing view of evangelicalism's effects, see Jon Butler, "Enthusiasm Described and Decried: The Great Awakening as Interpretative Fiction," *Journal of American History* 69, no. 2 (Sept. 1982): 320–21.

6. William Wirt Henry, *Patrick Henry: Life, Correspondence and Speeches* (New York, 1891), 1:15–16, 265–66; Edmund Randolph quoted in Isaac, *Transformation of Virginia*, 268, see also 267–69; Henry Mayer, *A Son of Thunder: Patrick Henry and the American Republic* (New York, 1991), 34–39; Charles L. Cohen, "The 'Liberty or Death' Speech: A Note on Religion and Revolutionary Rhetoric," *William and Mary Quarterly*, 3d ser., 38, no. 4 (Oct. 1981): 706. There has been debate about the authorship of the "Liberty or Death" speech, but Cohen argues that it at least originated with Henry (pp. 713–14).

7. Mark Noll, *Christians in the American Revolution* (Washington, D.C., 1977), 12.

8. William Sprague, ed., *Annals of the American Pulpit*, vol. 3 (repr. New York, 1969), 242–43.

9. William Tennent, *An Address, Occasioned by the Late Invasion of the Liberties of the American Colonists by the British Parliament* (Philadelphia, 1774), 5–6.

10. Oliver Hart diary transcription, Aug. 11, 23, 1775, South Caroliniana Library, University of South Carolina, Columbia; Walter Edgar, *Partisans and Redcoats: The Southern Conflict That Turned the Tide of the American Revolution* (New York, 2001), 30–32; Bonomi, *Under the Cope of Heaven*, 211; Thomas Little, "The Rise of Evangelical Religion in South Carolina during the Eighteenth Century," (Ph.D. diss., Rice University, 1995), 397–401; Rachel N. Klein, "Frontier Planters and

the American Revolution: The South Carolina Backcountry, 1775–1782," in Ronald Hoffman, Thad W. Tate, and Peter J. Albert, eds., *An Uncivil War: The Southern Backcountry during the American Revolution* (Charlottesville, Va., 1985), 44–45.

11. William Tennent, "A Fragment of a Journal Kept by the Rev. William Tennent," *Year Book* (Charleston, S.C., 1894), 298, 300, 302–3, 305; James H. O'Donnell, ed., "A Loyalist View of the Drayton-Tennent-Hart Mission to the Upcountry," *South Carolina Historical Magazine* 67, no. 1 (1966): 18.

12. Oliver Hart, *The Character of a Truly Great Man Delineated* (Charlestown, S.C., 1777), 25; Edgar, *Partisans and Redcoats*, 41; "Petition of the Dissenters" and "Mr. Tennent's Speech on the Dissenting Petition," in "Writings of the Rev. William Tennent," *South Carolina Historical Magazine* 61, no. 4 (1960): 194–95, 203, 209; Derek Davis, *Religion and the Continental Congress, 1774–1789: Contributions to Original Intent* (New York, 2000), 32.

13. Sprague, ed., *Annals of the American Pulpit*, 3:165–67, 208–9; Richard Warch, "The Shepherd's Tent: Education and Enthusiasm in the Great Awakening," *American Quarterly* 30, no. 2 (summer 1978): 185; Marjoleine Kars, *Breaking Loose Together: The Regulator Rebellion in Pre-Revolutionary North Carolina* (Chapel Hill, N.C., 2002), 214.

14. Ernest T. Thompson, *Presbyterians in the South*, vol. 1e: *1607–1861* (Richmond, Va., 1963), 64; Bonomi, *Under the Cope of Heaven*, 211; Leonard Trinterud, *The Forming of an American Tradition: A Re-Examination of Colonial Presbyterianism* (Philadelphia, 1949), 245; North Carolina Delegates to Elihu Spencer, Dec. 8, 1775, in Paul H. Smith, ed., *Letters of Delegates to Congress, 1774 to 1789*, vol. 2, Sept.-Dec. 1775 (Washington, D. C., 1977), 459; Sprague, ed., *Annals of the American Pulpit*, 3:167–68, 210.

15. [John Cleaveland], "NORTH-AMERICA", *Essex Gazette*, Nov. 1, 1768; Christopher Jedrey, *The World of John Cleaveland: Family and Community in Eighteenth-Century New England* (New York, 1979), 130–38.

16. "JOHANNES IN EREMO," [John Cleaveland], *Essex Gazette*, June 7, 1774.

17. "JOHANNES IN EREMO," [John Cleaveland], *Essex Gazette*, Apr. 25, 1775; "JOHANNES IN EREMO," [John Cleaveland], *Essex Gazette*, July 13, 1775.

18. Samuel Sherwood, *A Sermon, Containing Scriptural Instructions to Civil Rulers* (New Haven, 1774), vi; Nathan Hatch, "The Origins of Civil Millennialism in America: New England Clergymen, War with France, and the Revolution," *William and Mary Quarterly*, 3d ser., 31, no. 3 (July 1974): 407–9; Ruth Bloch, *Visionary Republic: Millennial Themes in American Thought, 1756–1800* (New York, 1985), 80, 93.

19. Samuel Sherwood, *The Church's Flight into the Wilderness* (New York, 1776), dedication; Sherwood, *Church's Flight*, in Ellis Sandoz, ed., *Political Sermons of the American Founding Era, 1730–1805*, 2d ed. (Indianapolis, 1998), 1:499, 502–3. All further references to *Church's Flight* are from the Sandoz edition. Stephen Stein, "An Apocalyptic Rationale for the American Revolution," *Early American Literature* 9, no. 3 (winter 1975): 214; Stephen A. Marini, "Uncertain Dawn: Millennialism and Political Theology in Revolutionary America," in Richard Connors and Andrew Colin Gow, eds., *Anglo-American Millennialism, From Milton to the Millerites* (Boston, 2004), 164–66.

20. Sherwood, *Church's Flight*, 1:522–23; Stein, "Apocalyptic Rationale," 215–16, 220–22; Susan Juster, "Demagogues or Mystagogues? Gender and the Language of Prophecy in the Age of Democratic Revolutions," *American Historical Review* 104, no. 5 (Dec. 1999): 1564–65; James West Davidson,

The Logic of Millennial Thought: Eighteenth-Century New England (New Haven, Conn., 1977), 250–51; Grasso, *Speaking Aristocracy,* 75–76.

21. Trinterud, *Forming of an American Tradition,* 223; Alexander Mackie, "George Duffield, Revolutionary Patriot," *Journal of Presbyterian History* 33, no. 1 (1955): 3–4; Sprague, ed., *Annals of the American Pulpit,* 3:190.

22. George Duffield, sermon on Isaiah 21:11–12, in George Duffield, Jr., *Courage in a Good Cause* (Philadelphia, 1861), 34–35; Keith Griffin, *Revolution and Religion: American Revolutionary War and the Reformed Clergy* (New York, 1994), 76.

23. Duffield, sermon on Isaiah 21:11–12, 36–37.

24. George Duffield, *A Sermon Preached on a Day of Thanksgiving* (Philadelphia, 1784), in Sandoz, *Political Sermons,* 775, 783–84; Catherine Albanese, *Sons of the Fathers: The Civil Religion of the American Revolution* (Philadelphia, 1976), 110–11; Heimert, *Religion and the American Mind,* 494–95.

25. John Witherspoon, *The Dominion of Providence over the Passions of Men* (Princeton, N.J., 1776), in Sandoz, ed., *Political Sermons,* 553–54; Jeffry Morrison, *John Witherspoon and the Founding of the American Republic* (Notre Dame, Ind., 2005), 24–36, 63; Wood, *Radicalism,* 104–6; Davis, *Religion and the Continental Congress,* 175–98; Joseph Tiedemann, "Presbyterianism and the American Revolution in the Middle Colonies," *Church History* 74, no. 4 (June 2005): 307.

26. Franklin B. Dexter, *Biographical Sketches of the Graduates of Yale College* (New York, 1896), 671; Ammi R. Robbins, *Journal of the Rev. Ammi R. Robbins, A Chaplain in the American Army* (New Haven, Conn., 1850), 10–11, 39; Charles Royster, *A Revolutionary People at War: The Continental Army and American Character, 1775–1783* (Chapel Hill, N.C., 1979), 166.

27. Robbins, *Journal,* 13–14, 16; Royster, *Revolutionary People at War,* 157.

28. Hezekiah Smith to Hephzibah Smith, Mar. 11, 1776, in Reuben Guild, *Chaplain Smith and the Baptists* (Philadelphia, 1885), 170–71; Hezekiah Smith journal, Oct. 26, 1777, in John David Broome, ed., *The Life, Ministry, and Journals of Hezekiah Smith* (Springfield, Mo., 2004), 454; Hezekiah Smith, sermon, Oct. 17, 1779, in Guild, *Chaplain Smith,* 227–30; Hezekiah Smith to Hephzibah Smith, July 14, 1780, in Guild, *Chaplain Smith,* 268–69.

29. David Levinson, "An Explanation for the Oneida-Colonist Alliance in the American Revolution," *Ethnohistory* 23, no. 3 (summer, 1976): 284–85; J. T. Headley, *Chaplains and Clergy of the Revolution* (New York, 1864), 240–42, 345; Terry Wolever, *The Life and Ministry of John Gano, 1727–1804* (Springfield, Mo., 1998), 78–79; Royster, *Revolutionary People at War,* 167; Alan Taylor, *The Divided Ground: Indians, Settlers, and the Northern Borderland of the American Revolution* (New York, 2006), 81–82.

30. Richard R. Beeman and Rhys Isaac, "Cultural Conflict and Social Change in the Revolutionary South: Lunenberg County, Virginia," *Journal of Southern History* 46, no. 4 (Nov. 1980): 537–39; Thomas E. Buckley, S.J., *Church and State in Revolutionary Virginia, 1776–1787* (Charlottesville, Va., 1977), 24.

31. Smith quoted in Preserved Smith, "Chronicles of a New England Family," *New England Quarterly* 9, no. 3 (Sept. 1936): 424; Janice Potter, *The Liberty We Seek: Loyalist Ideology in Colonial New York and Massachusetts* (Cambridge, Mass., 1983), 13; William McLoughlin, *Soul Liberty: The Baptists' Struggle in New England, 1630–1833* (Hanover, N.H., 1991), 134.

32. Isaac Backus, *An Appeal to the Public for Religious Liberty, against the Oppressions of the Present Day* (Boston, 1773), 19, 52, 54; William McLoughlin, "Isaac Backus and the Separation of Church

and State in America," *American Historical Review* 73, no. 5 (June 1968): 1404–5; William McLoughlin, "Massive Civil Disobedience as a Baptist Tactic in 1773," *American Quarterly* 21, no. 4 (winter 1969); 725; Noll, *Christians in the American Revolution*, 80–87.

33. William McLoughlin, ed., *The Diary of Isaac Backus*, vol. 2: 1765–1785 (Providence, R.I., 1979), 915–17; McLoughlin, *Isaac Backus*, 129–32; Thomas McKibbens, Jr., and Kenneth Smith, *The Life and Works of Morgan Edwards* (New York, 1969), 25–40.

34. Israel Holly, *An Appeal to the Impartial* (Norwich, Conn., 1778), 4, 6–8; Noll, *Christians in the American Revolution*, 88–92.

35. Jacob Green, *A Sermon Delivered at Hanover* (Chatham, N.J., 1779), 4; Mark Noll, "Observations on the Reconciliation of Politics and Religion in Revolutionary New Jersey: The Case of Jacob Green," *Journal of Presbyterian History* 54, no. 2 (summer 1976): 219–20.

36. Green, *Sermon*, 5, 12–13, 16; Noll, *Christians in the American Revolution*, 102.

37. John Zubly, *The Law of Liberty* (Philadelphia, 1775), in Randall Miller, ed., *"A Warm and Zealous Spirit": John J. Zubly and the American Revolution, A Selection of His Writings* (Macon, Ga., 1982), 126, also 17–19.

38. Miller, *John J. Zubly*, 20–23; Lilla Mills Hawes, ed., *The Journal of the Reverend John Joachim Zubly* (Savannah, Ga., 1989), 40.

39. "Helvetius," *Royal Georgia Gazette* 75, Aug. 3, 1780, in Miller, *John J. Zubly*, 178; Joel Nichols, "A Man True to His Principles: John Joachim Zubly and Calvinism," *Journal of Church and State* 43, no. 2 (spring 2001): 312–14; Daryl C. Cornett, "The American Revolution's Role in the Reshaping of Calvinistic Protestantism," *Journal of Presbyterian History* 82, no. 4 (winter 2004): 244–57.

40. Dee Andrews, *The Methodists and Revolutionary America, 1760–1800: The Shaping of an Evangelical Culture* (Princeton, N.J., 2000), 45–55; Robert M. Calhoon, "The Evangelical Persuasion," in Ronald Hoffman and Peter Albert, *Religion in a Revolutionary Age* (Charlottesville, Va., 1994), 164–65.

41. William H. Nelson, *The American Tory*, 2d ed. (Boston, 1992), 91; Robert M. Calhoon, *The Loyalist Perception and Other Essays* (Columbia, S.C., 1989), 4.

42. Miles quoted in Kars, *Breaking Loose Together*, 213–14; Childs quoted in George Paschal, *A History of North Carolina Baptists*, vol. 1: 1663–1805 (Raleigh, N.C., 1930), 472. Kars identifies the two separately, but Miles and Childs are identified as the same person in Jeffrey Crow and Paul Escott, "The Social Order and Violent Disorder: An Analysis of North Carolina in the Revolution and the Civil War," *Journal of Southern History* 52, no. 3 (Aug. 1986): 389.

43. John Rippon, "An Account of the Life of Mr. David George," *Baptist Annual Register for 1790, 1791, 1792, and part of 1793*, 476–77; Sylvia Frey, *Water from the Rock: Black Resistance in a Revolutionary Age* (Princeton, N.J., 1991), 63–80, 200; Simon Schama, *Rough Crossings: Britain, the Slaves and the American Revolution* (New York, 2006), 6–11.

44. Samson Occom to the Oneidas, 1775, in Samson Occom Papers, CHS, also in W. DeLoss Love, *Samson Occom and the Christian Indians of New England* (repr. Syracuse, N.Y., 2000), 228–29; Colin G. Calloway, *The American Revolution in Indian Country: Crisis and Diversity in Native American Communities* (New York, 1995), 28.

45. Samson Occom to John Bailey, 1783, Samson Occom Papers, CHS; Taylor, *Divided Ground*, 101, 208–13.

46. George Rawlyk, ed., *Henry Alline: Selected Writings* (New York, 1987), 10–12, 95–96; J. M. Bumsted, *Henry Alline, 178–1784* (Toronto, 1971), 48–49.

47. Rawlyk, *Alline*, 125; Gordon Stewart and George Rawlyk, *A People Highly Favoured of God: The Nova Scotia Yankees and the American Revolution* (Hamden, Conn., 1972), 157–61, 174–75; Stephen Marini, *Radical Sects of Revolutionary New England* (Cambridge, Mass., 1982), 46.

48. Hannah Heaton diary, Feb. 9, 1777, in Barbara Lacey, ed., *The World of Hannah Heaton: The Diary of an Eighteenth-Century New England Farm Woman* (DeKalb, Ill., 2003), 180–81; Jon F. Sensbach, *A Separate Canaan: The Making of an Afro-Moravian World in North Carolina, 1763–1840* (Chapel Hill, N.C., 1998), 91–93; John Howard Smith, "'The Promised Day of the Lord': American Millennialism and Apocalypticism, 1735–1783," in Connors and Gow, *Anglo-American Millennialism*, 143–44.

CHAPTER 19. "MANY THOUGHT THE DAY OF JUDGMENT WAS COME"

1. *A Few Lines Composed on the Dark Day, of May 19,* 1780 ([Boston? 1780?]), broadside.

2. Cora Lutz, "Ezra Stiles and the Dark Day," *Yale University Library Gazette* 54, no. 4 (1980): 164, 166; William McLoughlin, ed., *The Diary of Isaac Backus*, vol. 2: 1765–1785 (Providence, R.I., 1979), 1048; Barbara Lacey, ed., *The World of Hannah Heaton: The Diary of an Eighteenth-Century Farm Woman* (DeKalb, Ill., 2003), 197; Samuel Gatchel, *The Signs of the Times* (Danvers, Mass., 1781), 6–7; Josiah Litch, *Prophetic Expositions* (Boston, 1842), 1:151; Peter Eisenstadt, "The Weather and Weather Forecasting in Colonial America" (Ph.D. diss., New York University, 1990), 184–88.

3. Stephen Marini, *Radical Sects of Revolutionary New England* (Cambridge, Mass., 1982), 40; Mark Noll, *America's God: From Jonathan Edwards to Abraham Lincoln* (New York, 2002), 162–63.

4. James Beverly and Barry Moody, eds., *The Life and Journal of the Rev. Mr. Henry Alline* (Hantsport, N. S., 1982), 34, 36, 38, 47–49; J. M. Bumsted, *Henry Alline, 1748–1784* (Toronto, 1971), 36.

5. Beverly and Moody, *Life and Journal*, 50–51; Bumsted, *Henry Alline*, 37.

6. Beverly and Moody, *Life and Journal*, 57.

7. Ibid., 62; G. A. Rawlyk, *Ravished by the Spirit: Religious Revivals, Baptists, and Henry Alline* (Kingston, Ont., 1984), 4–5, 11.

8. Beverly and Moody, *Life and Journal*, 64, 75, 79, 84, 97; Bumsted, *Henry Alline*, 69–72.

9. Beverly and Moody, *Life and Journal*, 154.

10. Ibid., 166, 184, 209–10.

11. Ibid., 30–31; Henry Alline, *Two Mites on Divinity*, in George Rawlyk, ed., *Henry Alline: Selected Writings* (New York, 1987), 182; Bumsted, *Henry Alline*, 81–88.

12. Nathan O. Hatch, *The Democratization of American Christianity* (New Haven, Conn., 1989), 40–43; Bumsted, *Henry Alline*, 99–100; Maurice Armstrong, *The Great Awakening in Nova Scotia, 1776–1809* (Hartford, Conn., 1948), 128–29; Rawlyk, *Ravished by the Spirit*, 73–93.

13. David Avery to David McClure, June 26, 1779, David Avery to David McClure, Aug. 30, 1779, David Avery to John Witherspoon, Aug. 13, 1780, David Avery Papers, Princeton Theological Seminary.

14. Isaac Backus, *A History of New England* (Newton, Mass., 1871), 2:264–65; Marini, *Radical Sects*, 46.

15. Jonathan Jeffers to Isaac Backus, Apr. 21, 1778, PIB; Jonathan Jeffers to Isaac Backus, May 23, 1778, PIB; McLoughlin, ed., _Diary of Isaac Backus_, 2:982–83; Asa Hunt to Isaac Backus, May 31, 1780, PIB; Asa Hunt to Warren Association, Aug. 26, 1780, PIB.

16. Biel Ledoyt to Isaac Backus, June 13, 1780, PIB.

17. Backus, _History of New England_, 280; Marini, _Radical Sects_, 45; William Sprague, ed., _Annals of the American Pulpit_, vol. 6 (repr. New York, 1969), 135–36.

18. Asa Hunt to Isaac Backus, July 12, 1780, PIB; Asa Hunt to Warren Association, Aug. 26, 1780, PIB; Elkanah Ingalls to Isaac Backus, Jan. 21, 1781, PIB.

19. John Buzzell, _The Life of Elder Benjamin Randal_ (Limerick, Me., 1827), 10–13; Marini, _Radical Sects_, 64–65; Norman Allen Baxter, _History of the Freewill Baptists: A Study in New England Separatism_ (Rochester, N.Y., 1957), 3–9.

20. Buzzell, _Life of Elder Benjamin Randal_, 87–89; Marini, _Radical Sects_, 65–66; Baxter, _History of the Freewill Baptists_, 20–26.

21. William Hooper to Isaac Backus, May 3, 1780, PIB; Marini, _Radical Sects_, 67; Baxter, _History of the Freewill Baptists_, 27, 31.

22. McLoughlin, ed., _Diary of Isaac Backus_, 2:1034, 1045, 1049, 1058; Marini, _Radical Sects_, 70–71; Hatch, _Democratization_, 41–42.

23. Caleb Rich, "Memoir of Elder Riche," _Candid Examiner_ 2, no. 24 (May 14, 1827): 185–87; Marini, _Radical Sects_, 72–73; Hatch, _Democratization_, 40.

24. Rich, "Memoir," 2, no. 25 (May 28, 1827): 194–97; Marini, _Radical Sects_, 73–74.

25. Rich, "Memoir," 2, no. 25, and 2, no. 26 (May 28–June 18, 1827): 197, 201; Hatch, _Democratization_, 41; Marini, _Radical Sects_, 74–75.

26. Hugh McClellan, _History of Gorham, Maine_ (Portland, Me., 1903), 200–204; Marini, _Radical Sects_, 51–52.

27. Theodore Johnson, ed., "Biographical Account of the Life, Character, & Ministry of Father Joseph Meacham . . . by Calvin Green, 1827," _Shaker Quarterly_ 10 (1970): 23–25; Marini, _Radical Sects_, 52; Stephen Stein, _The Shaker Experience in America_ (New Haven, Conn., 1992), 11.

28. Johnson, "Joseph Meacham," 25–27; Valentine Rathbun, _An Account of the Matter, Form, and Manner of a New and Strange Religion_ (Providence, R.I., 1781), 4; Catherine Brekus, _Strangers and Pilgrims: Female Preaching in America, 1740–1845_ (Chapel Hill, N.C., 1998), 97–112; Marini, _Radical Sects_, 52–53, 78–79; Stein, _Shaker Experience_, 11–12.

29. David Hudson, _Memoir of Jemima Wilkinson_ (repr. New York, 1972), 23; Marini, _Radical Sects_, 48–50; Brekus, _Strangers and Pilgrims_, 80–86; Juster, _Doomsayers_, 123–27.

30. Brekus, _Strangers and Pilgrims_, 86–97; Susan Juster, _Doomsayers: Anglo-American Prophecy in the Age of Revolution_ (Philadelphia, 2003), 227–32.

31. Noll, _America's God_, 161–63; Jon Butler, _Awash in a Sea of Faith: Christianizing the American People_ (Cambridge, Mass., 1990), 223–24.

EPILOGUE

1. Warren Association, _Minutes of the Warren Association_ ([Boston?], 1784), 6–7; Mark Noll, _America's God: From Jonathan Edwards to Abraham Lincoln_ (New York, 2002), 166.

2. John H. Wigger, _Taking Heaven by Storm: Methodism and the Rise of Popular Christianity in America_ (repr. Urbana, Ill., 2001), 24–25; Dee E. Andrews, _The Methodists and Revolutionary_

America, 1760–1800: The Shaping of an Evangelical Culture (Princeton, N.J., 2000), 67–72; Noll, *America's God*, 166.

3. Noll, *America's God*, 434–35; Sylvia R. Frey and Betty Wood, *Come Shouting to Zion: African American Protestantism in the American South and British Caribbean to 1830* (Chapel Hill, N.C., 1998), 118.

4. Mark A. Noll, *The Rise of Evangelicalism: The Age of Edwards, Whitefield, and the Wesleys* (Downers Grove, Ill., 2003), 137.

INDEX